Review of Nursing for State Board Examinations

Second Edition

Sandra Fucci Smith, R.N., M.S.

National Nursing Review

Los Altos, California

International Standard Book Number: 0-917010-03-5

Copies of this book may be obtained @ $12.95/copy from:
National Nursing Review, Inc.
Box 806, Los Altos, CA 94022

Contributing Authors

Chapter Contributors

Barbara Devine Bode, R.N., M.N.
Loyola University

Juliet Marie Corbin, R.N., M.S.
University of California, San Francisco

Donna Johnson Duell, R.N., M.S.
San Jose State University

Dolores Hilden, R.N., M.S.
University of Pennsylvania

Beverly Smith Meyer, R.N., M.S.
San Jose State University

Sandra Fucci Smith, R.N., M.S.
Stanford University — Doctoral Program

Section Contributors

Lida G. Chase, R.N., M.S.
University of Hawaii

Lori Costa, R.N., J.D.
City College of San Francisco

Helen R. Di Croce, R.N., M.S.N.
St. Louis University

Kathleen Dooley, R.N., A.H.N.P.
Golden Gate University — MBA Program

Donna Johnson Duell, R.N., M.S.
San Jose State University

Vicki C. Edwards, R.N., M.S.
University of Hawaii

Cleora B. Horton, R.N., M.S.
San Jose State University

Sue A. Kelly, R.N., M.S.
Santa Cruz County Health Department

Lynn Messenger, R.N., M.S.
University of California, Los Angeles

Susan D. North, R.N., M.S.
University of Maryland

Virgil Parsons, R.N., D.N.Sc.
San Jose State University

Kate De Clue Schejbal, R.N., M.S.
St. Louis University — Doctoral Program

Dorothy Siegle, R.N., M.S.
San Jose State University

JoAnn Rupert Underwood, R.N., M.S.
President, Applied Medical Training

Gloria H. Vanisko, R.N., M.S.
San Jose State University

Judith A. Yanda, R.N., M.S.
West Valley Joint Community College

Preface

For several years you have been studying nursing theory and gaining clinical experience. Now you face an important challenge—scoring sufficiently high in five exams to qualify for R.N. licensure.

My experience in teaching student nurses and in formulating and conducting special nursing reviews for State Board Exams has made me aware of the problems that the graduate nurse encounters while preparing for these tests. Most students do not know how to review the vast amount of material to which they have been exposed during their nursing education. To help you prepare for the State Board Examinations in the most efficient manner is the objective of this book.

The best way to prepare for this test is to thoroughly review the material most likely to be covered on the exam and to take practice tests having similar questions. With this objective in mind, *Review of Nursing* is organized into eight chapters. To keep pace with nursing education and State Boards, we have added to the second edition two chapters (Emergency Interventions and Nursing Procedures, and Legal Issues), and new sections have been added to each of the original six chapters. The outline format is designed to help you review quickly, as well as to emphasize significant content.

The question and answer sections serve a dual purpose—to acquaint you with the type of questions to expect on the examination and to give you an opportunity to test and improve your knowledge of concepts and expertise in realistic nurse-patient situations. The answers and rationale sections are intended to discourage rote memorization and to reinforce learning by demonstrating the underlying principle which tells you why the answers are right or wrong. The selection and presentation of content in this edition are directed toward minimizing your review time and maximizing your test results.

Acknowledgments

I wish to extend my thanks to all of the contributing authors and to the many other people who helped with the development of this book. In particular, I want to thank Vi Sidre and Shirley Hoogeboom, whose dedicated work to edit and proofread greatly enhanced our efforts to clearly present the relevant content material. Because of the invaluable assistance of the editors, graphic designers, typesetters, and book manufacturer, this review book is available to help students prepare for the current State Board Examination.

Contents

Chapter Eight   Legal Issues in Nursing 489

Introduction

The second edition of *Review of Nursing for State Board Examinations* has been expanded and updated. The additional one hundred text pages add new content to each of the six original chapters. Two new chapters have also been included to assist the student in reviewing nursing content for R.N. Licensure: Emergency Interventions and Nursing Procedures, and Legal Issues in Nursing. The final addition to this review book is an extensive index that enables the student to locate several thousand topic areas quickly and efficiently.

The content and format of the book are planned to help the student utilize review time and effort more effectively. Nursing curriculum varies from school to school, and students may find that they are more knowledgeable in one content area than another. *Review of Nursing* will enable the student to quickly recognize her areas of expertise and concentrate on less familiar content. The review questions at the end of each chapter will also assist the student by testing mastery of basic nursing principles and their application to clinical situations.

State Board Examinations test the student's knowledge of nursing rather than physiology, chemistry, medicine, etc. The test questions focus on nursing knowledge, nursing techniques, and nursing interventions in varied clinical situations. *Review of Nursing* includes the subjects of anatomy and physiology as a general review source only for students unsure of basic principles. This book concentrates on pathophysiology, clinical manifestations and treatment of diseases and, most important, nursing management. The content was selected especially for student nurses to utilize in reviewing for both nursing tests at school and State Board Examinations.

The introduction to this book presents general background information on R.N. Licensure and State Board Examinations, previews the contents of *Review of Nursing,* and provides helpful techniques for studying and achieving positive test results. The introduction also provides guidelines for the most effective methods of using this review book.

R.N. Licensure Procedures

The purpose of the R.N. Licensure is to establish minimum levels of professional competency for nurses. All the states require nurses to pass a licensing examination to practice as a registered nurse. Today, emphasis on consumer protection affects the entire medical field and nearly all of its related professions. The system of licensure protects the general public and, at the same time, confirms for the registered nurses that they can embark on a career with professional confidence.

The State Board Test Pool Examination is the means by which each state evaluates the applicants' qualifications to practice nursing. The State Board Examination consists of five tests, one for each of the five main nursing subject areas: medical, surgical, maternity, pediatric, and psychiatric. The candidate must pass all five tests to receive the R.N. license. The same examination is given throughout the United States, and the five parts are usually administered over a two-day period. The examination is usually given in February and July. A candidate for the examination should contact the licensure authority in the state in which the candidate expects to practice nursing because each state sets its own standards for minimal scores and decides whether to accept test results from another state. Since most states require that the candidate's application be filed at least one month prior to examination, applicants should plan sufficiently ahead to assure that key dates are not missed.

A foreign-trained nurse must have her credentials evaluated by the state in which she wishes to practice. If she meets the requirements of the State Board of Licensure, she is then eligible to take the State Board Examination.

Organization and Presentation of Review Material

This book contains extensive coverage, in outline format, of nursing content oriented around five major subject areas which coincide with the five main sections of the State Board Examination:

1. Medical Nursing
2. Surgical Nursing
3. Maternity Nursing
4. Pediatric Nursing
5. Psychiatric Nursing

Each subject area contains material on both nursing theory and practical applications of this theory. The nursing theory section for each subject area includes pathophysiology, clinical manifestations of diseases, diagnosis and treatment of medical conditions, and the appropriate nursing management. Practical applications of the nursing theory to clinical situations are made by the student when answering the situational questions that follow each section. The remaining questions are factual and test the student's ability to recall specific data. The tables, appendices, and glossaries throughout the book will assist the student in reviewing such factual material.

Three additional chapters augment the basic five subject areas and review key content in several important interdisciplinary subjects. This material is presented as follows:

1. Nursing Through the Life Cycle
2. Emergency Procedures and Nursing Interventions
3. Legal Issues in Nursing

The multiple-choice questions at the end of each chapter are similar in format, subject matter, length, and degree of difficulty to those contained in the State Board Examinations. The answers to the multiple-choice questions are accompanied by rationale or an identification of the underlying principle. These sections provide the reviewer with an added learning experience; if the student understands the basic principles of nursing content, she can transfer them to the clinical situations contained in State Board Examinations. Furthermore, the sample tests will provide a basis for understanding the process of selecting the "best" answer to a question.

Finally, the annotated bibliography at the end of the book will serve as an excellent reference if further validation or information is needed to reinforce the student's present level of knowledge. The publications included in this bibliography were selected by the contributing authors both for their clarity of presentation and their coverage of material relevant to State Board Examinations.

Guidelines for Using This Review Book

This review book is organized in the same manner as the State Board Examinations; the five main subject areas of the tests and the book are the same. Each test integrates basic knowledge of the medical sciences, principles of nutrition and diet, and pharmacology. Each main chapter of the book also combines these subjects. The following procedure is recommended for effective utilization of this review text:

1. Review each of the major outlines and evaluate your knowledge and understanding of the main concepts and their clinical applications.
2. Study carefully the various glossaries, tables, and appendices. These sections contain information essential for mastery of the nursing subject areas.
3. Take the practice tests at the end of each section,

and using the answers provided, correct each question and read the rationale for the correct answer. This procedure will enable you to understand the underlying principle for each answer. These principles will apply to questions on the State Board Examinations that are similar to but worded in a slightly different way from the practice questions in this text.

Guidelines for Reviewing and Testing

Since most students have only a few weeks between final examinations at nursing school and the State Board Examinations, it becomes most important that the review process be conducted in an efficient manner. The following recommendations illustrate ways that the reviewer can achieve maximum results for the amount of time invested.

A. Use regularly scheduled periods for study and review.
   1. Arrange to study when mentally alert; if you study during periods of mental and physical fatigue, your efficiency is reduced.
   2. When studying, use short breaks at relatively frequent intervals. Breaks used as rewards for hard work serve as incentives for continued concentrated effort.

B. Analyze your own strengths and weaknesses.
   1. Consider your past performance on classroom tests and written clinical applications of factual material. Learn from past errors on tests by studying corrected material.
   2. Check your past performance on NLN Achievement Tests to identify areas in which you are not sufficiently knowledgeable and which will require more preparation.
   3. Systematically eliminate your weaknesses. Allow sufficient time for repeated review of those areas that continue to pose problems.

C. Become familiar with the examination format.
   1. Study the format used for State Board Examinations so you know the different ways in which questions are asked. For example, you must know how to deal with clinical situations and multiple-choice questions.
   2. Practice taking tests by answering the questions in *Review of Nursing*. Set time limits for covering a given unit of questions to establish the habit of working within a time frame.

D. Systematically study the material contained in each chapter of this book.

    1. First, gain a general impression of the content unit to be reviewed. Skim over the entire section and identify the main ideas.

    2. Then, carefully read and study the tables, glossaries, and appendices.

    3. Mark the key material which you do not know thoroughly.

E. Follow up on your priority areas.

    1. Set priorities on the material that is to be learned or reviewed. Identify the most crucial sections and underline the essential thoughts.

    2. Review what you have read. Ask yourself to think of examples that illustrate the main points you have studied. Recall examples from your own clinical experience or from clinical cases about which you have read.

    3. Solidify newly learned material by writing down the main ideas or by explaining the major points to another person.

F. Test yourself on what you have learned.

    1. Answer practice questions in this review book.

    2. Besides studying answers to practice questions, concentrate on understanding the underlying principles and reasons for the answers.

    3. Acquire the flexibility to answer questions phrased in different ways over the same wide range of content. Important concepts may be tested repeatedly in exams, but the questions will be phrased differently.

Effective Testing

Students who are relaxed and confident while taking tests have a distinct advantage over those who become extremely anxious when facing an important test. Achieving the maximum testing effectiveness involves your mental attitude as well as your knowledge of specific testing techniques.

The following suggestions will help you to maximize your testing effectiveness.

A. General readiness.

    1. The night before the test.

        a. Assemble the materials needed for the test as specified in your instruction booklet.

        b. Get a good night's rest. Don't stay up all night learning new materials.

        c. Avoid the use of stimulants or depressants, either of which may affect your ability to think clearly during the test.

        d. Approach the test with confidence and the determination to do your best. Think positively and concentrate on all you *do* know rather than on what you think you *do not* know.

    2. The day of the exam.

        a. Eat a good breakfast.

        b. Allow ample time to travel to the testing site, including time to park, to locate the proper room, etc.

        c. Choose a location in the testing room where you are least likely to be distracted and where you are away from friends.

    3. During the exam.

        a. Carefully read the directions for the test to avoid errors in understanding how to proceed.

        b. Review the scoring rules. You are usually penalized for incorrect answers on State Board Examinations; so, as a general rule, if you know nothing about a question, it is probably better to skip it. However, if you skip too many questions you may not accumulate enough points to pass the examination.

        c. Determine the total number of questions, and estimate how much time you have for each question to judge how best to use your time.

        d. Answer the practice questions to initiate the test-taking process.

B. Scoring well on the examination.

    1. Using your time wisely.

        a. Start at the beginning of the test, check the time periodically, and maintain a good rate of progression throughout the test. Do not spend too much time on any one question. If there is time left over, go back and spend time on questions about which you were uncertain.

        b. Attempt to answer all questions. If you do not know the answer, leave the question and return to it later. Do not waste time by struggling with questions which perplex you.

c. On multiple-choice questions, first eliminate the answers that you know are
wrong and then spend time deciding
among the answers that are left. If you
are not sure of an answer, pencil in the
answer you think is correct and go back
to it later if you have time.

2. Reading and understanding the question.

a. Carefully read each question. Determine what the question is really asking.
Sometimes details are extraneous. Mentally underline important factors; pay
attention to key terms and phrases. For
example, do not misread *grams* as *milligrams.*

b. Be alert and watch for questions that
ask which answers are *not* correct or
that say, "All the following are correct
except . . ." Read the question as it is
stated, not as you would like it to be
stated.

3. Selecting an answer.

a. Do not look for a pattern in the answer
key—there is none. For example, if you
have already answered several consecutive questions with a *B,* do not hesitate
to answer the next questions in sequence
with a *B* if you think that is the right
answer.

b. Evaluate the possible answers in relation
to the stem (the question), not to other
answers. Choose the answer that best
fits that question rather than an answer
that sounds good by itself.

c. When several alternatives are correct,
choose the answer that is broader or
more general. When several alternatives
look equally correct, compare them. Ask
yourself what the difference is between
the two alternative answers.

d. Recognize answers that are obviously
different from what is logically right,
such as an answer given in grams when
other choices are given in milligrams.

e. Be wary of possible answers that contain
specific qualifiers—words like *always* or
never. Remember, however, that sometimes qualifiers are correct. Some situations are true *only* when a qualifier is
added.

4. Conditions necessary for scoring well on nursing State Board Examinations.

a. When questions are given about a clinical situation, read the situation very
carefully. Identify the essential ideas.
Be careful of distractors that divert your
attention from key ideas. Be aware of
distractors that may in themselves be
correct, but that are not relevant to the
stem of the question or the main idea of
the clinical situation.

b. When questions refer to effective communication, apply your knowledge of
fundamental communication principles
to answer the question.

(1) Focus on the patient's feelings.
(2) Always accept the patient as he is.
(3) Be honest and consistent in approach.
(4) Attempt to establish a good relationship (rapport).
(5) Note other basic principles in the
chapter on psychiatric nursing (see
the table on effective communication).

c. Use information obtained from one
question to help answer other questions.

Nursing Through the Life Cycle

All topics in this chapter pertain to the nursing process. The first section examines general aspects of stress and the various body responses, encompassing Selye's primary principles of stress. Since all phases of illnesses are accompanied by stress, the nurse should have an understanding of the basic concepts and their application.

The effects of middle and old age upon normal and disease processes in the life cycle are summarized in the second section. A *new* section, Human Sexuality, has been added in recognition of today's emphasis on holistic nursing.

State Board Examinations emphasize nutrition. The final section provides data on basic diets, identifies foods high in essential vitamins and minerals, and discusses special diets for various disease processes.

Homeostasis: Stress and Adaptation

Homeostasis

Definition: Homeostasis is the maintenance of a constant state in the internal environment through self-regulatory techniques that preserve an organism's ability to adapt to stresses.

A. Dynamics of homeostasis.
1. Danger or its symbols, whether internal or external, result in the activation of the sympathetic nervous system and the adrenal medulla.
2. The organism prepares for flight or fight.
B. Adaptation factors.
1. Age—adaptation is greatest in youth and young middle life, and least at the extremes of life.
2. Environment—adequate supply of required materials is necessary.
3. Adaptation involves the entire organism.
4. The organism can more easily adapt to stress over a period of time than suddenly.
5. Organism flexibility influences survival.
6. The organism usually uses the adaptation mechanism that is most economical in terms of energy.
7. Illness decreases the organism's capacity to adapt to stress.
8. Adaptation responses may be adequate or deficient.
9. Adaptation may cause stress and illness (for example, ulcers, arthritis, allergy, asthma, and overwhelming infections).

Stress

A. Definitions of stress.
1. A physical, a chemical, or an emotional factor that causes bodily or mental tension and that may be a factor in disease causation; a state resulting from factors that tend to alter an existing equilibrium.
2. Selye's definition of stress.
a. The state manifested by a specific syndrome which consists of all the nonspecifically induced changes within the biologic system.
b. The body is the common denominator of all adaptive responses.
c. Stress is manifested by the measurable changes in the body.
d. Stress causes a multiplicity of changes in the body.
B. General aspects of stress.
1. Body responses to stress are a self-preserving mechanism that automatically and immediately becomes activated in times of danger.
a. Caused by physical or psychological stress: disease, injury, anger, or frustration.
b. Caused by changes in internal and/or external environment.
2. There are a limited number of ways an organism can respond to stress (for example, a cornered amoeba cannot fly).

Selye's Theory of Stress

A. General adaptive syndrome (G.A.S.).
1. Alarm stage (call to arms).
a. Shock—the body translates as sudden injury, and the ANS becomes activated.
b. Countershock—the organism restored to its pre-injury condition.
2. Stage of resistance—the organism is adapted to the injuring agent.
3. State of exhaustion—if stress continues, the organism loses its adaptive capability and goes into exhaustion, which is comparable to shock.
B. Local adaptive syndrome (L.A.S.).
1. Selective changes within the organism.
2. Local response can elicit general response.
3. Example of L.A.S.: a cut, followed by bleeding, followed by coagulation of blood, etc.
4. Ability of parts to the body to respond to a specific injury will be impaired if the whole body is under stress.
C. Whether the organism goes through all the phases of adaptation depends both upon its capacity to adapt and the intensity and continuance of the injuring agent.
1. Organism may return to normal.
2. Organism may overreact; stress decreases.
3. Organism may be unable to adapt or maintain adaptation, a condition which may lead to death.

D. Objective of stress response.
 1. To maintain stability of the organism during stress.
 2. To repair damage.
 3. To restore body to normal composition and activity.

Psychological Stress

Definition: Psychological stress includes all processes which impose a demand or requirement upon the organism, the resolution or accommodation of which necessitates work or activity of the mental apparatus.

A. May involve other structures or systems, but primarily affects mental apparatus.
 1. Anxiety is a primary result of psychological stress.
 2. Causes mental mechanisms to attempt to reduce or relieve psychological discomfort.
 a. Attack/fight.
 b. Withdrawal/flight.
 c. Play dead/immobility.
B. Causes of psychological stress.
 1. Loss of something of value.
 2. Injury/pain
 3. Frustrations of needs and drives.
 4. Threats to self-concept.
 5. Many illnesses directly cause stress.
 a. Disfigurement.
 b. V.D.
 c. Long-term or chronic diseases.
 d. Cancer.
 e. Heart disease.
 6. Conflicting cultural values (example: the American values of competition and assertiveness vs. the need to be dependent).
 7. Future shock: physiological and psychological stress resulting from an overload of the organism's adaptive systems and decision-making processes brought about by too rapidly changing values and technology.
 8. Cultural shock: stress developing in response to transition of the individual from a familiar environment to unfamiliar one.
 a. Involves unfamiliarity with communication, technology, customs, attitudes and beliefs.
 b. Examples: individual moving to new area from foreign country or individual placed in hospital environment.
C. Effects of psychological stress, future shock and cultural shock.
 1. Increased anxiety, anger, helplessness, hopelessness, guilt, shame, disgust, fear, frustration or depression.
 2. Behaviors resulting from stress.
 a. Apathy, regression, withdrawal.
 b. Crying, demanding.
 c. Physical illness.
 d. Hostility, manipulation.
 e. Senseless violence, acting out.

Nursing Management

A. Gather information about patient's internal and external environment.
B. Modify external environment of the patient so that adaptation responses are within the capacity of the patient.
C. Support the efforts of the patient to adapt or to respond.
D. Provide patient with the materials required to maintain constancy of his internal environment.
E. Understand body's mechanisms for accommodating stress.
F. Prevent additional stress.
G. Reduce external stimuli.
H. Reduce or increase physical activity depending on the cause of and response to stress.

Stress Model

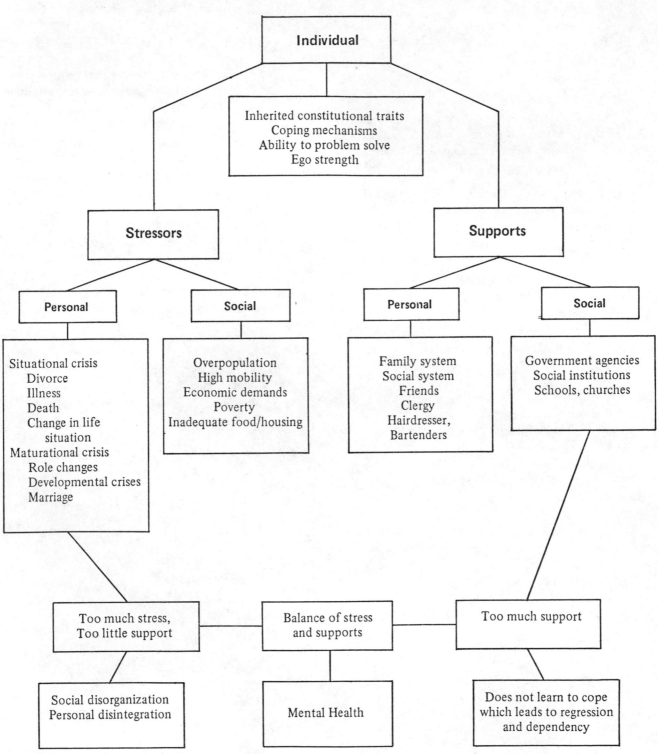

Considerations of Middle Adulthood

Definition: Middle adulthood is the time of life between young adulthood and old age, generally between forty-two years old and sixty-five years old.

Developmental Tasks of Middle Adulthood (Middle Age)

A. Achievement of generativity versus stagnation.
   1. Concern for establishing and guiding next generation.
   2. Includes productiveness, creativity, and an attitude of looking forward to the future.
   3. Stagnation results from the person's refusal to assume power and responsibility of the goals of middle age.
      a. Suffer pervading sense of boredom and impoverishment.
      b. Unresolved mid-life crisis.
B. Relaxed sense of competitiveness.
C. Opening up of new interests.
D. Moving from "us-ness" to "me-ness."
E. Values shifting away from physical attractiveness and strength to intellectual abilities.
F. May be most productive years of one's life.
G. Relationships may become more varied and satisfying.
H. No significant decline in learning abilities or sexual interests.
I. Sexual interests shift from physical performance to the individual's total sexuality and need to be loved and touched.
J. Changes in one's values.
   1. Middle-aged person becomes more introspective.
   2. Less concern as to what others think.
   3. Identifies self as successful even though all life goals may not be achieved.
   4. Outward manifestations of success become less important.
   5. Live more day-to-day and value life more deeply. Has faced one's finiteness and eventual death.
K. Assisting next generation to become happy, responsible adults.
L. Achieving mature social and civic responsibility.
M. Accepting and adjusting to physiological changes of middle life.
N. Satisfying use of leisure time.
O. Mid-life crisis: a normal stage in the ongoing life cycle in which the middle-aged person reevaluates his/her total life situation in relation to youthful achievements and actual accomplishments.
   1. Struggle to maintain physical attractiveness in relation to younger people.
   2. Partner or lover critical self-definition.
   3. Feelings that they have peaked in ability.
   4. Tendency to blame environment or others for failure to succeed.
   5. Increased interest in sexuality.
   6. Competitive in career plans.
   7. Unresolved crises result in stagnation, boredom, and decreased self-esteem and depression.
   8. Age for crisis varies.
      a. Women pass through it between 35 to 40 years old.
      b. Men experience the crisis between 40 to 45 years old.

Physiological and Psychological Health in Middle Age

A. Physiological changes.
   1. Male climacteric syndrome.
   2. Female menopause.
   3. General slowing down of organism.

B. Major health problems.
   1. Heart disease in both male and female.
   2. Diabetes.
   3. Hypertension.
   4. Accidents.
   5. Confrontation with the most acute psychological problems of any age group.
      a. Depression.
      b. Involutional psychosis.
   6. Cancer.

C. Failure to complete developmental tasks may cause the individual to approach old age with resentment and fear.
   1. Neurotic symptoms may appear.
   2. Increased psychosomatic disorders develop.

D. Major causes of psychological problems of middle age.
  1. Fear of loss of job.
  2. Competition with younger generation.
  3. Loss of job.
  4. Loss of nurturant functions.
  5. Loss of spouse, particularly females. Forty-five percent of women over sixty-five are widowed.
  6. Realization that person is not going to do some of the things that he wanted to do.
  7. Changes in body image.
  8. Illness.
  9. Role change within and outside of family.
  10. Fear of approaching old age.
  11. Physiological changes.

Considerations of the Aged

Definition: Old age is the time of life after sixty-five years of age or after retirement.

A. Maintaining ego integrity versus despair.
  1. Integrity results when an individual is satisfied with his own actions and life style, feels life is meaningful, remains optimistic, and continues to grow.
  2. Despair results from the feeling that he has failed and that it is too late to change.
B. Continuing a meaningful life after retirement.
C. Adjusting to income level.
D. Making satisfactory living arrangements with spouse.
E. Adjusting to loss of spouse.
F. Maintaining social contact and responsibilities.
G. Facing death realistically.

Physiological, Psychological, and Socio-economic Implications of Old Age

A. Physical changes.
  1. Decrease in physical strength and endurance.
  2. Decrease in muscular coordination.
  3. Tendency to gain weight.
  4. Loss of pigment in hair and skin.
  5. Increased brittleness of the bones.
  6. Greater sensitivity to temperature changes with low tolerance to cold.
  7. Degenerative changes in the cardiovascular system.
  8. Diminution of sensory faculties.
  9. Decreased resistance to infection and disease.
B. Developmental process retrogresses.
  1. Increasing dependency.
  2. Concerns focus increasingly on self.
  3. Interests may narrow.
  4. Needs tangible evidence of affection.
C. Major fears of the aged.
  1. Fear of physical and economic dependency.
  2. Fear of chronic illness.
  3. Fear of loneliness.
  4. Fear of boredom resulting from not being needed.
D. Major problems of the aged.
  1. Economic deprivation.
     a. Increased cost of living on a fixed income.
     b. Increased need for costly medical care.
  2. Chronic disease and disability.
  3. Social isolation.
  4. Blindness.
  5. Organic brain changes.
     a. Not all persons become senile.
     b. Most people have memory impairment.
     c. The change is gradual.
  6. Nutritional deprivation.
E. Death in the life cycle.
  1. In American culture, death is very distasteful.
  2. The elderly may see death as an end to suffering and loneliness.
  3. Death is not feared if the person has lived a long and fulfilled life, having completed all developmental tasks.
  4. Religious beliefs and/or philosophy of life important.
F. The elderly may provide knowledge and wisdom from their vast experiences, which can assist those at other developmental levels to grow and learn.
G. There will be approximately 20 million people over the age of sixty-five in the United States by 1980.

Human Sexuality

Definition: Difficult to define precisely, human sexuality is considered to be a pervasive life force, a person's total feelings, attitudes, and behavior related to gender identity, sex-role identity, and sexual motivation. Touching, intimacy, and companionship are included in this description as factors that have unique meaning for each person's sexuality.

Overview of Human Sexuality

A. Biological sexuality is determined at conception.
1. Male sperm contributes an X or a Y chromosome.
2. Female ovum has an X chromosome.
3. Fertilization results in either an XX (female) or an XY (male).
B. Preparation for adult sexuality originates in the sexual role development of the child.
1. Significant differences between male and female infants are observable even at birth.
2. Biological changes are minimal during childhood, but parenting strongly influences a child's behavior and sexual role development.
3. Anatomical and physiological changes occur during adolescence which establish biological sexual maturation.
C. Human sexuality pervades the whole of an individual's life.
1. More than a sum of isolated physical acts.
2. Functions as a purposeful influence in human nature and behavior.
3. Observable in everyday life in endless variations.
D. Each society develops a set of normative behaviors, attitudes, and values in respect to sexuality which are considered "right" and "wrong" by individuals.
E. Freud described the bisexual (androgynous) nature of the person.
1. Each person has components of maleness-femaleness, masculinity-femininity, and heterosexuality-homosexuality.
2. These components are physiological and psychological in nature.
3. All components influence an individual's sexuality and sexual behavior.
F. Gender identity refers to whether a person is male or female—usually identified at birth.
1. Cases of "ambiguous genitalia" are rare (1/3000 births), and require special care for the infant and parents.
2. Ambiguous genitalia is clinical label similar to slang term "morphodite," or biological term "hermaphrodite."
G. Sex role describes whether a person assumes masculine or feminine behaviors, usually a combination of both.
1. This role generally considered to be fairly established by age five.
2. Usually referred to by the concepts boy/girl and man/woman.

Sexual Object Choice

A. Sexual object choice is the selection of a mode of outlet for sexual desire, usually with another person.
1. Generally occurs during adolescence and beyond.
2. Includes heterosexuality, homosexuality, bisexuality, celibacy, and narcissism/onanism.
B. Sexual object choice has strong influence on the person's life style.
1. Individual must establish patterns of intimacy and sexual behavior that are acceptable to self, to significant others, and to society to a certain extent.
2. Psychological demands and expectations throughout life influence an individual's sexual interest, activity, and functional capacity.
3. Sexual object choice can affect a person's choices in life such as whether to be a parent, where to live, and what career to maintain.

Sexual Behavior

A. Sexual behavior is a composite of developed patterns of intimacy, psychological demands and expectations, and sexual object choice.
1. Can be genital (sexual intercourse), intimate (holding, hugging), or social (dating, choice of clothing) in nature.
2. Beyond the obvious examples, one never stops "behaving sexually."
3. Dress, communication, and activity are all expressions of sexuality.
4. Every person exhibits sexual behavior continually; no one is sexless.

B. "Transvestite" and "transsexual" are two terms that often cause confusion and need definition and differentiation.

1. Transvestite refers to one who enjoys wearing clothing of the opposite sex; may or may not be homosexual.
2. Transsexual is a person who chooses sexual reassignment: a complex physical (surgical), psychological, and social process of taking on the gender identity, sex role, sexual object choice, and sexual behavior of the opposite sex.

C. Sexuality, although difficult to define, is pervasive from birth to death, and nurses need to look beyond the framework of reproduction and procreation to understand the influence of sexuality on clients' health and illness.

Sexuality and the Nursing Process

A. Assessment can be as complex as a full sexual history, but should at least include consideration of each client's sexuality in assessing health and illness status.

1. An atmosphere should be created which is conducive to discussion of sexual concerns.
2. The nurse needs to "listen" for nonverbal cues of sexual problems and elicit verbalization of underlying concerns.

B. Problem identification can also be complex, but most common problem is the need for recognition of sexuality of each client and allowance of sexual expression within appropriate limits.

1. Clients need to be given "permission" to maintain and/or be concerned about sexuality and sexual behavior.
2. A common general problem is that many clients have incorrect information or misconceptions about sexuality.
3. The relationship between each client's health problems and his/her sexuality needs to be identified.
4. Most clients will not have major sexual problems that require complex intervention.

C. Interventions most commonly indicated are sex education and counseling.

1. Clients consider nurses to be experts in sexuality.
2. Intervention requires knowledge and skill.
3. Nurses need to know referral sources for inter-

ventions beyond their ability.

D. Evaluation should be done in terms of specific outcomes, such as:

1. Client freely expresses concerns related to sexuality.
2. Client verbalizes understanding of the effect of his illness on sexual behavior and functioning.

Common Problems and Implications for Nursing

A. Masturbation.

1. A common sexual outlet for many people.
2. For inpatient clients, particularly those requiring long-term care, masturbation may be only means for gratifying sexual needs.
3. Nurses frequently react negatively to any type of masturbatory activity, especially by male clients.
4. Clients should be allowed privacy; if nurse walks in on a client masturbating, she/he should leave with an apology for having intruded on the client's privacy.
5. Frequent or inappropriate masturbation that may be harmful to the client's health.
   a. Nurse should use team planning to identify what need the client is attempting to meet.
   b. Limits need to be set to protect client and other clients if behavior is inappropriate.

B. Homosexuality.

1. Homosexuality is accepted by many as a viable life style.
2. Nurses have tended to have negative attitudes and incorrect knowledge about homosexuality.
3. A client's homosexual (gay) life style should be accepted and respected.
4. As with any client, visitors should be encouraged as appropriate for the health/illness status, and these people should not be embarrassed or ridiculed.

C. Sexuality and aging.

1. Older people are sexual beings also.
2. There is no particular age at which a person's sexual functioning ceases.
3. Frequency of genital sexual behavior (intercourse) may tend to decline gradually in later years, but capacity for expression and enjoyment continue far into old age.
4. Touching and companionship are of importance for older people and should be encouraged.

5. For chronically ill clients, such as in a nursing home, it is essential that sexuality needs be considered in the total care plan and special efforts be made to have these needs met.

D. Inappropriate sexual behavior.
1. Difficult to precisely define "inappropriate" sexual behavior.
2. Determine if sexual activity or behavior is contrary to a professional nurse-client relationship.
3. Sometimes it is in reaction to unintentional "seductive" behavior of nurses.
4. Specific nursing interventions.
   a. Set limits to unacceptable behavior immediately.
   b. Interact without rejecting client.
   c. Help client express his feelings in an appropriate manner.
   d. Teach alternative behaviors that are acceptable.
   e. Provide acceptable outlets to sexual feelings.

E. Venereal disease.
1. Based on reported cases, the incidence of gonorrhea and syphilis is increasing slowly.
2. Both syphilis and gonorrhea can be cured with appropriate antibiotic therapy. (Recently there has occurred a strain of syphilis resistant to antibiotic therapy, so prevention is an important teaching concept.)
3. Treatment and care should be given without stigma.
4. Case finding and treatment are still very difficult, especially for adolescents who may need parental consent to obtain health services.

F. Contraception.
1. Nurses are considered experts on forms of birth control.
2. Nurse should be familiar with different methods and relative effectiveness of each one.
3. Clients should be assisted to make their own choices as to whether to use contraception and what method is best for them.
4. More detailed outline of contraception (control of parenthood) appears on pages 331–332.

G. Therapeutic abortion.
1. Clients need information about resources for and procedures of therapeutic abortions.
2. Clients should be given nonjudgmental assist-

ance and support in decision-making process.
3. If nurse cannot in good conscience assist the client, referral should be made to someone who can.
4. More detailed outline of abortion appears on pages 329–331.

H. Rape.
1. Rape is basically an act of violence; is only secondarily a sex act.
2. Treatment should consist of both medical and psychological intervention.
3. Sexual assault can have a long-term impact on the victim.
4. Victims may need encouragement and support to report rape occurrences to authorities.
5. Female nurses especially can play a valuable role in giving assistance and support to rape victims.
6. Many communities have "hot-lines" which offer telephone information and crisis counseling to victims of sexual assault and to professionals.

I. Child sexual abuse.
1. There is only a beginning awareness of this problem area.
2. Most child sexual abuse involves a male adult and female child, but male children can also be victims of female or male sexual abusers.
3. The child may need special protection or temporary placement outside the home, but often the family unit can be maintained.
4. Child sexual abuse is a form of child abuse, and nurses should know local regulations and procedures for case finding and reporting.

J. Sexuality and disability.
1. Physically and developmentally disabled persons are sexual beings also.
2. Developmentally disabled persons should be given sexuality education and counseling in preparation for responsible sexual expression and behavior.
3. After spinal cord injury, the level of the lesion and degree of interruption of nerve impulses influence sexual functioning; adaptation of previous sexual practices may be needed after the injury.
4. Fertility and the ability to bear children are usually not compromised in women with spinal cord injury.

5. Nurses working with disabled clients must make special effort to include sexuality in total health care and services.

Drugs and Medications

A. Nurses should be aware of the effect of medications on clients' sexuality and sexual functioning.

B. Oral contraceptives are considered by some to have played a major role in creating a sense of sexual freedom in contemporary society.

C. Drugs that decrease sexual drive or potency may act directly on the physiological mechanisms or may decrease interest through a depressant effect on the central nervous system.

D. Drugs with an adverse effect on sexual activity include antihypertensive drugs, antidepressants, antihistamines, antispasmodics, sedatives and tranquilizers, ethyl alcohol, and some hormone preparations and steroids.

E. There are no known drugs that specifically increase libido or sexual performance; those that seem to enhance sexual behavior do so indirectly through transient relaxation of tensions, alleviation of discomfort, or release of inhibitions.

F. Long-term use of any drug or medicine will likely have a negative effect on sexual interest and capability.

Nurses' Problems in the Area of Sexual Health Care

A. Sexual health care is as important a part of total health care as the physical, emotional, mental, and spiritual aspects.

B. Problems to which nursing personnel should direct themselves.
1. Attitudes.
   a. Nurses should increase their self-awareness of their own attitudes and the effect of these attitudes on the sexual health care of their clients.
   b. Nurses should suppress negative biases and prejudices and/or make appropriate referrals when they cannot give effective sexual health care.
2. Knowledge.
   a. May have to be actively sought although nursing programs are increasing the sexuality content in their curricula.
   b. Also available through books, journal articles, classes and workshops, and preparation for sexuality therapy on the graduate level.
3. Skills.
   a. Primary skills needed are interpersonal techniques such as therapeutic communication, interviewing, and teaching.
   b. As with any skill, practice is needed for proficiency in sexual-history taking, education, and counseling.

Nutritional Concepts and Selected Diets

Normal and Therapeutic Nutrition

A. Normal nutrition—guides for determination of adequate nutrition.
   1. Recommended daily dietary allowances—*Recommended Dietary Allowances,* revised 1974 (see Appendix).
      a. Scientifically designed for maintenance of nearly all healthy people in the United States.
      b. The values of the caloric and nutrient requirements given in this guide are used in assessing nutritional states.
      c. Stress periods in the life cycle, which require alterations in the allowances, should be considered when menus are planned for each age group.
   2. The basic four food groups—*A Daily Food Guide: the Basic Four* (see Appendix).
      a. Offers choices in four food groups to meet the nutrient recommendations during the life cycle. (Caloric requirement is not included.)
      b. Basic nutrients in each food group should be related to dietary needs during the life cycle when menus are planned for each age group.

B. Therapeutic nutrition.
   1. The therapeutic or prescription diet is a modification of the nutritional needs based on the disease condition and/or the excess or deficit nutrition state.
   2. Combination diets, which include alterations in minerals, vitamins, proteins, carbohydrates, fats, as well as fluid and texture, are prescribed in therapeutic nutrition.
   3. Although not all such diets will be included in this review, study of the selected diet concepts will enable you to combine two or more diets when necessary.

C. Normal and therapeutic nutrition considerations.
   1. Cultural, socioeconomic, and psychological influences, as well as physiological requirements, must be considered for effective nutrition.
   2. In any given situation, the nutrition requirements must be considered within the context of the bio-psycho-social needs of the individual.

Essential Body Nutrients

Water	
Fats	3 essential (polyunsaturated) fatty acids: Linoleic acid, Linolenic acid, Arachidonic acid
Carbohydrates	Monosaccharides Glucose, Fructose, Galactose Disaccharides Sucrose, Lactose, Maltose Polysaccharides Starch, Dextrin, Glycogen, Cellulose, Hemicellulose
Protein	Essential amino acids Phenylalanine-tyrosine, Isoleucine, Leucine, Methionine-cystine, Valine, Tryptophan, Threonine (possible essential: Histidine-arginine)
Minerals	Major elements Calcium, Chlorine, Iron, Magnesium, Phosphorus, Potassium, Sodium, Sulfur Trace elements

Therapeutic/Prescription Diets

Diets Associated with Carbohydrate Control

(Note the source of glucose from food: carbohydrate—100 percent; protein—58 percent; fat—10 percent. The control of glucose in diets is based on these three nutrients.)

A. Hypoglycemia diet.
   1. Utilized for hypoglycemia, postgastrectomy complex ("dumping" syndrome).
   2. Purpose of diet: to reduce stimulation of excessive insulin by avoiding highly concentrated carbohydrate foods.
   3. Diet allowances/requirements.
      a. Foods prescribed: high protein, high fat, low carbohydrate.
      b. Foods not allowed: high carbohydrate foods—for example, sugars, syrups, candy.

B. Diabetes mellitus diet.
   1. Purpose of diet: to maintain normal nutritional needs and achieve an ideal weight for the individual. The methods vary from strict control of glucose intake to free control, depending on the physician and the medication that may be ordered.
   2. Diet allowances/requirements.
      a. Diet prepared for individual usually uses exchange method.
      b. Diet is adjusted to normal nutritional and medical needs and must consider food preferences, ideal weight, height, activity, and life style.
C. Foods usually not allowed: refined sugars.
D. Example of exchange list.

Diabetic Exchange Diets

Food Group	Unit of Exchange	Calories	Foods Allowed
Milk:			
whole	1 cup	170	1 cup whole milk = 1 cup skim milk and 2 fat exchanges
skim	1 cup	80	
Fruit	Varies according to calories allotted	40	Fresh or canned without sugar or syrup
Vegetables:			
A	1 cup	Vary	Green, leafy vegetables, tomatoes
B	1/2 cup	35	Vegetables other than green, leafy
Bread	1 slice	70	Can exchange cereals, starch items, some vegetables
Meat	1 ounce	75	Lean meats, egg, cheese, seafood
Fat	1 teaspoon	45	1 teaspoon butter or mayonnaise = bacon, oil, olives, avocado

Unlimited foods:	Coffee, tea, bouillon, spices, flavorings

Diets Associated with Protein Control

A. Low protein diet.
   1. Utilized for renal impairments (uremia), hepatic coma, cirrhosis (according to individual requirements).
   2. Purpose of diet: to control by limiting protein intake the end (breakdown) products of protein metabolism which are disturbing the fluid and electrolytes and/or acid-base balances.
   3. Diet allowances/requirements.
      a. The number of grams of protein allowed is stated for each diet.
      b. Examples of high protein foods to be avoided: eggs, meat, milk and milk products.
B. High protein diet.
   1. Utilized for tissue building conditions, correction of protein deficiencies, burns, liver diseases, malabsorption syndromes, undernutrition, maternity.
   2. Purpose of diet: to correct protein loss, and/or maintain and rebuild tissues by increasing intake of high quality protein food sources.
   3. Protein supplements are ordered by physician for individual needs. Examples of protein supplements: Sustagen, Meritene, Proteinum.
C. Amino acid metabolism abnormalities diet.
   1. Utilized for phenylketonuria (PKU), galactosemia, lactose intolerance.
   2. Purpose of diet: to reduce and/or eliminate the offending enzyme in the food intake of protein and utilize substitute nutrient foods.
   3. The main source of enzymes for the three diseases is milk. Milk and milk products must be avoided and substitutes used to meet daily allowances.

Diets Associated with Fat Control

A. Restricted cholesterol diet.
   1. Utilized for cardiovascular diseases, diabetes mellitus, high serum cholesterol levels.
   2. Purpose of diet: to decrease the blood cholesterol level and/or maintain blood cholesterol at

a normal level by restricting foods high in cholesterol.

3. High cholesterol foods to be restricted or avoided (primarily originating from animal sources).
   a. Saturated fats.
   b. Examples: egg yolk, shell fish, organ meats, bacon, pork, avocado, olives.
4. Low cholesterol foods allowed (primarily originating from plant sources).
   a. Polyunsaturated fats.
   b. Examples: vegetable oils, raw or cooked vegetables, fruits, lean meats, fowl.

B. Modified fat diet.
1. Utilized according to individual tolerance in malabsorption syndromes, cystic fibrosis, gall bladder disease, obstructive jaundice, liver diseases.
2. Purpose of diet: to lower fat content in diet to stop contractions of diseased organs; to reduce fat content where there is inadequate absorption of fat.
3. Diet allowances/requirements.
   a. Moderate fat diet.
      (1) Foods to be avoided: gravies, fat meat and fish, cream, fried foods, rich pastries.
      (2) Foods allowed: eggs, lean meat, butter/ margarine, cheese.
   b. Low fat diet.
      (1) Foods to be avoided: gravies, fat meat and fish, cream, fried foods, rich pastries, whole milk products, cream soups, salad and cooking oils, nuts, chocolate.
      (2) Foods allowed: eggs (2 to 3 per week), lean meat, butter/margarine.
   c. Fat free diet.
      (1) No fat is allowed in diet; fatty meats are omitted from diet.
      (2) Foods to be avoided: eggs, butter/ margarine.
      (3) Foods allowed: vegetables, fruits, lean meats, fowl, fish, bread, cereal.

C. High polyunsaturated fat diet.
1. Utilized for cardiovascular diseases.
2. Purpose of diet: to reduce intake of saturated fats and to increase intake of foods rich in polyunsaturated fats. (Physician usually prescribes caloric level as well as restrictions.)
3. Foods to be avoided: foods originating from animal sources, selected peanuts, olives, avocado, coconuts, chocolate, cashew nuts.
4. Foods allowed: foods originating from vegetable sources (except for those named above); margarine, corn/soybean/safflower oil, fresh ground peanut butter, nuts (except cashews).
5. Frequently used in conjunction with restricted cholesterol diet.
   a. Select foods that are compatible with both diets.
   b. Shellfish is allowed in high polyunsaturated fat diet but is restricted in low cholesterol diet.

Diets Associated with Renal Disease

A. Low protein, essential amino acid diet (modified Giovannetti diet: 20 gm. protein, 1500 mg. potassium).
1. Utilized for renal failure.
2. Purpose of diet: to prevent electrolytes and by-products of metabolism from accumulating to a fatal level between artificial kidney treatments.
3. Foods allowed:
   a. Eggs (1 daily).
   b. Milk (6 ounces).
   c. Low protein bread.
   d. Fruit (2 to 4 servings): apples, peaches, pears, cherries, pineapple, strawberries, grapefruit, grapes.
   e. Vegetables (2 to 4 servings): usually any vegetable.
   f. Free list: for calories—butter, oil, jelly, candy with chocolate; tea, coffee.
4. Foods restricted or not allowed:
   a. Meat: chicken, roast beef, fish, lamb, veal.
   b. Peanuts; bread other than low protein bread.

B. Low calcium diet.
1. Utilized to prevent formation of renal calculi (96 percent calculi are calcium compounds).
2. Purpose of diet: to decrease the total daily intake of calcium to prevent further stone formation. Total 400 mg. calcium instead of normal 800 mg. calcium per day.

3. Foods allowed:
   a. Milk (1 cup daily).
   b. Fruit juices, tea, coffee.
   c. Eggs (1 daily); fats.
   d. Fresh fruits; vegetables (except dried).
4. Foods restricted:
   a. Rye and whole grain breads and cereals.
   b. Dried fruits and vegetables (peas and beans).
   c. Fish, shellfish, dried and cured meats.
   d. Cheese, chocolate, nuts.

C. Acid ash diet.
1. Utilized to prevent precipitation of stone elements.
2. Purpose of diet: to establish well-balanced diet with total acid ash greater than total alkaline ash daily.
3. Foods allowed:
   a. Breads and cereals of any type.
   b. Fats.
   c. Fruits (1 serving), except those restricted.
   d. Vegetables; potatoes, noodles, rice.
   e. Meat, eggs, cheese, fish, fowl (2 servings).
   f. Spices.
4. Foods restricted:
   a. Carbonated beverages.
   b. Foods containing baking powder or soda.
   c. Dried fruits, bananas, figs, raisins.
   d. Dried beans; carrots.
   e. Chocolate candy.
   f. Nuts, olives, pickles.

D. Low purine diet.
1. Utilized to prevent uric acid stones; also utilized for gout patients.
2. Purpose of diet: to restrict purine, which is the precursor of uric acid; 4 percent of urinary stones are composed of uric acid.
3. Foods allowed:
   a. Carbonated beverages, milk, tea, fruit juices.
   b. Breads, cereals.
   c. Cheese, eggs, fat.
   d. Most vegetables.
4. Foods restricted:
   a. Glandular meats, gravies.
   b. Fowl, fish, meat (restricted in amount).

Diets Associated with Surgery

A. Preoperative diet.
1. Purpose of diet.
   a. Maintenance of normal serum protein levels.
   b. Provide adequate carbohydrate to maintain liver glycogen.
   c. Provide adequate amino acids to promote wound healing.
   d. Restore nitrogen balance if protein-depleted (burn, elderly, severely debilitated patient).
2. Recommended nutrient requirements.
   a. 0.8 to 1.5 gm. of protein/kg. body weight/day.
   b. 25 to 50 Kcal./kg./day.
      (1) A calorie is a unit of heat measurement defined as the amount of heat required to raise 1 kg. of water 1°C.
      (2) One gram of protein equals 4 kilogram calories (Kcal.).
3. Recommended diet.
   a. 2500 Kcal.
   b. A high energy, moderate protein diet.
   c. High protein supplements.
4. Elemental diet.
   a. Low residue diet.
   b. Contains synthetic mixture of CHO, amino acids, essential fatty acids with added minerals and vitamins.
   c. Bulk free, easily assimilated and absorbed.
   d. Replace clear liquid diet for patients with colon surgery.
   e. Diet products: Vivonex and Precision.

B. Postoperative surgical diets.
1. Purpose of diet.
   a. Promote wound healing by adequate protein intake.
   b. Avoid shock from decreased plasma proteins and circulating red blood cells by increasing protein intake.
   c. Prevent edema by adequate protein intake (maintains colloidal osmotic pressure).
   d. Promote bone healing in orthopedic surgery by adequate protein and mineral replacement.
   e. Prevent infection by adequate amino acid replacement (amino acids are involved in

body defense mechanisms).

2. Recommended nutrient requirements.

    a. Total calories: 2800 for tissue repair; 6000 for extensive repair.

    b. Protein.

       (1) 50 to 75 g./day early in postoperative period.

       (2) 100 to 200 g./day if needed for new tissue synthesis.

    c. CHO—sufficient in quantity to meet calorie needs and allow protein to be used for tissue repair.

    d. Fat—not excessive as it leads to poor tissue healing and susceptibility to infection.

    e. Vitamins.

       (1) Vitamin C—up to 1 g./day.

       (2) Vitamin B—increased above normal.

       (3) Vitamin K—normal amounts.

    f. Fluid intake.

       (1) Uncomplicated surgery: 2000 to 3000/day.

       (2) Complicated surgery (sepsis, renal damage): 3000 to 4000/day.

       (3) Seriously ill with drainage: 7000/day.

C. Clear liquids.

  1. Water, tea, broth, jello, juices (avoid juices with pulp).

  2. 1000 to 1500 cc./day.

D. Full liquids.

  1. Clear liquids.

  2. Milk and milk products, custard, puddings, creamed soups, sherbet, ice cream, any fruit juice.

E. Soft diet.

  1. Full liquids.

  2. Pureed vegetables, eggs (not fried), mild cheese, fish, fowl, tender beef, veal, etc., potatoes, cooked fruit.

Diets Associated with Calorie Control

A. Restricted calorie diet.

  1. Utilized in obesity, overnutrition in the aged, and specific conditions requiring weight reduction.

  2. Purpose of diet: to reduce the caloric intake of food below the energy demands of the body so weight loss will occur. Psychological support

and exercise are important components of therapy along with diet.

3. Individual diet plan is based on nutritional requirements for age group. Low caloric intakes may require nutrient supplements.

    a. Food exchange patterns are widely used for weight control diets.

    b. Aging adult requires less calories to maintain normal weight.

4. Foods restricted.

    a. CHO.

    b. Fat.

B. Increased calorie diet.

  1. Utilized in burns, pregnancy, aging, childhood, surgery, undernutrition.

  2. Purpose of diet: to meet the increased metabolic needs of the body. There is usually an increase in protein and vitamins when increased calories are ordered.

  3. Foods allowed:

    a. Any food group.

    h CHO, particularly high calorie.

Diets Associated with Vitamin Control

A. Diets adequate in caloric and nutrient requirements usually contain adequate amounts of vitamins.

B. Increased vitamin diet.

  1. Utilized for treatment based on specific deficiencies of vitamins.

    a. Dietary increases are needed for patients with burns, healing wounds, raised temperatures, infections, pregnancy.

    b. Water-soluble vitamins may be prescribed for certain diseases such as cystic fibrosis and liver disease.

  2. Diet allowances/requirements.

    a. Examples of sources rich in fat soluble vitamins (A, D, E, K)—usually found in animal sources associated with fats.

       (1) Vitamin A—liver, egg yolk, whole milk, butter, fortified margarine, green and yellow vegetables, fruits.

       (2) Vitamin D—fortified milk and margarines, sunshine, fish oils.

       (3) Vitamin E—vegetable oils and green vegetables.

(4) Vitamin K—egg yolk, leafy green vegetables, liver, cheese.

b. Examples of foods rich in water soluble vitamins—C, Thiamine (B₁), Riboflavin (B₂), Niacin, B₆ and B₁₂.

(1) Vitamin C—citrus fruits, tomatoes, broccoli, cabbage.

(2) Thiamine (B₁)—lean meat such as beef, pork, liver; whole grain cereals and legumes.

(3) Riboflavin (B₂)—milk, organ meats, enriched grains.

(4) Niacin—meat, beans and peas, peanuts, enriched grains.

(5) Pyridoxine (B₆)—yeast, wheat, corn, meats, liver, and kidney.

(6) Cobalamin (B₁₂)—lean meat, liver, kidney.

(7) Folic acid—leafy green vegetables, eggs, liver.

C. There are no specific diets associated with low vitamin control.

Selected Diets Associated with Mineral Control

A. Restricted sodium diet.

1. Definitions of restrictions.

a. Mild: 2 to 3 g. sodium.

b. Moderate: 1000 mg. sodium.

c. Strict: 500 mg. sodium.

d. Severe: 250 mg. sodium.

2. Utilized for hypertension, hepatitis, congestive heart failure, renal deficiencies, cirrhosis of liver, adrenal corticoid treatment.

3. Purpose of diet: to correct and/or control the retention of sodium and water in the body by limiting sodium intake. May be done strictly by food restriction or in combination with medications.

4. Diet allowances/requirements.

a. Restriction varies from eliminating salt in cooking or at the table to strict food restrictions of any product containing sodium such as soda bicarbonate.

b. Foods high in sodium.

(1) Table salt and all prepared salts, such as celery salt.

(2) Smoked meats and salted meats.

(3) Most frozen vegetables or canned vegetables with added salt.

(4) Butter, margarines, cheese.

(5) Quick-cooking cereals.

(6) Shellfish, frozen or salted fish.

(7) Seasonings and sauces.

(8) Canned soups.

(9) Chocolates and cocoa.

(10) Beets, celery, and selected greens (spinach).

(11) Anything with salt added, such as potato chips, popcorn.

B. Increased or high potassium diet.

1. Utilized for diabetic acidosis, extended use of certain diuretic drugs, burns (after first 48 hours), vomiting, fevers.

2. Purpose of diet: to replace potassium loss from the body. (Severe potassium loss is managed with intravenous therapy.)

3. Diet allowances/requirements.

a. Foods high in potassium.

(1) Fruit juices such as orange, grapefruit, banana, raw apple.

(2) Instant, dry coffee powder.

(3) Egg, legumes, whole grains.

(4) Fish, fresh halibut, codfish.

(5) Pork, beef, lamb, veal, chicken.

(6) Milk, skim and whole.

(7) Dried dates, prunes.

(8) Bouillon and meat broths.

b. Foods to avoid: none, unless there is a sodium restriction; some foods high in potassium are also high in sodium.

C. High iron diet.

1. Utilized for anemias (hemorrhage, nutritional, pernicious), postgastrectomy syndrome, malabsorption syndrome.

2. Purpose of diet: to replace a deficit of iron due to either inadequate intake or chronic blood loss.

3. Foods high in iron content: organ meats (especially liver), meats, egg yolks, whole wheat, seafood, leafy green vegetables, nuts, dried fruit, legumes.

Diets Associated with Fiber Control

A. High residue (roughage) diets.

1. Prescribed for constipation and diverticulosis (prescription varies with physician).

2. Purpose of diet: to mechanically stimulate the gastrointestinal tract.
3. Diet allowances/requirements.
   a. Foods high in residue.
      (1) Any meat or fish—fried, canned, or smoked; any poultry with skin.
      (2) Cheese.
      (3) Fat in any form.
      (4) Milk and fruit juices.
      (5) Whole wheat breads, unrefined bran, cereals, shredded wheat.
   b. Foods low in carbohydrates are usually high residue.

B. Low residue (roughage) diets.

1. Utilized for ulcerative colitis, postoperative colon and rectal surgery, diverticulitis (when inflammation decreases diet may revert to high residue), rheumatic fever, diarrhea and enteritis.
2. Purpose of diet: to soothe and be non-irritating residue in the large intestine.
3. Diet allowances/requirements.
   a. Foods low in residue.
      (1) Ground, tender meat; fresh fish; any boiled, roasted, or broiled poultry without skin or fat.
      (2) Hard-boiled egg.
      (3) Creamed cottage cheese and mild cheeses.
      (4) Limited fat, crisp bacon, plain gravies.
      (5) Warm drinks (not iced); no milk.
      (6) Refined, strained, precooked cereals like pablum; enriched white bread; crackers; toast.
   b. Foods high in carbohydrates are low in residue.

Bland Food Diets

A. These diets are presented in stages, with gradual addition of specific foods.
B. Frequent, small feedings during active stress periods; then regular meals and patterns should be established.
C. Utilized for duodenal ulcer, gastric ulcers, postoperative stomach surgery.
D. Purpose of diet: to promote the healing of the gastric mucosa by eliminating food sources that are chemically and mechanically irritating.

E. Diet allowances/requirements.
   1. Foods allowed.
      a. Milk, butter, eggs (not fried), custard, vanilla ice cream, cottage cheese.
      b. Cooked refined or strained cereal, enriched white bread.
      c. Jello; homemade creamed, pureed soups.
      d. Baked or boiled potatoes.
   2. Examples of foods that are eliminated.
      a. Spicy and highly seasoned foods.
      b. Raw foods.
      c. Very hot and very cold foods.
      d. Gas-forming foods (varies with individuals).
      e. Coffee, alcoholic beverages, carbonated drinks.
      f. High fat contents (some butter and margarine allowed).

Appendix 1. The Basic Four Food Diet

Milk Group

Foods Included

Milk: fluid whole, evaporated, skim, dry, buttermilk.
Cheese: cottage; cream; cheddar-type—natural or processed.
Ice cream.

Contributions to Diet

Milk is our leading source of calcium, needed for bones and teeth. It also provides high quality protein, riboflavin, vitamin A (if milk is whole or fortified), and other nutrients.

Amounts Recommended

Some milk every day for everyone.

Recommended amounts are given below in terms of whole fluid milk:

	8-ounce cups
Children under 9	2 to 3
Children 9 to 12	3 or more
Teenagers	4 or more
Adults	2 or more

Pregnant women   3 or more
Nursing mothers   4 or more

Part or all of the milk may be fluid skim milk, buttermilk, evaporated milk, or dry milk.

Cheese and ice cream may replace part of the milk. The amount of either it will take to replace a given amount of milk is figured on the basis of calcium content. Common portions of various kinds of cheese and of ice cream and their milk equivalents in calcium are:

1-inch cube cheddar-type cheese	= ½ cup milk
½ cup cottage cheese	= 1/3 cup milk
2 tablespoons cream cheese	= 1 tablespoon milk
½ cup ice cream or ice milk	= 1/3 cup milk

Meat Group

Foods Included

Beef; veal; lamb; pork; variety meats, such as liver, heart, kidney.
Poultry and eggs.
Fish and shellfish.
As alternates—dry beans, dry peas, lentils, nuts, peanuts, peanut butter.

Contribution to Diet

Foods in this group are valued for their protein, which is needed for growth and repair of body tissues— muscle, organs, blood, skin, and hair. These foods also provide iron, thiamin, riboflavin, and niacin.

Amounts Recommended

Choose 2 or more servings every day.
Count as a serving: 2 to 3 ounces (not including bone weight) cooked lean meat, poultry, or fish. Count as alternates for ½ serving meat or fish: 1 egg; ½ cup cooked dry beans, dry peas, or lentils; or 2 tablespoons peanut butter.

Vegetable-Fruit Group

Foods Included

All vegetables and fruit. This guide emphasizes those that are valuable as sources of vitamin C and vitamin A.

Sources of Vitamin C

Good sources—Grapefruit or grapefruit juice; orange or orange juice; cantaloupe; guava; mango; papaya; raw strawberries; broccoli; brussels sprouts; green pepper; sweet red pepper.

Fair sources—Honeydew melon; lemon; tangerine or tangerine juice; watermelon; asparagus tips; raw cabbage; cauliflower; collards; garden cress; kale; kohlrabi; mustard greens; potatoes and sweetpotatoes cooked in the jacket; rutabagas; spinach; tomatoes or tomato juice; turnip greens.

Sources of Vitamin A

Dark-green and deep-yellow vegetables and a few fruits, namely apricots, broccoli, cantaloupe, carrots, chard, collards, cress, kale, mango, persimmon, pumpkin, spinach, sweetpotatoes, turnip greens and other dark-green leaves, winter squash.

Contribution to Diet

Fruits and vegetables are valuable chiefly because of the vitamins and minerals they contain. In this plan, this group is counted on to supply nearly all the vitamin C needed and over half the vitamin A.

Vitamin C is needed for healthy gums and body tissues. Vitamin A is needed for growth, normal vision, and healthy condition of skin and other body surfaces.

Amounts Recommended

Choose 4 or more servings every day, including:
1 serving of a good source of vitamin C or 2 servings of a fair source.
1 serving, at least every other day, of a good source of vitamin A. If the food chosen for vitamin C is also a good source of vitamin A, the additional serving of a vitamin A food may be omitted.

The remaining 1 to 3 or more servings may be of any vegetable or fruit, including those that are valuable for vitamin C and vitamin A.

Count as 1 serving: ½ cup of vegetable or fruit; or a portion as ordinarily served, such as 1 medium apple, banana, orange, or potato, half a medium grapefruit or cantaloupe, or the juice of 1 lemon.

Bread-Cereal Group

Foods Included

All breads and cereals that are whole grain, enriched,

or restored; *check labels to be sure.*

Specifically, this group includes breads; cooked cereals; ready-to-eat cereals; cornmeal; crackers; flour; grits; macaroni and spaghetti; noodles; rice; rolled oats; and quick breads and other baked goods if made with whole-grain or enriched flour. Parboiled rice and wheat also may be included in this group.

Contribution to Diet

Foods in this group furnish worthwhile amounts of protein, iron, several of the B-vitamins, and food energy

Amounts Recommended

Choose 4 servings or more daily. Or, if no cereals are chosen, have an extra serving of breads or baked goods, which will make at least 5 servings from this group daily.

Count as 1 serving: 1 slice of bread; 1 ounce ready-to-eat cereal; ½ to ¾ cup cooked cereal, cornmeal, grits, macaroni, noodles, rice, or spaghetti.

Other Foods

To round out meals and meet energy needs, almost everyone will use some foods not specified in the four food groups. Such foods included unenriched, refined breads, cereals, flours; sugars; butter, margarine, other fats. These often are ingredients in a recipe, or are added to other foods during preparation or at the table.

Try to include some vegetable oil among the fats used.

Appendix 2. Recommended Daily Dietary Allowances

DESIGNED FOR THE MAINTENANCE OF GOOD NUTRITION OF PRACTICALLY ALL HEALTHY PEOPLE IN THE U.S.A.

Age[2] (years)	Weight (kg)	Weight (lbs)	Height (cm)	Height (in.)	kcal	Protein (gm)	Fat-soluble vitamins			Water-soluble vitamins							Minerals				
							Vitamin A activity (IU)	Vitamin D (IU)	Vitamin E activity (mg)	Ascorbic acid (mg)	Folacin[3] (mg)	Niacin (mg equiv)[4]	Riboflavin (mg)	Thiamine (mg)	Vitamin B$_6$ (mg)	Vitamin B$_{12}$ (μg)	Calcium (g)	Phosphorus (g)	Iodine (μg)	Iron (mg)	Magnesium (mg)
Infants																					
0–⅙	4	9	55	22	kg × 120	kg × 2.2[5]	1,500	400	5	35	0.05	5	0.4	0.2	0.2	1.0	0.4	0.2	25	6	40
⅙–½	7	15	63	25	kg × 110	kg × 2.0[5]	1,500	400	5	35	0.05	7	0.5	0.4	0.3	1.5	0.5	0.4	40	10	60
½–1	9	20	72	28	kg × 100	kg × 1.8[5]	1,500	400	5	35	0.1	8	0.6	0.5	0.4	2.0	0.6	0.5	45	15	70
Children																					
1–2	12	26	81	32	1,100	25	2,000	400	10	40	0.1	8	0.6	0.6	0.5	2.0	0.7	0.7	55	15	100
2–3	14	31	91	36	1,250	25	2,000	400	10	40	0.2	8	0.7	0.6	0.6	2.5	0.8	0.8	60	15	150
3–4	16	35	100	39	1,400	30	2,500	400	10	40	0.2	9	0.8	0.7	0.7	3	0.8	0.8	70	10	200
4–6	19	42	110	43	1,600	30	2,500	400	10	40	0.2	11	0.9	0.8	0.9	4	0.8	0.8	80	10	200
6–8	23	51	121	48	2,000	35	3,500	400	15	40	0.2	13	1.1	1.0	1.0	4	0.9	0.9	100	10	250
8–10	28	62	131	52	2,200	40	3,500	400	15	40	0.3	15	1.2	1.1	1.2	5	1.0	1.0	110	10	250
Males																					
10–12	35	77	140	55	2,500	45	4,500	400	20	40	0.4	17	1.3	1.3	1.4	5	1.2	1.2	125	10	300
12–14	43	95	151	59	2,700	50	5,000	400	20	45	0.4	18	1.4	1.4	1.6	5	1.4	1.4	135	18	350
14–18	59	130	170	67	3,000	60	5,000	400	25	55	0.4	20	1.5	1.5	1.8	5	1.4	1.4	150	18	400
18–22	67	147	175	69	2,800	60	5,000	400	30	60	0.4	18	1.6	1.4	2.0	5	0.8	0.8	140	10	400
22–35	70	154	175	69	2,800	65	5,000	—	30	60	0.4	18	1.7	1.4	2.0	5	0.8	0.8	140	10	350
35–55	70	154	173	68	2,600	65	5,000	—	30	60	0.4	17	1.7	1.3	2.0	5	0.8	0.8	125	10	350
55–75+	70	154	171	67	2,400	65	5,000	—	30	60	0.4	14	1.7	1.2	2.0	6	0.8	0.8	110	10	350
Females																					
10–12	35	77	142	56	2,250	50	4,500	400	20	40	0.4	15	1.3	1.1	1.4	5	1.2	1.2	110	18	300
12–14	44	97	154	61	2,300	50	5,000	400	20	45	0.4	15	1.4	1.2	1.6	5	1.3	1.3	115	18	350
14–16	52	114	157	62	2,400	55	5,000	400	25	50	0.4	16	1.4	1.2	1.8	5	1.3	1.3	120	18	350
16–18	54	119	160	63	2,300	55	5,000	400	25	50	0.4	15	1.5	1.2	2.0	5	1.3	1.3	115	18	350
18–22	58	128	163	64	2,000	55	5,000	400	25	55	0.4	13	1.5	1.0	2.0	5	0.8	0.8	100	18	350
22–35	58	128	163	64	2,000	55	5,000	—	25	55	0.4	13	1.5	1.0	2.0	5	0.8	0.8	100	18	300
35–55	58	128	160	63	1,850	55	5,000	—	25	55	0.4	13	1.5	1.0	2.0	5	0.8	0.8	90	18	300
55–75+	58	128	157	62	1,700	55	5,000	—	25	55	0.4	13	1.5	1.0	2.0	6	0.8	0.8	80	10	300
Pregnancy					+200	65	6,000	400	30	60	0.8	15	1.8	+0.1	2.5	8	+0.4	+0.4	125	18	450
Lactation					+1,000	75	8,000	400	30	60	0.5	20	2.0	+0.5	2.5	6	+0.5	+0.5	150	18	450

Reprinted with permission from the U.S. Department of Agriculture, Revised 1973.

Medical
Nursing

Medical Nursing requires the broadest and most extensive mastery of nursing knowledge and expertise, for it encompasses every system of the body and includes all possible disease processes. We believe that the student can more easily accomplish a review of nursing content from a system point of view. Therefore, we have organized this chapter by systems instead of following the more contemporary conceptual or nursing process approach found in curricula across the country. However, it is important that the student approach the study of each system remembering that the body is an integrated whole; what is happening in one system will affect and be affected by all other systems in the body.

Each system in this chapter includes basic principles of physiology, pathophysiology, various disease processes, their treatment, and nursing interventions. The material is organized and presented to enable the student to transfer basic principles to any manifestation of illness, while understanding the total interaction which takes place inside the body.

Neurological System

The nervous system (together with the endocrine system) provides the control functions
for the body. Unique in its incredible ability
to handle thousands of bits of information
and stimuli from the sensory organs, this system of nerves and nerve centers coordinates
and regulates all of this data and determines
the responses of the body.

Anatomy and Physiology of the Nervous System

Structure and Function

Neuron

A Structure.
1. Cell body (gray matter).
2. Processes (nerve fibers).
   a. Axon conducts impulses from cell body.
   b. Dendrites receive stimuli from the body and transmit them to the axon.
3. Synapse—chemical transmission of impulses from one neuron to another.
B. Myelin sheath (white matter).
1. Surrounds axon.
2. Insulates; correlates with function and speed of conduction.
3. Produced by neurolemmal cells in peripheral nerve fibers (sheath of Schwann).
4. Produced by neuroglial cells in CNS fibers.
C Classification by function.
1. Sensory (afferent)—conducts impulses from end organ to CNS.
2. Motor (efferent)—conducts impulses from CNS to muscles and glands.
3. Internuncial (connector)—conducts impulses from sensory to motor neurons.
4. Somatic—innervates body wall.
5. Visceral—innervates the viscera.
D. Reflex arc (basic unit of function).
1. Receptor—receives stimulus.
2. Afferent pathway—transmits impulses to spinal cord.

3. CNS—integration takes place at synapse between sensory and motor neurons.
4. Efferent pathway—motor neurons transmit impulses from CNS to effector.
5. Effector—organ or muscle that responds to the stimulus.
E. Regeneration of destroyed nerve fibers.
1. Peripheral nerve—can regenerate, possibly due to neurolemma.
2. CNS—cannot regenerate; lacks neurolemma.

Central Nervous System—Brain and Spinal Cord

A. Brain.
1. Cerebrum (two hemispheres).
   a. Function.
      (1) Highest level of functioning.
      (2) Governs all sensory and motor activity, thought, and learning.
      (3) Analyzes, associates, integrates, and stores information.
   b. Cerebral cortex (outer gray layer)—divided into four major lobes.
      (1) Frontal.
         (a) Precentral gyrus—motor function.
         (b) Broca's area—motor speech area.
         (c) Prefrontal—controls morals, values, emotions, and judgment.
      (2) Parietal.
         (a) Postcentral gyrus—integrates general sensation.
         (b) Interprets pain, touch, temperature, and pressure.
         (c) Governs discrimination.
      (3) Temporal.
         (a) Auditory center.
         (b) Wernicke's area—sensory speech center.
      (4) Occipital—visual area.
   c. Basal ganglia.
      (1) Collections of cell bodies in white matter.
      (2) Control motor movement.
      (3) Part of extrapyramidal tract.
2. Diencephalon.
   a. Thalamus.

(1) Screens and relays sensory impulses to cortex.

(2) Lowest level of crude conscious awareness.

b. Hypothalamus—regulates autonomic nervous system, stress response, sleep, appetite, body temperature, water balance, and emotions.

3. Brainstem.

a. Midbrain—motor coordination, conjugate eye movements.

b. Pons.

(1) Contains projection tracts between spinal cord, medulla, and brain.

(2) Controls involuntary respiratory reflexes.

c. Medulla oblongata.

(1) Contains all afferent and efferent tracts.

(2) Decussation of most upper motor neurons (pyramidal tracts).

(3) Contains cardiac, respiratory, vomiting, and vasomotor centers.

4. Cerebellum.

a. Connected by afferent/efferent pathways to all other parts of CNS.

b. Coordinates muscle movement, posture, equilibrium, and muscle tone.

B. Spinal cord.

1. Structure.

a. Conveys messages between brain and the rest of the body.

b. Extends from foramen magnum to second lumbar vertebra.

c. Inner column of H-shaped gray matter which contains two anterior and two posterior horns.

d. Posterior horns—contain cell bodies which connect with afferent (sensory) nerve fibers from posterior root ganglia.

e. Anterior horns—contain cell bodies giving rise to efferent (motor) nerve fibers.

f. Lateral horns—present in thoracic segments; origin of autonomic fibers of sympathetic nervous system.

g. White matter of cord contains nerve tracts.

(1) Principal ascending tracts (sensory pathways).

(a) Lateral spinothalamic—governs pain, temperature (contralateral).

(b) Anterior spinothalamic—governs touch, pressure (contralateral).

(c) Posterior column to medial lemniscus—governs proprioception, vibration, touch, pressure (epsilateral).

(d) Spinocerebellar—governs bilateral proprioception to posterior and anterior portions of the cerebellum.

(2) Principal descending tracts (motor pathways).

(a) Pyramidal, upper motor neuron, or corticospinal—from motor cortex to anterior horn cell. Tract crosses in medulla.

(b) Extrapyramidal tracts consist of corticorubrospinal, corticoreticulospinal, and vestibulospinal. These tracts facilitate or inhibit flexor/extensor activity.

2. Protection for CNS.

a. Skull—rigid chamber with opening at the base (foramen magnum).

b. Meninges.

(1) Dura mater—tough, fibrous membrane—forms falx, tentorium.

(2) Arachnoid membrane—delicate membrane that contains subarachnoid fluid.

(3) Pia mater—vascular membrane.

(4) Subarachnoid space—formed by the arachnoid membrane and the pia mater.

c. Ventricles.

(1) Four ventricles.

(2) Communication between subarachnoid space.

(3) Produce and circulate cerebrospinal fluid.

d. Cerebral spinal fluid.

(1) Secreted from choroid plexuses in lateral ventricles, third ventricle, and fourth ventricle.

(2) Circulates within interconnecting ventricles and subarachnoid space.

(3) Protective cushion; aids exchange of nutrients and wastes.

(4) Normal pressure: 60-180 mm./H_2O.

(5) Volume: 125-150 cc.

e. Blood-brain barrier.

(1) CSF.

(2) Brain parenchyma.

f. Blood supply—conductor of oxygen vitally needed by nervous system.

(1) Internal carotids branch to form anterior and middle cerebral arteries.

(2) Vertebral arteries arise from the subclavians and merge to form the basilar arteries which then subdivide into the two posterior cerebral arteries.

(3) Circle of Willis—formed as the anterior communicating artery bridges the anterior cerebral arteries, and as the posterior communicating artery bridges each posterior and middle cerebral artery.

Peripheral Nervous System—Cranial and Spinal Nerves

A. Carries voluntary and involuntary impulses.

B. Lower motor neuron—motor cell in anterior horn and its peripheral processes (final common path).

C. Cranial nerves are 12 pairs of parasympathetic nerves with their nuclei along the brainstem.

1. Olfactory—sensory.

2. Optic—conducts sensory information from the retina.

3. Oculomotor—motor nerve that controls four of the six extraocular muscles. Raises eyelid and controls the constrictor pupillae and ciliary muscles of the eyeball.

4. Trochlear—a motor nerve that controls the superior oblique eye muscle.

5. Trigeminal nerve—a mixed nerve with three sensory branches and one motor branch. Corneal reflex is supplied by the opthalmic branch.

6. Abducens—controls the lateral rectus muscle of the eye.

7. Facial—a mixed nerve. The anterior tongue receives sensory supply. Motor supply to glands of nose, palate lacrimal, submaxillary, and sublingual. The motor branch supplies hyoid elevators and muscles of expression and closes eyelid.

8. Acoustic—a sensory nerve with two divisions—hearing and semicircular canals.

9. Glossopharyngeal—a mixed nerve. Motor innervates parotid gland and sensory innervates auditory tube and posterior portion of taste buds.

10. Vagus—a mixed nerve with motor branches to the pharyngeal and laryngeal muscles and to the viscera of the thorax and abdomen. Sensory portion supplies the pinna of the ear, thoracic, and abdominal viscera.

11. Accessory nerve—a motor nerve innervating the sternocleidomastoid and trapezius muscles.

12. Hypoglossal—a motor nerve controlling tongue muscles.

D. Spinal nerves (31 pairs).

1. All mixed nerve fibers formed by joining of anterior motor and posterior sensory roots.

2. Anterior root—efferent nerve fibers to glands and voluntary and involuntary muscles.

3. Posterior root—afferent nerve fibers from sensory receptors. Contains posterior ganglion—cell body of sensory neuron.

Autonomic Nervous System

A. Structure and function.

1. Part of peripheral nervous system controlling smooth muscle, cardiac muscle, and glands.

2. Two divisions make involuntary adjustments for integrated balance (homeostasis).

B. Sympathetic nervous system—thoracolumbar division.

1. Structure.

a. Long postganglionic (adrenergic) fibers.

b. Fibers arise in brainstem and descend to gray matter in spinal cord from C_8 to L_2.

2. Function.

a. Fight, flight, or freeze; diffuse response.

b. Increases heart rate, blood pressure.

c. Dilates pupils, bronchi.

d. Decreases peristalsis.

e. Increases perspiration.

f. Increases blood sugar.

3. Drug intervention.

a. Adrenaline stimulates sympathetic esponses.

b.   Ergotoxine inhibits responses.

C.   Parasympathetic nervous system—craniosacral division.

   1.   Structure.

      a.   Short postganglionic (cholinergic) fibers.

      b.   Cells lie in brainstem and sacral region of spinal cord.

   2.   Function.

      a.   Repair, repose; discrete response.

      b.   Decreases heart rate, blood pressure.

      c.   Constricts pupils, bronchi.

      d.   Increases salivation and peristalsis.

      e.   Dilates blood vessels.

      f.   Bladder contraction.

   3.   Drug intervention.

      a.   Acetylcholine stimulates responses.

      b.   Atropine inhibits responses.

Basic Neurological Assessment

Common Signs and Symptoms

A.   Numbness, weakness.

B.   Dizziness, fainting, loss of consciousness.

C.   Headache, pain.

D.   Speech disturbances.

E.   Visual disturbances.

F.   Disturbances in memory, thinking, personality

G.   Nausea, vomiting.

Level of Consciousness

A.   Most sensitive, reliable index of cerebral function.

B.   Assessment of consciousness.

   1.   Orientation of person, place, purpose, time.

   2.   Response to verbal/tactile stimuli or simple commands.

   3.   Response to painful stimuli: purposeful, nonpurposeful, decorticate, decerebrate, no response.

C.   Describe *behaviors* indicating levels of consciousness: clouding, confusion, delirium, stupor, coma.

Pupillary Signs

A.   Light reflex is most important sign differentiating structural from metabolic coma.

B.   Assessment.

   1.   Size—measure in millimeters.

   2.   Equality—equal, unequal, fluctuations.

   3.   Reactions to light—brisk, slow, fixed.

   4.   Unusual eye movements or deviations from midline.

C.   Pupillary abnormalities.

   1.   Unilateral dilation—pressure conus compression third cranial nerve.

   2.   Mid-position, fixed (often unequal)—midbrain.

   3.   Pinpoint, fixed—pontine.

Motor Function

A.   Pattern of motor dysfunction gives information about anatomic location of lesions, independent of level of consciousness.

B.   Assessment—face, upper and lower extremities.

   1.   Muscle tone, strength, equality.

   2.   Voluntary movement.

   3.   Involuntary movements.

   4.   Reflexes: Babinski, corneal, gag.

C.   Patterns of motor function.

   1.   Appropriate—spontaneous movement to stimulus or command.

   2.   Absence: hemiplegia, paraplegia, quadriplegia.

   3.   Inappropriate—nonpurposeful.

      a.   Posturing in response to noxious stimuli.

         (1)   Decorticate—nonfunctioning cortex, internal capsule (flexion, upper extremity).

         (2)   Decerebrate—brainstem lesion (total extension).

      b.   Involuntary.

         (1)   Choreiform (jerky, quick).

         (2)   Athetoid (twisting, slow).

         (3)   Tremors.

         (4)   Spasms.

         (5)   Convulsions.

   4.   Reflexes.

      a.   Babinski—dorsiflexion ankle and great toe with fanning of other toes; indicates disruption of pyramidal tract.

      b.   Corneal—loss of blink reflex indicates dysfunction of fifth cranial nerve (danger of corneal injuries).

      c.   Gag—loss of gag reflex indicates dysfunction of the 9th–10th cranial nerves (danger of aspiration).

Sensory Function

A. Assess general sensory function in all extremities: touch, pressure, pain.

B If no motor response to command, may elicit response by sensory stimuli such as supraorbital pressure.

C. Use minimal amount of stimulus necessary to evoke a response.

Vital Signs

A. Monitor for trends; changes often unreliable and occur late with increasing intracranial pressure.

B. Blood pressure and pulse.
1. Increasing blood pressure with reflex slowing of pulse—compensatory stage with increasing intracranial pressure.
2. Fall in blood pressure with increasing or irregular pulse—decompensation.

C. Respiration.
1. Rate, depth, and rhythm more sensitive indication of intracranial pressure than blood pressure and pulse.
2. Cheyne-Stokes.
   a. Rhythmically waxes and wanes, alternating with periods of apnea.
   b. Cerebral hemisphere, basal ganglia, or metabolic.
3. Neurogenic hyperventilation.
   a. Sustained regular, rapid, and deep.
   b. Low midbrain, middle pons.
4. Apneustic.
   a. Irregular with pauses at end of inspiration and expiration.
   b. Mid or caudal pons.
5. Ataxic.
   a. Totally irregular, random rhythm and depth.
   b. Medulla.
6. Cluster.
   a. Clusters of breaths with irregularly spaced pauses.
   b. High medulla, low pons.

D. Temperature—rectal.
1. Early rise may indicate damage to hypothalamus or brainstem.
2. Slow rise may indicate infection.

3. Elevated temperature increases brain's metabolic rate.

Signs of Meningeal Irritation

A. Brudzinski's sign—flexion of head causes flexion of both thighs at the hips and flexion of the knees.

B. Kernig's sign—supine position, thigh and knee flexed to right angles. Extension of leg causes spasm of hamstring, resistance, and pain.

Diagnostic Procedures

Radiologic Procedures

A. Skull series.
1. Procedure—X-rays of head from different angles.
2. Purpose—to visualize configuration, density, and vascular markings.
3. Tomograms—layered verticle or horizontal X-ray exposures.

B. Ventriculography.
1. Procedure—injection of air directly into lateral ventricles followed by X-rays.
2. Purpose—to visualize ventricles, localize tumors. May be used if increased intracranial pressure contraindicates pneumoencephalography.
3. Potential complications—headache, nausea and vomiting, meningitis, increasing intracranial pressure.
4. Nursing care.
   a. Monitor vital signs.
   b. Check neurological status.
   c. Elevate head.
   d. Administer icebag and analgesics for headache.

C. Myelography.
1. Procedure—injection of dye or air into lumbar or cisternal subarachnoid space followed by X-rays of the spinal column.
2. Purpose—to visualize spinal subarachnoid space for distortions caused by lesions.
3. Potential complications.
   a. Same as for lumbar puncture.
   b. Cerebral meningeal irritation from dye.

4. Nursing care.
   a. Same as for lumbar puncture.
   b. If dye is used, elevate head and observe for meningeal irritation.
   c. If air is used, keep head lower than trunk.

D. Cerebral angiography.
   1. Procedure—injection of radiopaque dye into carotid and/or vertebral arteries followed by serial X-rays.
   2. Purpose—to visualize cerebral vessels and localize lesions such as aneurysms, occlusions, angiomas, tumors, or abscesses.
   3. Potential complications.
      a. Anaphylactic reaction to dye.
      b. Local hemorrhage.
      c. Vasospasm.
      d. Adverse intracranial pressure.
   4. Nursing care.
      a. Prior to procedure.
         (1) Check allergies.
         (2) Take baseline assessment.
         (3) Measure neck circumference.
      b. During and post procedure.
         (1) Have emergency equipment available.
         (2) Monitor neurological and vital signs for shock, level of consciousness, hemiparesis, hemiplegia, and aphasia.
         (3) Monitor swelling of neck, difficulty in swallowing or breathing.
         (4) Administer ice collar.

E. Pneumoencephalography (PEG).
   1. Procedure—withdrawal of CSF and introduction of air through lumbar, cisternal puncture, followed by X-rays.
   2. Purpose.
      a. To visualize ventricles, aqueducts, and subarachnoid space.
      b. To demonstrate cerebral atrophy, hydrocephalus, and intracranial lesions.
   3. Potential complications—headache, shock, convulsions, increased intracranial pressure, and herniation of brainstem.
   4. Nursing care.
      a. Prior to procedure.
         (1) NPO.
         (2) Take baseline assessment.
         (3) Have emergency equipment available.

      b. During procedure—observe vital signs, hypotension, shock, headache, and level of consciousness.
      c. Post procedure.
         (1) Keep patient in a horizontal position and turn frequently.
         (2) Force fluids.
         (3) Monitor neurological and vital signs.
         (4) Give icebag and analgesics for headache.

F. Brain scan.
   1. Procedure—intravenous injection of radioactive isotope substance followed by anterior-posterior and lateral scanning. Concentration of substance is greatest in pathological areas.
   2. Purpose—to localize tumors with high degree of accuracy. Accuracy is increased if scanning is combined with arteriography or encephalography.
   3. No special preparation or aftercare.

G. Tomography.
   1. Type of brain scan which relies on tissue density and shadows to reflect internal state of brain tissue.
   2. EMI and/or CAT.

Electroencephalography (EEG)

A. Procedure—graphic recording of brain's electrical activity by electrodes placed on the scalp.
B. Purpose—to detect intracranial lesion and abnormal electrical activity (epilepsy).
C. Nursing care.
   1. Wash hair.
   2. Withhold sedatives or stimulants.
   3. Administer fluids as ordered.

Echoencephalogram

A. Procedure—recording of reflected ultrasonic waves from brain structures.
B. Purpose.
   1. To measure position and shifting of midline structures.
   2. To detect subdural hematoma or tumors.

Electromyography (EMG)

A. Procedure—recording of muscle action potential by surface or needle electrodes.
B. Purpose—to diagnose or localize neuromuscular disease.

Lumbar Puncture (LP)

A. Procedure—insertion of spinal needle through L_3-L_4 or L_4-L_5 interspace into lumbar subarachnoid space.

B. Purpose.
   1. To obtain cerebral spinal fluid (CSF).
   2. To measure intracranial pressure and spinal fluid dynamics.
   3. To instill air, dye, or medications.

C. Potential complications—headache, backache, and herniation with brainstem compression (especially if intracranial pressure is high).

D. Nursing care.
   1. Have patient empty bowel and bladder.
   2. Assist with specimens and spinal fluid dynamics.
   3. Maintain strict asepsis.
   4. Monitor vital signs.
   5. Have patient in horizontal position.
   6. Encourage fluids if not contraindicated.
   7. Inspect puncture site.

E. Spinal fluid dynamics—Queckenstedt-Stookey test.
   1. Normal—pressure increases with jugular compression and drops to normal ten to thirty seconds after release of compression.
   2. Partial block—slow rise and return to normal.
   3. Complete block—no rise.

Cisternal Puncture

A. Procedure—needle puncture into cisterna magna just below the occipital bone.

B. Purpose—same as for lumbar puncture. May be used if intracranial pressure is high or for infants.

C. Potential complications—respiratory distress.

D. Nursing care.
   1. Same as for lumbar puncture.
   2. Observe for cyanosis, dyspnea, and apnea.

Conditions of the Neurologic System

Increased Intracranial Pressure

Etiology

Trauma, hemorrhage, tumors, abscess, hydrocephalus, edema, or inflammation.

Pathology

A. Cranial cavity is a solid compartment with relatively little room for expansion.

B. Increased intracranial bulk due to blood, CSF, or brain tissue will increase intracranial pressure.

C. Increased pressure impedes cerebral circulation, absorption of CSF, and function of the nerve cells.

D. Increasing pressure is transmitted downward toward the brainstem with eventual tentorial herniation, brainstem compression, and death.

Clinical Manifestations

A. See section on basic neurological assessment.

B. Level of consciousness—most sensitive indication of increasing intracranial pressure—changes from restlessness to confusion to declining level of consciousness and coma.

C. Headache—tension, displacement of brain.

D. Vomiting—irritation vagal nuclei in floor of 4th ventricle.

E. Pupillary changes—unilateral dilation of pupil; slow reaction to light; fixed dilated pupil is ominous sign requiring immediate action.

F. Motor function—weakness, hemiplegia, positive Babinski, decorticate, decerebrate, seizure activity.

G. Vital signs—rise in blood pressure; widening pulse pressure; reflex slowing of pulse; abnormalities in respiration, especially periods of apnea; temperature elevation.

Nursing Management

A. Assess and treat cerebral edema/increased intracranial pressure.
   1. Give medications—osmotic diuretics, steroids.
   2. Limit fluid intake.
   3. Elevate head of bed; avoid Trendelenburg's position.
   4. Administer mechanical decompression.

B. Prevent further complications.
   1. Monitor neurological dysfunction versus cardiovascular shock.
   2. Prevent hypoxia—avoid morphine.
   3. Monitor fluid-electrolyte and acid-base balance.
   4. Prevent straining by the patient—avoid restraints, prevent coughing and vomiting.

C. Treat underlying cause.

Hyperthermia

Definition: Hyperthermia occurs when the temperature reaches 41°C (106°F); associated with increased cerebral metabolism, increasing risk of hypoxia.

Etiology

A. Dysfunction of thermoregulatory center—trauma, tumor, cerebral edema, CVA, intracranial surgery.

B. Prolonged exposure to high environmental temperatures—heatstroke.

C. Infections.

Treatment

A. Methods for inducing hypothermia.
1. External—cool bath, fans, ice bags, hypothermic blanket (most common).
2. Drugs.
   a. Chlorpromazine—reduces peripheral vasoconstriction, muscle tone, shivering; depresses thermoregulation in hypothalamus.
   b. Meperidine—relaxes smooth muscle, reduces shivering.
   c. Promethazine—dilates coronary arteries, reduces laryngeal and bronchial irritation.
3. Extracorporeal—usually reserved for surgery.

B. Effects of hypothermia.
1. Reduces cerebral metabolism and demand for oxygen.
2. Decreases cerebral and systemic blood flow.
3. Reduces CSF pressure.
4. Decreases endocrine, liver, and kidney function.
5. Decreases pulse, blood pressure, and respiration; may affect cardiac pacemaker.

Nursing Management

A. Prevent shivering.
1. Shivering increases CSF pressure and oxygen consumption.
2. Treatment: chlorpromazine.

B. Prevent trauma to skin and tissue.
1. Frostbite—crystallization of tissues with white or blue discoloration, hardening of tissue, burning, numbness.
2. Fat necrosis—solidification of subcutaneous fat creating hard tissue masses.

3. Initially give complete bath and oil the skin; during procedure, massage skin frequently with lotion or oil to maintain integrity of the skin.

C. Monitor and prevent respiratory complications.
1. Hypothermia may mask infection, cause respiratory arrest.
2. Institute measures to maintain open airway and adequate ventilation.

D. Monitor and prevent cardiac complications.
1. Hypothermia can cause arrhythmias and cardiac arrest.
2. Monitor cardiac status and have emergency equipment available.

E. Monitor renal function.
1. Insert Foley catheter.
2. Monitor urinary output, BUN; may monitor specific gravity.

F. Prevent vomiting and possible aspiration; patient may have loss of gag reflex and reduced peristalsis.

G. Monitor changes in neurological function during hypothermia.

Convulsions

Definition: Convulsions are the forceful involuntary contractions of voluntary muscles; may be one component of a seizure.

Etiology

Cerebral trauma, congenital defects, epilepsy, infection, tumor circulatory defect, anoxia, metabolic abnormalities, excessive hydration.

Classification

A. Tonic convulsion—sustained contraction of muscles.

B. Clonic convulsion—alternating contraction/relaxation of opposing muscle group.

C. Epileptiform—any convulsion with loss of consciousness.

Nursing Management

A. Protect patient from further injury.

B. Observe and record characteristics of seizure activity.
1. Level of consciousness.

2. Description of any aura.
3. Description of body position and initial activity.
4. Motor activity—initial body part involved, character of movements (tonic/clonic), progression of movement, duration, biting of the tongue.
5. Respiration, color.
6. Pupillary changes, eye movements.
7. Incontinence, vomiting.
8. Total duration of seizure.
9. Postictal state—loss of consciousness; sleepiness; impaired speech, motor or thinking; headache; injuries.
10. Neurological and vital signs post convulsion.
11. Frequency and number of convulsions.

C. Protect patient from trauma.
1. Maintain patent airway.
2. Keep padded tongue blade at bedside; do not force between teeth if they are already clenched.
3. Be sure side rails are padded and there is padding around head.
4. Avoid use of any restraints.
5. Remove any objects from environment that may cause injury.
6. Stay with patient.

D. Care after the seizure.
1. Maintain open airway—positioning, suction.
2. Reorient to environment; give reassurance and support.
3. Monitor clinical status.
4. Administer anticonvulsants.
5. Maintain quiet environment.

Assessment to Determine Comatose State

Definition: Coma is complete unconsciousness from which the patient cannot be aroused. Stupor refers to partial to almost complete loss of consciousness.

A. Glasgow Coma Scale is a functional measure to determine clinical status.
B. Determines comatose state based on three areas associated with level of consciousness.
C. Scoring system.
1. Based on a scale of 1 to 15 points.
2. Any score below 8 indicates coma is present.

D. Eye opening is the most important indicator.

Coma Scale

A. Motor response.   Points

		Points
1.	Obeys	6
2.	Localizes	5
3.	Withdrawn	4
4.	Abnormal flexion	3
5.	Extensor response	2
6.	Nil	1

B. Verbal response.   Points

		Points
1.	Oriented	5
2.	Confused conversation	4
3.	Inappropriate words	3
4.	Incomprehensible sounds	2
5.	Nil	1

C. Eye opening.   Points

		Points
1.	Spontaneous	4
2.	To speech	3
3.	To pain	2
4.	Nil	1

Etiology of Sustained Coma

A. Intracranial.
1. Supratentorium mass lesion compressing or displacing brainstem.
2. Infratentorium destructive lesions.
B. Extracranial.
1. Metabolic encephalopathy—most common.
2. Psychiatric conditions.

Treatment

A. Primary objective is to maintain life until a specific diagnosis has been made and the appropriate treatment instituted.
B. Other treatment measures are covered under "The Unconscious Patient" in the following section.

The Unconscious Patient

Definition: Unconsciousness is a state of depressed cerebral functioning with altered sensory and motor function.

Etiology

A. Inability to respond to sensory stimuli: cerebral

vascular disorders, intracranial mass, head trauma, toxins, metabolic disorders, acute infections.

Nursing Management

A. Maintain open airway and adequate ventilation.
  1. Airway obstruction.
     a. Can result in retention of carbon dioxide (with cerebral vasodilation, edema, and increased intracranial pressure).
     b. Hypoxia (with potential irreversible brain damage).
  2. Assessment.
     a. Color, chest expansion, deformities.
     b. Rate, depth, and rhythm of respirations.
     c. Air movement at nose/mouth or intratracheal tube.
     d. Breath sounds, adventitious sounds.
     e. Accumulation of secretions or blood in mouth.
     f. Signs of respiratory distress: hypoxemia, hypercapnia, infection, atelectasis.
  3. Airway.
     a. Head tilt; modified jaw thrust if cervical injury suspected.
     b. Cuffed endotracheal or tracheostomy tube (maintain airway, avenue for suctioning and/or mechanical ventilation).
  4. Assisted ventilation.
     a. If mechanical ventilator is used, insure proper functioning.
     b. Watch PO_2 and PCO_2.
  5. Positioning.
     a. Semiprone (to prevent tongue from occluding airway and secretions from pooling in pharynx).
     b. Frequent change of position.
  6. Bronchial hygiene.
     a. Deep breathing and coughing if not contraindicated.
     b. Suctioning of secretions as necessary.
  7. Emergency equipment available.
B. Maintain adequate circulation.
  1. Assessment.
     a. Blood pressure.
        (1) Hypertension—result of increased intracranial pressure.

(2) Hypotension—result of immobility.
  b. Pulse.
     (1) Check quality and presence of all pulses.
     (2) Check rate, rhythm of apical and/or radial pulse.
  c. Heart sounds.
     (1) Arrhythmias due to hypoxia.
     (2) Usually premature ventricular contractions.
  d. Skin.
     (1) Color.
     (2) Temperature.
  e. Edema.
     (1) Dependent areas.
     (2) Generalized.
  f. Signs of shock.
  2. Positioning.
     a. Perform passive ROM to all extremities.
     b. Change position at least every two hours.
     c. Avoid Trendelenburg's position.
C. Assess neurological status.
  1. Level of consciousness.
  2. Pupillary signs.
  3. Motor function.
  4. Sensory function.
D. Maintain nutrition, fluid, and electrolyte balance.
  1. NPO while unconscious (check for gag and swallowing reflex).
  2. Intravenous fluids, hyperalimentation as required.
  3. Use caution with I.V. rates in presence of increased intracranial pressure.
  4. Tube feeding for long-term management (see page 266).
  5. Monitor homeostasis.
     a. Intake—NPO oral, tube feedings, I.V.
     b. Output—urinary, feces; check emesis, nasogastric tube.
     c. Daily weight.
     d. Electrolyte studies.
     e. Clinical signs of hydration.
  6. Resume oral intake carefully as consciousness returns.
     a. Check gag reflex.
     b. Use ice chips or water as first liquid.
     c. Keep suction equipment ready.

E. Promote elimination.
  1. Urinary: retention catheter.
     a. Maintain daily hygiene of meatus.
     b. Insure patency to prevent bladder distention, urinary stasis, infection, and urinary calculi.
     c. Evaluate amount, color, consistency of output; check specific gravity.
     d. Specific orders for irrigation needed.
  2. Bowel: suppositories and enemas.
     a. Establish routine elimination patterns.
     b. Observe for complications.
     c. Paralytic ileus.
        (1) Abdominal distention and/or paralytic ileus.
        (2) Constipation and/or impaction.
        (3) Diarrhea.
F. Maintain integrity of the skin.
  1. High risk of decubitus ulcers due to:
     a. Loss of vasomotor tone.
     b. Impaired peripheral circulation.
     c. Paralysis, immobility, and loss of muscle assistance to blood flow.
     d. Hypoproteinemia.
  2. Loss of sensation of pressure, pain or temperature—decreased awareness of developing decubitus ulcers or burns.
  3. Skin care.
     a. Clean and dry skin; avoid powder because it may cake.
     b. Massage with lotion around and toward bony prominences once a day.
     c. Use alcohol to toughen skin.
     d. Alternate air mattress and sheepskin pad.
     e. Keep linen from wrinkling; avoid mechanical friction against linen.
G. Maintain personal hygiene.
  1. Eye—loss of corneal reflex may contribute to corneal irritation, keratitis, blindness.
     a. Assess corneal reflex and signs of irritation.
     b. Irrigate eyes, instill artificial tears or patch.
  2. Nose—trauma or infection in nose or nasopharynx may cause meningitis.
     a. Observe for drainage of CSF.
     b. Clean and lubricate nares; do not clean inside nostrils.
     c. Change nasogastric tube at intervals.
  3. Mouth—mouth breathing contributes to drying and crusting excoriation of mucous membranes, which may contribute to aspiration and respiratory tract infections.
     a. Examine the mouth daily with a good light.
     b. Clean teeth, gums, mucous membranes, tongue, and uvula to prevent crusting and infection; lubricate lips.
     c. Inspect for retained food in the mouth of patients who have facial paralysis; follow with mouth care.
  4. Ear—drainage of CSF from the ear indicates damage to the base of the brain and a danger of meningitis.
     a. Inspect ear for drainage of CSF.
     b. Loosely cover ear with sterile, dry dressing.
H. Maintain optimal positioning and movement.
  1. Prevent further trauma.
     a. Maintain body alignment, support head and limbs when turning, logroll.
     b. Do not flex or twist spine or hyperextend neck if spinal cord injury suspected.
  2. Positioning.
     a. Disuse of muscle leads to contractures, osteoporosis, and compromised venous return.
     b. Maintain and support joints and limbs in most functional anatomic position.
     c. Avoid improper use of knee gatch or pillows under knee.
  3. Avoid complete immobility.
     a. Perform ROM (against resistance if able), weight bearing, tilt table.
     b. Encourage self-help.
I. Provide psychosocial support for patient and family.
  1. Assume that an unconscious patient can hear; frequently reassure and explain procedures to the patient.
  2. Encourage family interaction.
J. Institute safety precautions.
  1. Use siderails at all times.
  2. Remove dentures and dental bridges.
  3. Remove contact lenses.
  4. Avoid restraints.
  5. Do not leave unattended when unstable for more than 15 to 30 minutes.

Head Injury

Definition: Head injury is a trauma to the skull resulting in varying degrees of injury to the brain by compression, tension, and/or shearing force.

Etiology

A. Auto accidents—acceleration/deceleration.
B. Falls, assaults, missiles, blunt objects.

Craniocerebral Injuries

A. Concussion—violent jarring of brain within skull; temporary loss of consciousness.
B. Contusion—bruising, injury of brain.
   1. Acceleration—slower moving contents of cranium strike bony prominences or dura (coup).
   2. Deceleration—moving head strikes fixed object and brain rebounds, striking opposite side of cranium (contrecoup).
C. Hemorrhage.
   1. Epidural hematoma—most serious; hematoma between dura and skull from tear in meningeal artery; forms rapidly.
   2. Subdural hematoma—under dura due to tears in veins crossing subdural space; forms slowly.
   3. Subarachnoid hematoma—bleeding into subarachnoid space.
   4. Intracerebral hematoma—usually multiple hemorrhages around contused area.
D. Fracture—linear, depressed, compound, comminuted.

Clinical Manifestations

A. Impaired level of consciousness, or unconsciousness; confusion.
B. Headache, nausea, vomiting.
C. Pupillary changes—epsilateral dilated pupil.
D. Changes in vital signs, reflecting increased intracranial pressure or shock.
E. Vasomotor or sensory losses.
F. Rhinorrhea, otorrhea, nuchal rigidity.
G. Overt scalp, skull trauma.

Nursing Management

A. Primary nursing goal is to recognize, prevent, and treat complications.

B. Maintain adequate respiratory exchange—increased CO_2 levels increase cerebral edema.
C. Assess and treat cerebral edema and increased intracranial pressure.
   1. Awaken the patient as completely as possible for assessment.
   2. See section on increased ICP (p. 32).
D. Monitor temperature.
E. Control pain and restlessness.
   1. Avoid morphine, a respiratory depressant which might increase ICP.
   2. Use codeine or other mild, safe analgesic.
F. Monitor and treat seizure activity.
G. Assess and treat other complications.
   1. Shock—significant cause of death.
   2. Cranial nerve paralysis.
   3. Rhinorrhea (fracture ethmoid bone) and otorrhea (temporal).
      a. Check discharge—bloody spot surrounded by pale ring; positive testtape reaction for sugar.
      b. Do not attempt to clean nose or ears.
      c. Do not suction nose.
      d. Instruct patient not to blow his nose.
   4. Ear—drainage of CSF from the ear indicates damage to the base of the brain and a danger of meningitis.
      a. Inspect ear for drainage of CSF.
      b. Loosely cover ear with sterile, dry dressing.
H. Prevent infection.
   1. High risk of meningitis, abscess, osteomyelitis, particularly in presence of rhinorrhea, otorrhea.
   2. Maintain strict asepsis.
I. Prevent complications of immobility.

Spinal Cord Injury

Definition: Partial or complete disruption of nerve tracts and neurons resulting in paralysis, sensory loss, altered reflex activity, and autonomic nervous system dysfunction.

Assessment of level of injury: A neurological examination for motor, sensory, and reflex loss is done from head to toe. The last cord segment in which normal motor, sensory, and reflex can be demonstrated is labeled "level of injury," i.e., "C_5 level of injury" means neurofunction is intact for C_5 but not C_6.

Etiology

A. Trauma associated with cord damage is usually related to vertebra fracture resulting from severe hyperflexion, extension, or rotation.

B. Common traumas.
   1. Automobile and motorcycle accidents.
   2. Sports and industrial injuries.
   3. Falls and crushing injuries.
   4. Gunshot or stab wounds.

C. Other conditions associated with spinal cord pathology.
   1. Infections, tumors.
   2. Disruption of blood supply to cord—thrombus.
   3. Degenerative diseases.
   4. Congenital or acquired anomalies—spina bifida, myelomeningocele.

Pathophysiology of Traumatic Spinal Cord Injury

A. Improper handling and transport may result in extension of cord damage.

B. Vascular disruption, biochemical changes, and direct tissue damage cause pathology associated with trauma.
   1. Inflammatory process leads to edema and neuronal dysfunction.
   2. Ischemia and hypoxia due to vasoconstriction, edema, and hemorrhage.
   3. Hypoxia of gray matter stimulates release of catecholamines which increases hemorrhage and necrosis.

C Systems affected.
   1. Spinal shock—absence of reflexes slightly above and completely below level of lesion.
      a. Temporary condition: lasts days to months.
      b. Initial flaccid paralysis, absent reflexes, loss of sensation, loss of urinary and bowel retention, hypotension (especially positional).
   2 Degree of sensory, motor, and reflex loss depends upon severity of cord damage.
   3. Autonomic dysfunction—absence of sweating below lesion, orthostatic hypotension, fluctuations in temperature, neurogenic bowel and bladder, and paralytic ileus.
   4. Respiratory insufficiency or failures occur in injuries above C_4 due to lack of diaphragm innervation.

D. Classification of cord involvement.
   1. Functional deficiencies.
      a. Quadriplegia (tetraplegia)—all four extremities functionally involved—cervical injuries (C_1 through C_8).
      b. Paraplegia—both lower extremities functionally involved—thoracic-lumbar region (T_1 through L_4).
   2. Partial or complete cord damage.
      a. Complete cord transection.
         (1) All voluntary motor activity below injury is permanently lost.
         (2) All sensation dependent on ascending pathway of segment is lost.
         (3) Reflexes may return if blood supply to cord below injury is intact.
      b. Incomplete injuries.
         (1) Motor and sensory loss varies and is dependent on degree of incompleteness.
         (2) Extent of reflex dysfunction dependent on location of neurological deficit.
      c. Central cord syndrome—leg function returns, arm function does not, as damage has occurred to peripheral cord which innervates arms.
      d. Brown-Séquard's syndrome—one side of cord damaged resulting in paralysis on one side of body and loss of sensation on the other side.
   3. Upper and lower motor neuron damage.
      a. Upper motor neuron originates in cerebral cortex and terminates at anterior horn cell in cord.
         (1) Post-spinal shock reflexes return resulting in spastic paralysis. No reflex return if blood supply to cord is lost.
         (2) Spasms and reflexes used to retrain activities of daily living—bowel evacuation and bladder control.
      b. Lower motor neuron begins at anterior horn cell and becomes part of peripheral nerve to muscle, motor side of reflex arc.
         (1) Aflexia continues, flaccid paralysis.
         (2) Usually cauda equina injuries.

Nursing Management

A. Emergency care—suspect spinal cord injury if neurological deficits are present in extremities.
   1. Immobilize entire body, especially head and neck; do not flex head.
   2. Transport log fashion with sufficient help.
   3. Maintain open airway and adequate ventilation—high cervical injuries can cause complete paralysis of muscles for breathing; observe for signs of respiratory failure.

B. Primary nursing goals.
   1. Prevent further injury or complications.
   2. Maintain optimal body functioning.
   3. Begin rehabilitation while patient is immobilized (see p. 35).

C. Immobilize patient, as ordered, to allow fracture healing and prevent further injury.
   1. Stryker frame permits change of position between prone and supine.
      a. Maintain optimal body alignment.
      b. Place patient in center of frame without flexing or twisting.
      c. Position arm boards, footboards, and canvas.
      d. Turn; reassure patient while turning.
      e. Free all tubings; secure bolts and straps.
   2. Regular hospital beds used in many rehabilitation centers.
   3. Halotraction with body cast allows early mobilization.
   4. Soft and hard collars and back braces used about six weeks post-injury.
   5. Maintain skeletal traction, if part of treatment.
      a. Cervical tongs for hyperextension (Crutchfield, Gardner-Wells, Vinke).
         (1) Apply traction to vertebral column by attaching weights to pair of tongs.
         (2) Insert tongs into outer layer of parietal area of skull.
      b. Facilitates moving, turning of patient while maintaining spine immobilization.
      c. Observe site of insertion for redness or drainage, alignment and position of traction, and pressure areas.

D. Take neurological assessment: note changes in muscle tone, motor movement, sensation, bladder and bowel function, presence or absence of sweating, temperature, and reflexes.

E. Monitor autonomic nervous system disturbances.
   1. Heart, lung, and bowel sounds for complications, such as embolus, ileus.
   2. Temperature fluctuations—unable to adapt to environmental changes or infection-related.
      a. Excessive perspiration causes dehydration.
      b. Absence of perspiration leads to hyperthermia.

F. Postural hypotension and syncope occur when head is elevated.
   1. Apply ace bandage or teds.
   2. Administer ephedrine p.o. one-half hour before patient is to get up.

G. Autonomic hyperreflexia (or dysreflexia).
   1. Signs and symptoms: extreme hypertension, flushing, bradycardia, headache (usually occipital), sweating, diplopia, convulsions.
   2. Caused by full bowel or bladder, urinary infection, kidney stones.
   3. Provide immediate treatment.
      a. Catheterize bladder or manually evacuate bowel.
      b. May administer parasympatholytic (Banthine) or ganglionic blocking agent (Hyperstat, Apresoline).
      c. If patient is lying down and fracture status permits, immediately elevate the head of bed or elevate patient to sitting position.
   4. Control factors that precipitate episode so it will not recur.
      a. Set up regular bowel and bladder programs.
      b. Apply nupercainal ointment prior to rectal stimulation.
      c. Administer alpha-adrenergic blocking agents (phenoxybenzamine) b.i.d.
   5. Prevent infections.
      a. Administer prophylactic antibiotics while on catheterizations.
      b. Evaluate elevated temperatures for urinary or respiratory infection.
   6. Prevent circulatory complications.
      a. Turn entire body every two hours. Give range-of-motion exercises to extremities.
      b. Apply ace bandages and teds to legs.
      c. Monitor for edema, thrombus, and emboli; provide prompt anticoagulant therapy if needed.
      d. Do not overhydrate based on blood pres-

sure (normal B.P. is 100/60 or below).

7. Maintain optimal positioning.
   a. Logroll with firm support to head, neck, spine, and limbs; do not allow neck flexion.
   b. Maintain good body alignment with 10 degree flexion of knees, heels off mattress or canvas, and feet in firm dorsiflexion.
   c. During convalescence, provide cervical collar, tilt table, wheelchair, braces, parallel bars.

8. Promote optimal physical activity.
   a. Provide physical therapy, exercises, range of motion.
   b. Encourage independent activity within limitations.
   c. Provide extensive program of rehabilitation and self-care.

9. Maintain integrity of the skin.
   a. Turn every two hours and check skin.
   b. Do not administer I.M. medication below a lesion due to impaired circulation and potential skin breakdown.
   c. Provide elastic stockings to improve circulation in legs.
   d. Later, instruct patient how to look for and prevent injury; reinforce the necessity for self-care.
   e. Provide prompt treatment of pressure areas.

10. Promote adequate nutrition, fluid, and electrolyte balance.
    a. Provide diet adequate in protein, vitamins, calories and bulk; limit milk.
    b. Avoid citrus juices which alkalize the urine, contributing to infection and renal calculi.
    c. Avoid gas-forming foods.
    d. Monitor calcium, electrolyte, and hemoglobin levels.
    e. Restrict fluids if patient is on intermittent catheterization.

11. Establish optimal bladder function.
    a. During spinal shock, bladder is atonic with urinary retention; danger of overdistention, stretching.
    b. Possible reactions.
       (1) Hypotonic, retention with overflow—sacral reflex center injury (lower motor neuron).
       (2) Hypertonic, sudden reflex voiding—injury above sacral area (upper motor neuron).
    c. Check for bladder distention, voiding, incontinence, and symptoms of infection.
    d. Provide aseptic intermittent catheterizations—prophylactic antimicrobials (nitrofurantoin).
    e. Prevent urinary tract infection, calculi.
       (1) Monitor urinary residuals.
       (2) Take periodic bladder and kidney function studies—I.V.P., cystogram.
    f. Initiate bladder retraining.
       (1) Hypertonic—sensation of full bladder, trigger areas, regulation of fluid intake.
       (2) Hypotonic—manual expression of urine (Crede).
    g. Administer medications to treat incontinence.
       (1) Hypertonic—propantheline bromide, diazepam.
       (2) Hypotonic—bethanechol chloride.

12. Establish optimal bowel function.
    a. Incontinence and paralytic ileus occur with spinal shock; later, incontinence, constipation, impaction.
    b. For severe distention, administer neostigmine methylsulfate and insert rectal tube, which decompresses intestinal tract.
    c. Give enema only if necessary. Excessive amount of fluid distends bowel. Manual evacuation is preferred.
    d. Initiate bowel retraining.
       (1) Record bowel habits before and after injury.
       (2) Provide well-balanced diet with bulky foods.
       (3) Encourage fluid intake.
       (4) Provide stool softeners, bulk producers, mild laxative.
       (5) Encourage the development of muscle tone.
       (6) Administer suppository (glycerin or Dulcolax) as indicated.
       (7) Emphasize importance of a regular, consistent routine.

H. Provide psychological support to patient and family.
   1. Support patient and family through grief process.

2. Promote sustained therapeutic relationships.
3. Provide diversionary activities, socialization.
4. Promote independence; teach patient to problem-solve.
5. Give encouragement and reassurance but never false hope.
6. Encourage family involvement in care.
7. Provide sexual counseling if needed.
   a. Patient should be aware of his sexual abilities post-injury.
   b. Role perception may need expansion.
8. During rehabilitation stage, provide employment counseling if needed.

Disorders of the Neurologic System

Cerebral Vascular Accident (CVA)

Definition: Cerebral vascular accident is a sudden focal neurological deficit due to cerebral vascular disease and is the most common cause of brain disturbances.

Etiology

A. Thrombosis.
B. Embolism.
C. Hemorrhage.
D. Compression or spasm.

Pathophysiology

A. Blood supply to brain via carotid and vertebral-basilar arteries.
B. Interruption of blood supply causes cerebral anoxia.
C. Cerebral anoxia longer than ten minutes to a localized area of brain causes cerebral infarction (irreversible changes).
D. Surrounding edema and congestion causes further dysfunction.
E. Lesion in cerebral hemisphere (motor cortex, internal capsule, basal ganglia) results in manifestations on the contralateral side.
F. Permanent disability unknown until edema subsides. Order in which function may return: facial, swallowing, lower limbs, speech, arms.

Clinical Manifestations

A. Depend on site and size of involved area.

1. Appear suddenly with embolism.
2. More gradually with hemorrhage and thrombosis.

B. Generalized—headache; hypertension; changes in level of consciousness, convulsions; vomiting, nuchal rigidity, slow bounding pulse, Cheyne-Stokes respirations.
C. Focal—upper motor lesion in motor cortex, and pyramidal tracts: hemiparesis, hemiplegia, central facial paralysis, language disorders, cranial dysfunction, conjugate deviation eyes toward lesion, flaccid hyporeflexia (later, spastic hyperreflexia).
D. Residual manifestations
   1. Lesion left hemisphere.
      a. Usually dominant, containing speech center; right hemiplegia; aphasia, expressive and/or receptive.
      b. Behavior is slow, cautious, disorganized.
   2. Lesion right hemisphere.
      a. Left hemiplegia; spatial-perceptual deficits.
      b. Behavior is impulsive, quick; unaware of deflcits; poor judge of abilities, limitations; neglect of paralyzed side.
   3. General.
      a. Memory deficits; reduced memory span; emotional lability.
      b. Visual deficits such as homonomous hemianopia (loss of half of each visual field).
      c. Apraxia (can move but unable to use body part for specific purpose).

Nursing Management

A. Initial nursing goal is to support life and prevent complications; long term goal is rehabilitation.
B. Give oxygen as needed.
C. Maintain patent airway and ventilation—elevate head of bed 20 degrees unless shock is present.
D. Monitor clinical status to prevent complications.
   1. Neurological.
      a. Include assessment of recurrent CVA, increased intracranial pressure, bulbar involvement, hyperthermia.
      b. Continued coma is a negative prognostic sign.
   2. Cardiovascular—shock and arrhythmias, hypertension.
   3. Lungs—pulmonary emboli.

E. Maintain optimal positioning.
1. During acute stages, quiet environment and minimal handling may be necessary to prevent further bleeding.
2. Upper motor lesion—spastic paralysis, flexion deformities, external rotation of hip.
3. Positioning schedule—two hours on unaffected side; twenty minutes on affected side; thirty minutes prone, b.i.d.-t.i.d.
4. Complications common with hemiplegia—frozen shoulder, footdrop.
F. Maintain skin integrity.
G. Maintain personal hygiene—encourage self-help.
H. Promote adequate nutrition, fluid, and electrolyte balance.
1. Encourage self-feeding.
2. Food should be placed in unparalyzed side of mouth.
I. Promote elimination.
1. Bladder control may be regained within three to five days.
2. Retention catheter may not be part of treatment regime.
3. Offer urinal or bedpan every two hours day and night.
J. Provide emotional support.
1. Behavior changes as consciousness is regained—loss of memory, emotional lability, confusion, language disorders.
2. Reorient, reassure, and establish means of communication.
K. Promote rehabilitation to maximal functioning.
1. Comprehensive program—begin during acute phase and follow through convalescence.
2. Guidelines to assist patient with lesion left hemisphere.
   a. Do not underestimate ability to learn.
   b. Assess ability to understand speech.
   c. Act out, pantomime communication; use patient's terms to communicate; speak in normal tone of voice.
   d. Divide tasks into simple steps; give frequent feedback.
3. Guidelines to assist patient with lesion right hemisphere.
   a. Do not overestimate abilities.
   b. Use verbal cues as demonstrations; pantomimes may confuse.
   c. Use slow, minimal movements and avoid clutter around patient.
   d. Divide tasks into simple steps; elicit return demonstration of skills.
   e. Promote awareness of body and environment on affected side.

Epilepsy

Definition: Epilepsy is a paroxysmal disturbance in consciousness, with autonomic, sensory, and/or motor dysfunction; a manifestation of excessive neuronal discharge in the brain.

Etiology

A. Congenital, genetic, trauma, tumors, infections, vascular disorders, ischemia, metabolic disorders, degenerative disorders.
B. Divisions.
1. Symptomatic—secondary to probable cause.
2. Idiopathic—primary epilepsy without definite, known cause.

Common Types of Seizures—Clinical Manifestations

A. Grand mal.
1. Generalized—symmetrical tonic-clonic movements without focal onset and involving entire body.
2. May be preceded by brief aura which is specific for each patient—visual, olfactory, auditory, gustatory, somatic.
3. Epileptic cry (result of expired air passing a spastic glottis) precedes loss of consciousness and convulsion.
4. Brief tonic phase—rigid extension, muscle contraction; cessation of respirations; dilated pupils; cyanotic, clenched jaws.
5. Clonic phase follows—alternating forceful contraction and relaxation of muscles creating jerking movements, stertorous respirations, excessive salivation, incontinence; tongue may be bitten.
6. Postictal period after seizure subsides—fatigue, headache, confusion, sleepiness, residual neurological deficit, amnesia.
B. Petit mal.
1. Generalized—frequent episodes of loss of consciousness for a matter of seconds, and cessa-

tion of motor activity; patient may stop in mid-sentence, stare, and then go on.

2. No change in muscle tone; falls seldom occur although patient may stagger in gait or lose bladder control.

3. Most common in children and may affect child's progress in school if attacks are frequent.

C. Myoclonic seizure.

1. Generalized—brief involuntary contractions of muscles in trunk or upper extremities.

2. Relatively rare and of short duration.

3. May occur in petit mal or grand mal.

D. Akinetic seizures.

1. Generalized—sudden brief loss of motor tone; "drop" attack.

2. May lose consciousness and recover immediately.

3. May occur in petit-mal or grand mal.

E. Jacksonian (focal) seizures.

1. Partial seizure with motor or sensory symptoms.

2. Precipitated by lesion in motor or sensory cortex area and may be identified by characteristics of the seizure.

3. Motor seizures begin with convulsion in particular body part and may progress centrally to other body parts.

4. Loss of consciousness occurs if seizures become generalized.

5. Sensory seizures involve transient numbness, tingling in particular areas.

F. Psychomotor seizures.

1. Partial seizure with complex symptoms involving the temporal lobe.

2. Brief lapses of consciousness; mental clouding lasts for a longer period than in petit mal and may continue after attack.

3. Wide range of automatic, repetitive motor activity occurs which may be inappropriate or asocial.

4. Psychic phenomena; visual, auditory, or olfactory hallucinations may occur.

5. Patient has amnesia during and after attack.

Nursing Management

A. Protect patient from injury.

1. Remove objects from environment which may cause injury.

2. Stay with patient during seizure.

3. Pad bedrails.

4. Lay patient flat and provide protection from injury if out of bed.

5. Have padded tongue blade available.

6. Avoid use of restraints.

7. If tongue is caught in teeth, do not attempt to pry mouth open.

B. Observe and record seizure pattern.

1. Precipitating factors.

2. Presence of aura.

3. Duration of unconsciousness.

4. Pattern of seizure activity.

5. Incontinence.

6. Postictal state.

C. Promote physical and mental health.

1. Establish regular routines for eating, sleeping, and physical activity (activity tends to inhibit seizure activity).

2. Provide appropriate safeguard during exercise and sports.

3. Avoid alcohol, stress, exhaustion.

4. Foster self-esteem and confidence; avoid overprotection of patient.

5. Instruct patient and family regarding epilepsy and its control.

   a. Recognition of impending seizure and care during seizure.

   b. Importance of carrying identification card in case of emergency.

   c. Organizations which provide services such as the National Epilepsy League and the National Association to Control Epilepsy.

D. Administer and monitor effects of medications.

1. Medication regime may require periods of adjustments and/or a combination of drugs.

2. Reinforce necessity for taking medication regularly as prescribed; observe response, any side effects, or seizure activity.

3. Administer anticonvulsants.

   a. Most common drugs: phenobarbital, diphenylhydantoin (Dilantin), mephenytoin (Mesantoin), primidone (Mysoline), paramethadione (Paradione), trimethadione (Tridione), ethosuximide (Zarontin).

   b. Usually used in combination—decreased dosage lessens side effects.

c. Hydantoins are used for grand mal seizures.

4. Monitor toxic side effects of drugs: drowsiness, skin rash, nervousness, nausea, ataxia, gum hyperplasia, blood dyscrasias.

5. Avoid sudden withdrawal of drugs—may precipitate status epilepticus.

E. Treatment of complicating status epilepticus.

1. Successive major convulsions without regaining consciousness between attacks are a medical emergency and may cause death.

2 Most frequent cause is sudden withdrawal of anticonvulsants; other factors include insulin, electroshock, acute infections, trauma, and metabolic disorders.

3. Management.

a. Maintain open airway.

b. Terminate seizure with I.V. medications: phenobarbital, diphenylhydantoin, diazepam, paraldehyde.

c. Monitor patient's condition frequently for complications: cardiac, respiratory, and neurological status; arterial blood gases, glucose, calcium, electrolytes, renal and liver function.

Multiple Sclerosis

Definition: Multiple sclerosis is a chronic, slowly progressive, noncontagious, degenerative disease of the CNS.

Etiology

A. Definite cause unknown; question autoimmunity or virus.

B. Incidence is greater in colder climate, equal in the sexes, and usually occurs between ages twenty to forty years.

Pathophysiology

A. Demyelination of nerve fibers within long conducting pathways of spinal cord and brain.

B. Lesions (plaques) are irregularly scattered—disseminated.

C. Destruction of myelin sheath creates patches of sclerotic tissue, degeneration of the nerve fiber, and disturbance in conduction of sensory and motor impulses.

D. Initially the disease is characterized by periods of remission with exacerbation and variable manifestations, followed by irreversible dysfunction.

E. Clinical course may extend over ten to twenty years.

Clinical Manifestations

A. Highly variable, depending on area of involvement: sensory fibers, motor fibers, brainstem, cerebellum, internal capsule.

B. Weakness, paralysis, incoordination, ataxia, intention tremor, bladder/bowel retention or incontinence, spasticity, numbness, tingling, analgesia, anesthesia, loss of position sense, impaired vision (diplopia, nystagmus), dysphagia, impaired speech, emotional instability, impaired judgment.

C. Charcot's triad—nystagmus, intention tremor, scanning speech.

Nursing Management

A. Avoid precipitation of exacerbations.

1. Avoid fatigue, stress, infection, overheating, chilling.

2. Establish regular program of exercise and rest.

3. Provide a balanced diet.

B. Administer and assess effects of medications.

1. Steroids—hasten remission.

2. Antibiotics, muscle relaxants, mood elevators, vitamin B.

C. Promote optimal activity.

1. Moderation in activity with rest periods.

2. Physical and speech therapy.

3. Diversionary activities, hobbies.

4. During exacerbation, patient is usually put on bed rest.

D. Promote safety.

1. Sensory loss—regulate bath water; caution with heating pads; inspect skin for lesions.

2. Motor loss—avoid waxed floors, throw rugs; provide rails and walker.

3. Diplopia—eye patch.

E. Promote regular elimination—bladder/bowel training programs.

F. Provide education and emotional support to patient and family.

1. Encourage independence and realistic goals; assess personality and behavior changes; observe for signs of depression.

2. Provide instruction and assistive devices; provide information about services of the National Multiple Sclerosis Society.

G. Assess and prevent potential complications.
   1. Most common: urinary tract infection, calculi, decubitus ulcers.
   2. Common cause of death: respiratory tract infection, urinary tract infection.
   3. Contractures, pain due to spasticity, metabolic or nutritional disorders, regurgitation, depression.

Parkinson's Disease

Definition: Parkinson's disease is a degenerative disease resulting in dysfunction of the extrapyramidal system.

Etiology

A. Idiopathic.
B. Other possible causes: atherosclerosis, drug induced, postencephalitis.

Pathophysiology

A. Degeneration of basal ganglia due to depleted concentration of dopamine.
B. Depletion of dopamine correlated with degeneration of substantia nigra (midbrain structures which are closely related functionally to basal ganglia).
C. Loss of inhibitory modulation of dopamine to counterbalance cholinergic system and interruption of balance-coordinating extrapyramidal system.
D. Slowly progressive disease with high incidence of crippling disability; mental deterioration occurs very late.

Clinical Manifestations

A. Five stages: unilateral, bilateral, impaired balance, fully developed severe disease, confinement to bed or wheelchair.
B. Initial symptoms.
   1. Slowing of all movements.
   2. Aching shoulders and arms.
   3. Monotonous and indistinct speech.
   4. Writing becomes progressively smaller.
C. Major symptoms.
   1. Tremor at rest—especially in hands and fingers (pill-rolling).
      a. Increases when stressed or fatigued.
      b. May decrease with purposeful activity or sleep.
   2. Rigidity—blank facial expression (mask-like).
      a. Drooling, difficulty swallowing or speaking.
      b. Short, shuffling steps with stooped posture.
      c. Propulsive gait.
      d. Immobility of muscles in flexed position, creating jerky cogwheel motions.
      e. Loss of coordinated and associated automatic movement and balance.
   3. Akinesia—difficulty initiating voluntary movement.
D. Associated symptoms—autonomic dysfunction: lacrimation, incontinence, decreased sexual function, intractable constipation.

Treatment

A. Medication—usual therapy.
B. Surgical intervention.
   1. Stereotactic surgery to reduce tremor.
      a. Pallidotomy—lesion in globus pallidus.
      b. Thalamotomy—lesion in ventrolateral portion of thalamus.
   2. Implantation of electrodes through burr holes into target area of brain; creation of lesion with high-frequency coagulation probe.

Nursing Management

A. Primary goals are to reduce muscle tremor and rigidity and prevent complications.
B. Administer and assess effects of medications.
   1. Anticholinergic drugs—inhibit action of acetylcholine; side effects include dry mouth, dry skin, blurring vision, urinary retention, and tachycardia.
   2. Antihistamines—reduce tremor and anxiety; side effect is drowsiness.
   3. Antispasmotics (Artane, Kemadrin) improve rigidity but not tremor.
   4. Levodopa.
      a. Reduces akinesia, tremor, and rigidity.
      b. Passes through blood-brain barrier.
      c. Side effects.
         (1) Anorexia, nausea, and vomiting (administer drug with meals or snack; avoid coffee, which seems to increase nausea).

(2) Postural hypotension, dizziness, tachycardia, and arrhythmias (monitor vital signs; caution patient to sit up or stand up slowly; have patient wear support stockings).

(3) Psychic manifestations of agitation, aggression, hypersexuality, depression, insomnia, paranoia, acute delirium (may need to reduce dose or give chlorpromazine).

(4) Confusion, hyperkinesis, or abnormal, exaggerated involuntary movements may occur.

5. Sinemet.
   a. Combination of carbidopa and levodopa.
   b. Inhibits enzyme dopadecarboxylase, allowing levodopa to reach brain.
   c. Has fewer side effects than levodopa.
   d. No dietary limitations.

6. Avoid the following drugs:
   a. Phenothiazines, reserpine, pyridoxine, vitamin B_6 (block desired action of levodopa).
   b. Monamine oxidase inhibitors—precipitate hypertensive crisis.
   c. Methyldopa—potentiate effects.

C. Maintain regular patterns of elimination.
   1. Constipation is often a problem due to side effects of medications, reduced physical activity, muscle weakness, and excessive drooling.
   2. Provide stool softeners, suppositories, mild cathartics.

D. Promote physical therapy and rehabilitation.
   1. Provide preventive, corrective, and postural exercises.
   2. Institute massage and stretching exercises, stressing extension of limbs.
   3. Encourage daily ambulation—have patient lift feet up when walking and avoid prolonged sitting.
   4. Facilitate adaptation for activities of daily living and self-care; encourage rhythmic patterns to attain timing; foster independence; utilize special aids and devices.
   5. Remove hazards that might cause falls.

E. Provide education and emotional support to patient and family.
   1. Remember, intellect is usually not impaired.
   2. Assess changes in self-consciousness, body image, sexuality, moods.

3. Instruct patient to avoid emotional stress and fatigue, which aggravate symptoms.
4. Instruct patient to avoid foods high in vitamin B_6 and monamine oxidase.

F. Provide appropriate nursing care following surgery.

Myasthenia Gravis

Definition: Myasthenia gravis is a neuromuscular disease characterized by marked weakness and abnormal fatigue of voluntary muscles.

Etiology

A. Unknown; question autoimmune reaction.
B. Patients with myasthenia have a high incidence of thymus abnormalities and frequently have systemic lupus erythematosus.

Pathophysiology

A. Basic pathology is a defect in transmission of nerve impulse at the myoneural junction, the junction of motor neuron with muscle.
B. Normally, acetylcholine is stored in synaptic vesicle of motor neurons to skeletal muscles.
C. Defect may be due to:
   1. Deficiency in acetylcholine/excess acetylcholinesterase.
   2. Defective motor-end plate and/or nerve terminals.
   3. Decreased sensitivity to acetylcholine.
D. Muscles supplied by bulbar nuclei (cranial nerves) are commonly involved.
E. Muscle involvement usually progresses from ocular to oropharyngeal, facial, proximal muscles, respiratory muscles.
F. Generally there is no muscle atrophy or degeneration; there may be periods of exacerbations and remissions.

Clinical Manifestations

A. Symptoms are related to progressive weakness and fatigue of muscles when used; muscles generally are strongest in the morning.
B. Eyes are affected first: ptosis, diplopia, and eye squint.
C. Impaired speech; dysphagia; drooping facies; diffi-

culty chewing, closing mouth, or smiling; breathing difficulty and hoarse voice.

D. Respiratory paralysis and failure.

E. Diagnosis confirmed with Tensilon test.
1. Positive for myasthenia—improvement in muscle strength.
2. Negative—no improvement or even deterioration.

Nursing Management

A. Primary goals are to improve neuromuscular transmission and prevent complications.

B. Administer and assess effects of medications.
1. Anticholinesterase drugs increase levels of acetylcholine at myoneural junction.
   a. Neostigmine, pyridostigmine, ambenonium —main difference is duration of effect.
   b. Edrophonium (Tensilon)—is a rapid, brief-acting anticholinesterase for testing purposes.
   c. Side effects.
      (1) Related to effects of increased acetylcholine in parasympathetic nervous system: sweating, excessive salivation, nausea, diarrhea, abdominal cramps; possibly bradycardia or hypotension.
      (2) Excessive doses lead to cholinergic crisis—atropine given as cholinergic blocker.
   d. Nursing measures.
      (1) Give medication exactly on time, thirty minutes before meals.
      (2) Give medication with milk and crackers to reduce GI upset.
      (3) Observe therapeutic or any toxic effects; monitor and record muscle strength and vital capacity.
2. Steroids.
   a. Suppress immune response.
   b. Usually the last resort after anticholinesterase and thymectomy.
3. The following drugs must be avoided.
   a. Streptomycin, kanamycin, neomycin, gentamicin—block neuromuscular transmission.
   b. Ether, quinidine, morphine, curare, procainamide, innovar, sedatives—aggravate

weakness of myasthenia.

C. Provide appropriate nursing measures following thymectomy surgery (significant correlation with improvement or remission of the disease).

D. Monitor patient's condition for complications.
1. Vital signs.
2. Respirations—depth, rate, vital capacity, ability to deep breathe and cough.
3. Swallowing—ability to eat and handle secretions.
4. Muscle strength.
5. Speech—provide method of communication if patient unable to talk.
6. Bowel and bladder function.
7. Psychological status.

E. Promote optimal activity.
1. Plan short periods of activity and long periods of rest.
2. Time activity to coincide with maximal muscle strength.
3. Encourage normal activities of daily living
4. Encourage diversionary activities.

F. Provide education and emotional support for patient and family.
1. Give reassurance and facts about the disease, medications and treatment regime, importance of adhering to medication schedule, difference between myasthenic/cholinergic crisis, and emergency care.
2. Instruct patient to avoid infection, stress, fatigue, and over-the-counter drugs.
3. Instruct patient to wear identification medal and carry emergency card.
4. Provide information about services of Myasthenia Gravis Foundation.

G. Prevent myasthenic or cholinergic crisis.
1. Myasthenic crisis.
   a. Acute exacerbation of disease may be due to rapid, unrecognized progression of disease; failure of medication; infection; or fatigue or stress.
   b. Myasthenic symptoms—weakness, dyspnea, dysphagia, restlessness, difficulty speaking.
2. Cholinergic crisis.
   a. Cholinergic paralysis with sustained depolarization of motor-end plates is due to over-medication with anticholinesterase.

b. Symptoms similar to myasthenic state—restlessness, weakness, dysphagia, dyspnea.

c. Cholinergic symptoms—fasciculations, abdominal cramps, diarrhea, nausea, vomiting, salivation, sweating, increased bronchial secretion.

3. Tensilon test to differentiate crises, as symptoms are similar.

a. Give Tensilon; if strength improves, it is symptomatic of myasthenic crisis and the patient needs more medication; if weakness is more severe, it is symptomatic of cholinergic crisis and overdose has occurred.

b. Be prepared for emergency with atropine, suction, and other emergency equipment for respiratory arrest.

4. Crisis with respiratory insufficiency—patient cannot swallow secretions and may aspirate.

a. Maintain bed rest.

b. May require endotracheal or tracheostomy tube to assist with ventilation.

c. Monitor vital capacity, blood gases.

d. Give atropine and may hold anticholinesterase (cholinergic).

e. Begin anticholinesterase (myasthenic).

Meningitis

Definition: Meningitis is an acute infection of the pia-arachnoid membrane.

Etiology

Organisms: meningococcus, staphylococcus, streptococcus, pneumococcus, Haemophilus influenzae, tuberculous.

Pathology

A. Inflammatory reaction with exudate in pia-arachnoid.

B. Degeneration of nerve cells.

C. Congestion of adjacent brain tissue.

Clinical Manifestations

A. Painful, stiff neck—nuchal rigidity, Kernig's and Brudzinski's signs.

B. Severe headache, photophobia.

C. Fever.

D. Irritability, stupor, coma, possible seizures.

Nursing Management

A. Maintain open airway.

B. Treat the infective organism—antimicrobial therapy by intravenous route.

C. Isolate for 48 hours after antibiotic therapy is initiated.

D. Assess and treat increased intracranial pressure or seizures.

E. Control body temperature.

F. Provide adequate fluid and electrolyte balance.

G. Provide quiet environment.

H. Prevent complications of immobility.

Cranial Nerve Disorders

Trigeminal Neuralgia (Tic Douloureux)

Definition: Trigeminal neuralgia is a sensory disorder of the fifth cranial nerve, resulting in severe, recurrent paroxysms of sharp facial pain along the distribution of the trigeminal nerve. Etiology and pathology are unknown; incidence is higher in older women.

Clinical Manifestations

A. Trigger points on the lips, gums, nose, or cheek.

B. May be stimulated by a cold breeze, washing, chewing, food/fluids of extreme temperatures.

C. Pain is limited to those areas innervated by the three branches of the fifth nerve.

Treatment

A. Medical.

1. Massive doses of B_{12}.

2. Inhalation: 10-15 drops of trichloroethylene on cotton.

3. Anticonvulsants: Dilantin and Tegretol.

4. Alcohol injections to produce anesthesia of the nerve.

B. Surgical.

1. Peripheral—avulsion of supraorbital, infraorbital, or mandibular division.

2. Intracranial.

a. Division of the sensory nerve root for permanent anesthesia.

b. Patient may experience numbness, stiffness, or burning after surgery.

c. Microsurgery allows for selective sectioning of the fifth nerve.

d. Pain and temperature fibers are destroyed, and sensation of touch and corneal reflex are preserved.

Nursing Management

A. Observe and record characteristics of the attack.

B. Record method patient uses to protect face.

C. Avoid extremes of heat or cold.

D. Provide small feedings of semi-liquid or soft food.

E. Administer medication and record effects.

F. Complete postoperative care.

1. Ophthalmic nerve—patient needs protective eye care.

2. Maxillary and mandibular nerves.

a. Avoid hot food and liquids which might burn.

b. Instruct patient to chew on unaffected side to prevent biting denervated portion.

c. Encourage patient to visit dentist within six months.

d. Provide frequent oral hygiene to keep the mouth free of debris.

Bell's Palsy (Facial Paralysis)

Definition: Bell's palsy is a lower motor neuron lesion of the seventh cranial nerve, resulting in paralysis of one side of the face.

Etiology

A. Etiology and pathology unknown.

B. May occur secondary to intracranial hemorrhage, tumor, meningitis, trauma.

C. Majority of patients recover in a few weeks without residual effects.

Clinical Manifestations

A. Flaccid muscles.

B. Shallow nasolabial fold.

C. Inability to raise eyebrows, frown, smile, close eyelids, or puff out cheeks.

D. Upward movement of eye when attempting to close eyelid.

E. Loss of taste in anterior tongue.

Nursing Management

A. Palliative.

B. Analgesics, steroids, physiotherapy, support of facial muscles, protection of cornea.

C. Provide face sling to prevent stretching of weakened muscles and loss of tone.

D. Promote active facial exercises to prevent loss of muscle tone.

E. Instruct to chew food on unaffected side.

F. Provide attractive, easy-to-eat foods to prevent anorexia and weight loss.

G. Provide special eye care to prevent keratitis.

H. Reassure and support.

Meniere's Disease

Definition: Meniere's disease consists of dilatation of the endolymphatic system causing degeneration of the vestibular and cochlear hair cells.

Etiology

A. Unknown.

B. Possible causes may include allergies, toxicity, localized ischemia, hemorrhage, viral infection, and edema.

Clinical Manifestations

A. Chronic, recurrent process.

B. Severe vertigo, nausea, vomiting, nystagmus, and loss of equilibrium.

C. Impaired hearing and tinnitus.

Treatment

A. Bedrest during acute attack.

B. Drug therapy.

1. Vasodilators (nicotinic acid).

2. Diuretics, antihistamines (Benadryl).

3. Sedatives.

C. Diet therapy.

1. Low sodium.

2. Lipoflavonoid vitamin supplement.

3. Restricted fluid intake.

D. Surgical division of vestibular portion of nerve or

destruction of labyrinth may be necessary for severe cases.

Nursing Management

A. Prevent injury during attack.
B. Provide side rails if necessary.
C. Keep room dark when photophobia present.
D. Assist with ambulation if necessary
E. Assess nutritional needs, which will depend on amount of nausea and vomiting.

Bulbar Palsy

Definition: Bulbar palsy is a dysfunction of the 9th and 10th cranial nerves. The disease is secondary to tumors, infections, vascular, or degenerative diseases.

Pathophysiology

A. Glossopharyngeal paralysis—absent gag reflex; difficulty swallowing, increased salivation; anesthesia posterior palate and base of tongue.
B. Vagal paralysis—difficulty with speech, breathing, and regurgitation.

Nursing Management

A. Medical/surgical treatment is directed toward underlying cause.
B. Nursing care is directed toward prevention of complications.
   1. Aspiration.
      a. Keep suction equipment at bedside.
      b. Elevate head of bed.
      c. Provide oral care.
   2. Difficulty breathing.
      a. Maintain open airway.
      b. Assess breathing capability.
      c. Have emergency equipment available.
   3. Difficulty swallowing.
      a. Avoid milk products and sticky carbohydrates.
      b. Use small cup instead of straw.
   4. Depression and fear.

Guillain-Barré Syndrome

Definition: An acute infectious neuronitis of cranial and peripheral nerves.

Etiology

A. Unknown.
B. Occurs at any age but increased incidence between thirty and fifty years of age.
C. Both sexes equally affected.
D. Presyndrome patients may report a mild upper respiratory infection or gastroenteritis.

Clinical Manifestations

A. Initial symptom weakness of lower extremities.
B. Gradual progressive weakness of upper extremities and facial muscles (24–72 hours).
C. Paresthesias may precede weakness.
D. Respiratory failure occurs in some patients.
E. Sensory changes are usually minor, but in some cases severe impairment of sensory information occurs.
F. Recovery is a slow process.

Nursing Management

A. No specific treatment available.
B. Carefully observe for respiratory paralysis and inability to handle secretions.
C. Prevent complications of immobility.
D. Provide appropriate diversion.
E. Reassure patient, especially during paralysis period.

Management of the Patient in Pain

Classification of Pain Fibers

A. Class A—large myelineated—fast pain.
B. Class B—smaller unmyelineated.
C. Class C—unmyelinated—slow pain.

The Experience of Pain

A. Pain source—direct causative factor.
B. Stimulation of pain receptor—mechanical, chemical, thermal, electrical, ischemic.
C. Pain pathway.
   1. Sensory pathways through dorsal root, ending on second order neuron in posterior horn.
   2. Afferent fibers cross over to anterolateral path-

way, ascend in lateral spinothalmic tract to thalamus.

3. Fibers then travel to postcentral gyrus in parietal lobe.

D. Pain perception—thalamus/awareness and parietal/integration.

E. Pain interpretation—cerebral cortex; delayed response influenced by previous experiences, culture, existing physical/psychological state.

F. Reactions—psychic and/or physiologic.

Types of Pain

A. Superficial—localized, shorter duration, sharp sensation.

B. Deep pain—long duration, diffuse, dull aching quality; associated autonomic responses, musculoskeletal tension, nausea.
1. Visceral—internal organs.
2. Somatic—neuromuscular, segmental distribution.
3. Referred—area stimulated (deep) and area pain referred to (superficial) are innervated by nerve fibers arising from same segment of spinal cord.
4. Secondary to skeletal muscle.

C. Central pain—autonomic reflex pain syndrome.
1. Causalgia—lesion peripheral nerve.
2. Phantom—after amputation.
3. Central—lesion in CNS, affecting pain pathway.

D. Psychogenic—due to emotional factors without anatomic or physiological explanation.

Assessment of Pain

A. Onset, location, intensity, character, precipitating factors, associated manifestations, alleviating or aggravating factors, duration.

B. Previous experiences, treatment.

Nursing Management

A. Nursing measures.
1. Assess pain before treating.
2. Give reassurance, reduce anxiety and fears.
3. Offer distraction.
4. Give comfort measures—positioning, rest, elevation, heat/cold applications; protect from painful stimuli.
5. Massage—but never massage calf due to danger of emboli.
6. Administer pain medication as needed—monitor therapeutic, toxic dose, and side effects.

B. Gate theory control.
1. Pain impulses can be modulated by a transmission blocking action within CNS.
2. Large diameter cutaneous pain fibers can be stimulated (rubbing, scratching) and may inhibit smaller diameter excitatory fibers and prevent transmission of that impulse.
3. Cerebral cortical mechanisms that influence perception and interpretation may also inhibit transmission.

C. Dorsal column stimulator—stimulation of electrodes at dorsal column of spinal cord by patient-controlled device to inhibit pain.

D. Analgesics—alter perception, threshold, and reaction to pain.

E. Anesthesia—block pain pathway.

F. Local nerve block.

G. Neurosurgical procedures—interrupt sensory pathways; usually also affect pressure and temperature pathways.
1. Neurectomy—interrupt cranial or peripheral nerves.
2. Sympathectomy—interrupt afferent pathways (ganglia).

Cardiovascular System

The heart and the circulatory system, both systemic and pulmonary, comprise one of the most essential parts of the body; failure to function results in death of the organism. The heart is a hollow muscular organ which, by contracting rhythmically, effectively pumps the blood through the circulatory system to nourish all of the body tissues.

Anatomy

Gross Structure of Heart

Layers

A. Pericardium.
  1. Fibrous pericardium—fibrous sac.
  2. Serous pericardium—allows for free cardiac motion.
B. Epicardium—covers surface of heart, extends onto great vessels, and becomes continuous with inner lining of pericardium.
C. Myocardium—muscular portion of heart.
D. Endocardium—thin, delicate layer of tissue that lines cardiac chambers and covers surface of heart valves.

Chambers of the Heart

Definition: The heart is a muscular organ divided by a septum into two halves—right or venous chamber and left or arterial chamber. The heart is actually a pump considered as two pumps working in sequence.

A. Right chamber.
  1. Right atrium (receiving chamber) is a thin-walled, distensible, low-pressure collecting chamber for systemic venous system.
    a. Inlets: superior vena cava, inferior vena cava, coronary sinus, thebesian veins.
    b. Outlet: tricuspid valve.
  2. Right ventricle (RV)—(ejecting chamber) is a thin-walled, low-pressure crescent-shaped pump for propelling blood into low resistance pulmonary circuit.

    a. Normal thickness: 0.5 cm.
    b. Type of contraction: bellows pumping action.
    c. Outlet: pulmonic valve into pulmonary artery.
B. Left chamber.
  1. Left atrium—(receiving chamber) is a thin-walled, medium-pressure collecting chamber for pulmonary venous system.
    a. Inlets: four pulmonary veins.
    b. Outlet: mitral valve.
  2. Left ventricle (LV)—(ejecting chamber) is a thick-walled, high-pressure cone-shaped pump for propelling blood into high resistance systemic circuit.
    a. Normal thickness: 1.5 cm.
    b. Type of contraction: spiral squeezing-type pumping action.
    c. Outlet: aortic valve into aorta.

Valves

Definition: Valves are strong membranous openings that provide one-way flow of blood.

A. Atrioventricular valves prevent backflow of blood from the ventricles to the atria during systole.
  1. Tricuspid—right heart valve.
    a. Three cusps or leaflets.
    b. Free edges anchored to papillary muscles in right ventricle by chordae tendineae which contract when the ventricular walls contract.
  2. Mitral—left heart valve.
    a. Two cusps or leaflets.
    b. Free edges anchored to papillary muscles in left ventricle by chordae tendineae which contract when the ventricular walls contract.
B. Semilunar valves prevent backflow from the aorta and pulmonary arteries into the ventricles during diastole.
  1. Pulmonic—three cusps or leaflets.
  2. Aortic—three cusps or leaflets; orifices for coronary arteries arise from wall of aorta above two of the three cusps.
C. Valves function passively.
  1. Close when backward pressure pushes blood backward.

2. Open when forward pressure forces blood in a forward direction.

Conduction System

Definition: Conduction system is composed of specialized tissue that allows rapid transmission of electrical impulses through the myocardium.

A. Sinoatrial (SA) node—main pacemaker of heart in which normal rhythmic self-excitatory impulse is generated.
   1. 60 to 100 electrical impulses/min.
   2. External control is through autonomic nervous system.
      a. Sympathetic—speeds rate.
      b. Parasympathetic—slows rate.
   3. Nerves affect cardiac pumping in two ways.
      a. Changes heart rate.
      b. Changes strength of contraction of the heart.
   4. Intrinsic automaticity—initiates electrical impulses automatically.
B. Internodal tracts—transmission of electrical impulses through atria from sinoatrial node to atrioventricular node.
C. Atrioventricular (AV) node—contains delay tissue to allow atrial contraction to eject blood into ventricle before ventricular contraction.
D. Bundle of His—conducts the electrical impulse from the atria into ventricles.
E. Left and right bundles to Purkinje's fibers—conduct impulses to all parts of the ventricles.

Coronary Blood Supply

Definition: Coronary blood flow is regulated by local blood flow regulation in the heart in response to needs of cardiac muscle for oxygen; thus, the rate of oxygen consumption is the major factor in determining coronary blood flow.

A. Arteries.
   1. Right coronary artery supplies mainly the right ventricle but also part of the left ventricle.
   2. Left coronary artery divides into two branches and supplies mainly the left ventricle.
      a. Left anterior descending artery.
      b. Circumflex artery.
B. Veins—generally parallel arterial system.

1. Coronary sinus veins empty into right atrium.
2. Thebesian veins empty into right atrium.

Gross Structure of Vasculature

Arteries

A. The function of the arteries is to transport blood under high pressure to the body tissues.
   1. Arteries have strong vascular walls.
   2. Blood flows rapidly to the tissues.
B. Precapillary sphincters.
   1. Offer most resistance to blood flow located between arterioles and capillary bed.
   2. Allow for local autoregulation of blood flow to meet individual tissue needs.
C. Arteriovenous shunts.
   1. Bypass capillary bed and provide direct communication between arterioles and venules.
   2. Normally are closed but in shock states are open.

Capillaries

Definition: Capillaries are minute passageways with the function of exchanging fluid and nutrients between blood and interstitial spaces.

A. Capillary walls are thin and permeable to small substances.
B. Blood flow is slowest in capillaries.

Veins

Definition: The primary function of veins is to act as conduits for transport of the blood from tissues back to the heart.

A. Venous system.
   1. Pressure is low.
   2. Walls are thin but muscular.
   3. Walls are able to contract or expand thereby storing a small or large amount of blood.
B. Factors influencing venous return.
   1. Muscle contraction.
   2. Gravity.
   3. Competent valves.
   4. Respiration.
      a. Inspiration increases venous return.
      b. Expiration decreases venous return.
   5. Compliancy of right heart.

Physiology

Regulation of Cardiac Function

Contraction

Definition: The heart muscle utilizes chemical energy to do the work of contraction—a shortening or increase in tension.

A. The sarcomere is the unit of contraction and contains the proteins actin and myosin.

B. Sliding theory of contraction.
    1. Actin slides inward on myosin causing shortening of sarcomere, resulting in systole.
    2. When calcium is used up, actin and myosin slide apart, resulting in diastole.

C. Each cardiac cell is composed of many sarcomeres.

Cardiac Muscle Principles

A. Frank-Starling law: the greater the heart is filled during diastole, within physiological limits, the greater the quantity of blood pumped into the aorta and pulmonary artery.
    1. The heart can pump a large amount of blood or a small amount depending on the amount that flows into it from the veins.
    2. It automatically adapts to whatever the load may be (within physiological limits of the total amount heart can pump).
    3. Decreased blood volume reduces cardiac output since muscle length is too short to perform properly.
    4. Factors affecting cardiac output.
        a. Length of diastole.
        b. Force of contractility of cardiac muscle.
        c. Venous return.
        d. Peripheral vascular resistance (blood pressure).
        e. Ventricular compliancy (distensibility).

B. All-or-none principle: cardiac muscle either contracts or does not contract when stimulated.

C. Two phases of contractility.
    1. Isometric—increasing tension while maintaining length of muscle fiber.
    2. Isotonic—shortening muscle fiber while tension remains constant.

Mechanisms of Cardiac Reserve

A. Response of increased stretch to increased force of contraction.

B. Alteration of heart rate.

C. Hypertrophy to meet increased demands.

D. Blood flow redistribution via sympathetic nervous system response.

Properties of Cardiac Cells

A. Automaticity: ability to initiate an electrical impulse without external stimuli.
    1. SA node.
    2. Junctional tissue.
    3. Bundle branch—Purkinje system.
    4. Phases—depolarization and repolarization.

B. Conductivity—ability to transmit electrical impulse.

C. Contractility—ability of muscle to shorten with electrical stimulation.

D. Excitability (irritability)—ability to be stimulated.

E. Refractoriness—ability to return cells to resting state.
    1. Absolute refractory period—no amount of electrical stimulation will cause contraction.
    2. Relative refractory period—strong enough electrical stimulation will cause contraction.

Pulse

Definition: Pulse is the rhythmic dilation of an artery caused by the contraction of the heart.

A. Pulse deficit—difference between apical and radial, due to weakened or ineffective contraction of heart.

B. Pulse pressure—difference between systolic and diastolic pressure.

C. Factors influencing blood pressure.
    1. Force of heart contractions.
    2. Volume of blood; for example, hemorrhage will decrease blood pressure.
    3. Diameter and elasticity of blood vessels; for example, arteriosclerosis will increase blood pressure.
    4. Viscosity of blood; for example, polycythemia vera will increase blood pressure.

Autonomic Nervous System Control

Cardiac Muscle

A. Sympathetic nervous system (adrenergic)—innervates all cardiac muscle.

1. Secretes epinephrine and norepinephrine.
2. Response to stress—excitatory.
   a. Increases SA node rate.
   b. Increases conductivity, especially AV node.
   c. Increases contractility of cardiac muscle.
B. Parasympathetic nervous system (cholinergic)—innervates all but ventricular muscle.
   1. Mediated via vagus nerve.
   2. Secretes acetylcholine.
   3. Maintenance of homeostasis—"brake of heart."
      a. Decreases SA node rate.
      b. Decreases conductivity, especially AV node.
      c. Decreases atrial contractility.

Systemic Blood Vessels

A. Sympathetic nervous system.
   1. Effect is vasoconstriction of blood vessels through action mainly on precapillary sphincter (one exception: vasodilation of coronary arteries).
   2. To obtain dilatation: sympathetic system inhibited.
B. Parasympathetic nervous system.
   1. Usually predominates so blood vessels not vasoconstricted.
   2. Effect is vasodilation in certain areas such as cerebrum, salivary glands and lower colon.

Baroreceptor Reflex

A. Most important circulatory reflex is called baroreceptor reflex.
   1. Initiated by baroreceptors (also called pressoreceptors) located in walls of large systemic arteries.
   2. Rise in pressure results in baroreceptors transmitting signals to CNS to inhibit sympathetic action.
   3. Other signals, in turn, sent to circulation reduce pressure back toward normal.
   4. Result is decreased heart rate, vasodilation, and decreased blood pressure.
B. Effect of decreased blood pressure.
   1. Sympathetic stimulation overrides vagal response.
   2. Result is increased heart rate, vasoconstriction, and increased blood pressure.

Other Chemical Controls of Blood Pressure

A. Kidney.
   1. Adrenal cortex releases aldosterone, causing sodium and water to be reabsorbed. This increases blood volume and blood pressure
   2. Juxtaglomerular apparatus releases renin which causes vasoconstriction to increase blood pressure.
B. Antidiuretic hormone (vasopressin)—acts on kidney tubules to reabsorb water, thereby increasing blood volume and blood pressure.
C. Histamine release.
   1. Arterioles dilate.
   2. Venules constrict.
D. Capillary fluid shift mechanism; for example, hemorrhage and decreased blood pressure allow capillaries to reabsorb interstitial fluid.

Cardiovascular Disease

Evaluation of Cardiovascular System

History of Patient

A. Pain—character, location, duration, intensity, precipitating or aggravating factors, and relieving factors.
   1. Ischemic type of pain: pain of angina or myocardial infarction.
   2. Pain from dissecting aorta: tearing or burning.
   3. Pericarditis pain: aggravated by deep breathing, supine position, turning from side to side.
B. Dyspnea—shortness of breath, feeling of inability to get enough air.
   1. Exertional dyspnea (DOE): occurs while exercising.
   2. Orthopnea: occurs while in a reclining position.
   3. Paroxysmal nocturnal dyspnea (PND): interrupts patient's sleep.
   4. Differentiations.
      a. Tachypnea: increase in rate of breathing.
      b. Hyperpnea: increase in depth and rate of breathing.
C. Fatigue—result of diminution of cardiac output.
D. Palpitations—patient aware of heartbeat, often with rapid heart rates.

E. Syncope—transient loss of consciousness due to inadequate cerebral blood flow.

F. Hemoptysis—cough accompanied by bloody sputum.

G. Edema—collection of fluid in interstitial spaces.

H. Condition of extremities—color, temperature, skin nutrition, presence of petechiae, presence of dryness or clamminess.

Physical Examination of Patient

A. Inspection and palpation of venous and arterial pulses.
  1. Veins.
     a. Neck veins—jugular venous pulsations.
        (1) Indirect measurement: height in cm. of jugular venous distention from sternal notch when patient is at a 45-degree angle.
        (2) Direct measurement through a central venous catheter placed in superior vena cava or right atrium.
     b. Arm and hand veins.
     c. Leg and feet veins.
  2. Arteries.
     a. Central (precordial).
     b. Peripheral pulses.
        (1) Presence or absence; character.
           (a) Small, weak: low stroke volume (for example, aortic stenosis); narrowed pulse pressure (for example, cardiac tamponade); increased systemic vascular resistance (for example, arteriosclerosis).
           (b) Large, bounding: water-hammer (for example, aortic insufficiency).
        (2) Pulsus alternans: alteration in height of pulse wave, usually in left ventricle failure.
        (3) Pulsus paradoxus: systolic blood pressure drop greater than 10 mm. Hg during inspiration, as in cardiac tamponade.

B. Auscultation.
  1. Heart sounds—frequency, pitch, intensity, duration, timbre.
     a. S_1—closure of mitral and tricuspid valve.
     b. S_2—closure of aortic and pulmonic valve.

c. S_3 and S_4—gallop sounds, usually indicative of heart failure.
   (1) S_3—rapid filling of ventricle in early diastole; may be heard normally; after S_2.
   (2) S_4—coincides with atrial contraction due to poorly compliant ventricle; prior to S_1.
d. Murmurs: turbulence of blood flow through narrowed lumen or incompetent valve, classified by their timing.
   (1) Systolic.
      (a) Mitral and tricuspid insufficiency.
      (b) Aortic and pulmonic stenosis.
      (c) Patent foramen ovale.
      (d) Ventricular septal defect.
   (2) Diastolic.
      (a) Mitral and tricuspid stenosis.
      (b) Aortic and pulmonic insufficiency.
e. Pericardial friction rub—timed with heart rate.
  2. Arteries.
     a. Measurement of blood pressure—indirect via cuff.
        (1) Both arms.
        (2) Both legs initially.
     b. Presence of bruits: turbulence of blood flow usually around obstruction.

Diagnostic Procedures

Electrocardiogram

Definition: An electrocardiogram (ECG or EKG) is a record of the electrical activity of the heart reflected by changes in electrical potential at skin surface.

A. Purpose—to determine types and extent of heart damage, cardiac irregularities, electrolyte imbalances.
  1. Nonpainful procedure but should be explained to patient.
  2. Relaxation of patient important to reduce electrical interference from muscle movement.

B. ECG interpretation.
  1. Normal cardiac cycle.
     a. P wave—atrial depolarization.
     b. P-R interval—atrial depolarization and atrial systole.

c. QRS wave—ventricular depolarization.

d. ST segment—ventricular repolarization and ventricular systole.

e. T wave—ventricular repolarization and ventricular diastole.

2. Interpretation of ECG.

a. Determine heart rate by calculating atrial rate (P-P interval) and ventricular rate (R-R interval). Normal pulse 60–100.

b. Determine regularity of rhythm (atrial and ventricular).

c. Measure P-R interval to determine conduction time in atria and AV junction (0.16–0.20 sec.).

d. Measure QRS duration to determine ventricular conduction (0.16 sec.). There are six complexes.

e. Measure Q-T interval (rate of 70 in one minute occurring 0.36 seconds apart).

f. Check configuration and placement of P waves, QRS complex, ST segment, and T wave.

g. Summarize findings to obtain interpretation.

3. Etiology of arrhythmias:

a. Heart failure, electrolyte imbalance, acidosis or alkalosis, hypoxemia, drugs, hypotension, emotional stress.

b. Precipitating or contributing diseases—infection, hypovolemia, anemia, thyroid disorders.

Cardiac Catheterization

A. Right placement: venous system into right atrium into right ventricle into pulmonary artery into pulmonary wedge position.

B. Left placement.

1. Retrograde entry into left ventricle via arterial puncture site into ascending aorta into left atrium and left ventricle.

2. Transeptal puncture via femoral vein into right atrium through interatrial septum into left atrium.

C. Data collected.

1. Pressure measurements of various chambers.

a. Shape of pressure waveforms determines type of pathology.

b. Evaluation of mean pressure indicates severity of pathology.

2. Blood oxygen measurements.

3. Determination of cardiac output.

D. Nursing management.

1. Monitor vital signs.

a. Observe for possible orthostatic hypotension due to reaction to dye, NPO, supine position.

b. Notify M.D. if B/P decreased 10 percent or arrhythmias are present.

c. Observe for signs of shock.

d. Observe for possible cardiac tamponade.

2. Check peripheral pulses distal to puncture site—indication of occlusion.

3. Observe puncture site for bleeding, edema, inflammation, and color.

E. Observe for complications.

1. Respiratory complications—hypoventilation, hypoxia, pulmonary edema, and pneumonia.

2. Hemorrhage—apply pressure dressing and elevate extremity.

3. Thrombosis at cannulations site—notify M.D. if peripheral pulse is lost or if numbness, tingling, or coldness occurs.

4. Arrhythmias—if PVC's present, notify M.D.

5. Cardiac tamponade—notify M.D. immediately.

Other Diagnostic Procedures

A. Routine chest films—silhouette of heart, chambers, and great vessels observed on X-ray.

B. Fluoroscopy—heart, lung, and vessel movements viewed on luminescent X-ray film screen in darkened room.

C. Angiography.

1. Injection of radiopaque compounds into circulation at appropriate sites.

2. Cineangiograms—dynamics of passage of contrast agent through vascular tree starting at injection site.

3. Angiograms into chamber.

4. Selective coronary arteriography.

D. Phonocardiogram—heart sounds translated into electrical energy by a microphone and recorded.

E. Echocardiography—records high-frequency sound vibrations.

Congestive Heart Failure

Definition: Congestive heart failure results from insufficient cardiac output to meet the metabolic needs of the body.

Left Ventricular Failure

Definition: Congestion occurs mainly in the lungs due to inadequate ejection of the blood into the systemic circulation.

Pathophysiology

A. Decreased cardiac output to systemic circulation.
B. Congestion in pulmonary circuit due to inability of left heart to accommodate pulmonary vein input.
C. Decrease in oxygen and carbon dioxide diffusion.

Etiology

A. Arteriosclerotic heart disease.
B. Acute myocardial infarction.
C. Tachyarrhythmias.
D. Myocarditis.
E. Increased circulating blood volume.
F. Valvular heart disease.

Clinical Manifestations

A. Symptoms primarily related to pulmonary system.
   1. Dyspnea, orthopnea, PND, DOE.
   2. Moist cough.
   3. Wheezing.
   4. Rales.
   5. Cyanosis or pallor.
   6. Increased pulmonary artery and/or pulmonary wedge pressure.
B. Other symptoms.
   1. Anxiety, weakness, and fatigue.
   2. Behavior changes.
   3. Palpitations and diaphoresis.
   4. Gallop rhythm—presence of S_3 or S_4 or both.
   5. Arrhythmias and cardiomegaly.

Acute Pulmonary Edema

Definition: Acute pulmonary edema is an excessive quantity of fluid in the pulmonary interstitial spaces or in the alveoli usually following severe left ventricular decompensation.

Pathophysiology

A. The most common cause is greatly elevated capillary pressure resulting from failure of left heart and damming of blood in lungs.
B. Alveoli filled with fluid and bronchioles congested.
C. Retention of fluid resulting from reduced renal function.

Clinical Manifestations

A. Primary symptoms are moist rales and frothy sputum.
B. Severe anxiety—feelings of impending doom.
C. Marked dyspnea.
D. Stertorous breathing.
E. Marked cyanosis.
F. Profuse diaphoresis—cold and clammy.
G. Tachyarrhythmia.
H. Gallop rhythm (S_3, S_4, or both).
I. Cardiomegaly.
J. Marked increase in pulmonary artery and/or pulmonary capillary wedge pressure.
K. Increased CVP and neck vein distention in severe cases.

Right Ventricular Failure

Definition: Congestion occurs when the blood is not pumped adequately from the systemic circulation into the lungs.

Pathophysiology

A. Inability to handle systemic venous return.
B. Systemic congestion.

Etiology

A. Any disease resulting in left ventricular failure.
B. Pulmonary embolism.
C. Fluid overload.
D. COPD.
   1. Pulmonary hypertension.
   2. Cor pulmonale.

E. Cirrhosis—portal hypertension.

Clinical Manifestations

A. Symptoms primarily related to systemic system.
  1. Peripheral edema in dependent parts (necessitating good skin care and positioning).
     a. Feet and legs.
     b. Sacrum, back, buttocks.
  2. Ascites.
  3. Anorexia and nausea due to congestion in liver and gut.
  4. Weight gain.
  5. Oliguria during day and polyuria at night.
  6. Hepatomegaly, liver congestion.
B. Other symptoms.
  1. Jugular venous distention at 45°
  2. Arrhythmias.
  3. Increased central venous pressure.

Nursing Management for CHF

A. Treat underlying cause.
B. Reduce pain and anxiety.
  1. Morphine sulfate.
  2. Physical and emotional rest; also decrease oxygen requirements.
C. Improve pulmonary ventilation and oxygenation.
  1. Oxygen—cannula usually better than mask since patient already feels as though he cannot breathe.
  2. IPPB—also decreases venous return.
  3. Bronchodilator therapy.
  4. Mechanical ventilation (pulmonary edema).
D. Reduce pulmonary and systemic venous congestion and blood volume.
  1. Diuretics.
  2. Fluid and sodium restriction—also prevents fluid retention.
  3. Rotating tourniquets (pulmonary edema).
  4. Fowler's position.
E. Monitor drug administration when digitalizing patient (improves myocardial contractility).
F. Prevent fluid retention.
  1. Record intake and output.
  2. Weigh daily.
G. Treat arrhythmias.
H. Provide support to patient.
I. Teach patient principles of care.
J. Contraindicated drugs.
  1. Propranolol (Inderal).
  2. Methyldopa (Aldomet).
  3. Guanethidine (Ismelin).

Complications of Treatment

A. Digitalis toxicity.
B. Electrolyte imbalance from diuretics, especially decreased potassium.
C. Pulmonary emboli from tourniquets and bed rest.
D. Oxygen toxicity, especially with COPD patients.

Cardiogenic Shock

Definition: Cardiogenic shock is a severe form of pump failure resulting in decreased cardiac output.

Pathophysiology

A. Decreased contractility.
B. Decreased arterial blood pressure causing sympathetic nervous system stimulation which produces vasoconstriction and opens AV shunts.
C. Oxygen transport impairment causes increased anaerobic metabolism.
  1. Result is increased lactate.
  2. Increased lactate causes metabolic acidosis.
D. Decreased cerebral perfusion.
E. Decreased renal perfusion, resulting in renal failure.
F. Myocardial ischemia leads to further pump failure.

Etiology

A. Massive myocardial infarction with 40 to 60 percent muscle damage.
B. Severe hemorrhage.
C. Inadequate blood supply, compensatory mechanism, or changes in microcirculation leads to clinical manifestations.

Clinical Manifestations

A. Cold and clammy skin—vasoconstriction.
B. Tachycardia—(weak and feeble) sympathetic stimulation.
C. Decreased blood pressure to less than 80 mm. Hg systolic.

D. Restlessness—cerebral anoxia due to decreased cardiac output.
E. Decreased urinary output to less than 30 ml./hour —poor renal perfusion, secretion of aldosterone retaining sodium and water.
F. Pallor or cyanosis.
G. Hypoxia.
H. Acidemia.
I. Signs of CHF due to inadequate ventricular emptying.
J. Differentiation from hypovolemic shock.
   1. Pulmonary capillary wedge pressure is increased in left ventricular failure in cardiogenic shock.
   2. Pulmonary capillary wedge pressure is normal or low in hypovolemic shock.

Nursing Management

A. Early recognition important.
B. Monitor improvement of left ventricular function.
   1. Digitalis (controversial)—increases oxygen consumption.
   2. Isuprel (beta stimulator)—increases oxygen consumption.
   3. Dopamine (precursor of norepinephrine)— causes vasoconstriction peripherally but increases renal perfusion.
C. Monitor Nipride.
   1. Drug lowers peripheral vascular resistance.
   2. Decreases cardiac workload and increases tissue perfusion.
D. Maintain arterial blood pressure—vasopressors.
   1. Intraarterial blood pressure monitoring necessary to obtain accurate reading.
   2. Cuff pressures may be low (false reading) due to vasoconstriction and poor Korotkov sounds.
E. Maintain ventilation and oxygenation.
   1. Airway.
   2. Oxygen.
   3. Artificial ventilation if necessary.
   4. Arterial blood gases, to determine effect of therapy.
F. Establish fluid and electrolyte acid-base balance.
   1. Replace fluid if hypovolemic.
   2. Correct acidosis—for example, $NaHCO_3$.
   3. Maintain urinary output—greater than 30 cc./hour.

G. Control pain and restlessness—I.V. analgesia most effective.
H. Treat arrhythmias—result of tissue hypoxia, acidosis, electrolyte imbalance, underlying disease, and drug therapy.
I. Decrease cardiac workload.
   1. Physical and emotional rest.
   2. Psychological support.
   3. Comfortable position—flat with pillow, or semi-Fowler's position if patient has difficulty breathing.

Major Valve Defects

Mitral Stenosis

Definition: Mitral stenosis is a progressive thickening of the valve cusps which results in the narrowing of lumen of mitral valve.

Etiology

A. Rheumatic heart disease.
B. Congenital disease.

Clinical Manifestations

A. Asymptomatic until valve area is less than 1.5 sq. cm. and tachycardia or atrial fibrillation occurs.
B. Signs of decreased cardiac output.
C. Left, and then right, ventricular failure.
D. Accentuated S_1 and opening snap; diastolic murmur.
E. Complications.
   1. Atrial fibrillation.
   2. Subacute bacterial endocarditis.
   3. Thrombi formation.

Treatment

A. Surgical replacement of the mitral valve.
B. Valvotomy if no calcification of valve.

Nursing Management

A. Treat heart failure and arrhythmias.
B. Decrease cardiac workload.

C. Prevent and/or treat infections.

D. Monitor administration of anticoagulants for treatment and/or prevention of thrombi in patients with atrial fibrillation.

E. Provide emotional support to patient.

Mitral Insufficiency

Definition: Mitral insufficiency is distortion of the valve that allows backward flow of blood from ventricle to atrium.

Etiology

A. Rheumatic heart disease.

B. Congenital disease.

C. Bacterial endocarditis.

D. Rupture of chordae tendineae.

E. Rupture or dysfunction of papillary muscle.

F. Dilatation of left ventricle.

Clinical Manifestations

A. Evidence of left, then right, heart failure.

B. Decreased intensity of S_1; pansystolic murmur, S_3.

C. Atrial fibrillation.

D. Systemic emboli and hemoptysis uncommon.

Nursing Management

Same as for mitral stenosis.

Aortic Stenosis

Definition: Aortic stenosis is the narrowing of the aortic valve opening due to fibrosis and calcification. This results in inadequate ejection of blood from the left ventricle.

Etiology

A. Rheumatic heart disease.

B. Arteriosclerosis.

C. Congenital defect.

Clinical Manifestations

A. Dizziness and syncope.

B. Angina.

C. Symptoms of congestive heart failure.

D. Systolic murmur; decreased S_2; gallop rhythm.

E. Heart block due to calcification in upper interventricular system.

Treatment

A. Replacement with prosthetic valve.

B. Same treatment as for congestive heart failure.

Nursing Management

Same as for congestive heart failure (see p. 59).

Aortic Insufficiency

Definition: Aortic insufficiency occurs when the blood flows back into the ventricle from aorta. It is usually the result of aortic valve disease or aortic root disease.

Etiology

A. Rheumatic heart disease.

B. Congenital disease.

C. Bacterial endocarditis.

D. Syphilitic aortitis.

E. Rheumatoid aortitis.

F. Medial necrosis of aorta.

G. Arteriosclerotic and hypertensive dilatation of aortic root.

H. Dissecting aneurysm.

Clinical Manifestations

A. Left, then right, heart failure.

B. Pounding arterial pulse (Corrigan-type arterial pulse).

C. Diastolic blood pressure falls and systolic blood pressure remains normal or rises.

D. Diastolic murmur.

Treatment

Replacement with prosthetic valve.

Nursing Management

Same as for congestive heart failure.

Tricuspid Stenosis

Definition: Tricuspid stenosis is the progressive narrowing of valve lumen.

Etiology

A. Rheumatic heart disease with mitral valve involvement.

B. Congenital disease.

C. Bacterial endocarditis.

Clinical Manifestations

A. Evidence of systemic venous congestion.

B. Diastolic murmur.

Treatment

A. Same treatment as for CHF.

B. Valve replacement or valvotomy.

Nursing Management

Same as for congestive heart failure.

Tricuspid Insufficiency

Definition: Tricuspid insufficiency occurs when blood flows back into atrium from ventricle.

Etiology

A. Functional lesion resulting from disease, which produces heart dilatation and failure.

B. Organic—same as tricuspid stenosis.

Clinical Manifestations

A. Pansystolic murmur, S_3 accentuated during inspiration.

B. Symptoms of right-sided heart failure.

Coronary Artery Disease

Definition: Coronary artery disease occurs as the result of accumulation of fatty materials (lipids, cholesterol being primary one), which narrows the lumen of coronary arteries. Clinical manifestations of disease reflect ischemia to myocardium, resulting from inadequate blood supply to meet metabolic demands.

Etiology

A. Unknown.

B. Incidence is of epidemic proportion in U.S.

Contributing Factors

A. Major—most amenable to prevention and control.
   1. Diet—increased intake of cholesterol and saturated fats.
   2. Hypertension—aggravates atherosclerotic process.
   3. Cigarette smoking.

B. Other risk factors.
   1. Diabetes mellitus—accelerates atherosclerotic process.
   2. Males more prone to disease.
   3. Lack of exercise; sedentary living.
   4. Psychosocial tensions—may precipitate acute events.
   5. Obesity—susceptibility to hypertension, diabetes mellitus, hyperlipidemia.

Clinical Manifestations

A. Asymptomatic—silent myocardial infarction; development of collateral circulation.

B. Symptomatic.
   1. Congestive heart failure.
   2. Arrhythmias.
   3. Sudden death.
   4. Angina.
   5. Myocardial infarction.

Angina

Definition: Angina is a severe chest pain due to temporary inability of coronary arteries to meet oxygen needs of myocardium. Pathophysiology involves narrowing of lumen of coronary artery, usually by atherosclerotic process.

Precipitating Factors

A. Increased need for oxygen due to:
   1. Exertion and effort.
   2. Emotional upsets.
   3. Tachyarrhythmias.
   4. Overeating.
   5. Extremes of temperature, especially cold.
   6. Smoking.

B. Associated disease states—anemia, polycythemia, syphilitic heart disease, rheumatic heart disease, mitral and aortic stenosis, tachyarrhythmias, hypertension, hypotension, thyrotoxicosis, hypoglycemia.

Clinical Manifestations

A. Pain.
   1. Location: precordial, substernal.
   2. Character: compressing, choking, burning, squeezing, crushing heaviness.
   3. Radiation: left arm or right arm, jaw, neck, back.
   4. Duration: usually five to ten minutes, relieved by rest or nitroglycerin.
B. Dyspnea.
C. ECG changes (may not be any at rest).
   1. ST segment depression during pain.
   2. T wave depressed or inverted.
D. Ninety percent of the time there are no physical signs.

Nursing Management

A. Decrease oxygen demand of myocardium (current approach to therapy).
B. Provide patient instruction.
   1. Learn to live in moderation—physical activity should be sufficient to maintain general physical state, but short of causing angina.
   2. Avoid stress and emotional upset.
   3. Reduce caloric intake if overweight.
   4. Refrain from smoking.
   5. Decrease use of stimulants (coffee, tea, cola).
C. Primary medication—nitroglycerine.
   1. Short-acting nitrite.
      a. Dilates coronary arteries that are not atherosclerotic to increase blood flow to myocardium.
      b. Lessens cardiac work by decreasing venous return and decreasing peripheral vascular resistance.
   2. Use: relief of pain from myocardial ischemia.
   3. Side effects: hypotension, headache.
   4. Important factors.
      a. Effective sublingually only.
      b. Dosage (one to two tablets) may be repeated at five-minute intervals.
      c. Physician should be called if no relief in fifteen minutes.
      d. No limit to number taken in twenty-four hour period.
      e. Is not addictive.
      f. May be used prophylactically before engaging in activity known to precipitate angina.
      g. Must be stored in closed, dark glass container, avoiding light, heat, and moisture.
D. Other medications.
   1. Long-acting nitrites (Isordil, cardilate).
   2. Propranolol (Inderal).

Treatment

Coronary artery bypass surgery.

Myocardial Infarction

Definition: Myocardial infarction is the process by which cardiac muscle is destroyed due to interruption of or insufficient blood supply for a prolonged period, resulting in sustained oxygen deprivation.

Etiology

A. Atherosclerotic heart disease.
B. Coronary artery embolism.
C. Decreased blood flow with shock and/or hemorrhage.
D. Direct trauma.

Diagnosis

A. History (very important).
B. Serial ECG's to observe for changes which reflect area of involvement.
   1. ST elevation.
   2. Development of Q waves.
   3. T wave inversion.
C. Laboratory studies.
   1. Serum enzymes—released with death of tissue.
      a. CPK—most valuable measurement—level rises within 6 hours.
      b. LDH—level rises 6-8 hours, persists longer.
      c. SGOT—not specific to heart disease alone, but serial determinations are helpful.
   2. Increased white blood cells.
   3. Increased sedimentation rate.

Clinical Manifestations

A. Pain—similar to angina but usually more intense and longer in duration (thirty minutes or longer).
   1. Location: left precordial, substernal.

2. Character: crushing, vise-like, tightness, burning.
3. Radiation: jaw, back, arms.

B. Anxiousness—feeling of doom.
C. Dyspnea or orthopnea.
D. Nausea and vomiting.
E. Diaphoresis.
F. Pallor or cyanosis.
G. Arrhythmias.
H. Signs of congestive heart failure.

Nursing Management

A. Treat death-producing arrhythmias immediately.
B. Administer I.V. or I.M. narcotic analgesics, as ordered, to relieve pain and anxiety.
C. Provide physical rest and emotional support.
   1. Sedation, graduated activity.
   2. Use of commode and self-feed.
D. Administer oxygen via cannula.
E. Maintain patient on stool softeners and soft diet to prevent increased workload on heart.
F. Provide low fat, low cholesterol diet.
G. Rehabilitate patient to enable him to return to physical level according to cardiac capability.
   1. Planned exercise.
   2. Provide psychological support.
   3. Avoid stressful environment.
   4. Possible change of life style.
   5. Long-term drug therapy might include anti-arrhythmics, anticoagulants, and antihypertensives.

Complications

A. Arrhythmias.
B. Congestive heart failure.
C. Cardiogenic shock.
D. Thrombophlebitis.
E. Papillary muscle dysfunction.
F. Pericarditis.
G. Ventricular aneurysm or rupture (late complication) due to weakened area of myocardium as result of myocardial infarction.

Bacterial Endocarditis

Definition: Bacterial endocarditis is an infection of the lining of the heart caused by pathogenic micro-organisms.

Types

A. Acute—fulminating disease due to organisms engrafted on normal or diseased valve.
B. Subacute—slowly progressive disease on rheumatic or congenital lesion.

Clinical Manifestations

A. Fever, chills, diaphoresis, lassitude, anorexia.
B. Preexisting valve disease or surgery for valvular defects.
C. History of recent infection, dental work, cystoscopy, I.V. drug addiction.
D. Splenomegaly; petechiae on skin or mucous membranes; tender, red nodules on fingers, palms or toes; changing heart murmurs.
E. Systemic emboli.
F. Heart murmurs.

Nursing Management

A. Maintain intensive chemotherapy with antibiotic drugs.
B. Follow general nursing measures.
   1. Decrease cardiac workload.
   2. Ensure physical and emotional rest.
C. Anticoagulant therapy contraindicated because of danger of cerebral hemorrhage.

Pericarditis

Definition: Pericarditis is the inflammation of the pericardium.

Etiology

A. Frequently the result of transmural infarction.
B. Infection.
C. Hypersensitivity.
D. Trauma.

Clinical Manifestations

A. Pain—stabbing and knife-like; aggravated by supine position, turning from side to side.
B. Dyspnea, especially with deep inspiration.

C. Pericardial friction rub.
D. Complications.
    1. Pericardial effusion leading to tamponade.
    2. Constrictive pericarditis—prevents adequate diastolic filling of ventricles leading to decreased cardiac output.

Nursing Management

A. Treat symptoms with bed rest and salicylates.
B. Take vital signs and observe for complications following pericardiocentesis.

Cardiovascular Drugs Commonly Used

Digitalis

A. Effects.
    1. Increases contractile force of heart (positive inotropism) which increases cardiac output in failing heart.
    2. Slows heart rate.
        a. Direct effect.
        b. Increases vagal tone and decreases sympathetic tone as heart failure lessens.
    3. Slows conduction through AV node.
    4. Increases automaticity which may cause many arrhythmias.
B. Uses.
    1. Congestive heart failure—increases contractility which in CHF reduces oxygen needs, increases cardiac efficiency, and reduces heart size.
    2. Supraventricular tachyarrhythmias—slows ventricular rate by slowing conduction of impulses through AV node.
C. Dosage—individualized to patient and clinical situation (usually 0.25 mg. q.d.).
D. Precautions.
    1. Hypokalemia predisposition.
    2. Renal failure predisposition to digitalis toxicity, especially with preparation of Digoxin.
    3. Generally should not be given with AV block.
E. Major side effects.
    1. Cardiac.
        a. Arrhythmias, due to increased automaticity.
        b. Conduction disturbances—AV block.
    2. Gastrointestinal.

a. Anorexia.
b. Nausea and vomiting.
c. Diarrhea.
3. Others.
    a. Gynecomastia.
    b. Allergic reactions.

Antiarrhythmic Drugs: Quinidine, Pronestyl, Lidocaine

A. Effects.
    1. Increases recovery time of atrial and ventricular muscle.
    2. Decreases myocardial excitability.
    3. Increases conduction in cardiac muscle, Purkinje's fibers, and AV junction (exception: lidocaine).
    4. Decreases contractility (exception: lidocaine).
    5. Decreases automaticity.
B. Uses.
    1. Quinidine—atrial fibrillation, atrial flutter, supraventricular and ventricular tachycardia, premature systoles.
    2. Procainamide hydrochloride (Pronestyl)—premature ventricular systoles.
    3. Xylocaine (lidocaine)—ventricular tachyarrhythmias.
C. Side effects.
    1. Quinidine.
        a. Hypersensitivity, thrombocytopenia.
        b. Cinchonism—nausea, vomiting, diarrhea, tinnitus, vertigo, visual disturbances.
        c. Sudden death from ventricular fibrillation.
        d. Worsened congestive heart failure due to negative inotropism.
        e. Conduction disturbances (not used in patients with conduction disturbances).
    2. Pronestyl.
        a. Anorexia, nausea, vomiting, diarrhea.
        b. Systemic lupus erythematosus and agranulocytosis.
        c. Cardiac AV block (not used in patients with AV block).
        d. May be used in congestive heart failure due to less negative inotropic effect.
    3. Lidocaine.
        a. CNS disturbances—drowsiness, paresthesias, slurred speech, blurred vision, seizures, coma.

b. Cautious use in patients with liver disease or low cardiac output (metabolism of drug slowed).

Epinephrine (Adrenalin)

A. Effect: beta stimulation—increases heart rate and contractility.

B. Use: cardiac arrest most common.

Propranolol (Inderal)

A. Effect: blocks beta stimulation.
    1. Decreases heart rate and contractility; that is, it decreases oxygen consumption.
    2. Depresses automaticity of pacemakers and AV conduction.
    3. Produces bronchoconstriction.

B. Uses.
    1. To decrease ventricular rate from atrial flutter, fibrillation, and tachycardia.
    2. To suppress ectopic arrhythmias, especially ventricular arrhythmias.
    3. For angina.

C. Side effects—should not be used in AV block, bradycardia, congestive heart failure, or lung disease (bronchospasm).

Atropine

A. Effects: anticholinergic.
    1. Increases rate of SA node.
    2. Increases conduction through AV node.

B. Uses.
    1. Symptomatic sinus bradycardia.
    2. Partial AV block.

C. Side effects.
    1. Inability to void, especially with prostate enlargement.
    2. Dry mouth, skin, flushing, dilation of pupil.
    3. Decrease in bronchial secretions.

Dopamine (Intropin)—Precursor of Norepinephrine

A. Effects.
    1. Increases myocardial contractility.
    2. Causes mild vasoconstriction.
    3. Increases cardiac output and stroke volume.
    4. Dilates renal vessels.

B. Uses.
    1. Cardiogenic shock.

2. Chronic cardiac failure with congestive heart failure.

Isoproterenol (Isuprel)

A. Effects: beta stimulation.
    1. Increases heart rate, contractility, and oxygen consumption.
    2. Decreases peripheral vascular resistance.

B. Uses.
    1. Cardiogenic shock with high peripheral vascular resistance.
    2. AV block—increases pacemaker automaticity and improves AV conduction.

C. Side effects.
    1. Tachyarrhythmias, especially ventricular tachycardia.
    2. Hypotension when hypovolemia is not corrected.
    3. Headache, skin flushing, angina, dizziness, weakness.

Norepinephrine (Levophed)

A. Effects.
    1. Alpha stimulation—peripheral vasoconstriction.
    2. Beta stimulation mild.

B. Uses: cardiogenic shock with low peripheral resistance and normal cardiac output; requires careful monitoring of blood pressure.

C. Side effects.
    1. Anxiety, headache.
    2. Severe hypertension from overdosage.
    3. Arrhythmias.
    4. Infiltration into tissues, causing sloughing.

Antihypertensive Drugs

A. Purpose: reduce blood pressure to normal or near-normal without side effects.

B. Drugs.
    1. Thiazides—when used in combination with other antihypertensive drugs, potentiate second drug.
    2. Hydralazine (Apresoline).
        a. Effect: adrenergic blocker.
        b. Side effects: headache, tachycardia, and postural hypotension.
    3. Methyldopa (Aldomet).
        a. Effect: decreases blood pressure.

b. Side effect: postural hypotension.
4. Ganglionic blocking agents—pentolinium tartrate (Ansolysen), mecamylamine (Inversine).
   a. Effect: blocks parasympathetic and sympathetic ganglia.
   b. Side effect: postural hypotension.
5. Postganglionic blocking agents—guanethidine (Ismelin).
   a. Effect: blocks norepinephrine.
   b. Side effect: postural hypotension.
6. Diazoxide (Hyperstat).
   a. Effects: decreases peripheral vascular resistance in all circulatory beds; affects arterial smooth muscles.
   b. Use: hypertensive crisis only.
   c. Administration: I.V., rapidly.
   d. Side effects: hypotension (rarely severe), GI disturbances, angina, atrial and ventricular arrhythmias, palpitations, headache, hyperglycemia, fluid retention due to reabsorption of sodium, propranolol potentiates action.
7. Sodium nitroprusside (Nipride).
   a. Effect: acts on vascular smooth muscle causing peripheral vasodilation. Effect occurs in two minutes but it is transitory.
   b. Administration: I.V. infusion.
   c. Side effects: restlessness, agitation, muscle twitching, vomiting, or skin rash.

Diuretics

A. Purpose: most diuretics block sodium reabsorption in proximal tubule of kidney and decrease ionic exchange of sodium in distal tubule, thereby eliminating water.
B. Drugs.
   1. Thiazides.
      a. Common preparations: chlorothiazide (Diuril), hydrochlorothiazide (Hydrodiuril), chlorthalidone (Hygroton).
      b. Administration: oral and parenteral.
      c. Advantages: potent by mouth; effective antihypertensives.
      d. Disadvantages: electrolyte imbalances; loss of potassium.
         (1) Hyperuricemia and secondary aldosteronism.

(2) Allergic reactions.
(3) Hyperglycemia.
(4) Hematologic complications.
2. Potassium-sparing agents.
   a. Common preparations: spironolactone (Aldactone), triamterene (Dyrenium).
   b. Administration: oral only.
   c. Advantages: conserve potassium.
   d. Disadvantages.
      (1) Usually not effective when used alone (best used with thiazides).
      (2) Electrolyte imbalance.
      (3) Gynecomastia and nitrogen retention.
3. Potent diuretics.
   a. Common preparations: furosemide (Lasix), ethacrynic acid (Edecrin).
   b. Administration: oral and parenteral.
   c. Advantages: rapid, potent action useful in cases of severe pulmonary edema and refractory edema.
   d. Disadvantages.
      (1) Allergic reactions.
      (2) Severe electrolyte imbalance (potassium and chloride loss).
      (3) Hypovolemia.
      (4) Hyperuricemia, secondary aldosteronism, hyperglycemia.

Peripheral Vascular Problems

Hypertension

Definition: Hypertension occurs when blood pressure is greater than 140 mm. Hg systolically and 90 mm. Hg diastolically.

Types

A. Primary (essential): no known etiology.
B. Secondary.
   1. Renal disease.
   2. Endocrine disorders.
      a. Pheochromocytoma.
      b. Adrenal cortex lesions—aldosteronism, Cushing's syndrome.
   3. Coarctation of aorta.

4. Toxemia of pregnancy.
5. Acute autonomic dysreflexia.
6. Increased intracranial pressure.

Clinical Manifestations

A. Asymptomatic (early).
B. Headache, dizziness, tinnitus.
C. Target organ involvement (later).
 1. Eyes—narrowing of arteries, papilledema (malignant hypertension), visual disturbances.
 2. Brain—mental and neurologic abnormalities, encephalopathy, CVA.
 3. Cardiovascular system—left ventricular hypertrophy and failure, angina, aggravation and acceleration of atherosclerotic process in coronary arteries and peripheral vessels.
 4. Kidneys—renal failure.

Medical Management

A. Treat secondary causes of hypertension.
B. Essential hypertension.
 1. Dietary restriction: decreased sodium and decreased calories (if overweight).
 2. Sympathectomy.
 3. Chemotherapeutic intervention.
 a. Vasodilator—hydralazine.
 b. Sympathetic inhibitors: reserpine (Serpasil), methyldopa (Aldomet), and propanolol (Inderal).
 c. Diuretics.

Nursing Management

A. Relieve patient's environmental stress and anxiety.
B. Suggest moderate activity.
C. Educate patient in importance of following medical treatment.

Thromboangiitis Obliterans (Buerger's Disease)

Definition: Thromboangiitis obliterans is the chronic inflammation of arteries and veins, and secondarily of nerves. Process affects males under 40.

Clinical Manifestations

A. Pain, temperature, and color changes (cyanosis); alterations in skin of lower extremities at rest and especially after exercise.

B. Intermittent calf claudication.
C. Decreased pulses.
D. Complications: swelling, ulceration, gangrene.

Medical Treatment

A. Cessation of smoking.
B. Bilateral sympathectomy.
C. Reduction of pain.
D. Medication—Vasodilan.

Arteriosclerosis Obliterans

Definition: Arteriosclerosis obliterans is the diminution of blood supply due to fatty substances and other substances being laid down in inner wall of arteries.

Clinical Manifestations

A. Asymptomatic until metabolic requirements of exercising limb are not met.
 1. Intermittent calf claudication.
 2. Pain at rest.
B. Diminished or absent pulses.
C. Complications: ulcerations.

Medical Treatment

Reconstructive arterial surgery via vein graft.

Raynaud's Disease

Definition: Raynaud's disease is a vasospastic condition of arteries that occurs with exposure to cold or to strong emotion and affects fingers, toes, ears, nose, cheeks. Most common in women.

Clinical Manifestations and Physical Signs

A. Blanching or cyanosis of extremities.
B. Numbness.
C. Pulses present and normal.
D. Gradual onset.
E. Complications: pulp ulceration and thickening of skin.

Medical Treatment

A. Conservative treatment: medication—Vasodilan.
B. Sympathectomy.

Thrombophlebitis

Definition: Thrombophlebitis is the inflammation of wall of vein resulting in venous obstruction by thrombus.

Precipitating Causes

A. Stagnation of blood flow; for example, from bed rest.
B. Change in clotting of blood.
C. Change in lining of blood vessel.

Clinical Manifestations

A. Superficial vein.
  1. Vein hard to the touch.
  2. Skin reddened, hot, tender.
B. Deep vein.
  1. Leg swollen, tender.
  2. Increased temperature, pulse, white blood count.

Medical Treatment

A. Prevention: exercise, nonconstrictive clothing, footboard walking, no gatching of bed, no pillows under knees, adequate hydration.
B. Proper fitting of elastic stockings.
C. Bed rest with elevation of affected limb.
D. Anticoagulant drug therapy
E. Heat.

Varicose Veins

Definition: Varicose veins is a condition in which the veins are dilated because of incompetent valves.

Precipitating Causes

A. Pregnancy.

B. Standing for long periods of time.
C. Poor venous return.
D. Heredity.

Clinical Manifestations

A. Ache in legs.
B. Edematous ankles.
C. Skin brown from blood which has escaped from overloaded veins.
D. Ulceration.

Medical Treatment

A. Prevention.
B. Elevation of legs; removal of constricting clothing; elastic stockings.
C. Vein stripping.

Nursing Management—Peripheral Vascular Problems

A. Limit disease and prevent complications.
B. Maintain adequate blood supply to affected areas.
  1. Warmth.
  2. Cleanliness.
  3. Infection control.
  4. Avoidance of heat and cold extremes.
C. Educate patient to see need for cessation of smoking.
D. Prevent constrictive clothing and positions; protect legs from pressure
E. Prevent emotional stress.
F. Teach patient to recognize extension of symptoms.
  1. Increase in pain in extremities.
  2. Changes in skin color
  3. Ulceration.
  4. Change in temperature in extremities.
G. Have patient recognize limitations caused by disease.

Respiratory System

The respiratory system is that body process which accomplishes pulmonary ventilation. The act of breathing involves an osmotic and chemical process by which the body takes in oxygen from the atmosphere and gives off end products, mainly carbon dioxide, formed by oxidation in the alveolar tissues.

Anatomy of Respiratory System

Upper Airway

A. Nasal passages.
  1. Filter the air.
  2. Warm the air.
  3. Humidify the air.
B. Nasopharynx.
  1. Tonsils.
  2. Eustachian tube—opens during swallowing to equalize pressure in the middle ear.
C. Oropharynx.
  1. Part of both the respiratory and digestive tract.
  2. Swallowing reflex initiated here.
  3. Epiglottis closes entry to trachea as foodstuff passes enroute to the stomach.

Lower Airway

A. Larynx.
  1. Protects the tracheobronchial tree from aspiration of foreign materials.
  2. Cough reflex initiated here, whether voluntary or involuntary.
  3. Houses the vocal cords, which are considered to be the dividing point between the upper and lower airways.
B. Trachea.
  1. Cylindrical structure.
  2. Extends from the cricoid cartilage into the thorax, branching into the right and left mainstem bronchi.
C. Right lung.
  1. Contains three distinct lobes: upper, middle, and lower.
  2. Lobes are divided by interlobar fissures.
D. Left lung.
  1. Contains two lobes: upper and lower.
  2. Lingula is part of the upper lobe but is sometimes referred to as the middle lobe of the left lung.
  3. Lobes are divided by one interlobar fissure.
E. Bronchi.
  1. Right mainstem bronchus (RMSB): shorter and wider than left bronchus; nearly vertical to trachea.
    a. Most frequent route for aspirated materials.
    b. Endotracheal tube might enter the RMSB if tube is passed too far.
  2. Left mainstem bronchus (LMSB): branches off the trachea at a 45-degree angle.
  3. The bronchi subdivide into bronchioles, terminal bronchioles, respiratory bronchioles, and alveoli.
F. Alveoli.
  1. Air cells in which gas exchange takes place: oxygen, carbon dioxide.
  2. House a substance known as surfactant, which keeps the alveoli expanded. Without surfactant the alveoli would collapse.
G. Pleura.
  1. The pleural fluid is a thin film of fluid encasing each lung, which allows for a smooth, gliding motion between the lung and the chest wall.
  2. Even though this fluid is film-like, it would be difficult to pull it away from the chest wall (analogous to two glass slides with fluid between them; the slides move back and forth easily but are difficult to pull apart).

Principles of Ventilation

Respiration

Definition: Respiration occurs when oxygen is transported from the atmosphere to the cells and carbon dioxide is carried from the cells to the atmosphere.

A. Respiration is divided into four phases.
  1. Pulmonary ventilation.

2. Diffusion of oxygen and carbon dioxide between alveoli and blood.
3. Transportation of oxygen and carbon dioxide in blood to and from cells.
4. Regulation of ventilation.

B. Respiratory cycle.
1. Inspiration (active process)—diaphragm descends and external intercostal muscles contract; alveolar pressure decreases, allowing air to flow into the lungs.
2. Expiration (normally a passive process)—alveolar pressure increases, allowing air to flow from the lungs.

Respiratory Pressures

A. At inspiration the intra-alveolar pressure is more negative than the atmospheric pressure.

B. At expiration the intra-alveolar pressure is more positive, thereby pressing the air out of the lungs.

C. A negative pressure exists in the intrapleural space and aids in keeping the visceral pleura of the lungs against the parietal pleura of the chest wall. Lung space enlarges as the chest wall expands.

D. Recoil tendency of the lungs is due to the elastic fibers in the lungs and the surfactant.

Surfactant

A. Surface-active material that lines the alveoli and changes the surface tension, depending on the area over which it is spread.

B. Surfactant in the lungs allows the smaller alveoli to have lower surface tension than the larger alveoli.
1. Therefore, the pressures within both are equal and prevent collapse.
2. Production of surfactant depends on adequate blood supply.

C. Conditions that decrease surfactant.
1. Hypoxia.
2. Oxygen toxicity.
3. Aspiration.
4. Atelectasis.
5. Pulmonary edema.
6. Pulmonary embolus.
7. Mucolytic agents.
8. Hyaline membrane disease.

Compliance

A. Relationship between pressure and volume: elastic resistance. This is determined by dividing the tidal volume by peak airway pressure (V_t PAP). Total compliance equals chest wall compliance plus lung compliance.

B. Conditions that decrease chest wall compliance.
1. Obesity—excess fatty tissue over chest wall and abdomen.
2. Kyphoscoliosis—marked resistance to expansion of the chest wall.
3. Scleroderma—expansion of the chest wall limited when the involved skin over the chest wall becomes stiff.
4. Chest wall injury—as in crushing chest wall injuries.
5. Diaphragmatic paralysis—as a result of surgical damage to the phrenic nerve, or disease process involving the diaphragm itself.

C. Conditions that decrease lung compliance.
1. Atelectasis—collapse of the alveoli as a result of obstruction or hypoventilation.
2. Pneumonia—inflammatory process involving the lung tissue.
3. Pulmonary edema—accumulation of fluid in the alveoli.
4. Pleural effusion—accumulation of pleural fluid in the pleural space compressing lung on the affected side.
5. Pulmonary fibrosis—scar tissue replacing necrosed lung tissue as a result of infection.
6. Pneumothorax—air present in the pleural cavity; lung is collapsed as volume of air increases.

Airway Resistance

A. Opposition or counterforce. Resistance depends on the diameter and length of a given tube (respiratory tract).
1. Flow may be laminar (smooth) or turbulent.
2. Resistance equals pressure divided by flow (Poiseuille's law).

B. Conditions that increase airway resistance.
1. Secretions.
2. Bronchial constriction.

Lung Volumes

A. Total lung capacity (TLC)—total volume of air that is present in the lungs after maximum inspiration.

B. Vital capacity (VC)—volume of air that can be expelled following a maximum inspiration.

C. Tidal volume (TV)—volume of air with each inspiration.

D. Inspiratory reserve volume (IRV)—volume of air that can be inspired above the tidal volume.

E. Inspiratory capacity (IC)—volume of air with maximum inspiration; comprises tidal volume and inspiratory reserve volume.

F. Expiratory reserve volume (ERV)—volume of air that can be expelled following a resting expiration.

G. Reserve volume (RV)—volume of air remaining in the lungs at the end of maximum expiration.

H. Functional reserve capacity (FRC)—volume of air remaining in the lungs at the end of resting expiration; comprises ERV and RV.

I. Forced expiratory volume$_1$ (FEV$_1$)—volume of air that is expelled within the first second of the vital capacity.

Alveolar Ventilation

Definition: The rate at which the alveolar air is renewed each minute by atmospheric air—the most important factor of the entire pulmonary ventilatory process.

A. Rate of alveolar ventilation.

1. Alveolar ventilation is one of the major factors determining the concentrations of oxygen and carbon dioxide in the alveoli.

2. Alveolar ventilation per minute is the total volume of new air entering the alveoli each minute equal to the respiratory rate times the amount of new air that enters the alveoli with each breath.

B. Dead space.

1. Dead space air is the air that fills the respiratory passages with each breath.

2. The volume of air that enters the alveoli with each breath is equal to the tidal volume minus the dead space volume.

3. Anatomical dead space refers to volume of all spaces of the respiratory system besides the gas exchange areas (the alveoli and terminal ducts).

4. Physiological dead space refers to alveolar dead space (occurring because of nonfunctioning or partially functioning alveoli) included in the total measurement of dead space.

5. In the normal person anatomical and physiological dead space are equal because all alveoli are functional.

Oxygen and Carbon Dioxide Diffusion and Transportation of Respiratory Gases

Ventilation

A. The first phase in respiration is ventilation, which is the constant replenishment of air in the lungs.

B. Composition of alveolar air.

1. Alveolar air is only partially replenished by atmospheric air each inspiratory phase.

   a. Approximately 350 cc. (tidal volume minus dead space) of new air is exchanged with the functional residual capacity volume each respiratory cycle (FRC = 2300 cc.).

   b. Sudden changes in gaseous concentrations are prevented when alveolar air is replaced slowly.

2. Alveolar air contains more carbon dioxide and water vapor than atmospheric air.

3. Alveolar oxygen concentration depends on the rate of oxygen absorbed into the blood and the ability of the lungs to take in carbon dioxide.

4. Carbon dioxide content is likewise affected by the rate carbon dioxide is passed into the alveoli from the blood and the ability of the lungs to expire it.

Diffusion of Gases

A. The next phase is movement of oxygen from the alveolar air to the blood and movement of carbon dioxide in the opposite direction.

B. Movement of gases through the respiratory membrane depends on the following factors.

1. Thickness of membrane.

2. Permeability of membrane (diffusion coefficient).

3. Surface area of the membrane.

4. Differences in gas pressures in the alveolar and blood spaces.

5. Rate of pulmonary circulation.

C. Blood low in carbon dioxide and high in oxygen leaves lungs.

D. Throughout the body there again is exchange of respiratory gases in the capillary beds.
1. Oxygen out of the blood and into the cells.
2. Carbon dioxide from cells into the blood.

Oxygen Transport in the Blood

A. About 3 percent of the oxygen is carried in a dissolved state in the water of plasma and cells.

B. About 97 percent is carried in chemical combination with hemoglobin in red blood cells.
1. The percent of oxygen combined with each hemoglobin molecule depends on the partial pressure of oxygen.
2. The relationship is expressed as the oxygen-hemoglobin dissociation curve.
   a. It shows the progressive increase in the percent of the hemoglobin that is bound with oxygen as the pO_2 increases.
   b. When the pO_2 is high, oxygen binds with the hemoglobin, but when pO_2 is low (tissue capillaries), oxygen is released from hemoglobin.
   c. This is the basis for oxygen transport from the lungs to the tissues.
3. Febrile states and acidosis permit less oxygen to bind with Hb, thereby limiting the amount of oxygen available for the tissues.
4. The amount of oxygen that is available to the tissues depends on the oxygen content of the blood and the cardiac output.

C Inadequate oxygen transport to the tissues—hypoxia.
1. Hypoxic hypoxia: low arterial pO_2.
   a. Alveolar hypoventilation.
   b. Ventilation-perfusion inequalities.
   c. Diffusion defects.
   d. Fraction of inspired oxygen (FIO_2) is less than atmosphere, such as in high altitudes.
2. Anemic hypoxia: decreased oxygen-carrying capacity to the blood.
   a. Anemia—less Hb; therefore, less oxygen is able to combine with it.
   b. Carbon monoxide poisoning—carbon monoxide combines with the Hb, preventing oxygen from combining with the Hb.

3. Circulatory hypoxia: circulatory insufficiency.
   a. Shock—decreased cardiac output.
   b. Congestive heart failure.
   c. Arterial vascular disease—localized obstruction to arterial blood flow.
   d. Tissue need for oxygen surpasses supply available.
4. Histotoxic hypoxia: prevents tissues from utilizing oxygen.

Carbon Dioxide Transport in the Blood

A. A small amount of carbon dioxide is dissolved in plasma and red blood cells in the form of bicarbonate.

B. Inside the red blood cells, carbon dioxide combines with water to form carbonic acid.
1. It is catalyzed by the enzyme called *carbonic anhydrase.*
2. The enzyme accelerates the rate to a fraction of a second.

C. In another fraction of a second carbonic acid dissociates to form hydrogen ions and bicarbonate in the red cells.

D. Carbon dioxide combines with the hemoglobin molecule.
1. The hemoglobin molecule has given off its oxygen to the tissues, and carbon dioxide attaches itself.
2. The venous system carries the combined carbon dioxide back to the lungs where it is expired.

Regulation of Respiration

A. Respiratory centers.
1. Pons—two respiration areas: pneumotaxic and apneustic.
2. Medulla oblongata—major brain area controlling rhythmicity of respiration.
3. Spinal cord—facilitory role in maintaining respiratory center.
4. Hering Breuer reflexes—stretch receptors located in lung tissue which assist in maintaining respiratory rhythm and prevent overstretch of the lung. Afferent fibers are carried in the vagus nerve.

B. Humoral regulation of respiration (chemical).
1. Central chemoreceptors.

a. Directly stimulated by an increase in hydrogen ion concentration (acidity) in the cerebral spinal fluid.

b. An increase in arterial pCO_2 effects a rapid change in pH of the cerebral spinal fluid, increases the depth and rate of respiration, and decreases the pCO_2 level.

c. Changes in hydrogen ion and bicarbonate ion concentrations are not as quickly recognized as changes in the pCO_2 by the central chemoreceptors; therefore, responses to metabolic imbalances are slower.

d. Receptors are located in the medulla oblongata and adjacent structures.

2. Peripheral chemoreceptors.

a. Receptor cells are located in the carotid body at the bifurcation of the common carotid arteries and at the aortic arch.

b. Impulses from the aortic arch are transmitted to the brain via the vagus nerve.

c. Impulses from the carotid body are transmitted to the brain via the glossopharyngeal nerve.

d. The peripheral chemoreceptors primarily respond quickly to a decreased pO_2 (below 50 mm. Hg) and to some extent to alteration of the pCO_2 and hydrogen ion concentration in the arterial blood.

Diagnostic Procedures

Radiologic Studies

A. Chest X-ray.

B. Lung scintigraphy—measures concentration of gamma rays from lung after intake of isotope.

C. Perfusion studies—outline pulmonary vascular structures after intake of radioactive isotopes I.V.

D. Bronchography.
1. An opaque substance is inserted into trachea, and an X-ray is taken of the tracheobronchial tree and lungs.
2. Patient is NPO to prevent dangers of regurgitation and aspiration.

Bronchoscopy

A. A tube-like lighted scope to visualize the interior of the tracheobronchial tree.

B. Used as a therapeutic tool to remove foreign materials.

C. Procedure and nursing care.
1. Place patient supine with neck hyperextended.
2. Post-procedure: check patient's ability to control secretions.
3. Observe for potential complications of laryngospasm, laryngeal edema, anesthesia complications, subcutaneous emphysema.
4. Inform patient to expect hoarseness and sore throat.

Biopsy of Respiratory Tissue

A. May be done by needle, via bronchoscope or an open lung procedure biopsy.

B. Nursing care: observe for hemothorax and/or pneumothorax.

Thoracentesis

A. A needle puncture through the chest wall to remove air or fluid.

B. Used for diagnostic and/or therapeutic purposes.

C. Nursing care: observe for possible pneumothorax post-procedure.

Pulmonary Function Tests

A. Measure body's ability to mechanically ventilate and to effect gaseous exchange.

B. See "Lung Volumes," p. 72.

Tuberculin Skin Test

A. Mantoux subcutaneous test (more reliable).
1. Tuberculin injected subcutaneously, intermediate PPD.
2. Test read 48 to 72 hours post-intradermal wheal production.
3. Erythema not important.
4. Area of induration more than 10 mm. indicates positive reaction (patient has had contact with the tubercle bacillus).
5. Reactions of 5-9 mm. require retest.

B. Tine test.
1. Not recommended for diagnosis.
2. Test read on third day.
3. Mantoux test if induration more than 2 mm.

Arterial Blood Studies

A. Arterial blood gases.
1. Indicate respiratory function by measuring:
    a. Oxygen (pO_2).
    b. Carbon dioxide (pCO_2).
    c. pH.
    d. Oxygen saturation and bicarbonate (HCO_3).
2. Determine state of acid-base balance.
3. Reveal the adequacy of the lungs to provide oxygen and to remove carbon dioxide.
4. Assess degree to which kidneys can maintain a normal pH (BE).

B. Normal arterial values.
1. Oxygen saturation: 93-98%.
2. PaO_2: 95 mm. Hg.
3. Arterial pH: 7.35-7.45 (7.4).
4. pCO_2: 35-45 mm. Hg (40).
5. HCO_3 content: 23-27 mEq. (25).
6. Base excess: -3 to +3 (0).

Respiratory Problems

Problems with Respiration

A. Dyspnea—labored or difficult breathing.
B. Hyperpnea—abnormal deep breathing.
C. Hypopnea—reduced depth of breathing.
D. Orthopnea—difficulty breathing in other than upright position.
E. Tachypnea—rapid breathing.
F. Stridor—noisy respirations as air is forced through a partially obstructed airway.
G. Cough.
1. Normally a protective mechanism utilized to keep the tracheobronchial tree free of secretions.
2. Common symptom of respiratory disease.
H. Bronchospasm.
1. Bronchi narrow and secretions may be retained.
2. Condition may lead to infection.
I. Hemoptysis—expectoration of blood or blood-tinged sputum.

Problems with Gaseous Exchange

A. Hypoxia (anoxia) is a deficiency of oxygen in body tissues.
B. Hypercapnia occurs when carbon dioxide is retained.
1. High levels of oxygen depress and/or paralyze the medullary respiratory center.
2. Peripheral chemoreceptors (sensitive to oxygen) become the stimuli for breathing.

Problems with Circulation

A. Cyanosis—late sign of hypoxia, due to large amounts of reduced hemoglobin in the blood (PaO_2 of about 50 mm. Hg.).
B. Polycythemia—increase in RBC's as a compensatory response to hypoxemia.
C. Clubbing of fingers—pathogenesis is not well understood.
D. Cor pumonale—enlargement of the right ventricle as a result of pulmonary arterial hypertension following respiratory pathology.
E. Chest pain.

Respiratory Acid-Base Imbalance

Respiratory Acidosis

A. Hypoventilation or decreased gaseous exchange leads to retained pCO_2.
B. Blood gas changes.
1. pH decreases.
2. pCO_2 increases.
3. HCO_3 normal.
C. Compensation.
1. Kidneys retain HCO_3 ion.
2. Kidneys excrete H+ ion.
3. pH returns more toward normal range.

	Respiratory Acidosis		Compensation
pH:	↓	< 7.40	7.40
pCO_2:	↑	> 40	
HCO_3^-: normal		24	↑ > 24

D. Etiology.
1. Obstructive lung disease.
2. Depression of the respiratory center: sedation.
3. Neurological dysfunction: Guillain-Barré syndrome, myasthenia gravis, Pickwickian syndrome.
E. Clinical manifestations.
1. Headache.
2. Dizziness.
3. Confusion.
4. Disorientation.
5. Tremor.
F Treatment.
1. Treat underlying cause.
2. Increase alveolar ventilation.

Respiratory Alkalosis

A. Hyperventilation leads to excessive loss of carbon dioxide through the lungs.
B. Blood gas changes in alkalosis.
1. pH increases.
2. pCO_2 decreases
3. HCO_3 normal.
C. Compensation.
1. Kidneys excrete HCO_3 ions.
2. Kidneys retain H+ ions.
3. pH returns more toward normal.

	Respiratory Alkalosis	Compensation
pH: ↑	> 7.40	7.40
pCO_2: ↓	< 40	
HCO_3^-: normal	24	↓ < 24

D. Etiology.
1. Hypoxia.
2. Anxiety.
3. Pregnancy.
4. Restrictive lung disease.
E. Clinical manifestations.
1. Vertigo.
2. Confusion.
3. Paresthesias.
4. Tachycardia.
5. Tetany.
6. Blurred vision.
7. Sweating.
8. Dry mouth.
F. Treatment.
1. Treat underlying cause.
2. Return carbon dioxide to blood.

Conditions Associated with Respiratory Failure

A. Infectious diseases.
1. Tuberculosis.
2. Pneumonia.
B. Obstruction of airway.
1. Pulmonary embolism.
2. Chronic bronchitis.
3. Bronchiectasis.
4. Emphysema.
5. Asthma.
6. Cardiac disorders leading to pulmonary congestion.
C. Restrictive lung disease.
1. Pleural effusion.
2. Pneumothorax.
3. Atelectasis.
4. Pulmonary tumors.
5. Obesity.
D. CNS depression.
1. Drugs.
2. Head injury.
3. CNS infection.
E. Chest wall trauma.
1. Flail chest.
2. Neuromuscular disease.
3. Congenital deformities.

Infectious Diseases

Pulmonary Tuberculosis

Definition: Tuberculosis is an infectious, communicable process which is caused by *Mycobacterium tuberculosis.* It may affect any part of the body but is most common in the lungs.

Characteristics of Tubercle Bacilli

A. Rod-shaped.

B. Gram-positive, acid-fast.

C. Aerobic (need oxygen).

D. Can live in dried sputum if in a dark area.

E. Destroyed by direct sunlight or ultraviolet rays.

F. Essentially an air-borne infection, although there are other avenues of entry.

Pathology

A. After entrance of tubercle bacilli, the body attempts to wall off the organism by phagocytosis and lymphocytosis.

B. If this fails, tubercles (gray transparent masses) form.

C. Caseation, a necrotic process of the tubercles, occurs. (Cells become an amorphous cheese-like mass—may be encapsulated to form a nodule.)

D. The caseous nodule erodes, and sputum is released leaving an air-filled cavity.

Clinical Manifestations

A. Pulmonary symptoms.
1. Cough (at cavitation stage).
2. Sputum production
3. Dyspnea.
4. Hemoptysis.
5. Pleuritic pain (with pleural involvement).

B. Systemic symptoms.
1. Fatigue, malaise.
2. Irritability, lassitude.
3. Night sweats, low-grade fever in late afternoon.
4. Tachycardia.
5. Weight loss.
6. Anorexia.

Diagnosis

A. Physical examination.

B. Chest X-ray.

C. Sputum examination.

D. Social and medical history.

E. Tuberculin test (refer to preceding Diagnostic Procedure section).

Treatment

A. Chemotherapy.
1. Drug resistance is a problem

2. Ischemic area in center of nodule reduces efficiency of medication.
3. Drugs are bacteriostatic.
4. Proper study of organisms in sputum important in choosing initial medications (susceptibilities and resistances).
5. Treatment long-term; may be life-long for some people.
6. Drugs are more effective when administered in a single daily dose.
7. Most common drugs.
   a. Isoniazid—300 mg. daily.
   b. Ethambutol—15 mg./kg. daily.
   c. Streptomycin—500 mg. daily.
   d. Rifampin—600 mg. daily.
   e. Para-aminosalicylic acid—8 to 15 grams.
8. Usually INH, ethambutol, rifampin, or streptomycin used in combination, once daily.
9. Other drugs sometimes utilized in resistant cases: viomycin, pyrazinamide, cycloserine, and kanamycin.
10. Corticosteroids are used along with antituberculosis agents in severe cases to reduce severe symptoms.

B. Chemoprophylaxis.
1. Isoniazid and vitamin B_6 therapy for one year.
2. Uses.
   a. Tuberculin converters without active disease.
   b. Individuals in close contact with untreated active tuberculosis.
   c. Individuals with silicosis.

C. Surgical resection when chemotherapy ineffective.

Nursing Management

A. Maintain respiratory isolation.
1. Strict isolation for at least 48 hours after medication is begun.
2. Masks necessary only for uncooperative patient.

B. Administer medications on time.

C. Instruct patient in ways to prevent spread of disease.
1. Cover nose and mouth with a few layers of disposable tissue when sneezing, coughing, laughing.
2. Expectorate into a disposable sputum container.
3. Maintain adequate air ventilation

D. Decontaminate infected air by non-recirculated air or ultraviolet rays.
E. Provide well-balanced diet.
F. Provide frequent oral hygiene.
G. Maintain bedrest only with weak or clinically ill patients.
H. Patient education.
  1. Relapsing disease.
  2. Preventing transmission.
  3. Understanding treatment.

Pneumonia

Definition: Pneumonia is an acute inflammatory process of the alveolar spaces that results in lung consolidation as the alveoli fill with exudate.

Etiology

A. Bacterial pneumonias.
  1. Lobar.
    a. Pneumococcus—most common organism.
    b. Communicable disease.
    c. Young males most affected.
    d. Clinical manifestations.
      (1) Rapid onset, severe chills, high temperature (103° to 106° F, reduced by crisis).
      (2) Constant dry, hacking cough.
      (3) Pleuritic pain.
      (4) Anxiety.
      (5) Dyspnea.
      (6) Sputum—watery to rust-colored.
  2. Bronchopneumonia.
    a. Strep and staph common organisms.
    b. Aspiration frequently of this type (food, chemical, smoke, oil).
    c. Secondary to other conditions such as age, debilitation, stasis.
    d. Common in very young and very old.
    e. Clinical manifestations.
      (1) Temperature—101° to 103° F (reduced by lysis).
      (2) Cough productive—yellow or green sputum.
B. Atypical pneumonia.
  1. Known etiology—rickettsial: Q fever, Rocky Mountain spotted fever, psittacosis.
  2. Nonspecific etiology—known as "walking pneumonia."
    a. Found in common living conditions.
    b. Most common in young adults.
    c. Temperature not usually above 99° F (reduced by lysis).
    d. Clinical manifestations.
      (1) Malaise.
      (2) Fatigue.
      (3) Chills.
      (4) Cough—usually nonproductive ("goose honk").
      (5) Sputum—clear or white (if productive).

Treatment

A. Throat, sputum, and blood cultures for specific organisms.
B. Specific antibiotic therapy (if indicated).
C. Oxygen therapy.
D. Hydration and nutrition.

Nursing Management

A. Maintain bedrest.
B. Limit visitors.
C. Force fluids to 3000 cc. or more.
D. Observe and record type and amount of sputum.

Chronic Restrictive Disorders

Pleural Effusion

Definition: Pleural effusion is a collection of non-purulent fluid in the pleural space. Many pathological processes can irritate the pleurae and cause effusion, but in older patients cancer is a common cause.

Clinical Manifestations

A. Symptoms.
  1. Dyspnea.
  2. Fatigue.
  3. Elevated temperature.
  4. Dry cough.
  5. Pleural pain.

B. Physical signs.
   1. Absence of movement on side of effusion.
   2. Percussion—dull.
   3. Decreased breath sounds.
   4. Pleural friction rub occurs in dry pleurisy, but as effusion develops, the friction rub disappears.
   5. Collapse of lung—when fluid increases in amount.
   6. Mediastinal structures shift position.
   7. Cardiac tamponade.

Treatment

A. Thoracentesis is used to aid in diagnosis and to relieve pressure by draining excess fluid.
B. Correct or treat underlying disorder.

Pneumothorax

Definition: Pneumothorax is a collection of air in the pleural cavity. As the air collects in the pleural space, the lung is collapsed and respiratory distress ensues. The condition occurs as a result of chest wall penetration by surgery or injury or when disease process interrupts the internal structures of the lung.

Clinical Manifestations

A. Symptoms.
   1. Sharp, sudden chest pain.
   2. Anxiety, vertigo.
   3. Hypotension, dyspnea, cough.
   4. Tachycardia.
   5. Elevated temperature, diaphoresis.
   6. Hypoxia, hypercapnia.
B. Physical signs.
   1. Paradoxical or diminished movement on the affected side.
   2. Percussion—hyperresonant.
   3. Absent breath sounds.
   4. Tactile fremitus decreased.

Treatment

A. Tension pneumothorax is a medical emergency.
   1. The mediastinum shifts away from the side of the pneumothorax compressing the unaffected lung.
   2. A large bore needle is introduced into the pleural cavity to release the pressure.

   3. A tube thoracostomy is then performed.
B. A small pneumothorax may reabsorb on its own.
   1. If the pneumothorax is large or increasing in size, closed tube thoracostomy is performed.
   2. Water-seal is utilized to reexpand the lung.
C. Hemothorax (blood in the thoracic cavity).
   1. Hemothorax occurs with pneumothorax, especially if trauma is the causative factor.
   2. Treatment: evacuate the blood through chest tube insertion.
D. Close observation of the patient, frequent auscultation of the chest, and monitoring of the vital signs are necessary.

Atelectasis

Definition: Atelectasis occurs when alveoli collapse, become airless, and shrink as a result of some form of bronchial obstruction. The obstruction may be produced by many disease entities, and eventually infection and impaired regional circulation occur in the lung.

Clinical Manifestations

A. Symptoms.
   1. Slowly developing atelectasis.
      a. Increased dyspnea.
      b. Weakness.
   2. Extensive atelectasis with infection.
      a. Severe dyspnea.
      b. Cyanosis.
      c. Hypotension, tachycardia.
      d. Shock, anxiety.
      e. Temperature elevation.
      f. Pain on affected side.
B. Physical signs.
   1. Reduced breath sounds.
   2. Decreased chest wall movement (affected side)
   3. Percussion dull over involved area.
   4. Elevated diaphragm on affected side in severe condition.
   5. Tracheal deviation toward atelectatic area.

Pulmonary Tumors

Definition: Pulmonary tumors are either primary or metastatic and interrupt the normal physiological functioning of the lung.

Pathology

A. Classification of lung cancer is designated by anatomic location or by histological pattern.
   1. Anatomic classification.
      a. Central lesions involve the tracheobronchial tube up to the distal bronchi.
      b. Peripheral lesions extend from the distal bronchi and includes the bronchioles.
   2. Four histologic types.
      a. Squamous cell (epidermoid).
         (1) Most frequent lung lesions.
         (2) Affects more men than women.
         (3) Associated with cigarette smoking.
         (4) Lesion usually starts in bronchial area and extends.
         (5) Metastasis not usually a rapid process.
      b. Adenocarcinoma.
         (1) Usually develops in peripheral tissue (smaller bronchi).
         (2) Metastasizes by blood route.
         (3) May be associated with focal lung scars.
         (4) Affects more women than men.
      c. Bronchiole-alveolar cell.
         (1) Rare multimodular lesion.
         (2) Affects bronchiolar or alveolar linings.
      d. Undifferentiated carcinoma.
         (1) Metastisizes early.
         (2) Affects younger age group.
         (3) Affects more men than women.
B. Pulmonary lesions are not usually detected by physical exam, and symptoms do not occur until process is extensive. Chest X-ray is very helpful in diagnosis.

Clinical Manifestations

A. Pulmonary symptoms.
   1. Persistent cough.
   2. Dyspnea.
   3. Bloody sputum.
   4. Long-term pulmonary infection.
   5. Atelectasis.
   6. Bronchiectasis.
   7. Chest pain.
   8. Chills, fever.

B. Systemic symptoms.
   1. Weakness.
   2. Weight loss.
   3. Anemia.
   4. Anorexia.
   5. Metabolic syndromes.
      a. Hypercalcemia.
      b. Inappropriate ADH.
      c. Cushing's syndrome.
      d. Gynecomastia.
   6. Neuromuscular changes.
      a. Peripheral neuropathy.
      b. Corticocerebellar degeneration.
   7. Connective tissue abnormalities.
      a. Clubbing.
      b. Arthralgias.
   8. Dermatologic abnormalities.
   9. Vascular changes.

Chronic Obstructive Pulmonary Disease (COPD)

Definition: COPD is a functional category that is applied to respiratory disorders that obstruct the pathway of normal alveolar ventilation, either by spasm of the airways, mucus secretions, or changes in airway and/or alveoli.

Pulmonary Embolism

Definition: Pulmonary embolism is an obstruction of the pulmonary arteries by emboli that originate and break free from the deep veins of the lower extremities, or emboli that originate from the right heart, pelvic veins, or upper extremities.

Clinical Manifestations

A. Symptoms.
   1. Classic pulmonary embolism (rare).
      a. Sudden pleuritic chest pain.
      b. Dyspnea, hemoptysis.
      c. Fever.
      d. Consolidation, pleural friction rub.
      e. Positive venous thrombosis site.
   2. Splinting.

3. Dyspnea, air hunger.
4. Cough on second or third day.
5. Hemoptysis.
6. Elevated temperature.
7. Acute pain when site of the chest pain is touched.
8. Tachycardia, arrhythmias.

B. Physical signs.
1. Diminished expansion.
2. Percussion—dull.
3. Diminished breath sounds, bronchial breath sounds.
4. Rales, pleural rub.
5. Tactile fremitus; breath sounds decreased if pleural effusion.
6. Circulatory collapse.

Treatment

A. Priority—place in high-Fowler's position.
B. Administer oxygen (may require mechanical ventilation).
C. Anticoagulation therapy.
D. Hydration.
E. Chest physiotherapy contraindicated over involved area.

Chronic Bronchitis

Definition: Chronic bronchitis is a long-term inflammation of the mucous membrane of the bronchial tubes with recurrent cough and sputum production.

Etiology

A. Cigarette smoking is probably the biggest culprit, inhibiting the ciliary activity of the bronchi, resulting in increased stimulation of the mucous glands to secrete mucus.
B. Immunological factors and familial predisposition may also be implicated for those individuals who do not smoke.

Clinical Manifestations

A. Symptoms.
1. Bronchoconstriction.
2. Malaise.
3. Exertional dyspnea.

4. Hemoptysis.
5. Cough—may not be productive but may be purulent.
6. Hypoxia.

B. Physical signs.
1. Atelectasis.
2. Percussion—hyperresonant.
3. Tactile fremitus decreased.
4. Prolonged expiratory phase.
5. Expansion decreased.
6. Trachea midline.
7. Wheezes, rales.

Note: Nursing management is in the section that follows pulmonary diseases.

Bronchiectasis

Definition: Thought to develop following airway obstruction or atelectasis as a result of diseases such as tuberculosis or of infections such as pneumonia.

Clinical Manifestations

A. Symptoms.
1. Frequent, severe paroxysms of coughing.
2. Hemoptysis.
3. Fetid breath.
4. Sputum—thick, profuse.
5. Breathlessness, fatigue.
6. Profuse night sweats.
7. Weight loss, anorexia.

B. Physical signs.
1. Trachea deviates to the affected side.
2. Decreased expansion.
3. Percussion—dull.
4. Vocal fremitus and breath sounds absent if bronchus occluded.
5. Vocal fremitus increased, bronchovesicular/bronchial breath sounds if bronchus open.
6. Rales, rhonchi.

Emphysema

Definition: Emphysema is the permanent overdistention of the alveoli with resulting destruction of the alveolar walls. (*Emphysema* is a Greek word meaning *overinflated.*)

Etiology (postulated)

A. Bronchiolar obstruction as a result of repeated in-flammatory processes with air trapping of the alve-oli and eventual rupture of the walls.

B. Obstruction of multiple pulmonary vessels.

C. Genetic predisposition.

D. Environmental pollution.

Clinical Manifestations

A. Symptoms.
  1. Cough—may be present many years before dyspnea.
  2. Dyspnea.
  3. Sputum production.
  4. Weight loss.
  5. Hypoxia, hypercapnia.

B. Physical signs.
  1. Barrel chest.
  2. Expansion decreased.
  3. Flat diaphragm.
  4. Accessory muscles of respiration.
  5. Tactile fremitus decreased.
  6. Percussion—hyperresonant.
  7. Distant breath sounds.
  8. Prolonged expiratory phase.
  9. Wheezes, forced expiratory rhonchi.

Complications

A. Pulmonary hypertension.

B. Right-sided heart failure.

C. Spontaneous pneumothorax.

Chronic Asthma

Definition: Chronic asthma is manifested by difficult breathing, characterized by generalized bronchocon-striction, excess mucus secretion, and mucosal edema.

Types

A. Specific etiology is unknown.

B. Extrinsic—early onset in life and often associated with history of allergy.

C. Intrinsic—usually adult onset and often associated with environmental factors.

Precipitating Factors

A. Emotion.

B. Infection.

C. Seasonal changes.

D. Pets.

E. Smoking.

F. Family history.

G. Occupational exposure to dusts or chemical irri-tants.

H. Drugs.

Clinical Manifestations

A. Symptoms.
  1. Respiratory distress.
  2. Air hunger.
  3. Tachypnea.
  4. Prolonged expiratory phase.
  5. Cough—may be nonproductive or very puru-lent.
  6. Tachycardia.
  7. Hypoxia, cyanosis, hypercapnia.

B. Physical signs.
  1. Retraction of intercostal and sternal muscles.
  2. Percussion—hyperresonant.
  3. Distant breath sounds.
  4. Rhonchi, wheezes, rales.

Treatment

A. Supportive respiratory care.

B. Drug therapy.
  1. Bronchodilators.
     a. Epinephrine and derivatives.
     b. Aminophylline and derivatives.
     c. Isuprel.
     d. Ephedrine.
  2. Antihistamines.
  3. Corticosteroids.

C. Sedatives and narcotics should be used with caution.

Right Ventricular Failure

Definition: Right ventricular failure occurs when blood from the right ventricle meets resistance from noncom-pliant lungs as it is pumped into the pulmonary artery, resulting in hypertrophy of the right ventricle and eventual failure of the pump mechanism.

Clinical Manifestations

A. Symptoms: severe exertional dyspnea.
B. Physical signs.
   1. Neck vein distention.
   2. Increased central venous pressure.
   3. Hepatomegaly.
   4. Ascites.
   5. Peripheral edema.
   6. Cyanosis.

Treatment

A. Rest.
B. Low sodium diet.
C. Diuretic therapy.
D. Digitalization.

Pulmonary Edema (Left Ventricular Failure)

Definition: Pulmonary edema is an excessive fluid accumulation in the alveoli, bronchioles, and bronchi from left-sided heart failure.

Clinical Manifestations

A. Symptoms.
   1. Sense of impending suffocation.
   2. Apprehension, restlessness.
   3. Orthopnea.
   4. Tachypnea—shallow and wet.
   5. Productive cough—pink and frothy.
   6. Tachycardia—bounding to thready.
   7. Pallor, diaphoresis.
   8. Elevated blood pressure until shock; then decreased blood pressure.
   9. Hypoxia, cyanosis.
B. Physical signs.
   1. Bibasilar rales—wet.
   2. Wheezes and gurgling sounds.

Treatment

A. Mild: rest, low sodium diet, diuretic therapy, digoxin.
B. Severe: morphine, bronchodilators, rotating tourniquets, oxygen therapy, IPPB, possible digitalization.

Respiratory Nursing Care

Principles and Treatment of Pulmonary Disease

Chest Physiotherapy

A. Postural drainage.
   1. Positions are utilized to promote gravitational drainage and mobilization of secretions of affected lung segments.
   2. This allows the patient to expectorate them.
   3. They may also be aspirated through a sterile suctioning procedure.
B. Cupping and vibration.
   1. Valuable and necessary adjunct to postural drainage.
   2. Vibration of the chest is performed only during the expiratory phase of respiration.
C. Deep breathing and coughing.
   1. Should be encouraged often.
   2. Patients with COPD should be taught the mechanics of an effective cough.
      a. Contract intercostal muscles.
      b. Contract diaphragm.
      c. Fill lungs with air.
D. Breathing exercises or exercise regimen—an integral part in the management of patients with pulmonary disease.
   1. Diaphragmatic breathing.
      a. Breathe in via nose.
      b. Exhale through slightly pursed lips.
      c. Contract abdominal muscles while exhaling.
      d. Chest should not move, but abdomen should do the moving. (Abdomen contracts at expiration.)
      e. Exercises can be learned with patient flat on back and then done in other positions.
   2. Accelerated diaphragmatic breathing.
   3. Chest expansion—apical, lateral (unilateral, bilateral), basal.
   4. Controlled breathing with daily activities and graded exercises to improve general physical fitness.
   5. Relaxation and stretching.
   6. General relaxation.
E. Intermittent positive pressure breathing (IPPB).
   1. Purposes.
      a. Improve oxygenation to the lungs.

b. Improve alveolar ventilation.
c. Deliver aerosolized bronchodilators.
d. Decrease the work of breathing.
e. Mobilize secretions.
f. Improve or prevent atelectasis.
g. Treat pulmonary edema.
2. IPPB treatments should be administered by a respiratory therapist or trained nursing personnel.
3. The patient should not be left unattended during the IPPB treatments.
4. Postural drainage, cupping and vibration, and coughing and deep breathing should follow each treatment.

Positions for Chest Physiotherapy

A. To affect RUL and LUL, place patient in upright position.
B. To affect RML, position patient on left side with head slanted down, right shoulder one-quarter turn onto pillow. Cup anteriorly over left nipple.
C. To affect lingula LL, position patient on right side with head slanted down, left shoulder one-quarter turn onto pillow. Cup anteriorly over left nipple.
D. To affect RLL and LLL, place patient in Trendelenburg position, alternating sides, or prone.

Hydration

A. Necessary to liquefy secretions present, or to prevent formation of thick, tenacious secretions in patients with pulmonary disease.
B. Modalities.
1. Oral intake of fluids.
2. I.V. administration of fluids.
3. Humidification to tracheobronchial tree via face tent or aerosol mask, using compressed air.
C. Humidification and aerosolization.
1. Humidity.
a. Water content of a gas at a given temperature.
b. Humidification can be delivered through humidifier or nebulizer.
2. Aerosol.
a. Suspension of water particles in a gas medium.
b. Nebulizers deliver aerosols.

3. Clinical implications.
a. Relief of bronchospasm and mucosal edema.
b. Mobilization of secretions.
c. Administration of medications such as bronchodilators, mucolytics, detergents, and selected antibiotics.
d. Humidification of the tracheobronchial tree.

Treatment of Infection

A. Respiratory infections frequently precipitate acute exacerbation of chronic obstructive pulmonary disease.
B. An increase in the amount of sputum.
1. Change in the character of sputum (particularly color—yellow to green).
2. Onset of malaise or febrility may indicate infection.
C. Antibiotics are instituted at onset of infection.
1. Given for a period of ten to fourteen days.
2. Antibiotics most commonly used are ampicillin and tetracycline.
D. Frequency of chest physiotherapy treatments is increased until phase has passed.

Chemotherapeutic Agents for Pulmonary Disease

Bronchodilators Commonly Used

A. Aminophylline.
1. Relaxes smooth muscle of the tracheobronchial tree.
2. Intravenous, oral, elixir.
3. Should be taken on an empty stomach since it is not absorbed well in an alkaline medium.
4. Side effects include gastric irritation, nausea, cardiac arrhythmias (tachycardia, ventricular ectopy).
B. Tedral.
1. Relaxes smooth muscle of the tracheobronchial tree, reduces congestion, and aids in preventing histamine-induced bronchospasm.
2. Tablet, elixir—contain phenobarbital (habit forming).
3. Caution necessary for patients with cardiovascular disease, hypertension, hyperthyroidism, prostatic hypertrophy, and glaucoma.

4. Side effects include drowsiness, epigastric distress, difficulty of urination, palpitations, insomnia, CNS stimulation.

C. Ephedrine.
   1. Relaxes smooth muscle of the tracheobronchial tree, reduces congestion, and acts as a vasoconstrictor.
   2. Tablet, parenteral.
   3. Side effects include anxiety, tremulousness, palpitations, insomnia, difficulty of urination, and CNS stimulation.

D. Isuprel.
   1. Relaxes smooth muscle of the tracheobronchial tree, relieves bronchospasm, and acts as a cardiac stimulant (increases cardiac output and venous return to the heart).
   2. Mistometer, solution for nebulization, I.V. (requires ICU).
   3. Caution necessary for patients with existing cardiac arrhythmias associated with tachycardias.
      a. It may result in aggravation of arrhythmias.
      b. Should not be used with epinephrine since both are cardiac stimulants and the combined effect may produce serious arrhythmias.
   4. Side effects include tachycardia, nervousness, palpitations, arrhythmias, nausea, headaches, flushing, tremor, dizziness, weakness, diaphoresis, chest pain.

E. Bronkosol.
   1. Relaxes smooth muscle of the tracheobronchial tree.
      a. Acts as bronchovasoconstrictor and reduces congestion.
      b. Less effective than Isuprel in its bronchodilating effect, but more potent than epinephrine.
   2. Hand nebulizer and solution for aerosolization.
   3. Precautions are the same as for Isuprel, but the side effects seem to appear less frequently.

F. Choledyl.
   1. Relaxes smooth muscle of the tracheobronchial tree.
      a. Relieves bronchospasm.
      b. Useful in long-term therapy of bronchospasm.
   2. Tablet, elixir.

3. Concomitant use with other bronchodilators may increase side effects, especially CNS stimulation.
   4. Side effects include gastric distress, palpitations, CNS stimulation.

G. Alupent.
   1. Relaxes smooth muscle of the tracheobronchial tree and relieves bronchospasm.
   2. Metered dose inhaler, tablets.
   3. Caution necessary for patients with hypertension, cardiovascular disease, congestive heart failure, hyperthyroidism, and diabetes.
   4. Side effects include tachycardia, sporadic hypertension, palpitations, nervousness, tremor, nausea, vomiting.

H. Prednisone.
   1. Indicated in the treatment of patients with bronchospasms not relieved by aminophylline or Isuprel.
      a. Also indicated for frequent recurrence of bronchospasm in spite of other bronchodilator therapy.
      b. Primarily used for its anti-inflammatory effects.
   2. Tablet, I.V.
   3. Caution necessary for patients with history of ulcer disease, diabetes.
   4. Side effects include increased appetite, sense of well-being, euphoria, and psychosis.

General Respiratory Drugs

A. Quibron.
   1. Relieves bronchiolar constriction and assists in removal of mucus.
   2. Capsule or elixir.
   3. Should not be given within twelve hours of rectal doses of theophylline.
   4. Side effects include GI upset, nausea, and vomiting.

B. Epinephrine.
   1. Acts directly on beta cells of the bronchi, increases title volume, and relieves congestion in bronchial mucosa and constricting pulmonary vessels.
   2. Used in anaphylaxis and asthma.
   3. Subcutaneous injection.
   4. Strong cardiotonic.
   5. Side effects include palpitations, tachycardia,

headache, tremor, weakness, and vertigo.
6. Vital signs should be monitored during use.

Mucolytics

A. Mucomyst.
1. Reduces viscosity of purulent and nonpurulent secretions by breaking disulfide bond; assists in removal of secretions.
2. Inhalation medication.
3. Side effects include stomatitis, hemoptysis, and nausea.
4. Inactivates many antibiotics, including penicillin.
B. Potassium iodide.
1. Expectorant liquefies tenacious bronchial secretions.
2. Enseal (enteric-release) capsule.
3. Not used in acute bronchitis.
4. Thyroid abnormalities can occur with use.

Oxygen Therapy

Hypoxic Condition

Definition: Oxygen deficiency—the primary indication for initiation of oxygen therapy.

Manifestations of Hypoxia

A. Early symptoms.
1. Restlessness.
2. Headache, visual disturbances.
3. Slight confusion.
4. Hyperventilation.
5. Tachycardia.
6. Hypertension.
7. Dyspnea.
B. Late symptoms.
1. Hypotension.
2. Bradycardia.
3. Metabolic acidosis (production of lactic acid).
C. Chronic oxygen lack.
1. Polycythemia.
2. Clubbing of fingers and toes.
3. Thrombosis.

Oxygen Administration

Aim of Administration

A. To deliver adequate FIO_2.
1. Provide adequate arterial pO_2 (enough oxygen for tissue needs).
2. Avoid levels which might produce toxicity or atelectasis.
B. Some patients with COPD have a ventilatory drive that is hypoxemic.
1. Oxygen administration requires critical observation. Starts at 2 L./minute.
2. Carbon dioxide narcosis can develop if hypoxic drive is removed by administering FIO_2 to return the arterial pO_2 to normal range.
3. Symptoms of carbon dioxide narcosis.
   a. Comatose.
   b. Flushed, pink skin.
   c. Flaccid (sometimes twitching) extremities.
   d. Shallow breathing.

Side Effects

A. Atelectasis.
1. Nitrogen is washed out of the lungs when a high FIO_2 is delivered to the patient.
2. In alveoli, free of nitrogen, oxygen diffuses out of the alveoli into the blood faster than ventilation can enter the alveoli.
3. This results in a collapse (atelectasis) of the affected alveoli.
B. Pulmonary oxygen toxicity.
1. High FIO_2 delivered over a long period of time (forty-eight hours) results in destruction of the pulmonary capillaries and lung tissue.
2. The clinical picture resembles that of pulmonary edema.
C. Retrolental fibroplasia.
1. Blindness resulting from high FIO_2 delivered to premature infants.
2. This condition is seen in prolonged FIO_2 of 100 percent.

Modes of Administration

A. Nasal prongs.
1. Easily tolerated by patients.
2. The FIO_2 will vary depending on the flow.
   a. FIO_2: 24-28%—flow: 1-2 L.

b. FIO_2: 30–35%—flow: 3–4 L.

c. FIO_2: 38–44%—flow: 5–6 L.

B. Mask without reservoir bag.

1. Requires fairly high flows to prevent rebreathing of carbon dioxide.

2. Accurate FIO_2 difficult to estimate.

a. FIO_2: 35–45%—flow: 5–6 L.

b. FIO_2: 45–55%—flow: 6–7 L.

c. FIO_2: 55–65%—flow: 7–8 L.

C. Mask with reservoir bag.

1. Higher FIO_2 is delivered because of the reservoir.

2. At flows less than 6 L./min., risk of rebreathing carbon dioxide increases.

a. FIO_2: 50–60%—flow: 6 L.

b. FIO_2: 60–70%—flow: 7 L.

c. FIO_2: 70–100%—flow: 8–10 L.

D. Venturi mask.

1. Delivers fixed or predicted FIO_2.

2. Utilized effectively in patients with COPD when accurate FIO_2 is necessary for proper treatment.

a. FIO_2: 24%—flow: 2–4 L.

b. FIO_2: 28%—flow: 4–6 L.

c. FIO_2: 35%—flow: 6–8 L.

E. Face tent.

1. Well tolerated by the patient but sometimes difficult to keep in place.

2. Convenient for providing humidification with compressed air in conjunction with nasal prongs.

3. FIO_2: 35–50%—flow: 8–10 L.

F. Mechanical ventilators.

1. Negative pressure ventilator.

a. Helpful in problems of a neuromuscular nature.

b. Not effective in the treatment of increased airway resistance.

c. Types—full body, chest, and chest-abdomen.

2. Positive pressure ventilator.

a. Uses positive pressure (pressure greater than atmospheric) to inflate lungs.

b. Types.

(1) Pressure cycle.

(a) Pressure ranges from 10 to 30 cm. of water pressure.

(b) Air is actively forced into lungs.

(c) Expiration is passive.

(2) Volume cycle.

(a) Uses physiological limits.

(b) Predetermined total volume is delivered irrespective of airway pressure.

(c) Positive end expiratory pressure (PEEP) utilized to maintain positive pressure between expiration and beginning of inspiration.

c. Complications of positive pressure therapy.

(1) Respiratory alkalosis.

(2) Gastric distention and paralytic ileus.

(3) GI bleeding.

(4) Diffuse atelectasis.

(5) Infection.

(6) Circulatory collapse.

(7) Pneumothorax progressive alveolar capillary block.

(8) Sudden ventricular fibrillation.

Gastrointestinal System

The alimentary tract's primary function is to provide the body with a continual supply of nutrients, fluids, and electrolytes for tissue nourishment. This system has three components: a tract for ingestion and movement of food and fluids; secretion of digestive juices for breaking down the nutrients; and absorption mechanisms for the utilization of foods, water, and electrolytes for continued growth and repair of body tissues.

Anatomy and Physiology

Main Organs

Description: The main organs of the gastrointestinal system include the mouth, pharynx, esophagus, stomach, small intestine, and large intestine.

Functions

A.   Normally, it is the only source of intake for the body.
B.   Provides the body with fluids, nutrients, and electrolytes.
C.   Provides means of disposal for waste residues.

Activities

A.   Secretion of enzymes and electrolytes to break down the raw materials ingested.
B.   Movement of ingested products through the system.
C.   Complete digestion of ingested nutrients.
D.   Absorption of the end products of digestion into the blood.

Coats Composing the Walls

A.   Mucous lining.
  1.   Rugae and microscopic gastric and hydrochloric acid glands in the stomach.
  2.   Villi, intestinal gland Peyer's patches, and lymph nodes.
  3.   Intestinal glands.
B.   Submucous coat of connective tissue, in which the main blood vessels are located.
C.   Muscular coat.
  1.   Digestive organs have circular and longitudinal muscle fibers.
  2.   The stomach has oblique fibers in addition to the circular and longitudinal fibers.
D.   Fibroserous coat, the outer coat.
  1.   In the stomach, the omentum hangs from the lower edge of the stomach, over the intestines.
  2.   In the intestines, it forms the visceral peritoneum.

The Mouth, Pharynx, and Esophagus

A.   The buccal cavity includes:
  1.   Cheeks.
  2.   Hard and soft palates.
  3.   Muscles.
  4.   Maxillary bones.
B.   The pharynx.
  1.   Tubelike structure that extends from the base of the skull to the esophagus.
  2.   Compound of muscle lined with mucous membrane, composed of the nasopharynx, the oropharynx, and the laryngopharynx.
  3.   Functions include serving as a pathway for the respiratory and digestive tracts, and playing an important role in phonation.
C.   The esophagus begins at the lower end of the pharynx and is a collapsible muscular tube about ten inches long.
  1.   It leads to the abdominal portion of the digestive tract.
  2.   The main portion is lined with many simple mucous glands; complex mucous glands are located at the esophagastric juncture.

The Stomach

A.   Elongated pouch lying in the epigastric and left hypochondriac portions of the abdominal cavity.
B.   Divisions are the fundus, the body, and the pylorus (the constricted lower portion).
C.   Curvatures are the lesser curvature and the greater curvature.
D.   Sphincters.
  1.   Cardiac sphincter—at the opening of the esophagus into the stomach.
  2.   Pyloric sphincter—guards the opening of the

pylorus into the duodenum.

E. Coats.

1. The mucous coat allows for distention and contains microscopic glands: gastric, hydrochloric acid, and mucous.

2. The muscle coat contains three layers.

    a. Circular—forms the two sphincters.
    b. Longitudinal.
    c. Oblique.

3. The fibroserous coat forms the visceral peritoneum; the omentum hangs in a double fold over the intestines.

F. Glands.

1. Mucous—secrete mucus.
2. Goblet cells—secrete viscid mucus.
3. Gastric glands.

    a. Parietal—secrete hydrochloric acid.
    b. Chief cells—secrete pepsin, lipase, amylase, and rennin.

G. Function: mechanical and chemical digestion.

1. Mechanical.

    a. Churning provides for forward and backward movement.
    b. Peristalsis moves material through the stomach and, at intervals with relaxation of the pyloric sphincter, squirts chyme into the duodenum.

2. Chemical.

    a. Hydrochloric acid provides the proper medium for action of pepsin and aids in the coagulation of milk in adults.
    b. Pepsin splits protein into proteoses and peptones.
    c. Lipase is a fat-splitting enzyme with limited action.
    d. Rennin coagulates or curdles the protein of milk.
    e. Intrinsic factor—acts on certain components of food to form the antianemic factor.

The Small Intestine

A. Approximately twenty feet in length.

B. Divisions.

1. The duodenum includes the Brunner's glands (the duodenal mucous digestive glands) and the openings for the bile and pancreatic ducts.

2. The jejunum is approximately eight feet long and the ileum is approximately twelve feet long. Both have deep circular folds that increase their absorptive surfaces.

    a. The mucous lining has numerous villi, each of which has an arteriole, venule, and lymph vessel that serve as structures for the absorption of digested food.
    b. The small intestine terminates by opening into the cecum (the opening is guarded by the ileocecal valve).

C. Intestinal digestion.

1. Intestinal juice has an alkaline reaction and contains a large number of enzymes.

2. Enzymes.

    a. Peptidase splits fragments of proteins into free amino acids.
    b. Amylase digests starch to maltase.
    c. Maltase reduces maltose to monosaccharide glucose.
    d. Lactase splits lactose into galactose and glucose.
    e. Sucrase reduces sucrose to fructose and glucose.
    f. Nucleoses split nucleic acids into nucleotides.
    g. Enterokinase activates trypsinogen to trypsin.

The Large Intestine

A. Approximately five to six feet in length, with a relatively smooth mucous membrane surface. The only secretion is mucus.

B. Muscle coats pucker the wall of the colon into a series of pouches (haustra) and contain the internal and the external anal sphincters.

C. Divisions.

1. The cecum (the first part of the large intestine) is guarded by the ileocecal valve, which prevents regurgitation of the cecal contents into the ileum.

2. Colon.

    a. Ascending—that portion of the colon extending from the ileocecal valve to the right hepatic flexure.
    b. Transverse—the largest, most mobile section extending from the right hepatic flexure to the left splenic flexure.

c. Descending—the narrowest portion of the large intestine, extending from the left splenic flexure to the brim of the pelvis.

d. Sigmoid—S-shaped portion of the colon, beginning at the brim of the pelvis and extending to the rectum.

D. Functions.

1. Absorption and elimination of wastes.
2. Formation of vitamins: K, B_{12}, riboflavin, and thiamin.
3. Mechanical digestion: churning, peristalsis, and defecation.
4. Absorption of H_2O from fecal mass.

Accessory Organs

Description: The accessory organs of the gastrointestinal system include the teeth, tongue, salivary glands, pancreas, liver, gallbladder, and appendix.

Tongue

A. A skeletal muscle covered with a mucous membrane that aids in chewing, swallowing, and speaking.
B. Papillae on the surface of the tongue contain taste buds.
C. The frenulum is a fold of mucous membrane that helps to anchor the tongue to the floor of the mouth.

Salivary Glands

A. Three pairs—the submaxillary, the sublingual, and the buccal glands.
B. Secretion.

1. Saliva is secreted by the glands when sensory nerve endings are stimulated mechanically, thermally, or chemically.
2. pH ranges: 6.0-7.9. Between 1000 and 1500 ml. are secreted in a 24-hour period in adults.
3. Contains amylase, an enzyme that hydrolyzes starch.

Teeth

A. Deciduous teeth (twenty in the set) and permanent teeth (thirty-two in the set).

B. The functions are mastication and mixing saliva with food.

Liver

A. Location and size.

1. Located in the right hypochondrium and part of the epigastrium.
2. It is the largest gland in the body, weighing three to four pounds.
3. It is protected by the lower ribs and is in contact with the undersurface of the dome of the diaphragm.

B. Lobes—right lobes (include the right lobe proper, the caudate, and the quadrate) and left lobe.

1. The lobes are divided into lobules by blood vessels and fibrous partitions.
2. The lobule is the basic structure of the liver and contains hepatic cells and capillaries.

C. Ducts include the hepatic duct from the liver, the cystic duct from the gallbladder, and the common bile duct (the union of the hepatic and cystic ducts).

Functions of the Liver

A. Metabolism of carbohydrates.

1. Converts glucose to glycogen and stores glycogen.
2. Converts glycogen to glucose.
3. Glycogenolysis—the supply of carbohydrate released into bloodstream.

B. Metabolism of fats.

1. Oxidation of fatty acids and formation of acetoacetic acid.
2. Formation of lipoproteins, cholesterol, and phospholipids.
3. Conversion of carbohydrates and protein to fat.

C. Metabolism of proteins.

1. Deamination of amino acids.
2. Formation of urea.
3. Formation of plasma proteins.
4. Interconversions among amino acid and other compounds.

D. Vascular functions for storage and filtration of blood.

1. Blood (200-400 ml.) can be stored by the liver.
2. Vitamins (A, D, and B_{12}) and iron are stored in the liver.

3. Detoxifies harmful substances in the blood.
4. Breaks down worn-out blood cells.
5. Filters blood as it comes through the portal system.

E. Secretory functions.
   1. Constant seccretion (500–1000 ml. in twenty-four hours) of bile, which is stored in the gall-bladder.
   2. Bile is a yellow-brown viscous fluid, alkaline in reaction, and consists of bile salts, bile pigments, cholesterol, and inorganic salts.
   3. Bile emulsifies fats.
   4. Red blood cell destruction releases hemoglobin which changes to bilirubin; bilirubin unites with plasma proteins and is removed by the liver and excreted in the bile.
   5. The bile pigment bilirubin is converted by bacterial action into urobilin and to urobilinogen (appears in urine and gives feces brown color).

F. Hepatic reticuloendothelial functions.
   1. Inner surface of the liver sinusoids contains Kupffer cells.
   2. Kupffer cells are phagocytic and are capable of removing bacteria in the portal venous blood.

The Gallbladder

A. Small sac of smooth muscle located in a depression at the edge of the visceral surface of the liver, which functions as a reservoir for bile.

B. Ducts.
   1. Cystic duct—the duct of the gallbladder joins the hepatic duct, which descends from the liver, to form the common bile duct.
   2. The common bile duct is joined by the duct of the pancreas (Wirsung's duct) as it enters the duodenum.
   3. The sphincter of Oddi guards the common entrance.

C. Secretion—the presence of fatty materials in the duodenum stimulates the liberation of cholecystokinin which causes contraction of the gallbladder and relaxation of the sphincter of Oddi.

The Pancreas

A. A soft, pink-white organ, six inches long and one inch wide, that adheres to the middle portion of the duodenum.

B. Divided into lobes and lobules.
   1. Exocrine portion secretes digestive enzymes, which are carried to the duodenum by Wirsung's duct.
   2. Endocrine secretion is produced by the islets of Langerhans; insulin is secreted into the bloodstream and plays an important role in carbohydrate metabolism.

C. Pancreatic juices contain enzymes for digesting proteins, carbohydrates, and fats.
   1. Enzymes are secreted as inactive precursors which do not become active until secreted into the intestine (otherwise they would digest the gland).
   2. Actions.
      a. Trypsinogen to trypsin to act on proteins producing peptones, peptides, and amino acids.
      b. Pancreatic amylase acts on carbohydrates, producing disaccharides.
      c. Pancreatic lipase acts on fats, producing glycerol and fatty acids.

D. Two regulatory mechanisms of pancreatic secretion.
   1. Nervous regulation—distention of the intestine.
   2. Hormonal regulation.
      a. Chyme in the intestinal mucosa causes the release of secretin (which stimulates the pancreas to secrete large quantities of fluid) and pancreozymin.
      b. Pancreozymin passes by way of the blood to the pancreas and causes secretion of large quantities of digestive enzymes.

Diagnostic Procedures

Roentgenography of the Gastrointestinal Tract

A. The gastrointestinal tract cannot be visualized unless a contrast medium is ingested or instilled into it.

B. Barium sulfate is normally used as a contrast medium. It is a white, chalky radiopaque substance that can be flavored.

C. For an upper gastrointestinal tract study, the patient ingests an aqueous suspension of barium. The progression of barium is followed by the fluoroscope.

D. Roentgenography of the upper tract reveals:
   1. Structure and function of the esophagus.
   2. Size and shape of the right atrium.
   3. Esophageal varices.
   4. Thickness of gastric wall.
   5. Motility of the stomach.
   6. Ulcerations, tumor formations, and anatomic abnormalities of the stomach.
   7. Pyloric valve patency.
   8. Emptying time of the stomach.
   9. Structural abnormalities of the small intestine.
E. X-rays are taken for permanent records.
F. Preparation of the patient for an upper G.I. roentgenograph.
   1. NPO after midnight, prior to the test.
   2. Withhold medication.
   3. Explain procedure.
G. The lower G.I. roentgenograph involves rectal instillation of barium, which is viewed with the fluoroscope. Then permanent X-rays are taken.
H. The lower G.I. roentgenograph reveals the following information:
   1. Abnormalities in the structure of the colon.
   2. Contour and motility of the cecum and appendix.
I. Preparation of the patient for a lower G.I. roentgenograph.
   1. Empty intestinal tract by giving an enema, laxatives, or suppositories as ordered.
   2. NPO after midnight, prior to the examination.
   3. Explain procedure.

Endoscopy

A. Visualization of the inside of a body cavity by means of a lighted tube.
B. Flexible scopes are used for these examinations; the scopes may be equipped with a camera.
C. Purposes.
   1. Direct visualization of mucosa to detect pathologic lesions.
   2. Obtaining biopsy specimens.
   3. Securing washings for cytologic examination.
D. Organs capable of being scoped: esophagus, stomach, duodenum, rectum, sigmoid colon, transverse colon, and right colon.
E. Nursing management.
   1. Explain the procedure.

   2. Have the patient fast, prior to the examination.
   3. Prepare the lower bowel with laxatives, enemas, or suppositories as ordered.
   4. Prior to gastroscopy, a local anesthetic may be used in the posterior pharynx. Withhold fluids and food after the procedure until the gag reflex has returned.
   5. Support the patient during the procedure. The muscles of the G.I. tract tend to go into spasm with the passage of the scope, causing pain.
   6. Following the endoscopy, observe for hemorrhage, swelling, or dysfunction of the involved area.

Analysis of Secretions

A. Contents of the G.I. tract may be examined for the presence or absence of digestive juices, bacteria, parasites, and malignant cells.
B. Stomach contents may be aspirated and analyzed for volume and free and total acid.
C. *Gastric analysis,* performed by means of a nasogastric tube.
   1. NPO six to eight hours prior to the test.
   2. Pass nasogastric tube; verify its presence in the stomach; tape to nose.
   3. Collect fasting specimens.
   4. Administer agents, as ordered, to stimulate the flow of gastric acid, such as alcohol, caffeine, histamine (0.2 mg. subcutaneous).
      a. Watch for side effects of histamine, including flushing, headache, and hypotension.
      b. Do not give drug to patients with a history of asthma or other allergic conditions.
   5. Collect specimens as ordered, usually at ten to twenty minute intervals.
   6. Label specimens and send to laboratory.
   7. Withdraw nasogastric tube; offer oral hygiene; make the patient comfortable.
   8. Gastric acid is high in the presence of duodenal ulcers, and is low in pernicious anemia.
D. *Tubeless gastric analysis.*
   1. Enables the determination of acidity or its absence.
   2. Have patient fast for six to eight hours prior to the examination.
   3. Administer gastric stimulant, followed by Azuresin or Diagnex Blue, as ordered.
   4. Acid in the stomach displaces the dye, which is

then released, absorbed by the bowel mucosa, and excreted in the urine.

5. The bladder is emptied; the specimen saved. One hour after taking dye resin the patient is instructed to void again. Urine is analyzed, and an estimation is made of the amount of free acid in the stomach.

E. Gastric washings for acid-fast bacilli.

1. Have patient fast six to eight hours prior to the procedure.

2. Insert nasogastric tube and secure gastric washings.

3. Send specimens to the laboratory to determine the presence of acid-fast bacilli.

4. Wash hands carefully and protect yourself from direct contact with specimens.

5. This procedure is performed on suspected cases of active pulmonary tuberculosis when it is difficult to secure sputum for analysis.

F. Analysis of stools.

1. Stool specimens are examined for amount, consistency, color, shape, blood, fecal urobilinogen, fat, nitrogen, parasites, food residue, and other substances.

2. Stool cultures are also done for bacteria and viruses.

3. Some foods and medicines can affect stool color: spinach, green; cocoa, dark red; senna, yellow; iron, black; upper G.I. bleeding, tarry black; lower G.I. bleeding, bright red.

4. Stool abnormalities.

   a. Steatorrhea—bulky, greasy and foamy, foul odor.

   b. Biliary obstruction—light gray or clay-colored.

   c. Ulcerative colitis—loose stools, with copious amounts of mucus or pus.

   d. Constipation or obstruction—small, hard masses.

5. Specimen collection.

   a. Specimens for detection of parasites should be sent to the laboratory while the stool is still warm and fresh.

   b. Examinations for blood are performed on small samples. A tongue blade may be used to place a small amount of stool in a disposable waxed container.

c. Stools for chemical analysis are usually examined for the total quantity expelled, so the complete stool is sent to the laboratory.

Biopsy and Cytology

A. Specimens for microscopic examination are secured by endoscopy examination, cell scrapings, and needle aspiration.

B. Specimens are examined, and the laboratory then determines their origin, structure, functions, and the presence of malignant cells.

Radionuclide Uptake

A. Radionuclides are used in diagnosis by measuring the localization of the substance, such as radioiodine in the thyroid, and the excretion of the material.

B. Various substances are studied, such as vitamin B_{12}, iron and fat and major organs can be scanned.

C. Substances are tagged with radioactive isotopes to assess the degree of absorption.

Blood Examinations

A. Hematologic studies and electrolyte determinations reveal information about the general status of the patient.

B. Results of these examinations in conjunction with other assessment procedures and clinical symptoms help to localize the disorder.

General Disorders

Definition: General symptoms of the gastrointestional tract which may occur singly or concurrently and may be due to a wide variety of causes.

Anorexia

Definition: Anorexia is loss of appetite.

Causes

A. Physiological.

1. Most illnesses, especially active stages of infections and disorders of the digestive organs.

2. Physical discomfort.

3. Constipation.

4. Fluid and electrolyte imbalances.
5. Oral sepsis.
6. Intestinal obstruction.
B. Psychological.
   1. Fear and anxiety.
   2. Depression.
   3. Anorexia nervosa.
C. Mechanical.
   1. Improperly fitting dentures.
   2. Excessive amounts of food.

Nursing Management

A. Be aware of patient's eating habits, food likes and dislikes, cultural and religious beliefs regarding food.
B. Permit choices of food when possible.
C. Show interest, but don't force the patient to eat.
D. Provide a pleasant environment.
E. Serve small, attractive portions of food.

Nausea and Vomiting

Definitions: Nausea is a feeling of revulsion for food, accompanied by salivation, sweating, and tachycardia. Vomiting is the contraction of the expiratory muscles of the chest, spasm of the diaphragm with contraction of the abdominal muscles, and subsequent relaxation of the stomach, allowing the gastric contents to be forced out through the mouth.

Characteristics

A. Accompanying symptoms: decreased blood pressure, increased salivation, sweating, weakness, faintness, paleness, vertigo, headache, and tachycardia.
B. Vomiting centers.
   1. Chemoreceptor emetic trigger zone.
   2. Vomiting center in the medulla.
C. Stimulation of vomiting centers.
   1. Impulses arising in the gastrointestinal tract.
   2. Impulses from cerebral centers.
   3. Chemicals via the bloodstream to the centers.
   4. Increased intracranial pressure.

Causes of Nausea and Vomiting

A. Cerebromedullary causes.
   1. Stress, fear, and depression.
   2. Neuroses and psychoses.
   3. Shock.

4. Pain.
5. Hypoxemia.
6. Increased intracranial pressure.
7. Anesthesia.
B. Toxic causes.
   1. Drugs.
      a. Direct action on the brain.
      b. Irritant effects on the stomach or the small bowel.
   2. Food poisoning.
   3. Acute febrile disease.
   4. Systemic diseases.
C. Visceral causes.
   1. Allergy.
   2. Intestinal obstruction.
   3. Constipation.
   4. Diseases of the stomach.
   5. Acute inflammatory disease of the abdominal and pelvic organs.
   6. Pregnancy.
   7. Cardiovascular diseases.
   8. Visceral disease.
D. Deficiencies that cause nausea and vomiting.
   1. Severe hypovitaminosis, especially B vitamins.
   2. Fasting and starvation.
   3. Endocrine disorders, such as hypothyroidism and Addison's disease.
   4. Motion sickness.
E. Implications of nausea and vomiting.
   1. Prolonged vomiting will result in dehydration and electrolyte imbalance, leading to alkalosis. Convulsions and tetany may occur in severe alkalosis.
   2. Prolonged vomiting, postoperatively, may cause wound dehiscence or hemorrhage.
   3. Aspiration of vomitus may cause asphyxia, atelectasis, or pneumonitis.

Nursing Management

A. Administer drugs: antiemetics, antihistamine, phenothiazines.
B. Monitor parenteral fluid and electrolyte replacements.
C. Gastric decompression.
D. Protect the patient from unpleasant sights, sounds, and smells.
E. Promptly remove used equipment.

F. Promptly change soiled linens and dressings.

G. Ventilate room and use unscented air fresheners.

H. Observe the character and quantity of emesis.

Constipation and Diarrhea

Definitions: Diarrhea is a condition characterized by loose, watery stools resulting from hypermotility of the bowel (not determined by frequency). Constipation is the undue delay in the evacuation of feces, with passage of hard and dry fecal material.

Causes

A. Constipation.
  1. Lack of regularity.
  2. Psychogenic causes.
  3. Drugs such as narcotics.
  4. Inadequate fluid and bulk intake.
  5. Mechanical obstruction.

B. Diarrhea.
  1. Fecal impaction.
  2. Ulcerative colitis.
  3. Intestinal infections.
  4. Drugs such as antibiotics.
  5. Neuroses.

C. Implications of constipation and diarrhea.
  1. Prolonged diarrhea may cause dehydration and metabolic acidosis.
  2. Prolonged fecal impaction may cause pain, obstruction, and rupture of the intestine.
  3. Chronic constipation may occur in neoplastic disorders of the intestine.

Nursing Management

A. Administer drugs.
  1. Laxatives may be used temporarily to relieve constipation, but regular use will cause loss of bowel tone.
  2. Antidiarrheals, such as absorbents, astringents, and antispasmodics, may relieve symptoms.

B. Provide fluid and electrolyte replacement therapy to correct imbalances.

C. Observe the condition of the stool, such as color, odor, shape, consistency, amount, and any unusual features, such as mucus, blood, or pus.

D. Prevent skin excoriation with emollients, powder, and cleanliness.

E. Assess all other systems of the body to determine causal factors.

Disorders of the Upper Gastrointestinal Tract

Oral Infections

Definitions: Stomatitis is an inflammation of the mouth; glossitis, an inflammation of the tongue; and gingivitis, an inflammation of the gums.

Causes of Oral Infections

A. Mechanical trauma: jagged teeth, mouth breathing.

B. Chemical trauma: foods, drinks, allergies.

C. Infection: viruses, bacteria, yeasts, molds.

Types

A. Herpes simplex—a group of vesicles on an erythematous base.
  1. Usually located at the mucocutaneous junction of the lips and face.
  2. Caused by a virus that may be activated by sunlight, heat, fever, digestive disturbances, and menses.
  3. Antimicrobial treatment is not effective unless there is secondary bacterial infection.
  4. Treated symptomatically.

B. Vincent's angina (trench mouth)—purplish-red gums covered by pseudomembrane.
  1. Caused by fusiform bacteria and spirochetes.
  2. Symptoms include: fever, anorexia, enlarged cervical glands, and foul breath.
  3. May be acute, subacute, or chronic.

Clinical Manifestations

A. Anorexia.

B. Excessive salivation.

C. Foul breath.

Treatment

A. Removal of cause.

B. Frequent, soothing oral hygiene.

C. Topical medications of systemic antibiotics.

D. Soft, bland diet.

E. Pain medications.

Disorder of the Salivary Glands

Definition: Salivary gland infection is an inflammation (parotitis or surgical mumps) usually caused by *Staphylococcus aureus.*

Clinical Manifestations

A. Pain.

B. Fever.

C. Enlargement and dysphagia.

Nursing Management

A. Preventive measures.
1. Keep the glands active; calculus or calculi (stones) form when the gland is inactive.
2. Provide adequate fluids.
3. Give oral hygiene.
B. Treatment.
1. Warm packs.
2. Antibiotics.
3. Hydration.
4. Possible incision and drainage.

Malignant Tumors of the Mouth

Definition: Cancer of the mouth is a malignant tumor (squamous cell carcinomas) and usually affects the lips, the lateral border of the tongue, or the floor of the mouth.

Characteristics

A. Lesions tend to be painless and hard, and ulcerate easily.

B. Contributing causes.
1. Poor oral hygiene.
2. Chronic irritation.
3. Chemical and thermal trauma (tobacco, alcohol, and hot, spicy foods).
C. Treatment is surgical incision or radiation.

D. Metastasis by local extension.
1. Cause symptoms by occupying space and exerting pressure.
2. Usually fibromas, lipomas, or neurofibromas.

Inflammation of the Esophagus

Definition: Esophagitis may be caused by local or systemic infection, or by chemical irritation from reflux of gastric juices into the lower esophagus.

Clinical Manifestations

A. Heartburn.

B. Intolerance of spices, alcohol and caffeine.

C. Dysphagia.

Treatment

A. Oral antacids.

B. Bland diet.

C. Elevation of bed.

Esophageal Varices

Definition: Tortuous dilated veins in the submucosa of the lower esophagus, possibly extending into the fundus of the stomach or upward into the esophagus; caused by portal hypertension and often associated with cirrhosis of the liver.

Clinical Manifestations

A. Usually no symptoms unless mucosa becomes ulcerated.

B. Bleeding.

C. Hypotension.

D. Neck vein distension.

E. Poor nutritional status.

F. Indications that lead to suspected varices.
1. Hematemesis.
2. Melena.
3. History of alcoholism.
G. Esophageal rupture precipitated by strain of coughing or vomiting.

Treatment

A. Lowering portal pressure by Pitressin administration.
1. Intravenous infusion.
   a. 20 to 50 units in 100–200 cc. D_5W over 20 minutes.
   b. Side effects.
      (1) Abdominal colic.

      (2) Bowel evacuation.

      (3) Facial pallor.

      (4) Arterial hypertension and reduced hepatic blood flow.

  2. Intra-arterial infusion.

    a. 0.05 to 0.1 unit per minute via the superior mesenteric artery.

    b. The rate of infusion may be increased up to a limit of 0.4 unit per minute.

    c. Side effects at the catheter insertion site.

      (1) Bleeding.

      (2) Thrombosis.

      (3) Embolism.

      (4) Infection.

    d. Major complication: bowel necrosis from altered perfusion.

B. Sengstaken-Blakemore tube for pressure application against varices.

  1. Tube has three openings.

    a. One opening to gastric balloon (inflated with 200 cc. of air).

    b. Second opening to esophageal balloon.

    c. Third opening for aspiration of gastric contents.

  2. Traction with a 3/4 to 1½ pound weight used to prevent downward movement.

  3. Ice gastric may be used to vasoconstrict the small collaterals.

C. Restoration of clotting factors.

  1. Vitamin K replacement.

  2. Platelet replacement (destroyed by damaged spleen).

  3. Fresh frozen plasma.

D. Surgical repairs.

  1. Direct ligation of varices.

  2. Portasystemic shunts.

    a. Portacaval.

      (1) End to side.

      (2) Side to side.

    b. Splenorenal.

      (1) End to side.

      (2) Side to side.

    c. Mesocaval.

      (1) End to side.

      (2) Use of synthetic graft.

E. Complications of active bleeding varices.

  1. Hypovolemia.

  2. Hepatic encephalopathy due to increased ammonia production as blood protein is metabolized.

  3. Metabolic imbalances due to acid-base and electrolyte disturbances.

Nursing Management

A. Carefully observe vital signs, watching for hemorrhage and shock.

B. Maintain prescribed pressure levels in esophagogastric balloons.

C. Provide frequent oral hygiene and aspiration of the mouth and throat since the patient cannot swallow saliva with the balloons in place.

D. Prevent esophageal erosion by deflating the balloons (only with physician's order).

E. Safety measure: keep scissors at bedside. If tube dislodges and causes obstruction, cut tube to deflate balloons.

F. Prevent nasal breakdown.

  1. Keep nostrils lubricated and clean.

  2. Provide foam rubber padding to reduce pressure.

G. Observe for sudden respiratory crisis, which may occur with aspiration or upward displacement of the balloons.

H. Maintain fluid and nutritional balance.

I. Comfort family and patient.

  1. Explain procedures and utilize nursing comfort measures.

  2. Use sedatives and narcotics judiciously because the liver is usually impaired in its ability to detoxify.

Esophageal Hernia (Hiatus Hernia)

Definition: In esophageal hernia, a portion of the stomach herniates through the diaphragm and into the thorax.

Causes

A. Congenital weakness.

B. Trauma.

C. Relaxation of muscles.

D. Increased intraabdominal pressure.

Clinical Manifestations

A. Range from no manifestations to acutely severe manifestations.
B. Heartburn and pain.
C. Dysphagia.
D. Vomiting.
E. Complications.
    1. Ulceration.
    2. Hemorrhage.
    3. Regurgitation and aspiration of gastric contents.
    4. Incarceration of stomach in the chest, with possible necrosis, peritonitis, and mediastinitis.

Treatment

A. Medical treatment.
    1. Reduction of stomach distension.
    2. Reduction of stomach acidity.
    3. Reduction of increased levels of intraabdominal pressure.
B. Surgical reduction of hernia, via a thoracic or abdominal approach.

Nursing Management

A. Provide small, frequent meals, avoiding highly seasoned foods.
B. Maintain upright position during and after meals.
C. Give antacids after meals and at bedtime.
D. Elevate head of bed to avoid regurgitation.
E. Avoid anticholinergic drugs so that emptying of stomach is delayed.
F. Prevent constricting clothing about the waist and sharp, forward bending.

Esophageal Neoplasms

A. Benign lesions.
    1. Leiomyoma most common type.
    2. Asymptomatic.
B. Malignant lesions.
    1. Usually occur in lower two-thirds of esophagus.
    2. Mainly affect men over fifty.
    3. Smoking and alcohol are risk factors.
        a. Poor prognosis (less than 5 years' survival) due to early lymphatic spread and late development of symptoms.
        b. Dysphagia most common symptom.
        c. Diagnosis made by barium swallow, esophagoscopy, biopsy.

Treatment

A. Surgical excision.
B. Radiation therapy (fistulas may be a complication).

Nursing Management

A. Maintain fluid and electrolyte balance.
B. Manage nutrition needs (hyperalimentation therapy may be used).
C. Administer gastrostomy (tube feedings), if needed.
D. Observe for complications of poor nutrition, ulceration and hemorrhage, fistula formation, and pneumothorax in end-stage disease.
E. Provide emotional support.

Gastric Disorders

Dyspepsia Indigestion

Definition: Indigestion caused by diseases of the G.I. system, eating too rapidly, emotional problems, inadequate chewing, eating improperly cooked foods, systemic diseases, food allergies, and altered gastric secretion or motility.

Clinical Manifestations

A. Heartburn.
B. Flatulence.
C. Nausea.
D. Eructations.
E. Feeling of fullness.

Nursing Management

A. Based on the cause of the disorder.
B. Antacids and bland diets.
C. Antispasmodics, and tranquilizers.
D. Altered eating habits.

Anorexia Nervosa

Definition: Underlying emotional disorders cause psychogenic aversion to food, with resulting emaciation. It usually occurs in females during the late teens or early twenties.

Clinical Manifestations

A. Loss of one-fourth to one-half or more of the body weight.
B. Amenorrhea.
C. Vomiting when food is forced.
D. Hypotension.
E. Anemia.
F. Hypoproteinemia.

Treatment

A. Supportive care.
B. Tube feedings.
C. Psychiatric treatment.

Acute Gastritis

Definition: Acute gastritis is an inflammation of the stomach.

Causes

A. Ingestion of infectious, corrosive or erosive substance (such as alcohol, aspirin and food poisoning).
B. Acute systemic infections.
C. Radiotherapy or chemotherapy.

Clinical Manifestations

A. Pain.
B. Nausea and vomiting.
C. Malaise.
D. Hemorrhage.
E. Anorexia.
F. Headache.

Treatment

A. Remove cause and treat symptomatically.
B. Drugs often include antacids and phenothiazines.

Chronic Gastritis

Definition: Chronic gastritis is nondescript upper abdominal distress with vague symptoms which indicate that other causes should be explored.

Types

A. Atrophic—decreased number of gastric cells, and shrinking of mucosa and muscular layers.
B. Hypertrophic—modular, thickened, irregular mucosa.
C. Superficial—edematous, reddened mucosa with erosions.

Clinical Manifestations

A. Vary greatly; majority of persons do not have symptoms.
B. Usually include dyspepsia, anorexia, and eructations.
C. Foul taste in mouth.
D. Nausea and vomiting.
E. Pain; mild epigastric tenderness.
F. Complications.
    1. Hemorrhage.
    2. Scarring of mucosa.
    3. Ulcer formation.
    4. Malnutrition.

Treatment

The same as for peptic ulcer.

Peptic Ulcer

Definition: Peptic ulcer is an ulceration in the mucosal wall of the stomach, pylorus, or duodenum, occurring in portions that are accessible to gastric secretions. Erosion may extend through the muscle to the peritoneum.

Pathophysiology

A. Any condition which upsets the balance between digestion and protection.
    1. Digestive balance: HCl and pepsin secretion.
    2. Protective balance: hormone mucin.
B. Predisposing factors.
    1. Emotional stress.

2. Excessive smoking.
3. Ingestion of steroids and ASA.
4. Irregular eating patterns.

Diagnostic Evaluation

A. Medical history and symptoms.
B. Upper G.I. series—most definitive.
C. Gastroscopy—fiberoptic panendoscopy.
D. Gastric analysis—helpful in atypical cases.
E. Laboratory examination of blood and stools.

Treatment

A. Medical management—duodenal and peptic ulcers.
   1. Antacids.
      a. Action.
         (1) Reduce gastric acidity.
         (2) Effects last longer if taken one hour after meals.
      b. Types of nonabsorbable antacids.
         (1) Calcium carbonate is most effective but may cause hypercalcemia, hypercalciuria, and constipation.
         (2) Magnesium oxide is more potent than either magnesium trisilicate or magnesium carbonate.
         (3) Aluminum hydroxide—high sodium content and constipation are disadvantages.
         (4) Sodium bicarbonate is absorbed and should be avoided to prevent systemic alkalosis.
      c. Side effects.
         (1) Diarrhea.
         (2) Constipation.
   2. Anticholinergic drugs—duodenal ulcers.
      a. Action.
         (1) Decrease effect of vagus nerve and increase neutralization of gastric juice by food and antacids.
         (2) Drug most effective if given thirty minutes before meals because it peaks in two hours, which covers the maximum secretory response to food (15 to 75 minutes).
         (3) Cannot be used in patients with glaucoma and prostatic hypertrophy.

b. Types.
   (1) Pro-banthine.
   (2) Belladonna.
c. Contraindications—gastric ulcers (stimulate gastrin because of prolonging emptying time of stomach).
d. Side effects are dry mouth, vertigo, blurred vision, urinary retention, flushed dry skin, and constipation.

B. Surgical treatment.
   1. Indications: perforations, intractable bleeding, organic obstruction, and nonresponse to medical treatment.
   2. Goals: permanent reduction in secretion of pepsin and hydrochloric acid.

C. Dietary.
   1. Three nutritious meals.
   2. Foods that are highly seasoned, rough, greasy, or fried should be avoided.
   3. Prolonged use of milk and cream may increase the incidence of atherosclerosis and actually stimulate acid production.
   4. Alcohol is contraindicated as it releases gastrin, stimulates the parietal cell, and may damage the mucosa.
   5. Tea, coffee, and cola should be avoided because caffeine stimulates gastric secretion.
   6. No bedtime snack (stimulates acid secretion).

D. Rest.
   1. Adequate sleep is strongly advised.
   2. Business and social responsibilities should be curtailed during acute phase.
   3. Hospitalization may be required if therapy is not effective in one week's time.
   4. Sedatives and tranquilizers may be helpful for the anxious, tense patient.
   5. Treatment aimed at stress control and tension-releasing activities.

Nursing Management

A. Overall goals are to promote healing and to avoid complications.
B. Promote relief of symptoms.
   1. Eliminate factors that stimulate gastric secretions, such as alcohol, cigarettes, coffee, tea, cola, and ulcerogenic drugs.

2. Administer medications.
   a. Antacids to neutralize hydrochloric acid.
   b. Anticholinergics (for duodenal ulcer) to decrease gastric motility and suppress gastric secretions.
   c. Iron and ascorbic acid to promote healing.
   d. Sedatives to decrease anxiety.
3. Avoid gas-forming foods, which cause pain.
4. Reduce stressful situations.
   a. Allow patient to care for important business obligations.
   b. Eliminate visitors or duties that increase stress.
   c. Teach autogenic methods of stress reduction and relaxation.
5. Provide patient and family instruction.
   a. Diet.
   b. Activity levels and rest.
   c. Correct use of medications.
   d. Potential complications and how to deal with them.

Complications

A. Hemorrhage, ranging from slight blood loss (revealed by occult blood in stool) to massive blood loss, which may lead to shock.
   1. Symptoms.
      a. Dark, granular (coffee ground) emesis is a result of acid digestion of blood in the stomach.
      b. Tarry, black stools result when blood is completely digested.
      c. Hematemesis (vomiting of bright red blood).
      d. Bright red blood from rectum. Occurs when bleeding is from high in the G.I. tract and there is concurrent rapid G.I. motility.
   2. Medical management.
      a. Bed rest.
      b. Frequent observation of vital signs.
      c. Observation of consistency, color, and volume of vomitus and stools.
      d. Nasogastric suction to empty the stomach of clots and blood and to watch the rate of bleeding.
      e. Blood, plasma, or I.V. fluids to support blood volume.
      f. Narcotics and/or tranquilizers to reduce restlessness and to relieve pain.
      g. Gavage with ice water to increase vasoconstriction.

B. Perforation—occurs almost exclusively in males twenty-five to forty years of age.
   1. Symptoms.
      a. Acute onset of severe, persistent pain that increases in intensity and can be referred to the shoulder.
      b. Tender, board-like rigidity of the abdomen.
      c. Free air visible on flat plate of the abdomen.
   2. Treatment: surgical intervention.
   3. If left untreated, perforations that seal off may cause abscess.

C. Pyloric obstruction.
   1. Causes: scarring, edema, or inflammation at the pylorus.
   2. Symptoms.
      a. Nausea and vomiting.
      b. Pain.
      c. Weight loss.
      d. Constipation.
      e. Persistent vomiting can lead to alkalosis.
   3. Treatment.
      a. Intravenous fluids with electrolytes.
      b. Gastric decompression.
      c. Surgery to release the obstruction.

Gastric Cancer

Definition: Carcinoma of the stomach is a common cancer of the digestive tract.

Incidence

A. Responsible for twenty thousand deaths annually in the United States.
B. Has decreased in incidence during the last twenty years, but is a significant cause of death because of low cure rate.
C. Occurs twice as often in males as in females, and more often in Blacks than in other races.
D. Found frequently in conjunction with pernicious anemia and atrophic gastritis.
E. Worldwide incidence varies.

Table 1. Comparison of Duodenal and Gastric Ulcer

	Chronic Duodenal Ulcer	Chronic Gastric Ulcer
Age	Usually twenty-five to fifty	Usually fifty and over
Sex	Male:female—3:1	Male:female—2:1
Blood group	Most frequently type O	No differentiation
Social class	Executives, leaders in competitive fields	Laborers
Incidence	80%	20%
General nourishment	Well nourished	Malnourished
Acid production in stomach	Hypersecretion	Normal to hyposecretion
Location	Within 3 cm. of pylorus	Lesser curvature
Pain	2–3 hours after meal; night and early morning. Ingestion of food relieves pain. (Pain is a gnawing sensation sharply localized in midepigastrium or in back.)	½–1 hour after meal; rarely at night. Relieved by vomiting. Ingestion of food does not help; sometimes causes pain.
Vomiting	Uncommon	Common—caused by pyloric obstruction by either muscular spasm of pylorus or by mechanical obstruction from scarring
Hemorrhage	Melena more common than hematemesis	Hematemesis more common than melena
Malignancy possibility	None	Usually less than 10 percent
Complications	Hemorrhage, perforation and obstruction	Hemorrhage and perforation

Clinical Manifestations

A. Vary according to location of tumor; early carcinoma causes no symptoms.
B. Weight loss and anorexia.
C. Feeling of vague fullness and sensation of pressure.
D. Anemia from blood loss.
E. Occult blood in stools.
F. Vomiting if pylorus becomes obstructed.
G. Late symptoms: ascites, palpable mass, and pain from metastasis.
H. Metastasis.
   1. Occurs by direct extension into surrounding tissue.
   2. Spreads through lymphatic and hematogenous systems.

Treatment

A. Surgical resection.
   1. Surgical mortality is 5 to 12 percent.
   2. Five-year survival rate is 5 to 15 percent.
B. Chemotherapy—response has not been consistent; may shorten lifespan if toxic effects occur.
C. Radiation not proven helpful.

Nursing Management (see p. 100).

Intestinal Disorders

Regional Enteritis (Regional Ileitis, Crohn's Disease)

Definition: Regional enteritis is an inflammatory disease of the small intestine that is chronic and relapsing. It results in thickening, scarring, and granulomas of intestinal tissues, which cause narrow lumen, fistulas, ulcerations, and abscesses. The etiology is unknown, but may be related to altered immunologic reactivity.

Incidence

A. Occurs at all ages.
B. Usually observed in second and third decade of life.
C. High incidence of familial occurrence.
D. High incidence in Jewish population; low in Blacks.

Clinical Manifestations

A. Cramp-like pain after meals.
B. Weight loss.
C. Malnutrition.
D. Secondary anemia.
E. Chronic diarrhea.
F. Fever.
G. Acute perforation, generalized peritonitis, and massive melena are sometimes present at onset.

Nursing Management

A. Diet: low residue, bland, with iron and vitamin supplements.
B. Medications.
   1. Antibiotics (nonabsorbable sulfonamides) to control infection.
   2. Antiinflammatory drugs to reduce swollen membranes.
   3. Antidiarrheal agents to control diarrhea.
   4. Sedatives and narcotics to reduce apprehension and pain.
C. Surgical intervention (ileostomy) for complications.

Malignant Tumors of Small Intestine

Incidence

A. Adenocarcinoma of the duodenum is the most common lesion.
B. In the United States, less than one percent of G.I. tract cancers arise in the small bowel.
C. Occurs in younger age group.
D. Twice as common in men.

Clinical Manifestations

A. Abnormal stools.
B. Weight loss.
C. Anorexia.
D. Vomiting.
E. Crampy pain.
F. Intestinal obstruction.
G. Biliary obstruction.
H. Malabsorption.
I. Intestinal bleeding.

Treatment

A. Surgical excision.
B. Prognosis poor.

Malignant Tumors of Large Intestine

Incidence

A. Second most frequent cause of death from cancer.
B. Men and women equally affected.
   1. CA colon more common in women.
   2. CA rectum more common in men.
C. Metastasis.
   1. By direct extension, usually to stomach from transverse colon, bladder, and bowel.
   2. Lymphatic and hematogenic.
   3. Seeding into peritoneal cavity.

Clinical Manifestations

A. G.I. bleeding.
B. Change in bowel habits.
C. Abdominal pain.
D. Weight loss.
E. Anorexia.
F. Nausea and vomiting.

Treatment

A. Surgical intervention—colostomy.

B. Cytotoxic drug therapy following surgery.

Nursing Management—Preoperative

A. Inform patient of colostomy procedure and care.

B. Provide psychological support.

C. Maintain low-residue or liquid diet.

D. Administer antibiotics.

E. Utilize G.I. decompression, if necessary.

Intestinal Obstructions

Definition: An intestinal obstruction is an impairment of the forward flow of intestinal contents by partial or complete stoppage.

Types

A. Mechanical.
   1. Adhesions—fibrous bands of scar tissue, following abdominal surgery, may become looped over a portion of the bowel.
   2. Hernias—incarcerated or strangulated.
   3. Volvulus—twisting of the bowel.
   4. Intussusception—telescoping of the bowel upon itself.
   5. Tumors.
   6. Hematoma.
   7. Fecal impaction.
   8. Intraluminal obstruction.

B. Neurogenic.
   1. Paralytic, adynamic ileus.
   2. Ineffective peristalsis due to toxic or traumatic disturbance of the autonomic nervous system.

C. Vascular—occlusion of the arterial blood supply to the bowel.
   1. Mesenteric thrombosis.
   2. Abdominal angina.

Pathophysiology

A. Fluids and air collect proximal to the obstruction.
   1. Peristalsis increases as the bowel attempts to force material through.
   2. Peristalsis ends and the bowel becomes blocked.

B. Pressure increases in the bowel and decreases the absorptive ability.

C. Circulating blood volume is reduced and shock may develop.

D. Location of the obstruction determines the symptoms and progression of the clinical course.

Clinical Manifestations

A. Small bowel obstruction.
   1. Cramp-like pain in midabdomen.
   2. Nausea and early severe vomiting.
   3. Reverse peristalsis.
   4. Dehydration.
   5. Abdominal distention.
   6. Shock and death.

B. Large bowel obstruction.
   1. Progression of symptoms is slower than with small bowel obstruction.
   2. Constipation.
   3. Abdominal distention.
   4. Cramp-like pain in lower abdomen.
   5. Fecal vomiting if ileocecal valve incompetent.

C. Paralytic ileus.
   1. Dull, diffused pain.
   2. Gaseous distention.
   3. Constipation.
   4. Vomiting after eating.

Treatment

A. Intestinal decompression to remove gas and fluid.

B. Parenteral fluids to replace fluids and electrolytes.
   1. Sodium, potassium, and chloride.
   2. Dextrose and water.

C. Antibiotics to prevent secondary infections (especially peritonitis).

Nursing Management

A. Observe and report the nature, duration, and character of pain.

B. Assess the presence and progression of distention and the absence of flatus and stool.

C. Observe for signs and symptoms of fluid and electrolyte imbalance.

D. Measure and record vital signs, intake and output, and emesis.

E. Save stool for testing.

F. Prepare patient for surgery, if indicated.

Diverticulosis and Diverticulitis

Definitions: Diverticulum is the outpouching of the intestinal mucosa which may occur at any point in the gastrointestinal tract but more commonly in the sigmoid colon. It is caused by congenital weakness and increased pressure in the lumen. Diverticulosis is the presence of multiple diverticula. Diverticulitis is the inflammation of diverticula.

Clinical Manifestations

A.   No symptoms unless complications develop.
B.   Large bowel diverticula are more apt to develop complications.
C.   Complications are perforation, hemorrhage, inflammation, fistulas, and abscess.
D.   Diverticulitis produces cramp-like pain, flatulence, nausea, fever, irregularity, irritability and spasticity of the intestine, urinary frequency, and dysuria associated with bladder involvement.
E.   Diagnosis.
   1.   Upper and lower G.I. series.
   2.   Sigmoidoscopy.

Treatment

A.   Acute phase.
   1.   Intravenous fluids with electrolytes.
   2.   Bed rest.
   3.   NPO.
   4.   Nasogastric decompression.
   5.   Drugs: antibiotics, analgesics, antispasmodics, and bulk former (Metamucil).
B.   Diet.
   1.   Current studies indicate a high residue diet using bran fiber for diverticulosis.
   2.   Low residue regime for severe inflammatory phase of diverticulitis.
C.   Surgery may be necessary.

Nursing Management

A.   Instruct patient and family in pathology and rationale for treatment.
B.   Maintain high residue diet with bulk additives and vitamin and iron supplements.
C.   Administer anticholinergics: Donnatol, Pro-banthine.
D.   Provide sedatives and tranquilizers for anxiety.
E.   Monitor stool normalization: bowel lubricant nightly, bulk preparation daily, evacuant suppository, vegetable oil, unprocessed bran in fruit juice daily.

Ulcerative Colitis

Definition: Ulcerative colitis is a chronic ulcerative and inflammatory disease of the colon and rectum, which commonly begins in the rectum and sigmoid colon and spreads upward. The disease is characterized by periods of exacerbations and remissions.

Etiology and Incidence

A.   Cause unknown, but theories include autoimmune factor, allergic reaction, specific vulnerability of colon, emotional instability, and bacterial infection.
B.   Most common in young adulthood and middle life. More prevalent among Jews; less common in Blacks than Whites.

Clinical Manifestations

A.   Types of onset.
   1.   Gradual onset.
      a.   Malaise.
      b.   Early—vague abdominal discomfort.
      c.   Later—crampy abdominal pain.
      d.   Bowel evacuation—pus, mucus, and blood.
      e.   Stools scanty and hard.
      f.   Painful straining with defecation.
   2.   Abrupt onset.
      a.   Severe diarrhea (15-20 watery stools a day that may contain blood and mucus).
      b.   Fever.
      c.   Anorexia.
      d.   Weight loss.
      e.   Abdominal tenderness.
      f.   Rectal and anal spasticity.
      g.   Consistency of stools vary with area of colon involved.
B.   Complications.
   1.   Dehydration.
   2.   Magnesium and calcium imbalances.
   3.   Anemia and malnutrition—malabsorption and iron and vitamin K deficiency.
   4.   Perforation, peritonitis, and hemorrhage.
   5.   Abscesses and strictures.
   6.   Carcinomatous degeneration (if more than ten years' duration).

7. Hemorrhoids and anal fissures.
8. Bleeding tendency.

C. Diagnosis.
   1. Medical history.
   2. Clinical manifestations.
   3. Lower G.I. series.
   4. Stool and blood examinations.
   5. Sigmoidoscopy.

Treatment

A. Sedatives and tranquilizers to relieve anxiety and to decrease peristalsis.
B. Antibiotics for secondary bowel inflammations.
C. Steroid therapy for inflammation, toxicity, and emotional symptoms.
D. Anticholinergic drugs to relieve cramps and to control diarrhea.
E. Surgical treatment when medical management fails.

Nursing Management

A. Major goal—prevent acute episodes and/or manage complications.
B. Maintain nutritional status.
   1. High protein, high calorie diet, if tolerated.
   2. Avoid gas-forming foods and milk products.
   3. All foods should be cooked to reduce cramping and diarrhea.
   4. Vitamin and iron supplements.
   5. Eating may increase diarrhea and anorexia.
C. Replace fluid and electrolytes.
   1. 3–4 liters/day.
   2. Added KCl.
D. Correct psychological disturbances.
   1. Allow patient to ventilate his feelings; accept him as he is.
   2. Help patient live with chronic disease (a change in life style may be necessary).
   3. Avoid emotional probing during periods of acute illness.
   4. Provide patient and family with instructions about pathology of the disease and rationale for treatment.
E. Administer drugs as ordered.
   1. Steroids.
      a. Induce remissions.
      b. Given I.V. in acute episode.
      c. Given rectally for long term.

2. Anti-infectives.
   a. Routine sulfonamides to reduce severity of attack.
   b. Antibiotic therapy for systemic infections.
3. Immunosuppressives.
4. Tranquilizers: e.g., phenobarbital.
5. Anticholinergics.
   a. Relieve abdominal cramps.
   b. Assist in controlling diarrhea.
6. In acute stages cathartics contraindicated.

F. Maintain bed rest during acute phase.

Hemorrhoids

Definition: Hemorrhoids are dilated varicose veins of the anal canal that may be internal or external.

Types

A. Internal hemorrhoids occur above the internal sphincter and are covered by mucous membrane.
B. External hemorrhoids occur outside the external sphincter and are covered by anal skin.
C. Thrombosed hemorrhoids are infected and clotted.

Causes

A. Portal hypertension.
B. Straining from constipation.
C. Irritation and diarrhea.
D. Increased venous pressure from congestive heart failure.
E. Increased abdominal pressure as from pregnancy.

Clinical Manifestations

A. Itching.
B. Pain.
C. Bleeding.
D. Incontinence.
E. Complications.
   1. Hemorrhage.
   2. Strangulation.
   3. Thrombosis.
   4. Prolapse.

Treatment

A. Medical or surgical injection of sclerosing substance.

B. Temporary relief from sitz baths or analgesic ointment.

Nursing Management

A. Treat constipation and other causes of increased pressure.

B. Maintain low roughage diet.

C. Provide nonirritating laxatives or mineral oil.

D. Provide suppositories, ointments, and systemic analgesics.

E. Administer hot sitz baths.

Disorders of Liver, Biliary, and Pancreatic Function

Diagnostic Evaluation Studies

Physical Examination

A. Palpation of the abdomen to determine tenderness, size, and shape of liver and spleen.

B. Visual inspection for ascites, venous networks, and jaundice.

Radiologic Techniques

A. Cholecystogram—to visualize the gallbladder for detection of gall stones, and to determine the ability of the gallbladder to fill, concentrate, contract, and empty normally.
   1. Organic radiopaque dye may be given by mouth ten to twelve hours before X-ray, or intravenously ten minutes before X-ray.
   2. Dyes taken orally (e.g., Telepaque, Priodax, Arografin) are given one at a time at three to five minute intervals with at least 240 cc. of water. A low-fat evening meal precedes the dye ingestion. Patients are NPO until after examinaation. An enema is given before test.

B. Cholangiography—the dye (e.g., Urokon Sodium) is injected directly into the biliary tree.
   1. May be injected into the common duct drain during surgery or postoperatively.
   2. Gallbladder disease is indicated by poor or absent visualization of the gallbladder.
   3. Stones will appear as shadows within the opaque medium.

C. Scanning of the liver—iodine 131 or other like substances are administered intravenously; then a scintillation detector is passed over the area.
   1. Lesions appear as filling defects.
   2. The isotopes are concentrated in functioning tissue.

D. Other procedures with contrast media: celiac angiography, hepatoportography, splenoportography, and pancreatic angiography.
   1. With all these procedures, organic iodine dye is injected into the vessel, flowing to and outlining the desired area.
   2. Reveals the patency of the vessels and the lesions that distort the vasculature.

Liver Biopsy

A. Sampling of liver tissues by needle aspiration to determine tissue changes and to facilitate diagnosis.

B. Nursing management prior to procedure.
   1. Verify test results of prothrombin times and blood typing. Low PT (prothrombin time) and an uncooperative patient are contraindications.
   2. Obtain baseline vital signs and written permission.
   3. Keep NPO and provide sedation as ordered.
   4. Assemble equipment, position patient, and assist with procedure.
   5. Support patient; let him verbalize fears.

C. Nursing management following procedure.
   1. Position patient on right side over biopsy site to prevent hemorrhage.
   2. Measure and record vital signs.
   3. Watch for shock.
   4. Observe for complications: hemorrhage, puncture of the bile duct, peritonitis, and pneumothorax.

Laboratory Tests

A. Biliary excretion.
   1. Serum bilirubin—abnormal in biliary and liver disease causing jaundice.
      a. Direct (conjugated)—normal: 0.2 mg./100 ml., soluble in H_2O.
      b. Indirect (unconjugated)—normal: 0.8 mg./100 ml., insoluble in H_2O.
      c. Total serum bilirubin—normal: 1.0 mg./100 ml.
   2. Urine bilirubin—normally none is found.
   3. Urine urobilinogen—0 to 4 mg./24 hours.

4. Fecal urobilinogen—40 to 280 mg./24 hours.
5. Serum cholesterol—150 to 250 mg./100 ml.

B. Protein studies.
1. Total protein—6 to 8 g./100 ml.
2. Serum albumin—3.5 to 5.56 m./100 ml.
3. Serum globulin—2.5 to 3.56 m./100 ml.
4. Prothrombin time—12 to 15 sec.
5. Cephalin—0 to 1+.
6. In liver damage, fewer plasma proteins are synthesized; thus, albumin synthesis is reduced.
   a. Serum globulins produced by the plasma cells are increased.
   b. PT is reduced in liver cell damage.

C. Fat metabolism—serum lipase 1.5 units.

D. Carbohydrate metabolism—glucose tolerance levels should return to normal in one to two hours.

E Liver detoxification.
1. Bromsulphalein excretion (BSP) should be less than five percent dye retention after one hour.
2. Dye is injected intravenously and removed by the liver cells, conjugated, and excreted.
3. Blood specimen is obtained at thirty-minute and one-hour intervals after injection.
4. Increased retention occurs in hepatic disorders.

F. Enzyme production—elevations reflect organ damage.
1. SGOT: 10 to 40 units.
2. SGPT: 5 to 35 units.
3. LDH: 165 to 400 units.

G. Alkaline phosphatase (2 to 5 units) elevated in obstructive jaundice and in liver metastasis.

H. Blood ammonia (20 to 50 mg. %/100 ml.)—ammonia level rises in liver failure since liver converts ammonia to urea. Metabolic alkalosis increases the toxicity of NH_3.

Jaundice

Definition: Jaundice is a symptom of a disease which results in yellow pigmentation of the skin due to accumulation of bilirubin pigment. Jaundice is usually first observed in the sclera of the eye.

Types

A. Hemolytic.
1. Results from rapid rate of red blood cell destruction which releases excessive amounts of unconjugated bilirubin.
2. Caused by hemolytic transfusion reactions, erythroblastosis fetalis, and other hemolytic disorders.
3. Findings: increased indirect (unconjugated) serum bilirubin, absence of bilirubin in urine, and increased urobilinogen levels.

B. Hepatocellular.
1. Results from inability of the diseased liver cells to clear the normal amount of bilirubin from the blood.
2. Caused by viral liver cell necrosis or cirrhosis of the liver.
3. Findings: increased bilirubin, SGOT, SGPT, alkaline phosphatase, and urobilinogen in urine; increased PT; decreased albumin.

C. Obstructive.
1. Caused by intrahepatic obstruction due to inflammation, tumors, or cholestatic agents.
2. Bile is dammed into the liver substance and reabsorbed into the blood.
3. Deep orange, foamy urine; white or clay-colored stools; and severe itching (pruritus).
4. Findings: increased bilirubin, alkaline phosphatase, and PT; decreased stool urobilinogen.

Nursing Management

A. Determine cause and treat.

B. Control puritus.
1. Starch or baking soda baths.
2. Soothing lotions, such as calamine.
3. Antihistamines, tranquilizers, and sedatives.
4. Cholestyramine—binds bile salt.

C. Provide emotional support.
1. Allow patient to ventilate feelings of altered body image.
2. Notify family and visitors of patient's appearance.

D. Provide dietary plan for anorexia and liver involvement.

Viral Hepatitis

Definition: Viral hepatitis is the inflammation of the liver; the most common infection of the liver, often becoming a major health problem in crowded living conditions.

Type A Hepatitis (Infectious Hepatitis)

A. Transmission.
1. Oral-anal route.
2. Blood transfusion with infected serum or plasma.
3. Contaminated equipment, such as syringes and needles.
4. Contaminated milk, water, and food (uncooked clams and oysters).
5. Respiratory route is possible, but not yet established.
6. Antibodies persist in serum.
B. Incubation period: twenty to fifty days. (Short incubation period.)
C. Incidence.
1. More common in fall and winter months.
2. Usually found in children and young adults.
3. Patient is infectious three weeks prior to and one week after developing jaundice.

Clinical Manifestations

A. Pre-icteric phase.
1. Headache.
2. Fever.
3. Nausea and vomiting.
4. Anorexia.
5. Pain and abdominal tenderness.
B. Icteric phase.
1. Jaundice.
2. Dark urine.
3. Enlarged liver.
4. Nausea.
5. Dyspepsia.
6. Flatulence.
C. Clinical recovery: three to sixteen weeks.

Nursing Management

A. Wash hands carefully and take precautions during stool and needle procedures.
B. Use disposable equipment or sterilized reusable equipment.
C. Provide diet.
1. High calorie, well balanced diet; modified servings according to patient response.

2. Protein decreased if signs of coma.
3. Ten percent glucose I.V. if not taking oral foods.
D. Instruct patient and family.
1. Stress the importance of follow-up care.
2. Stress the restricted use of alcohol.
3. Stress that patient never offer to be a blood donor.
4. Encourage gamma globulin for close contacts.
5. Advise correction if any unsanitary condition exists in the home.
E. Maintain bed rest during symptomatic stage.

Type B Hepatitis (Serum Hepatitis, SH Virus)

A. Transmission.
1. Oral or parenteral route with infusion, ingestion, or inhalation of the blood of an infected person.
2. Contaminated equipment, such as needles, syringes, and dental instruments.
3. Infected people can become carriers.
4. Caused by filtrable virus—Australian antigen.
B. Incubation period: forty to one hundred eighty days. (Long incubation period.)

Clinical Manifestations

A. Variable, ranging from asymptomatic to a fulminating disease.
B. Similar to infectious hepatitis but more severe.
C. Recovery: four months or more.

Nursing Management

A. Maintain bed rest until symptoms have decreased.
1. Activities restricted while liver is enlarged.
2. Activities discouraged until serum bilirubin is normal.
B. Provide well-balanced diet supplemented with vitamins.
C. Administer antacids for gastric acidity and soporifics for rest and relaxation.
D. Instruct patient and family in pathology of the disease and rationale for treatment.

Cirrhosis / Portal Hypertension

Definition: Cirrhosis is a progressive disease of the liver characterized by diffuse damage to the cells with fibrosis and nodular regeneration. The altered liver structure impedes blood flow via portal system leading to portal hypertension.

Types

A. Laennec's portal cirrhosis (alcoholic/nutritional).
1. Most common in the United States.
2. Scar tissue surrounds the portal areas.
3. Characterized by destruction of hepatic tissue, increased fibrous tissue, and disorganized regeneration.
B. Postnecrotic cirrhosis—a sequela to viral hepatitis in which there are broad bands of scar tissue.
C. Biliary cirrhosis.
1. Pericholangitic scarring as a result of chronic biliary obstruction and infection.
2. Least encountered of the three types.

Etiology

A. Repeated destruction of hepatic cells, replacement with scar tissue, and regeneration of liver cells.
B. Insidious onset with progression over a period of years.
C. Occurs twice as often in males; primarily affects forty- to sixty-year-old age group.

Clinical Manifestations

A. Long history of failing health, weakness, gastrointestinal distress, fatigue, weight loss, and low resistance to infections.
B. Emaciation and ascites due to malnutrition, portal hypertension, and hypoalbuminemia.
C. Hematemesis.
D. Lower leg edema from ascites obstructing venous return from legs.
E. Liver palpable and blunt.
F. Prominent abdominal wall veins from collateral vessels bypass.
G. Esophageal varices and hemorrhoids from portal hypertension.
H. Skin manifestations: spider angiomas, telangiectasia, vitamin deficiency, and alterations.
I. Laboratory tests.
1. Impaired hepatocellular function; elevated bilirubin, SGOT, SGPT, and LDH; reduced BSP; reduced albumin; and elevated PT.
2. Increased WBC, decreased RBC, coagulation abnormalities, increased gamma globulin, and proteinuria.
J. Pre-coma: tremor, delirium, and dysarthria.

Treatment

A. Maximize liver function.
1. Diet: ample protein to build tissue; carbohydrates to sustain weight and to provide energy.
2. Salt restriction in edema.
3. Multivitamin supplement (especially B).
4. Diuretics—spironolactones.
B. Eliminate hepatotoxin intake.
1. Completely restrict use of alcohol.
2. Lower the dosage of drugs metabolized by the liver.
3. Avoid sedatives and opiates.
4. Avoid all known hepatotoxic drugs (Thorazine, halothane).
C. Prevent infection by adequate rest, diet, and environmental control.
D. Restore plasma proteins.
E. Prevent and control complications.
1. Ascites.
2. Bleeding esophageal varices.
3. Hepatic encephalopathy.
4. Anemia.

Nursing Management

A. Maintain adequate rest during acute phase.
B. Monitor I & O due to fluid restriction.
C. Instruct, prepare, and support patient during diagnostic evaluation.
D. Provide good skin care and control pruritus.
E. Observe for signs of complications.
F. Evaluate nutritional status and response of the patient to diet therapy.
G. Measure, record, and compare vital signs.
1. Character of pain.
2. Progression of edema.
3. Character of emesis and stools.
H. Evaluate level of consciousness, personality changes, and signs of increasing stupor.
I. Instruct patient and family in pathology and rationale for treatment.

Hepatic Coma (Hepatic Encephalopathy)

Definition: Hepatic coma results from brain cell alterations due to build-up of ammonia levels.

Etiology

A. Increased blood ammonia levels.
   1. Normally, ammonia is formed in the intestines from the breakdown of protein and is converted by the liver to urea.
   2. In liver failure, ammonia is not converted into urea, and blood ammonia concentrations increase.
B. Any process that increases protein in the intestine, such as G.I. hemorrhage and high protein intake, will cause elevated blood ammonia.
C. Other factors involved in high ammonia levels.
   1. Electrolyte and acid-base imbalances. Alkalosis increases toxicity of NH_3.
   2. Constipation.
   3. Infectious diseases.
   4. Central nervous system depressants.
   5. Shunting of blood into systemic circulation without passing through the hepatic sinusoids.

Clinical Manifestations

A. Mental aberrations.
   1. Impaired memory, attention, concentration, and rate of response.
   2. Personality changes: untidiness, confusion, and inappropriate behavior.
B. Depressed level of consciousness and flapping tremor (liver flap) upon dorsiflexion of hand.
C. Disorientation and eventual coma.

Treatment

A. Eliminate precipitating cause.
B. Temporarily eliminate protein from the diet.
C. Give bile salts to assist absorption of vitamin A.
D. Administer antibiotics to destroy intestinal bacteria and to reduce the amount of ammonia formed.
E. Give folic acid and iron to prevent anemia.
F. Give enemas and/or cathartics to empty bowel and to prevent further ammonia formation.
G. Give salt-poor albumin to maintain osmotic pressure.
H. Use cation exchange resins to remove toxin substances from the bowel.
I. Correct fluid and electrolyte imbalances.
J. Avoid depressants which must be detoxified by the liver. Use agents such as phenobarbital that are excreted through the kidneys.

Nursing Management

A. Observe, measure, and record neurologic status daily.
   1. Test ability to perform mental tasks.
   2. Keep samples of handwriting.
B. Weigh daily.
C. Measure and record intake and output.
D. Prevent complications—decubitus, thrombophlebitis, pneumonia.
E. Give sedatives and analgesics sparingly.
F. With coma, utilize same nursing skills as with the unconscious patient.

Cholecystitis with Cholelithiasis

Definitions: Cholecystitis is an inflammation of the gallbladder; cholelithiasis indicates the presence of gallstones in common bile duct.

Incidence and Etiology

A. Four times more common in women.
B. Usually occurs during 40s.
C. Obesity predisposing factor.
D. Usually caused by strep, staph, or typhoid.

Clinical Manifestations

A. Cholecystitis.
   1. Epigastric distress—eructation after eating.
   2. Pain—localized in right upper quadrant because of somatic sensory nerves.
   3. Pain begins two to four hours after eating fried or fatty foods.
   4. Nausea, vomiting, and anorexia.
   5. Fever.
   6. Jaundice due to hepatocellular damage.
   7. Weight loss.
B. Cholelithiasis.
   1. Pain—excruciating, upper right quadrant—

radiates to right shoulder (biliary colic).

2. Pain—sudden, intense, paroxysmal—occurs with contraction of gallbladder.
3. Nausea and vomiting.
4. Jaundice due to obstructions and/or hepatocellular damage.

Treatment

A. Medical.
   1. Drug therapy.
      a. Chenodeoxycholic acid—bile acid dissolves cholesterol calculi (90 percent of stones).
      b. Nitroglycerin or papaverine to reduce spasms of duct.
      c. Synthetic narcotics (Demerol, methadone) to relieve pain.
      d. Antibiotics as needed.
      e. Questran to relieve pruritus in obstruction.
   2. Low fat diet; avoid alcohol and gas-forming foods.
   3. Bed rest.
B. Surgical—cholecystectomy.

Nursing Management

A. Provide relief from vomiting.
   1. Position nasogastric tube and attach to low suction. The tube reduces distention and eliminates gastric juices that stimulate cholecystokinin.
   2. Provide good oral and nasal care; assure patency of tube and flow of gastric secretions.

B. Maintain fluid and electrolyte balance.
   1. Monitor intravenous fluids.
   2. Measure and record intake and output.
   3. Observe serum electrolyte levels; watch for signs of imbalance.

C. Prevent infection.
   1. Administer broad spectrum antibiotics.
   2. Monitor patient response; be alert to toxic reactions.

D. Observe for biliary obstruction.
   1. Jaundice—yellow sclera.
   2. Urine—dark orange and foamy.
   3. Feces—clay colored.
   4. Pruritus.

Acute Pancreatitis

Definition: Acute pancreatitis is an inflammation of the pancreas with associated escape of pancreatic enzymes into surrounding tissue.

Etiology

A. Primary condition—etiology unknown.
B. Condition occurs as a result of prednisone or thiazide therapy.
C. The most common precipitating factor is alcoholic indulgence.
D. Biliary tract disease with blocking of ampulla of Vater by gallstones.
E. Cholecystitis with reflux of bile components into the pancreatic duct.
F. Spasm and edema of ampulla of Vater following inflammation of the duodenum.
G. Complication of a viral or bacterial disease.

Clinical Manifestations

A. Acute interstitial pancreatitis.
   1. Constant epigastric abdominal pain radiating to the back and flank. More intense in supine position.
   2. Nausea, vomiting, abdominal distention, and paralytic ileus.
   3. Elevation of temperature in a few days.
   4. Severe perspiration.
   5. Anxiety.
   6. Elevation of white count—20,000 to 50,000.
   7. Jaundice.
   8. Elevated blood lipase and amylase.
B. Acute hemorrhagic pancreatitis.
   1. Pancreatic enzymes erode major blood vessels causing hemorrhage into the pancreas and retroperitoneal tissues.
   2. Enzymatic digestion of the pancreas.
   3. Severe abdominal, back, and flank pain.
   4. Ascites.
   5. Shock.

Nursing Management

A. Alleviate pain.
   1. Give meperidine (Demerol) as ordered.
   2. Avoid opiates, which may cause spasm of biliary-pancreatic ducts.

3. Give antispasmodic—atropine.
B. Reduce pancreatic stimulus.
   1. NPO to eliminate chief stimulus to enzyme release.
   2. Nasogastric tube to low suction to remove gastric secretions.
      a. Record characteristics and amounts of secretions.
      b. Utilize good oral and nasal hygiene.
   3. Drugs to reduce pancreatic secretion.
      a. Anticholinergics (e.g., Pro-banthine).
      b. Antacids.
      c. Diamox to prevent carbonic anhydrase from catalyzing secretion of bicarbonate into pancreatic juice.
   4. Diet to avoid pancreatic secretion; low fat, no alcohol or caffeine.
C. Take vital signs every 15 to 30 minutes during acute phase.
D. Prevent or treat infection with broad spectrum antibiotics.
E. Replace and maintain fluids and electrolytes.
   1. Replacements based on intake, output, serum levels of electrolytes, and clinical symptoms.
   2. Blood and plasma may be necessary to maintain circulatory volume.
F. Prevent hyperglycemia.
   1. Monitor blood sugar levels, fractional urines, and clinical symptoms.
   2. Administer insulin as indicated.
G. Reduce body metabolism.
   1. Oxygen for labored breathing.
   2. Bed rest.
   3. Cool, quiet environment.
H. Provide patient and family instruction.
   1. Discuss pathology of disease.
   2. Give rationale for treatment.
   3. Instruct patient to avoid alcohol, coffee, heavy meals, and spicy foods.
   4. Encourage follow-up visits with the physician.

Chronic Pancreatitis

Definition: Chronic pancreatitis is the chronic fibrosis of the pancreatic gland with obstruction of ducts and destruction of secreting cells, following repeated attacks of acute pancreatitis.

Clinical Manifestations

A. Pain—persistent epigastric and left upper quadrant pain with referral to back.
B. Anorexia, nausea, vomiting, and constipation.
C. Disturbances of protein and fat digestion.
   1. Malnutrition.
   2. Weight loss.
   3. Abdominal distention with flatus and paralytic ileus.
   4. Foul, fatty stools (steatorrhea).
D. Hyperglycemia with symptoms of diabetes.
E. Calcification of pancreas with stone deposits in duct
F. Elevated serum amylase and lipase; fecal fat in stool specimens; X-ray often shows pancreatolithiasis and mild ileus, indicating fibrous tissue and calcification.

Nursing Management

A. Give bland, low fat diet in small, frequent feedings.
B. Administer antacids and anticholinergic agents to reduce pancreatic activity.
C. Instruct patient to avoid alcohol as it may precipitate an attack.
D. Administer pancreatic replacements, such as pancreatin, Cotazym, and Viokase.
E. Report diabetic symptoms. (Associated diabetes is treated the same as for any diabetic patient.)
F. Administer bile salts to prevent loss of fat and to promote absorption of vitamins A, D, E, and K.
G. Surgical treatment for specific complications and to relieve constant pain.

Genitourinary System

The genitourinary system—the kidneys and their drainage channels—is essential for the maintenance of life. This system is responsible for excreting the end products of metabolism as well as regulating water and electrolyte concentrations of body fluids.

Anatomy and Physiology

Kidney Structure

A. Paired organs located to the right and left of midline lateral to lower thoracic vertebrae.

B. Kidneys perform two major functions.
   1. Excrete most of the end products of body metabolism.
   2. Control the concentrations of most of the constituents of body fluids.

C. Composed of structural units, each of which functions the same as the total kidney and is capable of forming urine by itself.

D. The functional renal unit is called the nephron. Each nephron is composed of:
   1. A glomerulus (a network of many capillaries) which filters fluid out of the blood. It is encased by Bowman's capsule.
   2. Tubules (proximal, Henle's loop, distal) in which fluid is converted to urine as it goes to the pelvis of the kidneys.

E. Fluid from Bowman's capsule moves through the proximal tubule located in the cortex.

F. Fluid then flows through Henle's loop located in medulla of kidney.

G. Fluid flows from loop to the collecting tubule.

H. After flowing through many convolutions, the fluid goes into a collecting sac called the pelvis of the kidney.

I. From the pelvis, fluid flows through the ureter and empties into the bladder.

Kidney Function

A. Urine production.
   1. As the fluid filtrate flows through the proximal tubules, 80 percent of the water and solutes are reabsorbed into tubular capillaries.
   2. The water and solutes that are not reabsorbed become urine.
   3. The amount of fluid and solutes excreted is determined through selective reabsorption.

B. Nephron function.
   1. The basic function is to rid the body of unwanted substances, the end products of metabolism (fluid and electrolytes).
   2. The nephron filters much of the plasma through the glomerular membrane into the tubules.
   3. The tubules filter the wanted elements of the blood (e.g., water and electrolytes) from the unwanted elements and reabsorb them into the plasma through the peritubular capillaries.
   4. Reabsorption and secretion take place by both active and passive transport.

C. Tubular reabsorption and secretion.
   1. Three substances filtered at glomerulus.
      a. Electrolytes: Na^+, K^+, Ca^{++}, Mg^{++}, HCO_3^-, Cl^-, and HPO_4^{--}.
      b. Nonelectrolytes: glucose, amino acids, urea, uric acid, creatinine.
      c. Water.
   2. Proximal tubule reabsorption.
      a. 80% of filtrate reabsorbed actively through obligatory reabsorption.
      b. H_2O, Na^+, and Cl^- continue through loop of Henle where Cl^- is actively transported out of ascending loop followed passively by Na^+

D. Glomerular filtration.
   1. Glomerular membrane is semipermeable (proteins and glucose do not cross the membrane).
   2. Amount of filtration is determined by hydrostatic pressure.
   3. A decrease in blood pressure leads to a decrease in GFR and therefore a decrease in urine output.
   4. Approximately 1000-2000 ml. blood flows through kidney each minute to produce 60 cc. urine output per hour.

E. Concentrating and diluting mechanisms.
   1. Countercurrent flow of blood and tubular fluid increase concentration of NaCl and therefore H_2O reabsorption.

2. ADH (antidiuretic hormone) controls H_2O reabsorption at distal tubule.
   a. Concentrated urine leads to increased ADH secretion.
   b. Dilute urine leads to decreased ADH secretion.

3. Distal tubule and collecting duct.
   a. Secretion and reabsorption completed.
   b. Distal tubule—final regulation of H_2O balance and acid-base balance.
   c. Uric acid and K^+ secreted into distal tubules and excreted in urine.

4. Hormonal regulation.
   a. H_2O reabsorption depends on ADH.
   b. Na^+ and K^+ reabsorption influenced by aldosterone.
      (1) Increased aldosterone causes increased Na^+ reabsorption and increased K^+ secretion.
      (2) Decreased aldosterone exhibits opposite effect.
   c. Ca^{++} and HPO_4^{--} reabsorption regulated by parathyroid hormone.
      (1) Increased parathyroid hormone leads to increased Ca^{++} reabsorption and increased HPO_4^{--} excretion.
      (2) Decreased parathyroid hormone exhibits opposite effect.

5. Water balance maintained through homeostasis —all functions of kidney must be maintained.

F. Blood pressure regulation.
   1. Regulation occurs through release of renin from juxtaglomerular cells in response to low blood volume or ischemia.
   2. Renin stimulates conversion of angiotensinogen to angiotensin I in liver.
   3. Angiotensin I changed to angiotensin II in pulmonary capillary bed.
   4. Angiotensin II increases blood pressure by vasoconstriction of peripheral arterioles and secretion of aldosterone.
   5. Increased aldosterone stimulates Na^+ reabsorption.
   6. Increased Na^+ reabsorption causes increased H_2O retention and plasma volume, which leads to increased blood pressure.

Characteristics of Urine

A. Components of urine include organic and inorganic materials in urine solution.
B. Cloudy urine is of little significance and is usually the result of urates or phosphates which precipitate out.
C. Red blood cells in the urine or hematuria is significant and indicates the presence of some disease or disorder in the body.
   1. Acute nephritis or exacerbation of chronic nephritis.
   2. Neoplasms, vascular accidents, or infections.
   3. Renal stones.
   4. Renal tuberculosis.
   5. Trauma to the urinary tract.
   6. A manifestation of thrombocytopenia.
   7. May be the result of problems along the genitourinary tract, such as the ureter, the bladder, or the prostate gland.
D. The source of blood cells in urine must be determined.
   1. Blood during the initial period of voiding may be from the anterior urethra or prostate.
   2. Blood mixed with the total volume of urine may be from kidneys, ureters, or bladder.

Diagnostic Procedures

Renal Function Tests

Purpose: Recognition and evaluation of renal disease is largely dependent on laboratory tests.

A. PSP test indicates the functional ability of the kidney to:
   1. Excrete waste products.
   2. Concentrate and dilute urine.
   3. Carry on absorption and excretion activities.
   4. Maintain body fluids and electrolytes.
B. Renal concentration tests.
   1. Underlying principles.
      a. Evaluate the ability of the kidney to concentrate urine.
      b. As kidney disease progresses, renal function decreases. Concentration tests evaluate this process.

c. Renal concentration is measured by specific gravity readings (normal range is 1.022 to 1.035).

d. If specific gravity is 1.018 or greater, it may be assumed that the kidney is functioning within normal limits.

e. Specific gravity that stabilizes at 1.010 indicates kidney has lost ability to concentrate or dilute.

2. Concentration and dilution tests.

a. Fishberg concentration test—high protein dinner with 200 cc. fluid is ordered. Next A.M. on arising, patient voids q. 1/hr. One specimen should have specific gravity more than 1.025.

b. Dilution test—NPO after dinner. Morning voiding discarded. Patient drinks 1000 ml. in 30-45 minutes. Four specimens at one hour intervals are collected. One specimen will fall below 1.003.

c. Specific gravity—urine 1.003 to 1.030. Increased solutes cause increased specific gravity.

C. Glomerular filtration test (endogenous creatinine clearance).

1. Kidney function is assessed by clearing a substance from the blood (filtration in the glomerulus).

2. Common test is the amount of blood cleared of urea per minute.

3. Test done on 12-hour or 24-hour urine specimen.

4. Normal range is approximately 125 ml./minute (male) and 110 ml./minute (female).

D. Electrolyte tests.

1. Kidney function is essential to maintain fluid and electrolyte balance.

2. Tests for electrolytes (sodium, potassium, chloride, and bicarbonate) measure the ability of the kidney to filter, reabsorb, or excrete these substances.

3. Impaired filtration leads to retention, and impaired reabsorption leads to loss of electrolytes.

4. Tests are performed on blood serum, so venous blood is required.

Analysis of Urine

A. Urinalysis is a critical test for total evaluation of the renal system and for indication of renal disease.

B. Specific gravity shows the degree of concentration in urine.

1. Indicates the ability of the kidney to concentrate or dilute urine.

2. Change from normal range indicates diabetes mellitus (greater than 1.030) or kidney damage (less than 1.010).

3. Renal failure—specific gravity constant at 1.010.

C. Analysis of the pH of urine.

1. pH is the symbol for the logarithm of the reciprocal of the hydrogen ion concentration.

2. A measurement of hydrogen ion concentration is taken: the lower the number (1 to 14), the higher the acidity in urine.

a. Normal urine pH is 6 to 7.

b. Lower than 6 is acidic urine, and higher than 7 is alkaline urine.

3. Regulation of urine pH is important for treatment of certain conditions.

a. Above 6.0.

(1) Treatment of hypertension with mecamylamine hydrochloride.

(2) Management of blood transfusions.

(3) Streptomycin and sulfonamide therapy.

(4) Management of renal calculi.

b. Below 6.0—treatment of urinary tract infections.

D. Chemical analysis of urine.

1. Protein or albumin—normal for a twenty-four-hour specimen: zero.

a. Presence may indicate renal disease, such as nephritis or nephrosis.

b. Inflammatory processes any place in the body may result in proteinuria.

c. Toxemia of pregnancy yields a finding of proteinuria.

d. Renal calculi indicate positive test results.

e. Appearance in urine may be due to dehydration, strenuous exercise, high protein diet.

2. Glucose—normal range: zero.

a. Presence of glucose may indicate head

injury or diabetes.

    b. Test is usually done by test strips or tablets; change in color indicates presence of glucose.

3. Ketone bodies—normal range: zero.

    a. Ketonuria primarily indicates diabetic acidosis but is also present with starvation and pernicious vomiting.

    b. Test is usually done by strip or powder mixed with urine; purple color indicates positive test.

4. Bilirubin—normal range: zero.

    a. Presence in urine may indicate liver disease and may appear before the clinical symptom of jaundice.

    b. Detected in the urine by qualitative methods, such as inspection of color.

5. Blood—normal range: zero.

    a. If red blood cells present, may indicate disease of kidney or urinary tract, and the source of hemorrhage must be determined.

    b. Specific diagnosis is made by complete urine analysis for casts and epithelial cells.

E. Microscopic examination of urine.

  1. Evaluation of urinary sediment is important for diagnostic purposes.

  2. Test for cellular elements (epithelial cells, white and red blood cells).

  3. Test for casts, fat bodies, and crystals.

F. Levels of albuminuria.

    30 mg./100 ml. = 1+
    100 mg./100 ml. = 2+
    300 mg./100 ml. = 3+
    1000 mg./100 ml. = 4+

Renal Biopsy

A. Unless contraindicated, renal biopsy can indicate the presence of disease, confirm diagnosis and/or prognosis, and give evidence of response to treatment.

B. A needle is inserted through renal tissue, and tissue cells are examined for evidence of malfunction.

Renal Regulation of Fluid and Electrolytes

Composition of the Body

Body Water

Definition: Total body water represents the largest constituent (45 to 80 percent) of the total body weight, depending on the amount of fat present.

A. Intracellular—represents two-thirds of total body water fluid; contained inside the cell; includes the red blood cells.

B. Extracellular—represents one-third of total body water; includes remaining fluid not contained within the cell.

  1. Intravascular (plasma)—liquid in which the blood cells are suspended.

  2. Interstitial—liquid surrounding tissue cells.

Electrolytes

Definition: Electrolytes are compounds that dissolve in a solution to form ions; each particle then carries either a positive or negative electrical charge.

A. Types.

  1. Cations—positive charge (Na^+, K^+, Ca^{++}, Mg^{++}).

  2. Anions—negative charge (Cl^-, HCO_3^-, HPO_4^{--}, SO_4^{--}).

B. Concentration in solution is expressed in mEq./L. Total number of cations (mEq.) plus total number of anions (mEq.) will be the same in both the intracellular fluid and extracellular fluid, thereby rendering the body's fluid composition electrically **neutral**.

C. Compartment composition.

  1. Extracellular—large quantities of sodium, chloride, and bicarbonate ions.

  2. Intracellular—large quantities of potassium, phosphate, and proteins.

Dynamics of Intercompartmental Fluid Transfer

A. Osmosis—movement of water molecules across a semipermeable membrane in a direction that equalizes the concentration of water. The flow of water is into a solution that has a high solute concentration.

B. Diffusion—movement of a substance from an area of high concentration to an area of low concentration.

C. Facilitated diffusion—transport of molecules that are too large or insoluble across the membrane by means of a carrier molecule, creating a complex which is soluble in the membrane.

D. Active transport—transport (requiring energy—ATP) of substances across a membrane from an area of low concentration to an area of high concentration.

E. Oncotic pressure—osmotic pressure that results from dispersed colloid particles (the largest being proteins) in the blood capillaries; the pressure draws water back into the vascular system, thereby maintaining blood volume.

F Lymphatics—vessels responsible for returning the large molecules that have escaped from the blood capillaries (including protein molecules) to the bloodstream, returning them from the interstitial fluid and the gastrointestinal tract.

Balance of Body Fluid

A. Intake.
   1. Ingestion of foodstuff and water.
   2. Oxidation of foodstuff.
B Output.
   1. Skin and lungs.
      a. Water is lost through vaporization from the skin surface and through expired air from the lungs.
      b. The amount lost increases as metabolism increases.
   2. Gastrointestinal tract.
      a. Routes include saliva, gastric secretions, bile, pancreatic juices, and intestinal mucosa.
      b. A volume in excess of seven liters is transferred from the extracellular fluid (ECF) into the gastrointestinal tract, only to be reabsorbed, excepting some 200 ml. which is passed with feces.
   3. Kidneys.
      a. Carry the heaviest load.
      b. Through glomerular filtration and tubular reabsorption, the kidneys maintain homeostasis.
      c. Three hormones influence the kidneys in fluid balance.
         (1) Antidiuretic.
         (2) Aldosterone.
         (3) Thyroid.

Major Electrolyte Disorders

Hyponatremia

Definition: Hyponatremia is caused by a very low concentration of sodium in extracellular fluid.

A. Etiology.
   1. Skin—excessive sweating, burns, fibrocystic disease.
   2. Gastrointestinal tract—severe vomiting, diarrhea, pancreatic and biliary fistulas.
   3. Kidneys—diuretic therapy, adrenal insufficiency, I.V. fluids free of sodium.
B. Clinical manifestations.
   1. Anorexia, nausea.
   2. Muscular weakness.
   3. Abdominal cramps.
   4. Orthostatic syncope.
   5. Convulsions.
   6. Circulatory collapse.
C. Treatment—reestablishment of sodium concentration through I.V. administration of sodium chloride solutions.

Hypernatremia

Definition: Hypernatremia is caused by a very high concentration of sodium in extracellular fluid.

A. Etiology—gastrointestinal tract: severe diarrhea, decreased water intake, febrile state, ingestion of sodium chloride, and excessive loss of water through rapid and deep respiration.
B. Clinical manifestations.
   1. Dry, sticky mucous membranes.
   2. Flushed skin.
   3. Depressed lacrimation.
   4. Dry tongue, thirst.
   5. Hypertension.
C. Treatment—water by mouth or I.V. to reestablish the normal level of water to electrolytes.

Hypokalemia

Definition: Hypokalemia is a very low concentration of potassium ions in extracellular fluid.

A. Etiology.
1. Loss of potassium due to diuretic therapy, endocrine disorders, trauma, gastrointestinal disorders, or renal disease.
2. Increased use of potassium by the body through sweat, gastric and intestinal juices, or excretion.

B. Clinical manifestations.
1. Generalized weakness, fatigue.
2. Weak pulse.
3. Vomiting.
4. Shortness of breath, shallow respirations.
5. Depression, mental dullness.
6. ECG changes.
   a. Presence of U wave.
   b. T wave depression.
   c. ST segment depression.

C. Treatment—replacement of potassium orally or parenterally.

Hyperkalemia

Definition: Hyperkalemia is an excess of potassium in extracellular fluid.

A. Etiology.
1. Renal failure.
2. Adrenal insufficiency.
3. Overtreatment with potassium salts.
4. Respiratory or metabolic acidosis.

B. Clinical manifestations.
1. Diarrhea, nausea.
2. Weakness, dizziness.
3. Muscle cramps.
4. Peaked T waves on ECG.
5. Apprehension.
6. Cardiac arrest

C. Treatment.
1. Potassium intake decreased.
2. I.V. infusion of sodium chloride, providing kidney function is normal.
3. Kayexalate enemas.
4. Dialysis.
5. I.V. glucose and insulin.

Hypocalcemia

Definition: Hypocalcemia results from a deficit of calcium in the extracellular fluid.

A. Etiology.
1. Acute pancreatitis.
2. Chronic renal insufficiency.
3. Burns.
4. Removal of parathyroid glands.
5. If transfused with over 2000 cc. of blood requires calcium supplement.
6. Malabsorption syndrome.

B. Clinical manifestations.
1. Abdominal cramps, muscle cramps.
2. Tetany, carpopedal spasms.
3. Circumoral tingling, especially in fingers.
4. Convulsions.

C. Treatment.
1. Calcium gluconate I.V.
2. Serum albumin if condition due to low serum albumin concentration.

D. Diagnostic tests.
1. Trousseau test positive.
2. Chvostek test positive.

Hypercalcemia

Definition: Hypercalcemia results from an excess of calcium in the extracellular fluid.

A. Etiology.
1. Excessive intake of vitamin D (milk).
2. Hyperparathyroidism, neoplasm of parathyroids.
3. Thyrotoxicosis.
4. Immobilization.
5. Paget's disease.

B. Clinical manifestations.
1. Anorexia, nausea.
2. Lethargy, weight loss, polydipsia, polyuria.
3. Flank pain, bone pain, decreased muscle tone.

C. Treatment.
1. Treat the underlying cause of the high serum calcium level.
2. Immediate reversal—sodium salts I.V. and diuretics (Lasix).

Hypomagnesemia

Definition: Deficit of Mg^{++} due to chronic alcoholism, starvation, malabsorption, or vigorous diuresis.

A.   Decreased serum level.
1.   Low intake.
2.   Abnormal loss—diarrhea.
3.   Chronic nephritis.
4.   Diuretic phase of renal failure.

B.   Clinical manifestations.
1.   Neuromuscular irritability.
a.   Jerks, twitches.
b.   Hyperactive reflexes.
c.   Convulsions.
d.   Tetany.
2.   Cardiovascular changes.
a.   Tachycardia.
b.   Hypotension.

C.   Treatment.
1.   Magnesium sulfate.
a.   Administer I.V. or I.M. slowly.
b.   Observe for adequate urine output.
2.   Antidote: calcium gluconate.

Hypermagnesemia

Definition: An excess of Mg^{++} as a result of renal insufficiency or inability to excrete Mg^{++} absorbed from food.

A.   Increased serum level.
1.   Renal insufficiency.
2.   Overdose.
3.   Severe dehydration.
4.   Overuse of antacids with Mg^{++} (Gelusil).

B.   Clinical manifestations.
1.   Hypotension.
2.   Curare-like paralysis.
3.   Sedation.
4.   Decreased respiration function.
5.   Cardiac arrhythmias.
6.   Warm sensation in body.

C.   Treatment: calcium gluconate.
1.   Administer I.V. slowly.
2.   Give in peripheral veins (not IVP line).

Renal Regulation of Acid-Base Balance

Kidney Function

A.   Kidney most efficient regulatory mechanism.
B.   Begins to function within hours to days.
C.   Blood pH is maintained by balance of twenty parts of bicarbonate to one part carbonic acid.
D.   Four processes are involved in acid-base regulation.
1.   Disassociation of H^+ from H_2CO_3. (H^+ and HCO_3.)
2.   Reabsorption of Na^+ from urine filtrate. (Na^+ and H^+ change places.)
3.   Formation and conservation of $NaHCO_3$. (Na^+ and HCO_3^-.)
4. NH_3 from metabolic process (Krebs cycle) enters kidney's tubular cell and adds a H^+ ion and then exchanges as ammonium with Na^+. (Na^+ and NH_4.)
E.   Hydrogen and potassium compete with each other in exchange for Na^+ in the tubular urine.
1.   In acidosis the H^+ ion concentration is increased and K^+ ion must wait to be excreted as hydrogen has preference.
2.   In alkalosis the H^+ ion is low and K^+ is excreted in larger amounts

Metabolic Acidosis

A.   Etiology.
1.   Occurs when kidney function decreases or fails.
2.   Excess metabolic acids are formed.
a.   Diabetes—keto acids.
b.   Hypoxia—lactic acid.
3.   Loss of alkali.
a.   Severe vomiting of intestinal contents.
b.   Biliary fistula.
c.   Diarrhea.
d.   Intestinal fistula draining large amounts of fluid.

B.   Blood gas changes.
1.   pH decreases.
2. HCO_3^- decreases.
3. PCO_2 normal.

C.   Compensation.
1.   Kidney excretes H^+.
2.   Kidney conserves HCO_3^-.
3   Lungs blow off CO_2.

Metabolic Acidosis		Compensation
pH: ↓	<7.40	7.40
HCO_3^-: ↓	< 24	
BE: ↓	< 0	
pCO_2: normal	40	↓<40

Base excess (BE): reflection of HCO_3

Metabolic Alkalosis

A. Etiology.
1. Vomiting of stomach contents where HCl is lost. (Prolonged vomiting may lead to loss of $NaHCO_3$—acidotic condition.)
2. Excess NG suction.
3. Ingestion of alkaline drugs (ulcer patients).
4. Excess diuretics—as chloride follows Na^+, HCO_3^- increases in plasma to maintain electroneutrality.
B. Blood gas changes.
1. pH increases.
2. PCO_2 normal.
3. HCO_3^- increases.
C. Compensation.
1. Kidney excretes HCO_3^-.
2. Kidney retains H^+.
3. Lungs retain CO_2.

Metabolic Alkalosis		Compensation
pH: ↑	>7.40	7.40
HCO_3^-: ↑	> 24	
BE: ↑	> 0	
pCO_2: normal	40	↑>40

Other Acid-Base Regulatory Mechanisms

A. Chemical buffers.
1. Function continuously to maintain acid-base balance.
2. Types.
a. Phosphate.
b. Protein.
c. Bicarbonate.
d. Hemoglobin.
B. Lungs (see Respiratory System, p. 75–76).

Dysfunctions of Genitourinary Tract

Pain Associated with Genitourinary Disorders

A. Ureteral pain is related to obstruction and is usually an acute manifestation.
1. Site of obstruction may be found by tracing the location of radiation of pain.
2. Pain may be severe and usually radiates down ureter into scrotum or vulva and to the inner thigh.
B. Bladder pain is due to infection and overdistention of the bladder in urinary retention.
C. Testicular pain is caused by inflammation or trauma, and is acute and severe.
D. Pain in the lower back and leg may be caused by prostate cancer with metastasis to pelvic bones.
E. Pain caused by renal disease.
1. Dull ache in flank, radiating to lower abdomen and upper thigh.
2. Pain may be absent if there is no sudden distention of kidney capsules.

Injuries to the Kidney

Definition: Injury to the kidney includes any trauma that bruises, lacerates, or ruptures any part of the kidney organ.

Clinical Manifestations

A. Hematuria.
B. Shock, if hemorrhage has occurred.
C. Pain over costovertebral area.
D. Gastrointestinal symptoms of nausea and vomiting.

Nursing Management

A. Promote bed rest.
B. Monitor vital signs frequently for possible hemorrhage.

C. Monitor blood work and laboratory examination of urine, to assess hematuria.

D. Prevent infection.

E. Frequently monitor the total status of the patient following injury.
  1. Observe for pain and tenderness.
  2. Observe any sudden change in status.

F. Prepare for surgery (nephrectomy) if health status deteriorates (shock indicating severe hemorrhage).

Urinary Tract Infections

Definition: Urinary tract infection is a term that refers to a wide variety of conditions affecting the urinary tract in which the common denominator is the presence of microorganisms.

Pathophysiology

A. Urine is sterile until it reaches the distal urethra.

B. Any bacteria can be introduced into the urinary tract, resulting in infection which may spread to any other part of the tract. Escherichia coli most frequent organism.

C. The most important factor influencing ascending infection is obstruction of free urine flow.
  1. Free flow, large urine output, and pH are antibacterial defenses.
  2. If defenses break down, the result may be an invasion of the tract by bacteria.

Examination of Urine

A. Urine cultures and chemical tests to determine presence and number of bacteria.

B. Microscopic examination for detailed identification of the organism (especially important in chronic infections).

C. Colony count of over 100,000/ml. most important lab finding.

Nursing Management

A. Force fluids to 3000 cc.

B. Administer urinary antiseptics as ordered.
  1. Antibacterial effects occur in genitourinary tract and are not systemic.
  2. Common drugs—Gantrisin, NegGram, Mandelamine, Furadantin.

3. Usual side effects—nausea, vomiting, diarrhea, rash pruritus, urticaria.

C. Administer systemic antibiotics as ordered.
  1. Specific for causative bacteria (given one to two weeks).
  2. Common drugs—streptomycin, kanamycin, neomycin, gentamicin.
  3. Usual side effects—vertigo, nausea, vomiting, rash.

D. Obtain sterile urine specimens.

E. Provide warm sitz baths.

Cystitis

Definition: Cystitis is an inflammation of the bladder from infection or from obstruction of the urethra, the most common cause.

Clinical Manifestations

A. Frequency, urgency, and burning sensation on urination.

B. Lower abdominal discomfort.

C. Dark and odorous urine (often a manifestation).

D. Laboratory findings indicating presence of bacteria and hematuria.

Treatment

A. Identification and removal of the cause of the condition (infection, obstruction, etc·).

B. Antibiotic therapy.

C. Maintenance of fluid and electrolyte balance.

D. Prevention of infection.

E. Symptomatic relief for chronic conditions.

Nursing Management

A. Collect an uncontaminated urine specimen (midstream specimen is an optional method).

B. Maintain adequate fluid intake.
  1. Force fluids only if specifically ordered.
  2. Check and record intake and output.

C. Encourage bed rest or a decrease in activity during the acute stage.

D. Maintain acid urine (pH 5.5).

E. Monitor antibiotic therapy if instituted.

F. Instruct patient in follow-up urinary tests for pH.

Pyelonephritis

Definition: Pyelonephritis is an acute or chronic infection and inflammation of one or both kidneys that usually begins in the renal pelvis. Women are more commonly affected. Gram-negative organisms are most often responsible, especially E. coli.

Clinical Manifestations

A. Attacks of chills, fever, malaise, GI upsets.

B. Tenderness and dull, aching pain in back.

C. Frequent and burning urination (more common in lower tract involvement).

D. Pus and bacteria in urine on exam.

E. May have normal renal function except for the inability to concentrate urine.

F Renal insufficiency may develop.

   1. Progressive destruction of renal tubules and glomeruli.

   2. Inability of kidneys to excrete large amounts of electrolytes.

G. Hypertension in presence of bacterial pyelonephritis.

H. Overt symptoms disappear in a few days but urine is still infected.

Treatment

A. Drug therapy.

   1. Antibiotic therapy (organism-specific for infection).

   2. Urinary antiseptics.

   3. Analgesics and sedatives as needed.

B. Bed rest until asymptomatic.

C. Force fluids to maintain urine output of 1500 cc./day.

D. Continued monitoring for presence of bacteria.

E. Prevention of chronic renal insufficiency.

Nursing Management

A. Monitor course of antibiotic therapy.

B. Monitor urinalysis.

   1. Check urine concentration.

   2. Check electrolytes.

C. Provide special diet—high calorie, vitamin supplements, and protein restriction if oliguria is present.

D. Give fluid intake sufficient to maintain adequate urine volume.

E. Observe for edema and signs of renal failure.

F. Instruct patient in good hygiene to prevent further infections.

Glomerulonephritis

Definition: A variety of nephritis caused by inflammation of the capillary loops in the glomeruli of the kidney.

Pathophysiology

A. The kidney's glomeruli are affected by an immunological disorder.

B. Most frequently follows infections with group A beta-hemolytic streptococcus.

C. Upper respiratory infections, skin infections, other autoimmune processes (systemic lupus), acute infections predispose to glomerulonephritis.

D. Glomerulonephritis symptoms appear seven to fourteen days after original infection.

Clinical Manifestations

A. Pharyngitis, fever, malaise as initial symptoms.

B. Weakness, anorexia, mild anemia.

C. Edema—leg, face or generalized.

D. Oliguria.

E. Abdominal pain, nausea, vomiting.

F. Hypertension, headache, convulsion.

G. Hypoalbuminemia due to increased loss via urine. (Proteinuria, 2–8 g. daily.)

H. Hematuria.

I. High specific gravity.

J. Congestive heart failure.

K. Increased BUN.

Treatment

A. Bed rest.

B. Penicillin for residual infection.

C. Diuretics and antihypertensives if necessary.

D. Symptomatic treatment of CHF, hypertension, and anemia.

E. Diet.

   1. Proteins restricted if oliguria is severe. Otherwise 40 g. protein maximum (normal 60 to 80 g./day).

2. BUN level watched for protein determination.
3. Protein should be of the complete type (milk, eggs, meat, fish, poultry).
4. High carbohydrate to spare protein.
5. Potassium usually restricted.
6. Sodium restriction for hypertension and CHF. If diuresis is great, sodium replacement may be necessary.
7. Fluid restriction: replacement is based on insensible loss plus measured sensible loss of previous day or hour.
8. Vitamin replacement.

Nursing Management

A. Encourage complete bed rest during acute stage of disease.
  1. Continue until clinical signs abate.
  2. Start activity when blood pressure and blood urea nitrogen (BUN) normal for one to two weeks.
  3. If sedimentation rate increases or urinary findings indicative, return to bed rest regimen.
B. Constant monitoring of vital signs.
C. Encourage diet maintenance.
D. Allow person to verbalize feelings on body image changes (due to edema), loss of health, fear of death.
E. Monitor fluid intake.
  1. Measure fluids according to urinary output.
  2. Record intake and output.
  3. Weigh daily.
F. Observe for signs of overhydration.
G. Observe for hypertension.
H. Observe for symptoms of renal failure.
  1. Oliguria.
  2. Azotemia.
  3. Acidosis.

Nephrotic Syndrome

Definition: Nephrosis is a term that refers to renal disease characterized by massive edema and albuminuria.

Etiology

A. The syndrome is seen in any renal condition that has damaged glomerular capillary membrane: glomerulonephritis, lipoid nephrosis, syphilitic nephritis, amyloidosis, or systemic lupus erythematosus.

B. A specific form of intercapillary glomerulosclerosis is associated with diabetes mellitus (Kimmelstiel-Wilson syndrome).
C. Occurrence thought to be related to thyroid function.

Clinical Manifestations

A. Edema (at first, dependent; later, generalized).
B. Proteinuria (20 to 30 g./day).
C. Decreased serum albumin.
D. Elevated serum cholesterol, triglycerides, hyperlipemia.
E. Hypertension related to function of renin angiotensin system.
F. Decreased cardiac output secondary to fluid loss.
G. Pallor.
H. Malaise, anorexia, lethargy.

Treatment

A. Directed toward control of edema.
  1. Sodium restriction in diet.
  2. Avoidance of sodium-containing drugs.
  3. Diuretics (Lasix and Edecrin) that block aldosterone formation.
  4. Salt-poor albumin.
B. Dietary treatment.
  1. High protein to restore body proteins—100 g.
  2. High calorie.
  3. 500 mg. sodium.
C. Drug therapy.
  1. Adrenocortical therapy (prednisone prevents sodium retention).
  2. Immunosuppressives.
    a. Cyclophosphamide, drug of choice.
    b. Side effects: alopecia, hemorrhagic cystitis, increased susceptibility to infection.
D. Bed rest until edema has reached stable minimum.

Nursing Management

A. Support and instruct patient in dietary regime.
B. Instruct patient in the maintenance of general health status, as the disorder may persist for months or years.
  1. Avoidance of infections.
  2. Nutritious diet (low sodium, high protein).
  3. Activity as tolerated.

C. Maintain fluid balance.
   1. Daily weights.
   2. I and O.

Tuberculosis of the Kidney

Definition: Tuberculosis of the kidney is an infection caused by Mycobacterium tuberculosis which is usually blood-borne from other foci such as the lungs, lymph nodes, or bone.

Clinical Manifestations

A. Frequency and pain on urination.
B. Burning, spasm, and hematuria.
C. Fatigue and weight loss.
D. Tuberculous nodules may be present in the prostate.

Treatment

A. Diagnostic studies.
   1. Urine cultures to isolate the tubercle bacilli.
   2. X-ray to reveal lesions.
   3. Cystoscopic examination.
B. Drug therapy aimed at treating the original focus of infection as well as the genitourinary involvement.
   1. Isoniazid, sodium PAS, and cycloserine.
   2. Usually given together in a single daily dose.
C. Possible nephrectomy.
D. Improvement of general health status.

Nursing Management

A. Administer drugs and observe patient for side effects and drug intolerance.
   1. Skin rash.
   2. Bloating.
   3. Loose stools.
B. Improve general health status.
   1. Good dietary habits.
   2. Adequate rest.

Renal Failure

Acute Renal Failure

Definition: Acute renal failure is the sudden loss of kidney function caused by failure of renal circulation or damage to the tubules or glomerulus. Condition may be reversible. If reversed, diuresis follows oliguria.

Etiology

A. Conditions which lead to acute renal failure.
   1. Damage (injury) to the kidney.
   2. Bacterial infection.
   3. Dehydration (water and electrolyte depletion).
   4. Kidney stones.
   5. Toxic agents (e.g., carbon tetrachloride, sulfonamides, arsenic, etc.).
   6. Hemolytic transfusion reaction.
   7. Allergic conditions.
   8. Shock.
   9. Cardiopulmonary bypass.
   10. Collagen diseases.
B. Characteristics.
   1. Prerenal.
      a. Severe dehydration.
      b. Circulatory collapse.
   2. Renal.
      a. Acute glomerulonephritis.
      b. Vascular disorders.
      c. Nephrotoxicity.
      d. Severe infection.
   3. Postrenal—obstruction.
   4. Anemia—packed cells.
   5. Infection control.
   6. Dialysis.

Nursing Management

A. Monitor urinary output.
   1. Record intake and output.
   2. Weigh daily (lack of weight loss indicates retention of too much fluid).
B. Monitor fluid intake (observe for signs of CHF).
C. Observe for complications of electrolyte imbalances.
D. Allow patient to verbalize concerns.
E. Encourage the prescribed diet.
F. Provide good mouth care.
G. Take caution in using antibiotics and other drugs.
H. Continually assess status of patient.
   1. Dyspnea.
   2. Tachycardia.
   3. Signs of pulmonary edema.
   4. Distended neck veins.
   5. Signs of cardiac failure.

Chronic Renal Failure

Definition: Chronic renal failure is the progressive impairment of kidney functioning that, without intervention, ends fatally in uremia.

Pathophysiology (3 stages)

A. Diminished renal reserve.
   1. Renal function test abnormal.
   2. No accumulation of metabolic waste.
   3. Presence of polyuria, nocturia, and polydipsia.
B. Renal insufficiency.
   1. Metabolic waste begins to accumulate.
   2. Increased BUN.
   3. Stress poorly tolerated (e.g., infection).
   4. Chemical abnormalities resolve slowly.
C. Uremia.
   1. Homeostasis lost.
   2. Poor urine output.
   3. Severe alterations of electrolytes.
   4. Increased BUN to high levels.

Clinical Manifestations

A. Weakness, fatigue, and headaches.
B. Anorexia, nausea, and vomiting.
C. Hypertension with renal failure and heart failure.
D. Anemia, azotemia (nitrogen retention in the blood), and acidosis.
E. Nervous system signs (e.g., anxiety, irritability, hallucinations, convulsions, and coma).
F. Low and fixed specific gravity of urine.

Treatment

A. Diet and fluids (same as for acute renal failure).
B. Electrolyte replacement.
   1. Sodium supplements provided.
   2. Potassium restricted or supplemented.
   3. Acidosis treated.
C. Treatment for hypertension and heart failure.
D. Dialysis or kidney transplant.

Nursing Management (see Care Acute Failure, p. 125).

Uremia

Definition: Uremia is the accumulation of nitrogenous waste products in blood due to inability of kidneys to filter out waste products.

Etiology

A. May occur after acute or chronic renal failure.
B. Increased urea (200 mg.), creatinine, uric acid.
C. Extensive electrolyte imbalances (increased K^+, decreased Cl^-, decreased Ca^{++}).
D. Acidosis—bicarbonate cannot be maintained at adequate level.
E. Difficulty in concentrating or diluting urine.
F. Affects all body systems.

Clinical Manifestations

A. Oliguria for one to two weeks (produces less than 400 cc./day).
B. Urine changes.
   1. Urine contains protein, red blood cells, casts.
   2. Specific gravity of 1.010.
   3. Rise in urine solutes (e.g., urea, uric acid, potassium, and magnesium).
C. Increased BUN and H_2O output in diuretic phase.
D. Metabolic acidosis increases hydrogen concentration.
E. Increased potassium.
F. Hypotension or hypertension.
G. Gastrointestinal problems: stomatitis, nausea, vomiting, and diarrhea or constipation.
H. Respiratory complications.
I. Wound healing impaired.
J. Anemia.
K. Coma—with alterations of blood chemistry and acid load.
L. Altered blood chemistries: increased BUN, increased creatinine, increased uric acid.

Treatment

A. Immediate treatment of the cause of oliguria.
B. Restoration of blood volume.
C. Fluid and electrolyte balance.
D. Dietary regulation.
   1. Limited protein (20 to 60 g.). Reduced nitrogen, potassium, phosphate, and sulfate.
   2. Limited sodium intake.
   3. Glucose to prevent ketosis.

4. Vitamin supplements.
5. Control of potassium balance to prevent hyperkalemia.
6. Carbohydrate intake 100 g. daily.

Dialysis: Treatment for Acute or Chronic Renal Failure

Peritoneal Dialysis

Definition: Peritoneal dialysis is a method of separating substances by interposing a semipermeable membrane. The peritoneum is used as the dialyzing membrane and substitutes for kidney function during failure.

Principles of Peritoneal Dialysis

A. Usually temporary; can be used for patients in acute, reversible renal failure.
B. Most common causes for decreased renal perfusion.
  1. Decreased cardiac output due to myocardial infarction, cardiac arrhythmias, and cardiac tamponade.
  2. Altered peripheral vascular resistance.
  3. Hypovolemia.
C. Renal perfusion is compromised when increased size of the intravascular compartment and redistribution of blood volume result from:
  1. Gram-negative sepsis.
  2. Overdoses of some drugs.
  3. Anaphylactic shock.
  4. Electrolyte disturbances, such as acidosis.
D. Drugs are used to check for renal failure before patient is placed on dialysis.
  1. In most cases, Mannitol is tried before dialysis.
    a. Small molecular size.
    b. Has great osmotic effect and increases urinary flow.
    c. Administration.
      (1) Give it quickly in order to get higher blood level and then, in turn, filtered load.
      (2) If infusion is too slow, changes in the urinary flow rate will be delayed as urine flow depends on the amount of Mannitol filtered.
      (3) Give 12.5 gm. of a 25 percent solution in three minutes; if flow rate can be increased to 40 cc./hour, the patient is in reversible renal failure.
      (4) Keep urine at 100 cc./hour with Mannitol.
  2. Drugs such as Lasix (furosemide) and Edecrin (ethacrynic acid) may be used if Mannitol does not work.
    a. If the patient does not respond to Lasix or Edecrin, diagnosis of acute tubular necrosis is stated.
    b. If the patient has increased urine output with drugs, be sure to check electrolytes, as sodium and potassium depletion occurs along with water loss.
    c. In renal disease, make sure that drugs that depend on kidneys for secretion are not given.

Peritoneal Dialysis Function

A. Works on diffusion and osmosis, similar to hemodialysis; however, in this instance, the peritoneum is the semipermeable membrane.
B. Peritoneum is impermeable to large molecules (proteins).
C. Permeable to low molecular weight molecules (urea, sugar, electrolytes).
D. Cannot be used with patients who have the following conditions:
  1. Peritonitis.
  2. Recent abdominal surgery.
  3. Abdominal adhesions.
  4. Impending renal transplant.
E. Dialysate.
  1. Contains electrolytes but no urea, creatinine, etc.
    a. Common electrolytes in dialysate in mEq./liter.
      Na^+ 140–141 CL^- 101–102
      Ca^{++} 3.5–4.0 Lactate/acetate (base) 43–45
      Mg^{++} 1.5
    b. Osmolarity.
      1.5% = 365 mOsm.
      425% = 504 mOsm.
  2. Sterile.

3. Solutions vary in dextrose concentration.
    a. 1.5 percent solution used for drug intoxication and acute renal failure if large amounts of fluid are not required to be removed.
    b. 4.25 percent solution used for removal of excessive fluid.
4. If hyperkalemia is not a problem, 4 mEq. of potassium chloride is added to each solution.
5. Heparin is added to bottles to prevent clotting of the catheter.

Dialysis Procedure

A. Preliminary to procedure.
    1. Empty bladder before peritoneal catheter trocar is inserted.
    2. Prep and shave abdomen.
    3. Warm dialysate.
    4. Take baseline vital signs (including weight).
B. Dialysis process (see procedure, p. 266).
    1. Dialysis fluid instilled in abdominal cavity.
    2. Occurrence of osmosis, diffusion, and filtration via peritoneal membrane (called equilibration).
    3. Fluid drained from abdominal cavity.
    4. Process repeated with a time sequence allowed for each step. Period of time and number of cycles will vary according to patient problem, tolerance, response, and type of solution.
C. Peritoneal clearance rates.
    1. Peritoneal membrane only about 50% as efficient as normal kidney function.
    2. Flow rate of dialysate affects peritoneal clearance.
    3. Optimal flow rate suggested is 2.5 L./hour.
    4. Usual cycle to maintain 2.5 L./hour flow: 5–10 minutes in flow time, 20 minutes of equilibration, and 20 minutes for drainage (when using 2 liters of dialysate).
    5. Increased levels of glucose in dialysate increase area clearance.
    6. Dialysate perfused at body temperature increases urea clearance by 35%.

Nursing Management

A. Each morning, send culture on returning dialysate solution to observe for signs of infection.
B. Each day at the same time, weigh patient with abdomen empty of solution.

C. Monitor vital signs to observe for complications.
D. Monitor dialysis exchange.
    1. Keep exchange on time.
    2. Maintain aseptic technique when changing bottles and tubing.
    3. Record accurate intake and output on flow sheet.
E. Interventions to assist in returning dialysate from peritoneal cavity.
    1. Turn patient on side and prop with pillows.
    2. Place in Fowler's position after solution is infused into abdomen.
    3. Ambulate and/or seat in chair if patient is able.
    4. Palpate abdomen.
    5. Place pillow or bath blanket under small of back (this also assists in relieving hiccoughs).
F. Test urine for sugar.

Major Complications of Peritoneal Dialysis

A. Peritonitis.
    1. Diffuse abdominal pain.
    2. Palpation tenderness.
    3. Abdominal wall rigidity.
    4. Cloudy outflow.
B. Hypertension.
C. Pulmonary edema.
D. Hyperglycemia (insulin may be needed).
E. Hyperosmolar coma.
F. Protein loss (0.5 to 1.0 g. per liter of drainage).
G. Intestinal perforation.

Hemodialysis

Definition: Hemodialysis is the diffusion of dissolved particles from one fluid compartment into another across a semipermeable membrane. In hemodialysis, the blood is one fluid compartment while the dialysate is another.

Principles of Hemodialysis

A. The semipermeable membrane is a thin, porous cellophane.
B. The pore size of the membrane permits the passage of low molecular weight substances such as urea, creatinine, and uric acid to diffuse through the pores of the membrane.
C. Water molecules are also very small and move freely through the membrane.

D. Most plasma proteins, bacteria, and blood cells are too large to pass through the pores of the membrane.

E. The difference in the concentration of the substances in the two compartments is called the concentration gradient.

F. The blood, which contains the waste products, flows into the dialyzer where it comes in contact with the dialysate.

G. A maximum gradient is established so that movement of these substances occurs from the blood to the dialysate.

H. Dialysate (bath).
   1. Composed of water and major electrolytes.
   2. Tap water can be used (need not be sterile because bacteria are too large to pass through membrane).

Hemodialysis Function

A. Removes byproducts of protein metabolism: urea, creatinine, and uric acid.

B. Removes excessive fluid by changing osmotic pressure (this is done by adding high concentrations of dextrose to dialysate).

C. Maintains or restores body buffer system.

D. Maintains or restores level of electrolytes in the body.

Nursing Management

A. Take vital signs to observe for shock and hypovolemia.
   1. Hypotension is caused by:
      a. Fluid loss, initially.
      b. Decreased blood volume, especially if hematocrit is low.
      c. Use of antihypertensive drugs between dialyses.
   2. Plasma or volume expanders can be used to increase blood pressure; sometimes blood is used while the patient is on dialysis.

B. Check serum electrolytes frequently (pre-, mid-, and post-dialysis).

C. Weigh patient before and after dialysis to determine fluid loss.

D. Watch for leakage around trocar (catheter) site.

E. Observe for dialysis disequilibrium syndrome.
   1. Cerebral dysfunction symptoms.
      a. Nausea and vomiting.
      b. Headache.
      c. Hypertension leading to agitation.
      d. Twitching, mental confusion, and convulsions.
   2. Syndrome is caused by rapid, efficient dialysis, resulting in shifts in water, pH, and osmolarity between fluid and blood.
   3. In acutely uremic patients, avoid this syndrome by dialyzing slowly, for short periods of time over two to three days.
   4. Use Dilantin to prevent this syndrome in new patients.

F. Heparinizing while off dialysis machine.
   1. Take clotting time about one hour before patient comes off the machine. If less than thirty minutes, do not give protamine (heparin antagonist).
   2. Keep clotting time at thirty to ninety minutes while on dialysis (normal six to ten minutes).

G. Shunt care.
   1. Scribner-type shunt.
      a. Clean every day.
      b. Check for clotting.
         (1) Watch for clots which appear as dark spots in shunt, seen when flashlight is used.
         (2) Sound of rushing can be heard by stethoscope if the shunt is patent.
         (3) If thrill or bruit is loud, palpate to feel that shunt is patent.
         (4) Shunt is warm if patent.
         (5) Serum and cells separate if shunt is clotted.
      c. When necessary, declot shunt with flushing heparin solution or with aspiration via syringe.
   2. Arterial-venous fistula.
      a. Anastomosis of an artery and vein creates a fistula.
      b. Arterial blood flowing into the venous system results in marked dilation of veins which are then easily punctured with a 14-gauge needle.
      c. Two venipunctures are made at the time of dialysis.
         (1) One for blood source.
         (2) One for return.

      (3) Arterial needle is inserted to within 1 to 1½ inches from fistula and venous needle is directed away from fistula.

    d. Observe for patency of graft site.

      (1) Check for bruit with stethoscope.

      (2) Observe for signs of infection.

3. Bovine graft.

    a. Graft from neck of cow.

    b. Venipuncture same as for A-V fistula.

General Principles of Nursing Management

A. Limit fluid intake (400 cc. over previous day's output); provide accurate intake and output.

B. Diet: low sodium (20-40 g.), low protein, high carbohydrate, high fat, and foods low in potassium.

C. Check vital signs for hypovolemia; check temperature for infection.

D. Ascultate lungs for signs of pulmonary edema.

E. Provide shunt care for patients on hemodialysis.

F. Observe level of consciousness—indicative of electrolyte imbalance or thrombus.

G. Administer antihypertensive drugs between dialysis if ordered.

H. Administer diuretics if ordered.

I. Administer blood if ordered (cellular portion only is needed because of low hematocrit).

J. Weigh daily to assess fluid accumulation.

K. Prevent use of soap (urea causes dryness and itching, and soap will just add to this problem).

L. Provide continued emotional support.

    1. Allow for expression of feelings around change in body image.

    2. Encourage expression of fears of death especially during dialysis.

    3. Encourage family cooperation.

    4. Support required change in life style.

Disorders of the Blood and Spleen

The circulatory system, a continuous circuit, is the mechanical conveyor of the body constituent called blood. Blood, composed of cells and plasma, circulates through the body and is the means by which oxygen and nutritive materials are transported to the tissues and carbon dioxide and metabolic end products are removed for excretion.

Blood and Blood Factors

Blood Components

Plasma

A. Accounts for 55 percent of the total volume of blood.
B. It is comprised of 92 percent water and 7 percent proteins.
   1. Proteins include serum, fibrinogen, albumin, gamma globulin.
   2. Less than one percent organic salts, dissolved gases, hormones, antibodies, and enzymes.

Solid Particles

A. Comprise 45 percent of the total blood volume.
B. Blood cells.
   1. Erythrocytes (red blood cells).
      a. Normal count in an adult is 5 to 5½ million cells.
      b. They contain hemoglobin which carries oxygen to cells and carbon dioxide from cells to lungs.
      c. Red blood cells originate in bone marrow and are stored in the spleen.
      d. Average life span is 10 to 120 days.
   2. Leukocytes (white blood cells).
      a. Normal count in an adult is five to eight thousand.
      b. Primary defense against infection.
      c. Neutrophils play an active role in the acute inflammatory process and have phagocytic action.
      d. Macrophages—both fixed and wandering cells—act as scavengers and phagocytize foreign bodies, cellular debris, and more resistant organisms, i.e., fungi and *Mycobacterium tuberculosis*.
      e. Lymphocytes play an important role in immunologic responses.
      f. Monocytes are the largest of the leukocytes and are less phagocytic than macrophages.
   3. Platelets (thrombocytes). 250,000 to 450,000/cu. mm. needed for clot retraction.

Blood Coagulation

A. Clotting takes place in three phases.
   1. Phase I. Prothrombin activator formed in response to ruptured vessel or damage to blood.
   2. Phase II. Prothrombin activator catalyzes conversion of prothrombin into thrombin.
   3. Phase III. Thrombin acts as an enzyme to convert fibrinogen into fibrin thread.
B. Types of clotting factors.
   1. Calcium ions.
      a. Cofactor in coagulation.
      b. Does not enter into reaction.
      c. If absent, neither extrinsic or intrinsic system will operate.
   2. Phospholipids.
      a. Necessary for formation of final prothrombin activator.
      b. Thromboplastin is phospholipid in extrinsic system.
      c. Platelet factor 3 is phospholipid for intrinsic system.
   3. Plasma protein—all clotting factors from V to XIII.
C. Coagulation mechanisms.
   1. Extrinsic mechanisms.
      a. Extract from damaged tissue is mixed with blood.
      b. Trauma occurs to tissue or endothelial surface of vascular wall, releasing thromboplastin.
   2. Intrinsic mechanisms.
      a. Blood itself comes into contact with roughened blood vessel wall.
      b. Platelets adhere to vessel and disintegrate, which releases blood factor 3 containing thromboplastin.

D. Fibrinolytic system.
  1. Adequate function is necessary to maintain hemostasis.
  2. Dissolves clots through formation of plasmin.

Blood Grouping

Major Blood Groups

A. ABO blood group.
  1. A.
  2. AB.
  3. B.
  4. O.

B. Rh blood group.
  1. Positive (85 percent of the population).
  2. Negative (15 percent of the population).

Antigens and Antibodies

A. Based on type of antigens present in red blood cells as well as type of antibodies in the serum.

B. A and B antigens.
  1. Patients with type A blood have antigen A present; patients with type B blood have antigen B present.
  2. Patients with type AB blood have both A and B antigens present.
  3. Patients with type O blood have no antigens present.

C. Anti-A and anti-B antibodies present.
  1. Patients with type A blood do not have anti-A antibodies because the blood cells would be destroyed by agglutination.
    a. They have anti-B antibodies.
    b. Type B blood has anti-A antibodies.

Table 1. Blood Coagulation

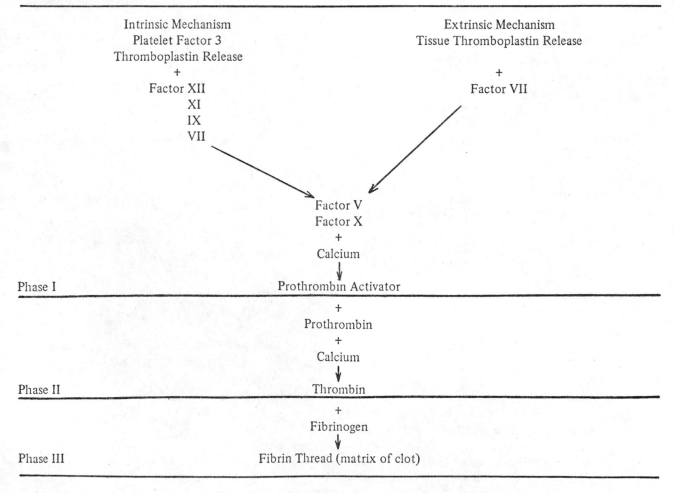

Intrinsic Mechanism Platelet Factor 3 Thromboplastin Release + Factor XII XI IX VII	Extrinsic Mechanism Tissue Thromboplastin Release + Factor VII

Factor V
Factor X
+
Calcium
↓
Phase I   Prothrombin Activator

+
Prothrombin
+
Calcium
↓
Phase II   Thrombin

+
Fibrinogen
↓
Phase III   Fibrin Thread (matrix of clot)

Summary of ABO Blood Grouping

Blood Type	Antigen in RBC's	Antibodies in Plasma	Incompatible Donor Blood	Compatible Blood Donor
A	A	Anti-B	AB and B	A and O
B	B	Anti-A	A and AB	B and O
AB	A and B	None	None	All blood groups
O	None	Anti-A and Anti-B	All blood groups	None

2. Patients with type AB blood have no antibodies; therefore, they are considered *universal recipients.*

    a. Their plasma contains no antibodies.

    b. It cannot destroy donor's red cells.

3. Patients with type O blood have both anti-A and anti-B antibodies.

    a. Therefore, they are *universal donors.*

    b. Their red cells do not contain antigens that could be destroyed by antibodies in the recipients' blood.

Blood-Forming Organs

Spleen

Definition: The spleen is a glandlike organ located in the left upper part of the abdominal cavity; it is a storage organ for red corpuscles and, because of a large number of macrophages, acts as a blood filter.

Functions

A. Acts as a blood reservoir.

B. Purifies blood by removing waste and infectious organisms.

C. Is the primary source of antibodies in infants and children.

D. Produces lymphocytes, plasma cells, and antibodies in adults.

E. Produces erythrocytes in fetus.

F. Destroys erythrocytes when they reach the end of their life span.

Disorders of the Spleen

Hypersplenism

Definition: Hypersplenism is the excessive destruction of erythrocytes, leukocytes, and platelets.

A. The most common form of hypersplenism is congestive splenomegaly, usually due to portal hypertension secondary to cirrhosis.

B. Other causes are idiopathic thrombocytopenia, thrombosis, stenosis or atresia.

C. Secondary hypersplenism occurs in association with leukemias, lymphomas, Hodgkin's disease, and tuberculosis.

D. Treatment: correct underlying condition and/or splenectomy (see p. 233).

Rupture of the Spleen

Definition: Traumatic rupture following violent blow or trauma to the spleen.

Clinical Manifestations

A. Weakness due to blood loss.

B. Abdominal pain and muscle spasm particularly in the left upper quadrant.

C. Depression of abdominal bleeding.

D. Rebound tenderness.

E. Referred pain to left shoulder.

F. Palpable tenderness.

G. Leukocytosis well over twelve thousand.

H. Progressive shock with rapid, thready pulse; drop in blood pressure; and pallor.

Disorders of the Blood *

Purpuras

Definition: Purpura refers to the extravasation of blood into the tissues and mucous membranes.

Types

A. Idiopathic thrombocytopenic purpura is characterized by platelet deficiency due to either hypoproliferation, excessive destruction or excessive pooling of platelets in the spleen.
B. Vascular purpura is characterized by weak, damaged vessels which rupture easily.

Clinical Manifestations

A. Petechiae.
B. Postsurgical bleeding.
C. Increased bleeding time.
D. Abnormal platelet count.
E. Ecchymosis.

Treatment

A. Remove underlying cause if possible.
B. Control bleeding; physician may order corticosteroids.
C. Transfusion of platelets.
D. Splenectomy for idiopathic thrombocytopenia.

Agranulocytosis

Definition: An acute, potentially fatal blood disorder characterized by profound neutropenia and most commonly caused by drug toxicity or hypersensitivity.

Clinical Manifestations

A. Chills and fever.
B. Sore throat.
C. Prostration.
D. Ulceration of oral mucosa and the throat.

Treatment

A. Discontinue suspected chemical agents or drugs.
B. Isolate the patient to reduce exposure to infections.

See also Hemophilia (p. 386) and Disseminated Intravascular Coagulation (p. 194).

C. Administer corticosteroids only if the patient appears to be toxic.

Polycythemia Vera

Definition: Polycythemia vera is a chronic disease of unknown etiology characterized by overactivity of bone marrow with overproduction of red cells and hemoglobin.

Clinical Manifestations

A. Reddish-purple hue to the skin.
B. Increased blood volume.
C. Capillary engorgement.
D. Hemorrhage.
E. Venous thrombosis.
F. Arterial hypertension.
G. Hepatomegaly and splenomegaly.

Treatment

A. Radiophosphorus in dosages based on body weight; initially I.V., then orally.
B. Phlebotomy to remove 500–2000 ml. of blood per week until hematocrit reaches 50 percent; repeated when hematocrit rises.

Anemia

Definition: Anemia occurs when there is a decrease in either quantity or quality of blood. The deficiency may be a decrease in erythrocytes or a reduction in hemoglobin.

Common Causes of Anemia

A. Blood loss.
B. Destruction of red blood cells (hemolysis).
C. Abnormal bone marrow function.
D. Decreased erythropoietin due to renal damage.
E. Inadequate maturation of red blood cells.

Classifications

A. Normocytic normochromic.
   1. Chronic infection.
   2. Cancer.
   3. General debilitation.

B. Macrocytic normochromic.
  1. Vitamin B_{12} deficiency.
  2. Folic acid deficiency.
  3. Iron deficiency.
C. Microcytic hypochromic.

Common Clinical Manifestations

A. Related to tissue hypoxia.
  1. Weakness and fatigue.
  2. Need for sleep and rest.
  3. Lethargy.
  4. Dyspnea.
  5. Tachycardia, tachypnea.
  6. Pallor.
  7. Cold extremities.
B. Related to central nervous system.
  1. Vertigo.
  2. Irritability.
  3. Depression.
C. Poor wound healing.
D. Dietary deficiencies.

Nursing Management

A. Provide diet high in protein, iron, and vitamins to increase production of erythrocytes; remember that patient is sensitive to hot, cold, and spicy foods.
B. Maintain adequate fluid intake.
C. Protect from infection.
D. Provide complete bed rest.
E. Promote good skin care to prevent decubiti.
F. Protect from falls and injury (due to vertigo).
G. Avoid extremes of heat and cold (due to disturbance in sensory perception.
H. Provide good mouth care with diluted mouthwash and soft toothbrush.
I. Provide emotional support for long-term therapy.

Iron Deficiency Anemia (Microcytic Hypochromic)

Etiology

A. Most common type.
B. Results from inadequate intake, defective absorption, and improper utilization of iron.

Clinical Manifestations

A. Cheilosis.
B. Dysphagia.
C. Glossitis.
D. Papillae atrophy of tongue.
E. Pica syndrome (abnormal craving for sand and clay).

Nursing Management

A. Provide diet high in iron: liver, lean meats, egg yolk, dried fruit, whole wheat bread.
B. Administer iron preparations.
  1. Oral.
    a. Ferrous sulfate, 300 mg. t.i.d.
    b. Liquid iron (give with straw to avoid staining of teeth).
    c. Administer oral iron on empty stomach to increase absorption.
    d. Iron absorption is aided with vitamin C (give iron with orange juice).
    e. Side effects: epigastric distress, abdominal cramps, nausea, and diarrhea or constipation.
  2. Parenteral.
    a. Imferon (I.V., I.M.), Sorbitex (I.M.).
    b. Administer with Z track to prevent pain and discoloration.
C. Observe for signs of anaphylactic shock.
  1. Observe particularly with I.V. medications.
  2. Signs and symptoms: headache, urticaria, hypotension.

Pernicious Anemia

Definition: Pernicious anemia is a chronic and, if untreated, progressive macrocytic anemia caused by the failure of gastric mucosa to produce an intrinsic factor essential for absorption of vitamin B_{12}. RNA is altered.

Etiology

A. Total gastrectomy.
B. Surgical resection of small intestine.
C. Atrophy of gastric mucosa.
D. Malabsorption disease—sprue.
E. Bacterial or parasitic infections.
F. May be autoimmune difficulty.
G. Genetic predisposition (especially in northern Europe).

Clinical Manifestations

A. Negative effect on CNS by decreasing RNA production.
   1. Neurological disturbance—tingling of extremities.
   2. Symptoms of spinal cord degeneration—alterations in gait.
   3. Loss of finger movement.
   4. Personality and behavioral changes.
B. Glossitis—beefy, red tongue.
C. Anorexia.
D. Fatigue, weakness, pallor.
E. Yellow cast to skin.

Nursing Management

A. Obtain blood work for RBC count and megaloblastic maturation.
B. Patient teaching and nursing responsibility for:
   1. Bone marrow aspiration (assist physician during test).
   2. Upper GI series—administer bowel prep.
   3. Schilling test—instruct in NPO for 12 hours, collect 24-hour urine.
   4. Gastric analysis—insertion of NG tube, collection of aspirant, injection of histamine.
C. Provide emotional support during bone marrow aspiration.
D. Provide safety measures if neurological deficiency (assist with ambulation).
E. Avoid pressure on lower extremities due to circulatory changes (foot cradle, etc.).
F. Avoid extremes of heat and cold.
G. Provide support and explain behavior changes to patient and family.
H. Administer B_{12} deep I.M.
I. Instruct in oral administration of B_{12}—lifelong therapy.

Aplastic Anemia

Definition: Deficiency of circulating RBC's resulting from bone marrow suppression. Pancytopenia frequently accompanies RBC deficiency.

Etiology

A. Toxic action of drugs (Chloromycetin, sulfonamides, Dilantin, etc., alkylatiny and antimetabolites).
B. Exposure to radiation.
C. Diseases that suppress bone marrow activity (leukemia and metastatic cancer).

Clinical Manifestations

A. Onset insidious or rapid.
B. Increased fatigue.
C. Lethargy.
D. Dyspnea.
E. Cutaneous bleeding.
F. Low platelet and leukocyte count.

Treatment

A. Withdraw causative agent from therapy.
B. Avoid use of toxic chemical agents—DDT, carbon tetrachloride, etc.
C. Administer androgens and/or corticosteroids.
D. Transfuse with fresh platelets (RBC transfusion may be introduced also).
E. Splenectomy (especially in severe thrombocytopenia).
F. Administer antibiotics when infection occurs.
G. Bone marrow transplant and WBC transfusion are becoming more prevalent.

Nursing Management

A. Carry out reverse isolation procedure.
B. Protect from infections.
C. Provide for adequate rest periods.
D. Observe for complications.
E. Provide physical comfort measures.
F. Provide emotional support for patient and family, especially while in isolation.
G. Educate public in use of toxic pesticides and chemicals.

See also Hemolytic Anemia (p. 134) and Sickle Cell Anemia (p. 385).

Nursing Care of Patients with Blood Disorders

Prevention of Infections

A. Reverse isolation, and meticulous medical asepsis.
B. Bed rest.

C. High protein, high vitamin, and high caloric diet.

D. Antibiotics as ordered.

Fatigue and Weakness

A. Conservation of the patient's strength.

B. Frequent rest periods.

C. Ambulation activities as tolerated.

D. Decreased disturbing activities and noise.

E. Provision of optimal nutrition.

Hemorrhagic Tendencies

A. Provide rest during the bleeding episodes.

B. Apply gentle pressure to the bleeding sites.

C. Apply cold compresses to the bleeding sites when indicated.

D. Do not disturb clots.

E. Use small gauge needles to administer medications by injection.

F. Support the patient during transfusion therapy.

G. Observe for symptoms of internal bleeding.

H. Have a tracheostomy set available for the patient who is bleeding from the mouth or the throat.

Ulcerative Lesions of the Tongue, the Gums, and/or the Mucous Membranes

A. Provide nonirritating foods and beverages.

B. Give frequent oral hygiene with mild, cool mouthwash and solutions.

C. Use applicators or soft-bristled toothbrush.

D. Lubricate the lips.

E. Give mouth care both before and after meals.

Dyspnea

A. Elevate the head of the bed.

B. Support the patient in the orthopneic position

C. Administer oxygen when indicated.

D. Prevent unnecessary exertion.

E. Avoid gas-forming foods.

Bone and Joint Pains

A. Use cradle to relieve pressure of bedding.

B. Apply hot or cold compresses as ordered.

C. Immobilize joints when ordered.

Fever

A. Apply cool sponges.

B. Administer antipyretic drugs as ordered.

C. Encourage fluid intake unless contraindicated.

D. Maintain a cool environmental temperature.

Pruritus and/or Skin Eruptions

A. Keep the patient's fingernails short.

B. Use soap sparingly, if at all.

C. Apply emollient lotions in skin care.

Anxiety of the Patient

A. Explain the nature, the discomforts, and the limitations of activity associated with the diagnostic procedures and treatments.

B. Listen to the patient.

C. Treat the patient as an individual.

D. Allow the family to participate in the patient's care.

E. Encourage the family to visit with the patient; provide privacy for the family and patient.

Neoplastic Blood Disorders

Leukemia

Definition: Leukemia is a disorder of blood-forming tissue characterized by neoplastic proliferation of hematopoietic cells or their precursors.

Characteristics

A. The increased proliferation process alters the cell's ability to mature and/or function correctly.

B. In acute processes the predominant cell is poorly differentiated but in chronic processes the leukemic cell is well defined.

C. Usually there is an increased number of white blood cells which are immature and do not function normally, and a decreased number of red blood cells, hemoglobin and platelets, which results in anemia.

D. Diagnostic tests.

   1. Bone marrow aspiration/biopsy.

   2. Differential count.

Etiology

A. Excess radiation exposure.
B. Viral factors.
C. Immune alteration.
D. Noxious chemicals and drugs.
E. Bone marrow alterations.

Clinical Manifestations

A. Anemia.
B. Hemorrhage.
C. Infection.

Chemotherapy Principles

A. Combination of drugs used.
   1. Limits toxicity of individual drugs.
   2. Increases destruction of cells sensitive to various agents.
B. Induction therapy used after initial diagnosis.
C. Maintenance therapy used during remission.

Chemotherapeutic Agents

A. Antimetabolites—interfere with cellular metabolic process, thereby stopping synthesis of cell protein.
   1. Common drugs: cytosine arabinoside, thioguanine, 6-mercaptopurine, nuorauracil (5-FU), methotrexate.
   2. Toxic effects: anorexia, nausea, vomiting, diarrhea, skin rash, alopecia, hyperuricemia, stomatitis, depression of bone marrow.
B. Alkylating agents damage the cells' DNA production.
   1. Common drugs: thio-tepa, nitrogen mustard, Cytoxan Leukeran, Busulfan, Alkeran, Myleran.
   2. Toxic effects: stomatitis, alopecia, anorexia, nausea, vomiting, bone marrow depression, skin reactions.
C. Antibiotic agents—interfere with synthesis of RNA.
   1. Common drugs: Adriamycin, daunomycin, Dactinomycin, bleomycin, Mithramycin, Mitomycin.
   2. Toxic effects: nausea, vomiting, alopecia, stomatitis, skin rash, bone marrow depression, fever.
D. Plant alkaloids.
   1. Common drugs: Vincristine, Vinblastine.
   2. Toxic effects: nausea, vomiting, alopecia, stomatitis, bone marrow depression, paralytic ileus, peripheral neuritis.
E Enzymes.
   1. Common drug: L-Asparaginase.
   2. Toxic effects: nausea, vomiting, hyperglycemia, hypersensitivity reactions, bone marrow depression.
F. Hormones.
   1. Common drugs:
      a. Estrogens—DES, Estinyl.
      b. Progestins—Delalutin, Megace, Provera.
      c. Androgens—testosterone.
      d. Adrenocorticosteroids—Meticorten.
      e. Dexamethasone—Decadron.
   2. Toxic effects: edema, increased susceptibility to infection, sex characteristic alterations, electrolyte alterations.
G. Combination drugs.
   1. VAMP—Vincristine, amethopterin, 6-MP, prednisone.
   2. POMP—prednisone, Oncovin, methotrexate, 6-MP.
   3. COAP—Cytoxan, Oncovin, Ara-C, prednisone.

Nursing Management in Chemotherapy

A. Prevent complications related to the side effects of drugs.
   1. Proper mouth care (ulcerations and bleeding).
   2. Anorexia.
B. Maintain fluid and electrolyte balance.
C. Administer Allopurinol to combat problems associated with increased serum uric acid (from rapid destruction of body tissue).
D. Provide diet—high calorie, high vitamin to prevent weight loss, weakness, debilitation.
E. Provide emotional support.
   1. Alopecia.
   2. Altered body image.
   3. Fear of dying.
   4. Depression.
   5. Financial burden.
F. Provide patient education.
   1. Drugs—dosage and side effects.
   2. Associated treatments.
   3. Disease process.
G. Prevent infections, ulcerations, hemorrhage.

Acute Myelogenous Leukemia (AML)

Characteristics

A. Incidence—occurs more commonly after age 40, slightly higher incidence in males. Onset can be insidious or rapid.

B. Pathophysiology—stem cell of WBC proliferates, decreasing stem cells availability for RBC's and platelets.

Clinical Manifestations

A. Anemia leads to dyspnea, fatigue, pallor, palpitations.

B. Platelet deficiency leads to epistaxis, gingival bleeds, purpura, petechiae on bleeding in major systems.

C. Neutropenia leads to local abscesses, elevated temperature, chills.

D. Splenomegaly.

E. Lymph node enlargement leading to difficulty with respiration and swallowing.

F. Bone pain.

G. CNS involvement with signs of increased ICP.

H. Hyperuricemia.

Treatment

A. Drugs.
 1. Cytarabine and thioguanine.
 2. COAP.

B. Local irradiation for lymph node enlargement and bone pain.

C. Antibiotics for increased temperature.

D. Platelet administration when bleeding occurs.

E. Allopurinol when hyperuricemia occurs.

Chronic Myelocytic Leukemia (CML)

Characteristics

A. Incidence—primarily a disease of young adults. Thought to have a genetic origin. Philadelphia chromosome is involved.

B. Pathophysiology—marked increase of granulocytes and megakaryocyte (platelet cell). The mature neutrophil is the cell which is predominant.

Clinical Manifestations

A. Early signs: splenomegaly, fatigue, malaise, pallor, heat intolerance, retinal hemorrhage, increased perspiration, purpura, skin nodules, abdominal discomfort.

B. Late signs: bone pain, anemia, fever, increased uric acid.

Treatment

A. Oral alkylating agent (Myleran).

B. Spleen or total irradiation.

Chronic Lymphocytic Leukemia (CLL)

Characteristics

A. Incidence—insidious onset, most common in ages 50 to 70.

B. Pathophysiology—the small lymphocyte (B cell) is the predominant cell type and eventually leads to decreased production of other hematopoietic cells.

Clinical Manifestations

A. Classic signs: anemia, weight loss, abdominal discomfort with hepatomegaly/splenomegaly, palpable lymph nodes.

B. Less common signs: excessive diaphoresis, malaise, fatigue, infection.

Treatment

A. Drugs: chlorambucil (Leukeran), cyclophosphamide (Cytoxan).

B. Some physicians feel that premature exposure to oxytocic drugs aggravate the condition.

C. Splenectomy in some cases.

Acute Lymphocytic Leukemia (ALL)

Characteristics

A. Incidence—usually appears before age 15 but is highest in 3- to 4-year-olds. Males slightly more at risk.

B. Pathophysiology—the lymphoblasts are most responsible for the pathogenesis with eventual reduction of other blood cells.

Clinical Manifestations

A. Malaise, fatigue, and fever.

B. Bone involvement and lymph and spleen alterations.

C. Bleeding gums, skin and nose.

D. CNS symptoms, especially stiff neck and headache.

Treatment

A. Induction chemotherapy.

B. Maintenance therapy when in remission.

C. Drugs: methotrexate, daunomycin, Oncovin.

Malignancy of the Lymph System

Hodgkin's Disease

Definition: Hodgkin's disease is a chronic, progressive, neoplastic, invariably fatal reticuloendothelial disease involving the lymphoid tissues of the body. It is most common between the ages of twenty and forty. While the exact etiology is unknown, the suspected sources are: viral, environmental, genetic, and immunologic.

Clinical Manifestations

A. Usually insidious onset starting in upper half of body, particularly cervical lymph nodes.

B. Painless enlargement of the lymph nodes.

C. Severe pruritus.

D. Irregular fever, night sweats.

E. Splenomegaly and hepatomegaly.

F. Jaundice, weight loss.

G. Edema and cyanosis of the face and neck.

H. Pulmonary symptoms including dyspnea, cough, chest pain, cyanosis, and pleural effusion.

I. Progressive anemia with resultant fatigue, malaise, and anorexia.

J. Bone pain and vertebral compression.

K. Nerve pain and paraplegia.

L. Laryngeal paralysis.

M. Increased susceptibility to infection.

Staging

A. Stage I—disease is restricted to single anatomic site, or is localized in a group of lymph nodes; asymptomatic.

B. Stage II(a)—two or three adjacent lymph nodes in the area on the same side of the diaphragm are affected.

C. Stage II(b)—symptoms appear.

D. Stage III—disease is widely disseminated on both sides of diaphragm into the lymph areas and organs.

E. Stage IV—involvement of bone, bone marrow, pleura, liver, skin, GI tract, CNS, and gradually the entire body.

Treatment

A. Radiation is used for stages I, II, and III in an effort to eradicate the disease.

B. Wide-field megavoltage radiation with doses of 3500–4000 roentgens over a four- to six-week period.

C. Chemotherapy with Cytoxan, nitrogen mustard, thio-tepa, TEM, Velban, Oncovin, prednisone, and Matulane.

D. Diagnostic laparotomy.

Nursing Management

A. Supportive relief from effects of radiation and chemotherapy.
   1. Side effects include nausea and vomiting.
   2. Controlled by premedication of sedatives and antiemetic agents.

B. Assisting patient to maintain as normal a life as possible during course and treatment of disease.
   1. Counseling of patient and family to accept process of treatment.
   2. Supportive assistance in dealing with feelings of anger, depression, fear, and loneliness.

C. Prevention of infection as body's resistance is lowered.

D. Continued observation for complications—pressure from enlargement of lymph glands on vital organs, especially the respiratory tree.

Integumentary System

The integumentary system comprises the enveloping membrane, or skin, of the body and includes the epidermis, the dermis, and all the derivatives of the epidermis, such as hair, nails, and various glands. It is indispensable for the body as it forms a barrier against the external environment and participates in many vital body functions.

Anatomy and Physiology

Skin

Definition: Skin is the organ that envelops the body, comprises about 15 percent of the body weight, and forms a barrier between the internal organs and the external environment.

Characteristics and Functions

A. Consists of three layers: epidermis, dermis, and subcutaneous.
B. Largest sensory organ, equipped with nerves and specialized sensory organs sensitive to pain, touch, pressure, heat, and cold.
C. Chief pigment is melanin, produced by basal cells.
D. Functions of skin.
   1. Protection.
   2. Temperature regulation.
   3. Sensation.
   4. Storage.

Bacterial Flora on the Skin

A. Normally present in varying amounts are coagulase positive staphylococcus, coagulase negative staphylococcus, mycobacterium, Pseudomonas, diphtheroids, nonhemolytic streptococcus, hemolytic streptococcus (group A).
B. The organisms are shed with normal exfoliation of skin; bathing and rubbing may also remove bacteria.
C. Normal pH of skin (4.2–5.6) retards growth of bacteria.

D. Damaged areas of skin are potential points of entry for infection.

Hair

Definition: Hair is a threadlike structure developed from a papilla in the corium layer.

A. Hair goes through cyclic changes: growth, atrophy, and rest.
B. Melanocytes present in the bulb of each hair account for color.
C. All parts of the body except the palms, soles of the feet, distal phalanges of fingers and toes, and the penis are covered with some form of hair.

Sweat Glands

Definition: Sweat glands are aggregations of cells that produce a liquid (perspiration) having a salty taste and a pH which varies from 4.5–7.5.

Types

A. Eccrine sweat glands.
   1. Located in all areas of the skin except the lips and part of the genitalia.
   2. Open onto the surface of the skin.
   3. Activity controlled by the sympathetic nervous system.
   4. Secrete sweat (perspiration).
      a. The chief components of sweat are water, sodium, potassium, chloride, glucose, urea, and lactate.
      b. Concentrations vary from individual to individual.
B. Apocrine sweat glands.
   1. Located in the axilla, genital, anal, and nipple areas.
   2. Located in ear and produce ear wax.
   3. Develop during puberty.
   4. Respond to adrenergic stimuli.
   5. Produce an alkaline sweat.

Sebaceous Glands

A. Develop at base of hair follicle.

B. Secrete sebum.

C. Hormone controlled. Increased activity with androgens; decreased activity with estrogens.

Definitions of Skin Disorders

A. Macule: a flat, circumscribed discolored lesion less than 1 cm. in diameter.

B. Papule: a raised, solid lesion less than 1 cm. in diameter.

C. Nodule: similar to a papule except greater depth.

D. Vesicle: an elevated lesion of skin or mucous membrane filled with fluid.

E. Pustule: a pus-filled vesicle.

F. Wheal: an irregularly shaped and elevated lesion of skin or mucous membrane due to edema.

G. Plaque: a collection of papules.

H. Erosion: a moist depressed area due to partial or full loss of epidermis.

I. Ulcer: the complete loss of dermis leaving irregular depression; scars on healing.

J. Fissure: a line-like split through the epidermis into the dermis.

Common Skin Lesions

Paronychia

Definition: Infection and inflammation of the tissue around the nailplate.

Clinical Manifestations

A. Acute infection from a hangnail.

B. May develop into cellulitis.

C. High incidence in middle-age women.

D. High incidence in diabetics.

Treatment

A. Warm soaks.

B. Antibiotic or fungicidal ointment.

C. Incision and drainage of affected area.

Acne Vulgaris

Definition: A disorder of the skin with eruption of papules or pustules primarily due to increased production of sebum from the sebaceous glands.

Clinical Manifestations

A. Affects adolescents and young adults.

B. Noninflammatory type composed of whiteheads and blackheads in the follicular duct.

C. Inflammatory acne pustules with possible scarring.

D. Affected by hormone levels (androgen).

Treatment

A. Estrogen therapy.

B. Desquamation preparations, which allow free flow of sebum.

C. Complete cleansing with regular or Neutrogena soap and clean towels.

D. Mild facial erythema via sunlight or lamp.

E. Removal of blackheads and whiteheads.

F. Topical antibiotics.

G. Systemic tetracycline for some cases.

H. Dermabrasion for selected cases.

Nursing Management

A. Teach good skin and scalp hygiene.

B. Avoid squeezing, rubbing, picking.

C. Avoid greasy cleansing creams and cosmetics.

D. Maintain high protein, low fat diet.
   1. Fatty foods, white sugar, nuts, and chocolate should be avoided.
   2. Diet not as important a therapy as in the past.

E. Provide adequate rest and sunshine.

F. Provide emotional support for body image and relationship problems.

Impetigo

Definition: Impetigo is a bacterial disease caused by streptococcus or staphylococcus or both.

Clinical Manifestations

A. Lesions are intraepidermal vesicles.

B. Lesions progress to pustules which become crusted.

Treatment

A. Most important intervention is the prevention of the spread of the disease: complete cleansing with hexachlorophene soap and other hygienic care materials; separate towels.

B. Lesions dried by exposure to air; compresses of Burow's solution used to remove the crusts to allow faster healing.

C. Antibiotic ointments; bland emollients to prevent cracking and fissures.

Furuncle (Boil)

Definition: Furuncle is a bacterial disease caused by staphylococcus pyrogen infection of a hair follicle.

Clinical Manifestations

A. Onset is sudden; the skin becomes red, tender, and hot around the hair follicle.

B. The center forms pus, and the core may be extruded spontaneously or by excision and manipulation.

C. Diabetes mellitus may be suspected and should be ruled out only after tests prove negative.

Treatment

A. Scrupulous cleanliness is necessary; isolation of towels, soap, and clothing.

B. Systemic antibiotics if a series of carbuncles occur.

Herpes Simplex

Definition: Herpes simplex is a viral disease (coldsore) caused by herpes virus, hominis types I and II.

Types of Virus

A. Herpes I.
   1. Most common type.
   2. Causes burning, tingling, and itching, soon followed by tiny vesicles on an erythematous base.
   3. Most frequently occurs on lips, but can occur on the face and around the mouth.
B. Herpes II.
   1. Most often the cause of genital infection.

2. Transmitted primarily through sexual contact.
3. Difficult to treat and to prevent recurrence.

Treatment

A. Area kept dry and clean.
B. Frequent applications of ether.
C. Avoidance of sexual contact.

Herpes Zoster

Definition: Herpes zoster is an acute viral invasion of the central nervous system.

Clinical Manifestations

A. Pain and discomfort.
B. Cutaneous lesions.

Treatment

A. Drying lotions.
B. Analgesics to control pain.
C. Prevention of infection.

Venereal Diseases and Cutaneous Lesions

Syphilis

Definition: Syphilis is a contagious venereal disease that leads to many structural and cutaneous lesions, caused by the spirochete *Treponema pallidum*. The disease is transmitted by direct, intimate contact or in utero.

Early Syphilis—Two Stages

A. Primary stage.
   1. Incubation period is ten days to three weeks.
   2. Characteristic lesion is red, eroded, indurated papule; the sore or ulcer at the site of the invasion by the spirochete is called a *chancre*.
   3. Accompanied by enlarged lymph node in drainage area of chancre.
   4. May be painless or painful.
   5. This stage is highly infectious.

B. Secondary stage.
1. Develops if the individual is not treated in the primary stage. Occurs in two to six months and may last two years.
2. May be mild enough to pass unnoticed or may be severe, with a generalized rash on skin and mucous membrane.
3. Headache, fever, sore throat, and general malaise are common.
4. Disappears by itself if untreated in three to twelve weeks.

Late Syphilis—Tertiary Stage

A. Symptoms may develop soon after stage two or lie hidden for years.
B. Blood test may be negative.
C. Less contagious but very dangerous to individual.
D. If untreated, cardiovascular problems may ensue.
E. Blindness or deep ulcers may occur.
F. May be treated with antibiotics but cure is more difficult.

Characteristics

A. Transmitted most commonly by sexual intercourse, but infants may become infected during the birth process.
B. No age or race is immune to the disease.
C. Diagnosed by serum studies and/or dark field examination of secretions of the chancre.
1. Wassermann test.
2. Kahn test.

Treatment

A. Long-acting Bicillin is still the primary treatment in the early stages.
B. Avoidance of sexual contact until clearance is given by physician.
C. No immunity develops and reinfection is common.

Nursing Management

A. Advise patient that strict personal hygiene is an absolute requirement.
B. Most importantly, educate patient in prevention: symptoms, mode of transmission, and treatment.
C. Assist in case finding; encourage use of clinics for diagnosis and treatment.

Allergic Responses

Eczema

Definition: Eczema is a superficial inflammatory process involving primarily the epidermis.

Clinical Manifestations

A. Eruptions occur that are erythematous, papular, or papulovesicular.
1. May be edematous, weeping, eroded, and/or crusted.
2. Chronic form may cause skin to be thickened, scaling, and fissured.
B. Regional lymph nodes swell.
C. Irritability is present, running a chronic course with remission and exacerbation.
D. Response occurs at all ages, and is common in infancy.

Treatment

A. Depends on cause (foods, emotional problems, familial tendencies).
B. Child is isolated from recently vaccinated children; child is *not* vaccinated.

Nursing Management

A. Have patients keep fingernails short; restrain or provide gloves to prevent scratching.
B. Apply wet dressings or therapeutic baths (no soaps during acute stages).
C. Apply mild lotion (calamine) when no oozing or vesiculation is present.
D. Use cornstarch paste to remove crusts.
E. Rub cornstarch into bed linen, and do not use woolen blankets.

Contact Dermatitis

Definition: Contact dermatitis is a skin reaction caused by contact with an agent to which the skin is sensitive.

Characteristic Causes

A. Clothing (especially woolens).

B. Cosmetics.

C. Household products (especially detergents).

D. Industrial substances (i.e., paints, dyes, cements).

Treatment

A. Avoidance of irritant or removal of irritating clothing.

B. Avoidance of contact with detergent (use of rubber gloves for household chores).

C. Avoidance of contact with industrial agent (use of protective clothing or, for highly sensitive individuals, change of job locations).

Poison Oak or Poison Ivy

Definition: Poison oak or poison ivy is a dermatitis caused by contact with poison oak, poison ivy, or poison sumac, which contain urushiol, a potent skin-sensitizing agent.

Clinical Manifestations

A. Papulovesicular lesions.

B. Severe itching.

Treatment

A. Skin cleansed of plant oils.

B. Lotion.

C. Steroids for severe reactions.

D. Cold, wet dressings of Burow's solution to relieve itching.

Nursing Management for Allergic Responses

A. Observe skin condition carefully.
   1. Texture.
   2. Hydration.

B. Describe lesion(s).
   1. Areas affected.
   2. Onset of symptoms (local and/or systemic).

C. Prevent infection of skin by careful handwashing and skin care.

D. Educate public about preventive measures.

Malignant Skin Tumors

Basal-Cell Epithelioma

Definition: Basal-cell epithelioma is a tumor arising from the basal layer of the epidermis formed because of basal cell keratinization. The typical lesion is a small, smooth papule with telangiectasis and atrophic center.

Clinical Manifestations

A. Starts as a papule and spreads; central area may become depressed and ulcerated.

B. It is locally invasive and if neglected may cause extensive local destruction.

C. Death may take place as a result of invasion of vital structures.

Treatment

A. Surgical excision is the most effective treatment.

B. Radiation therapy is administered for lesions of the eyelid and nose.

Nursing Management

A. Educate the patient to avoid exposure to sun.

B. Watch for potential malignancy in other locations.

Squamous Cell Carcinoma

Definition: Squamous cell carcinoma is a tumor of the epidermis that frequently comes from keratosis and is considered an invasive cancer. The lesion begins as erythematous macules or plaques with indistinct margins, and the surface often becomes crusted.

Clinical Manifestations

A. The lesions enlarge more rapidly than in basal-cell epithelioma, and can metastasize.

B. A nodular tumor appears, usually on the lower lip, tongue, head, or neck.

Treatment

A. Excision is the most effective treatment.

B. Irradiation.

Melanoma

Definition: Melanoma is the most malignant of all cutaneous lesions. It arises from melanocytes and is often fatal. It occurs most frequently in light-skinned people when they are exposed to sunlight.

Treatment

A. Surgical excision is the most effective treatment.
B. Cancer drugs may be used for treatment.

Nursing Management

A. Advise patient to prevent occurrence by using sun-screening devices.
B. Advise patient to avoid prolonged exposure to sun.
C. Educate patient to observe any changes in color or form of moles.

Collagen Diseases

Definition: Connective tissue disorders which have common wide-spread immunological and inflammatory alteration of connective tissue.

Common Clinical Manifestations

A. Skin changes.
B. Joint involvement.
C. Muscle involvement.

Etiology

A. Possible autoimmune disturbance.
B. Hereditary predisposition.

Lupus Erythematosus

Definition: Lupus erythematosus is a collagen disease of the connective tissue that may involve any organ of the body.

Clinical Manifestations

A. Discoid eruption—a chronic, localized scaling erythematous skin eruption over the nose, cheeks, and forehead, giving a characteristic "butterfly" appearance.

B. Fever, malaise and weight loss.
C. Exacerbation and remission of symptoms.
D. Sensitivity to sunlight.
E. Systemic (disseminated) lupus erythematosus may have multiple organ involvement that can lead to death.

Treatment

A. Avoidance of sunlight and local antibiotic ointments that spread the lesions.
B. Steroid treatment to prevent progression of the disease.

Nursing Management

A. Apply topical sunscreen preparations (i.e., Covermark, Pabanol, etc.).
B. Advise patient of possible side effects of prescribed medications; advise patient to notify physician promptly if side effects occur so drugs may be discontinued before serious complications.
C. Cover up disfigurement from scarring with opaque or tinted cosmetics as recommended by physician.

Joint Diseases

Rheumatoid Arthritis

Definition: Chronic systemic inflammatory disease affecting the joints. Usual onset is from 20 to 40 years of age.

Clinical Manifestations

A. Bilateral joint involvement (erythema, warm, tender, painful).
B. Insidious onset of malaise, weight loss, paresthesia, stiffness.
C. Pain and stiffness early in morning, subsides with moderate activity.
D. Subcutaneous nodules.
E. Low grade temperature.
F. Fatigue and weakness.

Treatment

A. Chemotherapy to reduce inflammation and relieve pain.

1. Salicylates.
   a. ASA most common.
   b. Side effects include tinnitus, GI upset, prolonged bleeding time.
2. Anti-inflammatory drugs.
   a. Phenylbutazone, indomethacin, Motrin.
   b. Side effects include GI disturbances, CNS manifestations, skin rashes.
3. Gold salts (chrysotherapy).
   a. Three to four months before effective.
   b. Expensive.
   c. Toxicity can be severe.
4. Corticosteroids.
   a. Adjunct therapy only.
   b. Used during exacerbations or severe involvement.
   c. Low dose to prevent toxicity.

B. Preserve joint function.
C. Prevent deformity.
D. Diet control.
E. Surgery if severe joint involvement.
   1. Synovectomy.
   2. Joint replacement.

Nursing Management

A. Provide rest periods throughout day.
B. Provide psychological support for altered body image and living with chronic disease.
C. Prevent flexion contractures and promote exercise.
   1. Initiate ROM exercises.
   2. Avoid weight bearing for inflamed joints.
   3. Give warm baths and exercise.
D. Administer medications as ordered and instruct patient as to side effects.

Osteoarthritis

Definition: Hypertrophic degeneration of joints that is part of the normal aging process. The cartilage that covers the ends of the bones disintegrates.

Clinical Manifestations

A. Strikes the joints that receive the most stress, e.g., knees, toes, lower spine. Distal finger joint involvement is usually seen in women.

B. Pain and stiffness in the joints.

Treatment

A. Physical therapy.
   1. Dry, moist heat.
   2. Exercise to maintain ROM and prevent complications.
B. Medications.
   1. Salicylates most common for pain relief.
   2. Steroids for reduction of inflammation.
C. Well-balanced diet.

Nursing Management

A. Prevent permanent disability.
   1. Plan exercise to prevent joint fixation.
   2. Provide exercise periods to increase muscle tone.
   3. Control exercise periods to prevent fatigue.
B. Maintain proper positioning.
   1. Align and frequently change position to prevent complications.
   2. Encourage and support patient as frequent movements cause pain.
C. Apply heat for relief of pain.
   1. Dry heat with a heat lamp to relieve stiffness.
   2. Moist heat with hot tubs, hot towels, or paraffin baths for the hands.
D. Provide adequate rest—10 to 12 hours a day.
E. Administer medications as ordered and teach about side effects.
   1. Salicylates most common for relief of pain.
   2. Side effects of ASA include tinnitus, nausea, and prolonged bleeding time.
   3. Anti-inflammatory drugs (cortisone) reduce the effect of inflammation thus decreasing pain, swelling and stiffness.
F. Provide psychological support and/or psychotherapy.

Burns

Definition: Destruction of layers of the skin by thermal, chemical, or electrical agents.

Classification of Burns

A. Degree of burn—determined by layers involved.

1. First degree.
   a. Involves epidermis.
   b. Area is red or pink.
   c. Moderate pain.
   d. Spontaneous healing.
2. Second degree.
   a. Involves epidermis and dermis to the basal cells.
   b. Blistering.
   c. Severe pain.
   d. Regeneration in one month.
   e. Scarring may occur.
3. Third degree.
   a. Involves epidermis, dermis, and subcutaneous tissue and may extend to the muscle in severe burns.
   b. White, gray, or black in appearance
   c. Absence of pain.
   d. Edema of surrounding tissues.
   e. Eschar formation.
   f. Grafting needed due to total destruction of dermal elements.
4. Fourth degree.
   a. Involves muscle and bone.
   b. Increased destruction of RBC's.

B. Methods for determining percent of body burned.
   1. Rule of Nines—good for rapid estimation.
      a. Head and neck   9%
      b. Anterior trunk   18%
      c. Posterior trunk   18%
      d. Arms (9% each)   18%
      e. Legs (18% each)   36%
      f. Perineum   1%
   2. Lund/Browder Method.
      a. More accurate and appropriate to use when calculating fluid replacement.
      b. A chart is necessary to compute percentages assigned to body areas.
      c. Percentages vary for different age groups.

C. Associated factors which determine seriousness of burn.
   1. Age.
      a. Below 18 months.
      b. Above 65 years.
   2. General health.
   3. Site of burn.
   4. Associated injuries (fractures).

5. Causative agents.

D. Classification according to the percentage of body area destroyed.
   1. Critical burns: 30 percent or more of the body has sustained second degree burn, and 10 percent has sustained third degree burn; further complicated by respiratory involvement, smoke inhalation, fractures, and other tissue injury.
   2. Moderate burns: less than 10 percent of the body has sustained third degree burn, and 15 to 30 percent has sustained second degree burn.
   3. Minor burns: less than 15 percent of the body has sustained second degree burn, and less than 2 percent has sustained third degree burn.

E. Classification according to cause.
   1. Thermal burns.
      a. Flame burns.
      b. Scalding with hot liquids.
      c. Radiation.
   2. Chemical burns.
      a. Strong acids.
      b. Strong alkali solutions.
   3. Electrical burns.
      a. Most serious type of burn.
      b. Body fluids may conduct an electrical charge through body (look for entrance and exit area).
      c. Cardiac arrhythmias may occur.
      d. Toxins are created post-burn which injure kidneys.
      e. Voltage and ampere information important in history taking.

Treatment

A. Immediate care.
   1. Iced water for brief duration in second degree burn if seen within 10 minutes of injury.
   2. No ointments.
   3. Burns covered with sterile or clean cloth.

B. Emergency room care.
   1. Establish and maintain patent airway.
   2. 100% O_2 if burn occurred in enclosed area.
   3. Determine degree and extent of burn.
   4. Manage fluid balance.
      a. Calculate fluid needed to maintain adequate circulation.
         (1) Brooks Evans or Parkland formula.

(2) 1.5 ml./kg./hr.

   b. Monitor urine output for fluid adequacy (Foley catheter).

   c. Vital signs—CVP line usually inserted.

5. Ng tube to prevent paralytic ileus.
6. Tetanus toxoid.
7. Escharotomy if needed.

C. Long-term care.
 1. Wound debridement.
 2. Wound care—ointment and/or dressing.
 3. Skin grafting.
    a. Homografts—from cadaver or other person.
    b. Xenografts—from an animal.
    c. Autografts—from self.

Management of Burns

A. Maintain patent airway.

B. Maintain aseptic area.

C. Provide fluid replacement therapy.
 1. Shock phase.
    a. First twenty-four to forty-eight hours post-burn, fluid shifts from plasma to interstitial space.
    b. Potassium levels rise in plasma; blood hemo-concentration and metabolic acidosis occur.
    c. Fluid loss is mostly plasma.
    d. Nursing responsibilities.
      (1) Monitor vital signs frequently.
      (2) Monitor urinary output (50–100 cc./hour).
      (3) Give 1/2 of total fluids in first eight hours.
 2. Post-shock phase (diuretic phase).
    a. Capillary permeability stabilizes and fluid begins to shift from interstitial spaces to plasma.
    b. Hypokalemia, hypernatremia, hemodilution, and pulmonary edema are potential dangers.
    c. Nursing responsibilities.
      (1) Monitor CVP.
      (2) Observe lab values.
      (3) Maintain adequate urine output.

D. Relieve pain with morphine sulfate, I.V. as ordered. Give small doses frequently.

E. Assess peripheral circulation.

F. Provide adequate heat to maintain patient's temperature.

G. Promote good body alignment—begin range of motion early.

H. Administer antacids to prevent stress ulcer.

I. Maintain reverse isolation.

J. Maintain wound care.
 1. Initial excision—mainly for electrical burns.
 2. Occlusive dressings.
    a. Painful and costly.
    b. Decreases water loss.
    c. Limits range-of-motion exercises.
    d. Helps to maintain functional position.
    e. Advent of topical antibiotics has led to decreased use.
 3. Exposure method.
    a. Allows for drainage of burn exudate.
    b. Eschar forms protective covering.
    c. Use of topical therapy.
    d. Skin easily inspected.
    e. Range-of-motion exercises easier to perform.

K. Apply topical preparations to wound area.
 1. Silver nitrate.
    a. 0.5% solution on dressings, which are changed b.i.d.; dressings must be kept moist at all times.
    b. Sodium chloride, which is lost due to hypotonicity of solution, is replaced, as ordered.
    c. Used if patient is allergic to Sulfamylon.
    d. Disadvantages.
      (1) Poor penetration.
      (2) Discoloration obscures wound.
 2. Mafenide (Sulfamylon).
    a. Exerts bacteriostatic action against many organisms.
    b. Penetrates tissue well.
    c. Dressings not needed when used.
    d. Breakdown of drug provides heavy acid load. Inhibition of carbonic anhydrase compounds situation. Individual compensates by hyperventilating.
    e. Alternate use with Silvadene.
 3. Gentamicin.
    a. 0.1% concentration of ointment with dressings; no dressings with cream.

       b.   Cream penetrates well.

       c.   Renal function must be monitored.

       d.   Not widely used.

   4.   Silvadene.

       a.   Broad antimicrobial activity.

       b.   Effective against yeast.

       c.   Inhibits bacteria resistant to other antimicrobials.

          (1)   Not usually used prophylactically.

          (2)   Given for specific organism.

          (3)   Not helpful first 48 hours due to vessel thrombosis.

       d.   Can be washed off with water.

L.   Administer systemic antibiotics.

M.   Debridement and eschar removal daily.

N.   Provide long-term care.

   1.   Maintain good positioning to prevent contractures.

   2.   Provide adequate rest.

   3.   Prevent infection.

   4.   Maintain adequate protein and caloric intake to promote healing.

   5.   Monitor hydration status.

   6.   Protect skin grafts.

   7.   Provide psychological support (as important as physical care).

       a.   Deal with the patient's fear of disfigurement and immobility from scarring.

       b.   Provide constant support, as plastic repair is lengthy and painful.

       c.   Involve the family in long-term planning and day-to-day care.

Endocrine System

The endocrine system consists of a series of glands that function individually or conjointly to integrate and control innumerable metabolic activities of the body. These glands automatically regulate various body processes by releasing chemical signals called hormones.

Anatomy and Physiology

Function

A. Maintenance and regulation of vital functions.
   1. Response to stress or injury.
   2. Growth and development.
   3. Reproduction.
   4. Fluid, electrolyte, and acid-base balance.
   5. Energy metabolism.
B. Endocrine glands.
   1. Have specific functions.
   2. Influence each other.
   3. Secrete hormones.
   4. Controlled by autonomic nervous system.
   5. Located in various parts of body.
C. Hormones.
   1. Proteins or steroids.
   2. Chemical messengers which stimulate or inhibit life processes.
   3. Transmitted via the bloodstream to target tissues.
   4. Regulated through negative feedback control system (hypothalamic-pituitary axis). For example, the TSH-releasing hormone (TRH) is secreted by the hypothalamus, which causes the pituitary to secrete TSH. TSH stimulates the thyroid to secrete thyroxine. Thyroxine feeds back on the pituitary and inhibits production of TSH.
   5. Also regulated by renin-angiotensin-aldosterone, insulin-glucose, and calcium-parathormone.
   6. Endocrine disorders caused by a deficit or excess in hormone production.

Structure

A. Hypothalamus connects pituitary gland to central nervous system.
B. Pituitary gland divided into three lobes.
   1. Anterior pituitary control (master gland).
      a. Tropic hormones exert effect through regulation of other endocrine glands—ACTH, TSH, FSH, LH.
      b. Target tissues: hormones have direct effect on tissues—growth hormone, prolactin, MSH.
   2. Posterior lobe (neurohypophysis)—ADH, oxytocin, melanophore stimulating hormone.
   3. Intermediate lobe.

Conditions Associated with Hormonal Imbalances

A. Tumors of the glands.
   1. Benign (common).
   2. Malignant (rare).
   3. Ectopic.
B. Absence of gland.
C. Autoimmune factors.
D. Infections.
E. Side effects of replacement hormones.
F. Dysfunction of the pituitary gland, which affects functioning of the target glands.

General Signs of Hormonal Imbalance

A. Growth imbalance.
   1. Excessive growth.
      a. Pituitary or hypothalamic disorders.
      b. Excess adrenal, ovarian, or testicular hormone.
   2. Retarded growth.
      a. Endocrine and metabolic disorders; difficult to distinguish from dwarfism.
      b. Hypothyroidism.
B. Obesity.
   1. Sudden onset suggests hypothalamic lesion (rare).
   2. Cushing's syndrome (with characteristic buffalo hump).

Endocrine System

Endocrine Gland	Hormones Produced	Function	Endocrine Disorder

Pituitary
 	
Location: Base of the brain
	Anterior Lobe
	  Adrenocorticotropic hormone (ACTH)
	  Thyrotropic hormone (TSH)
	  Somatotropic hormone growth—(STH)
	  Gonadotropic hormones (FSH, LH, LTH)
	Posterior Lobe
	  Vasopressin (ADH)
	  Oxytocin
	  Melanophore stimulating hormone (MSH)
		Termed "master gland" as it directly affects the function of other endocrine glands.
		Controls sexual development and function.
		Promotes growth of body tissues.
		Influences water absorption by kidney.
		Influenced by hypothalamus.
			Anterior pituitary
			  Giantism
			  Acromegaly
			  Cushing's disease
			  Dwarfism
			Posterior pituitary
			  Diabetes insipidus

Adrenal
 	
Location: On top of each kidney
	Cortex
	  Glucocorticoids
	    Cortisol
	    Cortisone
	    Corticosterone
	  Mineralocorticoids
	    Aldosterone
	    Deoxycorticosterone
	    Corticosterone
	  Sex hormones
	    Androgens
	    Estrogens
	Medulla
	  Epinephrine
	  Norepinephrine
		Regulates sodium and electrolyte balance.
		Affects carbohydrate, fat, and protein metabolism.
		Influences the development of sexual characteristics.
		Stimulates "fight or flight" response to danger.
			Addison's disease
			Cushing's syndrome
			Pheochromocytoma
			Primary aldosteronism

Thyroid Location: Anterior part of the neck	Thyroxine Triiodothyronine Thyrocalcitonin	Controls rate of body metabolism, growth, and nutrition.	Goiter Cretinism Myxedema Hyperthyroidism (Graves' disease)
Parathyroid Location: Near thyroid	Parathormone (PTH)	Controls calcium and phosphorus metabolism.	Hypoparathyroidism Hyperparathyroidism
Pancreas Islets of Langerhans Location: Posterior to stomach and liver	Insulin Glucagon	Influences carbohydrate metabolism. Indirectly influences fat and protein metabolism.	Diabetes mellitus Hyperinsulinism
Ovaries Location: Pelvic cavity Testes Location: Scrotum	Estrogen and progesterone Testosterone	Controls development of secondary sex characteristics.	Lack of acceleration or regression of sexual development

C. Abnormal skin pigmentation.
1. Hyperpigmentation may coexist with depigmentation in Addison's disease.
2. Thyrotoxicosis may be associated with spotty brown pigmentation.
D. Hirsutism.
1. Normal variations in body occur on nonendocrine basis.
2. First sign of neoplastic disease.
3. Indicates changes in adrenal status.
E. Appetite changes.
1. Polyphagia is a common sign of uncontrolled diabetes.
2. Indicates thyrotoxicosis.
3. Nausea and weight loss may indicate addisonian crisis or diabetic acidosis.
F. Polyuria and polydipsia.
1. Symptoms usually of nonendocrine etiology.
2. If sudden onset, suggest diabetes mellitus or insipidus.
3. May be present with hyperparathyroidism or hyperaldosteronism.
G. Mental changes.
1. Though often subtle, may be indicative of underlying endocrine disorder.
   a. Nervousness and excitability may indicate hyperthyroidism.
   b. Mental confusion may indicate hypopituitarism, Addison's disease, or myxedema.
2. Mental deterioration is observed in untreated hypoparathyroidism and hypothyroidism.

Disorders Associated with the Pituitary Gland

Acromegaly (Hormone Excess)

Definition: Acromegaly is the hypersecretion of growth hormone by the anterior pituitary, which occurs in adulthood after closure of the epiphyses of the long bones.

Clinical Manifestations

A. Excessive growth of short, flat bones.
1. Large hands and feet.
2. Thickening and protrusion of the jaw and orbital ridges that cause teeth to spread.
3. Increased growth of soft tissue.
4. Coarse features.
5. Pain in joints.
B. Voice becomes deeper.
C. Increased diaphoresis.
D. Oily, rough skin.
E. Increased hair growth over the body.
F. Menstrual disturbances; impotence.
G. Symptoms associated with local compression of brain by tumor.
1. Headache.
2. Visual disturbances; blindness.
H. Related hormonal imbalances.
● 1. Diabetes mellitus (growth hormone is insulin antagonist).
2. Cushing's syndrome.
I. Laboratory values—increased growth hormone level.

Treatment

A. Irradiation of pituitary.
B. Hypophysectomy.

Nursing Management

A. Provide emotional support.
1. Encourage patient's expression of feelings.
   a. Loss of self-image and self-esteem.
   b. Fears about brain surgery.
   c. Consequences of surgery (sterility and lifetime hormone replacement).
2. Avoid situations which may be embarrassing.
3. Encourage support of and communication with family.
B. Provide frequent skin care.
C. Position and support painful joints.
D. Test urine for sugar and acetone.

Giantism (Hormone Excess)

Definition: Giantism is the hypersecretion of growth hormone by the anterior pituitary, which occurs in childhood prior to closure of the epiphyses of the long bones.

Clinical Manifestations

A. Symmetrical overgrowth of the long bones.

B. Increased height in early adulthood (eight to nine feet).

C. Deterioration of mental and physical processes, which may occur in early adulthood.

D. Other tissue response similar to acromegaly.

Treatment

A. Irradiation of pituitary.

B. Hypophysectomy.

Panhypopituitarism (Hormone Deficit)

Definition: Dwarfism is the hyposecretion of growth hormone by the anterior pituitary. Growth is symmetrical but decreased.

Clinical Manifestations

A. Retarded physical growth.

B. Premature body-aging processes.

C. Pale, dry, smooth skin.

D. Poor development of secondary sex characteristics and external genitalia.

E. Slow intellectual development.

Treatment—Human growth hormone injections (HGH) are given if the imbalance is diagnosed and treated in early stage.

Diabetes Insipidus (Hormone Deficit)

Definition: Diabetes insipidus, usually seen in young adults, is an antidiuretic hormone (ADH) deficiency resulting from damage or tumors in the posterior lobe of the pituitary gland. May develop following brain surgery or head injury.

Clinical Manifestations

A. Severe polyuria and polydipsia.

B. Fatigue and muscle pain.

C. Dehydration.

D. Weight loss, muscle weakness, headache.

E. Laboratory values—low urinary specific gravity (<1.006).

F. Inability to concentrate urine.

Treatment

A. Vasopressin tannate (Pitressin tannate), I.M., or nasal spray.

B. Benzothiodiazide diuretics for mild cases.

C. Diabinese to potentiate vasopressin or act as antidiuretic.

D. Irradiation of tumor.

E. Hypophysectomy for tumors.

Nursing Management

A. Maintain adequate fluids.

B. Measure intake and output and weight.

C. Stress importance of medic-alert band.

D. Avoid liquids or foods with diuretic-type action.

E. Provide comfort measures if patient is on radiation therapy.

F. Provide preop and postop care if hypophysectomy.

Disorders Associated with the Adrenal Gland

Addison's Disease (Hormone Deficit)

Definition: Addison's disease is the hypofunction of the adrenal cortex of the adrenal gland, resulting in deficiency of the steroid hormones: glucocorticoids, mineralocorticoids, and androgens.

Clinical Manifestations

A. Slow and insidious onset; eventually fatal if untreated.

B. Lassitude, lethargy, and generalized weakness.

C. Gastrointestinal disturbances, nausea, diarrhea, and anorexia.

D. Hypotension.

E. Increased pigmentation of the skin in 15% of cases, especially skin of nipples, buccal mucosa, and scars.

F. Emotional disturbances.

G. Weight loss.

Laboratory Values

A. Elevated potassium; decreased sodium; elevated BUN levels due to decreased glomerular filtration rate.

B. Low blood sugar.

C. Lack of normal rise in urinary output of 17-keto-steroids and 17-hydroxycorticosteroids following I.V. administration of ACTH over eight hours.

D Lack of normal rise in blood level of plasma cortisol following I.M. injection of ACTH.

Treatment

A. Lifelong replacement therapy with synthetic corticosteroid drugs.
   1. Cortisone acetate.
   2. Hydrocortisone.
   3. Fludrocortisone acetate (Florinef).
   4. Desoxycorticosterone (Cortate, DOCA-A).
B. High protein, high carbohydrate diet.

Nursing Management

A. Take daily weight and keep accurate I & O records.
B. Take vital signs q.i.d.
C. Observe for side effects of replacement hormones.
   1. Cortisone and hydrocortisone.
      a. Sodium and water retention.
      b. Potassium depletion.
      c. Drug-induced Cushing's syndrome.
      d. Gastric irritation (give medication with meal or antacid).
      e. Mood swings.
      f. Local abscess at injection site when given I.M. (inject deeply into gluteal muscle).
      g. Addisonian crisis, which might be produced by sudden withdrawal of medication.
   2. Fludrocortisone acetate—the same side effects as cortisone and hydrocortisone, particularly sodium retention and potassium depletion.
   3. Desoxycorticosterone—sodium retention and potassium depletion.
D. Protect from exposure to infection and from stress.
E. Provide frequent small feedings.
F. Provide emotional support.
G. Provide patient education.
   1. Safe self-administration of replacement hormones.
   2. Avoidance of over-the-counter drugs.
   3. Care to avoid infections; report promptly to physician if infections appear.
   4. Medic-alert band.
   5. Regular exercise; avoid strenuous activity, particularly in hot weather.
   6. Importance of continuous medical supervision.
   7. Avoidance of stress.

Addisonian Crisis (Hormone Deficit)

Definition: Addisonian crisis is a condition caused by adrenal insufficiency, which may be precipitated by infection, trauma, stress, surgery, or diaphoresis with excessive salt loss.

Clinical Manifestations

A. Severe headache; abdominal, leg, and lower back pain.
B. Extreme, generalized muscular weakness.
C. Severe hypotension and shock.
D. Irritability and confusion.
E. Death from shock, vascular collapse, or hyperkalemia.

Treatment

A. I.V. fluid replacement: restoration of electrolyte balance.
B. Steroid replacement.

Nursing Management

A. Administer parenteral fluids and adrenocorticosteroids; do not vary dosage or time from that ordered.
B. Continually monitor vital signs and intake and output until crisis passes.
C. Protect patient from infection.
D. Keep patient immobile and as quiet as possible; avoid unnecessary nursing procedures.

Cushing's Syndrome (Hormone Excess)

Definition: Clinical condition resulting from the combined metabolic effects of persistently elevated blood levels of glucocorticoids.

Etiology

A. Overactivity of adrenal cortex.
B. Benign or malignant tumor of adrenal gland.

C. Iatrogenic—drug therapy for other conditions.

Clinical Manifestations

A. Abnormal adipose tissue distribution.
   1. Moon face.
   2. Buffalo hump.
   3. Obese trunk with thin extremities.
B. Florid facies.
C. Red striae of skin stretched with fat tissue.
D. Fragile skin—easily bruised.
E. Osteoporosis—susceptible to fractures, renal stones.
F. Hyperglycemia—may eventually develop diabetes mellitus.
G. Mood swings—euphoria to depression.
H. High susceptibility to infections; diminished immuno-response to infections once they occur.
I. Lassitude and muscular weakness.
J. Masculine characteristics in females.
K. Thin extremities.
L. Hypertension.
M. Potassium depletion.
N. Sodium and water retention.

Laboratory Values

A. Elevated blood sugar and glycosuria.
B. Elevated white blood count with depressed eosinophils and lymphocytes.
C. Elevated plasma cortisone levels.
D. Elevated 17-hydroxycorticosteroids in urine.

Treatment

A. Adrenalectomy, unilateral or bilateral, for tumors.
   1. Bilateral—lifetime replacement of steroids.
   2. Unilateral—temporary steroid replacement (6 to 12 months).
B. Chemotherapy for inoperable, cancerous tumors (Metopirone).
C. Cobalt irradiation of pituitary.
D. Hypophysectomy.

Nursing Management

A. Protect from infections.
B. Protect from accidents or falls.
C. Provide meticulous skin care, avoiding harsh soaps.

D. Provide low calorie, high protein, high potassium diet.
E. Provide emotional support.
   1. Allow for ventilation of patient's feelings.
   2. Avoid reactions to patient's appearance.
   3. Anticipate the needs of the patient.
   4. Explain that changes in body appearance and emotional lability should improve with treatment.
F. Measure intake and output and daily weights; test for urinary sugar.
G. Follow specific nursing measures postsurgery.
H. Provide comfort measures during radiation therapy.
I. Educate patient.
   1. Importance of continuous medical supervision.
   2. Safe self-administration of replacement hormones.
   3. Side effects of medications.
   4. Avoidance of infections and stress.
   5. Need for adequate nutrition and rest.

Primary Aldosteronism (Hormone Excess)

Definition: Primary aldosteronism is a disorder due to the hypersecretion of aldosterone from the adrenal cortex of the adrenal gland. It is usually caused by tumors. Females are more at risk.

Clinical Manifestations

A. Hypokalemia.
   1. Weakness of muscles.
   2. Excessive urine output (polyuria); excessive thirst (polydipsia).
   3. Metabolic alkalosis.
B. Hypertension, postural hypotension, headache.
C. Positive Chvostek's sign (muscle twitching when area over facial nerves is tapped).

Laboratory Values

A. Lowered potassium level.
B. Elevated serum sodium level.
C. Increased urinary output of aldosterone.
D. Alkalosis.

Treatment

A. Surgical removal of tumors.

B. Potassium salts.

C. Spironolactone.

Nursing Management

A. Provide quiet environment.

B. Measure I and O and daily weights.

C. Check muscular strength and presence of Chvostek's sign.

D. Measure blood pressure in supine and standing positions.

E. Provide same postoperative care as for adrenalectomy.

Pheochromocytoma

Definition: Pheochromocytoma is a small tumor in the adrenal medulla of the adrenal gland that secretes large amounts of epinephrine and norepinephrine. Familial autosomal dominant.

Clinical Manifestations

A. Occurs primarily in children and middle-aged women.

B. Hypertension is primary manifestation.

C. Sudden attacks resemble overstimulation of the sympathetic nervous system.

1. Hypertension.
2. Severe headache.
3. Excessive diaphoresis.
4. Palpitation, tachycardia.
5. Nervousness and hyperactivity.
6. Nausea, vomiting, and anorexia.
7. Dilated pupils.
8. Cold extremities.
9. Cardiac failure or cerebral hemorrhage leading to death if not treated.

D. Increased rate of metabolism and loss of weight.

E. Hyperglycemia.

Laboratory Values

A. Findings common to hypertension, cardiac disease, and loss of kidney function.

B. Elevated vanillylmandelic acid (VMA) and catecholamine levels in urine.

C. Elevated blood levels of catecholamines.

D. Elevated blood sugar and glycosuria.

E. Presence of tumor on X-rays.

Treatment

A. Surgical excision of tumor.

B. Drugs: alpha blocker; phentolamine, phenoxybenzamine.

Nursing Management

A. Provide high calorie, nutritious diet omitting stimulants.

B. Promote rest and reduce stress.

C. Provide preoperative care.

1. Give Regitine one to two days before surgery to counteract hypertensive effects of epinephrine and norepinephrine.
2. Closely monitor BP during interval of phentolamine administration.

D. Provide postoperative care—observe for precipitous shock, hemorrhage, persistent hypertension.

Disorders Associated with the Thyroid Gland

Cretinism (Hormone Deficit)

Definition: Cretinism is a condition caused by severe hypofunction of the thyroid gland in the fetus, inutero or soon after birth.

Clinical Manifestations

A. Severe retardation of physical development, resulting in grotesque appearance, sexual retardation.

B. Severe mental retardation, apathy.

C. Dry skin; coarse, dry, brittle hair.

D. Constipation.

E. Slow teething.

F. Poor appetite.

G. Large tongue.

H. Pot belly with umbilical hernia.

I. Sensitivity to cold.

J. Yellow skin

Laboratory Values

A. T$_4$ under 3 μg./100 ml.

B. Elevated serum cholesterol.

C. Low radioactive iodine uptake.

Treatment

A. Desiccated thyroid.

B. Synthroid is drug of choice.

C. Cytomel used when rapid response is needed.

Myxedema (Hormone Deficit)

Definition: Myxedema is the decreased synthesis of thyroid hormone in adulthood, resulting in a hypothyroid state.

Clinical Manifestations

A. Occurs primarily in older age group, five times more frequent in women than in men.

B. Slowed rate of body metabolism.
   1. Lethargy, apathy, and fatigue.
   2. Intolerance to cold.
   3. Hypersensitivity to sedatives and barbiturates.
   4. Weight gain.
   5. Cool, dry, rough skin.
   6. Coarse, dry hair.

C. Personality changes.
   1. Forgetfulness and loss of memory.
   2. Complacency.

D. Anorexia, constipation, and fecal impactions.

E. Interstitial edema.
   1. Nonpitting edema in the lower extremity.
   2. Generalized puffiness.

F. Decreased diaphoresis.

G. Menstrual disturbances.

H. Cardiac complications.
   1. Coronary heart disease.
   2. Angina pectoris.
   3. MI and congestive heart failure.

I. Anemia.

Laboratory Findings

A. Low serum thyrotoxin concentration.

B. Hyponatremia.

Treatment

A. Thyroid replacement (initial small dosage, increased gradually).

B. Individualized maintenance dosage.
   1. Desiccated thyroid.
   2. Thyroxine (Synthroid).
   3. Triiodothyronine (Cytomel).

Nursing Management

A. Allow time for patient to complete activities.

B. Provide warm environment: extra blankets, etc.

C. Provide meticulous skin care.

D. Orient patient as to date, time, and place.

E. Prevent constipation.

F. If sedatives or narcotics are necessary, give 1/2 to 1/3 normal dosage, as ordered by physician.

G. Observe for overdosage symptoms of thyroid preparations.
   1. Myocardial infarction and angina and cardiac failure, particularly in patients with cardiac problems.
   2. Restlessness and insomnia.
   3. Headache and confusion.

Myxedema Coma

Definition: Coma results from persistent low thyroid production.

Clinical Manifestations

A. Large weight gain.

B. Cardiac abnormalities.

C. Cold sensitivity.

D. Drug sensitivities.

E. Mood swings.

Nursing Management

A. Provide total hygienic care.

B. Provide psychological support.
   1. Body image change.
   2. Complete dependency.
   3. Mental depression.

C. Closely observe hormone replacement.

D. Provide low calorie diet.

E. Provide ventilatory support if needed.

F. Measure vital signs frequently, especially temperature.

G. Monitor fluid intake to prevent dilutional hyponatremia.

H. Avoid use of sedatives and hypnotics.

Hyperthyroidism Thyrotoxicosis/ Graves' Disease

Definition: Hyperthyroidism results from the increased synthesis of thyroid hormone.

Clinical Manifestations

A. Occurs four times more frequently in women than in men; usually occurs between twenty to forty years of age.

B. Increased rate of body metabolism.
1. Weight loss despite ravenous appetite and ingestion of large quantities of food.
2. Intolerance to heat.
3. Nervousness, jitters, and fine tremor of hands.
4. Smooth, soft skin and hair.
5. Tachycardia and palpitation.
6. Diarrhea.
7. Diaphoresis.

C. Personality changes.
1. Irritability and agitation.
2. Exaggerated emotional reactions.
3. Mood swings—euphoria to depression.
4. Quick motions, including speech.

D. Enlargement of the thyroid gland (goiter).

E. Exophthalmos.
1. Fluid collects around eye sockets, causing eyeballs to protrude.
2. Not always present.
3. Usually does not improve with treatment.

F. Cardiac arrhythmias.

G. Difficulty focusing eyes.

Laboratory Values

A. Above normal test results.
1. PBI.
2. 131_I.
3. T_3 and T_4.

B. Relatively low serum cholesterol.

Treatment

A. Antithyroid drugs.
1. Propylthiouracil.
2. Methimazole (Tapazole).
3. Side effect: agranulocytosis.

B. Iodine preparations.
1. Saturated solution of potassium iodide (SSKI).
2. Lugol's solution.

C. Propranolol.
1. Rapidly reverses toxic manifestations.
2. Used preoperatively.

D. Radioiodine therapy.
1. Useful in patients who are poor surgical risks.
2. Uptake of 131_I by thyroid gland results in destruction of thyroid cells.
3. Mxyedema may occur as complication.

E. Thyroidectomy.
1. Subtotal or total removal of thyroid gland.
2. Required preoperative state.
   a. Return of thyroid function tests to normal.
   b. Adequate nutritional status.
   c. Marked decrease in signs of thyrotoxicosis.
   d. Absence of cardiac problems.
3. Complications.
   a. Hemorrhage.
   b. Respiratory distress.
   c. Laryngeal nerve injury.
   d. Tetany and hypocalcemia.
   e. Thyroid storm.

Nursing Management

A. Provide adequate rest.
1. Bed rest.
2. Diversionary activities.
3. Sedatives.

B. Provide cool, quiet, stable environment.

C. Maintain high calorie, protein, carbohydrate, vitamin diet without stimulants.

D. Take daily weights.

E. Provide emotional support.
1. Be aware that exaggerated emotional responses are a manifestation of hormone imbalance.
2. Be sensitive to needs.
3. Avoid stress-producing situations.

F. Adhere to regular schedule of activities.

G. Provide patient education.
   1. Protection from infection.
   2. Safe self-administration of medications.
   3. Importance of adequate rest and diet.
   4. Avoidance of stress.

Thyroid Storm or Thyroid Crisis

Definition: Thyroid storm is an acute, potentially fatal hyperthyroid condition which may occur as a result of surgery, inadequate preparation for surgery, severe infection, or stress.

Clinical Manifestations

A. High fever (may rise to 106° F).
B. Tachycardia.
C. Irritability and restlessness proceeding to delirium and coma.
D. Vomiting, diarrhea.
E. Dehydration.

Treatment

A. Hypothermia.
B. Hydration.
C. Antithyroid drugs and iodine preparations.
D. Adrenergic and catecholamine blocking agents.
E. Corticosteroids.
F. Propranolol.

Nursing Management

A. Monitor vital signs and intake and output.
B. Provide hypothermic measures as ordered.
C. Take safety measures as indicated.
D. Provide calm, quiet environment.
E. Give medications as ordered.

Disorders Associated with the Parathyroid Glands

Hypoparathyroidism

Definition: Hypoparathyroidism is a condition caused by acute or chronic deficient hormone production by the parathyroid gland. Usually occurs following thyroidectomy.

Clinical Manifestations

A. Acute hypocalcemia.
   1. Numbness, tingling, and cramping of extremities.
   2. Acute, potentially fatal tetany.
      a. Painful muscular spasms.
      b. Seizures.
      c. Irritability.
      d. Positive Chvostek's sign.
      e. Positive Trousseau's sign.
      f. Laryngospasm.
      g. Cardiac arrhythmias.
B. Chronic hypocalcemia.
   1. Poor development of tooth enamel.
   2. Mental retardation.
   3. Muscular weakness with numbness and tingling of extremities.
   4. Loss of hair and coarse, dry skin.
   5. Personality changes.
   6. Cataracts.
   7. Cardiac arrhythmias.
   8. Renal stones.

Laboratory Values

A. Low serum calcium levels.
B. Increased serum phosphorous level.
C. Low urinary calcium and phosphorous output.
D. Increased bone density on X-ray examination.

Treatment

A. Acute.
   1. Slow drip of I.V. calcium gluconate or calcium chloride.
   2. Anticonvulsants and sedatives (phenytoin and phenobarbital).
   3. Parathyroid hormone I.M. or sub q.
   4. Aluminum hydroxide (decreases phosphate level).
   5. Rebreathing bag to produce mild respiratory acidosis.
   6. Tracheostomy if laryngospasm causes obstruction.
B. Chronic.
   1. Oral calcium carbonate (OS CAL).

2. Vitamin D preparations (calciferol).

3. High calcium, low phosphorous diet.

Nursing Management

A. Same as for convulsions and epilepsy.

B. Frequently check for increasing hoarseness.

C. Observe for irregularities in urine.

D. Force fluids as ordered.

E. Observe for dystonic reactions if on phenothiazines.

F. Provide psychological support.
   1. Altered body image.
   2. Emotional instability.
   3. Extreme weakness.

Hyperparathyroidism

Definition: Hyperparathyroidism is caused by excessive hormone production of the parathyroid gland.

Clinical Manifestations

A. Bone demineralization with deformities; pain; high susceptibility to fractures.

B. Hypercalcemia.
   1. Calcium deposits in various body organs: eyes, heart, lungs, and kidneys (stones).
   2. Gastric ulcers.
   3. Personality changes, depression, and paranoia.
   4. Nausea, vomiting, anorexia, and constipation.
   5. Polydipsia and polyuria.

Laboratory Values

A. Elevated serum calcium level.

B. Low to normal serum phosphorous level.

C. Elevated urinary calcium and phosphorous levels.

D. Evidence of bone changes on X-ray examinations.

E. Normal to increased alkaline phosphatase.

Treatment

A. Subtotal surgical resection of parathyroid glands.

B. Additional oral calcium for bone rebuilding processes (several months).

Nursing Management

A. Force fluids: include juices to make urine more acidic.

B. Provide normal saline I.V. infusion.

C. Observe for electrolyte imbalance with Lasix administration.

D. Measure intake and output.

E. Closely observe urine for stones and gravel.

F. Observe for digitalis toxicity if patient is taking digitalis.

G. Provide a high phosphorous, low calcium diet.

H. Prevent accidents and injury through safety measures.

Disorders Associated with the Pancreas

Diabetes Mellitus

Definition: Diabetes mellitus is a condition caused by the absence or relative lack of insulin secretion by the beta cells in the islets of Langerhans of the pancreas gland.

Clinical Manifestations

A. Classification according to age of onset.
   1. Juvenile onset diabetes.
      a. Onset in children or adolescents; usually acute with ketoacidosis.
      b. Absent or inadequate insulin.
      c. Insulin injections required to maintain life.
   2. Mature onset diabetes.
      a. Onset in adulthood; usually insidious.
      b. Lack of effective insulin (blood insulin levels may be higher than normal).
      c. Obesity usually present.
      d. Treatment by diet only, or diet and medication, or insulin injections.

B. Classification according to measurement of glucose tolerance.
   1. Prediabetes.
      a. No clinical symptoms.
      b. Normal glucose tolerance test.
      c. Predisposition to develop disease.
   2. Subclinical diabetes.
      a. No clinical symptoms.
      b. Normal glucose tolerance test.
      c. Abnormal cortisone induced glucose tolerance test.

3. Latent or chemical diabetes.
   a. No clinical symptoms.
   b. Abnormal glucose tolerance test.
4. Overt diabetes.
   a. Clinical symptoms present.
   b. Abnormal glucose tolerance test.

C. General symptoms.
   1. Polyuria.
   2. Polydipsia.
   3. Polyphagia.
   4. Weight loss (juvenile onset diabetes).

D. Complications.
   1. Ketoacidosis.
      a. Onset.
         (1) Acute or over several days.
         (2) Result of stress, infection, surgery, or lack of effective insulin.
         (3) Overeating may contribute to but does not cause onset.
         (4) Life-threatening situation.
      b. Hyperglycemia, glucosuria, ketosis, ketonuria, and low CO_2 combining power.
      c. Polyuria, polydipsia, and dehydration.
      d. Nausea, vomiting, and anorexia.
      e. Flushed, warm skin.
      f. Blurred vision.
      g. Acetone odor (sweet) on breath.
      h. Kussmaul respirations (rapid, deep).
      i. Cardiac failure and coma.
   2. Infections.
   3. Vascular disease.
      a. Microangiopathy.
         (1) Affects basement membrane of almost all small vessels throughout body.
         (2) Retinopathy.
         (3) Nephropathy.
      b. Large vessel.
         (1) Coronary heart disease.
         (2) Athlerosclerosis, arteriosclerosis.
   4. Neuropathy.
   5. Cataracts.

Laboratory Values

A. Elevated fasting blood sugar; postprandial blood sugar; glucose tolerance test or tolbutaimide (Orinase) tests.

B. Clinitest and Testape.
   1. Indicate presence of sugar in urine, i.e., 1+ to 4+.
   2. Clinitest: 2-drop and 5-drop method.
   3. Values of the two tests are not interchangeable.

C. Acetest and Ketostix—may be positive for presence of acetone in urine.

D. Elevated cholesterol and triglyceride blood levels.

Treatment

A. Diet.
   1. The cornerstone of management, interdependent with medication and exercise.
   2. Attainment of normal weight may clear symptoms.
   3. Types of diet.
      a. ADA exchange diet (see p. 16).
         (1) Milk, vegetables (A and B), fruit, bread, meat, fat.
         (2) Prescribed as to total calories and number of exchanges from each group.
      b. Gram weight diet.
         (1) Total calories and number of grams of carbohydrate are calculated.
         (2) Food portions are weighed.
      c. Free diet.
         (1) Food as desired.
         (2) Used primarily by children.
      d. Modified free diet.
         (1) Food as desired.
         (2) Exceptions: avoidance of concentrated sugars and saturated fats.

B. Medications.
   1. Insulin (see chart, p. 390).
      a. Types.
         (1) Short acting.
            (a) Regular.
            (b) Semilente.
         (2) Intermediate acting.
            (a) NPH.
            (b) Lente.
         (3) Long acting.
            (a) PZI.
            (b) Ultralente.
         (4) Available in U–40, U–80, U–100 (measured by units of insulin per cc.).

b. Insulin reaction—hypoglycemia.
(1) Excessive insulin due to decreased food intake, increased exercise, and decreased body need for insulin replacement.
(2) Clinical manifestations.
(a) Low blood sugar and lack of sugar in urine.
(b) Nervousness, apprehension, personality changes, and confused behavior.
(c) Nausea, hunger, and yawning.
(d) Tachycardia.
(e) Cold, clammy, pale skin and numbness or tingling.
(f) Progresses to convulsive seizures.
(3) Treatment—oral concentrated sugar, I.M. injection of Glucagon, I.V. glucose if hospitalized.
2. Oral hypoglycemic drugs.
a. Sulfonylureas.
(1) Thought to stimulate beta cells to increase insulin release.
(2) Tolbutamide (Orinase), short acting.
(3) Chlorpropamide (Diabinese), long acting.
(4) Acetohexamide (Dymelor), intermediate acting.
(5) Tolazamide (Tolinase), intermediate acting.
b. Biguanides—taken off U.S. market in 1977.
C. Exercise.
1. Decreases body's need for insulin.
2. Regular, ongoing activities important.
3. Sporadic, vigorous exercise dangerous.

Nursing Management

A. Give I.V. fluids, medications, as ordered.
B. Test urine (second voided specimen).
C. Adhere to procedures for other laboratory tests.
D. Provide meticulous skin care, particularly lower extremities.
E. Protect from infection, injury, stress.
F. Observe for signs of insulin reactions and ketoacidosis.
G. Measure intake and output.

H. Provide emotional support.
1. Allow for verbalization of patient's feelings.
a. Necessary changes in life style, diet, and activities.
b. Change in self-image and self-esteem.
c. Fear of future and complications.
2. Encourage involvement of family.
I. Provide patient education (key to effective self-management).
1. Assessment.
a. Level of knowledge.
b. Cultural, socio-economic, and family influences.
c. Daily dietary and activity patterns.
d. Emotional and physical status and effect on patient's current ability to learn.
2. Insulin and insulin injections.
a. Keep insulin at room temperature; refrigerate extra supply of insulin.
b. Rotate insulin bottle gently prior to drawing up insulin.
c. Use sterile injection techniques.
d. Rotate injection sites to prevent injection in dystrophied areas.
e. Watch for signs of under- and over-dosage.
3. Oral medications.
a. Take medications regularly.
b. Watch for hypoglycemic reactions occurring with sulfonylureas).
c. Remember that alcohol ingestion in conjunction with sulfonylureas brings Antabuse effects.
4. Avoidance of infection and injury.
a. Report infection or injury promptly to physician.
b. Maintain meticulous skin care.
c. Maintain proper foot care.
d. Be aware that insulin requirements may increase with infections.
e. Be prepared for healing process impairment.
f. Avoid tight-fitting garments and shoes.
g. Avoid "bathroom surgery" for corns and callouses.
5. Diet.
a. Do not vary meal times.
b. Incorporate diet into individual needs, life style, cultural and socio-economic patterns.

c. Increase intake in proportion to vigorous exercise, but sporadic exercise is dangerous.

6. Exercise.
    a. Regulate time and amount.
    b. Avoid sporadic, vigorous activities.
    c. With careful planning, participate in most activities and sports.
    d. Increase or decrease food intake according to level of activity.
7. Medic-alert band.
8. Provide constant availability of source of concentrated sugar.

Ketoacidosis

Definition: The two major metabolic problems that are the source of this condition are hyperglycemia and ketoacidemia, both due to insulin lack associated with hyperglucagonemia.

Pathophysiology

A. Without insulin, carbohydrate metabolism is affected.
B. Hyperglycemia results from increased liver production of glucose and decreased glucose uptake by peripheral tissues.
C. The liver oxidizes fatty acids into:
    1. Acetoacidic acid (increased ketone bodies leads to ketoacidosis).
    2. Beta-hydroxybutyric acid (acetone is volatile and is blown off by lungs).
    3. As glucose levels increase, there is osmotic overload in kidney resulting in dehydration and electrolyte losses.
    4. As ketone bodies increase, acidosis and comatose states occur.

Clinical Manifestations

A. Ketoacidotic coma is usually preceded by a few days of polyuria and polydipsia with associated symptoms.
    1. Fatigue.
    2. Nausea and vomiting.
    3. Mental stupor.
B. Physical assessment indicates dehydration, rapid breathing, and fruity odor of acetone to breath.

Nursing Management

A. Maintain fluid and electrolyte balance.
    1. Normal saline I.V. until blood sugar reaches 250-300 mg.%; then a dextrose solution is started.
    2. Potassium added to I.V. after renal function is evaluated and hydration is adequate.
B. Provide insulin management.
    1. Give ½ dose I.V. and ½ dose sub q.
    2. Give with small amounts of albumin as insulin adheres to I.V. tubing.
    3. Hourly dosage depends on S & A and blood sugar levels.
C. Provide patent airway and adequate circulation to brain.
D. Obtain hourly sugar and acetone urine tests.
E. Test blood sugar level q. 1-2 hours. Keep sugar and acetone at 1+.
F. Maintain personal hygiene.
G. Protect from injury if comatose.

Functional Hyperinsulinism/Hypoglycemia

Definition: Hyperinsulinism occurs as the result of excess secretion of insulin by the beta cells of the pancreas gland.

Clinical Manifestations

A. Personality changes.
    1. Tenseness.
    2. Nervousness.
    3. Irritability.
    4. Anxiousness.
    5. Depression.
B. Excessive diaphoresis.
C. Excessive hunger.
D. Muscle weakness and tachycardia.
E. May be associated with "dumping syndrome" following gastrectomy.
F. May occur prior to development of diabetes mellitus.
G. Laboratory values—low blood sugar during hypoglycemic episodes.

Treatment

A. High protein, low carbohydrate diet.
B. Counseling may reduce anxiety and tenseness.

General Concepts in Oncology Nursing

Neoplastic Diseases

Definition: Cancer is a group of neoplastic diseases in which there is a new growth of abnormal cells.

Etiology

A. Unknown.
B. Environmental factors (50 to 80 percent of cases).
C. Biological factors.
D. Heredity.
E. Theory—caused by a virus.

Pathophysiology

A. Cell growth is unregulated and there is uncontrolled division.
B. Cells reproduce and divide at a greater rate than normal cells until a tumor mass is formed.
C. Tumors grow in a disorganized fashion, interrupting bodily function.
D. Malignant cells metastasize by:
    1. Direct extension into adjacent tissue.
    2. Permeating along lymphatic vessels.
    3. Traveling through lymph system to nodes.
    4. Entering blood circulation.
    5. Diffusing into body cavity.

Differentiation of Benign and Malignant Tumors

	Malignant	Benign
Cell type	Abnormal from those of original tissues	Close to those of original tissues
Growth	Rapid, infiltrates surrounding tissue in all directions	Slow and noninfiltrating
Encapsulated	Infrequent	Frequent
Metastasis	Through blood, lymph, or new tumor sites	Remains localized
Effect	Terminal without treatment	Can become malignant or obstruct vital organs

Classification of Cancers

A. Classed according to type of tissue from which they evolve.
    1. Carcinomas.
        a. Begin in epithelial tissue.
        b. Example: skin, gastrointestinal tract lining, lung, breast, uterus.
    2. Sarcomas.
        a. Begin in nonepithelial tissue.
        b. Example: bone, muscle, fat, lymph system.
B. Type of cell in which they arise.
    1. Cell type affects appearance, rate of growth, and degree of malignancy.
    2. Carcinomas.
        a. Epithelial basal cells are basal cell carcinomas.
        b. Bone cells—osteogenic carcinoma.
        c. Gland epithelium—adenocarcinoma.

Staging

A. Describes extent of tumor.
B. Basic components.
    1. T—primary tumor.
    2. N—regional nodes.
    3. M—metastasis.
C. Subscripts.
    1. Describe extent to which malignancy has increased in size.
        a. T0: no evidence of primary tumor.
        b. TIS: carcinoma in situ.
        c. T_1, T_2, T_3, T_4: progressive increase in tumor, size, and involvement.
        d. TX: tumor cannot be assessed.
    2. Involvement of regional nodes.
        a. N0: regional lymph nodes not abnormal.
        b. N_1, N_2, N_3, N_4: increasing degree of abnormal regional lymph nodes.
        c. NX: regional lymph nodes cannot be assessed clinically.
    3. Metastatic development.
        a. M0: no evidence of distant metastasis.
        b. M_1 to M_3: increasing degree of distant metastasis.

Safeguards Against Cancer

A. Monthly breast self-examination.

B. Annual pap smear.

C. Annual colon-rectum exam for patients over forty.

D. Annual chest X-ray; eliminate smoking.

E. Annual exam of mouth and teeth.

F. Avoid unnecessary sunlight exposure.

G. Annual physical exam (include urine and blood work).

Warning Signs

A. Open sore or wound that does not heal.

B. Indigestion or difficulty swallowing.

C. Change in normal bowel or bladder habits.

D. Obvious change in moles or warts.

E. Unusual bleeding or discharge.

F. Thickening or lump in breast or other tissue.

G. Nagging cough or hoarseness.

Medical Treatment

A. Radiotherapy.

B. Chemotherapy.

C. Surgical interventions.

Radiation Therapy

A. Categories.
   1. Curative (primary treatment for Hodgkin's disease).
   2. Palliative (reduces pain from breast tumor).
   3. Adjunctive therapy (used with surgery and/or chemotherapy).

B. Types.
   1. External—gamma rays delivered via machine to lesion on body.
   2. Internal—isotope placed into a body cavity or interstitially.

C. Side effects.
   1. Severe nausea and vomiting.
   2. Diarrhea.
   3. Hematuria.
   4. Anemia.
   5. Skin—scaling and dryness; "wet" reaction.
   6. Body systems involved depends on area of radiation.
      a. Pneumonia.
      b. Myocarditis.

c. Tooth decay.

d. Loss of hair—alopecia.

D. External radiation.
   1. Types.
      a. Cobalt-60 unit.
      b. Linear accelerator.
   2. Nursing interventions.
      a. Psychological support.
      b. Patient education.
         (1) What to expect from treatment.
         (2) Explanation of radiotherapy room.
         (3) Possible side effects and ways to minimize them.
      c. Diet: high protein, high carbohydrate, fat free, and low residue.
         (1) Foods to avoid: tough, fibrous meat; poultry; shrimp; all cheeses (except soft); coarse bread; raw vegetables; irritating spices.
         (2) Foods allowed: soft-cooked eggs, ground meat, pureed vegetables, milk, cooked cereal.
         (3) Increase fluids.
         (4) Diet supplement to increase calorie and fluid intake.
         (5) Do not eat several hours before treatment.
      d. Medications.
         (1) Compazine—nausea.
         (2) Lomatil—diarrhea.
      e. Skin care—radiodermatitis occurs three to six weeks after start of treatment.
         (1) Avoid creams, lotions, perfume to irradiated areas.
         (2) Wash with lukewarm water, pat dry (some physicians allow mild soap).
         (3) Avoid exposure to sunlight or artificial heat such as heating pad.
         (4) Baby oil may be ordered t.i.d.
      f. "Wet" reaction.
         (1) Weeping of skin due to loss of upper layer.
         (2) Rest from therapy.
         (3) Cleanse area with warm water and pat dry b.i.d.
         (4) Apply antibiotic lotion or steroid cream if ordered.

(5) Expose site to air.

E. Internal radiation.

1. Types.

   a. Ionizing radiation—can destroy tissue lining.

   b. Cesium needles—usual method.

2. Precautions to excessive exposure.

   a. Distance.

      (1) Work as far away from source as possible.

      (2) Intensity of radiation decreases rapidly the further away from source.

   b. Shielding.

      (1) Lead shield—keep between source and staff.

      (2) Radioactivity material stored in lead-shielded container when not in use.

      (3) Do not touch radioactive material with hand.

   c. Time.

      (1) Work efficiently.

      (2) Review procedures before beginning them.

      (3) Trade-off between distance and time (the further away from source, the more time that can be spent around source).

3. Cumulative dose (measured in millirems) not to exceed 1,250 mrem every three months.

4. Nursing interventions.

   a. Maintain bed rest when radiation source in place.

   b. Restrict movement to prevent dislodging radiation source.

   c. Do not turn or position patient except on back (when cesium needle in tongue or cervix).

   d. Administer range-of-motion exercise q.i.d.

   e. Avoid direct contact around implant site; avoid washing areas, etc.

   f. Take vital signs q. 4 hours (report temperature over 100°F).

   g. Observe for dehydration or paralytic ileus (if cervical implant).

   h. Observe and report skin eruption, discharge, abnormal bleeding.

   i. Diet: clear liquid (low residue is sometimes ordered) and force fluids.

   j. Insert Teflon Foley catheter (radiation decomposes rubber) to avoid necessity of bedpan.

   k. Observe frequently for dislodging of radiation source (especially linen and dressings).

   l. When radiation source falls out:

      (1) Do not touch with hands.

      (2) Pick up source with foot-long applicator.

      (3) Put source in lead container and call the physician.

      (4) If unable to locate source, call physician immediately and bar visitors from room.

   m. After source removed:

      (1) Administer Betadine douche if cervical implant.

      (2) Give Fleets enema.

      (3) Patient may be out of bed.

      (4) Avoid direct sunlight to radiation areas.

      (5) Administer cream to relieve dryness or itching.

      (6) Patient may resume sexual intercourse within seven to ten days.

      (7) Notify physician if nausea, vomiting, diarrhea, frequent urination or bowel movements, or temperature above 100°F is present.

Chemotherapy

A. Purpose.

1. Interferes with cell doublings.

2. Destroys all cancer cells.

B. Action.

1. Damages cells only during process of dividing.

2. To eradicate malignant tumor, large doses are administered or treatment started when the number of cells is small enough to allow tumor destruction.

3. Used in conjunction with surgery and/or radiotherapy early in disease process.

4. Combination of antineoplastics frequently used for synergistic effect.

5. Sequential antineoplastic therapy may be used, particularly with remissions.

C. Factors for deciding dosage and timing of drugs.

1. Dosage calculated on body surface area and kilograms of body weight.
2. Time lapse between doses to allow recovery of normal cells.
3. Side effects of each drug and when they are likely to occur.
4. Liver and kidney function, as most antineoplastics are metabolized in one of these organs.

D. Common side effects.

1. Damage to rapidly growing normal cells.
   a. Bone marrow (most serious damage).
      (1) Infection.
      (2) Abnormal bleeding.
   b. Hair follicles—alopecia.
   c. Mucous lining of GI tract.
      (1) Nausea, vomiting, anorexia.
      (2) Fluid and electrolyte imbalances.
      (3) Dietary deficiency.
      (4) Stomatitis.
2. Elevated uric acid, crystal and urate stone formation.
3. Time of most severe depression of cells (termed nadir); different for each type of cell.
4. Chemotherapeutics—have specific side effects in addition to these.

E. Classification of chemotherapeutic agents.

1. Alkylating agents—nitrogen mustard, cyclophosphamide.
2. Antimetabolites—5-FU, methotrexate.
3. Antibiotics—Adriamycin, Bleomycin, Dactinomycin.
4. Plant alkaloids (antimitotics)—Vincristine, Vinblastine.
5. Hormones—estrogens, progestins.
6. Miscellaneous—decarbazine, procarbazine, platinium.

F. Baseline nursing assessment.

1. Nutritional status.
   a. Weight.
   b. Muscle tone.
   c. Skin turgor.
   d. Oral mucosa.
2. Skin condition.
   a. Skin lesions.
   b. Infection.
3. Mobility.
   a. Activity level.
   b. Indications of hypoxia on exertion.
4. Psychological status.
   a. Emotional state.
   b. Family interactions.
5. Laboratory values.
   a. X-rays.
   b. Blood studies.
   c. Bone marrow aspiration.

G. Nursing care.

1. Minimize scalp hair loss by tourniquet application around scalp during I.V. administration and for 15 minutes after dose.
2. Observe frequently for signs of bleeding or infection.
3. Provide emotional support for alteration in body image or grieving process.
4. Administer I.V. dose slowly to prevent toxic effects.
5. Discontinue I.V. administration of drug if extravasation occurs, as tissue damage will result.
6. Maintain I&O to observe kidney function.
7. Force fluids to increase uric acid excretion and decrease crystal and urate stone formation.
8. Administer allopurinol to lower uric acid.
9. Provide small, frequent meals with nutritious snacks with main meal early in morning.
10. Provide high calorie dietary supplements.
11. Provide frequent oral hygiene to decrease severity of stomatitis.
12. Diet for diarrhea: bland, low residue, high in constipating food.
13. Avoid exposure to infected persons.

Guideline to Oncological Diseases

Medical Chapter

A. Disorders of the blood and spleen.

1. Leukemias.
2. Hodgkin's disease.

B. Integumentary system.

1. Malignant tumors of the skin.

C. Gastrointestinal system.

1. Malignant tumors of the mouth.
2. Gastric cancer.
3. Malignant tumors of the small intestine.
4. Malignant tumors of the large intestine.

Surgical Chapter

A. Laryngectomy—removal of larynx due to cancer.
B. Radical neck dissection.
C. Prostatic malignancy.
D. Tumors of the breast.
E. Tumors of the reproductive system.
F. Cancer of the vulva.
G. Cystectomy.

Pediatric Chapter—Oncology Section

A. Wilm's tumor.
B. Hodgkin's disease.
C. Leukemia.
D. Brain tumors.
E. Bone tumors.
F. Chemotherapy and radiation.

Review Questions

1. The intracellular fluid contains large quantities of

   A. Na, K, Mg, PO_4.
   B. K, Mg, PO_4, proteins.
   C. K, Cl, HCO_3, proteins.
   D. K, Mg, Na, HCO_3.

2. If the extracellular fluid becomes hypotonic, water shifts

   A. From the extracellular fluid into the intracellular fluid to equalize the concentration of water through the process of osmosis.
   B. From the intracellular fluid into the extracellular fluid to equalize the concentration of water through the process of osmosis.
   C. From the extracellular fluid into the intracellular fluid to equalize the concentration of water through the process of diffusion.
   D. From the extracellular fluid into the intracellular fluid to equalize the concentration of water through the process of facilitated diffusion.

3. Routine testing of the patient's urine for sugar and acetone is part of nursing care for all of the following conditions except

   A. Diabetes mellitus.
   B. Cushing's syndrome.
   C. Acromegaly.
   D. Diabetes insipidus.

4. Ms. Jones is being admitted to a medical-surgical unit. She has Addison's disease, has been taking her medications as ordered, and is scheduled for a bilateral adrenalectomy. To which of the following patients' rooms would it be inappropriate to assign Ms. Jones?

   A. Ms. R., a forty-five-year-old female, five days postoperative gastrectomy.
   B. Ms. S., a thirty-four-year-old female, ten days postoperative craniotomy.
   C. Ms. T., a fifty-eight-year-old female, diabetic, admitted yesterday, leg ulcer with drainage (culture and sensitivity not reported yet).
   D. Ms. U., a thirty-year-old female, with breast cancer.

5. Which of the following skin cancers has the poorest prognosis because it metastasizes so rapidly and extensively via the lymph system?

   A. Basal cell epithelioma.
   B. Squamous cell epithelioma.
   C. Malignant melanoma.
   D. Sebaceous cyst.

6. Which of the following statements best describes a guiding principle in treating dermatoses?

   A. It is better to leave the skin alone than to experiment with several interventions.
   B. Use heat for the first twenty-four hours; then apply tepid compresses.
   C. Debridement of pustules is essential before applying a topical substance.
   D. Irritants frequently are valuable to produce erythema and an increased blood supply.

7. Select the best explanation of a buffer system.

   A. Kidneys do most of the work in maintaining body pH.
   B. A mixture of an acid and base.
   C. A solution of two or more chemicals which minimize changes in pH.
   D. The amount of hydrogen ion required to bring about a specific pH change in the blood.

8. After the lungs, the kidneys do the work to maintain body pH. The best explanation of how they accomplish this regulation of pH is that they

   A. Secrete hydrogen ion and sodium.
   B. Secrete ammonia.
   C. Exchange hydrogen and sodium in the kidney tubules.
   D. Decrease sodium ions, hold on to hydrogen ions, and then secrete sodium bicarbonate.

9. Hemodialysis works on the principle that

   A. Diffusion of dissolved particles can move across a semipermeable membrane.
   B. Pore size of the membrane permits passage of high molecular weight substances.
   C. Water, being a large molecule, is unable to move freely through the membrane.
   D. Plasma proteins are large and, therefore, can move easily through the membrane.

10. Mr. Williams is a thirty-five-year-old patient with an admitting diagnosis of head injury following an auto accident. What is the most sensitive indication of a patient's clinical condition following a head injury?

    A. Pupillary changes.
    B. Level of consciousness.
    C. Blood pressure and pulse.
    D. Motor function.

11. Which vital sign is the most sensitive index of increasing intracranial pressure?

    A. Pulse.
    B. Blood pressure.
    C. Respiration.
    D. Temperature.

12. Mr. Williams has all of the following needs, but which one should receive first priority?

    A. Control of pain and restlessness.
    B. Maintenance of open airway.

C. Maintenance of fluid-electrolyte balance.
D. Monitoring of neurological status, including vital signs.

13. Mr. Williams is complaining of a severe headache and demonstrates nuchal rigidity and Kernig's sign. Which complication is most likely?

A. Subdural hemorrhage.
B. Increased intracranial pressure.
C. Shock.
D. Subarachnoid hemorrhage.

14. One of the most serious consequences of agranulocytosis is

A. The potential danger of excessive bleeding even with minor trauma.
B. Generalized ecchymosis on exposed areas of the body.
C. High susceptibility to infection.
D. Extreme prostration.

15. Mr. Sundstrom, a fifty-eight-year-old vice-president of a bank, began having intermittent chest discomfort over the past three weeks but did not seek medical attention. However, it finally interrupted his activities during the day so he went to his physician. After a work-up, a diagnosis of angina pectoris due to atherosclerotic heart disease was made. The pain in angina is due to

A. Spasm of coronary arteries.
B. Inability of coronary arteries to meet oxygen requirements of myocardium.
C. Rubbing of epicardium against pericardial sac.
D. Irritation of cardiac nerve endings.

16. Angina may be brought on by many things, but the most common cause is

A. Rest.
B. Sudden change in position.
C. Physical exertion.
D. Severe depression.

17. Nitroglycerin was prescribed to control the frequency of Mr. Sundstrom's attacks. Nitroglycerin acts by causing

A. Dilation of atherosclerotic arteries to increase blood flow to the myocardium where it is compromised.
B. Reduction of venous return to lessen cardiac workload.
C. Increase in cardiac contractility.
D. Increase in peripheral vascular resistance (BP).

18. Nitroglycerin should be taken

A. Every two to three hours during the day.
B. Before every meal and at bedtime.
C. At the first indication of chest pain.
D. Only when chest pain is not relieved by rest.

19. Mr. Sundstrom is able to return to his work with some modification of his activities. Anginal attacks were infrequent and when they did occur, they always were relieved by rest and nitroglycerin. However, one evening, he had some indigestion after supper, took some bicarbonate of soda, and went to bed early. Around midnight he was awakened by severe substernal chest pressure and dyspnea. He took two nitroglycerin tablets without relief. In five minutes, he took two more without relief. He called his physician to come to his home but the physician instructed him to go directly to the hospital. The rationale for this instruction is that sudden death (outside the hospital) in association with coronary artery disease is due to

A. Acute myocardial infarction.
B. Pump failure accompanied by pulmonary congestion.
C. Arrhythmias.
D. Papillary muscle dysfunction.

20. Mr. Sundstrom is diagnosed as having an anterior myocardial infarction, which is

A. Necrosis of myocardium.
B. Substernal chest pain.
C. Irregular pulse.
D. Papillary muscle dysfunction.

21. Diagnosis of an MI is made from

A. The patient's history.
B. ECG's.
C. Enzyme studies.
D. All of the above.

22. Four days after admission, Mr. Sundstrom says to the nurse that he might as well have died because now he won't be able to do anything. The nurse can best respond by saying

A. "Don't worry about it, Mr. Sundstrom. Everything will be all right."
B. "You shouldn't be thinking about that because you are doing so well now."
C. "What do you mean about not being able to do anything, Mr. Sundstrom?"
D. "Take life one day at a time, Mr. Sundstrom."

23. The occlusion of the left anterior descending coronary artery, which supplies a large percentage of ventricular muscle mass, results in an anterior MI. Left ventricular heart failure can complicate this type of an MI. All the following may be evident in left ventricular heart failure except

A. Dyspnea, orthopnea.
B. Pulmonary rales.
C. Gallop rhythm.
D. Pedal and sacral edema.

24. Dyspnea of CHF is due to

A. Blockage of a pulmonary artery by an embolus.

B. Accumulation of fluid in the interstitial spaces and alveoli of the lungs.

C. Blockage of bronchi by mucous secretions.

D. Compression of lungs by the dilated heart.

25. The leukocytes' ability as a primary defense system against infection is due primarily to

A. The mobility and phagocytic action of various types of leukocytes.

B. The large numbers of leukocytes present in the body at all times.

C. The ability of leukocytes to multiply rapidly.

D. The high composition of polymorphonuclear leukocytes.

26. Mr. More is noted to have a normal blood pressure of 130/90. His heart rate is 110/minute and his skin is clammy. Rales are heard in the lower lung fields and a low urine output of 15 cc./hour is recorded. Which of the following statements most accurately accounts for these findings?

A. Both cardiac output and peripheral vascular resistance are low.

B. The patient has a low cardiac output and a high peripheral vascular resistance.

C. Cardiac output is normal with an elevated peripheral vascular resistance.

D. Both cardiac output and peripheral vascular resistance are normal.

27. Prolonged bed rest, as sometimes required by heart patients like Mr. More, may result in thrombophlebitis. This is due to all of the following except

A. A decrease in viscosity of the blood.

B. A slowing of blood flow to the heart.

C. A change in the lining of the vessel wall due to inflammation.

D. Hypercoagulability.

28. Thrombophlebitis is prevented by

A. Rubbing calves of legs strenuously with lotion several times a day.

B. Gatching of knee while patient is in bed.

C. Footboard walking and tightening and relaxing leg muscles several times a day.

D. The use of anticholinergic drugs.

29. The electrolyte most responsible for fluid distribution is

A. Potassium.

B. Calcium.

C. Sodium.

D. Magnesium.

30. If a patient has an external shunt in place for use in hemodialysis, which of the following will be included in the teaching plan?

A. Blood going through the shunt needs to be observed for possible clotting only immediately following the dialysis run.

B. If a bruit is heard over the shunt area, it is probably clotted.

C. A patent shunt is cool to the touch, like that of the forearm.

D. Dark spots visualized in the shunt represent clot formation.

31. The availability of oxygen to the tissues

A. Depends on adequate cardiac output and the oxygen content of the blood.

B. Is enhanced in a febrile state.

C. Remains unchanged with anemia.

D. Is increased at high altitudes.

32. Surfactant

A. Is a substance produced by and contained in the alveoli, which prevents them from collapsing.

B. Production is increased in atelectasis.

C. Increases surface-tension in the alveoli.

D. Production is increased during hypoventilation.

33. What effect will infectious processes occurring in a person who is taking steroid replacements have on the medication dosage?

A. Increased dosage needed.

B. Decreased dosage needed.

C. Decreased, then increased dosage needed.

D. No change in dosage needed.

34. Mrs. Jones, seventy years old, was admitted to the hospital following complaints of a headache and loss of consciousness. Shortly after admission, she regained consciousness but was confused. Physical examination findings included paralysis on the right side. A diagnosis of CVA with right-sided hemiparesis was made. Loss of motor function in the right arm and leg indicates a lesion in which of the following structures?

A. Motor nerve fibers in the anterior horn.

B. Pyramidal tract in the right hemisphere.

C. Pyramidal tract in the left hemisphere.

D. Spinocerebellar tract.

35. All the following are appropriate nursing measures to maintain optimal positioning and function after a CVA except

A. Placing patient in prone position fifteen to thirty minutes three times a day.

B. Conducting passive ROM exercises four times daily.

C. Encouraging self-care activities as soon as possible.

D. Changing position between affected and unaffected side every two hours.

36. Mrs. Jones has some residual expressive aphasia. Which of the following would be the most therapeutic nursing action?

A. Anticipate her needs and requests.
B. Encourage communication by writing or using an alphabet board.
C. Encourage every attempt to communicate without correcting words or usage.
D. Use and encourage pantomime.

37. The nurse noted that Mrs. Jones seemed to be unaware of objects on her right side. Examination revealed a visual loss in the right half of each visual field. Which of the following is the most important in assisting the patient to compensate for this loss?

A. Place on the unaffected side those items that are used frequently.
B. Position the patient so that her unaffected side is toward the activity in the room.
C. Frequently encourage the patient to position and turn her head to scan the environment on the affected side.
D. Approach the patient on the unaffected side.

38. Mrs. Jones is due to be discharged from the rehabilitation center. She has regained partial use of her arm and almost full use of her leg. Home visits are being planned by the nurse for the primary purpose of

A. Assisting the patient in activities of daily living.
B. Assessing the home for safety hazards.
C. Assisting the patient in transferring learning from the hospital environment to the home.
D. Assisting the patient in performing prescribed physical therapy.

39. Mr. Raggers was admitted to the hospital with a diagnosis of acute glomerulonephritis. His symptoms were mild and consisted of fatigue, anorexia, mild hypertension, and a slight edema of the extremities. Mr. Raggers had had a routine physical examination performed as a part of a company program to keep their executives in good health. The disease, acute glomerulonephritis, was suspected after the results came back from which of the following tests?

A. Blood work-up.
B. Routine urinalysis.
C. Blood pressure and vital signs.
D. Renal biopsy.

40. One of the primary objectives of treatment for Mr. Raggers' illness would be to

A. Restore fluid and electrolyte balance.
B. Encourage bed rest during the acute phase.
C. Give high protein diet to restore nutritional status.
D. Treat hypertension.

41. Mr. Raggers' condition suddenly worsens, and renal failure is suspected. All of the following symptoms would be present except

A. Hypertension.
B. Proteinuria.
C. Hypotension.
D. Azotemia.

42. Mr. Raggers is put on Lasix. The main action of this drug is to

A. Increase blood flow to the renal cortex.
B. Increase intrarenal vascular resistance.
C. Restore circulating blood volume.
D. Prevent infection.

43. Mr. Raggers is put on a special diet. The main objective of dietary control during the acute stage of renal failure is to

A. Increase sodium intake to hold more fluids in the body.
B. Reduce protein intake to a minimum to reduce nitrogenous waste products.
C. Reduce calories so the body will not have to work so hard to burn off the energy.
D. Force fluids with potassium for the oliguria.

44. Mr. Raggers is to undergo peritoneal dialysis to aid in the removal of toxic substances and metabolic wastes, and to restore fluid balance in his body. The primary nursing responsibility during this procedure is to

A. Monitor vital signs frequently.
B. Observe for infection.
C. Allow the fluid to remain in the peritoneal cavity for a maximum of sixty minutes.
D. Promote patient comfort during dialysis therapy.

45. Peritoneal dialysis is utilized for all of the following reasons except

A. Long-term dialysis for chronic patients.
B. Drug overdose for some drugs.
C. Electrolyte disturbances.
D. Gram-negative sepsis.

46. Severe vomiting will result in

A. Acidosis.
B. Alkalosis.
C. Achlorhydria.
D. Base bicarbonate deficit.

47. Bile salts may be administered

A. To control hemorrhage.
B. To increase prothrombin time.
C. To improve absorption of vitamin K.
D. When diet lacks foods rich in vitamin K.

48. Which of the following activities is contraindicated in infantile eczema?

A. Have child vaccinated to prevent childhood diseases.

B. Cover hands and feet with cotton materials.
C. Apply open wet dressings or corn starch paste.
D. Adhere strictly to elimination diet.

49. The loss of fluids in diarrhea results in

A. Metabolic alkalosis.
B. Hypokalemia.
C. Metabolic acidosis.
D. Hyperkalemia.

50. All of the following diseases are caused by viruses except

A. Herpes simplex.
B. Warts.
C. Rubeola.
D. Tinea capitis.

51 If a child has impetigo contagiosa, to prevent the further spread of the disease the nurse should ask the mother to

A. Strictly isolate this child from others in his family.
B. Wash toys and other objects the child uses with soap and very hot water.
C. Take all other children to the physician for vaccination for this disease.
D. Not take any special precautions.

52. A patient with epilepsy should be advised by the nurse to avoid all of the following except

A. Emotional stress.
B. Physical activity.
C. Physical exhaustion.
D. Alcoholic beverages.

53. Of the following nursing actions, which one should receive priority during a grand mal seizure?

A. Place padding under and around the patient's head.
B. Restrain the patient.
C. Monitor the respirations.
D. Monitor the pupillary reactions.

54. Mr. Wood has Parkinson's disease with progressive disability. The primary goal of nursing interventions should be that Mr. Wood

A. Maintain a cheerful, positive outlook.
B. Be physically active and independent.
C. Be in a quiet environment without excessive external stimuli.
D. Maintain good personal hygiene.

55. Myasthenic crisis and cholinergic crisis are the major complications of myasthenia gravis. Which of the following is essential nursing knowledge when caring for a patient in crisis?

A. Weakness and paralysis of the muscles for swallowing and breathing occur in either crisis.

B. Cholinergic drugs should be administered to prevent further complications associated with the crisis.
C. Clinical condition usually improves after several days of treatment.
D. Loss of body function creates high levels of anxiety and fear.

56. Mr. Smith is a diabetic and takes forty-five units of NPH insulin every morning. He has developed flu-like symptoms; he has been vomiting and has had diarrhea since 4:00 A.M. He will probably need

A. No insulin.
B. His regular dose of NPH insulin.
C. A smaller dose of his NPH insulin.
D. An increased dose of his NPH insulin.

57. Ms. White is admitted with a diagnosis of Cushing's syndrome. Which of the following interventions is most important in her care?

A. Careful administration of steroids.
B. Accurate monitoring of fluid and electrolyte balance.
C. Acceptance of her appearance.
D. A high protein, high carbohydrate diet.

58. Ms. Black has been admitted with a diagnosis of severe hyperthyroidism. Which aspect of her nursing care do you anticipate will be most difficult?

A. Adequate rest.
B. Eye care.
C. Diet.
D. Skin care.

59. Which of the following items constitutes one meat exchange on the ADA exchange diet?

A. One cup of whole milk.
B. Two ounces of cheddar cheese.
C. One-fourth cup tuna fish.
D. Ten small nuts.

60. Inspiration is an active process requiring contraction of the

A. Diaphragm and intercostal muscles.
B. Abdominal muscles.
C. Diaphragm, intercostal, and sternocleidomastoid muscles.
D. Diaphragm, intercostal, and abdominal muscles.

61. Central chemoreceptors in the medulla are stimulated primarily

A. When there is an increase in the arterial pCO_2 level.

B. When there is an imbalance in the metabolic state.

C. When there is a decrease in the arterial pO_2 level.

D. By any metabolic or respiratory imbalance.

62. Peripheral chemoreceptors are stimulated primarily

A. When there is an increase in the arterial pCO_2 level.

B. When there is an imbalance in the metabolic state.

C. When there is a decrease in the arterial pO_2 level.

D. By any metabolic or respiratory acid-base imbalance.

63. Blood that finds its way back to the arterial vascular system without going through ventilated areas of the lung is referred to as

A. Alveolar dead space ventilation.
B. Shunting.
C. Physiologic dead space ventilation.
D. Anatomic dead space ventilation.

64. The patient with gastric pain is advised to take any one of the following antacids except

A. Aluminum hydroxide.
B. Amphojel.
C. Maalox.
D. Soda bicarbonate.

65. A patient with peritonitis is placed in semi-Fowler's position because

A. It decreases the pain from the infection.
B. It localizes the infection to the pelvic cavity rather than the diaphragm.
C. It facilitates breathing as the diaphragm is relieved of pressure.
D. It makes the patient more comfortable.

66. John, age 35, was admitted to the dialysis unit in chronic renal failure as a result of polycystic kidneys. He will be on dialysis until a transplant is available. The most important nursing intervention at this time would be to

A. Monitor fluid intake.
B. Maintain complete bed rest.
C. Encourage diet maintenance.
D. Encourage verbalization of feelings about illness and change in body image.

67. A patient who is vomiting and a patient with a paralytic ileus have all of the following physiological alterations in common except

A. Dehydration.
B. Metabolic alkalosis.

C. Hypokalemia.
D. Deficiency of ADH.

68. Which of the following is characteristic of a third-degree burn?

A. Numerous blisters and tissues are moist.
B. Skin appears reddened and soft.
C. Extremely painful when exposed to air.
D. No pain response when involved hair follicle is pulled out.

69. Which one of the following statements related to the pathophysiology of burns is not true?

A. Pathological changes depend upon the intensity of heat and the length of time applied.
B. Loss of fluid from the capillaries results in an overload of the lymphatic system.
C. Loss of fluid from the capillaries continues until the healing process is well established.
D. RBC's may be destroyed after the initial burn injury.

70. Which one of the following statements about burns is not true?

A. Rate of healing depends upon the depth of skin destruction and whether infection has occurred.
B. Deep dermal burns are injuries that extend into the corium.
C. Epithelial regeneration takes place principally from the epithelial lining of the sweat glands and hair follicles.
D. Systemic effects are easily controlled in deep dermal burns.

71. Vitamin B_{12} injections are best administered by which method?

A. Subcutaneously in the deltoid.
B. Intramuscularly in the gluteus.
C. Intramuscularly in the lateral thigh.
D. Intramuscularly in the deltoid.

72. Trigeminal neuralgia results in severe recurrent paroxysms of pain on one side of the face. Which of the following nursing measures would probably not be helpful in preventing onset of pain?

A. Provide small feedings of soft foods.
B. Protect the patient's face from drafts.
C. Place a cold compress on the affected side.
D. Phrase questions that may be answered by gestures or short answers.

73. A chordotomy is a procedure which may be used in the management of intractable pain. Which of the following statements is true in relation to the effect on the sense of temperature?

A. Would be impaired on both sides below the level of the procedure.
B. Would be impaired on the opposite side of the procedure.

C. Would be impaired on the same side as the procedure.

D. Would not be impaired.

74. Mr. Jones, a fifty-two-year-old man with emphysema, was admitted to the hospital with recent onset of malaise and productive cough of green sputum. An arterial blood gas was obtained on admission, oxygen via nasal prongs at 6 l./minute was started, and a repeat arterial blood gas after one hour was obtained. Following are the ABG results:

	FIO_2	pH	pCO_2	HCO_3	pO_2
ABG 1:	21%	7.35	50	27	48
ABG 2:	6 l. O_2 NP	7.20	75	29	140

The acid-base abnormality demonstrated with ABG 1 is

A. Respiratory acidosis.

B. Respiratory alkalosis.

C. Metabolic acidosis.

D. Metabolic alkalosis.

75. Identify some of the changes you might observe in Mr. Jones at the time the second ABG sample was obtained.

A. Improvement of hypoxemia, decreased cyanosis, increased alertness.

B. Increase in acid-base imbalance, improvement of hypoxemia, somnolence, and coma.

C. Decreased cyanosis, agitation, improvement of acid-base imbalance.

D. Increase in acid-base imbalance, somnolence, increased cyanosis.

76. Mrs. Rush went to her doctor for an annual physical. He discovered that her blood pressure was 150/95. He asked her to return once a week for three weeks to determine if the high reading was temporary. The third week, her blood pressure remained elevated but she denied experiencing any uncomfortable symptoms. The best rationale for treating Mrs. Rush's hypertension is

A. To prevent uncomfortable symptoms from appearing.

B. To prevent the occurrence of a myocardial infarction which occurs in eighty-two percent of the cases.

C. To avoid side effects affecting her ability to exercise or engage in moderately strenuous activities.

D. To prevent the development of or to arrest the progress of vascular damage.

77. A patient comes into the out-patient clinic where you are working. While giving you a history, he tells you that he has leg pains that begin when he walks but that cease when he stops walking. Which of the following conditions would you suspect?

A. An acute obstruction in the vessels of the legs.

B. Peripheral vascular problems in both legs.

C. Diabetes.

D. Calcium deficiency.

78. Mrs. James has to receive medication I.V. every twelve hours. To prevent constant venipunctures, the physician has ordered a heparin lock. The nurse's clearest explanation of this procedure to the patient is

A. To explain that a special needle will remain in the patient's arm in between giving the patient medication twice a day.

B. To show the needle to the patient and explain that it is a special needle inserted into the vein where medication will be injected.

C. To explain that this special needle will cut down on the risk of infiltration, thrombophlebitis, and circulatory overload.

D. To tell the patient that a heparin lock is like a scalp vein needle, capped by a resealable rubber diaphragm that is further enforced by a plastic seal around the hub.

79. Roberta Brown has been admitted to the unit with a tentative diagnosis of urinary tract infection. You know that the most important factor influencing ascending infection is

A. Not enough fluid intake.

B. Obstruction of free urine flow.

C. A change in pH.

D. Presence of microorganisms.

80. Mr. Swanson was put on Quinidine (which decreases myocardial excitability) to prevent atrial fibrillation. He also has kidney disease. The nurse must be aware of the dangers of this drug in relation to kidney disease because

A. It can cause cardiac arrest.

B. It can cause hypotension.

C. It produces mild bradycardia.

D. It is very toxic even in small doses.

81. Drugs that are commonly given for peptic ulcer disease (relax smooth muscle and inhibit secretions of the duct glands) are classified as

A. Antiinflammatory.

B. Adrenergic.

C. Anticholinergic.

D. Cholinergic.

82. In treatment of pancreatitis, which of the following drugs would be contraindicated?

A. Opiates.

B. Meperidine.
C. Antibiotics.
D. Anticholinergics.

83. The underlying cause of esophageal varices is

    A. Loss of hepatic cellular regeneration.
    B. Dilated veins and varicosities.
    C. Elevated blood ammonia levels.
    D. Portal hypertension.

84. Common symptoms associated with Addison's disease include

    A. Generalized weakness, increased pigmentation of the skin, hypotension, and emotional disturbances.
    B. Buffalo hump, weight gain, and striae of the skin.
    C. Hyperglycemia, increased frequency of infections, and polyuria.
    D. Grotesque appearance, increased oiliness of skin and hair, headaches, and impotence.

85. Following a hypophysectomy, the nurse would observe signs for all of the following except

    A. Adrenal insufficiency.
    B. Acute thyroid crisis.
    C. Hypoglycemia.
    D. Hypertension.

86. When teaching the patient safe, self-administration of steroid therapy, which of the following would the nurse not include?

    A. The medication should never be stopped abruptly.
    B. The medication should be taken with a meal or snack.
    C. The patient should protect himself from contracting infections.
    D. The patient may need to increase his salt intake.

87. Which of the following diets is appropriate for hyperinsulinism (hypoglycemia)?

    A. High fat, high carbohydrate.
    B. Low protein, high carbohydrate.
    C. Low carbohydrate, high protein.
    D. Low fat, low protein.

88. Mr. McKay is being treated with chemotherapy and radiation therapy (for cancer of the lung) as an outpatient in the clinic where you are working. Which of the following patient teaching instructions should be included in the initial discussion period before radiation therapy is begun?

    A. Radiation therapy can cause pneumonitis.
    B. Radiation ionizes atoms in the chemical systems of the cell.
    C. Radiodermatitis occurs later in the course of therapy.
    D. Radiation therapy causes cell damage which results in gastrointestinal side effects.

89. As Mr. McKay's treatment proceeds, he comes in for his usual treatment and the nurse notices his skin appears wet and there is a weeping of the skin. Her intervention would be

    A. Do not give the treatment and explain to Mr. McKay to not bathe the skin until the weeping is stopped.
    B. Give the treatment and make a note on his record concerning the skin condition.
    C. Do not give the treatment and notify the physician.
    D. Give the treatment and instruct him to use antibiotic lotion to the lesions.

90. Mr. McKay should be instructed to avoid eating the following foods.

    A. Cheese, fried eggs, nuts, raw fruit.
    B. Beef, pork, bread, cooked vegetables.
    C. Lunch meat, canned soups, tomatoes, yellow vegetables.
    D. Milk, eggs, canned vegetables, fish.

91. Mrs Jones states that rather than take the antacid as prescribed, she eats something to eliminate the gastric distress. The nurse tells Mrs. Jones that foods should not be used in place of antacids. The principle underlying this teaching is that

    A. The neutralization produced by food is always followed by increased secretion.
    B. Foods involve more calories, and she does not need them to maintain nutritional status.
    C. If foods contain caffeine, they stimulate acid.
    D. Gastric distress will not be eliminated, only briefly avoided.

92. Mr. Alles is about to be discharged on the drug Dicumarol. Of the principles below, which one is the most important to teach the patient before discharge?

    A. He should be sure to take the medication before meals.
    B. He should shave with an electric razor.
    C. If he should miss a dose, double the dose at the next scheduled time.
    D. Nothing, for it is the responsibility of the doctor to do the teaching.

93. When a patient is scheduled for bowel surgery, which of the following should be administered to prevent anemia?

    A. Vitamin B_{12} and vitamin K.
    B. Antibiotics.
    C. High dosages of vitamin C.
    D. Bland foods with high vitamin content.

94. Signs of right ventricular failure would include

   A. Bibasilar rales, and frothy pink sputum.
   B. Neck vein distention, peripheral edema, and bibasilar rales.
   C. Increased CVP, frothy pink sputum, and hepatomegaly.
   D. Neck vein distention, peripheral edema, increased CVP, and hepatomegaly.

95. Symptoms of hypercarbia (increased CO_2) would include

   A. Headache, dizziness, confusion, tremor, and somnolence.
   B. Tachycardia, anxiety, and paresthesias.
   C. Tetany, headache, and confusion.
   D. Disorientation, anxiety, and paresthesias.

96. With a severely burned patient, the nurse must know that the major loss to the body is

   A. Electrolytes.
   B. Water.
   C. Blood.
   D. Skin.

97. The practice of cautious administration of fluids to a burned patient who is hypovolemic is based on a major principle that

   A. Fluids by themselves do not contain the necessary electrolytes.
   B. Fluids are given to maintain kidney perfusion.
   C. When fluids move back into the vascular compartment, there is a danger of congestive heart failure from too much fluid.
   D. There is an extracellular fluid volume shift occurring after twenty-four hours.

98. Mr. Brynes, a fifty-year-old Caucasian, came into the emergency room with the following symptoms: fever, painful cough, chest pain aggravated by coughing and breathing, tachycardia, and muscle aches and pains. These symptoms would lead you to suspect which of the following conditions?

   A. Influenza—severe.
   B. Pneumonia.
   C. Congestive heart failure.
   D. Chronic bronchitis.

99. Mr. Brynes was experiencing tachycardia. Your understanding of the physiological bases for this symptom is explained by which of the following statements?

   A. The demand for oxygen is decreased because of pleural involvement.
   B. The inflammatory process causes the body to demand more oxygen to meet its needs.
   C. The heart has to pump faster to meet the demand for oxygen in the face of lowered arterial oxygen tension.

   D. Respirations are labored.

100. Mr. Brynes' treatment regime included antimicrobials to fight the infection, oxygen to treat his hypoxemia, I.V. fluids for dehydration and hyponatremia, and suctioning to evacuate secretions. Chest physiotherapy is a crucial aspect of care for pneumonia. The best underlying principle explaining the objective of this regime is that

   A. The patient has difficulty coughing on his own.
   B. Removal of collected secretions opens up the airways.
   C. The program includes principles of postural drainage.
   D. The program lessens the possibility of pleural friction rub.

Answers and Rationale

1. (B) Intracellular fluid contains large quantities of the following electrolytes: K, Mg, PO_4, proteins. Extracellular fluid contains large quantities of the following electrolytes: Na, Cl, HCO_3. The concentration in solution is expressed in mEq./L. The total number of electrolytes in the ICF and ECF will be equal, thereby rendering the fluid composition electrically neutral.

2. (A) The flow of water is from an area of low concentration to a high *solute* concentration.

3. (D) The sugar content of urine in diabetes insipidus is not of concern.

4. (C) Mrs. Jones' medication therapy includes steroids; she needs protection from infections and potential infections.

5. (C) Basal cell epithelioma and squamous cell epithelioma are both superficial, easily excised, slow-growing tumors. A sebaceous cyst is a benign (non-malignant) growth.

6. (A) Until a condition is specifically diagnosed, the treatments described in answers B, C, and D can exacerbate the disease and cause disfigurement and/or spreading of dermatoses.

7. (C) This is the most complete answer as the other alternatives only partially define the concept of buffer system.

8. (D) This is the most complete answer, and while this buffer system is slowest, it can completely compensate for acid-base imbalance.

9. (A) The principle underlying the way dialysis works is the ability of fluid to move between compartments across a semipermeable membrane. When blood moves through the dialysate, the waste products, such as urea, are removed because they are low

weight molecules and can be diffused through the membrane; water, being a larger molecule, is unable to move across the membrane.

10. (B) Highly specialized tissue in the cerebral cortex is most sensitive to a lack of oxygen.

11. (C) Respiration is controlled by many different areas of the brain.

12. (B) A patent airway is always a priority need, particularly in the patient with a head injury, because hypoxia and hypercapnia cause cerebral edema with increasing intracranial pressure.

13. (D) Blood in the CSF, within the subarachnoid space, is irritating to the meninges causing headache and nuchal rigidity.

14. (C) Agranulocytosis is characterized by neutropenia (decreased number of lymphocytes) which lowers the body defenses against infection. Granulocytes are the first barrier to infection in the body.

15. (B) Temporary ischemia of myocardium causes anginal pain due to inadequate oxygen to meet increased myocardial metabolic needs.

16. (C) Exertion increases myocardial oxygen needs.

17. (B) Atherosclerotic vessels are unable to dilate although nonaffected arteries will dilate. Decreasing venous return decreases blood volume and therefore less cardiac work is needed. Nitroglycerin also decreases peripheral vascular resistance.

18. (C) Nitroglycerin should be taken whenever the patient feels a full, pressure feeling or tightness in his chest, not waiting until chest pain is severe. It can also be taken prophylactically before engaging in an activity known to cause angina to prevent an anginal attack.

19. (C) About fifty percent of the people who do die outside the hospital have a fatal arrhythmia, usually shortly after experiencing the onset of symptoms.

20. (A) Myocardial infarction is death of myocardium.

21. (D) History is of paramount importance in diagnosis; patients are admitted to CCU many times on this basis alone since ECG's and enzyme changes may not be present immediately, but they confirm the diagnosis.

22. (C) By keeping the lines of communication open, Mr. Sundstrom can cope with his condition and continue in the rehabilitative process.

23. (D) If left ventricular failure produces right ventricular failure, pedal edema will result. Therefore, it is important to detect left heart failure before it causes right heart failure.

24. (B) Failure of left ventricle to pump effectively causes damming of blood back into pulmonary circuit, increasing the pressure and causing extrav-asation of fluid into interstitial spaces and alveoli.

25. (A) The ability of the leukocytes to travel quickly to the site of infection and ingest the invading bacteria is the main line of defense against infection in the body.

26. (B) Low cardiac output is reflected in the decreased urinary output; with low cardiac output, the sympathetic nervous system is stimulated, resulting in increased pulse rate and blood pressure.

27. (A) As blood becomes more viscous it flows more easily through vessels preventing stasis and clotting.

28. (C) The treatment described in the first answer should never be used since small clots may have formed and become dislodged. Gatching of the knee restricts venous return. Footboard walking and tightening and relaxing of leg muscles promote venous return.

29. (C) Sodium transport system is very important to many different functioning systems of the body. Called the *sodium pump*, one of its most important functions is to prevent continual swelling of the cells by transporting sodium to the exterior; this initiates an opposite osmotic tendency to move water out of the cell.

30. (D) Shunts should be inspected several times each day for presence of possible clotting. Dark spots will quickly be followed by separation of the sera and cells if clotting becomes complete. When dark spots appear, patients should be instructed to immediately seek treatment for declotting.

31. (A) The amount of oxygen which is available to the tissues depends on the oxygen content of the blood; i.e., the amount of oxygen that is dissolved in the plasma, the amount of oxygen that combines with the hemoglobin molecules and an adequate cardiac output to deliver oxygenated blood to the tissues. Febrility decreases the amount of oxygen available for the tissues to draw from. Anemia results in less hemoglobin, therefore less oxygen is able to bind. At high altitudes the FIO_2 is less than atmospheric.

32. (A) Surfactant changes the surface tension of the alveoli. The smaller alveoli have a lower surface tension than the larger alveoli, thereby preventing the alveoli from collapsing.

33. (A) Infectious processes increase the body's need for steroids due to the additional stress.

34. (C) The manifestations of a CVA are due to an upper motor neuron lesion. The motor (pyramidal) tracts cross over to the opposite side in the medulla; therefore, a lesion in the cerebral hemisphere results in manifestations on the opposite side.

35. (D) Prolonged pressure on the affected side contributes to contractures, deformities, and decubitus ulcers due to loss of motor tone and circulation.

Patients can be positioned on the affected side for 10–15 minutes but no longer.

36. (C) Recovery of language is related to frequent attempts to communicate with a responsive listener. Allowing the patient to use his jargon to express his needs encourages further attempts to communicate.

37. (C) Homonymous hemianopsia is a common visual deficiency associated with hemiplegia. Loss of the visual field must be compensated for by the patient's increased conscious awareness of hazards to personal safety.

38. (C) Patients with brain damage following a CVA may have difficulty with new learning and generalization. Home visits may be necessary to aid in the transfer of learning from the hospital to the home.

39. (B) Frequently the disease is not discovered until a routine urinalysis is done. It will show hematuria, proteinuria, and casts.

40. (B) Bed rest would protect the poorly functioning kidneys (protein breakdown which will result in an extra workload for the kidney) as well as facilitate diuresis.

41. (C) Patients in early stages of renal failure are hypertensive due to poor kidney perfusion and function, probably caused by renal ischemia.

42. (A) I.V. fluids and Lasix are given to increase blood flow to the kidneys. Answer B is wrong because the action is to decrease intrarenal vascular resistance and Lasix by itself will not restore blood volume (answer C).

43. (B) Protein free diet is important, for damaged kidneys may not be able to eliminate nitrogenous waste products. Low sodium, high calorie, and potassium-free fluids are other important components of the dietary regime.

44. (A) Vital signs must be monitored for impending shock, overhydration, or cardiac arrhythmias.

45. (A) Not as efficient as hemodialysis, it may have more complications. Patients are less comfortable during this procedure. It is used for a temporary situation unless no shunt site available.

46. (B) Alkalosis occurs due to loss of HCL from the stomach. Prolonged, severe vomiting could result in hypochloremic acidosis.

47. (C) The absorption of vitamin K in oily solution is facilitated by bile.

48. (A) The vaccine can cause vaccinia which can superimpose the pustular eruptions of the viral infection on the eczema.

49. (C) Acidosis occurs through loss of electrolytes, leading to imbalance. Sodium increases, chloride decreases, and potassium loss varies.

50. (D) Tinea capitis (ringworm of scalp) is a fungus that occurs almost exclusively in children.

51. (B) Washing with soap and hot water keeps the objects relatively free of streptococci and lessens the danger of spread of the disease.

52. (B) Regular physical activity tends to inhibit seizure activity.

53. (A) The primary nursing goal during a seizure is to protect the patient from physical injury and to maintain a patent airway if possible.

54. (B) Physical activity is necessary to maintain function and to prevent deformities in relation to immobility of muscles. Independent function also fosters self-esteem.

55. (A) The patient cannot handle his own secretions, and respiratory arrest may be imminent. Atropine may be administered to prevent crisis.

56. (C) Although he is unable to eat, Mr. Smith still needs insulin for body metabolism processes; insulin requirements increase with infectious processes.

57. (B) It is important to monitor fluids and electrolytes as K^+, Na^+, and water retention occur.

58. (A) Persons with hyperthyroidism are hyperactive, nervous, and irritable; provision for adequate rest is a major nursing challenge.

59. (C) All other responses are incorrect. Milk is from the milk exchange; nuts are from the fat exchange; one ounce of cheese is equivalent.

60. (A) Inspiration requires contraction of the diaphragm and intercostal muscles. In patients with COPD, the accessory muscles of respiration play an important role. In patients with emphysema, the diaphragms are usually flat, barely participating in the act of inspiration.

61. (A) Central chemoreceptors are located in the medulla as well as adjacent structures. They respond immediately to an increase in the arterial pCO_2 level. They respond less readily to metabolic imbalances and hypoxia.

62. (C) Peripheral chemoreceptors are located in the carotid arteries and aorta arch. They respond primarily to a decrease in the arterial pO_2 level. In patients with chronic hypercarbia (increased pCO_2), the central chemoreceptors are dulled so that the peripheral chemoreceptors are the main stimulus for ventilation. When a patient with COPD, who is hypoxic and hypercarbic, is given high oxygen concentrations, the hypoxic drive to breathe is removed, resulting in correction of the hypoxemia but in an increase of the CO_2 level.

63. (B) Shunting is defined as blood which finds its way back to the arterial vascular system without going through ventilated areas of the lung. Alveolar dead space ventilation is that portion of the ventilated alveoli that is not perfused. Anatomic dead space ventilation is that portion of ventilation that is not available for gas exchange; it includes the

physiological dead space ventilation which is the volume ventilating alveoli but which is ineffective in removing carbon dioxide.

64. (D) Soda bicarbonate is absorbed into the system and destroys acid balance; it can lead to acidosis.

65. (B) It is important to contain and localize the infection as much as possible, so positioning is important.

66. (D) He will already have been on a limited fluid intake and diet management. It is now important to allow him to express his feelings about his illness.

67. (D) ADH promotes the absorption of sodium. Hypokalemia may result because of a shift of potassium ion from intracellular to extracellular fluid to compensate for loss of potassium. Dehydration occurs because of loss of fluid intake in vomiting, and in paralytic ileus there is interruption of the normal pathways of intestinal propulsion and liquid absorption. Metabolic alkalosis is the loss of extracellular fluid and of sodium and chloride ions.

68. (D) In a third-degree burn, the nerve endings are destroyed and the wound is usually without pain sensation.

69. (C) The loss of fluid from capillaries ceases as soon as healing starts; new skin will immediately seal the exposed capillaries. The healing area is vulnerable to further damage if handled roughly, however.

70. (D) Deep dermal burns cause widespread shock which may precipitate renal shutdown, fluid and electrolyte imbalance, and RBC destruction with subsequent anemia.

71. (B) Vitamin B_{12} should be given deep intramuscular as it is painful and allows for better absorption.

72. (C) Sensitive trigger zones are present in the cheek and may be stimulated by cold temperatures or even washing.

73. (B) Pain and temperature are transmitted in the anterolateral ascending tract, which crosses to the opposite side after entering the spinal cord.

74. (A) Respiratory acidosis represents an increase in the acid component, carbon dioxide, and an increase in the hydrogen ion concentration (decreased pH) of the arterial blood.

75. (B) Mr. Jones' drive to breathe is hypoxia. When he was given an FIO_2 to return his arterial pO_2 level to above normal, the peripheral chemoreceptors no longer could respond to hypoxia. The central chemoreceptors had been dulled over the years by the constant increased CO_2 level so they did not respond to an increasing pCO_2 level. Hypercarbia (increased pCO_2) exhibits symptoms of somnolence and coma in the acute situation.

76. (D) The higher the pressures and the longer they

remain elevated, the more the damage to the vascular network, which can result in strokes, heart failure, loss of vision, or kidney failure.

77. (B) Intermittent claudication is a condition that indicates vascular deficiencies in the peripheral vascular system. If an obstruction were present, the leg pain would persist when the patient stops walking. Low calcium level may cause leg cramps but would not necessarily be related to walking.

78. (B) Be simple, clear, and precise in an explanation, and do not introduce possible complications or technical information that the patient neither wants nor needs.

79. (B) Free flow of urine together with large urine output and pH are antibacterial defenses. If free flow is obstructed the infection will most likely ascend up the urinary tract.

80. (A) Kidney disease interferes with metabolism and excretion of Quinidine, resulting in higher drug concentrations in the body. Quinidine can depress myocardial excitability enough to cause cardiac arrest.

81. (C) Anticholinergics decrease gastric motility and suppress gastric secretions (used in the treatment of peptic ulcer).

82. (A) Opiates are contraindicated as they may produce spasm of the biliary-pancreatic ducts.

83. (D) The underlying cause is portal hypertension which usually results from obstruction of the portal venous circulation and cirrhosis of the liver.

84. (A) Answer B is associated with Cushing's syndrome; answer C is associated with diabetes mellitus; answer D is associated with acromegaly.

85. (D) Hypotension is most likely to occur.

86. (D) The patient may need to decrease his salt intake.

87. (C) This diet tends to inhibit stimulation of insulin release.

88. (D) All of the information is accurate regarding radiation; however, the patient's initial symptoms usually are related to GI function. He should not be told about pneumonitis but could be told about reporting any unusual symptoms. Answer B is technical and not necessary for patient understanding of the disease process.

89. (C) During the time the reaction occurs patients are taken off radiation therapy and instructed to use antibiotic lotion and steroid cream to prevent infection.

90. (A) These foods can be irritating to the GI tract leading to additional GI symptoms.

91. (A) Antacids absorb the acid secretions in the stomach and alleviate the gastric distress.

92. (B) Dicumarol is an anticoagulant drug and one of the dangers involved is bleeding. Using a safety razor is a potential cause of bleeding.

93. (A) Preparation for bowel surgery predisposes the patient to anemia, thus vitamins are necessary.

94. (D) RVF: backward failure. The RV is attempting to pump blood forward in spite of noncompliant lungs, resulting in eventual failure of the RV. Clinical manifestations include increased CVP, neck vein distention, hepatic congestion and peripheral edema.

95. (A) Respiratory acidosis (hypercarbia or increased CO_2) exhibits the following manifestations: headache, dizziness, confusion, tremor, somnolence. Respiratory alkalosis (hyperventilation or decreased CO_2) exhibits the following manifestations: paresthesias, tetany, anxiety, tachycardia.

96. (B) Water loss occurs from fluid moving from vascular compartment in burned area to interstitial tissues surrounding the burned area, causing edema.

97. (C) After forty-eight hours, fluids from interstitial tissues around the burned area start to move back into the vascular compartment, and an overload can result in congestive heart failure.

98. (B) Mr. Brynes is experiencing the classic symptoms of pneumonia, an infectious disease. Ninety percent of pneumonia cases are pneumococcal in origin.

99. (C) The arterial oxygen supply is lowered and the demand for oxygen is increased, which results in the heart's having to beat faster to meet body needs for oxygen.

100. (B) Removal of secretions is important to open up obstructed airways as well as to prevent further inhalation of infected material.

Surgical Nursing

The chapter on surgical nursing, like the medical chapter, is divided by systems to help the nurse review the pathophysiology as well as the disease processes associated with each system. Since we are concerned with surgical conditions, the emphasis will be on the surgical interventions into illness, pre- and post-operative procedures, and signs and symptoms of postoperative complications.

Both the content and questions are oriented towards nursing management for surgical procedures since the primary tasks of the nurse consist of observation, assessment, intervention, and evaluation. Although medical and surgical principles of care are clearly integrated in the nursing process, the two subjects are treated in separate chapters to facilitate review and to be consistent with the format of State Boards.

Operative Care Concepts

Preoperative and Postoperative Care

Routine Preoperative Care

Psychological Support

A. Reinforce the physician's teaching regarding the surgical procedure.

B. Identify patient's anxieties; notify physician of extreme anxiety.

C. Listen to patient's verbalization of fears.

D. Provide support to the patient's family (where family can wait during surgery, approximately how long the surgery takes, etc.).

Preoperative Teaching

A. Postoperative exercises: leg, coughing, deep breathing, etc.

B. Equipment which will be utilized during postoperative period: intermittent positive pressure breathing machine (IPPB), NG tube to suction, etc.

C. Pain medication and when to ask for it.

D. Explanation of NPO.

Physical Care

A. Completed night before surgery.
   1. Observe and record patient's overall condition.
      a. Nutritional status.
      b. Physical defects, such as loss of limb function, skin breakdown.
      c. Hearing or sight difficulties.
   2. Obtain chest X-ray, ECG, and blood and urine samples, as ordered.
   3. Take preoperative history and assess present physical condition.
   4. Determine if any drug allergies.
   5. Perform skin prep and shave when necessary; have patient shower with antibacterial soap, if ordered.
   6. Give enema, if ordered.

B. Completed one to two hours before surgery.

1. Insert indwelling catheter, NG tube, I.V.
2. Administer preoperative medications.
3. Provide quiet rest with side-rails up and curtains drawn.

Nurse's Responsibility

A. Perform or supervise skin prep and shave.

B. Carry out preoperative nursing interventions.

C. Notify physician of drug allergies, overwhelming anxiety, unusual ECG findings, abnormal lab findings.

D. See that consent form is signed.

E. Administer preoperative medications on time.

F. Complete preoperative checklist.

G. Check if history and physical exam is on chart.

H. Chart preoperative medications.

I. Check Identaband, provide quiet environment.

J. Remove dentures, nail polish, hairpins, etc.

Recovery Room

A. Immediate postoperative care.
   1. Maintain patent airway.
   2. Administer oxygen by mask or nasal cannula.
   3. Check gag reflex. Leave airway in place until patient pushes it out.
   4. Position patient for adequate ventilation.
   5. Observe for adverse signs of general anesthesia or spinal anesthesia.
      a. Level of consciousness.
      b. Movement of limbs.
   6. Monitor vital signs every ten to fifteen minutes.
      a. Pulse—check rate, quality, and rhythm.
      b. Blood pressure—check pulse pressure and quality as well as systolic and diastolic pressure.
      c. Respiration—check rate, rhythm, depth, and type of respiration (abdominal breathing, nasal flaring).
      d. Vital signs are sometimes difficult to obtain due to hypothermia.
      e. Movement from operating room table to guerney can alter vital signs significantly, especially with cardiovascular patients.
   7. Maintain temperature (operating room is usually cold)—apply warm blankets.
   8. Maintain patent I.V.

a. Check type and amount of solution being administered.

b. Adjust correct flow rate.

c. Check I.V. site for signs of infiltration.

d. Check blood transfusion.

(1) Blood type and blood bank number. Time transfusion started.

(2) Patient's name, identification number, expiration date.

(3) Amount in bag upon arrival in recovery room. Color and consistency of blood.

9. Observe dressings and surgical drains.

a. Mark any drainage on dressings and note time by drawing a line around the drainage.

b. Note color and amount of drainage on dressings and in drainage tubes.

c. Ensure that dressing is secure.

d. Reinforce dressings as needed.

B. Overall observations of condition.

1. Check skin for warmth, color, and moisture.

2. Check nailbeds and mucous membranes for color and blanching; report if cyanotic.

3. Observe for return of reflexes.

C. Medications.

1. Begin routine drugs and administer all STAT drugs.

2. Pain medications are usually administered sparingly and in smaller amounts.

D. Assessment for return to room.

1. Be sure vital signs are stable and within normal limits for at least one hour.

2. See if patient is awake and reflexes are present (gag and cough reflex). Check for movement and sensation in limbs of patients with spinal anesthesia.

3. Take oral airway out (if not out already). Observe for cyanosis.

4. Be sure dressings are intact and there is no excessive drainage.

E. Recovery-room nurse's responsibility for discharging patient.

1. Call anesthesiologist to discharge patient from recovery room (if appropriate).

2. Give report on patient's condition to floor nurse receiving patient.

3. Ensure I.V. is patent.

4. Reinforce or change dressings as needed.

5. Ensure all drains are functioning.

6. Record amount of I.V. fluid remaining and amount absorbed.

7. Record amount of urine in drainage bag.

8. Record all medications administered in recovery room.

9. Clean patient as needed (change gown, wash off excess surgical scrub solution).

Surgical Floor

A. Assessment.

1. Maintain patent airway; administer oxygen as necessary.

2. Take vital signs—usual orders are V.S. q. 15 minutes until stable; then q. ½ hour X 2, q. hour X 4; then q. 4 hours for 24–48 hours.

3. Check I.V. site and patency frequently.

4. Observe and record urine output.

5. Keep accurate records of intake and output.

6. Observe skin color and moisture.

B. Nursing management.

1. Position patient for comfort and maximum airway ventilation.

2. Turn q. 2 hours and p.r.n.

3. Give back care at least every four hours.

4. Encourage coughing and deep breathing every two hours (may use IPPB or blow bottles).

5. Keep patient comfortable with medications.

6. Check dressings and drainage tubes q. 2–4 hours; if abnormal amount of drainage, check more frequently.

7. Give oral hygiene at least q. 4 hours; if NG tube, nasal oxygen, or endotracheal tube inserted, q. 2 hours.

8. Bathe patient when temperature can be maintained—bathing removes the antiseptic solution and stimulates circulation.

9. Keep patient warm and avoid chilling, but do not increase temperature above normal.

a. Increased temperature increases metabolic rate and need for oxygen.

b. Excessive perspiration causes fluid and electrolyte loss.

10. Irrigate NG tube q. 2 hours and p.r.n. with normal saline to keep patent and to prevent electrolyte imbalance.

11. Maintain dietary intake—type of diet depends on type and extent of surgical procedure.

a. Minor surgical conditions—patient may drink or eat as soon as he is awake and desires food or drink.
b. Major surgical conditions.
   (1) NPO until bowel sounds return.
   (2) Clear liquid advanced to full liquid as tolerated.
   (3) Soft diet advanced to full diet within three to five days (depending on type of surgery and physician's preference).
12. Place on bedpan two to four hours postoperatively if catheter not inserted.
13. Start activity, as tolerated and dictated by surgical procedure. Most patients are dangled within first twenty-four hours.

Anesthesia

Preoperative Medications

General Action

A. Decreases secretions of mouth and respiratory tract.
B. Depresses vagal reflexes—slows heart and prevents complications with excitation during intubation.
C. Produces drowsiness and relieves anxiety.
D. Allows anesthesia to be induced more smoothly and in smaller amounts.

Types of Drugs

A. Barbiturates.
   1. Intermediate-acting barbiturate at bedtime (seconal or nembutal).
   2. Short-acting barbiturate one hour preoperatively (decreases blood pressure and pulse and relieves anxiety).
B. Belladonna alkaloids.
   1. General action.
      a. Decreases salivary and bronchial secretions.
      b. Allows inhalation anesthetics to be administered more easily.
      c. Prevents postoperative complications such as aspiration pneumonia.
   2. Scopolamine is used in conjunction with morphine or Demerol to produce amnesic block.

3. Atropine blocks the vagus nerve response of decreased heart rate, which can occur as a reaction to some inhalation anesthetics.

Anesthetic Agents

A. Anesthesia produces insensitivity to pain or sensation.
B. Dangers associated with anesthesia depend on overall condition of patient.
   1. High risk if associated cardiovascular, renal, or respiratory conditions.
   2. High risk for unborn fetus and mother.
   3. High risk if stomach full (chance of vomiting and aspiration).
C. Types of anesthesia.
   1. General—administered I.V. or by inhalation. Produces loss of consciousness and decreases reflex movement.
   2. Local—applied topically or injected regionally. Patient is alert, but pain and sensation is decreased in surgical area.

General Anesthesia

A. Balanced anesthesia (combination of two or more drugs) is used to decrease side effects and complications of anesthetic agents.
B. Goals of general anesthesia.
   1. Analgesia.
   2. Unconsciousness.
   3. Skeletal muscle relaxation.
C. Stages of general anesthesia.
   1. Stage one: early induction—from beginning of inhalation to loss of consciousness.
   2. Stage two: delirium or excitement.
      a. No surgery is performed at this point—dangerous stage.
      b. Breathing is irregular.
   3. Stage three: surgical anesthesia.
      a. Begins when patient stops fighting and is breathing regularly.
      b. Four planes, based on respiration, pupillary and eyeball movement, and reflex muscular responses.
   4. Stage four: medullary paralysis—respiratory arrest.
D. Classifications of general anesthesia.
   1. Potent (halothane, ether, chloroform)—capable

of achieving all three goals of general anesthesia but with severe side effects.

2. Nonpotent (nitrous oxide).
   a. If given in large dose, can achieve all three goals of general anesthesia but produces toxicity.
   b. When given in smaller doses, lacks analgesia or skeletal muscle relaxation.
3. Basal anesthesia (thiopental, Pentothal).
   a. Ultra short-acting barbiturate so high doses needed for prolonged deep anesthesia, which can lead to respiratory depression.
   b. Used for induction—effects are rapid, allowing for less inhalation anesthesia.
4. Dissociative anesthesia (Ketamine HCl and Innovar).
   a. Used with nitrous oxide and oxygen for short anesthesia.
   b. Patient is awake but unaware of what is actually happening.
   c. Useful for burn dressings.

E. Adjuncts for general anesthesia.
   1. Preoperative medications (see p. 186).
   2. Neuromuscular blocking agents (Anectine, Pavulon, Flaxedil) used to facilitate intubation.

Local Anesthesia

A. Topical anesthetics.
   1. Poorly absorbed through skin but usually rapid through mucous membranes (mouth, GI tract, etc.).
   2. Systemic toxicity is rare but local reactions common, especially if used for long periods of time on patients allergic to chemicals.
   3. Used for hemorrhoids, episiotomy, nipple erosion, and minor cuts and burns.
   4. Used on eye procedures extensively—removing foreign bodies and tonometry.
B. Infiltrated local anesthesia (or field block).
   1. Anesthesia directly applied to surgical area.
   2. Drug is injected into bloodstream.
   3. Can have systemic effects if injected into highly vascular area.
C. Regional anesthetics (central nerve blocks).
   1. Types—spinal, caudal, saddle, epidural.
   2. Precautions.
      a. Spinal and epidural anesthesia: position

patient with head and shoulder elevated (prevents diffusion of anesthesia to the intercostal muscles which could produce respiratory distress).
      b. Epidural (continuous anesthesia used in O.B.): make sure catheter is securely fastened to prevent it from slipping out.

Nursing Care

A. General anesthesia.
   1. Maintain patent airway.
   2. Promote adequate respiratory function (position patient for lung expansion).
   3. Have patient deep breathe and cough frequently, especially if inhalation anesthesia used, to promote faster elimination of gases.
   4. Turn frequently to promote lung expansion and to prevent hypostatic pneumonia and venous stasis.
B. Spinal and epidural anesthesia.
   1. Take precautions to prevent injury to lower extremities (watch heating pad, position limb correctly, etc.).
   2. Provide gentle passive range of motion to prevent venous stasis.
   3. Keep head flat or slightly elevated to prevent spinal headache (all right for patient to turn head from side to side).
   4. Increase fluid intake, if tolerated, to increase cerebral spinal fluid.

Postoperative Medications

Narcotic Analgesics

A. Pharmacological action—reduces pain and restlessness.
B. General side effects.
   1. Drowsiness.
   2. Euphoria.
   3. Sleep.
   4. Respiratory depression.
   5. Nausea and vomiting.
C. Given at three to four hour intervals for first 24 to 48 hours for better action and pain relief.
D. Types of analgesics.
   1. Opiates.
      a. Morphine sulfate—potent analgesic.

(1) Specific side effects: miosis (pinpoint pupils) and bradycardia.

(2) Usual dosage: 1/4 to 1/6 gr. I.M. q. 3–4 hours p.r.n.

b. Codeine sulfate—mild analgesic.

(1) Specific side effect: constipation.

(2) Usual dosage: 30 mg. to 60 mg. q. 3–4 hours I.M.

2. Synthetic opiate-like drugs.

a. Demerol (meperidine)—potent analgesic.

(1) Specific side effects: miosis or mydriasis (dilation of pupils), hypotension, and tachycardia.

(2) Usual dosage: 25 mg. to 100 mg. q. 3–4 hours I.M.

b. Talwin (pentazocine)—potent analgesic.

(1) Specific side effects: gastrointestinal disturbances, vertigo, headache, and euphoria.

(2) Usual dosage: 50 mg. oral tablets q. 3–4 hours; 30 mg. I.M. q. 3–4 hours p.r.n.

3. Nonnarcotic pain relievers.

a. Salicylates (aspirin).

(1) Decrease pain perception without causing drowsiness and euphoria. Act at point of origin or pain impulses.

(2) Side effects.

(a) GI irritation (give patient milk and crackers).

(b) GI bleeding.

(c) Increased bleeding time (watch if patient is on anticoagulants).

(d) Hypersensitivity reactions to aspirin.

(e) Tinnitus indicates toxic level reached.

(f) Thrombocytopenia can occur with overdose (especially in children).

(3) Usual dosage: 300 to 600 mg. q. 3–4 hours, orally or rectally.

b. Nonsalicylate analgesics (acetaminophen).

(1) Action similar to aspirin.

(2) Side effects: hemolytic anemia and kidney damage.

(3) Usual dosage: 325–650 mg. q. 3–4 hours orally.

Antiemetics

A. Pharmacological action.

1. Reduces the hyperactive reflex of the stomach.

2. Makes the chemoreceptor trigger zone of medulla less sensitive to nerve impulses passing through this center to the vomiting center.

B. General side effects.

1. Drowsiness.

2. Dry mouth.

3. Nervous system effects.

C. Common drugs.

1. Phenothiazines.

a. Compazine (prochlorperazine).

(1) Specific side effects: amenorrhea, hypotension, and vertigo.

(2) Normal dosage: 5–10 mg. q. 3–4 hours I.M.

b. Phenergan (promethazine).

(1) Specific side effects: dryness of mouth and blurred vision.

(2) Normal dosage: 12.5–50 mg. q. 4 hours p.r.n.

2. Nonphenothiazines.

a. Dramamine (dimenhydrinate).

(1) Specific side effect: drowsiness.

(2) Normal dosage: 50 mg. I.M. q. 3–4 hours.

b. Tigan (trimethobenzamide).

(1) Specific side effects (rare): hypotension and skin rashes.

(2) Normal dosage: 200 mg. (2 cc.) t.i.d. or q.i.d. I.M.

Common Postoperative Complications

Respiratory Complications

Clinical Manifestations

A. Complaint of tightness or fullness in chest.

B. Cough, dypsnea, or shortness of breath.

C. Increased vital signs, particularly temperature and respiratory rate.

D. Restlessness.

Prevention

A. Turn, cough, hyperventilate at least q. 2 hours.
B. Have patient use mechanical interventions to provide a means of forced-expiration exercise, especially with respiratory and cardiovascular associated conditions.
    1. Spirometers.
    2. Blow bottles and blow gloves.
    3. IPPB.
C. Provide pharmacological therapy (through nebulization or oral route).
    1. Antibiotics—to fight infection by causative organism.
    2. Bronchodilators—to act on smooth muscle to reduce bronchial spasm.
        a. Sympathomimetics (Adrenalin, Isuprel, ephedrine sulfate).
        b. Theophylline (aminophylline).
    3. Adrenocorticosteroids—to reduce inflammation (prednisone).
    4. Enzymes—to liquefy thick, purulent secretions through digestion.
        a. Dornavac.
        b. Varidase.
    5. Expectorants—to aid in expectoration of secretions.
        a. Mucolytic agents reduce viscosity of secretion (Mucomyst).
        b. Detergents liquefy tenacious mucus (Tergemist, Alevaire).
D. Medicate for pain to facilitate TCH and use of mechanical devices.

Pneumonia (see p. 78)

Atelectasis

Definition: Collapse of pulmonary alveoli caused by mucus plug or inadequate ventilation.

Clinical Manifestations

A. Usually develops 24 to 48 hours postoperative.
B. Most common cause of early postoperative temperature increase.
C. Asymmetrical chest movement.
D. Decreased or absent breath sounds over affected area; bronchial breathing over affected area.

E. Shortness of breath leading to cyanosis.
F. Painful respirations; splinting of diaphragm.
G. Increased vital signs: temperature, respiration, pulse.
H. Anxiety and restlessness.

Nursing Management

A. Auscultate breath sounds every two to four hours and report unusual occurrences.
B. Encourage coughing and deep breathing exercises; splint incision.
C. Administer oxygen if necessary.
D. Instruct in proper use of mechanical measures (blow bottles, etc.).
E. Turn frequently and position to facilitate expectoration.
F. Do clapping, percussion, vibration, postural drainage every four hours.
G. Administer expectorants and other medications, as ordered.
H. Suction as necessary.
I. Encourage oral fluid intake to reduce tenacious sputum and to facilitate expectoration.
J. Place patient in cool room with mist mask or vaporized steam.
K. Mobilize patient as soon as possible.
L. Medicate for pain to allow for respiratory ventilation.

Deep Vein Thrombophlebitis

Definition: Thrombophlebitis is the formation of a clot in a vein. It occurs most often in the left leg (due to right common iliac artery compressing the left common iliac vein). Most prevalent sites are the soleal, **poste**rior tibial, and peroneal veins.

Etiology

A. Persons most vulnerable are from forty-five to sixty-five years of age.
B. Dehydration leads to increased cellular components in vessel.
C. Decreased blood flow due to hypothermia and/or decreased metabolic rate during surgery.
D. Injury to vessel during surgery.
E. Incidence most common following abdominal or circulatory surgery or fractures of leg or pelvis.

F. Use of oral estrogens.

Clinical Manifestations

A. Red, tender calf, especially painful when climbing stairs.
B. Edema of affected ankle.
C. Increased temperature in affected area as well as generalized elevation of temperature.
D. Shiny, taut skin.
E. Homan's sign (only 60 percent accurate for diagnosis).

Nursing Management

A. Maintain strict bed rest for seven to ten days.
B. Do not use knee gatch or pillows under knees.
C. Elevate lower extremities slightly, if ordered; raise entire foot of bed.
D. Administer anticoagulants only after checking lab values.
E. Check for extension of clot.
   1. Breath sounds for possible emboli.
   2. Tenderness further up leg or in groin.
   3. Circulatory difficulties.
F. Position patient to avoid venous stasis and turn every two hours.
G. Take vital signs at least every four hours.
H. Apply hot packs, if ordered, for two to three days.
I. Use range-of-motion exercises on unaffected limbs only.
J. Do not massage or exercise affected leg unless specified by physician.
K. Apply antiembolic stocking to unaffected leg.
L. Have patient begin exercise gradually: first leg raises, then stand briefly every hour, then ambulate.
M. Medicate with salicylates and Butazolidin for pain control; watch for synergistic effect if anticoagulants are used.

Patient Education

A. Avoid standing in one position for any length of time (either walk or lie flat).
B. Avoid wearing constrictive clothing or garments.
C. Keep extremities at consistent, moderate temperature.
D. Wear support hose consistently.

E. Understand correct use of anticoagulants and the necessity for lab tests.
F. Do leg exercises when in bed.
G. Do not smoke.

Anticoagulant Therapy

A. Specific chemotherapeutic agents used to prevent intravascular thrombosis by decreasing blood coagulability.
B. Keep clotting time at 1½ to 2½ times normal.
C. Usual agents.
   1. Heparin (I.V. sub q.).
   2. Coumadin (p.o.).
D. Pharmacological action.
   1. Prevents fibrin deposits.
   2. Prevents extension of a thrombus.
   3. Prevents thromboembolic complications.
E. Major side effects of agents.
   1. Hematuria.
   2. Epistaxis.
   3. Ecchymosis.
   4. Bleeding gums.
F. Contraindications for use of drug.
   1. Blood dyscrasia.
   2. Liver and kidney disease.
   3. Peptic ulcer.
   4. Chronic ulcerative colitis.
   5. Active bleeding (except DIC).
   6. Spinal cord or brain injuries.
G. Drugs and foods to avoid when on anticoagulant therapy.
   1. Leafy green vegetables and foods high in vitamin K.
   2. Salicylates.
   3. Phenylbutazone.
   4. Reserpine.
   5. Steroids.
   6. Barbituates.
H. Safety precautions.
   1. Observe for signs of bleeding (gums, hematoma, etc.).
   2. Carry I.D. card.
   3. Keep antagonist in close proximity.
   4. Keep appointments for blood work.
   5. Do not use straight edge razors or work with equipment that could cause injuries.

Heparin

A. Mode of administration: I.V. or sub q. due to inactivation of drug when given orally.

B. Action.

1. Interferes with formation of thrombin from prothrombin.
2. Prevents thrombin from converting fibrinogen to fibrin.
3. Prevents agglutination and disintegration of platelets.
4. Dose lasts three to four hours if given I.V.

C. Lab findings.

1. Keep PTT (partial thromboplastin time) at 50 to 80 seconds (normal 39 to 53 seconds).
2. Keep clotting time at 15 to 20 minutes (normal 9 to 12 minutes).

D. Antagonist.

1. Protamine sulfate: 1 mg. protamine sulfate for each 100 u. of heparin in last dose.
2. Effective within minutes.
3. Anticoagulation therapy is reinstituted when needed.

E. Nursing management.

1. Check PTT or clotting time before administration.
2. Check patency of I.V.
3. Take following precautions when administering drug sub q. into abdomen:

   a. Use small needle.
   b. Form pouch of skin no closer than two inches around umbilicus.
   c. Administer injection at 90-degree angle.
   d. Do not aspirate syringe and needle or massage skin around injection site to prevent ecchymosis.
   e. Keep protamine sulfate easily accessible.

Coumadin

A. Mode of administration: oral.

B. Action.

1. Decreases prothrombin activity.
2. Depresses hepatic synthesis of several clotting factors.
3. Prevents utilization of vitamin K by liver.
4. Takes 24 to 72 hours for action to develop and continues for 24 to 72 hours after last dose.

C. Lab findings.

1. Keep pro time at 18 to 30 seconds (normal is 12 to 14 seconds).
2. 15 to 30 percent of normal activity.

D. Antagonist.

1. Vitamin K—aqua Mephyton I.M. or I.V.
2. Returns to hemostasis within six hours.
3. Blocks action of Coumadin for one week.

E. Nursing management.

1. Check pro time before giving.
2. Give at same time each day.
3. Teach patient to avoid foods high in vitamin K (cabbage, cauliflower, spinach, and leafy vegetables).

Types of Emboli

Pulmonary Embolism

Definition: Pulmonary embolism is caused by the movement of a thrombus from site of origin to lung.

Clinical Manifestations

A. Mild condition (involves smaller arteries).

1. Signs mimic pleurisy or bronchial pneumonia.
2. Transient dyspnea.
3. Mild pleuritic pain.
4. Tachycardia.
5. Increased temperature.
6. Cough with hemoptysis.

B. Severe condition (involves pulmonary artery).

1. Chest pain.
2. Severe dyspnea leading to air hunger.
3. Shallow, rapid breathing.
4. Sharp substernal chest pain.
5. Vertigo leading to syncope.
6. Hypovolemia.
7. Cardiac arrhythmias.
8. Generalized weakness.
9. Feelings of doom.
10. Hypotension.

Nursing Management

A. Provide patent airway.

1. Position in semi- to high-Fowler's position if vital signs allow.

2. Administer oxygen as needed (nasal cannula).
3. Assist with intubation as needed.
4. Auscultate breath sounds every one to two hours.
5. Obtain arterial blood gases to ascertain acid-base imbalance.
6. Check sputum for presence of blood or blood-tinged mucus.
7. Administer diuretics or cardiotonics, as necessary.
8. Observe for signs of shock.

B. Administer anticoagulants (check lab values each day before administering medication, following initial anticoagulation).
C. Give narcotics for pain (watch for respiratory depression).
D. Take vital signs every two to four hours.
E. Turn as directed by physician; do not do percussion or clapping or administer back rubs.
F. Encourage patient to cough and deep breathe every one to two hours.
G. Maintain bed rest; have patient avoid sudden movements.
H. Give emotional support.
I. Observe for possible extension of emboli or for occurrence of other emboli.
    1. Check urine for hematuria or oliguria.
    2. Check legs, especially calf.

Surgical Intervention

A. Surgical intervention carries high risk.
B. Types of surgery.
    1. Femoral vein ligation.
    2. Ligation of inferior vena cava.
    3. Pulmonary embolectomy.

Fat Embolism

Definition: Release of medullary fat droplets into bloodstream following trauma.

Etiology

A. Embolism occurs after long bone or sternum fractures (particularly from mishandling of patient or incorrect splinting of fracture).
B. Fat droplets which are released from the marrow enter the venous circulation, and usually become lodged in the lungs. If the fat droplets become lodged in the brain, the embolism is severe and usually fatal.
C. Usually occurs within first twenty-four hours following injury.
D. Major cause of death from fractures.
E. Prevent by adequate splinting at accident scene.

Clinical Manifestations

A. Classical sign: petechiae from fat globule deposits across chest, shoulders, and axilla. Do not blanch, but fade out within hours. Can involve conjunctiva.
B. Related pulmonary signs: shortness of breath, leading to pallor, cyanosis, and hypoxemia.
C. Related brain involvement: restlessness, memory loss, confusion, headache, hemiparesis.
D. Related cardiac involvement.
    1. Tachycardia.
    2. Right ventricular failure.
    3. Decreased cardiac output.
E. Other signs and symptoms.
    1. Diaphoresis.
    2. Change in level of consciousness.
    3. Shock.
    4. Increased temperature (if involvement of hypothalamus).

Nursing Management

A. Position patient in high-Fowler's position to allow for respiratory exchange. Maintain bed rest.
B. Administer oxygen to decrease anoxia and to reduce surface tension of fat globules (IPPB may be needed).
C. Obtain arterial blood gases to maintain sufficient pO_2 levels.
D. Physician may intubate and place on respirator if respirations are severely compromised.
E. Institute preventive treatment to avoid further complications, such as shock and heart failure.
F. Monitor administration of medications.
    1. Alcohol drip.
    2. Cortisone therapy to reduce inflammation.
    3. Decholin to emulsify fat.
    4. Antihyperlipemic drugs.
    5. Heparin to decrease platelet aggregation.
    6. Dextran to improve blood flow.

Shock Lung (Adult Respiratory Distress Syndrome, or Wet Lung)

Etiology

A. Can be secondary to viral pneumonia.

B. Massive trauma and hemorrhagic shock.

C. Fat emboli.

D. Neurological injuries

E. Sepsis.

Clinical Manifestations

A. Usually seen within first twenty-four hours following shock.

B. Pathophysiology—damage to pulmonary capillary membrane which produces a leak and diffuse interstitial edema and intra-alveolar hemorrhage.

C. Decrease in surfactant.

D. Intrapulmonary shunting with decreased oxygen saturation—hypoxia.

E. Decreased lung compliance.

F. Extreme dyspnea, tachypnea, and cyanosis.

G. Pulmonary edema.

H. Atelectasis (many small emboli throughout lungs).

I. Blood gas alterations.

   1. pO_2 decreased.

   2. pCO_2 normal or decreased due to tachypnea.

   3. pH normal to slightly alkalotic.

Nursing Management

A. Prevent overhydration in severe trauma cases.

B. Provide early treatment of severe hypoxemia.

C. Keep patients "dry," as they have excess fluids in their lungs. (Restrict fluid intake.)

D. Administer medications.

   1. Corticosteroids to reduce inflammation and to prevent further capillary membrane deterioration.

   2. Diuretics to decrease fluid overload.

   3. Sedatives to prevent patient from resisting respirator.

   4. Heparin to reduce platelet aggregation.

   5. Antibiotics.

E. Maintain adequate ventilation and oxygenation.

   1. Provide intubation and mechanical ventilation with volume respirator.

   2. Obtain frequent arterial blood gases.

   3. Suction frequently with "bagging." Ambu bag increases alveolar expansion.

F. Provide tracheostomy care, if necessary, every four hours.

G. Provide oral hygiene every four hours.

H. Prevent further complications, such as shock and septicemia.

I Provide adequate nutrition.

Wound Infections

Etiology

A. Usual causative agents.

   1. Staphylococcus.

   2. Pseudomonas aeruginosa.

   3. Proteus vulgaris.

   4. Escherichia coli.

B. Usually occur within five to seven days of surgery.

Clinical Manifestations

A. Slowly increasing temperature and tachycardia.

B. Pain and tenderness surrounding surgical site.

C. Edema and erythema surrounding suture site.

D. Increased warmth around suture site.

E. Purulent drainage.

   1. Yellow if staphylococcus.

   2. Green if Pseudomonas.

Nursing Management

A. Take all cultures before starting medication.

B. Administer specific antibiotics for causative agent.

C. Irrigate wound with solution as ordered (usually hydrogen peroxide and normal saline).

D. Keep dressing and skin area dry to prevent skin excoriation and spread of bacteria.

E. Use sterile technique in changing dressings.

F. If excoriation occurs, use karaya powder and drainage bags around area of wound.

Wound Dehiscence and Evisceration

Definition: Dehiscence is the splitting open of wound edges. Evisceration is the extensive loss of pinkish fluid (purulent if infection is present) through a wound and the protrusion of a loop of bowel through an open wound. Patient feels like "everything is pulling apart."

Etiology

A. Usual causes.
   1. General debilitation.
      a. Poor nutrition.
      b. Chronic illness.
      c. Obesity.
   2. Inadequate wound closure.
   3. Wound infection.
   4. Severe abdominal stretching (by coughing or vomiting).
B. Occurs about seventh postoperative day.

Nursing Management—Wound Dehiscence

A. Apply butterfly tapes to incision area.
B. Increase protein in diet.
C. Observe for signs of infection and treat accordingly.
D. Apply scultetus binder when ambulating.

Nursing Management—Evisceration

A. Lay patient in supine position.
B. Cover protruding intestine with moist, sterile, normal saline packs; change packs frequently to keep moist.
C. Notify physician.
D. Take vital signs for baseline data and detection of shock.
E. Notify operating room for wound closure.
F. Provide patent I.V.

Disseminated Intravascular Coagulation

Definition: Simultaneous activation of the thrombin (clotting) and fibrinolytic system.

Pathophysiology

A. Excessive intravascular thrombin is produced, which converts fibrinogen to fibrin clot.
B. After fibrinogen is used up, circulating thrombin continues to be present and will continue to convert any form of fibrinogen to fibrin.
C. Fibrinogen enters system by transfusion or by body production of fibrinogen. This process intensifies the hemorrhagic state.
D. DIC is associated with extracorporeal circulation and obstetric complications.

Clinical Manifestations

A. Arterial hypotension results in arterial vasoconstriction and capillary dilatation; this causes a shunting of blood which leads to acidotic blood formed from blood stagnation.
B. Stress is the primary cause of increased fibrinolysis.
C. Excessive bleeding (caused by depletion of clotting factors) through genitourinary tract, following injections, etc.
D. Low hemoglobin, low platelets.
E. Acidosis.
F. Skin lesions, such as petechiae, purpura, subcutaneous hematomas.

Nursing Management

A. Treat cause of DIC symptomatically.
   1. Antibiotics for infections.
   2. Fluids and colloids for shock.
   3. Steroids for endotoxins.
   4. Dialysis for renal failure.
B. Administer heparin I.V. to stop cycle of thrombosis—hemorrhage.
   1. Neutralizes free circulating thrombin.
   2. Inhibits blood clotting in vivo, due to effect on factor IX.
   3. Prevents extension of thrombi.
   4. Keep clotting time 2 to 3 times normal.
   5. Give 10,000 to 20,000 units every 2 to 4 hours.
C. Give transfusion of platelets and fresh-frozen plasma to replace clotting factors.
D. Administer oxygen as needed.
E. Take precautions to prevent additional hemorrhage.
   1. Avoid chest tube "milking."
   2. Take temperature orally or axillary, not rectally.
   3. Avoid administration of parenteral medications if possible.
   4. Avoid trauma to mucous membranes.
   5. If nasogastric tube inserted, prevent bleeding by administering antacids and keeping NG tube connected to low suction. Do not irrigate unless absolutely necessary.

Shock

Definition: Shock is an abnormal physiological state in which there is insufficient circulating blood volume for the size of the vascular bed, thereby resulting in circulatory failure and tissue anoxia.

Classifications of Shock

A. Hypovolemic.
1. Definition: decreased intravascular fluid volume.
2. Etiology.
   a. Blood loss (hematogenic)—from trauma, surgery, etc.
   b. Plasma and/or fluid loss.
      (1) Plasma loss—burns.
      (2) Fluid loss—diarrhea, vomiting, diabetes.

B. Neurogenic.
1. Definition: massive vasodilation and pooling of blood due to failure of sympathetic nerve impulses to produce vasoconstriction.
2. Etiology.
   a. Drug overdose, especially narcotics.
   b. Severe pain.
   c. Damage to medulla.
   d. Deep anesthesia.

C. Vasogenic.
1. Definition: massive vasodilation and pooling of blood due to failure of peripheral vessels to react to neural stimuli.
2. Etiology.
   a. Antigen—antibody reaction causes anaphylactic shock.
      (1) Insect stings.
      (2) Allergies to drugs, particularly antibiotics.
      (3) Blood transfusions.
      (4) Vaccines.
   b. Bacterial invasion causes gram negative sepsis (septic shock).
      (1) Following urinary tract instrumentation.
      (2) Overwhelming bacterial invasion of an "at risk" patient.

D. Cardiogenic.
1. Definition: left ventricular pump failure which results in circulatory inadequacy.

2. Etiology.
   a. Myocardial infarction.
   b. Congestive heart failure.
   c. Cardiac arrest.

Clinical Manifestations of Early Shock

A. Early stages, regardless of cause.
1. Decreased tissue perfusion.
2. Cellular hypoxia.
3. Increased sympathetic nervous system activity.

B. Oliguria—usually the first sign of shock.
1. Decreased blood volume through kidneys.
2. Decreased urine output; hyperkalemia can be a problem.

C. Hypotension.
1. Due to compensatory peripheral vasoconstriction (not evident initially, but it does appear in late shock).
2. Narrowing pulse pressure—due to systolic pressure falling and diastolic pressure being maintained.
3. Traditional criteria—systolic blood pressure below 70 mm. Hg.

D. Tachycardia—due to heart's responding to increased sympathetic activity.

E. Tachypnea.
1. Medulla is stimulated by buildup in lactic acid through anaerobic metabolism.
2. As blood pH is lowered, the respiratory rate increases in an effort to blow off excess carbon dioxide and return body to acid-base balance.

F. Cool, dry, or moist skin.
1. Caused by peripheral vasoconstriction.
2. Blood is supplied to vital organs rather than to skin.

G. Sensorium changes—due to brain cell hypoxia.
1. Restlessness.
2. Apprehension and anxiety.
3. Lethargy.
4. Confusion.
5. Semiconsciousness to coma.

H. Excessive thirst—due to loss of fluids or blood volume as well as peripheral vasoconstriction, which decreases salivary secretions.

I. Fatigue and muscle weakness—result of shift from aerobic to anaerobic metabolism leading to lactic acid buildup.

Clinical Manifestations of Severe Shock

A. Blood pressure below 70 mm. Hg and narrowing of pulse pressure (body loses ability to compensate and blood pressure drops rapidly).

B. Shallow, irregular respirations.

C. Tachycardia.

D. Unconsciousness progressing to coma as blood supply to brain cells decreases.

E. Dilated, fixed pupils due to decreased oxygen to brain.

F. Anuria as blood supply to kidneys decreases sharply.

G. Cyanotic skin, mucous membranes, and nailbeds.

Hypovolemic Shock

Degrees of Shock

A. Slight—approximately 20 percent of blood volume is lost.

B. Moderate—approximately 35 percent of blood volume is lost.

C. Severe—approximately 45 percent of blood volume is lost.

Nursing Management

A. Secure patent I.V. for drug (vasodilator), plasma expanders, I.V. fluid, or blood replacement.

B. Start I.V. fluid with D_5W. When adequate kidney function is assessed, change to Ringer's lactate (more isotonic).

C. Place patient in supine position with feet and/or head slightly elevated (Trendelenburg's position compromises venous return as well as respirations).

D. Provide oxygen via nasal catheter, mask, or cannula.

E. Record vital signs every fifteen minutes. Changes take place slowly except in massive hemorrhage.

1. Blood pressure.
   a. Decreased BP is usually late sign of shock.
   b. Orthostatic hypotension develops before systemic hypotension.
   c. Systolic BP below 80 mm. Hg. indicates inadequate coronary artery blood flow.
   d. Progressive drop in BP with a thready, increasing pulse indicates fluid loss.
   e. Decreased BP with strong, irregular pulse indicates heart failure.

2. Respirations.
   a. Become rapid and shallow early in shock (compensation for tissue anoxia).
   b. Slow breathing (below four per minute) appears late in shock after compensatory failure.
   c. Emergency respiratory equipment (ventilator, trach tubes, etc.) should be available.

3. Temperature.
   a. Below normal with hemorrhagic shock.
   b. Gradually increasing temperature indicates sepsis.

4. Central venous pressure.
   a. CVP line should be inserted in subclavian vein.
   b. If below 5 cm. H_2O indicates shock condition.
   c. If CVP decreases early it is usually a sign of shock.

F. Insert Foley catheter for hourly urine volumes.

1. Record intake and output.
2. Notify physician if total urine output is below 30 cc./hour.

G. Observe skin changes.

1. Change in skin temperature and color reflect changes in tissue oxygenation and perfusion.
   a. Cold, clammy skin indicates peripheral vascular constriction.
   b. Flushing and sweating reflects overheating, which indicates increased metabolic rate and the need for oxygen.
   c. Pallor and cyanosis indicate tissue hypoxia.
2. Observe for restlessness—indicates hypoxia.

H. Place enough light covering over patient to prevent chilling, but not enough to cause vasodilatation.

I. Treat the cause of the shock (stop bleeding, prepare for surgery, etc.).

Vasogenic Shock

A. Septic shock (warm, or toxic, shock).

1. Mortality—60 to 82 percent.
2. Caused by bacterial toxins (gm. - or +)—leads to vasodilatation.
3. Conditions leading to septic shock.
   a. Peritonitis.
   b. Urinary tract manipulations.
   c. Gas gangrene.

4. Signs/symptoms of mild infection.
   a. Fever; warm, pink face.
   b. Perspiration.
   c. Weakness, generalized aching.
5. Signs/symptoms of severe infection.
   a. High temperature (over 104°); sudden violent chills.
   b. Hemorrhage into tissue.
   c. Muscular pain.
   d. Rapid, deep respirations.
   e. Confusion and disorientation.
   f. Warm, dry skin.
6. Treatment.
   a. Broad spectrum antibiotics and then organism specific antibiotics.
   b. Systemic supportive management.
B. Anaphylactic shock.
   1. Caused by hypersensitivity to an allergen (allergic reaction to medication, bee sting, etc.).
   2. Antigen—antibody reaction.
   3. Increased cell membrane permeability—histamine is released, causing marked vasodilation.
   4. Bronchiolar constriction.
   5. Pooling of blood, causing decreased venous return.
   6. Decreased cardiac output and hypoxia.
   7. Signs/symptoms.
      a. Local edema.
      b. Urticaria (at times).
      c. Flushed face.
      d. Apprehension.
      e. Dyspnea, respiratory difficulty, cyanosis, wheezing.
      f. Vertigo, decreased blood pressure, increased pulse.
   8. Treatment.
      a. Identify causative agent.
      b. Patient positioned for optimal cerebral perfusion (flat or 30-degree elevation if dyspneic).
      c. Patent airway.
      d. Epinephrine, sub q.
         (1) Dilates bronchioles and constricts arterioles.

(2) Side effects: tachycardia, CNS stimulation.
(3) Rapid acting.
   e. Oxygen.
   f. Antihistamine (Benadryl).
      (1) Relieves itching, wheals, congestion of nasal mucosa.
      (2) Side effect: dries mucous membranes.
   g. I.V. of D_5W—as much as 2000 cc. in one hour.
   h. Corticosteroids.
      (1) Reduce formation of cellular proteins and decrease edema.
      (2) Side effects: same as any steroids.
   i. Aminophylline—bronchodilator; controls bronchospasms.

Cardiogenic Shock

Clinical Manifestations

A. Specific symptoms related to severe shock.
B. These symptoms may occur in addition to common symptoms of shock.
   1. Cardiac arrhythmias leading to cardiac arrest.
   2. CVP above 15 cm. water pressure.
   3. Heart failure symptoms.
      a. Orthopnea.
      b. Cyanosis.
      c. Dyspnea.
      d. Pitting edema.
      e. Distended neck veins.
      f. Pulmonary congestion.
   4. Acidosis.
   5. Hypokalemia.

Nursing Management (see p. 196)

A. Administer digitalis preparation in addition to diuretics.
B. Watch for hypokalemia and arrhythmias.
C. Administer vasodilators or vasopressors, as ordered.
D. Check arterial blood gases frequently.
E. Utilize intra-aortic balloon.

Homeostatic Mechanisms

Body Fluids and Electrolytes

Physiology

A. Body fluids (including excesses and deficits).
   1. Intracellular—fluid within the cell (40 percent).
   2. Extracellular—fluid outside of the cell (5 percent).
   3. Interstitial—fluid between the cells (15 percent).
   4. Percent varies with age and amount of fat.
       a. Newborn—83 percent of baby's weight is water.
       b. Thin person has more water.

B. Electrolytes.
   1. Anions—negatively charged ions (Cl^-, HCO_3^-).
   2. Cations—positively charged ions (Na^+, K^+, Ca^{++}).
   3. Equal number of cations and anions (154 each).

C. Transport of fluids and electrolytes.
   1. Diffusion—movement of solutes (substances that are dissolved in a solution) or gases from an area of higher concentration to an area of lower concentration; a passive transport system.
   2. Filtration—passage of fluids through a semipermeable membrane as a result of a difference in hydrostatic pressures (pressure exerted by a fluid within a closed system).
   3. Osmosis—passage of water or solvent through a semipermeable membrane from an area of lesser concentration to an area of greater concentration of solute; a passive transport system.

Fluid Imbalances

Dehydration and Circulatory Overload

A. Dehydration (extracellular fluid volume deficit).
   1. Causes.
       a. Vomiting, diarrhea.
       b. Increased urine output.
       c. Diuretics.
       d. Excessive loss through respiration.
       e. Insufficient I.V. replacement.
   2. Clinical manifestations.
       a. Loss of skin turgor (after being pinched and lightly pulled upward, skin returns to normal very slowly).
       b. Thirst.
       c. Dry, warm skin.
       d. Febrile (usually means there is fluid loss through perspiration).
       e. Cracked lips, dry mucous membranes.
       f. Decreased urinary output (normal output is 30 cc./hr.).
       g. Concentrated urine—dark amber color and odorous.
       h. Weight loss.
       i. Low central venous pressure.
       j. Increased respiration.

B. Circulatory overload (extracellular volume excess).
   1. Causes.
       a. Excessive I.V. fluids.
       b. Inadequate kidney function.
   2. Clinical manifestations.
       a. Headache.
       b. Flushed skin.
       c. Tachycardia.
       d. Venous distention, particularly neck veins.
       e. Increased blood pressure and CVP.
       f. Tachypnea (increased respiratory rate), coughing, dyspnea (shortness of breath), cyanosis, and pulmonary edema.

Electrolyte Imbalances

Potassium Imbalance

A. Normal serum level is 3.5–5.5 mEq./l.

B. Potassium deficiency and excess is a common problem in fluid and electrolyte imbalance.

C. Major cell cation.

D. Signs and symptoms of potassium excess (*hyperkalemia*).
   1. Weakness, flaccid paralysis.
   2. Hyperreflexia proceeding to paralysis.
   3. Bradycardia, arrhythmias.
   4. Ventricular fibrillation.
   5. ECG changes depict elevated or tented T wave; widened QRS; complex, prolonged P-R interval; and flattened P wave with depressed S-T segment.
   6. Oliguria.

E. Causes of excess potassium levels.
  1. Usually renal disease (cannot excrete potassium).
  2. Burns (due to cellular destruction releasing potassium from cells into extracellular space).
  3. Crushing injuries (due to cellular breakage releasing potassium from cells).
F. Nursing management of hyperkalemia.
  1. Administer diuretics if kidney function adequate.
  2. Administer hypertonic I.V. glucose with insulin.
  3. Provide exchange resins through NG or enema (Kayexalate).
  4. Provide calcium I.V. to stimulate heart if depressed action.
G. Signs and symptoms of potassium deficiency (*hypokalemia*).
  1. Muscle weakness, muscle pain, hyporeflexia.
  2. Hypotension.
  3. Arrhythmias—PVC's particularly.
  4. Anorexia advancing to nausea, vomiting.
  5. Apathy, drowsiness leading to coma.
  6. ECG changes include peaked P wave, flat T wave, depressed S-T segment, and elevated U waves.
  7. Paralytic ileus.
H. Causes of hypokalemia.
  1. Renal loss most common (usually caused by use of diuretics).
  2. Insufficient potassium intake.
  3. Loss from gastrointestinal tract via NG tube placement without replacement electrolyte solution, or from vomiting or diarrhea.
I. Nursing management of hypokalemia.
  1. Maintain I.V.'s with KC1 added.
  2. Replace K^+ when excess loss occurs (NG tubes, diarrhea, etc.).
  3. Replace no more than 20 mEq./KCl in one hour; observe ECG monitor if possible.
  4. Dilute KC1 in 30-50 cc. I.V. fluid via volutral.
  5. Observe for adequate urine output.
J. General nursing management related to potassium imbalances.
  1. Observe ECG tracings for change in T wave, S-T segment, or QRS complex.
  2. Measure intake and output accurately.
  3. Draw frequent blood specimens for potassium level.

  4. Observe for signs of metabolic acidosis and alkalosis.

Sodium Imbalance

A. Normal serum level is 135-145 mEq./l.
B. Sodium deficiency and excess is a common problem in fluid and electrolyte imbalance.
C. Causes of hypernatremia.
  1. Excessive administration of sodium chloride.
  2. Renal failure.
  3. Cirrhosis of liver.
  4. Congestive heart failure.
  5. Overproduction of aldosterone.
  6. Steroid administration.
D. Signs and symptoms of excessive sodium levels (*hypernatremia*).
  1. Signs and symptoms are same as for extracellular fluid excesses.
    a. Pitting edema.
    b. Excessive weight gain.
    c. Increased blood pressure.
    d. Dyspnea.
  2. If hypernatremia is due to dehydration, in which there is a loss of fluid thereby increasing the number of ions, the signs and symptoms include:
    a. Concentrated urine and oliguria.
    b. Dry mucous membranes.
    c. Thirst.
    d. Flushed skin.
    e. Increased temperature.
    f. Tachycardia.
E. Signs and symptoms of sodium deficiency (*hyponatremia*).
  1. Signs and symptoms are the same as those for extracellular fluid deficiency.
    a. Weakness.
    b. Restlessness.
    c. Delirium.
    d. Hyperpnea.
    e. Oliguria.
    f. Increased temperature.
    g. Flushed skin.
    h. Abdominal cramps.
    i. Convulsions.
  2. If sodium is lost but fluid is not, the following signs and symptoms will be present (similar to those of water excess).

a. Mental confusion.
b. Headache.
c. Muscle twitching and weakness.
d. Coma.
e. Convulsions.
f. Oliguria.

F. Causes of hyponatremia.
1. Excessive perspiration.
2. Use of diuretics.
3. Gastrointestinal losses.
4. Lack of sodium in diet.
5. Burns.
6. Excessive I.V. administration without NaC1.
7. Diabetic acidosis.

G. Nursing management related to sodium imbalances.
1. Hypernatremia.
   a. Record intake and output.
   b. Restrict sodium in diet.
   c. Weigh daily.
   d. Observe vital signs.
2. Hyponatremia.
   a. Administer I.V. fluids with sodium.
   b. Maintain accurate intake and output.

General Nursing Management for Fluid and Electrolyte Imbalance

A. Take central venous pressure to determine fluid balance if CVP catheter is in place. The CVP reflects the competency of the heart (particularly the right side) to handle the volume of blood returning to it.
1. CVP indicates the comparison of the pumping capacity of the heart and the volume of the circulating blood.
2. Normal CVP reading: 5-10 cm. H_2O.
3. Increased CVP (above 15 cm. H_2O) can be indicative of congestive heart failure or circulatory overload.
4. Decreased CVP (below 5 cm. H_2O) is indicative of hypovolemia (decreased fluid volume) whether from blood loss or other fluid losses.

B. Observe patient's condition every two hours.
1. Check condition of skin.
   a. Dry, warm, cracked lips.
   b. Elasticity.
2. Check body temperature—fever suggests loss of body fluids.
3. Check for venous distention.

4. Ask patient about unusual related symptoms, if possible, such as headache, shortness of breath.
5. Check urine output at least every eight hours for maintenance I.V. therapy, or as often as every hour for replacement fluid administration.
6. Check for symptoms of electrolyte disturbances at least every four hours.

Acid-Base Regulation

Normal Acid–Base Balance

Principles

A. Acid-base balance is the ratio of acids and bases in the body necessary in order to maintain a chemical balance conducive to life.
B. Acid-base ratio is 20 base to 1 acid.
C. Acid-base balance is measured by arterial blood samples and recorded as blood pH. Range is 7.35 to 7.45.
D. Acids are hydrogen ion donors. They release hydrogen ions to neutralize or decrease the strength of the base.
E. Bases are hydrogen ion acceptors. They accept hydrogen ions to convert strong acids to weak acids (for example, hydrochloric acid is converted to carbonic acid).

Regulatory Mechanisms

A. The body controls the pH balance by use of:
1. Chemical buffers.
2. Lungs.
3. Cells.
4. Kidneys.
B. The chemical buffer system works fastest, but other regulatory mechanisms provide more reliable protection against acid-base imbalance.
1. A buffer is a substance that reacts to keep pH within normal limits. It functions only when excessive base or acid is present.
2. Chemical buffers are paired (for example weakly ionized acid or base is balanced with a fully ionized salt).
   a. Pairing prevents excessive changes in normal acid-base balance.

b. The buffers release or absorb hydrogen ions when needed.

3. The buffer systems in the extracellular fluid react quickly with acids and bases to minimize changes in pH.

   a. Once they react, they are used up.
   b. If further stress occurs, the body is less able to cope.

4. There are three primary buffer systems.

   a. Bicarbonate—maintains blood pH at 7.4 with ratio of 20 parts bicarbonate to 1 part carbonic acid.
   b. Plasma proteins—vary the amounts of hydrogen ions in the chemical structure of the protein (along with liver). They can both attract and release hydrogen ions.
   c. Hemoglobin—maintains the balance by the chloride shift. Chloride shifts in and out of red blood cells according to the level of oxygen in the blood plasma. Each chloride ion that leaves the cell is replaced by a bicarbonate ion.

C. Lungs.

1. Next to react are the lungs.
2. It takes ten to thirty minutes for lungs to inactivate hydrogen molecules by converting them to water molecules.
3. The carbonic acid that was formed by neutralizing bicarbonate is taken to lungs.

   a. There it is reduced to carbon dioxide and water and exhaled.
   b. Therefore, when there is excessive acid in the body, the respiratory rate increases in order to blow off the excessive carbon dioxide and water.

4. When there is too much bicarbonate or base in the body, the respiration becomes deeper and slower.

   a. This process builds up the level of carbonic acid.
   b. The result is the strength of the excessive bicarbonate is neutralized.

5. Lungs can only inactivate the hydrogen ions carried by carbonic acid. The other ions must be excreted by the kidneys.

D. Cells.

1. They absorb or release extra hydrogen ions.
2. They react in two to four hours.

E. Kidneys.

1. They are the mainstay of regulatory mechanisms.
2. Excretion of excessive acid or base is slow. Compensation takes a few hours to several days, but it is more effective.
3. Primary function of kidneys is bicarbonate regulation. They restore bicarbonate by releasing hydrogen ions and holding bicarbonate ions.

Acid-Base Imbalances

Metabolic Acidosis

Definition: Metabolic acidosis occurs when there is a deficit of bases or an accumulation of fixed acids.

A. Changes in pH and serum carbon dioxide.

1. The pH will become acidotic as a result of insufficient base.

   a. Therefore, it falls below 7.35.
   b. There are either more hydrogen ions or less bicarbonate ions present in the blood.

2. The serum CO_2 level will be below 22 mEq./l (normal range of CO_2 is 26-28 mEq./l).

   a. Serum CO_2 measures the amount of circulating bicarbonate.
   b. Serum CO_2 will be decreased due to the depletion of the bicarbonate ion in the neutralization process of the extra acids.
   c. In lab reports, the CO_2 may be reported as: HCO_3, CO_2 content, or CO_2 combining power, depending on the laboratory.
   d. Laboratory values will vary depending on the methods used for analysis.
   e. Normal ranges:

      (1) HCO_3: 22-26 mEq./l.
      (2) CO_2 content: 26-28 mEq./l.
      (3) CO_2 combining power: 58 volume percent.

B. Compensatory mechanisms.

1. When compensating for metabolic acidosis the one clinical manifestation usually observed is: "blowing off" excessive acids. This can be noted by a respiratory rate increase.
2. The lungs are the fastest mechanism used to compensate for metabolic acidosis.

   a. If the lungs are involved, as in respiratory

acidosis, they cannot function as a compensatory mechanism.

   b. Therefore, the kidneys must take over and the process is much slower.

C. Laboratory values.

   1. The partial pressure of the blood gas carbon dioxide (pCO_2) will decrease below 35 mm. of pressure when the patient is compensating. (Normal values: 35–45 mm. pressure.)

   2. The partial pressure of oxygen (pO_2) is usually increased due to increased respiratory rate. (Normal values pO_2: 90–100 mm. of pressure.)

   3. The serum potassium level is increased with acidosis, due primarily to the cause of the acidosis.

     a. For example, patients can go into metabolic acidosis from severe diarrhea.

     b. When this condition is present, the potassium moves out of the cell and into the extravascular space due to the dehydration process.

   4. Sodium and chloride levels may be decreased. Again, this is usually due to excessive loss through urine or gastrointestinal disorders.

   5. Laboratory values when a patient is in metabolic acidosis and in the compensatory state.

     a. Metabolic acidosis.
       (1) pH: 7.30.
       (2) HCO_3: 16 mEq./l.
       (3) pCO_2: 38 mm.
       (4) pO_2: 95 mm.
       (5) Cl: 120 mEq./l.
       (6) K: 5.5 mEq./l.

     b. Compensated metabolic acidosis.
       (1) pH: 7.40.
       (2) HCO_3: 16 mEq./l.
       (3) pCO_2: 20 mm.

D. Causes of metabolic acidosis (seen particularly in the surgical patient).

   1. Diabetes—diabetic ketoacidosis.

     a. When insufficient insulin is produced or administered to metabolize carbohydrates, increased fat metabolism will result, thus producing excess accumulations of ketones and other acids.

     b. This is the most common problem associated with metabolic acidosis in the surgical patient.

   2. Renal insufficiency—kidneys retain the products of protein metabolism, thereby decreasing the bicarbonate that is available to maintain an acid-base balance.

   3. Diarrhea—excessive amounts of base are lost from the intestines and pancreas, resulting in acidosis.

E. Clinical manifestations.

   1. Headache.
   2. Drowsiness.
   3. Nausea, vomiting, diarrhea.
   4. Stupor, coma.
   5. Twitching, convulsions.
   6. Kussmaul's respiration (increased respiratory rate).
   7. Fruity breath (as evidence in diabetic ketoacidosis as a result of improper fat metabolism).

F. Nursing and medical management.

   1. Administer sodium bicarbonate intravenously to alkalize the patient and return patient to normal acid-base balance as quickly as possible.

     a. Usual dosage: 1–3 ampules of 50 mEq. bicarbonate/ampule.

     b. This is usually the immediate treatment rendered for metabolic acidosis.

   2. Administer sodium lactate solution to increase the base level.

     a. Sodium lactate is converted to bicarbonate by the liver.

     b. Lactated Ringer's I.V. solution may be used.

   3. In ketoacidosis, administer insulin, which will move glucose out of the blood serum and into the cell, thereby decreasing ketosis. Insulin decreases ketones by decreasing the release of fatty acids from fat cells.

   4. Watch laboratory values closely while treating metabolic acidosis.

   5. Watch for signs of hyperkalemia and dehydration in the patient (oliguria, vital sign changes, etc.).

   6. Record intake and output.

Metabolic Alkalosis

Definition: Metabolic alkalosis is a malfunction of metabolism, causing an increase in blood base or a reduction of available acids in the serum.

A. Changes in pH and serum carbon dioxide.

1. The pH will become more alkaline; therefore, it will be above 7.45.
2. The CO_2 will also increase above 35 mEq./l. Note that this measures the amount of circulating bicarbonate or the base portion of the plasma. (A good way to remember these acid-base values is to recall that as the pH increases, so does the CO_2. The reverse is true for acidosis.)
3. The pCO_2 will not change unless the lungs attempt to compensate.
4. Serum potassium and chloride levels will decrease, due to the basic cause of the alkalosis, whether it be excessive vomiting or the use of diuretics.

B. Compensatory mechanisms.
1. The lungs will attempt to hold on to the carbonic acid in an effort to neutralize the base state; therefore, the rate of respiration will decrease.
2. When the lungs are compensating for the alkalotic state, the pCO_2 will increase above 45 mEq./l.

C. Laboratory values when patient is in metabolic alkalosis and compensatory states.
1. Metabolic alkalosis.
   a. pH: 7.50.
   b. HCO_3: 38 mEq./l.
   c. pCO_2: 38 mm. pressure.
   d. pO_2: 95 mm. pressure.
   e. K: 3.0 mEq./l.
   f. Cl: 88 mEq./l.
2. Compensated metabolic alkalosis.
   a. pH: 7.40.
   b. HCO_3: 38 mEq./l.
   c. pCO_2: 50 mm. pressure.
   d. pO_2: 95 mm. pressure.

D. Causes of metabolic alkalosis.
1. Ingestion of excessive soda bicarbonate (used by individuals for acid indigestion).
2. Excessive vomiting which results in the loss of hydrochloric acid and potassium.
3. Placement of NG tubes which causes a depletion of both hydrochloric acid and potassium.
4. Use of potent diuretics, particularly by cardiac patients. They tend to lose not only potassium but also hydrogen and chloride ions, causing an increase in the bicarbonate level of the serum.

E. Clinical manifestations.
1. Nausea, vomiting, diarrhea.
2. Irritability, agitation, coma, convulsions.
3. Restlessness and twitching of extremities.
4. ECG changes indicate tachycardia, with the T wave running into the P wave.

F. Nursing management.
1. Maintain diet of foods high in potassium and chloride (bananas, apricots, dried peaches, Brazil nuts, dried figs, oranges).
2. Administer I.V. solution of added electrolytes.
   a. Estimate the potassium loss from gastric fluid at 5-10 mEq. for each liter lost.
   b. In many institutions, the gastric fluid loss is replaced cc. for cc. every two to four hours.
   c. In other institutions, the approximate electrolyte loss is calculated and this amount is added to the twenty-four hour I.V. solution.
3. Give Diamox to promote kidney excretion of bicarbonate.
4. Administer potassium chloride maintenance doses to patients on long-term diuretics.
5. Give ammonium chloride to increase the amount of available hydrogen ions, thereby increasing the availability of acids in the blood.
6. Check laboratory values frequently to watch for electrolyte imbalance.
7. Watch patient for physical signs indicative of hypokalemia or metabolic alkalosis.
8. Keep accurate records of intake and output and vital signs.

Respiratory Acidosis

Definition: Respiratory acidosis refers to increased carbonic acid concentration (accumulated CO_2 which has combined with water) caused by retention of carbon dioxide through hypoventilation. Differs from metabolic acidosis in that it is caused by defective functioning of the lungs.

A. Changes in pH, pCO_2, and pO_2.
1. With an increased acidic state, the pH will fall below 7.35.
2. The pCO_2 will be increased above 50 mm. Hg.
3. The pO_2 will be normal (90-100 mm. Hg) or it can be decreased as hypoxia increases.

4. The HCO_3 will be normal if respiratory acidosis is uncompensated.

B. Compensatory mechanisms.

1. Because the basic problem in respiratory acidosis is a defect in the lungs, the kidneys must be the major compensatory mechanism.

   a. The kidneys work much slower than the lungs.

   b. Therefore, it will take from hours to days for the compensation to take place.

2. The kidneys will retain bicarbonate and return it to the extracellular fluid compartment.

3. The bicarbonate level will be elevated with partial or complete compensation.

C. Laboratory values when patient is in respiratory acidosis and compensated acidosis.

1. Respiratory acidosis.

   a. pH: 7.32.

   b. pCO_2: 52 mm. Hg.

   c. pO_2: 90 mm. Hg.

   d. HCO_3: 24 mEq./l.

2. Compensated acidosis.

   a. pH: 7.35.

   b. pCO_2: 50 mm. Hg.

   c. pO_2: 90 mm. Hg.

   d. HCO_3: 36 mEq./l.

D. Causes of respiratory acidosis.

1. Sedatives.

2. Over-sedation with narcotics in postoperative period.

3. A chronic pulmonary disorder such as emphysema, asthma, bronchitis, or pneumonia leading to:

   a. Inability of the lungs to expand and contract adequately.

   b. Difficulty in the expiratory phase of respirations, leading to retention of carbon dioxide.

4. Poor gaseous exchange during surgery.

E. Clinical manifestations.

1. Dyspnea after exertion.

2. Hyperventilation when at rest.

3. Cyanosis.

4. Sensorium changes (drowsiness leading to coma).

5. Carbon dioxide narcosis.

   a. When body has adjusted to higher carbon dioxide levels, the respiratory center loses its sensitivity to elevated carbon dioxide.

   b. Medulla fails to respond to high levels of carbon dioxide.

   c. Patient is forced to depend on anoxia for respiratory stimulus.

   d. If a high level of oxygen is administered, patient will cease breathing.

F. Nursing and medical management.

1. Turn, cough, and hyperventilate patient at least every two to four hours postoperatively. Use oralpharyngeal suction if necessary.

2. When pulmonary complications present a threat, do postural drainage, percussion, and vibration, followed by suctioning.

3. Keep patient well hydrated to facilitate removal of secretions. If patient is dehydrated, secretions become thick and more difficult to expectorate.

4. Watch vital signs carefully, particularly rate and depth of respirations.

5. Teach pursed-lip breathing to chronic respiratory patients.

6. If oxygen is administered, watch carefully for signs of carbon dioxide narcosis.

7. Place patient on mechanical ventilation if necessary.

8. Administer aerosol medications through IPPB.

   a. Bronchodilators (aminophylline)—relieve bronchospasms.

   b. Detergents (tergemist)—liquefy tenacious mucus.

   c. Antibiotics specific to causative agent.

9. Drug therapy.

   a. Sodium bicarbonate I.V. (0.25 gm./Kg. body weight).

   b. Sodium lactate I.V.

   c. Ringer's lactate I.V. to replace electrolyte loss.

Respiratory Alkalosis

Definition: Respiratory alkalosis occurs when an excessive amount of carbon dioxide is exhaled, usually caused by hyperventilation. The loss of carbon dioxide results in a decrease in H^+ concentration along with a decrease in pCO_2 and an increase in the ratio of bicarbonate to carbonic acid. The result is an increase in the pH level.

A. Changes in pH, pCO_2, and pO_2.

1. With an increased alkalotic state, the pH will increase above 7.45, indicating there is a decreased amount of carbonic acid in the serum.
2. The pCO_2 will be normal-to-low, as this measures the acid portion of the acid-base system (30–45 mm. Hg).
3. The pO_2 should be unchanged.
4. The bicarbonate level (HCO_3 or CO_2 content) should be normal unless the patient is compensating.

B. Compensatory mechanisms.

1. Since the basic problem is related to the respiratory system, the kidneys will compensate by excreting more bicarbonate ions and retaining H^+.
2. This process will return the acid-base balance to a normal ratio.

C. Laboratory values when patient is in respiratory alkalosis and compensated alkalosis.

1. Respiratory alkalosis.
   a. pH: 7.51.
   b. pCO_2: 32 mm. pressure.
   c. pO_2: 95 mm. Hg.
   d. HCO_3: 24 mEq./l.
2. Compensated alkalosis.
   a. pH: 7.45.
   b. pCO_2: 30 mm. pressure.
   c. pO_2: 95 mm. Hg.
   d. HCO_3: 18 mEq./l.

D. Causes of respiratory alkalosis.

1. Hysteria —patient hyperventilates and exhales excessive amounts of carbon dioxide.
2. Hypoxia—stimulates patient to breathe more vigorously.
3. Following head injuries or intracranial surgery.
4. Increased temperature.
5. Salicylate poisoning.
   a. Stimulation of respiration causes alkalosis through hyperventilation.
   b. Acidosis may occur from excessive salicylates in the blood.

E. Clinical manifestations—increased neuromuscular irritability.

1. Hyperreflexia.
2. Muscular twitching.

3. Convulsions.
4. Gasping for breath.

F. Nursing and medical management.

1. Eliminate cause of hyperventilation.
2. Remain with patient and be supportive to reduce anxiety.
3. Use rebreathing bag to return patient's carbon dioxide to self (paper bag works just as well).

Neurological System

Intracranial Surgery

Preoperative and Postoperative Care

Preoperative Care

A. Observe and record neurological symptoms relative to site of problem (clot, lesion, aneurysm, etc.); for example:

1. Paralysis.
2. Seizure foci.
3. Pupillary response.

B. Prepare patient physically and psychologically for surgery.

1. Prep and shave cranial hair (save hair).
2. Apply scrub solution to scalp, as ordered.
3. Avoid using enemas unless specifically ordered; the strain of defecation can lead to increased intracranial pressure.
4. Explain postoperative routine orders such as neurological checks and headaches.
5. Administer steroids or mecurial diuretics as ordered, to decrease cerebral edema.
6. Insert NG tube and/or Foley catheter, as ordered.

General Postoperative Care

A. Observe neurological signs.

1. Evaluate level of consciousness.
   a. Orientation to time and place.
   b. Response to painful stimuli.

(1) Pinching Achilles tendon.

(2) Testing with safety pin.

   c. Ability to follow verbal command.

2. Evaluate pupil size and reactions to light.

   a. Are pupils equal, not constricted or dilated.

   b. Do pupils react to light.

   c. Do pupils react sluggishly or are they fixed.

3. Evaluate strength and motion of extremities.

   a. Are handgrasps present and equal.

   b. Are handgrasps strong or weak.

   c. Can patient move all extremities on command.

   d. Are movements purposeful or involuntary.

   e. Do the extremities have twitching, flaccid, or spastic movements (indicative of a neurological problem).

B. Observe vital signs.

1. Keep patient normothermic to decrease metabolic needs of the brain.

2. Observe respirations for depth and rate to prevent respiratory acidosis from anoxia.

3. Observe blood pressure and pulse for signs of shock or increased intracranial pressure.

C. Evaluate reflexes.

1. Babinski—positive Babinski is elicited by stroking the lateral aspect of the sole of the foot, backward flexion of the great toe or spreading of other toes.

   a. Most important pathological reflex in neurology.

   b. If positive, indicative of pyramidal tract involvement (usually upper motor neuron lesion).

2. Romberg—when patient stands with feet close together, he falls off balance. If positive, may have cerebellar, proprioceptive, or vestibular difficulties.

3. Kernig—patient is lying down with thigh flexed at a right angle; extension of the leg upward results in spasm of hamstring muscle, pain, and resistance to additional extension of leg at the knee (indicative of meningitis).

D. Watch for headache, double vision, nausea, or vomiting.

Nursing Management

A. Maintain patent airway.

1. Oxygen deprivation and an increase of carbon dioxide may produce cerebral hypoxia and cause cerebral edema.

2. Intubate if values indicate to be necessary:

   a. pO_2 below 80 mm. Hg.

   b. pCO_2 above 50 mm. Hg.

B. Suction if necessary, but not through nose without specific order.

C. Maintain adequate oxygenation and humidification.

D. Place patient in semi-prone or semi-Fowler's position (or totally on side). Turn every two hours, side to side.

E. Maintain fluid and electrolytes.

1. Do not give fluid by mouth to semiconscious or unconscious patient.

2. Weigh to determine fluid loss.

3. Administer I.V. fluids slowly; overhydration leads to cerebral edema.

F. Record accurate intake and output.

G. Watch serial blood and urine samples; sodium regulation disturbances accompany head injuries.

H. Keep temperature down with cooling blanket if necessary. If temperature is down, the metabolic requirement of brain as well as oxygen requirements are less.

I. Take vital signs and neuro signs every fifteen to thirty minutes until stable.

J. Use seizure precautions.

K. Provide hygienic care, including oral hygiene.

L. Observe dressing for unusual drainage (bleeding, cerebral spinal fluid).

M. Prevent straining with bowel movements.

Medications Frequently Used

A. Steroids.

1. Decreases cerebral edema by their antiinflammatory effect.

2. Decrease capillary permeability in inflammatory process, thus decreasing leakage of fluid into tissue.

B. Mannitol.

1. Decreases cerebral edema.

2. Diuretic action by carrying out large volume of water through the nephron.

3. Complications of therapy are fluid and electrolyte imbalance.

C. Dilantin.

1. Prevents seizures through depression of the motor areas of the brain.
2. Side effects include gastrointestinal symptoms and rash.

D. Valium.

1. For relief of restlessness.
2. To decrease seizure activity.

E. Phenobarbital.

1. Reduces responsiveness of normal neurons to the nervous impulses arising in the focal site.
2. Side effects are drowsiness, ataxia, nystagmus.
3. Toxic effects produce rash but usually no nausea and vomiting.

Neurosurgical Postoperative Complications

Increased Intracranial Pressure

A. Clinical manifestations.

1. As intracranial pressure increases, brain becomes compressed.
2. Change in level of consciousness—observe for responsiveness.
3. Watch for lethargy, slurring speech, slow response.
4. Changes in condition (often rapid change).
   a. Patient becomes restless.
   b. Patient becomes confused.
   c. Increased drowsiness.
   d. Stupor to coma.
5. Changes in vital signs.
   a. Pulse decreases to 60 (or occasionally increases above 100).
   b. Respiratory irregularities—decreased rate with lengthening periods of apnea progresses to Cheyne-Stokes or Kussmaul.
   c. Blood pressure increases with wide pulse pressure (difference between systolic and diastolic).
   d. Moderately elevated temperature.
6. Headache.
7. Vomiting.
8. Pupil changes—increasing pressure or an expanding clot can displace the brain against the oculomotor or optic nerve.

B. Nursing management.

1. Inform physician of any vital sign changes or sensorium changes.
2. Observe intake and output for possible fluid overload leading to cerebral edema.
3. Observe surgical incision site for sign of edema.
4. Administer diuretics or steroids to decrease edema.
5. Administer anticonvulsant drugs if ordered.
6. Have spinal or ventricular puncture tray available to drain off cerebral spinal fluid if necessary.

Seizures

A. Grand mal.

1. Jacksonian or focal—precipitated by organic lesions in motor or sensory cortex.
   a. Watch carefully when these seizures start, in order to find focal point.
   b. Begins with convulsive twitching starting in distal portion of one part of extremity, moving centrally to other areas of body.
2. Typical grand mal seizures.
   a. Tonic-clonic type.
      (1) Clonic—alternating between contraction and relaxation of muscle.
      (2) Tonic—tension or contraction of muscle.
   b. Usually have prodromal stage in which patient experiences vague changes.
   c. Aura.
      (1) Brief sensory experience in beginning of seizure.
      (2) Usually related to area of the origin of seizure.
   d. Epileptic cry.
   e. Convulsion.
   f. Postictal state.

B. Petit mal (usually not seen in neurosurgical patients).

1. Usually starts between ages three to ten; seldom starts past age twenty.
2. Manifestations.
   a. Brief loss of consciousness.
   b. Person stops whatever he is doing, stares blankly, then eyes deviate slightly.
   c. Person may stagger but usually does not fall.

d. Person may lose bladder and bowel control.

e. Following the episode, person is alert.

f. Seizure lasts one to two seconds up to 90 seconds.

3. Nursing management.

a. Administer drugs as a preventative measure for further episodes (Dilantin, phenobarbital, etc.).

b. Provide safe environment.

(1) Pad side rails.

(2) Position person on floor with head protected.

(3) Do not restrain during seizure.

(4) Use tongue blade to prevent tongue from falling back into throat.

c. Observe and record.

(1) Activities preceding the seizure (aura, movements, etc.).

(2) Type of movements and area of body involved.

(3) Incontinence.

(4) Any unconsciousness during seizure.

(5) Length of seizure.

(6) Conditions following seizure.

(a) Somnolent.

(b) Continuation of previous activities.

(c) Awareness of seizure activity.

d. Provide privacy during seizure.

Hemorrhage

Clinical manifestations same as for increased intracranial pressure or seizures, depending on cause and area involved.

Brain Abscess or Wound Infection

A. Clinical manifestations.

1. Increased temperature unless abscess walled off, in which case temperature can be subnormal.

2. Headache.

3. Neurological deficits relative to area involved (focal seizures, blurred vision, etc.).

4. Increased intracranial pressure.

B. Nursing management.

1. Observe neurological signs.

2. Decrease temperature.

a. Sponge bath.

b. Antipyretic drugs (Tylenol).

c. Cooling blanket.

3. Administer appropriate antibiotics for causative agent.

Precautions for Care of Neurosurgical Patient

A. Do not lower head in Trendelenburg position or place in supine position.

B. Do not suction through nose without specific order.

C. Be careful when administering sedations and narcotics.

1. Cannot evaluate neurological status.

2. May cause respiratory embarrassment.

D. Do not give oral fluids unless patient fully awake.

E. Do not administer enemas or cathartics (may cause straining, therefore increasing intracranial pressure).

F. Do not place on operative side if large tumor or bone removed.

Eye and Ear

Eye Surgery

Cataract Surgery

Etiology

A. Clouding, or opacity, of the lens that leads to blurring vision and eventual loss of sight.

B. Opacity is due to chemical changes in the protein of the lens caused by the slow degenerative changes of age, by injury, poison, or intraocular infection.

Surgical Procedure

A. Usually based on individual needs, that is, how much the patient can see out of the other eye.

1. If any inflammation is present, surgery is not performed.

2. Cataracts are removed under local anesthesia.

3. Some simple cataracts are removed by use of alpha-chymotrypsin, which weakens the zonular fibers that hold the lens in position.

4. Surgery is performed on one eye at a time.

B. Types of surgery.

1. Intracapsular technique of removal: the lens is removed within its capsule.

2. Extracapsular: an opening is made in the capsule and the lens is lifted out without disturbing the membrane.

3. Cryoextraction: the lens is frozen with a probe —cooled to a temperature of –35°C or lower— and then lifted from its position in the eye.

C. All surgeries are preceded by an iridectomy, which creates an opening for the flow of aqueous humor.

Nursing Management of Postoperative Care

A. Prevent clinical manifestations of:
1. Nausea and vomiting.
2. Restlessness.
3. Coughing.

B. Observe for:
1. Shock.
2. Hemorrhage from the eye.
3. Sudden pain in the eye.

C. Apply dressing and shield to prevent injury to the operative eye. The unoperative eye is usually left uncovered.

D. Dressing is changed by the doctor on the first to third postoperative day; the dressing is removed on the seventh to tenth day.

E. Keep patient flat or in low-Fowler's position the day of surgery.

F. Get patient out of bed the first postoperative day.

G. Turn patient on unoperative side if ordered; if patient cannot be turned, use sandbags to position head. Do not allow patient to bend over.

H. Temporary glasses are prescribed, one to four weeks postoperatively.

Specific Adjustment Problems

A. When the lens is removed, the eye cannot accommodate and glasses must be worn at all times.

B. Cataract glasses magnify so that everything appears to be one-fourth closer than it is, so the patient must be taught to accommodate to this situation.
1. It takes time to learn to judge distance and climb stairs.
2. Color as seen by the eye from which a cataract has been removed is slightly changed.
3. If the patient has had the lens removed from one eye only, he will use only one eye at a time and not both together unless he is fitted with a contact lens for the operative eye.

C. The patient should wait three months before getting permanent glasses.

Retinal Detachment

Etiology

A. The retina is the part of the eye that perceives light; it coordinates and transmits impulses from its seeing nerve cells to the optic nerve.

B. There are two primitive retinal layers: the outer pigment epithelium and an inner sensory layer.

C. Retinal detachment occurs when:
1. The two primitive layers of the retina separate, due to the accumulation of fluid between them.
2. Both retinal layers elevate away from the choroid, due to a tumor.

D. As the detachment extends and becomes complete, blindness occurs.

Clinical Manifestations

A. Opacities before the eyes.

B. Flashes of light.

C. Floating spots—blood and retinal cells that are freed at the time of the tear and that cast shadows on the retina as they drift about the eye.

D. Progressive constriction of vision in one area.
1. The area of visual loss depends on the location of detachment.
2. When the detachment is extensive and rapid, the patient feels as if a curtain has been pulled over his eyes.

Nursing Management in the Preoperative Period

A. Keep patient on bed rest.

B. Cover both eyes with patches to prevent further detachment.

C. Position patient's head so the retinal hole is in the lowest part of the eye.

D. Immediate surgery with drainage of fluid from subretinal space so that retina returns to normal position.

E. Retinal breaks are sealed by various methods that produce inflammatory reactions (chorioretinitis).
1. Adhesions will form between the edges of the break and the underlying choroid to obliterate the opening.
2. Laser beam can also be used to produce the chorioretinitis.

Nursing Management in Postoperative Care

A. Observe for hemorrhage which is a common complication. It can result from cryosurgery, diathermy, or from puncture of the choroid to obtain release of fluid.

B. Routine postoperative care (the same as for detached retina, enucleation, and corneal transplant).

C. Prevent clinical manifestations.
1. Nausea and vomiting (straining can cause hemorrhage).
2. Restlessness.

D. Observe for shock and sudden eye pain.

E. Cover the eye. If both eyes are covered, provide audible stimulation. Warn patient as you enter the room and always speak before you touch patient.

F. Keep bed flat or in low-Fowler's position.

G. Encourage patient to do deep breathing but to avoid coughing.

H. If patient is able to turn, usually position on unoperative side.

I. Avoid external eye pressure.

Patient Instruction

A. Convalescent period.
1. Wear patch at night to prevent rubbing of eyes.
2. Wear dark glasses.
3. Avoid squinting.

B. Postconvalescent period.
1. Avoid straining and constipation.
2. Avoid lifting heavy objects for six to eight weeks.
3. Avoid bending from the waist.

Ear Surgery

Stapedectomy

Etiology

A. Surgery performed when the patient has otosclerosis.

B. Otosclerosis is a condition in which the normal bone of the inner ear is replaced by abnormal osseous tissue.
1. The new growth of bone forms about the oval window and then about the stapes.
2. It blocks the movements of the stapes so that it is unable to vibrate effectively in response to sound pressure.

Surgical Procedure

A. An incision is made deep in the ear canal, close to the eardrum, so that the drum can be turned back and the middle ear exposed.

B. The surgeon frees and removes the stapes and the attached footplate, leaving an opening in the oval window.

C. The patient can usually hear as soon as this procedure has been completed.

D. The opening in the oval window is closed with a plug of fat or Gelfoam, which the body eventually replaces with mucous membrane cells.

E. A steel wire or a Teflon piston is inserted to replace the stapes.
1. It is attached to the incus at one end and to the graft or plug at the other end.
2. The wire transmits sound to the inner ear.

Nursing Management of Postoperative Care

A. Keep patient in supine position or as ordered by doctor.

B. Do not turn the patient.

C. Put side rails up.

D. Have patient deep breathe every two hours until ambulatory, but do not allow patient to cough.

E. Check for drainage; report excessive bleeding.

F. Prevent vomiting.

G. Give antibiotics as ordered.

H. Patient may have vertigo when ambulatory; stay with the patient and avoid quick movements.

I. Advise patient that he is not to smoke.

Respiratory System

Chest Injuries

Assessment of Respiratory Function

A. Check for airway patency.
1. Clear out secretions.
2. Insert oral airway if necessary.
3. Position patient on side if there is no cervical spine injury.
4. Place hand or cheek over nose and mouth of patient to feel if patient is ventilating.

B. Inspect thoracic cage for injury.
   1. Inspect for contusions, abrasions, and symmetry of chest movement.
   2. If open wound of chest, seal off immediately with a pressure dressing to prevent air from entering thoracic cavity.
   3. Watch for symmetrical movement of chest. Asymmetrical movement indicates:
      a. Flail chest.
      b. Tension pneumothorax.
      c. Hemothorax.
      d. Fractured ribs.
   4. Observe color; cyanosis indicates decreased oxygenation.
   5. Observe type of breathing; stertorous breathing usually indicates obstructed respiration.
C. Listen to lung sounds.
   1. Absence of breath sounds indicates lungs not expanding, due either to obstruction or deflation.
   2. Rales (crackling sounds) indicate vibrations of fluid in lungs.
   3. Rhonchi (coarse sounds) indicate partial obstruction of airway.
   4. Decreased breath sounds indicate poorly-ventilated lungs.
   5. Detection of bronchial sounds which are deviated from normal position indicates mediastinal shift due to collapse of lung.
D. Determine level of consciousness; decreased sensorium can indicate hypoxia.
E. Observe sputum or tracheal secretions; bloody sputum can indicate contusions of lung or injury to trachea and other anatomical structures.

General Nursing Management

A. Take history from patient to aid in total evaluation of patient's condition.
B. Administer electrocardiogram to establish if there is associated cardiac damage.
C. Maintain patent airway.
   1. Suction.
   2. Intubation.
      a. Oral airway.
      b. Endotracheal intubation.
D. Maintain adequate ventilation.
E. Maintain fluid and electrolyte balance.

   1. When blood and fluid loss is replaced, watch carefully for fluid overload which can lead to pulmonary edema.
   2. Record intake and output.
F. Maintain acid-base balance; make frequent blood gas determination as acid-base imbalances occur readily with compromised respirations or with mechanical ventilation.
G. Provide for relief of pain.
   1. Analgesics should be used with caution as they depress respirations. (Demerol is the drug of choice.)
   2. Atropine, morphine sulfate, and barbiturates should be avoided.
   3. Nerve block may be used.

Types of Traumatic Injury

Open Wounds of the Chest

A. Pathophysiology.
   1. Air from the atmosphere entering the pleural cavity causes collapse of lung.
   2. Air entering and leaving the wound during inspiration and expiration can be detected.
   3. Intrapleural negative pressure is lost, thereby embarrassing respirations, which leads to hypoxia and death if not corrected promptly.
B. Nursing management.
   1. Apply vaseline gauze to wound with pressure dressing.
   2. Place patient on assisted ventilation if necessary.
   3. Prepare for insertion of chest tubes.
   4. Place patient in high-Fowler's position (unless contraindicated) to assist in adequate ventilation.

Hemothorax or Pneumothorax

Definition: Hemothorax refers to blood in pleural space. Pneumothorax refers to air in pleural space.

A. Etiology: as air or fluid accumulates in pleural space, positive pressure is built up, collapsing the lung.
B. Clinical manifestations.
   1. Pain.
   2. Decreased breath sounds.
   3. Tracheal shift to unaffected side.

4. Dyspnea and respiratory embarrassment.

C. Nursing management.

1. Emergency treatment includes the insertion of a number 18 needle into the second intercostal space, midclavicular line, followed by aspiration of the fluid or air by means of a thoracentesis.
2. Insertion of chest tubes and connection to closed-chest drainage.
3. Continuous observation of vital signs for complications such as shock and cardiac failure.

Fractured Ribs

A. Clinical manifestations.

1. Pain and tenderness over fracture area.
2. Bruising at injury site.
3. Respiratory embarrassment occurring from splinters puncturing lung and causing pneumothorax.
4. Splinting of chest, causing shallow respirations, can cause a reduction in lung compliance as well as respiratory acidosis.

B. Nursing management.

1. Patient is treated for relief of pain by administering mild analgesic, like small doses of Demerol. (*Caution:* Narcotics can depress respiration and the cough reflex.)
2. Encourage deep breathing and coughing to prevent respiratory complications such as atelectasis and pneumonia.
3. Observe for signs of hemorrhage and shock.
4. Intercostal nerve block is administered if necessary to decrease pain.

Flail Chest

Definition: Multiple rib fractures that result in an unstable chest wall.

A. Clinical manifestations.

1. Pain.
2. Dyspnea leading to cyanosis.
3. Detached portion of flail chest moving in opposition to other areas of chest cage and lung.
   a. On inspiration, the affected chest area is depressed; on expiration, it is bulging outward.
   b. This causes poor expansion of lungs, which results in carbon dioxide retention and respiratory acidosis.

4. Inability to cough effectively, which leads to accumulation of fluids and respiratory complications such as pneumonia and atelectasis.
5. Cardiac failure, due to impaired filling of right side of heart as a result of high venous pressure caused by paradoxical breathing.
6. Rapid, shallow, and noisy respirations.

B. Nursing management.

1. Prepare for tracheotomy with a cuffed trach tube.
2. Place patient on volume-set respirator (MA-I), which delivers the same amount of tidal volume with each breath, not dependent on patient's respirations.
3. Suction frequently to prevent respiratory complications.
4. Prevent pain by administering nerve block or Demerol as ordered.
5. Observe for signs of shock and hemorrhage.
6. For patient on ventilator, use nasogastric tube to prevent abdominal distention and emesis, which can lead to aspiration.
7. For patient not on mechanical ventilator:
   a. Encourage turning, coughing, and hyperventilating every hour.
   b. Administer oxygen.
   c. Maintain IPPB therapy.
   d. Suction as needed.

Cardiac Tamponade

Definition: Acute accumulation of blood or fluid in the pericardial sac. Can occur from blunt or penetrating chest wounds (interferes with diastolic filling).

A. Clinical manifestations.

1. Increased CVP.
2. Decreased blood pressure.
3. Narrowed pulse pressure.
4. Paradoxical pulse (pulse disappears on inspiration and is weak on expiration, due to a changed intrathoracic pressure).
5. Distended neck veins (jugular vein cannot empty properly).
6. Distant heart sounds.
7. Agitation.
8. Cyanosis.

B. Nursing management.

1. Large needle (16–18 gauge) is inserted by M.D.

into pericardium and blood is withdrawn.

2. Continuous cardiac monitoring to observe for arrhythmias due to myocardial irritability.
3. Have cardiac defibrillator and emergency drugs available to treat cardiac arrhythmias.
4. Monitor vital signs and watch for shock.

Thoracic Surgical Procedures

Types

A. Exploratory thoracotomy—incision of the thoracic wall, performed to locate bleeding, injuries, tumors.
B. Thoracoplasty—removal of ribs or portions of ribs to reduce the size of the thoracic space.
C. Pneumonectomy—removal of entire lung.
D. Lobectomy—removal of a lobe of the lung (three lobes on right side, two on the left).
E. Segmented resection—removal of one or more segments of the lung (right lung has ten segments and left lung has eight).
F. Wedge resection—removal of a small, localized area of disease near the surface of the lung.

Postoperative Nursing Management

A. Closed chest suction is employed in all but pneumonectomy. In pneumonectomy, it is desirable that the fluid accumulate in empty thoracic space. Eventually the thoracic space fills with serous exudate which consolidates, preventing extensive mediastinal shifts.
B. Maintain patent chest tube drainage by chest tube stripping. (Not all patients with pneumonectomies have chest tubes.)
C. Maintain respiratory function.
   1. Have patient turn, cough, and deep breathe.
   2. Suction if necessary.
   3. Provide oxygen therapy.
   4. Provide IPPB therapy.
   5. Ventilate mechanically if necessary.
D. Ambulate early to encourage adequate ventilation and prevent postoperative complications. (Ambulate patients with pneumonectomies in two or three days due to need for cardiopulmonary adjustment.)
E. Provide range-of-motion exercises to all extremities to promote adequate circulation.
F. Monitor central venous pressure with vital signs—watch for indications of impaired venous return to heart.
G. Position patient correctly.
   1. Use semi-Fowler's position when vital signs are stable to facilitate lung expansion.
   2. Turn every one to two hours.
   3. Pneumonectomy.
      a. Position on operative side for back care only.
      b. Position on back or unoperative side only. (Some physicians will allow positioning on either side after twenty-four hours.)
   4. Segmental resection or wedge resection—position on back or unoperative side (aids in expanding remaining pulmonary tissue).
   5. Lobectomy—turn to either side (can expand lung tissue on both sides).
H. Maintain fluid intake, as tolerated. Watch for overload in pneumonectomy patients.
I. Provide arm and shoulder postoperative exercises—prevent adhesion formation.
   1. Put affected arm through both active and passive range of motion every four hours.
   2. Start exercises within four hours after patient has returned to room following surgery.

Prevention of Postoperative Complications

A. Respiratory complications.
   1. Causes of inadequate ventilation:
      a. Airway obstruction due to secretion accumulation.
      b. Atelectasis due to underexpansion of lungs and anesthetic agents during surgery.
      c. Hypoventilation and carbon dioxide build-up due to incisional splinting because of pain.
      d. Depression of CNS from overuse of medications.
   2. Tension pneumothorax.
      a. Caused by air leak through pleural incision lines.
      b. Can cause mediastinal shift.
   3. Pulmonary embolism.
   4. Bronchopulmonary fistula.
      a. Air escapes into pleural space and is forced into subcutaneous tissue around incision, causing subcutaneous emphysema.

b. Caused by inadequate closure of bronchus when resection is done.

c. Another cause is alveolar or bronchiolar tears in surface of lung (particularly following pneumonectomy).

5. Atelectasis and/or pneumonia—caused by airway obstruction or as result of anesthesia.

6. Respiratory arrest can occur.

B. Circulatory complications.

1. Hypovolemia due to fluid or blood loss.

2. Arrhythmias due to underlying myocardial disease.

3. Cardiac arrest can occur from either of these conditions.

4. Pulmonary edema can occur due to fluid overload of circulatory system.

Tracheostomy

Rationale for Procedure

A. Easy removal of tracheobronchial secretions when patient is unable to cough adequately.

B. Use with mechanical ventilators.

C. Unconscious patients.

Nursing Management

A. Cuffed tracheostomy tube.

1. Provide for release of cuff pressure for five minutes out of every hour. Hyperventilate patient before and after cuff is deflated with ambu bag.

2. Tracheal suction as ordered or p.r.n.

a. Always apply oral or nasal suction first so that when cuff is deflated, secretions will not fall into lung from area above cuff.

b. Catheter must be changed before doing trach suctioning.

3. Provide humidity by using trach mist mask, if patient is not on ventilator.

4. Observe for hemorrhage around tracheostomy site.

5. Change dressings (nonraveling type) and cleanse surrounding area with hydrogen peroxide at least every four hours.

B. Silver tracheostomy.

1. Remove inner cannula and soak in hydrogen peroxide solution to loosen mucus accumulation.

2. Use brush to cleanse inner and outer aspects of tube.

3. Rinse in sterile saline or water.

4. Suction outer cannula before reinserting.

5. Some orders state that tube is boiled for 5 minutes to disinfect it.

a. Other orders will prescribe leaving tube in disinfectant solution for varying lengths of time.

b. If this is the case, usually inner cannula is replaced by an interchangeable part every four hours.

Laryngectomy

Surgical Procedure

A. Removal of larynx due to malignant tumors.

B. Total laryngectomy and radical neck dissection procedure of choice for cancer under following circumstances:

1. If tumor does not extend more than 5 mm. up base of tongue or below upper edge of cricopharyngeus muscle.

2. If there is no evidence of distant metastases.

C. Epiglottis, thyroid cartilage, hyoid bone, cricoid cartilage, and part of trachea are removed.

D. Stump of trachea is brought out to neck and sutured to skin. The pharyngeal portion is closed and breathing through nose is eliminated.

E. Accompanied by radical neck dissection of neck tissue and lymph nodes are involved (see Gastrointestinal System).

Nursing Management

A. Suction frequently with sterile technique until area has healed; then use clean technique.

B. Observe for hemorrhage around site.

C. Instruct patient regarding means for communication, as he will not be able to speak immediately postoperatively.

D. Speech rehabilitation is utilized after surgical area has healed.

Cardiovascular System

Surgical Procedures

Cardiac Catheterization

Definition: Visualization of right and left sides of heart; visualization of coronary vessels (coronary angiography).

Purpose of Catheterization

A. Measure cardiac output and shunt flow.
B. Obtain oxygenation saturation of the chambers and of the pulmonary system.
C. Obtain chamber pressures and pulse configurations.
D. Measure pulmonary vascular resistance.
E. Observe coronary blood flow.

Types of Catheterizations

A. Right heart.
   1. Catheter is inserted through venous cutdown in antecubital vein or through femoral cutdown.
   2. Catheter is threaded into right side of heart by way of superior vena cava.
      a. Measure oxygen saturation.
      b. Observe functioning of valves.
      c. Take pulmonary wedge pressure.
B. Left heart—can be done by two methods.
   1. Transarterial left catheter may be advanced retrograde across the aortic valve into left ventricle through the mitral valve into left atrium.
   2. Brockenbrough transeptal catheter may be advanced through the femoral and external iliac veins and the inferior vena cava, to the right atrium, and across the left atrium.
      a. The needle inside the catheter penetrates the atrial septum to cross over from right to left atrium.
      b. Measurement is the same as for right heart catheterization.
      c. Selected coronary angiography may also be done.

Nursing Management Postcatheterization

A. Compare data with baseline data obtained prior to procedure.
   1. Notify physician if blood pressure is decreased by 10 percent from baseline.
   2. Take apical pulse to determine if arrhythmia is present.
   3. Record temperature and respirations to prevent infection and hemorrhage or cardiac tamponade.
B. Observe site of cutdown for presence of hematoma or hemorrhage.
C. Observe for signs of allergies to dye.
   1. Tachycardia.
   2. Erythema surrounding cutdown site.
   3. Nausea and vomiting.
   4. Shortness of breath.
D. Palpate pulses distal to catheter insertion site to observe for thrombophlebitis and vessel occlusion.
   1. Palpable pulses—bilateral and strong.
   2. Color—no cyanosis or blanching.
   3. Temperature of skin—warm.

Pacemaker Insertion

Definition: Pacemaker is inserted as a temporary or permanent device to initiate and maintain heart rate when patient's pacemaker is nonfunctioning.

Clinical Conditions Requiring Pacemakers

A. Conduction defect following open heart surgery.
B. Heart block (usually third degree).
C. Tachyarrhythmias.
D. Stokes-Adams syndrome.
E. Bradyarrhythmias.

Types of Pacemakers

A. Demand—functions only if patient's own pacemaker fails to discharge.
   1. The pacemaker is set at a fixed rate and will discharge only if patient's own rate falls below it.
   2. Used mainly in Adams-Stokes or bradyarrhythmias, or following cardiac surgery.
B. Asynchronous.
   1. Fixed rate—the pacemaker is set at a fixed rate

and will fire regardless of patient's own rhythm.

2. Variable rate—rate can be varied.

Placement of Pacemaker

A. Epicardial—electrodes are implanted on outside of left ventricle, and they barely penetrate myocardium. Battery pack is placed subcutaneously in a skin pocket.

B. Endocardial implantation—pacing electrode inserted through neck vein and placed near the apex of right ventricle.
   1. Permanent—battery is implanted beneath skin.
   2. Temporary—battery is located outside of skin.

Nursing Management

A. Observe for battery failure (pacemaker not firing as set).
   1. Faints easily.
   2. Hiccoughs.
   3. Rhythm change.

B. Observe for hematoma at site of insertion.

C. Observe for arrhythmias via cardiac monitoring.
   1. Competition from patient's own pacemaker evidenced on rhythm strip.
   2. Absence of pacemaker artifact on rhythm strip.
   3. Premature ventricular contractions (PVC's) and ventricular tachycardia.

D. Monitor vital signs.
   1. Hemorrhage and shock.
   2. Cardiac tamponade.
   3. Infection.

E. Observe for pacemaker failure.
   1. Decreased urine output.
   2. EKG pattern changes.
   3. Decreased blood pressure.
   4. Cyanosis.
   5. Shortness of breath.

Acquired Heart Disease

Coronary Artery Disease

Definition: Caused by atherosclerosis from lipoid changes. Clot or plaque can cause occlusion of vessel or vessels. This usually leads to angina and/or complete occlusion of vessel leading to muscle damage.

Surgical Procedure

A. Saphenous vein bypass is usual surgical approach to coronary artery disease.

B. Patient is placed on cardiopulmonary bypass during grafting of vein.

Nursing Management Postoperative

A. Observe for fluid and electrolyte imbalance.
   1. Obtain frequent lab specimens for hypokalemia and hyperkalemia.
   2. Measure CVP for hypovolemia and hypervolemia.
   3. Measure blood gases for acidosis and alkalosis.
   4. Measure hematocrit and hemoglobin for blood balance.
   5. Weigh daily.

B. Observe respiratory function.
   1. Place patient on respirator for varying lengths of time postoperatively.
      a. Use endotracheal intubation with cuffed trach tube.
      b. Deflate cuff for five minutes each hour to prevent tracheal stricture.
   2. Suction at least every hour.
   3. Hyperinflate the lungs to prevent atelectasis (from anesthesia) every hour with respirator or ambu bag.
   4. Take frequent tidal volumes.
   5. Auscultate for abnormal lung sounds.
      a. Rales.
      b. Rhonchi.

C. Observe for cardiogenic shock.
   1. Decreased blood pressure.
   2. Tachycardia—thready pulse.
   3. Absence of peripheral pulses.
   4. Cardiac arrhythmias leading to arrest.
   5. Decreased urine output.
   6. Skin—cool, clammy, cyanotic.
   7. Restlessness.
   8. Central venous pressure above 15 cm. water pressure (pulmonary edema).
   9. Electrolyte imbalance.

D. Observe for signs of hemorrhage due to bleeders or coagulation disorders.

E. Place in semi-Fowler's position to facilitate cardiac and respiratory function.

F. Pain medication such as morphine sulfate I.V.

G. Administer muscle relaxants such as Valium.
H. Monitor I.V. fluid and blood requirements by use of CVP, blood pressure readings, urine output.
    1. Keep CVP between 5-15 cm. water pressure or as directed by physician.
    2. Keep urine above 30 cc./hour.
    3. Hematocrit maintained at 35-40.
I. Maintain cardiac rhythm by use of antiarrhythmic drugs as necessary; Lidocaine prevents premature ventricular contractions.
    1. Side effects include convulsions, respiratory arrest, and hypotension.
    2. 50-100 mg. I.V. bolus or 250-1000 mg. in 500 cc. D_5W. Do not administer more than 3-4 mg./min.
J. Maintain blood pressure.
    1. Sympathomimetics increase blood pressure.
        a. Adrenalin.
            (1) Increases cardiac output by increasing heart rate and myocardial contractility.
            (2) I.V. drip of 2-4 mg. of Adrenalin in 500 cc. D_5W titrated to keep blood pressure at desired level.
        b. Dopamine.
            (1) Stimulates heart by beta-adrenergic action.
            (2) Constricts resistance vessels by acting on alpha receptors.
            (3) Has a direct vasodilating effect on the kidneys and splenetic vascular bed.
        c. Isuprel.
            (1) Lowers peripheral resistance.
            (2) Causes increase in venous return leading to increase in cardiac output.
            (3) I.V. drip of 2-4 mg. in 500 cc. D_5W titrated to desired effect.
    2. Antihypertensives (Arfonad).
        a. Quick-acting.
        b. Inhibits the transmission of nerve impulses through the sympathetic and parasympathetic ganglia.
        c. Produces peripheral vasodilatation.
        d. Administered via infusion pump in solution of 500 mg. Arfonad to 500 cc. D_5W. Begin at 0.08 to 0.1 mg./min.
K. Maintain kidney function.
    1. Keep urine output above 30 cc. per hour with I.V. fluids or plasma expanders.
    2. Administer diuretics to increase excretion of hemolyzed red cells caused by breakdown of the cell from cardiopulmonary bypass.
    3. Maintain blood pressure above 90 systolic.
L. Maintain patent chest tubes.
    1. Used to remove excessive fluid and air from chest cavity.
    2. Connected to water-seal system.
    3. Tubes should be stripped frequently.
M. Maintain body temperature.
    1. To raise body temperature.
        a. Thermal blankets, following hypothermic surgical procedure.
        b. Aqua K pads.
    2. To decrease body temperature.
        a. Antipyretics to keep temperature below 100°F to prevent demands for increased cellular oxygen.
        b. Hypothermia blankets.
N. Assess level of consciousness.
    1. Complications of coronary pulmonary bypass are air embolism or thrombus.
    2. Depending on type of anesthesia used, patient might awaken immediately upon return to recovery room or cardiac care unit, or remain unconscious up to several hours postoperatively.
        a. Neurological signs should be checked.
        b. All extremities should be checked for movement.

Valvular Disease

Mitral Stenosis

Definition: Thickening and loss of pliability of the valve leaflets, usually due to rheumatic heart disease. Valvular dysfunction is caused by narrowing of valvular orifice from scarring.

Surgical Corrections

A. Closed mitral commissurotomy—finger inserted to dilate valvular opening.

B. Open mitral commissurotomy—dissection of scarred area by means of scalpel.

C. Valve replacement.
1. Artificial, or prosthetic valves.
   a. Caged ball and caged disc.
   b. Eccentric monocusp disc.
2. Heterografts.
   a. Graft from porcine or bovine.
   b. Problem with sterilization and preparation.
3. Homografts.
   a. Graft from human cadaver donor.
   b. Only the aortic valve is retrieved, which can be used for mitral valve by turning it upside down.
4. Autografts—use of patient's own tissue.
5. Postoperative complications—same as for any open heart surgery plus the following:
   a. Conduction defects leading to arrhythmias.
   b. Embolism resulting from the break-off of calcium deposits or from thrombus.
   c. Hemorrhage.
   d. Cardiac tamponade.
   e. Supraventricular tachyarrhythmias.
   f. Heart block.

Aortic Stenosis

Definition: Narrowing of aortic valve orifice due to rheumatic heart disease.

A. Valve replacement treatment of choice.
B. Same type valves used in mitral replacement.
C. Postoperative complications.
1. Most common are heart block and congestive heart failure.
2. Complications occur less frequently than in mitral valve.

Nursing Management for Valve Replacements

A. Routine care as for coronary artery bypass.
B. Special nursing problems.
1. Observe cardiac monitor for tachyarrhythmias.
2. Observe monitor for heart block.
3. Auscultate for valvular competency of replacement valve.
4. Administer anticoagulant therapy to prevent clot formation on artificial valve.

a. Observe lab values for anticoagulation—partial thromboplastin time or Lee-White clotting for Heparin administration.
b. Observe lab values for prothrombin time for Dicumarol therapy.

Note: For medical management of valvular diseases, see Cardiovascular System, p. 59.

Aortic Aneurysms

Definition: A localized abnormal dilatation of the vascular wall occurring most often in the ascending aorta and secondly in the aortic arch.

Etiology

A. Arteriosclerosis and syphilis.
B. Infections within vessel, trauma.
C. Highest incidence in older men.
D. High mortality if not surgically treated.
E. Major cause of death is spontaneous rupture.

Clinical Manifestations

A. Result from compression or erosion of surrounding structures.
B. Symptoms vary according to location and size of lesion.
1. Pain results from pressure on spine, intercostal nerves, or various organs.
2. Cough and dyspnea due to tracheobronchial compression.
3. Hoarseness from pressure on laryngeal nerve.
4. Dysphagia from esophageal compression.
5. Persistent or intermittent pain in middle or lower abdomen—often referred to back.
C. Dissecting aneurysms—simulate coronary occlusion.
1. Originate in ascending aorta.
2. Usually associated with severe hypertension.
3. Pain described as tearing, referred pain.

Medical Management for Dissecting Aneurysms

A. Immediate reduction of blood pressure via medication—Arfonad.
B. Myocardial depressants—propranolol.
C. Surgical intervention—dacron graft or end-to-end anastomosis.
D. Cardiopulmonary bypass for lesions of ascending aorta.

Postoperative Nursing Management

A. Follow same procedures as for open heart surgery.
B. Observe circulatory status distal to graft site.
C. Observe all peripheral pulses and temperature of extremities.
D. Monitor renal function with accurate intake and output (cross clamp of aorta during surgery).
E. Observe for emboli.

Complications

A. Hypertensive preoperatively, but can easily become hypotensive postoperatively due to excessive bleeding.
B. Acute renal failure.
C. Hemorrhage from graft site.
D. Cerebral vascular accident.
E. Paraplegia.

Femoral Popliteal Bypass Graft

Definition: Prosthetic graft is anastomosed to the artery proximal and distal to the obstruction.

Postoperative Nursing Management

A. Observe peripheral pulses for patency of graft.
   1. Check for presence of distal pulses.
   2. Check that extremities are warm and pink.
   3. Compare both extremities.
B. Monitor vasopressors for at least twelve hours.
C. Maintain blood pressure approximately 20 mm. Hg. above normal (keep suture line taut to prevent leakage).
D. Elevate foot of bed to prevent edema and promote arterial blood flow.
E. Do not allow flexion at hips (decreases blood flow).
F. Provide good skin care to prevent decubiti (poor vascularization).
G. Record accurate intake and output hourly for twenty-four hours.

Vein Stripping and Ligation

Definition: The ligation and removal of affected veins in the legs. Usually affects greater and lesser saphenous veins.

Medical Management

A. Frequent rest periods with legs elevated.
B. Exercise and warm baths.
C. Elastic support stockings.
D. Injections of sclerosing solutions.

Postoperative Nursing Management

A. Observe feet for edema, warmth, color (tight elastic bandages applied following surgery can impede circulation).
B. Elevate feet above level of heart.
C. Position flat in bed or have patient walk. Do not allow patient to dangle legs or to sit in a chair for at least one week.
D. Ambulate early—five minutes every hour.
E. Following bandage removal, utilize elastic stockings.

Gastrointestinal System

Surgical Intervention for Neck Tumors

Radical Neck Dissection

Definition: Removal of cancerous lymph nodes in the neck.

Nursing Management

A. Maintain adequate respiratory functions.
   1. Place in high-Fowler's position.
   2. Observe dressings for hemorrhage which could lead to respiratory embarrassment.
   3. Suction to prevent aspiration and pneumonia.
   4. Administer oxygen as needed.
   5. Observe for edema which could constrict trachea.
   6. Provide care for laryngectomy (frequently performed with radical neck dissection).
      a. Use mist mask.
      b. Clean tube as you would tracheostomy tube.

B. Watch for difficulty in swallowing if allowed oral fluids. If radical procedure, patient will probably be fed through either nasogastric tube, gastrostomy, or I.V. therapy.

C. Change dressings frequently to prevent infection.
   1. Drains are frequently placed in surgical site— Hemovac most common.
   2. Observe for unusual drainage (amounts and type, as well as odor).

D. Give oral hygiene every two to four hours.

E. Develop means to communicate as patient will not be able to talk postoperatively if laryngecotomy was also performed.

F. Provide general postoperative care.

Surgical Intervention for Gastrointestinal Diseases

Peptic Ulcer Disease

Definition: Peptic ulcer is an excavation formed in mucosal wall of stomach, in pylorus, or in duodenum. It is usually located in duodenum rather than in stomach, and almost always located around pylorus. The erosion may extend to muscle layer or through to peritoneum.

Predisposing Factors

A. Stress; eating hurriedly; irregular meals; excessive smoking.

B. Drugs such as salicylates, reserpines, and steroids that irritate the mucous lining of the stomach.

Pathophysiology

A. Occurs only in areas of GI tract that are exposed to hydrochloric acid and pepsin.

B. The gastroduodenal mucosa is unable to withstand action of gastric acid and pepsin.

C. This is due either to an increase in concentration or activity of acid and pepsin, and/or a decrease in normal resistance of mucosa.

Drug Therapy

A. Antacids.
   1. Mylanta, Gelusil, Maalox, Amphojel.
      a. Given one to three hours after meals.
      b. Contain mixture of aluminum and magnesium hydroxide.
      c. Capable of preventing rebound hyperacidity and systemic alkalosis.
   2. Delcid, Camalox, Ducon.
      a. Given one hour after meals and at bedtime.
      b. Exert neutralizing effects longer than others.
      c. Cannot be given to kidney patients because of calcium content.
   3. If diarrhea occurs, antacids containing aluminum are given.
   4. If constipation occurs, antacids containing magnesium are given.

B. Anticholinergics.
   1. Types.
      a. Pro-banthine.
      b. Banthine.
      c. Pamine.
   2. Effects.
      a. Block vagal stimulation of parietal cells to decrease acid secretion.
      b. Decrease gastric motor activity, allowing antacid to remain in stomach longer.
      c. Side effects: dry mouth and throat, excessive thirst, difficulty in swallowing, flushed dry skin, increased pulse and respiration, dilated pupils, and emotional excitement.

Nursing Management

A. Control gastric acidity and reduce emotional stress— the two major objectives.

B. Ensure mental and physical rest.

C. Rest motor and secretory activities of stomach through therapeutic diet.
   1. Provide three regular meals with snack between.
   2. Avoid gas-forming foods.
   3. Avoid alcohol and caffeine.

D. Relieve pain and discomfort; promote healing.
   1. Antacids—neutralize gastric secretions and afford symptomatic relief.
   2. Anticholinergics—decrease gastric motility and decrease volume of gastric secretions.
   3. Adequate hydration—relieves side effects of anticholinergic drugs.
   4. Diet.

E. Observe for complications.
  1. Hemorrhage (see p. 208).
  2. Perforation. Clinical manifestations are:
     a. Acute surgical abdomen.
     b. Sudden, severe upper abdominal pain, persisting and increasing in intensity.
     c. Pain accompanied by vomiting and collapse.
     d. Pain referred to shoulders by irritation of phrenic nerve in diaphragm.
     e. Abdomen tender and board-like.
     f. Signs of shock developing.
     g. Chemical peritonitis occurs within hours.
  3. Pyloric obstruction (see p. 104).

Surgical Treatment

A. Vagotomy and gastroenterostomy or pyloroplasty.
  1. Vagus nerve is cut.
  2. Provide for drainage of stomach.
     a. Drainage operation necessary because vagotomy is often followed by gastric retention.
     b. Vagus nerve provides the motor impulses to the gastric musculature, whose division is often followed by gastric atony.
  3. The pyloroplasty or gastroenterostomy also reduces the stimulation of gastric acid by reducing the formation of gastrin produced in the antral area of the stomach.
B. Vagotomy and antrectomy.
  1. Decrease production of acid to a point where ulcers will not recur.
  2. Remove acid-stimulating mechanism of stomach (that is, divide vagus nerve and remove antral portion of stomach).
C. Partial gastrectomy and possible vagotomy.
  1. Billroth I—partial gastrectomy with remaining segment of stomach anastomosed to duodenum.
  2. Billroth II—remaining segment of stomach is anastomosed to jejunum. (Usual for duodenal ulcer.)

Postoperative Nursing Management

A. After anesthesia recovery, place in modified Fowler's for comfort and easy stomach drainage.
B. Prevent pulmonary complications—medicate before turning, coughing, or hyperventilating.
C. Institute nasogastric suction; drainage contains some blood first twelve hours.
  1. Physician inserts tube.
  2. Keep patent by irrigating with NaC1.
D. See that patient has nothing by mouth (no peristalsis).
E. Give intravenous fluids with KC1 added.
F. After nasogastric tube is out, give small sips of clear water. (Do not use straw.)
  1. Do not give cold fluids (cause distress); give warm, weak tea.
  2. Offer bland foods to where patient eats six small meals a day and drinks 120 cc. fluid between meals.
G. Promote ambulation on first postoperative day unless contraindicated by physician.
H. Check drainage tubes if inserted. (Serosanguineous drainage is normal.)

Postoperative Complications

A. Shock (from hypovolemia).
B. Vomiting—usually due to blood left in stomach. (Nasogastric tube prevents vomiting.)
C. Hemorrhage.
D. Pulmonary complications.
E. Large fluid and electrolyte losses.
F. Dumping syndrome—due to rapid emptying of gastric contents into small intestine, which has been anastomosed to the gastric stump.
  1. Mechanical result of surgery in which a small gastric remnant remains after surgery.
  2. From this there is a large opening from the gastric stump into the jejunum.
  3. Foods that are high in carbohydrates and electrolytes must be diluted in the jejunum before absorption can take place.
  4. The ingestion of fluid at mealtime is another factor in the rapid emptying of the stomach into the jejunum.
  5. Symptoms are caused by rapid distention of jejunal loop anastomosed to stomach.
     a. There is a withdrawal of water from the circulating blood volume into the jejunum to dilute the high concentration of electrolytes and sugars.
     b. A rapid movement of extracellular fluids into the bowel occurs and converts the

hypertonic material to an isotonic mixture.

c. This rapid shift decreases the circulatory blood volume, like a hypovolemic shock.

6. Foods high in sugars and salt produce the symptoms.

a. Palpitation.

b. Perspiration.

c. Faintness.

d. Weakness that lasts from a few minutes to as long as thirty minutes, causing the patient to lie down.

7. Prevention of dumping syndrome.

a. Avoid sugar and salt; maintain a high protein, high fat, low carbohydrate diet.

b. Avoid drinking fluids with meals, thereby delaying gastric emptying.

c. Lie down after meals.

d. Physicians can prevent symptoms by forming smaller stomas and larger gastric stump.

e. Syndrome usually subsides in six months.

G. Diarrhea—complication of vagotomy (use Kaopectate).

H. Vitamin B_{12} deficiency.

1. Production of "intrinsic factor" is halted. (The gastric secretion that is required for the absorption of vitamin B_{12} from the gastrointestinal tract.)

2. Unless supplied by parenteral injection throughout life, patient suffers vitamin B_{12} deficiency.

Colon Surgery

Ulcerative Colitis

Definition: Ulcerative and inflammatory disease of rectum and colon, spreading upward from rectum. It is characterized by exacerbations and remissions.

A. Etiology unknown; thought to be autoimmune or psychosomatic.

1. Ten to fifteen percent of patients will develop cancer.

2. Sigmoidoscopy and barium enema used for diagnosis.

B. Nursing management.

1. Do not administer cathartics, which can cause severe exacerbations of disease and megacolon

(excessive dilation of colon), perforation, and death.

2. Provide psychological care—determine environmental factors that distress patient.

C. Drug therapy.

1. Steroid therapy—ACTH and corticosteroids.

a. Effective early in course of disease (acute inflammatory phase rather than chronic).

b. Act to reduce inflammation, decrease temperature, and eliminate bloody stool.

2. Sedation and antidiarrheal medications—decrease colonic peristalsis to rest infected bowel.

3. Tincture of belladonna—decreases gastric motility.

4. Sulfonamides (Axulfidine and Gantrisin) for mild or moderate infection; antibiotics for severe infection.

Surgical Corrections of Colon

A. Ileostomy.

1. Causes.

a. Ulcerative colitis.

b. Crohn's disease (regional ileitis).

2. Procedure.

a. Total colectomy and ileostomy (anything less gives only temporary relief).

b. Portion of ileum brought through abdominal wall.

3. Preoperative care.

a. Provide intensified fluid, blood, and protein replacement.

b. Administer chemotherapy and antibiotics.

c. If on steroids, maintain therapy after surgery and then gradually decrease.

d. Provide low residue diet in small, frequent feedings.

e. Administer neomycin enemas.

4. Postoperative care.

a. Contents always liquid (from small intestine).

b. More chance of excoriation of skin around stoma.

c. Provide increased fluids because of excessive fluid loss through stoma.

d. Provide a low residue, high caloric diet until patient is accustomed to new arrangement for bowel evacuation.

B. Continent ileostomy.
   1. Internal reservoir created by short segment of small intestines.
   2. Nipple valve is formed from terminal ileum.
   3. As reservoir fills, fecal pressure closes valve.
   4. Patient catheterizes stoma two to four times a day.
   5. No appliance needed.
C. Colostomy.
   1. Causes.
      a. Cancer of colon—permanent colostomy.
      b. Traumatic or congenital disruption of intestinal tract (permanent or temporary).
      c. Diverticulitis (double barrel)—can be put back after inflammatory process healed.
   2. Procedure—portion of colon brought through abdominal wall.
   3. Preoperative care.
      a. Provide high calorie, low residue diet for several days.
      b. Administer intestinal antiseptics with sulfa and neomycin (p.o.) to decrease bacterial content of colon and to soften and decrease bulk of contents of colon.
      c. Cleanse bowel by administering laxatives and enemas.
      d. Provide adequate fluids and electrolytes.
   4. Postoperative care.
      a. Depends on which part of colon involved; contents are liquid to formed.
      b. Patient has no voluntary control of bowel evacuation.
      c. Ascending colostomy is hard to train for evacuation.
      d. Evacuate bowel every twenty-four to forty-eight hours.
      e. Control with diet and/or irrigation.
      f. Maintain skin care around stoma.
      g. Assure proper fit and placement of appliance.
      h. Increase fluid intake.
      i. Provide emotional support.
      j. Instruct patient in colostomy care.

Appendicitis

Definition: Appendicitis is an inflammation of the appendix due to infection.

Clinical Manifestations

A. Generalized, severe upper abdominal pain that localizes in the right lower quadrant.
B. Anorexia.
C. Slightly increased temperature.
D. Nausea and vomiting.

Postoperative Nursing Management

A. Place in semi-Fowler's position to relieve abdominal strain.
B. Give nothing by mouth until bowel sounds present.
C. Insert nasogastric tube as required.
D. Ensure adequate bowel evacuation with enema, if necessary.
E. Insert rectal tube for flatus.
F. Follow routine postoperative nursing care for any abdominal surgery.

Splenectomy

Definition: Excision of the spleen.

Function of Spleen

A. Destroys old red blood cells.
B. Produces lymphocytes, plasma cells, and antibodies.

Indications for Surgical Intervention

A. Trauma.
B. Hypersplenism.
C. Idiopathic thrombocytopenia.
D. Hodgkin's disease.
E. Lymphoma.
F. Preceding renal transplantation (reduces rejection).

Postoperative Nursing Management

A. Prevent thrombus formation.
   1. Initiate bed exercises.
   2. Ambulate early.
   3. Hydration.
B. Prevent respiratory complications due to reduced expansion of left lung and location of spleen near diaphragm.
   1. TCH q. 2 hours.
   2. IPPB if prone to URI.

C   Prevent infection if rupture occurred.
  1.   Observe for signs of infection.
  2.   Administer antibiotics.

Abdominal Herniorrhaphy

Definition: A hernia is a protrusion of the intestine through an opening in the abdominal wall.

Four Types

A.   Femoral—below groin.
B.   Umbilical—around umbilicus, due to failure, of orifice to close.
C.   Incisional—due to weakness in incisional area from infection or poor healing.
D.   Inguinal—weakness in abdominal wall where round ligament is located in female and where spermatic cord emerges in male.

Treatment

A.   Reducing hernia—place an appliance over hernia area to prevent abdominal contents from entering hernia area and strangulating.
B.   Surgical intervention.

Postoperative Nursing Management

A.   Maintain routine postoperative care.
B.   Ambulate day of surgery or next morning.
C.   Provide ice pack or scrotal support if inguinal hernia in male.
D.   Prevent urine retention.

Anorectal Surgery

Types

A.   Hemorrhoids or varicose veins of anal canal.
  1.   External—outside rectal sphincter.
  2.   Internal—above internal sphincter.
B.   Pilonidal cyst—cyst located on lower sacrum with hair protruding from sinus opening.
C.   Anal fissure—crack in the anal canal.
D.   Anal fistula—abnormal opening near the anus and continuing into the anal canal.

Nursing Management

A.   Give routine postoperative care.
B.   Keep perineal and rectal area clean by providing sitz baths (after first day) or irrigations.
C.   Apply spray analgesics when needed to ease pain.
D.   Medicate for pain but avoid codeine preparations as they are constipating.
E.   Place in prone position or side-lying position for at least four hours to prevent hemorrhage.
F.   Prevent urinary retention.
  1.   Keep accurate intake and output.
  2.   Observe for frequent, small voidings.
G.   Patients usually have packing inserted with pressure dressing applied.
  1.   Reinforce dressing as needed to apply pressure.
  2.   Keep area clean.
H.   Apply ice packs immediately postoperatively.
  1.   Prevents edema formation.
  2.   Provides vasoconstriction.
I.   When patient able to ambulate, encourage small steps; increase activity gradually.
J.   When patient sitting in chair, use flotation pads, not rubber rings; limit sitting to short periods of time.
K.   Force fluids to aid in keeping bowel movements soft.
L.   Administer stool softeners and laxatives every day.
M.   Before first bowel movement, medicate for pain. Sometimes enemas are ordered on second day.
  1.   Medicate for pain.
  2.   Administer with pliable, soft, well-lubricated tube.
  3.   Place in sitz bath to expel enema (will prevent excessive pain by relaxing anal area).

Gallbladder Disease

Types of Gallbladder Disease

A.   Cholecystitis—inflammation of gallbladder.
B.   Cholelithiasis—stones in gallbladder.
C.   Choledocholithiasis—stones in common bile duct.

Surgical Interventions

A.   Cholecystectomy—removal of gallbladder after ligation of the cystic duct and vessels. A penrose drain is usually inserted to allow for drainage.

B. Cholecystostomy—removal of bile, pus, or gall-stones through an incision in the gallbladder. A tube is then sutured into gallbladder for drainage.

C. Choledochostomy—opening into common bile duct for removal of stones. A drainage T-tube is inserted into duct and must be connected to drainage bottle.

Nursing Management

A. Prevent respiratory complications (the most common postoperative complication).
  1. Turn, cough, hyperventilate every two hours.
  2. Use IPPB or blow-bottles every two hours.
  3. Auscultate for abnormal breath sounds.
  4. Observe for signs of respiratory distress.
  5. Ambulate and activate as early as allowed.

B. Nasogastric tube inserted to relieve distention and increase peristalsis; irrigate tube every four hours and p.r.n.

C. If T-tube placed:
  1. Place in semi-Fowler's position to facilitate drainage.
  2. Measure amount and record character and color of drainage.
  3. Protect skin around incision and cleanse surrounding area.

D. Observe for wound infections; patients tend to be obese and therefore healing is often delayed.

E. Prevent thrombophlebitis.
  1. Encourage range of motion.
  2. Ambulate early.
  3. Provide antiembolic stockings.

F. Provide low fat diet high in carbohydrates and protein.
  1. Instruct patient to maintain diet for at least two or three months postoperatively.
  2. May require continuance of vitamin K as dietary supplement.

G. Observe for signs of biliary obstruction—jaundice.
  1. Skin.
  2. Sclera.
  3. Clay-colored stools.

H. Prepare patient for T-tube removal.
  1. As T-tube is clamped, observe for:
    a. Abdominal discomfort and distention.
    b. Chills and fever; nausea.
  2. Unclamp tube if any nausea or vomiting.
  3. Clamp tube before eating.

Genitourinary System

Surgical Interventions for Urinary System

Cystostomy

Definition: Suprapubic drainage.

Purpose

A. Diverts urine flow from urethra.

B. Empties bladder (similar for Foley catheter, but catheter is inserted in suprapubic area rather than through urinary meatus).

C. Provides less risk of infection for patient.

D. Used for:
  1. Urethral stricture.
  2. Following vaginal surgery.
  3. Neurogenic bladder.
  4. Following surgery on prostate and bladder.

Nursing Management

A. Same as for any patient with indwelling catheter.

B. Catheter is clamped and then patient is allowed to void on his own (through urinary meatus).

C. When able to void on own, catheter is clamped and then removed after a few hours.

Cystoscopy

Definition: Cystoscopy is the inspection of the bladder by means of a cystoscope.

Purpose

A. Inspect bladder for stones, etc.

B. Obtain biopsy for tissue examination.

Nursing Management

A. Watch for urethral bleeding.

B. Chart intake and output and consistency of urine.

C. Observe for signs of infection.

1. Frequency.
2. Urgency.
3. Burning during urination.
D. Observe for perforation of bladder.
  1. Sharp abdominal pain.
  2. Anuria.
  3. Board-like abdomen.
E. Maintain patient on bed rest for four to six hours; then ambulate if no complications.
F. Monitor vital signs for shock and infection.

Cystectomy (or Urinary Diversion)

Definition: Cystectomy is the removal of the bladder for cancer by anastomosing ureters into loop of ileum, which is then brought through abdominal wall.

Purpose

A. Cancer of neck of bladder or ureters.
B. Cancer of pelvic area.
C. Neurogenic bladder.

Treatment

A. Superficial low grade tumors—TUR.
B. Monthly bladder instillations of thio-tepa for one year for superficial tumors.
C. Radon seeds for vesical tumors.
D. Cystectomy for extensive tumors which are curable.
E. High voltage radiotherapy in conjunction with radical surgery.
F. Radiotherapy and chemotherapy (fluorouracil) for inoperable tumors.

Nursing Management

A. Secure tight-fitting ostomy bag around opening to prevent skin irritation.
B. Measure intake and output.
C. Observe for fluid and electrolyte imbalance.
D. Observe for complications related to surgical intervention.
  1. Urinary fistula (urine around incision).
  2. Bowel fistula (feces from incision).
  3. Wound complications (dehiscence or evisceration).
E. Provide range-of-motion exercise.

F. If nasogastric tube is inserted, irrigate when necessary.
G. Provide routine abdominal postoperative care.
H. Provide psychological support for altered body image, change in life style, chronic disease.
I. Refer to cancer society for help with ostomy care.

Urolithiasis

Definition: Urolithiasis refers to the presence of stones in any portion of the urinary system.

Causes

A. Dehydration.
B. Immobilization.
C. Hypercalcemia.
D. Excessive uric acid excretion.
E. Obstruction and urinary stasis.

Clinical Manifestations

A. Pain starting low in back and radiating around front down the ureter.
B. Nausea, vomiting, and diarrhea.
C. Hematuria.
D. Chills and fever.

Surgical Interventions

A. Ureterolithotomy—removal of stone from ureter.
B. Pyelolithotomy—removal of stone from kidney pelvis.

Nursing Management

A. Force fluids.
B. Record intake and output.
C. Strain all urine for stones.
D. Send stones to laboratory for chemical analysis.
E. Administer appropriate antibiotics (infections occur especially when stones block off a portion of kidney).
F. Provide diet therapy, depending on chemical composition of stones.
G. Place heating pad on affected area.
H. Watch vital signs for signs of infection.
I. Prevent urolithiasis.

1. Provide adequate fluid intake.
2. Immediately treat urinary tract infection with appropriate antibiotics.
3. Ambulate patients to prevent urinary stasis (or reposition in bed frequently).

Nephrectomy

Definition: Nephrectomy is the surgical removal of a kidney.

Etiology

A. Polycystic kidneys.
B. Stones.
C. Preparation for transplantation.
D. Injury.
E. Infection which has destroyed kidney function.

Nursing Management

A. Keep an accurate record of intake and output (anuria can result if remaining kidney is damaged).
B. Obtain urine specimens as ordered to detect renal function of remaining kidney.
C. Force fluids.
D. Observe for signs of hemorrhage or shock.
E. Turn, cough, and hyperventilate every two hours (turn to operative side and back).
F. Administer IPPB if necessary.
G. Begin range-of-motion exercises immediately.
H. Check for bowel sounds (paralytic ileus may be a complication).
I. Encourage early ambulation.
J. Observe that Foley or suprapubic catheter is draining adequately.
   1. Tape catheter to leg or abdomen to prevent trauma to bladder.
   2. Position catheter bag below bed level to facilitate drainage.
K. If nephrostomy tube is inserted, measure drainage and record characteristics of drainage (drains kidney after surgery).
   1. Do not clamp tubes unless ordered.
   2. Do not irrigate tubes unless ordered.

Surgical Interventions for Male Genital Disorders

Prostatic Surgery

Types Requiring Surgery

A. Benign prostatic hypertrophy.
   1. Enlargement of prostate gland from normal tissue; causes narrowing of urethra if large enough, which results in obstruction.
   2. Clinical manifestations.
      a. Recurring infection and urinary stasis.
      b. Nocturia.
      c. Frequency.
      d. Dysuria.
B. Prostatic malignancy.
   1. Etiology is from parenchyma of prostate.
   2. Clinical manifestations.
      a. Urinary obstruction late in disease.
      b. Early symptoms similar to benign prostatic hypertrophy.
      c. Symptoms due to metastatic state.
         (1) Weight loss.
         (2) Nausea.
         (3) Oliguria.
         (4) Pain radiating from lumbosacral area down legs.

Treatment

A. Medical.
   1. Estrogen therapy may be given to slow rate of growth and extension of tumor.
   2. Radiation to local lesion to reduce size of tumor.
   3. Cryosurgery results in death of obstructive tissue.
B. Surgical.
   1. Transurethral resection (most common intervention)—removal of the prostatic tissue by instrumentation through urethra.
   2. Suprapubic prostatectomy—removal of prostate by abdominal incision.
   3. Retropubic prostatectomy—removal of prostate through an incision in its capsule.

Postoperative Nursing Management

A. Maintain adequate bladder drainage via catheter.
1. Suprapubic catheter used following suprapubic prostatectomy.
2. Continuous bladder irrigation (or triple lumen catheter) is used following transurethral resection.
   a. One lumen is used for inflating bag (usually 30 cc. bag), one for outflow of urine, and one for irrigating solution instillation.
   b. Function:
      (1) Continuous antibacterial irrigation of solution which prevents infection.
      (2) Continuous saline irrigation to rid the bladder of tissue and clots following surgery.
   c. Nursing interventions.
      (1) Run solution in rapidly if bright red drainage or clots are present; when drainage clears, decrease to about 40 drops/minute.
      (2) If clots cannot be rinsed out with irrigating solution, irrigate with syringe as ordered.
B. Provide fluids to prevent dehydration (2 to 3 liters).
C. Provide high protein, high vitamin diet.
D. Observe for signs of hemorrhage and shock.
E. Traction is applied to Foley catheter (if not connected to three-way drainage) to help in hemostasis.
1. Catheter is pulled on and taped to leg.
2. Do not release traction without order (traction released after bright red drainage has diminished).
F. Instruct patient in perineal exercises to regain urinary control.
1. Tense perineal muscles by pressing buttocks together; hold for as long as possible.
2. Repeat this process ten times every hour.
G. Ambulate early (after urine has returned to nearly normal color).
H. Observe for complications.
1. Epididymitis (most frequent).
2. Gram negative sepsis.
I. Administer urinary antiseptics or antibiotics to prevent infection.
J. Administer anticholinergics, if necessary, to relieve smooth muscle spasms.
K. Provide wound care for suprapubic and retropubic prostatectomies (similar to that for abdominal surgery).
L. Provide sitz bath and heat lamp treatments to promote healing.

Surgical Interventions for Female Reproductive System

Tumors of the Breast

Clinical Findings

A. Nontender lump in breast, usually in upper outer quadrant.
B. Dimpling of breast tissue surrounding nipple.
C. Asymmetry with affected breast being higher.
D. Nipple bleeding or retraction.

Types of Surgery

A. Simple mastectomy—removal of breast. No lymph nodes removed.
B. Radical mastectomy—removal of breast and muscle layer down to chest wall. Lymph nodes in axillary region also removed.

Nursing Management

A. Begin emotional support preoperative and continue in postoperative period.
1. Patient will have altered body image.
2. Patient may be extremely depressed.
B. Place in semi-Fowler's position with affected arm elevated to prevent edema.
C. Turn, cough, and hyperventilate to prevent respiratory complications.
D. Turn only to back and unaffected side.
E. Hemovac placed frequently.
1. Maintain suction.
2. Record amount of drainage.
3. Record drainage characteristics.
F. Prevent complications of contractures and lymphedema by encouraging range-of-motion exercises early in postoperative period.

G. I.V. fluids should not be administered in affected arm.

H. Monitor vital signs for prevention of complications such as infection and hemorrhage. Take blood pressure on unaffected arm only.

I. Pressure dressings should be reinforced. Observe for signs of restriction from dressing.
    1. Impaired sensation.
    2. Color changes of skin.

J. If skin grafts were applied, treat as for any other graft.

K. Encourage visit from Reach for Recovery Group.

Tumors of the Reproductive System

Definition: Tumors or neoplasms are composed of new and actively growing tissue. They are classified in many ways, the most common according to origin and whether they are malignant or benign. The second highest cause of death in the female is caused by malignant tumors of the reproductive system.

Cancer of the Cervix

A. Most common type of cancer in the reproductive system.

B. Usually appears in females between the ages of thirty to fifty.

C. Signs and symptoms include bleeding between periods—may be noted especially after intercourse or douching; leukorrhea.

D. May become invasive and include tissue outside the cervix, fundus of the uterus, and the lymph glands.

E. Treatment—depends upon extent of the disease.
    1. Hysterectomy.
    2. Radiation.
    3. Radical pelvic surgery in advanced cases.

Cancer of the Endometrium, Fundus, or Corpus of Uterus

A. Usually not diagnosed until symptoms appear—Pap smear inadequate for diagnosis.

B. Progresses slowly—metastasis occurs late.

C. Treatment.
    1. Early—hysterectomy.
    2. Late—radium and X-ray therapy.

Cancer of the Vulva

Clinical Manifestations

A. Long-standing pruritus (itching) and local discomfort.

B. Foul-smelling and slightly bloody discharge.

C. Early lesions may appear as chronic vulval dermatitis.

Treatment

A. Vulvectomy is the preferred treatment.

B. Radiation therapy is used in the inoperable lesions.

Postoperative Nursing Management

A. Immediate care.
    1. Observe dressings for signs of hemorrhage.
    2. Check vital signs until stable.
    3. Assist patient to turn, cough, and deep breathe every two hours.
    4. Give pain medications as ordered.
    5. Observe drainage and empty Hemovac as necessary.
    6. Record intake and output.
    7. Maintain I.V.
    8. Maintain catheter care to reduce incidence of infection.
    9. Position for comfort.

B. Convalescent care.
    1. Encourage verbalization regarding change in body image.
    2. Irrigate wound as ordered, using solution as prescribed (usual solution is sterile saline hydrogen peroxide), which cleans area and improves circulation.
    3. Prevent wound infection.

C. Discharge teaching.
    1. Signs of infection—foul-smelling discharge, elevated temperature, swelling.
    2. Nutritious diet and planned rest periods.
    3. Wound irrigation and dressing change.
    4. Importance of follow-up care by physician.

Hysterectomy

Types

A. Total—removal of the entire uterus; Fallopian tubes and ovaries remain.

B. Panhysterectomy—involves removal of the entire uterus, ovaries, and Fallopian tubes.

C. Radical hysterectomy—wide removal of vaginal, cervical, uterosacral and other tissue along with the uterus.

Nursing Management

A. Abdominal hysterectomy.

1. Clinical manifestations.
   a. Hemorrhage—vaginal and at the incision site.
   b. Signs of infection—elevated temperature, foul-smelling vaginal discharge, and pelvic congestion.
   c. Changes in body image—feelings of loss.
   d. Pneumonia.
   e. Paralytic ileus.
   f. Thrombophlebitis.

2. Immediate postoperative care.
   a. Observe incision site for bleeding and reinforce dressings as needed.
   b. Monitor vital signs frequently.
   c. If patient has nasogastric tube to suction, keep NPO and observe amount, color, and consistency of drainage.
   d. Administer pain medications as ordered.
   e. Administer I.V. fluids as ordered.
   f. Provide for hygienic care.
   g. Catheter care to prevent infection—observe amount and color of drainage.
   h. Assist patient to cough, turn, and deep breathe.
   i. Promote methods to decrease pelvic congestion.
      (1) Apply antiembolic stockings.
      (2) Avoid high-Fowler's position.
   j. Measure intake and output.
   k. Apply R.O.M. exercises.

3. Convalescent care.
   a. Increase activity as tolerated.
   b. Ambulate with assistance.
   c. Auscultate chest for breath sounds.
   d. Auscultate abdomen for bowel signs.
   e. Allow patient to verbalize feelings of loss of feminity, childbearing ability, disfigurement, fear of cancer.
   f. Provide for emotional support.
   g. Increase diet as tolerated.

   h. Administer laxatives and stool softeners as ordered and rectal tubes or Harris flush for flatus.

B. Preparing the patient for discharge.

1. Encourage expression of feelings with significant other.
2. Explain that menstruation will no longer occur.
3. Explain that estrogen therapy may be ordered by the physician if the ovaries were removed to control menopausal symptoms.
4. Instruct the patient to observe for signs of complications.
   a. Elevation of temperature.
   b. Foul-smelling vaginal discharge.
   c. Redness, swelling, or drainage from the incision site.
   d. Abdominal cramping.
5. Explain the importance of follow-up visits with the physician.
6. Explain the importance of taking medications as ordered.
7. Douching and coitus are usually avoided for six weeks.

Anterior and Posterior Colporrhaphy

A. Purpose.

1. Repair of cystocele—downward displacement of the bladder towards the vaginal entrance, caused by tissue weakness, injuries in childbirth, and atrophy associated with aging.
2. Repair of rectocele—anterior sagging of rectum and posterior vaginal wall caused by injuries to the muscles and tissue of the pelvic floor during childbirth.

B. General postoperative care of the patient with "A and P" repair.

1. Observe for foul-smelling discharge from vaginal area or operative site.
2. Care of perineal sutures—two methods:
   a. Sutures left alone until healing begins, thereafter daily vaginal irrigations with sterile saline.
   b. Sterile saline douches twice daily, beginning with the first postoperative day.
3. Observe for urinary retention and catheterize as necessary.
4. Preparation of patient for discharge. Patient should be instructed in perineal hygiene (no

douching or coitus until advised by physician), and to watch for signs of infection.

Pelvic Exenteration

Definition: Pelvic exenteration is a surgical procedure that is performed when cancer is widespread and cannot be controlled by other means.

A. There are three types of pelvic exenteration:
1. Anterior pelvic exenteration—the removal of the reproductive organs, pelvic lymph nodes, adnexa, pelvic peritoneum, bladder, and lower ureter. Ureters are implanted in the small intestines or the colon.
2. Posterior pelvic exenteration—removal of the reproductive organs, vagina, adnexa, colon, and rectum. Pelvic lymph nodes may be removed.
3. Total pelvic exenteration—removal of the reproductive organs, pelvic floor, pelvic lymph nodes, perineum, bladder, rectum, and distal portion of sigmoid colon. A substitute bladder is made from a segment of the ileum. Patient will have a permanent colostomy.

B. Care of the patient undergoing pelvic exenteration.
1. General postoperative procedures.
2. Observe surgical site for drainage and reinforce dressings as necessary; patient may have drainage tubes connected to suction from incision area.
3. Apply antiembolic stockings.
4. Encourage patient to express feelings.

Endocrine System

Surgery Associated with Endocrine Disorders

Adrenalectomy

Definition: Surgical removal of an adrenal gland when overproduction of adrenal hormone is evident (Cushing's syndrome, pheochromocytoma) or in metastatic breast or prostatic cancer.

Treatment

A. Bilateral adrenalectomy.
B. Replacement therapy with adrenal corticosteroids.

Nursing Management

A. Preoperative care.
1. Provide general preoperative care.
2. Administer exogenous glucocorticoids.
B. Postoperative care.
1. Monitor vital signs and intake and output.
2. Administer parenteral fluids.
3. Strictly adhere to sterile techniques when changing dressings.
4. Observe for shock, hypoglycemia.
5. Maintain hydrocortisone therapy.

Complications

A. Wound infections.
B. Hemorrhage.
C. Peptic ulcers.
D. Pulmonary disorders.

Hypophysectomy

Definition: Removal of pituitary gland due to tumor formation.

Treatment

A. Craniotomy.
B. Microsurgery.
C. Cryohypophysectomy.
D. Hormone replacement.

Nursing Management

A. Preoperative care.
1. Provide general preoperative care.
2. Provide emotional support.
B. Postoperative care.
1. Administer corticosteroids on time.
2. Monitor fluid and electrolyte balance.
   a. Hyponatremia due to ADH disturbance and vasopressin alterations.
   b. Avoid water intoxification.
3. Carefully monitor vital signs.
4. Monitor blood gas determinations.

5. Provide routine care for craniotomy. Observe for:
   a. Vital signs.
   b. Increased intracranial pressure.
   c. Shock.
   d. LOC.
6. Initiate patient education.
   a. Compensate for altered stress response.
   b. Avoid contact with infectious individuals.
   c. Carry emergency adrenal hormone drugs.
   d. Use medic-alert arm band.

Complications

A. Craniotomy—bleeding in acromegaly (due to excessive growth of frontal bones).
B. Microsurgery—rhinorrhea and meningitis (due to interruption of CSF during surgery).
C. Cryohypophysectomy—probe hits other vital structures.

Thyroidectomy

Definition: Removal of thyroid gland for persistent hyperthyroidism.

Treatment

A. Total resection of gland.
B. Subtotal resection.
C. Hormone replacement therapy.

Nursing Management

A. Preoperative care—prevent thyrotoxicosis.
   1. Administer antithyroid drugs to deplete iodine and hormones (5–7 days).
   2. Administer iodine to decrease vascularity and increase size of follicular cells (5–7 days).
   3. Provide routine preoperative teaching.
   4. Reassure patient.
B. Postoperative care.
   1. Maintain semi-Fowler's position to avoid strain on suture line.
   2. Observe for bleeding.
      a. Vital signs—tachycardia, hypotension.
      b. Pressure on larynx.
      c. Hematoma around wound.
   3. Observe for damage to recurrent laryngeal nerve.

a. Respiratory obstruction.
b. Dysphonia.
c. High-pitched voice.
d. Stridor.
e. Dysphagia.
f. Restlessness.
g. Anxiety.
4. Keep tracheostomy set at bedside.
5. Observe for signs of hypoparathyroidism.
   a. Chvostek's sign.
   b. Muscle cramps.
   c. Dysphagia.

Thyroid Crisis

Etiology

A. Cause not known; symptoms reflect exaggerated thyrotoxicosis.
B. Infrequent due to premedication of iodine and antithyroid drugs.
C. Can be precipitated by stressors.
   1. Infection.
   2. Abrupt withdrawal of medication.
   3. Metabolic causes.
   4. Emotional stress.
   5. Pulmonary embolism.

Clinical Manifestations

A. Increased temperature ($>100°$).
B. Diaphoresis.
C. Cardiopulmonary symptoms.
   1. Tachycardia (>120).
   2. Arrhythmias.
   3. Congestive heart failure.
   4. Pulmonary edema.
D. Gastrointestinal symptoms.
   1. Abdominal pain.
   2. Nausea, vomiting, and diarrhea.
   3. Jaundice.
E. Central nervous system symptoms.
   1. Tremors.
   2. Severe agitation.
   3. Apathy leading to coma.

Treatment

A. Adrenergic blocking agents to decrease heart activity.

B. Glucocorticoids to allay stress effects.

C. Sodium iodide to slow I.V. infusion.

D. SSKI p.o.

E. Antithyroid drugs.

Nursing Management

A. Do not palpate thyroid gland (stimulus increases symptoms).

B. Decrease temperature: ASA, external cold (ice packs, cooling blanket).

C. Protect from infection, especially pneumonia.

D. Maintain fluid and electrolyte balance.
1. Electrolyte shifts cause brittle situation of over and under hydration.
2. Maintain adequate output.
3. Observe for Na^+ and K^+ imbalance due to vomiting and diarrhea.
4. Observe for signs of overhydration if cardiopulmonary complications are evident.

E. Monitor ECG for arrhythmias if:
1. Adrenergic blockers are used.
2. Diuretics are given.
3. Electrolyte imbalance is present.
4. Cardiovascular medication is given.

F. Administer I.V. glucose diet with glucose and large doses of vitamin B complex.

G. Protect for safety if agitated or comatose.

H. Reassure patient and family.

Parathyroidectomy

Definition: Removal of one or more of the parathyroid glands, usually as a result of thyroidectomy.

Treatment

A. Intravenous administration of calcium gluconate.

B. Check Chvostek's and Trousseau's signs.

Nursing Management

A. Observe for tetany and treat accordingly.

B. Maintain patent airway.

C. Provide diet high in calcium, vitamin D, and magnesium salts.

D. Increase fluids to prevent formation of urinary stones.

Musculoskeletal System

Fractures

Definition: A break in the continuity of bone caused by trauma, twisting or as a result of bone decalcification.

Specific Types of Fractures

A. Greenstick.
1. A crack; the bending of a bone with incomplete fracture. Only affects one side of the periosteum.
2. Common in young children when bones are pliable, or in skull fractures.

B. Comminuted.
1. Bone completely broken in a transverse, spiral, or oblique direction (indicates the direction of the fracture in relation to the long axis of the fracture bone).
2. Bone broken into several fragments.

C. Open, or compound.
1. Bone is exposed to the air through a break in the skin.
2. Can be associated with soft tissue injury as well.
3. Infection is common complication due to exposure to bacterial invasion.

D. Closed, or simple.
1. Skin remains intact.
2. Chances are greatly decreased for infection.

E. Compression.
1. Frequently seen with vertebral fractures.
2. Fractured bone has been compressed by other bones.

F. Complete—bone is broken with a disruption of both sides of the periosteum.

G. Impacted—one part of fractured bone is driven into another.

H. Depressed fracture.
1. Usually seen in skull or facial fractures.
2. Bone or fragments of bone are driven inward.

I. Pathological—break caused by disease process.

Causes of Fractures

A. Fatigue—muscles are less supportive to bone and

therefore cannot absorb the force being exerted.

B. Bone neoplasms—cellular proliferations of malignant cells replace normal tissue causing a weakened bone.

C. Metabolic disorders—poor mineral absorption and hormonal changes decrease bone calcification which results in a weakened bone.

D. Bedrest or disuse—atropic muscles and osteoporosis cause decreased stress resistance.

Assessment of Fracture

A. Cardinal signs of a fracture.
  1. Pain or tenderness over involved area.
  2. Loss of function of the extremity.
  3. Deformity.
     a. Overriding.
     b. Angulation—limb is in an unnatural position.
B. Crepitation—sound of grating bone fragments.
C. Ecchymosis or erythema.
D. Edema.
E. Muscle spasm.

Emergency Care of Fractures

A. Immobilize affected extremity to prevent further damage to soft tissue or nerve.
B. If compound fracture is evident, do not attempt to reduce it.
  1. Apply splint.
  2. Cover open wound with sterile dressing.
C. Splinting.
  1. External support is applied around a fracture to immobilize the broken ends. Materials used: wood, plastic (air splints), magazines.
  2. Function.
     a. Prevents additional trauma.
     b. Reduces pain.
     c. Decreases muscle spasm.
     d. Limits movement.
     e. Prevents complications, such as fat emboli if long bone fracture.

Treatment of Fractures

A. Traction (see Care of Patient in Traction, p. 235).
B. Reduction (restoring bone to proper alignment).
  1. Closed reduction.

     a. Manual manipulation.
     b. Usually done under anesthesia to reduce pain and relax muscles, thereby preventing complications.
     c. Cast is usually applied following closed reduction.
  2. Open reduction.
     a. Surgical intervention.
     b. Usually treated with internal fixation devices (screws, plates, wires, etc.).
     c. Following surgery, patient can be placed in traction; however, patient is usually placed in cast.
     d. Nursing management: provide care of suture site and follow procedures for general postoperative care.

Traction

Definition: Traction is force applied in two directions to reduce and/or immobilize a fracture, to provide proper bone alignment and regain normal length, or to reduce muscle spasm.

Skeletal Traction

A. Mechanical applied to bone, using pins (Steinmann), wires (Kirschner), tongs (Crutchfield).
B. Most often used in fractures of femur, tibia, humerus.

Nursing Management

A. Observe pin or tong insertion site for drainage, odors, erythema, edema (usually indication of inflammatory process or infection).
B. Watch for skin breakdown if bandage is used to apply traction.
C. Cover end of pins or wires with rubber stoppers or cork to prevent puncture of nursing personnel or patient.
D. Cleanse area surrounding insertion site of pin or tongs with hydrogen peroxide or Betadine. Some physicians order antibiotic ointments to be applied to area.

Balanced Suspension Traction

A. Thomas's splint with Pearson attachment is used in

conjunction with skin or skeletal traction (used particularly with skeletal traction for fractured femur).

B. Balanced suspension traction is produced by a counterforce other than the patient.

Nursing Management

A. Maintain proper alignment.

B. Protect skin from excoriation, particularly around the top of Thomas's splint. Pad with cotton wadding or ABD's.

C. Prevent pressure points around the top of Thomas's splint by keeping patient pulled up in bed.

D. Maintain at least 20-degree angle from thigh to the bed.

E. Provide foot plate to prevent foot drop.

F. Keep heels clear of Pearson attachment to prevent skin breakdown and decubitus.

G. Position patient frequently from side to side (as ordered).

H. Unless contraindicated, head of bed can be elevated for comfort and facilitating adequate respiratory functions.

I. Place overbed table on unaffected side.

Skin Traction

A. Traction applied by use of elastic bandages, moleskin strips, or adhesive.

B. Used most often in alignment or lengthening (for congenital hip displacement, etc.).

C. Most common types.
   1. Russell traction.
   2. Buck's extension (most common).
      a. Pull is exerted in one plane.
      b. Used for temporary immobilization.
      c. Apply moleskin or adhesive material to leg (after it has been wrapped in ace bandage).
      d. Attach a foot block with a spreader and rope which goes into a pulley.
      e. Attach weight to pulley and hang freely over edge of bed. (Not more than eight to ten pounds of weight can be applied.)
      f. Observe and readjust bandages for tightness and smoothness (can cause constriction which leads to edema or even nerve damage).

D. Cervical traction (used for whiplashes and cervical spasm).
   1. Use head harness (or halter).
      a. Pad chin.
      b. Protect ears from friction rub.
   2. Elevate head of bed and attach weights to pulley system over head of bed.
   3. Observe for skin breakdown.
      a. Powder areas encased in the halter.
      b. Place back of head on padding.

E. Pelvic traction (used for low back pain).
   1. Apply girdle snugly over patient's pelvis and iliac crest; attach to weights.
   2. Observe for pressure points over iliac crest.
   3. Keep patient in good alignment.
   4. May raise foot of bed slightly (12 inches) to prevent patient from slipping down in bed.

Care of Traction Apparatus

A. Weights should hang freely and not touch the floor.

B. Pulleys should not be obstructed.

C. Ropes in the pulley should move freely.

D. Knot should be secured in rope to prevent slipping.

E. Proper body alignment (up in bed, in direct line with traction) and proper countertraction should be maintained.

F. Weights should not be removed or lifted without specific order. (Exceptions are pelvic and cervicle traction that patients can remove at intervals.)

G. Sharp edges from traction apparatus should be covered with hollowed out rubber balls to prevent injury to nursing personnel if they bump into equipment.

Care of Patient in Traction

A. Maintain correct alignment.

B. Maintain counterbalance or correct pull.
   1. Pull is exerted against traction in opposite direction (balanced suspension).
   2. Pull is exerted against a fixed point.
   3. Bed is elevated under area involved to provide the countertraction.

C. Provide firm mattress or bedboards.

D. Observe for complications.
   1. Osteomyelitis (infections of bone).
   2. Bone deformities.

3.   Skin breakdown.

E.   Provide range-of-motion exercises for unaffected extremities.

F.   Observe for circulatory impairment.
1.   Blanching of nailbeds (color should return quickly when nailbeds are depressed).
2.   Extremity should be pink and warm.
3.   Check for edema in affected extremity.
4.   Patient should be able to wiggle finger or toes.
5.   Patient should not have tingling or loss of sensation in affected extremity.

G.   Prevent foot drop.
1.   Provide footplate.
2.   Encourage dorsiflexion exercises.

H.   Provide overhead trapeze to allow patient to assist in activities (turning, moving up in bed, using bedpan, etc.).

I.   Prevent postoperative complications (see General Postoperative Complications in this chapter).

Principles of Cast Care

A.   After application of cast, allow twenty-four to forty-eight hours for drying.
1.   Cast will change from dull to shiny substance when dry.
2.   Heat can be applied to assist in drying process.

B.   Do not handle cast during drying process as indentations from fingermarks can cause skin breakdown under cast.

C   Keep extremity elevated to prevent edema.

D.   Provide for smooth edges surrounding cast.
1.   Prevents crumbling and breaking down of edges.
2.   Stockinet can be pulled over edge and fastened down with adhesive tape to outside of cast.

E.   Observe casted extremity for signs of circulatory impairment. Cast may have to be cut if edematous condition continues.

F.   If there is an open, draining area on affected extremity, a window (cut out portion of cast) can be utilized for observation and/or irrigation of wound.

G.   Keep cast dry; it can break down when water comes in contact with plaster. Plastic bags or plastic coated bed chux can be utilized during the bath or when using bedpan, to protect cast material.

H.   Utilize isometric exercises to prevent muscle atrophy and to strengthen the muscle. Isometrics prevent joint from being mobilized.

I.   Position patient with pillows to prevent strain on unaffected areas.

J.   Turn every two hours to prevent complications. Encourage to lie on abdomen four hours a day.

The Immobilized Patient

A.   Prevent respiratory complications.
1.   Have patient cough and deep breathe every two hours.
2.   Turn every two hours if not contraindicated.
3.   Provide suction if needed.

B.   Prevent thrombus and emboli formation.
1.   Apply antiembolic stockings.
2.   Initiate isometric and isotonic exercises.
3.   Start anticoagulation therapy, if indicated.
4.   Turn every two hours.
5.   Observe for signs and symptoms of pulmonary and/or fat emboli.

C.   Prevent contractures.
1.   Start range-of-motion exercises to affected joints q.i.d., all joints b.i.d.
2.   Provide foot board and/or foot cradle.
3.   Position and turn every two hours.

D.   Prevent skin breakdown.
1.   Massage with lotion once a day to prevent drying.
2.   Use alcohol for back care to toughen skin.
3.   Massage elbows, coccyx, heels b.i.d.
4.   Turn every two hours.
5.   Alternate pressure mattress, sheepskin.
6.   Use stryker boats or heel protectors.
7.   Use elbow guards.

E.   Prevent urinary retention and calculi.
1.   Force fluids.
2.   Monitor intake and output.
3.   Administer urinary antiseptic (Mandelamine, etc.).
4.   Offer bedpan every four hours.

F.   Prevent constipation.
1.   Force fluids.
2.   Provide high fiber diet.
3.   Administer laxative or enema.
4.   Offer bedpan at same time each day—encourage to establish good bowel habits.

G. Provide psychological support.

1. Allow patient to ventilate feelings of dependence.
2. Encourage independence when possible (bathing, self feeding, etc.).
3. Encourage visitors for short time periods.
4. Provide diversionary activities (television, newspapers, etc.).

Fractured Ribs

A. Prevent shock if trauma is cause.

1. Assessment.
   a. Monitor vital signs every hour until stable.
   b. Check color and warmth every two hours.
   c. Check LOC.
   d. Observe for restlessness.
   e. Auscultate breath sounds.
2. Nursing management.
   a. Administer oxygen as indicated.
   b. Administer I.V. if signs of shock present.
   c. Keep lightly covered.
   d. Have chest tube insertion tray available.

B. Relieve pain from muscle spasms and fractures.

1. Give pain medication ½ hour before any movement.
2. Change position every two hours.
3. Use pillows for support.
4. Place patient in semi-Fowler's position.

C. Prevent complications of immobility.

1. Cough and deep breathe every two hours to prevent hypostatic pneumonia.
2. Turn to unaffected side and back every two hours.
3. Maintain skin care to prevent decubiti and circulatory impairment.
   a. Back care.
   b. Heel, elbow, coccyx massage.
4. Institute leg exercises to prevent circulatory impairment.
5. Prevent constipation and flatus.
   a. Insert rectal tube (no more than 20 min./time).
   b. Provide stool softener.
   c. Maintain diet high in bulk.
   d. Force fluids.

Hip Conditions

Types of Fractures

A. Intracapsular (neck)—bone broken inside the joint.

1. Treated by internal fixation—insertion of pins or nails; replacement of femoral head with prosthesis.
   a. Smith-Peterson nail.
   b. Austin Moore's prosthesis.
2. Usually placed in skeletal balanced suspension traction first for reduction of fracture.
3. Patient can be out of bed without weight-bearing in one to two days postoperatively (depending on other physical problems).

B. Extracapsular—trochanteric fracture outside the joint.

1. Fracture of greater trochanter.
   a. Can be treated by balanced suspension traction if little displacement of bone. Full weight-bearing usually in six to eight weeks, when healing takes place.
   b. Surgical intervention is necessary if large displacement or extensive soft tissue damage; usually internal fixation with wire.
2. Intertrochanteric fracture.
   a. Extends from medial region of the junction of the neck and lesser trochanter toward the summit of the greater trochanter.
   b. Treated initially by balanced suspension traction.
   c. Surgically treated early due to debilitated physical condition of most of these patients (usually seventy years and older with other system diseases like diabetes, hypertension, etc.).
   d. Internal fixation used with nail-plate, screws, and wire.
3. Not allowed to flex hip to the side, on the side of the bed, or in a low chair. When hip is flexed displacement can occur.

Nursing Management for Hip Surgery (Other Than Hip Prosthesis)

A. Hemovac will usually be in place to drain off excessive blood and fluid accumulation.

1. Compute intake and output.
2. Keep Hemovac compressed to facilitate drainage.

B. Have patient perform bed exercises at least four times a day.
   1. Flex and extend foot, tense muscles, and straighten knee.
   2. Tighten buttocks, straighten knee, and push leg down in bed.
   3. Tighten stomach muscles by raising neck and shoulders.
   4. Stretch arms to head of bed and deep breathe.
C. Change positions by raising head of bed.
   1. Gatch knees slightly to relieve strain on hips and back.
   2. Turn to unaffected side.
   3. Pivot into chair within one to two days postoperatively.
   4. Have patient avoid full weight-bearing until fracture has healed.
D. Perform routine postoperative nursing interventions (respiratory care, etc.).
E. Observe for adequate bowel and bladder function.
F. Observe for complications (infection, hemorrhage).

Hip Prosthesis

A. Replacement of head of femur by Austin Moore prosthesis.
B. Nursing management.
   1. Keep affected leg abducted and externally rotated with abductor splints, pillows, or sandbags.
   2. Make sure hip flexion angle does not exceed 60–80 degrees.
   3. Forbid patient to flex hip on the side of the bed or in low chair.
      a. Use high stools.
      b. Use wheelchairs with backs that are adjustable.
      c. Use commode extenders.
   4. Elevate head of bed 30 to 40 degrees for meals only.
   5. Turn patient to unaffected side with pillow support between legs.
   6. Ambulate in two to four days with partial weight-bearing.

Total Hip Replacement

A. Replacement of both the acetabulum and the head of the femur with metal or plastic implants.
B. Used in degenerative diseases of both aspects or when fracture of head of femur has occurred with nonunion.

Nursing Management

A. Initially suspend the operative leg in a Marmar sling with five pounds of Buck's extension. Maintain until hip can be put through full range of motion.
B. Keep the operative leg in abduction and externally rotated at all times by use of pillows or abductor splints.
C. Keep Hemovac in place until drainage has substantially decreased (twenty-four to ninety-six hours).
   1. Check dressing to ensure patency of Hemovac.
   2. Observe drainage for signs of hemorrhage or infection.
D. Keep patient in supine position until prosthesis is stable.
   1. Some physicians allow turning, but pillows must always be kept between legs and legs kept uncrossed.
   2. Do not turn to affected side.
E. Prevent edema.
   1. Readjust antiembolic stockings at least every four to eight hours.
   2. Change position frequently by raising and lowering head of bed. When ordered, tilt bed to change positions.
F. Prevent thrombus formation.
   1. Have patient wear antiembolic stockings.
   2. Promote leg exercises.
   3. Administer anticoagulants (usually ASA).
G. Prevent flexion contracture of hip.
H. Within first two days, instruct patient on bed exercises (see Nursing Management for Hip Surgery in this section).
I. Use Nelson bed, which prevents hip flexion by allowing patient to be tilted and to walk off end of bed.
J. Ambulate as early as seven to ten days postoperatively.
K. Instruct patient not to use low chairs or to sit on edge of bed.
   1. Use extended commode.

2. Use wheelchair that tilts back.
3. Use high stools.

Knee Surgery

Arthrotomy

Definition: Arthrotomy is the cutting into the joint for the removal of cartilage or meniscus.

Nursing Management

A. Begin quad setting, straight leg raising exercises. Should be done for five minutes every half hour.
   1. Quad setting exercises—tightening or contracting the muscles of anterior thigh (knee cap is drawn up toward thigh).
   2. Straight leg raising—lifting leg straight off the bed, keeping knee extended and foot in neutral position.
B. Perform bed exercises.
C. Do dorsiflexion and plantar flexion of feet and ankles.
D. Can apply ice bags to knee to reduce edema.
E. Patient can be out of bed first postoperative day without weight-bearing (use three point crutch walking gait).
F. In addition, give routine postoperative care.

Total Knee Replacement

Definition: Implantation of a metallic upper portion which substitutes for the femoral condyles and a high polymer plastic lower portion which substitutes for the tibial joint surfaces.

Nursing Management

A. Quad setting and straight leg raising exercises every hour.
B. General bed exercises.
C. Cast or splint is usually applied. (Nursing care is same as for any patient in a cast.)
D. To prevent dislocation, leg is not to be dangled.

E. Hemovac should be inserted to drain excessive blood and drainage.
   1. Accurate intake and output.
   2. Observe for hemorrhage and infection.
F. Instruct patient in crutch walking.
G. Patient will be out of bed in two to three days.
H. General postoperative care.

Spinal Surgery

Laminectomy

Definition: Laminectomy is the excision of a vertebral posterior arch.

Nursing Management

A. Observe for circulatory impairment—check blanching, color, warmth of lower or upper extremities (depending on surgical site).
B. Observe for sensations in lower extremities (checking for nerve root damage).
   1. Sensation.
   2. Ability to wiggle toes and move feet—record ability to do plantar flexion, dorsiflexion of feet, toes, and ankles.
C. Observe dressings for spinal fluid leak as well as hemorrhage and infection.
D. Change patient's position every two hours by log-rolling for at least forty-eight hours.
   1. Turn patient as one piece by using draw sheet (or pull sheet), placing pillows between legs.
   2. Turn patient to either side and back (unless contraindicated). Use support mechanisms when on side.
E. Promote general bed exercises—plantar flexion, dorsiflexion.
   1. Have patient come to a sitting position by lying on side, with bed in flat position.
   2. Have patient push up with arms, keeping back straight, and push legs over bed to a sitting position.
F. Patient should either ambulate or lie in bed, as sitting puts strain on surgical site.

G. Ambulate in one to two days postoperatively, unless contraindicated.

H. Instruct patient in application of back brace or corset. (Decreases strain and reduces muscle spasm.)

I. Provide general postoperative care.

J. Administer stronger pain medicines if on medication for long time preop (at least 48 hours postop).

Spinal Fusion

Definition: Spinal fusion is the fusion of spinous processes, stabilizing the spine by removal of bone chips from iliac crest and grafting them to fusion site.

Nursing Management

A. Postoperative positioning.
1. Some physicians keep patient supine for first eight hours to reduce possibility of compression.
2. Most physicians keep patient off back for first forty-eight hours.

B. Brace is applied when patient is ambulated. Start of ambulation varies with physicians, from three to four days to eight weeks, depending on extent of fusion.
1. Takes six to eight weeks of immobilization for early healing of bone graft and for new callus to form.
2. Patient is not to lift, bend, stoop, or sit for prolonged periods for at least three months.
3. Grafts are stable by one year.
4. Some limitation to flexion of spine, depending on extent of fusion.

C. Additional interventions are the same as for laminectomy.

Fusion with Harrington Rod

A. Keep flat in bed (no leg dangling or head elevation).

B. Cast care for full body cast.

C. Log roll every hour, 30 degrees to either side for at least four days.

D. Observe for circulatory impairment.

E. Assist in pain tolerance.
1. Severe pain first few days.
2. Pain for several weeks.
3. Pain medication routinely every three to four hours for five days.

4. Positioning.
5. Relaxation exercises.

F. Prevent complications of immobility.

G. Observe for signs of fluid and electrolyte imbalance, record I & O.

H. Provide diet high in protein, iron, and thiamin and low in calcium.

Amputation

Definition: Amputation is the surgical removal of a limb, a part of a limb, or a portion of a bone elsewhere than at the joint site. Removal of a bone at the joint site is termed disarticulation.

Preoperative Nursing Management

A. Have patient practice lifting buttocks off bed while in sitting position.

B. Provide range of motion to unaffected leg.

C. Inform patient about phantom limb sensation.
1. Pain and feeling that amputated leg is still there.
2. Caused by nerves in the stump.
3. Exercises lessen sensation.

Postoperative Nursing Management

A. Observe stump dressing for signs of hemorrhage and infection.
1. Keep tourniquet at bedside to control hemorrhage if necessary.
2. Mark bleeding by circling drainage with pencil and marking date and time.
3. Elevate foot of bed to prevent hemorrhage and to reduce edema first 24 hours. (Elevating the stump itself can cause a flexion contracture of hip joint.)

B. Observe for symptoms of a developing necrosis or neuroma in incision.

C. Provide stump care.
1. Rewrap ace bandage three to four times daily.
2. Wash stump with mild soap and water.
3. If skin dry, apply lanolin or vaseline to stump.

D. Teaching related to stump care.
1. Below knee amputation—prevent edema formation.

    a.   Do not hang stump over edge of bed.

    b.   Do not sit for long periods of time.

2. Above knee amputation—prevent external or internal rotation of limb.

    a.   Rolled towel can be placed along outside of thigh to prevent rotation.

    b.   Low Fowler's can be used to provide change in position.

3. Position patient with either type of amputation in prone position to stretch flexar muscles and to prevent flexion contractures of hip. Done usually after first twenty-four to forty-eight hours postoperative.

    a.   Place pillow under abdomen and stump.

    b.   Keep legs close together to prevent abduction.

4. Teach crutch working and wheelchair transfer.

5. Prepare stump for prosthesis.

    a.   Stump must be conditioned for proper fit.

    b.   Shrinking and shaping stump to conical form by applying bandages or an elastic stump shrinker.

    c.   A cast readies stump for the prosthesis.

6. Provide care for temporary prosthesis which is applied until stump has shrunk to permanent state.

E. Recognize and respond to patient's psychological reactions to amputation.

1. Feelings of loss.

2. Lowered self-image.

3. Depression.

4. Phantom limb pain.

Review Questions

1. John Thomas was admitted to the ICU following a car accident. He had multiple injuries, the most serious being a flail chest. John's hypoventilation due to the flail chest could cause

   A. Respiratory acidosis.
   B. Respiratory alkalosis.
   C. Metabolic acidosis.
   D. Metabolic alkalosis.

2. John had chest tubes inserted. Which of the following nursing interventions would not be carried out for him?

   A. Place hemostats on bed as a safety measure in case of air leaks.
   B. Milk (or strip) the chest tubes every two or four hours to maintain patency.
   C. Report chest drainage in excess of 200 cc./hour to the physician.
   D. Keep the patient flat in bed to avoid the formation of leaks and to promote drainage.

3. Nursing responsibilities associated with John's chest tubes will include

   A. Keeping the chest tubes free of kinking and obstruction by coiling them loosely to the bed.
   B. Keeping bottles at bed level to prevent backflow.
   C. Checking that water fluctuation is continuous in the trap bottle.
   D. Checking that the amount of pressure does not exceed 5 cm. water in the pressure chamber.

4. John is placed on ventilatory assistance. Which of the following statements is correct?

   A. A volume set or control respirator is the type that is usually used.
   B. A pressure set respirator is the type that is usually used.
   C. The ventilatory rate is measured with a gas meter.
   D. An uncuffed tracheostomy tube should be inserted.

5. Nursing care for patients with a cuffed tracheostomy tube will include which of the following?

   A. Keeping the tube inflated at all times.
   B. Suction tracheostomy at least every four hours.
   C. Auscultate breath sounds every one to two hours.
   D. Deflate tracheostomy tube when feeding patient.

6. Mrs. Garcia is scheduled for a radical mastectomy in the morning. Breast cancers are most common in which area of the breast?

   A. The region of the nipples.
   B. Lower outer quadrant.
   C. Upper outer quadrant.
   D. Upper inner quadrant near the sternum.

7. Following her radical mastectomy, which position would be most therapeutic?

   A. Positioned on operative side.
   B. Positioned on unoperative side.
   C. Positioned in semi-Fowler's with affected arm flat on bed.
   D. Positioned in semi-Fowler's with affected arm elevated.

8. Nursing interventions would include which of the following?

   A. Encourage deep breathing and coughing exercises.
   B. Place prosthesis as soon as dressing is removed.
   C. Keep affected arm immobile until sutures are removed.
   D. Delay all arm exercises until incision is healed.

9. Joan Carlson was diagnosed as having cholelithiasis. She had been having several episodes of gallbladder attacks over the past year. Which of the following symptoms would most likely bring Joan to the doctor?

   A. Chronic pain in lower right abdomen.
   B. Chronic pain in lower left abdomen.
   C. Fatty food intolerance while eating.
   D. Fatty food intolerance several hours after eating.

10. The major postoperative complication following a cholecystectomy is

    A. Paralytic ileus.
    B. Thrombophlebitis.
    C. Pneumonia.
    D. Hemorrhage.

11. A T-tube was placed in the common bile duct at the time of surgery. Which of the following statements are correct concerning the T-tube?

    A. It prevents backflow of bile into the liver.
    B. Patient is positioned in a prone position to promote bile drainage.
    C. The T-tube is connected to the drainage bottle at the level of the bed to prevent bile backflow.
    D. The T-tube is not to be clamped.

12. Which of the following clinical manifestations would Joan exhibit due to an obstruction of the biliary tract?

    A. Black tarry stools.
    B. Tachycardia.
    C. Prolonged bleeding time.
    D. Pain in the epigastric region.

13. Joan's biliary pain is best controlled by which one of the following medications?

    A. Thorazine.
    B. Codeine.
    C. Morphine.
    D. Demerol.

14. Nursing interventions most likely carried out during the preoperative period for Joan would include all except

    A. Administration of vitamin K.
    B. Administration of nitroglycerine.
    C. Provision of diet low in fat and protein, and high in carbohydrates.
    D. Provision for relief of pruritus.

15. Mrs. Johnson, twenty-three years old, was admitted to the hospital at 8:00 P.M. with the diagnosis of appendicitis. On admission she stated that she had been vomiting and experiencing pain all day. Which of the following signs and symptoms are indicative of appendicitis?

    A. High fever.
    B. Anorexia.
    C. Tenderness localized in the lower left quadrant.
    D. Nausea and vomiting only when eating.

16. Mrs. Johnson's I.V. orders were as follows: 3000 cc. D_5.2NS over twenty-four hours. The administration set delivers 15 gtts./minute. Calculate the number of drops that will be administered per minute.

    A. 20 gtts./minute.
    B. 31 gtts./minute.
    C. 125 gtts./minute.
    D. 187 gtts./minute.

17. Nursing interventions for Mrs. Johnson during the preoperative period will include

    A. Keeping her flat in bed.
    B. Allowing only sips of water.
    C. Using a heating pad on the tender area to decrease pain.
    D. Using an ice bag on the tender area to decrease pain.

18. When suctioning a patient with a cuffed tracheostomy tube, which of the following nursing measures should be included?

    A. Oral suctioning should be carried out after the trach tube is deflated.
    B. The size of the suction catheter should not exceed half the diameter of the trach tube.
    C. Suctioning should not exceed thirty seconds at a time.
    D. Apply suction when inserting as well as when removing the catheter.

19. Which of the following interventions are carried out when taking a CVP reading?

    A. Place patient in semi-Fowler's position while taking the reading.
    B. The "O" point of the manometer should be placed at the level of the subclavian artery.
    C. The patient should be kept on the respirator for a more accurate reading.
    D. The infusion set can be primed with a heparinized solution to ensure patency.

20. Which of the following signs and symptoms would indicate thrombophlebitis?

    A. Bluish discoloration along vein.
    B. Severe cramping.
    C. Varicosities.
    D. Surrounding area cool to the touch.

21. Which of the following manifestations would indicate a possible wound infection?

    A. Increased temperature within the first twenty-four hours after surgery.
    B. Serosanguineous drainage on dressing.
    C. Erythema surrounding suture line three to four days postoperatively.
    D. Bright red drainage on dressing the night of surgery.

22. The initial nursing intervention for a patient in hypovolemic shock would include:

    A. Place in Trendelenburg position.
    B. Administer intravenous fluids to maintain a CVP reading of 5–9 cm. of water pressure.
    C. Place several blankets on the patient to increase temperature.
    D. Administer vasodilator drugs.

23. Hemorrhage, a frequent postoperative vascular complication, can be prevented by administering which of the following medications?

    A. Protamine sulfate.
    B. Heparin sulfate.
    C. Vitamin D.
    D. Vitamin B.

24. A critical postoperative complication is hypovolemic shock. Which of the following signs would be seen initially by the nurse?

    A. Hypotension.
    B. Cyanosis.
    C. Oliguria.
    D. Tachypnea.

25. Postoperative pain can be controlled by all of the following nursing interventions except

    A. Avoiding unnecessary movements by having the patient positioned for at least four hours at a time.
    B. Medicating for the pain at least every four hours for the first twenty-four hours.

C. Keeping bed linens free of wrinkles.

D. Keeping the bladder empty.

26. Which one of the following medications would most likely be used to control postoperative nausea and vomiting?

   A. Compazine.
   B. Demerol.
   C. Talwin.
   D. Codeine.

27. A patient with a CVP reading of 19 cm. of water would most likely have the following condition.

   A. Left ventricular failure.
   B. Cardiac valve disease.
   C. Anemia.
   D. Hypovolemia.

28. Patients who develop atelectasis postoperatively will exhibit which one of the following signs or symptoms?

   A. Flushed face.
   B. Dyspnea.
   C. Decreased temperature.
   D. Severe cough.

29. Following oral Demerol for pain to a patient who had a herniorrhaphy, the patient vomits and states that he feels that he has to vomit again. You would carry out all of the following nursing interventions except

   A. Have patient take slow, deep breaths.
   B. Offer carbonated uncola beverages if not NPO
   C. Administer I.M. Demerol to relieve his pain.
   D. Splint the incisional area.

30. Esophageal varices are frequently a complication associated with Laennec's cirrhosis of the liver. Which of the following statements is true about this condition?

   A. The veins of the esophagus and stomach are dilated extensively, and this results in large amounts of blood being vomited when varices occur.
   B. The treatment of choice is an esophageal Teflon graft.
   C. The bleeding can be controlled by administering large amounts of vitamin K to raise the prothrombin level of the blood.
   D. The veins become distended due to pressure from the abdominal ascites.

31. The usual treatment of choice for patients with esophageal varices is

   A. Placement of a Miller-Abbott tube.
   B. Placement of a Levine tube.
   C. Placement of a Sengstaken-Blakemore tube.
   D. Placement of a Johnston tube.

32. Nursing interventions for patients having lumbar laminectomy surgery include which of the following?

   A. Supine position for twenty-four hours.
   B. Observation for spinal fluid leak.
   C. Observation for sensation in the upper extremities.
   D. Ambulation five to seven days postoperatively.

33. Jack Hanson was admitted to the hospital with ulcerative colitis. He has had the disease for eight years. He has been poorly controlled on a medical regime and is now scheduled for surgical correction. The usual surgical intervention for ulcerative colitis is

   A. Colostomy.
   B. Ileostomy.
   C. Abdominal perineal resection.
   D. Ureteroileostomy.

34. Mr. Hanson's symptoms include which one of the following?

   A. Abdominal cramping.
   B. Constipation.
   C. Normally formed stools with blood streaks.
   D. Tarry stools.

35. Preoperatively, Mr. Hanson's medications will include which one of the following classifications?

   A. Antibiotics.
   B. Antihistamines.
   C. Diuretics.
   D. Anticholinesterose.

36. Preoperatively, his diet will consist of a

   A. Bland, high residue, high protein diet.
   B. Bland, low residue, high protein diet.
   C. Bland, low residue, low protein diet.
   D. Bland, high residue, low fat diet.

37. Postoperatively, Mr. Hanson's nursing care plan will include all of the following interventions except

   A. Daily stoma irrigations.
   B. Appliance secured closely around stoma.
   C. Good skin care around stoma.
   D. Force fluids.

38. Mr. Swen Olsen was admitted for a gastric resection, to be performed in a few days. Which of the following observations of Mr. Olsen's pain pattern, indicating a probable duodenal ulcer, will be included in your nursing assessment?

   A. Pain is constant over epigastric area when eating.
   B. Pain is experienced about two to three hours after eating.

C. Pain occurs about one-half hour after eating.
D. There is no correlation between food intake and pain.

39. Your nursing assessment should include observations for possible complications associated with duodenal ulcer disease. Which of the following manifestations would indicate a complication has occurred.

A. Pain in lower right quadrant.
B. Expulsion of flatus.
C. Bright red bloody stools.
D. Tarry stools.

40. Anticholinergic drugs are used to treat patients with peptic ulcer diseases prior to surgery. Which of the following pharmacological actions is indicative of anticholinergic drugs?

A. Increase gastric emptying.
B. Interfere with histamine formation.
C. Block the effects of vagus nerve impulses on smooth muscle.
D. Decrease the responsiveness of the patient.

41 A side effect commonly seen in patients taking anticholinergic drugs orally is

A. Dryness of mouth.
B. Vertigo.
C. Become sedated.
D. Constricted pupils.

42. Insertion of a nasogastric tube in the postoperative patient can lead to which of the following complications?

A. Electrolyte imbalance.
B. Gastric distention.
C. Ulcerative colitis.
D. Infection.

43. Paralytic ileus is a frequent cause of postoperative abdominal surgery. Which of the following interventions would not be carried out for a patient with a paralytic ileus?

A. Administer P.O. fluids only.
B. Insert nasogastric tube.
C. Administer anticholinesterose drugs, such as Prostigmin.
D. Placement of a rectal tube.

44. An early complication following gastric resection is

A. Constipation.
B. Intractable pain.
C. Infection.
D. Pneumonia.

45. The most common late-occurring complication following a subtotal gastric resection is

A. Adhesions.
B. Hemorrhage.
C. Dumping syndrome.
D. Intractable pain.

46. To assist the patient in decreasing the chance of postoperative feeding complications, your patient teaching will include which of the following statements?

A. Increase fluid intake at meal time.
B. Exercise moderately following meals.
C. Decrease sodium and carbohydrate intake.
D. Increase carbohydrate intake at meals.

47. Negative nitrogen balance can occur following surgery. Which of the following clinical manifestations will be indicative of negative nitrogen balance?

A. Dehydration leading to poor skin turgor.
B. Edema or ascites of the abdomen and flank.
C. Jaundice.
D. Diarrhea.

48. Inhalation anesthetics are commonly used for major surgical interventions. Which one of the following statements is not true?

A. They prevent pain.
B. They relax smooth muscle.
C. They decrease respiratory rate.
D. They produce a state of amnesia during surgery.

49. Instructions to a patient receiving preoperative atropine would include the fact that

A. He might experience ringing in his ears.
B. He will become drowsy.
C. His mouth will feel dry.
D. His pain will be decreased.

50. Analgesics such as Demerol, given preoperatively, are used to

A. Decrease pain.
B. Decrease anxiety.
C. Decrease tracheobronchial secretions.
D. Reduce the amount of general anesthesia needed.

51. Preoperative teaching for a patient about to have a laryngectomy should include the fact that

A. He will continue to be able to breathe and smell through the nose.
B. He will be fed through a permanent gastrostomy tube.
C. He will be able to speak again, but it will not be the same as before surgery.
D. Oral fluids will be eliminated for the first week following surgery.

52. Mr. Marks is seen in the emergency room with the diagnosis of ruptured abdominal aortic aneurysm. His primary presenting symptom would be

A. Persistent pain in the epigastrium.
B. Abdominal spasms.
C. Lower back pain.
D. Intermittent pain in the lower right abdomen.

53. Mr. Marks needs whole blood transfusions immediately. His type and cross match is not completed. Therefore, which of the following blood groups would most likely be administered?

   A. O.
   B. A.
   C. AB.
   D. B.

54. Patients who have undergone thoracic surgery would have which of the following interventions carried out?

   A. Morphine administered for pain.
   B. Positioned in supine position.
   C. Bed rest for four to five days.
   D. Aerosol respiratory therapy to reduce viscosity of secretions.

55. Thrombophlebitis can occur following surgical intervention. A thrombus in the calf of the leg can be identified by which one of the following signs?

   A. Doll's sign.
   B. Kernig's sign.
   C. Hegar's sign.
   D. Homans' sign.

56. Nursing interventions carried out within an hour prior to any major surgery would be likely to include

   A. Putting siderails up following preoperative medication.
   B. Enema.
   C. Preoperative shave and scrub.
   D. Checking that history and physical are on the chart.

57. Nursing responsibilities for the preoperative period would include notifying the physician if

   A. The erythrocyte count is 6 mil./cc. mm.
   B. The temperature is 99.6°F orally.
   C. The hemoglobin is 14 gm./100 ml.
   D. The urine report indicates ketonuria.

58. Preoperative care for any surgical patient should include all of the following except

   A. Increasing the protein intake to help prevent postoperative protein depletion.
   B. Providing for adequate elimination.
   C. Ensuring that the patient is psychologically prepared for surgery.
   D. Making sure that a nurse explains the surgical procedure prior to carrying out the surgical skin prep.

59. Nursing care for a patient with a suprapubic cystostomy would include

   A. Placing a urinal bag around the tube insertion to collect the urine.
   B. Clamping the tube and allowing the patient to void through the urinary meatus before removing the tube.
   C. Catheter irrigations every four hours to prevent formation of urinary stones.
   D. Limiting fluid intake to 1500 cc. per day.

60. Which of the following clinical manifestations is not an indication of a possible wound infection?

   A. Serous drainage from a Penrose drain.
   B. Low grade temperature.
   C. Erythema surrounding incisional site.
   D. Tenderness of the incisional area.

61. Which one of the following nursing interventions will a first day postoperative retinal detachment patient have on his care plan?

   A. Turn, cough, hyperventilate every two hours.
   B. Up ad. lib.
   C. Remove eye patch during day.
   D. Complete bed bath.

62. Preoperative nursing interventions for patients having cataract surgery will include

   A. Instillation of mydriatic drugs.
   B. Instillation of miotic drugs.
   C. Instillation of topical anesthetics.
   D. Instillation of cryogenic drugs.

63. Instructions given to patients following cataract surgery include the information that

   A. The eye patch will be removed in three to four days, and they will be able to use the eye without difficulty.
   B. They must use only one eye at a time to prevent double vision.
   C. They will be able to judge distances without difficulty.
   D. Contact lenses will be fitted before discharge from the hospital.

64. Patient teaching in preparation for discharge after insertion of a pacemaker should include all of the following except

   A. Taking their blood pressure every day.
   B. Advising them to report signs and symptoms of dizziness, fainting, palpitations, and chest pain.
   C. Avoid working around microwave ovens or faulty electrical wiring.
   D. Wear loose fitting clothing around area of pacemaker implantation.

65. Jill Adams, a twenty-one-year-old patient, is admitted to the hospital with the diagnosis of possible

brain tumor. Soon after admission, Jill has a grand mal seizure. Which one of the following interventions would you carry out?

A. Go out and call the doctor immediately.
B. Restrain her to prevent injury.
C. Record the type of muscular activity involved in the seizure.
D. Place tongue blade between teeth, even if force is necessary.

66. Following surgery for a brain tumor near the hypothalmus, which one of the following clinical manifestations might be exhibited by Jill?

A. Inability to regulate body temperature.
B. Bradycardia.
C. Visual disturbances.
D. Inability to perceive sound.

67. The presence of which of the following reflexes is the most important indicator of neurological pathology?

A. Homans.
B. Babinski.
C. Gag.
D. Moro.

68. Postoperative nursing care for Jill will include

A. Placing her in supine position.
B. Administering morphine sulfate for pain.
C. Restraining her with posey belt and soft wrist restraints.
D. Recording rectal temperatures frequently.

69. Jill develops increased intracranial pressure. Which of the following clinical manifestations is indicative of intracranial pressure?

A. Vomiting.
B. Decreased blood pressure.
C. Increased pulse rate.
D. Agitation.

70. Which one of the following measures would not be effective for preventing increased intracranial pressure?

A. Administration of hypotonic I.V. solutions.
B. Restricting intake to 1200 cc. per day.
C. Administering osmotic diuretics, such as mannitol.
D. Administering corticosteroids, such as Decadron.

71. John Petry was admitted to the hospital with a head injury incurred when he fell off a ladder. John's restlessness is probably caused by

A. Decreased ocular pressure.
B. Cerebral anoxia.
C. Dehydration.
D. Decreased pain sensation.

72. John developed increased intracranial pressure due to a blood clot at the injury site. Which one of the following clinical manifestations is not indicative of increased intracranial pressure?

A. Pulse rate of 56.
B. Respiratory rate of 10 and irregular.
C. Blood pressure 100/80.
D. Temperature 100°F orally.

73. John is scheduled for a craniotomy. Which of the following would be included in preoperative preparation?

A. Give soapsuds enema.
B. Hydrate with 3000 cc.'s I.V. fluid.
C. Administer steroids.
D. Insert NG tube.

74. Immediate postoperative nursing care will include

A. Keeping temperature below 97°F to decrease metabolic needs.
B. Place in supine position.
C. Maintain fluid and electrolyte balance by administering at least 3000 cc. D_5 lactated Ringer's every twenty-four hours.
D. Obtain serial blood and urine samples.

75. John is placed on several intravenous medications postoperatively. Which one of the following would least likely be ordered?

A. Mannitol.
B. Solu cortef.
C. Dilantin.
D. Glucagon.

76. Marie Valdez underwent mitral valve replacement twelve hours ago. She is still on a respirator for assistance. Her laboratory values are:

Hct.	30.6	pO_2	300 mm. Hg.
WBC	8000/cc.	pCO_2	30 mm. Hg.
K^+	3.0 meg./l.	pH	7.30
Na^{++}	138 meg./l.		

The usual reason for mitral valve replacement is

A. Electrical conduction abnormalities.
B. Valvular regurgitation.
C. Inflammation of pericardium.
D. Left ventricular atrophy.

77. Which of the following orders would be carried out, based on Marie's laboratory values?

A. Administer fluids I.V. to increase HCT.
B. Administer potassium chloride I.V. volutrol.
C. Maintain oxygen concentration via respirator.
D. Decrease respiratory rate to retain carbon dioxide.

78. If Marie's blood transfusion reaction is due to a hemolytic reaction, your first nursing intervention will be to

A. Call the doctor.
B. Administer Benadryl I.V.
C. Stop the transfusion.
D. Obtain a urine specimen to check for hematuria.

79. Marie was given several blood transfusions following surgery. Which one of the following clinical manifestations is an early indication of a transfusion reaction?

A. Urticaria.
B. Dyspnea.
C. Hematuria.
D. Cyanosis.

80. Permanent pacemakers are inserted for each of the following reasons except

A. Adams-Stokes syndrome.
B. Tachyarrhythmias.
C. Premature atrial contractions.
D. Arrhythmias following myocardial infarctions.

81. Discharge instructions for patients with a spinal fusion will include the instruction

A. To keep brace on at all times.
B. To avoid heavy lifting or straining for two weeks.
C. To sit in soft chair only during the day.
D. That the graft may not be stable for one year.

82. Mrs. Marsh has been admitted for urological surgery. Choose the one nursing objective that is least appropriate in this situation.

A. Assess the functional status of the urinary tract and kidneys through evaluation studies.
B. Assess cardiopulmonary status of the patient.
C. Give inhalation therapy (IPPB) to encourage deep respiratory movements.
D. Recognize and try to allay fear and anxiety.

83. The main complication following a nephrostomy that the nurse must be aware of is

A. Bleeding from the nephrostomy site.
B. Cardiopulmonary involvement following the procedure.
C. Difficulty in restoring fluid and electrolyte balance.
D. Contamination.

84. Hemorrhage is a major complication following mouth surgery and radical neck dissection. If this condition occurs, the most immediate intervention of the nurse would be to

A. Notify surgeon immediately.
B. Treat the patient for shock.
C. Put pressure over the common carotid and jugular vessels in the neck.
D. Immediately put the patient in high Fowler's position.

85. All of the following factors would affect wound healing except

A. Proper diet.
B. Edema.
C. Age.
D. Iron administration.

86. Following a left leg amputation, you will instruct Inez Gomez in all of the following except

A. Rewrapping of the ace bandage four times a day.
B. Washing the stump with mild soap and water.
C. Keeping the legs elevated.
D. The likelihood of feeling the need to scratch the missing toes.

87. Patients undergoing a transurethral resection will be particularly prone to

A. Hemorrhage.
B. Fluid and electrolyte imbalance.
C. Cerebral vascular accidents.
D. Pneumonia.

88. John Wiser, age thirty-six, was admitted following a skiing accident. He suffered a compound fracture of the right femur. In which of the following tractions will he most likely be placed?

A. One-way pull.
B. Bryant's.
C. Balanced suspension.
D. Crutchfield.

89. Which nursing intervention would be included for patients in traction?

A. Place patient in supine position in bed for better traction.
B. Maintain countertraction.
C. Provide range-of-motion to affected limb.
D. Instruct not to turn side to side.

90. To ensure that John's traction is working properly, which of the following principles should be utilized?

A. Do not tie knots in the rope as it will not allow the rope to move freely on the pulley.
B. If the weights are positioned so that they gently touch the floor, it will prevent them from pulling the leg if accidentally hit.
C. Pulleys should be utilized only if the patient is allowed to move up in bed by aid of a trapeze.
D. Pulleys should not be obstructed by knots.

91. To observe for signs of circulatory impairment, John should be asked to

A. Cough and deep breathe.
B. Turn himself in bed.
C. Perform bicep exercises.
D. Wiggle his toes.

92. After an open reduction, John was placed in a long leg cast. Which of the following interventions would be indicated in his immediate postoperative care?

    A. Apply heat to assist in drying cast.
    B. Keep cast leg supine to prevent pressure points from developing.
    C. Observe for circulatory impairment.
    D. Handling of cast while drying.

93. A compound fracture is defined as

    A. A completely broken, fragmented bone.
    B. A bone that has been compressed onto another bone.
    C. A bone that has been exposed through a break in the skin.
    D. A break that has remained intact.

94. Emergency treatment for compound fractures should consist of

    A. Reducing the fracture if possible.
    B. Leaving the wound open to allow fluid to escape and to prevent a hematoma.
    C. Immobilizing the fracture.
    D. Immobilizing the fracture only after you clean out the wound.

95. Bessie Smith fell while shopping and came home complaining of her hip hurting. Bessie is eighty-five years old and is very self-sufficient. When brought to the hospital for X-rays, it was found that she had a fractured right hip which was only slightly displaced. Which type of hip fracture did Bessie most likely have?

    A. Intertrochanteric.
    B. Intracapsular.
    C. Extracapsular.
    D. Compound.

96. Her immediate treatment will likely consist of

    A. Bed rest with feet elevated.
    B. Surgical reduction.
    C. Balanced suspension traction.
    D. Internal fixation.

97. Full weight-bearing will probably be allowed in

    A. Six to eight weeks.
    B. Three to four days.
    C. One week.
    D. Probably not at all.

98. Initial postoperative orders will mostly include

    A. Supine position only for three days.
    B. Turn to operative side only for three days.
    C. Keep NPO until able to turn and sit up.
    D. Begin flexion and extension exercises of foot and knee the same day or first postoperative day.

99. Which one of the following orders would likely be written for a patient having total hip replacement, immediately postoperative?

    A. Head of bed elevated to 45° angle.
    B. Operative leg maintained in adduction.
    C. Buck's traction until hip can be put through range of motion.
    D. Dressing changes daily.

100. Which one of the following orders would be included in rehabilitation programs for total hip replacement?

    A. Ambulate first postoperative day.
    B. Dangle evening of surgery.
    C. Sit in chair second postoperative day.
    D. Use high extended commode when up.

Answers and Rationale

1. (A) Due to hypoventilation and poor respiratory exchange, the patient holds on to carbon dioxide which, when combined with water, forms carbonic acid.

2. (D) Patient must be in a semi-Fowler's position to assist in respiratory exchange by increasing lung expansion and allowing him to cough and deep breathe easier.

3. (A) This will allow the nurse to strip the chest tubes easily and thereby prevent clots from obstructing the tube as well as facilitate drainage.

4. (A) In order to deliver a pre-set amount of oxygen, it will be necessary to administer it through a volume-set machine. The patient will be unable to exert enough pressure to trigger off the pressure-set monitor.

5. (C) Auscultating the lungs will aid in detecting possible pulmonary complications to ensure early treatment and prevent serious complications. The tracheostomy should be suctioned at least every one to two hours to prevent pulmonary complications. It is necessary to deflate the cuff every hour for five to ten minutes to prevent tracheal strictures from occurring. Inflating the trach tube when feeding is necessary to prevent aspiration.

6. (C) Fifty percent of all cancers occur in the upper outer quadrant. Females should be informed of this when doing self-examinations.

7. (D) This will aid in lymphatic and venous drainage of fluid.

8. (A) Prosthesis are not fitted until the suture line is healed or after completion of radiation therapy. Exercises are usually started right after surgery to assist in lymphatic drainage. If skin grafting is done, exercise will be delayed.

9. (D) Pain is due to contraction of the gallbladder, which has stones present. The gallbladder empties when fat is present in the stomach. The gallbladder is located in the upper right side of the abdomen along the side of the liver.

10. (C) Patients with high abdominal incisions tend to splint and do not like to cough and deep breathe because of the pain associated with it.

11. (A) Patients are positioned in a semi-Fowler's position to assist in drainage. The T-tube can be clamped before meals to accumulate enough bile for digestion. The drainage bottle is positioned below the level of the bed to facilitate drainage.

12. (C) The bleeding time is prolonged due to a deficient prothrombin formation which occurs in liver cell damage. Pain is in upper right abdomen radiating to the back of right shoulder. Clay-colored stools are common in obstructive disease as they do not contain bile pigments.

13. (D) If narcotics are used, such as morphine, they can cause bilary colic. Thorazine is used to control anxiety or nausea.

14. (C) Diet must be high in protein in order to aid in wound healing. Increased carbohydrates are needed to build up glycogen stores in the liver. Low fat is used to decrease the contractility of the gallbladder, thereby decreasing the need for bile.

15. (B) Patients will have a low grade temperature, tenderness in lower right quadrant, and nausea and vomiting without reference to eating. Pain starts in the upper abdomen and progresses to the right quadrant.

16. (B) 31 gtts./minute.

$$= \frac{\text{Total vol. infused X drops/ml.}}{\text{Total time for infusion(min.)}}$$

$$31.25 = \frac{3000 \text{ X } 15}{24 \text{ X } 60}$$

17. (D) Semi-Fowler's position relieves abdominal pain and tension. They are NPO to decrease peristalsis. Heat is never used because it could cause the appendix to rupture, thus causing peritonitis.

18. (B) This allows for adequate oxygenation during suctioning. Oral suctioning must be done before the trach tube is deflated to prevent mucus from flowing into the lungs.

19. (D) There is a chance of clotting off the catheter and then having to replace it. The small amount of heparin will not interfere in blood coagulation.

20. (B) The surrounding area would be warm to the touch, and red, indicating an inflammatory response. There is no relationship between varicosities and thrombus formation.

21. (C) Erythema is usually one of the first signs of a possible wound infection. An increased temperature the first twenty-four hours usually indicates dehydration or possibly pulmonary complications.

22. (B) Vasodilators are administered to reduce peripheral resistance to blood flow and to increase capillary perfusion after the intravascular space has been expanded.

23. (A) Protamine sulfate is the antagonist for heparin. In vascular surgery the patient is frequently heparinized to prevent clot formation. Bleeding occurs when insufficient protamine has been administered at the end of the surgery to reverse the effects of heparin.

24. (C) In shock, decreased blood volume moves though the kidneys. This is evidenced by a decrease in the amount of urine excreted. The body has numerous compensatory mechanisms built in which assist in keeping the blood pressure elevated for a short time.

25. (A) They need to be turned and coughed at least every two hours to prevent pulmonary complications.

26. (A) Compazine is a psychotrophic drug, but in small doses, it tends to control nausea and vomiting. The other drugs are central nervous system depressants.

27. (B) A high CVP reading indicates either fluid overload or valve incompetence. Hypovolemia is a state of low fluid levels in the body or shifts in the fluid level.

28. (B) Patients become short of breath and usually experience severe pain but do not have a severe cough.

29. (C) There is a good possibility that the vomiting was caused from an allergic reaction to the Demerol, so it should not be administered again.

30. (A) The liver cells have been destroyed due to the cirrhosis. When this occurs portal hypertension usually follows. Vitamin K will not stop the bleeding at this point as the problem is directly related to the distended and dilated veins which have ruptured.

31. (C) This provides pressure in both the upper or cardiac portion of the stomach and the esophagus by means of a double lumen ballone.

32. (B) Lumbar laminectomy patients must be checked for sensation in the lower extremities to test for nerve root damage. They are logrolled every two hours.

33. (B) An ileostomy. A colostomy would be only a palliative measure as the disease progresses from anal area backward through the colon. More than likely the disease process would not be arrested by a colostomy as the most universally accepted theory of cause is autoimmunity. This indicates the patient is allergic to his own mucosal cells in the G.I. tract.

34. (A) Due to constant irritation of the colon, the stools are frequent and bloody and often contain mucus and pus. Abdominal cramps are associated with the irritated bowel.

35. (A) Antibiotics are ordered to prevent infection of the gastrointestinal tract before surgery.

36. (B) High protein diet will assist in preventing nitrogen imbalances following surgery and in tissue repair. The low residue diet prevents the need for excessive peristalsis. Bland diet is less irritating to tissue.

37. (A) Ileostomy patients do not have irrigations performed as the contents are liquid and contain few formed stool particles. Irrigations are utilized for complete evacuation of colostomy.

38. (B) Pain is reduced upon eating when patient has duodenal ulcer. When the duodenum is empty, about two to three hours after eating, the pain recurs.

39. (D) Bright red bloody stools indicate a bleeding problem low down in the gastrointestinal tract. A bleeding duodenal ulcer would have tarry stools as the blood has been digested by the action of the intestinal juices on free blood.

40. (C) Usually sedatives are administered with anticholinergic drugs, and these decrease the responsiveness of the patient. They increase gastric emptying and suppress gastric secretions.

41. (A) Pupils are dilated with the use of anticholinergic drugs when administered in the form of eye drops, such as atropine. There should be little or no effect to the eyes when anticholinergics are administered orally. When a side effect or toxic level is reached, the eye responds by pupil dilation. They become emotionally excited. Dries secretions.

42. (A) Nasogastric intubation leads to electrolyte imbalance through the suctioning out of the gastric contents. Large amounts of sodium and potassium are lost through the suctioning and, if not replaced via I.V. fluids, can lead to serious electrolyte imbalance.

43. (A) Prostigmin is used for relief of abdominal distention caused by accumulation of gas and insufficient peristaltic action following surgery. The patient will not be fed until bowel sounds are present, abdominal distention relieved, and flatus is passed.

44. (D) Patients undergoing anesthesia frequently have accumulation of fluid in the lungs which can lead to pneumonia if not coughed, hyperventilated, and turned frequently to rid the lungs of the fluid.

45. (C) Dumping syndrome is likened to hypovolemic shock. As increased amounts of food, particularly high in carbohydrates, enter the jejunum, the patient becomes weak, nauseated, dizzy, and perspires profusely. Symptoms are due to a form of hypoglycemia.

46. (C) Dumping syndrome can be prevented by decreasing fluid intake at meal times, taking in six small feedings per day, lying down following meals, and decreasing carbohydrates and salt intake. The hypoglycemic state which causes the syndrome arises from the pancreas responding by increasing the insulin output when large amounts of carbohydrates are introduced into the jejunum.

47. (B) Edema is due to insufficient nitrogen for synthesis which then leads to a change in the body's osmotic pressure resulting in oozing of fluids out of the vascular space. This phenomena results in the formation of edema in the abdomen and flanks.

48. (D) Inhalation drugs render a patient totally unconscious during the procedure. They do not remember the procedure based on this fact rather than it being just a period of forgetfulness.

49. (C) Atropine is administered to inhibit parasympathetic stimulation. It also reduces tracheobronchial secretions which results in dry mucous membranes. This aids in preventing postoperative respiratory complications.

50. (B) Demerol is given in this case to decrease anxiety, usually not pain. It does not dry up secretions and has relatively little effect on reducing the amount of general anesthesia.

51. (C) They will use an esophageal speech or mechanical device for communication. They can usually begin to take oral fluids sometime after forty-eight hours. They are usually fed by an intravenous or nasogastric tube prior to oral feedings. Because the larynx is removed, it will be impossible to breathe through the nose.

52. (C) When patient presents with a ruptured aneurysm, the pain is felt in the lower back. If the aneurysm has not ruptured, the pain would be persistent (sometimes intermittent) and located in middle or lower abdomen to the left of the midline.

53. (A) Blood type O is considered the universal donor because the cells do not agglutinate with any serum. Type O has no antigens present in the red cells which could be destroyed by antibodies in a recipient's blood when transfused.

54. (D) Patients are ambulated as soon as the respiratory and cardiovascular system are compensated.

They can walk around the bed usually in a day or two. Semi-Fowler's position facilitates expansion of lungs as well as permitting residual air to rise to the upper portion of the pleural space and be removed through the chest tube. Morphine sulfate depresses the respiratory system and should be avoided. Other narcotics are better, such as Demerol or Talwin.

55. (D) On dorsiflexion of the foot, the patient will experience upper posterior pain in the calf if a clot is present. This is termed Homans' sign.

56. (A) For all the other answers, even though they will be carried out preoperatively, they need to be done much earlier than one hour prior to surgery. The enema, for example, would probably not be expelled completely by the time the patient should be going to the O.R. If the history and physical is not on the chart, the patient will not be allowed to go to the O.R.

57. (D) All the other reports are within normal range. The ketonuria indicates a probable diabetic complication or other metabolic condition.

58. (D) The physician is the one who should initially instruct the patient in the surgical procedure. The nurse only reinforces teaching and explains areas which were unclear to the patient. The surgical preparation should not be carried out until the physician has discussed the procedure with the patient.

59. (B) This will be done prior to removal of the catheter to ensure adequate emptying of the bladder. They are always connected to a closed drainage system such as a Foley catheter inserted through a urethral opening. Irrigations are not recommended as they increase the chances of the patient developing a urinary tract infection. Any time a patient has an indwelling catheter in place, fluids should be forced (unless contraindicated) to prevent stone formation.

60. (A) This is the normal expected drainage from a Penrose drain. The drain is placed for evacuation of accumulated fluid to prevent complications.

61. (D) Patient is to be kept at rest to prevent possible complications such as hemorrhage or further detachment. Patients should be kept on bed rest for several days. They are turned according to physician's orders. They are not allowed to cough, as this can cause increased intraoccular pressure which could lead to hemorrhage.

62. (A) Mydriatic drugs are used to dilate the pupils in order to facilitate easy removal of the lens. Cryogenic just refers to low temperature; it is not a classification of drugs. Topical anesthetics would be instilled at the time of surgery, not preoperatively by the nurse.

63. (B) The function of the lens is that of accommodation, the focusing of near objects on the retina by the lens. Therefore, only the remaining lens will function in this capacity, dependent on whether a cataract is present.

64. (A) The most important vital sign to watch is the pulse. If it is below where the pacemaker has been set, it is an indication of a faulty pacemaker or that a battery replacement is necessary.

65. (C) Recording preconvulsive signs will assist the physician in determining the location of the tumor. Restricting patient's movements may cause serious injury to him. It is best to move objects away from him. If the jaw if forcibly opened, you can actually break it.

66. (A) The hypothalmus controls some of the emotions, such as pleasure and fear. It controls water balance, body temperature, sleep, and appetite. The visual area is controlled by the occipital lobe. The temporal lobe contains the auditory center. Bradycardia can be caused by a problem in the medulla oblongata.

67. (B) Moro's reflex, also called the startle reflex, is present in normal newborn infants. The gag reflex can be absent, but it can be an indication of many other conditions, such as oversedation; it is certainly not the most important sign of neurological pathology. A positive Babinski is indicative of pyramidal tract involvement, usually upper motor neuron lesion.

68. (D) Because Jill has a tumor near the hypothalmus, it is important to observe for signs of regulatory difficulties in the temperature regulating center. Increased temperatures increase the metabolic demands of the brain, which will lead to deterioration of brain circulation as well as increase the body's metabolic processes which utilize more oxygen.

69. (A) The blood pressure is increased and pulse rate decreased. Lethargy is the earliest sign of increased intracranial pressure. It is due to compression of the brain from edema or hemorrhage (or both).

70. (A) Administration of hypertonic Mannitol is used as it is relatively impermeable to the blood-brain barrier. The hypertonic solution reduces edema by a rapid movement of water out of the ventricles into the blood. Corticosteroids also reduce pressure but have a much slower action.

71. (B) Cerebral anoxia occurs frequently in severe trauma to the brain. A blood clot or edema can cause an interruption of the blood circulation, which leads to anoxia.

72. (C) Blood pressure is increased with a wide pulse pressure (the difference between the systolic pressure and the diastolic pressure). The cerebrospinal fluid pressure may cause elevated blood pressure by reducing oxygen supply to the hypothalmic vaso-

motor center. The excess of carbon dioxide which then forms will stimulate the center and cause an increase in the blood pressure.

73. (C) Enemas are usually not administered as they tend to cause straining which can lead to increased intracranial pressure. Steroid administration is frequently ordered to decrease edema and prevent inflammation. Nasogastric tubes, if inserted, are done under sedation in order to prevent increased intracranial pressure. I.V. fluid is usually limited for the same reason.

74. (D) Serial blood and urine samples are collected as sodium regulation disturbances frequently accompany head injury. The temperature should be kept at normal to avoid increasing the metabolic needs, but at 97°F the patient would probably shiver, causing not only increased intracranial pressure but an increased metabolic rate. Fluids are kept at a minimum to prevent overhydration, which can lead to cerebral edema.

75. (D) Glucagon is one of the principal hormones controlling carbohydrate metabolism. It promotes a rise in blood sugar. It would not be used in a patient with a head injury. Mannitol is an osmotic diuretic and so it decreases cerebral edema. Solu cortef, a corticosteroid, will assist in decreasing cerebral edema through its anti-inflammatory of fect. Dilantin is used to prevent seizure activity.

76. (B) Mitral valve disease is usually a result of rheumatic fever. It can leave the valve stenotic (narrowed) or incompetent where it allows blood to leak or regurgitate back into left atrium. The heart can compensate for this for a period of time, but eventually congestive heart failure results. When this happens, the usual treatment is the surgical approach.

77. (B) You would want to increase the respiratory rate in order to blow off carbon dioxide, thereby decreasing the accumulation of carbon dioxide which, when combined with water, forms carbonic acid and leads to acidosis. Decrease O_2 concentration and administer packed cells to increase HCT.

78. (C) Your first action would be to stop the transfusion to avoid administering any additional incompatible cells. The incompatible cells can lead to agglutination, oliguric renal failure, pulmonary emboli, and death if administered in large quantities. Some resources state that as little as 50 cc. of incompatible blood can lead to severe complications and death.

79. (A) If the patient is cyanotic, he probably has other complications associated with his illness such as respiratory involvement. If the transfusion is greatly advanced, it may cause laryngeal edema or perhaps even a blood clot to the lung if a hemolytic reaction has occurred. Hematuria is not an initial symptom.

80. (C) Premature atrial contractions are not indicative of heart failure which can lead to heart block. They represent atrial irritability, and if they continue at regular frequent intervals, medication therapy can be utilized.

81. (D) It is necessary to avoid straining, heavy lifting, sitting, etc., for a long period of time because the graft is not stable for at least one year.

82. (C) IPPB therapy would be used postoperatively to increase respiratory movement and aid in the expectoration of secretions.

83. (A) While all of the other conditions may be complications, bleeding from the site is the main concern as the procedure is done to get relief from (infection) urinary stasis which may have resulted in kidney congestion.

84. (C) Putting pressure over the vessels in the neck may be life-saving as severe blood loss can occur rapidly leading to shock and death.

85. (D) Iron by itself would probably not be effective. Whole blood is usually given to maintain adequate levels of red blood cells.

86. (C) Legs should not be elevated as the stump can get a flexion contracture of the hip joint. It is better to raise the foot of the bed on blocks to decrease edema.

87. (A) Hemorrhage can occur following any instrumentation. With this type of surgery, it is not uncommon for hemorrhage to occur.

88. (C) Balanced suspension traction will maintain proper alignment and provide immobilization and/or reduction of the fracture.

89. (B) To provide for countertraction, the patient should be placed in an elevated bed under the area involved. For example, the foot of the bed should be elevated in John's case. One reason for this type of traction is to allow patient to move in bed.

90. (D) The pulleys should be free to move in order to maintain the traction and to allow for movement. Knots should be tied in the rope near the Thomas splint or Pearson attachment to prevent slippage of the rope. If the weights are resting on the floor, they will provide no traction.

91. (D) The only activity that will indicate a complication that is directly related to impairment in circulation due to a fractured femur is the inability to wiggle his toes.

92. (C) Leg should be elevated to prevent edema formation. Unrelieved swelling may cause vascular insufficiency to the point of gangrenous necrosis. Symptoms would include numbness and no pulse.

93. (C) The term *compound* indicates that the bone has pierced the skin; this usually increases the possibility of infection.

94. (C) You should cover the wound with a sterile dressing and immediately immobilize it. Do not attempt to clean out the wound or to reduce it.

95. (A) Most people over age fifty have this type of fracture.

96. (C) Balanced suspension traction is needed to reduce the fracture if only slightly displaced; surgical intervention will usually follow in a few days.

97. (A) After healing takes place, full weight-bearing will usually be possible about six weeks after surgery.

98. (D) It is important that exercises be started early to prevent foot drop and circulatory complications, and to strengthen muscles for ambulation.

99. (C) This will assist in preventing dislocation of the new hip until the hip is able to move through range of motion. The leg must be kept in abduction to prevent it from dislocating. Dressings are not changed daily, thereby reducing chance of infection.

100. (D) Activity allowed varies among institutions; however, patients usually do not ambulate the first day. They all use some method of preventing flexion of the hip while hospitalized.

Emergency
Interventions
and
Nursing Procedures

A new chapter in this edition, Emergency Interventions and Nursing Procedures focuses on assisting the student to assess and intervene in emergency conditions. CPR, trauma assessment and thoracic procedures are a sampling of the first section, all presented with an emphasis on critical decision-making as a basis for nursing interventions.

The second section, Nursing Procedures, provides a valuable base of knowledge that can be applied to nursing performance in all clinical areas. These basic skills are important to review prior to taking State Board Examinations.

Emergency Interventions

Cardiopulmonary Resuscitation (CPR)

Suspect Unconsciousness

A. Call out for help.

B. Quickly approach victim.

C. Check responsiveness.
1. Shake shoulders.
2. Shout, "Are you OK!?"

D. Obtain proper position.
1. Victim: flat on firm surface.
2. Rescuer: next to victim at approximately the same level.

Respiratory Management

A. Airway obstruction.
1. Food or other foreign body aspirant (if known cause of unconsciousness).
   a. Tilt head—hyperextend neck and chin forward.
   b. One attempt to ventilate will not be successful if obstructed.
   c. If not successful, reposition head and reattempt to ventilate.
   d. Deliver four back blows.
   e. Deliver four abdominal thrusts.
   f. Finger probe for obstruction.
   g. Repeat steps until foreign body is removed.
2. Oral airway obstructants (if obvious and copious, i.e., blood, emesis, mucus, water).
   a. Turn head to side.
   b. Suction (if available).
   c. Finger swoops.

B. Open airway.
1. Adult.
   a. Head-tilt method.
   b. Jaw-thrust or chin-lift method (if neck injury even remotely possible).
2. Infant or toddler.
   a. Tilt head back without hyperextension.
   b. Normal, horizontal alignment, flat surface.

C. Evaluate respiratory function.
1. Maintain open airway.
2. Observe for respiratory activity.
   a. Rescuer puts ear down near mouth.
   b. Look for chest movement.
   c. Feel for air flow with cheek.
   d. Listen for exhalation.

D. Intervention.
1. Maintain open airway.
2. Form tight seal.
3. Adult management.
   a. Replace victim's dentures (if any).
   b. Pinch off nostrils.
   c. Fit mouth-to-mouth seal.
4. Infant or toddler management.
   a. Encircle nose and mouth.
   b. Maintain tight seal.
5. Administer four quick, full breaths.
   a. Give breaths as fast as you can.
   b. Between breaths, release seal for exhalation.
   c. Take fresh breath; do not allow complete deflation of lungs (stairstep volume).
   d. Maintain position.
   e. Volume: adult, 800 cc. minimum; infant, cheek full puffs.

Circulatory Management

A. Take major pulse.
1. Adult: carotid preferably and femoral as alternate.
2. Palpate one side, with two fingers, for five seconds.

B. Intervention (if pulseless).
1. Precordial thump (ON ADULTS MONITORED BY ECG ONLY).
   a. Midline, lower ½ sternum, two finger breadths above xiphoid process.
   b. Single sharp blow from 8 to 12 inches above sternum.
   c. Use fleshy side of fist.
   d. Evaluate effectiveness immediately on ECG and confirm with pulse, or proceed with CPR as indicated.
2. Cardiac compressions (firm surface or cardiac board needed).

3. Procedure for adult.
   a. Midline, lower ½ sternum, two fingers above xiphoid.
   b. Heel of one hand fixed on sternum, other hand superimposed.
   c. Fingers interlaced or extended off rib cage.
   d. Rate 60 to 80 per minute, depth 1½ to 2 inches.
   e. Count compressions: one-and, two-and, etc.
   f. Release pressure between compressions for cardiac refilling.
4. Procedure for child.
   a. Midline sternum, midway between xiphoid process and cricothyroid notch.
   b. Heel of one hand only.
   c. Rate 80 to 100 per minute, depth ¾ to 1½ inches.
5. Procedure for infant.
   a. Midline sternum, midway between xiphoid process and cricothyroid notch.
   b. Two fingers only.
   c. Rate 100 to 120 per minute, depth ½ to ¾ inches.
   d. Count compressions: one, two, three, four, five.

Interpolation (Compressions: Ventilations)

A. Lone rescuer: (15:2 for adults; 5:1 for infants).
B. Two rescuers: (5:1 adults).
C. Changing roles.
   1. Compressor sets pace (one, one thousand, two, one thousand, three, one thousand, four, one thousand, breath).
   2. Compressor observes for need and institutes change.
   3. Compressor states, "Change, one-thousand; two, one-thousand."
   4. Rescuer giving breaths gets into position to give compressions.
   5. Rescuer giving compressions moves to victim's head after fifth compression, counts pulse for five seconds.
   6. If no pulse, rescuer checking pulse states "No pulse, start CPR," gives a breath and CPR is begun again.

CPR Evaluation

A. In process.

1. Check major pulse after one minute of CPR.
   a. Equal to 4 sets of 15:2 by one rescuer.
   b. Equal to 12 sets of 5:1 by two rescuers.
2. Check major pulse every 4 to 5 minutes thereafter.
3. Pupil check every 4 to 5 minutes optional if third trained person present (not always a conclusive indicator).
4. Observe for abdominal distention (all age groups).
   a. If evident, reposition airway and reduce force of ventilation.
   b. Maintain a volume sufficient to elevate ribs.
5. Ventilator must check carotid pulse frequently between breaths to evaluate perfusion.
6. Ventilator must observe each breath for effectiveness.
7. If respiratory arrest only, check major pulse after each minute (12 breaths) to assure continuation of cardiac function.

B. After termination.
   1. Diagnosis made (no pulse, no respirations) and intervention instituted within one minute after unconsciousness.
   2. Assistance summoned and entry into Emergency Medical System done promptly and efficiently.
   3. Proper CPR performed until acceptable termination.
   4. No delay in CPR longer than five seconds (except extraordinary circumstances).
   5. No delay in CPR longer than fifteen seconds for extraordinary circumstances (intubation, transportation down stairs).
   6. Victim outcome.
      a. Condition.
      b. Potential for cardiac rehabilitation.
      c. Secondary complications (fractured ribs, ruptured spleen, lacerated liver, etc.).

Termination of CPR

A. Successful resuscitation.
   1. Spontaneous return of adequate life support.
   2. Assisted life support.
B. Transfer to emergency vehicle (other trained rescuers assume care).
C. Pronounced dead by physician.
D. Exhaustion of rescuer(s).

Trauma Assessment

A. Systemic evaluation completed to prevent concealed injury.

B. Priority of needs.
1. Respiratory difficulty.
   a. Observe for:
      (1) Patent airway.
      (2) Adequacy and symmetry of ventilation.
      (3) Unconsciousness.
      (4) Accumulation of secretions.
      (5) Bleeding in mouth.
   b. Insert naso- or oropharyngeal airway to prevent tongue occluding airway.
   c. Apply sterile vaseline gauze or pressure dressing to open wounds of chest.
   d. Stabilize chest wall and intubate if flail chest present.
   e. Remove air with No. 18 gauge needle if tension pneumothorax present.
   f. When multiple injuries or spinal injury suspected, do not turn on side.
2. Circulatory difficulty.
   a. Control bleeding.
      (1) Apply direct pressure on wound (if no glass in wound).
      (2) Apply pressure at pressure point area between heart and injury site.
      (3) Apply pressure dressing.
      (4) Use tourniquet only in life-threatening situations.
   b. Insert I.V.—usual solutions: lactated Ringer's or D_5W.
   c. Send blood work to lab for type and cross-match, electrolytes, hematocrit.
   d. Observe for signs of shock.
   e. Insert indwelling catheter if ordered (observe for adequate cardiac output).
   f. Elevate head 30 degrees, elevate feet with knees straight. Do not place in Trendelenburg position.
3. Neurological damage.
   a. Observe level of consciousness.
      (1) Type of physical activity (thrashing, no spontaneous movement).
      (2) Ability to respond appropriately to questions.
      (3) Vital signs, pupil size, and reactions.
   b. Monitor motor or sensory loss.
   c. Observe for seizure activity, vertigo, visual disturbances, headache.
4. Abdominal trauma.
   a. Observe for abdominal contusions, abrasions or wounds.
   b. Observe for distention, rigidity, absence or hyperactivity of bowel sounds.
   c. Question about abdominal pain.
      (1) Location.
      (2) Duration.
      (3) Intensity.
      (4) Associated with abdominal distention and rigidity.
   d. Insert nasogastric tube to detect upper G.I. bleeding.
   e. Perform rectal exam if detect lower G.I. bleeding.
5. Skeletal system damage.
   a. Observe all extremities for:
      (1) Edema.
      (2) Pain.
      (3) Obvious deformities.
   b. Immobilize all injured extremities.
   c. Do not remove air splints once applied. (Removal can cause simple fracture to become compound.)

Snake Bite and Bee Sting

A. Snake bite.
1. Assess extent of envenomation.
   a. Rattlesnakes, copperheads, cottonmouths (pitvipers) are responsible for 98 percent of venomous bites.
   b. Observe for:
      (1) Blood oozing from wound.
      (2) One or two distinct puncture wounds.
      (3) Edema and discoloration.
      (4) Numbness around bite within 5 to 15 minutes.
      (5) Painful and enlarged lymph nodes.
   c. Reactions to poisonous snakes occur within 30 to 60 minutes.
   d. Advanced signs indicating shock:

(1) Nausea, vomiting.
(2) Ecchymosis, blebs, blisters.
(3) Bleeding.
(4) Weakness, vertigo, clammy skin.

2. Emergency treatment: within 30-60 minutes of medical help.

   a. Immobilize area with support or sling.
   b. Apply tourniquet.
   c. Do not run or physically exert self as this hastens spread of venom.
   d. Seek medical help immediately.

3. Emergency treatment: when medical help not available within 30-60 minutes.

   a. Apply nonocclusive tourniquet or constriction band 2 to 5 inches above wound.
      (1) Adjust to allow for venous and lymphatic flow restriction but allow for arterial flow.
      (2) Loosen, but do not remove, for 1½ minutes every 15 minutes.
   b. Wash around bite with alcohol, hydrogen peroxide, or soap and water.
   c. Sterilize knife with match flame, alcohol, or soap and water, make longitudinal incision (not cross marks) 1/8 to 1/4 inch long and no more than 1/8 inch deep through each fang mark.
   d. Apply suction over incision site.
   e. Procedure must be done within 10 minutes of bite. After 30-60 minutes, little venom will be extractable.

4. In-hospital treatment.

   a. Within 30-60 minutes, make incisions and use suction intermittently for at least one hour.
   b. Test for sensitivity to horse serum.
   c. Judge severity of envenomation before giving antivenin.
      (1) Minimal pitviper bite: 1-5 ampules of antivenin (Crotalidae) I.M.
      (2) Moderate bite: 5-9 ampules I.V. drip.
      (3) Severe bite: 9 ampules I.V. drip immediately and up to 20 ampules over next 4 to 24 hours, until edema ceases and symptoms improve.
   d. Administer tetanus toxoid.
   e. Administer analgesics for pain.
      (1) ASA for mild pain.

      (2) Codeine or Demerol for severe pain.
   f. Administer antibiotics.
      (1) Initial dose: ampicillin, erythromycin, or tetracycline 500 mg.
      (2) Maintain 250 mg. every 4 hours for 24 hours.

B. Bee sting.

   1. Assessment.
      a. Generalized itching.
      b. Erythema and hives.
      c. Feeling of heat throughout body.
      d. Weakness, vertigo.
      e. Nausea, vomiting, abdominal cramps.
      f. Tightness in chest, difficulty swallowing or breathing.

   2. Treatment.
      a. Remove stinger with tweezers or by scraping motion with fingernail. Do not squeeze venom sac.
      b. Immediately administer epinephrine 1:1000 solution sub. q.
         (1) Adult. 0.25-0.3 ml. at sting site and same amount in unaffected arm.
         (2) Child: 0.01 ml./kg. (maximum 0.25 ml. at each site).
      c. Repeat injections 1 to 3 times at 20-minute intervals until blood pressure and pulse rise toward normal.
         (1) Adult: 0.3-0.4 ml.
         (2) Child: less than 20 kg., 0.10-0.15 ml.; over 20 kg., 0.15-0.3 ml.
      d. Apply tourniquet above sting on an extremity. Loosen every 3 to 5 minutes to allow venom to slowly enter circulation.
      e. Cleanse sting area and apply ice to relieve pain and edema.
      f. Administer pressor agents if blood pressure not stabilized following 2-3 subq. injections of epinephrine.
         (1) Aramine or levophed drugs of choice.
         (2) Administer I.V. drip at 30 to 40 drops per minute.
      g. Begin I.V. solution of D_5W with 250 mg. aminophylline and 30-40 mg. Solu-Cortef to support circulation and prevent shock.
      h. Observe for signs of laryngospasm or bronchospasm. Be prepared to assist with a tracheostomy.

i. Keep patient warm and positioned supine with head and feet slightly elevated.

j. Administer rapid-acting antihistamine: Benadryl 50 mg. I.M.

Application of Rotating Tourniquets

A. Purpose.
   1. Reduce venous return to heart.
   2. Pool blood temporarily in extremities.
   3. Treatment for pulmonary edema.
B. Procedure.
   1. Take blood pressure to determine midway between systolic and diastolic reading.
   2. Apply 4 pressure cuffs high up on all four extremities.
   3. Inflate 3 cuffs to pressure midway between systolic and diastolic pressure.
   4. Rotate the tourniquets every 15 minutes, using clockwise rotation.
   5. Release one tourniquet and then inflate the next tourniquet.
   6. Observe for presence of arterial blood flow by checking peripheral pulses. Arterial pulses should be present, venous pulses absent.
   7. Take frequent blood pressure readings to readjust cuff pressure.
   8. Continue treatment for prescribed time, usually when diuretic has adequately functioned and signs of pulmonary edema lessened.
   9. Discontinue tourniquets one at a time continuing the cuff deflation in clockwise manner, and every 15 minutes.

Thoracic Procedures

Chest Tubes

A. Placed in the pleural cavity following thoracic surgery to provide for removal of air and serosanguineous fluid from pleural space.
B. Attached to water-seal suction—maintains closed system.
   1. Tape all connectors.
   2. Ensure that all stoppers in bottles are tight fitting.
C. Suction.
   1. Keep bottles below level of bed.

2. Keep suction level where ordered (be sure that bubbling is not excessive in the pressure-regulating bottle).
   3. Maintain water level in bottle.
D. Patency.
   1. Milk chest tubes every thirty to sixty minutes.
      a. Milk away from patient toward the drainage receptable (pleur-Evac or bottles).
      b. Pinch tubing close to the chest with one hand as the other hand milks the tube. Continue going down tube in this method until coming to the drainage receptacle.
   2. Use lotion or alcohol swipes to provide ease of stripping.
E. Safety procedures.
   1. Keep rubber-tipped hemostats at bedside so that tube can be clamped off nearest to chest insertion site. (If air leak develops in tube, lung may collapse.) Some physicians do not allow clamping.
   2. Clamp if drainage system is interrupted.
F. Intake and output.
   1. With pleur-Evac suction equipment, visually measure chest drainage (holds up to 2800–3000 cc. drainage). With two- or three-bottle suction, tape or bottle markings may approximate the amount of drainage (similar to pleur-Evac).
   2. Change equipment only when the drainage chamber is full.

Water-seal Chest Drainage

A. Three types—one-, two-, or three-bottle drainage.
B. General principles.
   1. Used after some intrathoracic procedures.
   2. Chest tubes placed intrapleurally.
   3. Breathing mechanism operates on principle of negative pressure (pressure in chest cavity is lower than pressure of atmosphere, causing air to rush into chest cavity when injury such as stab wound occurs).
   4. When chest has been opened, vacuum must be applied to chest to reestablish negative pressure.
   5. Closed water-seal drainage is method of reestablishing negative pressure.
      a. Water acts as a seal and keeps the air from being drawn back into pleural space.
      b. Open drainage system would allow air to

be sucked back into chest cavity and collapse lung.

6. Closed drainage is established by placing catheter into pleural space and allowing it to drain under water.

    a. The end of the drainage tube is always kept under water.

    b. Air will not be drawn up through catheter into pleural space when tube is under water.

C. Different bottle suction types.

THREE-BOTTLE SUCTION SYSTEM

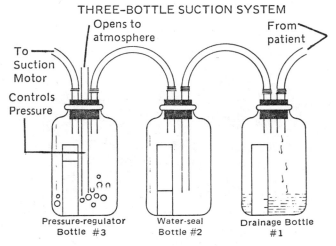

1. Three-bottle suction.

    a. One bottle is connected to suction motor—called mechanical suction.

    b. Bottle number three regulates the amount of pressure in the system.

    c. Three tubes.

       (1) Short tube, above water level, comes from water-seal bottle.

       (2) Short tube connected to suction motor.

       (3) Third tube, below water level in bottle, opens to the atmosphere outside of bottle.

       (4) The depth to which third tube is submerged in the water determines the pressure within the drainage system.

    d. When drainage system pressure becomes too low, outside air is sucked into the system. Results in constant bubbling in the pressure-regulator bottle.

    e. Whenever the motor is off, drainage system must be open to the atmosphere.

       (1) Intrapleural air can escape from the system.

       (2) Detach the tubing from the motor to provide the vent.

TWO-BOTTLE SUCTION SYSTEM

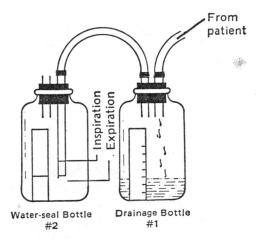

2. Two-bottle suction.

    a. Same as three-bottle suction except that the bottle connected to mechanical suction is not included.

    b. Drainage bottle (bottle number one) is connected from patient and is between the patient and the water-seal bottle (or bottle number two).

       (1) Short tube goes from patient into drainage bottle (not to extend below drainage level).

       (2) Mark drainage level on outside of bottle.

       (3) Short tube with rubber tubing goes from the drainage bottle to water-seal bottle.

       (4) This tube extends below water level in the water-seal bottle.

    c. Bottle number two.

       (1) The long tube extends below water level (from bottle number one).

       (2) A second short tube provides an air vent.

       (3) Water in this bottle goes up the tube when patient inhales and down the tube when patient exhales.

       (4) Water in this bottle should not bubble constantly

ONE-BOTTLE SUCTION SYSTEM

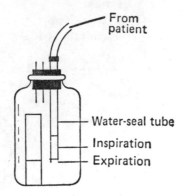

Water-seal and Drainage Bottle

3. One-bottle suction.
   a. There is only one bottle; it functions as a collection bottle for drainage as well as a pressure regulator.
   b. As the drainage increases in amount, the water-seal tube (immersed in the drainage), is pulled up slightly to decrease the amount of force that is required to permit the fluid to be drained from the pleural space.
   c. The depth to which the water-seal tube is immersed below the fluid in the bottle determines the pressure exerted by the water.
   d. Drainage is measured in the same way as two-bottle or three-bottle suction.

Suctioning

A. Nasotracheal.
   1. Equipment needed.
      a. Sterile suction catheter, usually No. 14 or No. 16 French.
      b. Sterile saline.
      c. Suction machine.
      d. Sterile gloves.
   2. Procedure.
      a. Lubricate catheter with normal saline.
      b. Insert catheter into the nose for 6 to 8 inches.
      c. To introduce catheter into right and left main branches, turn head in opposite direction of bronchus to be suctioned.
      d. Do not apply suction while introducing catheter.

   e. When advanced as far as possible, begin suctioning by withdrawing catheter slowly, rotating it with pressure applied. (Usually have a whistle tip catheter or Y connector tube which is used to apply pressure.)
   f. Hypoxia can occur when suctioning is carried out using incorrect procedure.
      (1) Excess of 15 seconds suctioning—oxygen decreased in respiratory tree.
      (2) Causes chemoreceptors to respond by increasing ventilation rate.

B. Tracheotomy.
   1. Equipment needed.
      a. Same equipment as for nasotracheal.
      b. Sterile syringe (5 cc.) and sterile saline for instillation into trach tube.
   2. Procedure.
      a. Be sure that suction catheter is not more than half the diameter of the trach tube.
      b. Lubricate with sterile saline.
      c. Insert catheter through trach tube for 8 to 12 inches with suction turned off.
      d. Do not suction for more than 10 seconds.
      e. Rotate catheter while withdrawing it.
      f. Do not repeat procedure for at least 3 minutes, unless necessary to withdraw more secretions to permit adequate ventilation.
      g. If secretions are very tenacious, 3-5 cc. of sterile saline may be inserted through tube and allowed to remain for a few seconds before suctioning (this increases viscosity of secretions and facilitates removal).
      h. To remove secretions from right bronchus, turn patient's head to left, vice versa for left bronchus.

Common Nursing Procedures

Fluid Replacement

Intravenous Regulation

A. Calculation of drip factor.
   1. Microdrop—60 gtt./cc. fluid.
   2. Adult drop factor usually depends on administration set 10-20 gtt./cc. fluid.

B. General formula.

$$\text{Drops/min.} = \frac{\text{Total volume infused X drops/cc.}}{\text{Total time for infusing in minutes}}$$

Example: Ordered 1000 cc. D_5W administered over 8-hour period of time.

1. With microdrip, it is easy to remember that the number of drops per minute equals the number of cc.'s or ml.'s to be administered per hour.

Example: $\frac{1000}{8} = 12.5$ cc./hour

Using Formula: (8 x 60) $\frac{1000 \times 60}{480} = \frac{60,000}{480} = 12.5$ gtt./min.

2. With administration set that delivers 10 gtt./min.

$$\frac{1000 \times 10}{480} = \frac{10,000}{480} = 20.8 \text{ or } 21 \text{ gtt./min.}$$

3. With administration set that delivers 15 gtt./min.

$$\frac{1000 \times 15}{480} = \frac{15,000}{480} = 31 \text{ gtt./min.}$$

Intravenous Calorie Calculation

A. 1000 cc. D_5W provides 50 g. of dextrose.

D. 50 g. of dextrose provides 4 calories per gram (actually 3.4 calories).

C. 1000 cc. D_5W provides 200 calories.

D. Usual I.V. total/day is 3000 cc. (600 calories/day).

Fluid Replacement Solutions

A. Types of I.V. solutions.

1. Hypertonic solution—a solution with higher osmotic pressure than blood serum.
   a. Cell placed in solution will crenate.
   b. Used in severe salt depletion.
   c. Common types of solution: normal saline, dextrose 10% in saline, dextrose 10% in water, and dextrose 5% in saline.
   d. Should not be administered faster than 200 cc./hr.

2. Hypotonic solution—a solution with less osmotic pressure than blood serum.
   a. Causes cells to expand or increase in size.
   b. Used in diarrhea and dehydration.
   c. Common types of solution: dextrose 5% in ½ strength (0.45%) N.S., dextrose 5% in ¼ strength (0.2) N.S., and dextrose 5% in water.
   d. Should not be administered faster than 400 cc./hr.

3. Isotonic solution—a solution with the same osmotic pressure as blood serum.
   a. Cells remain unchanged.
   b. Used for replacement or maintenance.
   c. Common type of solution: lactated Ringer's solution.

B. Choice of fluid replacement solution—depends on patient's needs.

1. Fluid and electrolyte replacement only.
   a. Saline solutions.
   b. Lactated Ringer's solution.
2. Calorie replacement—dextrose solutions.
3. Restriction of dietary intake, such as low sodium.
4. I.V. medications which are insoluble in certain I.V. fluids.
5. Rate of administration of I.V. solution to correct fluid imbalance.
6. Dextrose plays no part in tonicity. It is metabolized off.

C. Purpose of fluid and electrolyte therapy.

1. To replace previous losses.
2. To provide maintenance requirements.
3. To meet current losses.

D. Nursing management of I.V. therapy.

1. Check circulation of immobilized extremity.
2. Check label of solution against physician's order.
3. Check rate of infusion.
4. Observe vein site for signs of swelling.
5. Take vital signs at least every fifteen minutes for replacement fluid administration.

Parenteral Hyperalimentation Therapy

Principles of Therapy

A. Purpose of therapy is to supply nutrients via I.V. route.

1. Calories are provided.
2. Nitrogen is provided.
3. If body does not have calories or nitrogen, body begins to convert protein to CHO by gluconeogenesis.

B. Calorie requirements of normal adult.

1. Average adult postoperative requires 1500 cal./day to spare body protein.
2. If patient has temperature or hypermetabolic disease, can require up to 10,000 additional cal./day.
3. If enough fluids cannot be given to supply necessary calories, CHF or pulmonary edema can result.

C. Composition of I.V. fluid.
1. Hypertonic glucose used to meet calorie requirements, to allow amino acids to be released for protein synthesis rather than being utilized for energy.
2. Potassium added to provide electrolyte balance and to transport glucose and amino acids across the cell membrane.
3. Calcium, phosphorous, magnesium, sodium chloride added to prevent deficiencies and fulfill requirements for tissue synthesis.

D. Preparation of solution.
1. Solution prepared under sterile or aseptic technique under a filtered air laminar flow hood.
2. Solution: 25 percent glucose and synthetic amino acids (Fre Amine) provides 1000 calories and 6 gm. nitrogen/liter.
3. Electrolytes based on serum electrolyte levels.

E. Administration—through C.V.P. (subclavian vein into superior vena cava).

Nursing Management

A. Nursing responsibilities.
1. Avoid contamination by retaining sterility.
2. Maintain patency of indwelling catheter.
3. Administer at prescribed flow rate.

B. Nursing interventions.
1. Keep dressing on catheter site for forty-eight hours before removing.
2. Allow patient to ambulate with I.V. pole.
3. Check flow rate every thirty minutes; keep patient on I.V. monitor such as IVAC.
   a. If rate is too rapid, hyperosmolar diuresis occurs (excess sugar will be excreted); if severe enough, can cause intractable seizures, coma, death.
   b. If rate is too slow, no benefit derived from calories and nitrogen.
   c. Use clinitest every six hours to check for excessive sugar.

4. Weigh every day.
5. Record intake and output.
6. Measure vital signs (particularly temperature) every four hours.
7. Change dressing every two days; use sterile technique, cleansing solution, and apply antibiotic ointment.
8. Do not use I.V. catheter for administration of drugs.

Transfusion Administration

Procedure

A. Check carefully for correct name, ID numbers, blood group donor number (double check—have two persons check the information).
B. Do not warm blood as bacteria thrives in this medium.
C. Do not administer blood that has been out from refrigeration for over five hours.
D. Use blood filter to prevent fibrin and other materials from entering the bloodstream.
E. Start transfusion with normal saline or another electrolyte solution; blood will agglutinate without the presence of electrolytes.

Nursing Management

A. Start transfusion at 20 to 40 drops per minute and observe for transfusion reactions as they usually occur during the first fifteen minutes.
B. Take baseline vital signs and again five minutes after the start of the transfusion.
C. Complete the transfusion in no less than two hours and in no more than five hours.
1. Usually administered at a rate of 60 to 80 drops per minute. (Administration set—10 gtt./cc.)
2. If patient is hypovolemic, blood can be administered at the rate of 500 cc. in ten minutes by use of a blood pump. Observe for pulmonary edema and hypervolemia.

Transfusion Reactions

A. Hemolytic or incompatibility reaction.
1. Most severe complication.
2. Caused by mismatched blood.
3. Clinical manifestations.
   a. Increased temperature.

b. Decreased blood pressure.

c. Pain across the chest and at the site of needle insertion.

d. Chills.

e. Hematuria.

f. Backache in the kidney region.

g. Dyspnea and cyanosis.

h. Jaundice can occur in severe cases.

4. The reaction is caused by agglutination of the donor's red cells.

a. The antibodies in the recipient's plasma react with the antigens in the donor's red cells.

b. The clumping blocks off capillaries and therefore obstructs the flow of blood and oxygen to cells.

5. Nursing management.

a. Stop transfusion immediately upon appearance of symptoms.

b. Return remaining blood and the patient's blood sample to the laboratory for type and cross match.

c. Keep I.V. patent after changing blood tubing with either normal saline or preferably D_5W.

d. Take vital signs every fifteen minutes.

e. Insert Foley catheter for a urine sample for red blood cells and an accurate output record.

f. Check for oliguria.

g. Administer medications such as vasopressors if indicated.

h. Administer oxygen as necessary.

B. Bacterial contamination.

1. Check blood for discoloration, cloudiness, and bubbles, which are indicative of contamination.

2. If the blood is grossly contaminated with gram negative organisms, it can lead to death (more than half of the patients who receive contaminated blood die).

3. Clinical manifestations.

a. Sudden increase in temperature.

b. Sudden chill.

c. Headache.

d. Peripheral vasodilatation.

e. Malaise.

f. Lumbar pain.

4. Nursing management.

a. Do not use blood that is cloudy, dis-colored, or that appears to have bubbles present.

b. If transfusion has been started, discontinue immediately.

c. Send remaining blood to laboratory for culture and sensitivity. It is usually advisable to send patient's blood sample as well, if transfusion has been started.

d. Change I.V. tubing and keep it patent.

e. Check vital signs, including temperature, every fifteen minutes.

f. Insert Foley catheter for accurate output and urine specimen as ordered.

g. Control hyperthermia, if present, with antipyretics, cooling blankets, or sponge baths.

C. Allergic reactions.

1. Allergic response to any type of allergen in the donor's blood.

2. Common reaction, usually mild in nature.

3. Clinical manifestations.

a. Hives.

b. Urticaria.

c. Wheezing.

d. Laryngeal edema.

4. Nursing management.

a. Administer an antihistamine like Benadryl to control itching and to relieve edema.

b. If reaction is severe, discontinue the transfusion; otherwise, decrease the flow rate.

Transmission of Viral Hepatitis

A. Donors are screened to prevent transmission.

1. If blood shows positive for Australia antigen, donor is rejected.

2. If donor has had jaundice or hepatitis, donor is rejected permanently.

B. Usually hepatitis transmitted through blood is not fatal.

C. Nursing management is related to the care of patients with hepatitis (see medical section of this book), based on the seriousness of the condition.

Circulatory Overload

A. Causes.

1. Transfusion is administered too rapidly.

2. Quantity is in excess of what the circulatory system can accommodate.

3. Usually occurs when transfusion is administered

to debilitated patients, elderly or young patients, and patients with cardiac or pulmonary disease.

B. Clinical manifestations.
   1. Increased CVP reading.
   2. Tachycardia.
   3. Respiratory difficulty, i.e., dyspnea, shortness of breath, cough, rales, rhonchi.
   4. Hemoptysis and/or pink frothy sputum.
   5. Edema, especially pulmonary edema.
C. Nursing management.
   1. Discontinue transfusion.
   2. Provide for patent airway and adequate ventilation.
      a. Administer oxygen p.r.n.
      b. Intubate as needed.
   3. Place patient in semi- to high-Fowler's position to facilitate respiration.
   4. Give diuretics as ordered.
   5. If patient is in congestive heart failure, may need to digitalize.

Tube Feeding Procedure

A. Diet order.
   1. High in protein and calories.
   2. Feedings individualized according to patient need and type of supplement.
   3. Patient fed every 4 to 6 hours.
B. Check for presence of bowel sounds.
C. Position.
   1. Semi-Fowler's.
   2. Turned slightly to right side.
   3. Maintain position one-half to one hour following feeding.
D. Procedure for tube feeding.
   1. Insert tube or check patency of existing tube (intermittent tube insertion preferable).
   2. Aspirate and measure gastric contents.
   3. Warm feeding and dilute if not pre-mixed.
      a. Higher water volume—less possibility of vomiting and diarrhea.
      b. Higher water volume—less insult to kidney and liver.
   4. Give slowly by gravity flow—20-30 minutes.
   5. Flush tubing with water; prevent air from entering stomach via tubing.

E. Maintain oral and nasal hygiene.

Peritoneal Dialysis Procedure

A. Patient preparation.
   1. Patient voids before catheter insertion to prevent bladder damage.
   2. Abdominal skin is prepped.
   3. The area between the umbilicus and the pubic bone near the midline is most often used for catheter insertion.
   4. Weigh patient before procedure.
   5. The cycle used is described on p. 128.
B. Duration of dialysis depends on the following factors:
   1. Patient's size and weight.
   2. Severity of uremia.
   3. Physical state of patient.
   4. Usual time period for dialysis is 24 to 72 exchanges or runs.
C. Monitoring the procedure.
   1. Patient's electrolyte status is monitored during the process.
   2. Periodic samples of the return dialysate are sent for culture.
   3. Compare patient's weight before and after procedure to assess effectiveness.
   4. Vital signs must be monitored closely.
D. Care of equipment during procedure.
   1. Tubing should be changed every 8 hours when the procedure continues for days.
   2. Warming the dialysate not only improves area clearance but also maintains patient's body temperature and comfort.
   3. Avoid getting air into tubing as this is uncomfortable for the patient and impedes smooth and easy return of flow.
E. Quality and quantity of return.
   1. Initial few outflows may be slightly bloody due to insertion process.
   2. Cloudy fluid is usually an indication of peritonitis.
   3. Bowel perforation should be suspected if flow is brown.
   4. Record amount and type of solution for each inflow. This includes the medications added (e.g., KCl, heparin, antibiotics).
   5. Record outflow amount and characteristics.

6. Duration of each phase of the process should be recorded.
7. Keep a total net balance (difference between input and output for each exchange) and of cumulative net balance.
8. Inform physician if patient loses or retains large volumes of fluid.
   a. Periodic urine testing for presence of sugar which may be absorbed from dialysate.
   b. Heparin helps prevent drainage problems.
F. Procedures to check when drainage slows.
   1. Check proper position of clamps.
   2. Look for kinking in tubes.
   3. Milk the drainage tube.
   4. Observe air vent in drainage bottle for patency.
   5. Flush catheter.
   6. Reposition direction of catheter within means.
   7. Have patient change positions.
   8. Have physician change catheter.

Removal of Foreign Body From Eye

A. Have patient look upward, expose lower lid to expose conjunctival sac by everting lower lid.

B. Wet cotton applicator with sterile normal saline and gently twist swab over particle and remove it.
C. When particle unable to be found have patient look downward, place cotton applicator horizontally on outer surface of upper lid.
D. Grasp eyelashes with fingers and pull upper lid outward and upward over cotton stick.
E. With twisting motion upward, loosen particle and remove.

Irrigation of External Auditory Canal

A. Remove any discharge on outer ear.
B. Place emesis basin under ear.
C. Gently pull outer ear upward and backward for adult, or downward and backward for child.
D. Place tip of syringe or irrigating catheter at opening of ear.
E. Gently irrigate with solution at 95–105° F., directing flow toward the sides of the canal.
F. Dry external ear.
G. If irrigation does not dislodge wax, instillation of drops will need to be carried out.

Maternity
Nursing

This chapter is designed to give the nurse an understanding of the important phases and processes related to pregnancy. Key topics covered in a comprehensive manner include female anatomy, the health status of the female before and through pregnancy, labor and delivery, complications and postpartum adjustment, fetal development and care of the newborn.

Consistent with the other chapters, strong emphasis is placed on nursing interventions. To intervene effectively the nurse must have the theoretical background as well as the knowledge of emotional and psychological aspects of pregnancy, labor and delivery. To help the nurse integrate nursing content, the psychosocial aspects of maternal-child nursing are covered in detail.

The nursing content in this chapter is broad in scope so all technical information is presented in outline format. In addition to the questions and answers at the end of the chapter, several tables and appendices are included to facilitate learning.

Anatomy and Physiology of Female Reproductive Organs

Anatomy

Female Reproductive Organs

A. Usually divided into two groups, the external and internal genitalia.

B. External genitalia are collectively called the vulva, which consist of:
1. Mons veneris or mons pubis.
2. Labia majora.
3. Labia minora.
4. Clitoris.
5. Vestibule.
6. Urinary meatus.
7. Skene's ducts and Bartholin's glands.
8. Hymen.
9. Perineum.

C. Internal organs of reproduction—located in the pelvic cavity.
1. Uterus—muscular organ.
   a. Two major functions.
      (1) Organ in which fetus develops.
      (2) Organ from which menstruation occurs.
   b. Consists of two major parts.
      (1) Corpus (body), which has three layers.
         (a) Perimetrium—external layer.
         (b) Myometrium—middle layer.
         (c) Endometrium—internal layer.
      (2) Cervix, composed of three parts.
         (a) Internal os—opens into body of uterine cavity.
         (b) Cervical canal—located between internal and external os.
         (c) External os—opens into vagina.
2. Fallopian tubes—two slender muscular tubes that extend laterally from the cornu of the uterine cavity to the ovaries; they are the passageways through which the ova reach the uterus.
3. Ovaries—two flat, oval-shaped organs located on each side of the uterus. (Correspond to the testes in the male.) Two major functions are:
   a. Development and expulsion of ova.
   b. Secretion of certain hormones.
4. Vagina—canal that extends from lower part of the vulva to the cervix—serves three functions for the body:
   a. Passageway for menstrual blood.
   b. Passageway for fetus.
   c. Organ of copulation.

Skeletal Features of the Pelvis

A. The pelvis is important in obstetrics because it is the passage through which the baby passes during birth. Disproportions between fetus and size of pelvis may make vaginal delivery difficult or impossible.

B. Four bones form the pelvis—two innominate bones, the sacrum, and the coccyx.

C. Divisions of pelvis.
1. False pelvis—shallow extended portion above brim that supports abdominal viscera.
2. True pelvis—portion that lies below pelvic brim and is divided into three sections—the pelvic inlet, the mid-pelvis, and the pelvic outlet.
3. Four main types of pelves.
   a. Gynecoid—inlet nearly round or blunt, heart-shaped (45 percent of women).
   b. Android—inlet wedge-shaped (15 percent of women).
   c. Anthropoid—inlet oval-shaped (35 percent of women).
   d. Platypelloid—inlet oval-shaped, transversely (5 percent or less of women).

D. Measurements of the pelvis.
1. Diagonal conjugate (C.D.)—distance between sacral promontory and lower margin of symphysis pubis. Measurement greater than 11.5 cm. adequate.
2. True conjugate, or conjugate vera (C.V.)—distance from upper margin of symphysis to sacral promontory. Measurement greater than 11 cm. adequate.
3. Tuberischial diameter (T.I.)—transverse diameter of outlet. Measurement greater than 8 cm. adequate.
4. Size determination.
   a. X-ray pelvimetry is most accurate means of determining size of pelvis.
   b. X-ray pelvimetry is contraindicated to avoid undue exposure of mother and infant unless pelvic contraction is suspected.

Physiology

Menstruation and the Menstrual Cycle

Definition: Menstruation is the periodic discharge of blood, mucus, and epithelial cells from the uterus.

A. Menstrual cycle—usually lasts twenty-eight days, but may vary from twenty-one to thirty-five days with ovulation occurring about fourteen days before menstruation begins. Usually occurs between the ages of twelve to forty-five.

B. Hormonal control—depends upon adequate functioning of pituitary, ovaries, and uterus. Hypothalamus exerts control through releasing and inhibiting factors.

1. Proliferative phase.
   a. Follicle stimulating hormone (FSH), released by anterior pituitary, stimulates the development of the graafian follicle.
   b. As graafian follicle develops it produces increasing amounts of follicular fluid containing a hormone called estrogen.
   c. Estrogen stimulates build-up or thickening of the endometrium.
   d. As estrogen increases in the bloodstream, it suppresses secretion of FSH and favors the secretion of the luteinizing hormone (LH).
   e. LH stimulates ovulation and initiates development of the corpus luteum.

2. Secretory phase.
   a. Follows ovulation, which is the release of mature ovum from the graafian follicle.
   b. Rapid changes take place in the ruptured follicle under the influence of LH.
   c. Cavity of the graafian follicle is replaced by the corpus luteum (mass of yellow-colored tissue).
   d. Main function of the corpus luteum is to secrete progesterone and some estrogen.
   e. Progesterone acts upon the endometrium to bring about secretory changes that prepare it for pregnancy. Also, progesterone maintains the endometrium during the early phase of pregnancy, should a fertilized ovum be implanted.

3. Menstrual phase.
   a. Corpus luteum degenerates in about eight days unless the ovum is fertilized.
   b. There is a cessation of progesterone and estrogen produced by corpus luteum and blood levels drop.
   c. Endometrium degenerates and menstruation occurs.
   d. The drop in blood levels of estrogen and progesterone stimulate production of FSH and a new cycle begins.

Development of the Fetus

Fertilization

Definition: A gamete is a sex cell—ovum or spermatozoon—that has undergone maturation and is ready for fertilization.

A. Fertilization takes place when two essential cells—sperm and ovum—unite.

B. Each reproductive cell (one gamete) carries 23 chromosomes.

C. Sperm carries two types of sex chromosomes, X and Y, which when united with female X chromosome, determines the sex of the child (XY—male; XX—female).

D. The site of fertilization is usually in the outer third of the fallopian tubes, and the fertilized egg then descends to the uterus.

Fetal Development

Definition: Embryo is the fertilized ovum during the first two months of development. Fetus is product of conception from two months to time of birth.

A. Implantation occurs about the seventh day after fertilization.

B. First eight weeks, when all major organs are developing, is the period of greatest vulnerability.

C. Embryonic development—cells arrange themselves into three layers:

1. Ectoderm—outer layer—gives rise to skin, salivary and mammary glands, nervous system, and other external parts of the body.
2. Endoderm—inner layer—gives rise to thymus, thyroid, bladder, and other small organs and tubes.
3. Mesoderm—layer between the other two—gives rise to urinary and reproductive organs, circula-

tory system, connective tissue, muscle, and bones.

D. Fetal membranes and amniotic fluid.

1. Fetal membranes—membranes which surround the fetus—are composed of two layers:
   a. Amnion—glistening inner membrane—forms early, about the second week of embryonic development; encloses the amniotic cavity.
   b. Chorion—outer membrane.

2. Amniotic fluid—forms within the amniotic cavity and surrounds the embryo. Usually consists of 500 to 1000 ml. of fluid at the end of pregnancy.
   a. Amniotic fluid contains fetal urine, lanugo from fetal skin, epithelial cells, and subaqueous materials.
   b. Function of the fluid is to provide an optimum temperature and environment for fetus and provide a cushion against injury; fetus also drinks the fluid, probably as much as 450 ml. a day near term.
   c. Source is uncertain. Probably maternal exudate, fetal urine, or secretion of the amniotic membrane. Replaced continuously at a rapid rate.

E. Placental function.

1. Placenta—organ that provides for the exchange of nutrients and waste products between mother and fetus and acts as an endocrine organ.
   a. Provides oxygen and removes carbon dioxide from the fetal system.
   b. Maintains fetal fluid and electrolyte, acid-base balance.

2. Placenta develops by the third month.
   a. Formed by union of chorionic villi and decidua basalis.
   b. Fetal surface smooth and glistening.
   c. Maternal surface red and fleshlike.

3. Exchange takes place between mother and fetus through diffusion.

4. Placental function is dependent upon maternal circulation.

5. Materials passed through placenta in addition to nutrients are drugs, antibodies to some diseases, and certain viruses. Large particles such as bacteria cannot pass through barrier.

6. Placental transfer of maternal immunoglobulin (G) gives the fetus passive immunity to certain diseases for the first few months after birth.

7. Hormones produced by the placenta.
   a. Chorionic gonadotropin (HCG)—detected in urine fifteen days after implantation. Hormone stimulates the corpus luteum to maintain endometrium and is basis of immunological test of pregnancy.
   b. Human placental lactogen (HPL)—effect similar to growth hormone.
   c. Estrogen and progesterone.

8. The umbilical cord extends from the fetus to the center of the fetal surface of the placenta.
   a. Contains two arteries and one vein.
   b. Is protected by mucoid connective tissue termed Wharton's jelly.

F. Fetal circulation.

1. Arteries carry venous blood.

2. Vein carries oxygenated blood.

3. Fetal circulation bypass.
   a. Bypass due to nonfunctioning lungs: ductus arteriosus (between pulmonary artery and aorta) and foramen ovale (between right and left atrium).
   b. Ductus venosus bypass—due to fetal liver not being used for exchange of waste.
   c. Bypasses must close following birth to allow blood to flow through the lungs for respiration and through the liver for waste exchange.

G. Calculation of expected date of delivery or confinement (EDC).

1. Nägele's rule—count back three months from first day of last menstrual period and add seven days.

   Example: LMP July 18
             EDC April 25

2. Pregnancy usually does not terminate on the exact EDC. It may vary from one week before to two weeks after the expected date.

H. Multiple pregnancies (uterus contains two or more embryos). May be the result of fertilization of a single ovum or two separate ova. If division takes place very early in monozygotic twins, two placentas and two chorions are formed.

Multiple Pregnancies

Double Ovum	Single Ovum
Dizygotic or fraternal twins	Monozygotic or identical twins
Ova from same or different ovaries	Union of a single ovum and a single sperm
Same or different sex	Same sex
Brother or sister resemblance	Identical genetic pattern
Two placentas but may be fused	One placenta
Two chorions and two amnions	One chorion and two amnions

Maternal Changes During Pregnancy

Physiological Changes

Reproductive Organs

A. Uterus—increases in weight from two ounces to about two pounds at the end of gestation and in size from five to six times larger.
   1. Changes in tissue.
      a. Hypertrophy of muscle cells and development of new muscles.
      b. Development of connective and elastic tissue, which increases contractility.
      c. Increase in the size and number of blood vessels.
      d. Hypertrophy of the lymphatic system.
      e. Growth of the uterus is brought about by the influences of estrogen during the early months and the pressure of the fetus.
   2. Other changes.
      a. Contractions occur throughout pregnancy, starting from very mild to increased strength.
      b. As the uterus grows, it rises out of the pelvis displacing intestines and may be palpated above the symphysis pubis.

B. Ligaments.
   Broad ligaments in the pelvis become elongated and hypertrophied to help support and stabilize uterus during pregnancy.
C. Cervix.
   1. Becomes shorter, more elastic, and larger in diameter.
   2. Marked thickening of mucous lining and increased blood supply.
   3. Edema and hyperplasia of the cervical glands and increased glandular secretions.
   4. Mucous plug expelled from cervix as cervix begins to dilate at onset of labor.
D. Vagina.
   1. Increased vascularity, deepening of color to dark red or purple—Chadwick's sign.
   2. Hypertrophy and thickening of muscle.
   3. Loosening of connective tissue.
   4. Increased vaginal discharge.
   5. Secretions have high pH.
E. Perineum.
   1. Increased vascularity.
   2. Hypertrophy of muscles.
   3. Loosening of connective tissue.
F. Ovaries and tubes.
   1. Usually one large corpus luteum present in one ovary.
   2. Ovulation does not take place.

Breast

A. Changes in tissue.
   1. Extensive growth of alveolar tissue, necessary for lactation.
   2. Montgomery's glands enlarge.
B. Other changes.
   1. Increases in size and firmness and becomes nodular.
   2. Nipples become more prominent and areola deepens in color.
   3. Superficial veins grow more prominent.
   4. At the end of third month, colostrum appears.
   5. After delivery, anterior pituitary stimulates production and secretion of milk.

Abdomen

A. Contour changes as the enlarging uterus extends into the abdominal cavity.

Table 1. Fetal Growth

Age	Development
End of one month or four weeks	Form of embryonic disc No clearly defined features Body systems rudimentary form Cardiovascular system functioning
End of two months or eight weeks	Head greatly enlarged, about the size of rest of body Some fetal movement due to beginning neuromuscular development Facial features becoming distinct Body covered with thin skin
End of three months or twelve weeks	Teeth forming under gums Center ossification appearing in most bones Fingers and toes are differentiated and bear nails Kidneys able to secrete Eyes have lids which are fused shut until six months Fetus swallows Sex distinguishable
End of four months or sixteen weeks	Lanugo appears over body Meconium in intestines Face has human appearance Size: about six inches long; weight: about 3.5 oz.
End of five months or twenty weeks	Skeleton begins to harden Buds of permanent teeth develop Vernix caseosa makes appearance Fetal movements stronger and felt by mother Fetal heart rate heard Size: about ten inches long; weight: about 11 oz.
End of six months or twenty-four weeks	Fat beginning to deposit beneath skin Body and head better proportioned Eyebrows and eyelashes appear Size: about twelve inches long; weight: about 1½ lbs.
End of seven months or twenty-eight weeks	Skin reddish and covered with vernix Size: about fourteen inches long; weight: about 2½ lbs. May be viable if born at this time, though still immature
End of eight months or thirty-two weeks	Nails are firm and extend to end of digits Lanugo begins to disappear Size: about sixteen inches long; weight: about 4 lbs. Increased chance for survival if born at this time
End of nine months or thirty-six weeks	Increased fat deposits under skin Increased development Size: about eighteen inches long; weight: about 5 lbs. Good chance of survival
End of ten months or forty weeks	Full term Little lanugo Smooth skin Size: about twenty inches long; weight 7–7½ lbs. Optimum time for survival

B Striae gravidarum usually appear on the abdomen as pregnancy progresses.

Skin

A. Pigmentation increases in certain areas of the body.
1 Breast—primary areola deepens in color.
2 Abdomen—linea nigra, dark streak down the midline of the abdomen, especially prominent in brunettes.
3. Face—chloasma, the "mask of pregnancy" pigmentation distributed over the face. Usually disappears after pregnancy.
4. Face and upper trunk—occasionally spider nevi or palmar erythema develops with the increase in estrogen.

B Pigmented areas on abdomen and breast usually do not completely disappear after delivery.

Circulatory System

A. Considerable increase (about 30 percent) in volume as a result of:
1. Increased metabolic demands of new tissue.
2. Expansion of vascular system, especially in the reproductive organs.
3. Retention of sodium and water.

B. Increase in plasma volume is greater than increase in red blood cells and hemoglobin.
1. Dilution is usually not sufficient to cause anemia.
2. Low hemoglobin in pregnancy, below 11.5 percent, usually caused by iron-deficiency anemia.

C. Iron requirements are increased to meet demands of increased blood supply and growing fetus (need cannot be met by diet alone; supplement usually given).

D. Heart increases in size. Cardiac output is increased (25 to 50 percent); peaks at end of second trimester then levels off.

E. Blood pressure *should not* rise during pregnancy.

F. Fibrinogen concentration increases to term.

G. Palpitations may be experienced during pregnancy due to sympathetic nervous disturbance and intra-abdominal pressure caused by enlarging uterus.

Respiratory System

A. Thoracic cage is pushed upward and diaphragm is elevated as uterus enlarges.

B. Thoracic cage widens to compensate, so vital capacity remains the same or is increased.

C. Oxygen consumption is increased to support fetus.

D. Shortness of breath may be experienced in latter part of pregnancy due to pressure upon diaphragm caused by enlarging uterus.

Digestive System

A. Nausea, vomiting, and poor appetite are present in early pregnancy because of a decreased gastric motility.

B. Constipation is due to a decrease in gastrointestinal motility, reduced peristaltic activity, and the pressure of the uterus; it may be present in latter half of pregnancy.

C. Flatulence and heartburn may be present, due to decreased gastric acidity and decreased motility of the gastrointestinal tract.

Urinary System

A. Kidneys.
1. Kidney and renal function increase.
2. Renal blood flow and glomerular filtration increase.
3. Renal threshold for sugar is reduced in some women.

B. Bladder and ureters.
1. Blood supply to the bladder and pelvic organs is increased.
2. Early pregnancy—pressure of the uterus on the bladder causes frequent urination.
3. Atonia of smooth muscles during pregnancy leads to dilatation of ureters and renal pelvis, and may cause urine stasis.
4. A decrease in bladder tone is caused by hormonal influences, and a decrease in bladder capacity occurs because of crowding; may lead to complications during pregnancy and in the postpartum period.

Joints, Bones, and Teeth

A. Softening of pelvic cartilages occurs, probably due to the hormone relaxin.

B. Posture changes as upper spine is thrown forward to compensate for increased abdominal size.

C. Demineralization of teeth does not occur as a result of normal pregnancy but may be related to poor dental hygiene.

Endocrine System

A. Placenta produces hormones human chorionic gonadotropin (HCG) and placental lactogen (HPL).
   1. Production of estrogen and progesterone is taken over from the ovaries by the placenta after the second month.
   2. Normal cycle of production of estrogen and progesterone is suspended until after delivery.
B. Anterior lobe of pituitary gland enlarges slightly during pregnancy.
C. Adrenal cortex enlarges slightly.
D. Thyroid enlarges slightly and thyroid activity increases.
E. Aldosterone levels gradually increase beginning about the fifteenth week.

Metabolism

A. Increase in body weight—a twenty-five-pound weight gain usually recommended.
B. Some of the weight gain is caused by retention of fluid and by deposits of fatty tissue.
C. Water metabolism.
   1. Tendency to retain fluid in body tissues, especially in the last trimester.
   2. Reversal of fluid retention usually takes place in the form of diuresis in the first twenty-four hours postpartum.
D. Basal metabolic rate increases 20 percent.

Emotional Changes

Altered Emotional Characteristics

A. Pregnancy may be viewed as a developmental process involving endocrine, somatic, and psychological changes, a period of increased "susceptibility to crises," and an "altered state of consciousness."
B. Emotional reactions to pregnancy may vary from early rejection to elation.
C. Mother may be puzzled by changes in her feelings; needs reassurance from the nurse that these are normal reactions and that she need not feel guilty.
D. Mother may have fears and worries about the baby and herself and needs to be able to express her feelings to the nurse.
E. Quick mood changes are common; some emotional instability usually occurs.

F. Mother may become more passive and introverted.
G. Husband needs to be informed that wife's emotional lability, attitudes, and feelings toward sex are emotional reactions of pregnancy and are temporary.

Taking on the Parental Role

A. Pregnant woman may fantasize or daydream to "experience" the role of mother before the actual birth.
B. Takes on adaptive behaviors that are best suited to her own personality and situation.
C. Experiences a "letting go" of her former role (e.g., as a career woman).
   1. May experience ambivalence about letting go of her old role to take on the new one.
   2. Desire to have a baby influences adjustment.
D. Concerns.
   1. First and second trimester—concerns about body changes; fear of labor and delivery; beginning conceptualization of fetus as separate individual.
   2. Third trimester—more confident about labor and delivery; shows readiness to assume care of infant; incorporation of concept of fetus as a separate individual should be complete.
E. Father may also experience ambivalence at taking on new role, assuming increased financial responsibility, and sharing wife's attention with child.
F. Father may experience physiologic changes, such as weight gain, nausea, and vomiting.

Childbirth Preparation

Theories of Childbirth

A. Factors that influence pain in labor.
   1. Preconditioning—by "old wives' tales," fantasies, and fears. Accurate information about the childbirth process can often alleviate effects of preconditioning.
   2. Pain produces stress, which in turn affects the body's functioning. Interpretations of and reactions to pain can be altered by a refocusing of attention and by conditioning.
   3. Feelings of isolation. Social expectations and tension may also increase feelings of pain.

B. Childbirth education.

1. Each method varies somewhat but basic underlying concepts are similar. Birth is viewed as a natural occurrence. Knowledge about the birth experience dispels fears and tension, and distraction and concentration during labor and delivery modify the pain experience.

2. Purpose—to promote relaxation enabling the mother to work with the labor process. Allows parents to take an active part in the birth process, thereby increasing self-esteem and satisfaction.

3. Goals accomplished by means of:

   a. Education—anatomy and physiology of reproductive system, and the labor and delivery process; replacement of misinformation and superstition with facts. May include classes on nutrition, discomforts of pregnancy, breast-feeding, infant care, etc.

   b. Training—controlled breathing and neuromuscular exercises.

   c. Presence of father, or significant other, in labor and delivery rooms to serve as coach and lend support.

4. Common methods presently available.

   a. Read method (*Natural Childbirth*) introduced by Grantly Dick-Read in England. Believed pain in childbirth was psychological rather than physiological. Pain brought about by fear and tension.

   b. Lamaze method.

   c. Bradley method.

   d. Scientific relaxation for childbirth.

5. LeBoyer technique—used in delivery room to reduce stress of birth upon infant.

   a. Includes increasing room temperature to one comfortable for infant, reducing external stimuli by dimming lights, keeping noise level to a minimum.

   b. Infant is placed in skin-to-skin contact on mother's abdomen and gently stroked; cord clamping is delayed until pulsation stops.

   c. Infant is submerged up to head in a bath of warm water until it appears relaxed, then is dried and wrapped snugly in a warm blanket.

6. Classes are emerging for parents expecting delivery by C-section.

C. Nursing measures.

1. Support parents in method chosen.

2. Provide emotional and physical support during labor process.

3. Leave option open for mother to choose medication should she so desire.

Prenatal Instructions

Nutrition

A. It is important that mother maintain adequate nutrition.

B. See appendix for specific guidelines (pp. 340-342).

Use of Drugs

A. All drugs can be expected to cross the placenta and affect the fetus.

B. Greatest danger in first trimester, especially when organs are developing.

C. Many other effects of drugs on the fetus are unknown and may not be evident for years.

D. Pregnant women should refrain from taking drugs during pregnancy, even commonly used drugs such as aspirin.

E. Nicotine—current research indicates that smoking retards the growth of fetus.

   1. Vasoconstriction of mother's vessels, resulting in decreased placental flow.

   2. Increase in carbon dioxide levels in mother's blood and reduction of oxygen-carrying capacity.

Daily Activities

A. Exercise in moderation is beneficial—but should never be carried on past the point of fatigue.

B. Sports may be participated in if they are part of the mother's usual activity and there are no complications present.

C. Fatigue is common in early pregnancy.

D. Frequent rest periods, at ten- to fifteen-minute intervals, are helpful in avoiding needless fatigue.

E. Dental hygiene should be maintained daily and infections treated promptly.

F. Tub baths may be taken. Water enters vagina under pressure only. Baths contraindicated after membranes have ruptured.

G. Travel—may travel with physician's permission.
   1. Airlines discourage travel after the eighth month.
   2. When traveling, elevate feet and walk around periodically to decrease pedal edema.

Employment

A. May be continued as long as it does not cause over-fatigue.
B. Avoid areas where chemicals or gases are used—may cause congenital malformations in infant.
C. Avoid heavy lifting and individuals with contagious diseases.

Sexual Intercourse

A. May be carried on without fear unless bleeding or premature contractions develop.
B. May need to vary usual positions as pregnancy advances.

Signs and Discomforts of Pregnancy

Signs of Pregnancy

Definition: The signs of pregnancy are divided into three groups: presumptive, probable, and positive. Positive signs cannot be detected until after the fourth month.

Presumptive Signs

A. Cessation of menstruation—amenorrhea.
B. Breast changes—increased size and feeling of fullness, nipples more pronounced, areola darker.
C. Nausea and vomiting—"morning sickness"—appears in about 50 percent of pregnant women and usually disappears at the end of the third month.
D. Frequent urination—frequent desire to void—usually occurs in the first three to four months. Pressure on the bladder from an enlarged uterus gives the sensation of a distended bladder.
E. Quickening—first perception of fetal movement—occurs between sixteenth and eighteenth week.
F. Increased pigmentation of skin, chloasma, linea nigra, and striae gravidarum.
G. Fatigue—periods of drowsiness and lassitude during first three months.
H. Vaginal changes—Chadwick's sign, discoloration, and thickening of vaginal mucosa.

Probable Signs

A. Enlargement of the abdomen—usually occurs after the third month when the fetus rises out of the pelvis into the abdominal cavity.
B. Changes in internal organs.
   1. Change in shape, size, and consistency of the uterus.
   2. Hegar's sign—softening of the isthmus of the uterus—occurs about sixth week.
   3. Goodell's sign—softening of the cervix—occurs beginning of the second month.
C. Braxton Hicks contractions—usually not felt by the mother until seven months, but contractions begin in the early weeks of pregnancy and continue through gestation.
D. Ballottement—giving a sudden push to the fetus and feeling it rebound in a few seconds to the original position is usually possible in the fourth to fifth month.
E. Outline of the fetus by abdominal palpation (a probable sign, because a tumor may simulate fetal parts).
F. Positive pregnancy test is based upon the secretion of chorionic gonadotrophin in the urine of a pregnant woman; it is usually detectable ten days after the first missed period. Test is 95 percent effective.

Positive Signs

A. Apparent after eighteenth to twentieth week.
B. Auscultation of fetal heart rates with stethoscope or ultrasonic equipment (rates: 120-160). (Note: with ultrasonic equipment, FH rate may be heard at twelve weeks.)
C. Active fetal movements are perceptible by the physician.
D. X-ray or sonogram examination, showing fetal outline. X-ray not visible until fourteenth week or later, when bone calcification occurs.

Pseudocyesis/Pseudopregnancies

Definition: Pseudocyesis is the emotional control of physiological functioning, psychological in origin. Woman believes she is pregnant when she is not.

Table 2. Major Discomforts and Relief Measures

Discomfort	Trimester Most Prominent	Relief Measures
Nausea and vomiting	1st	Eat five or six small, frequent meals. In between meals, have crackers without fluid. Avoid foods high in carbohydrates, fried and greasy, or with a strong odor. Antinausea drug may be prescribed.
Frequency	1st and 3rd	Wear perineal pads if there is leakage.
Heartburn	2nd and 3rd	Avoid fatty, fried, and highly spiced foods. Have small frequent feedings. Use an antacid—*avoid* sodium bicarbonate.
Abdominal distress	1st, 2nd, and 3rd	Eat slowly, chew food thoroughly, take smaller helpings of food.
Flatulence	2nd and 3rd	Maintain daily bowel movement. Avoid gas-forming foods. Take antiflatulents as prescribed by physician.
Constipation	2nd and 3rd	Drink sufficient fluids. Eat fruit and foods high in roughage. Exercise moderately. Take stool softener if prescribed by physician. *Do not* use mineral oil.
Hemorrhoids	3rd	Apply ointments, suppositories, warm compresses. Avoid constipation and get adequate rest.
Insomnia	3rd	Exercise moderately to promote relaxation and fatigue. Change position while sleeping. If severe, take medication as prescribed by physician.
Backaches	3rd	Rest and improve posture—use a firm mattress. Use a good abdominal support, wear comfortable shoes. Do exercises such as squatting, sitting, and pelvic rock.
Varicosities, legs and vulva	3rd	Avoid long periods of standing or sitting with legs crossed. Sit or lie with feet and hips elevated. Move about while standing to improve circulation. Wear support hose; *avoid* tight garters.
Edema of legs and feet	3rd	Elevate feet while sitting or lying down. Avoid standing or sitting in one position for long periods.
Cramps in legs	3rd	Extend cramped leg and flex ankles, pushing foot upward with toes pointed toward knee. Increase calcium intake.
Pain in thighs or aching of perineum	3rd	Alternate periods of sitting and standing. Rest.
Shortness of breath	3rd	Sit up. Lie on back with arms extended above bed.
Breast soreness	1st, 2nd, and 3rd	Wear brassiere with wide adjustable straps that fits well.
Supine hypotensive syndrome	3rd	Change position to left side to relieve pressure of uterus on inferior vena cava.
Vaginal discharge	3rd	Practice proper cleansing and hygiene. Avoid douche unless recommended by physician. Observe for signs of vaginal infection common in pregnancy.

A. Clinical manifestations.
 1. Amenorrhea, breast changes, and secretion of colostrum.
 2. Enlargement of abdomen.
 3. Reports of quickening.
 4. Appears any age, but common in older women.
B. Treatment.
 1. Treatment aimed at uncovering underlying emotional problem.
 2. Important for nurse to offer continued emotional support.

Physical Examinations

A. Initial examination.
 1. Complete history is recorded—past pregnancies, medical history, and family history.
 2. Physical examination is made—pelvic, breast, abdomen, urinalysis, blood work, slides for pap and gonorrhea, Rh factor, blood pressure, weight, and serology for syphilis.
 3. Diet and health instructions given to patient.
B. Subsequent examinations—usually done once a month until the last trimester, then more frequently.
 1. Weight, blood pressure, and urinalysis tests for protein and sugar content.
 2. Palpation of abdomen.
 3. Auscultation of fetal heart tones.
 4. Observation for untoward signs and symptoms.
 5. Continuing health care and instructions.

High Risk Pregnancy

Definition: A patient is identified as "high risk" when there is an increased chance of morbidity and/or mortality to the mother, fetus, or both.

Related Factors

A. Age—under 17, over 35.
B. Parity—five or more pregnancies.
C. Previous conditions.
 1. Previous infant death, premature birth, or congenital malformations.
 2. History of cardiac disease, diabetes, renal disease, or other maternal condition.
 3. Difficulty in conceiving.

 4. Narcotic or alcohol addiction.
 5. Less than a year since last pregnancy.
 6. Rh incompatibility and sensitization.

Conditions Leading to High Risk

A. Infection.
B. Bleeding.
C. Toxemia.

Intrapartum Conditions

A. Premature labor.
B. Abnormal fetal positions.
C. Premature rupture of membranes.

Pregnancy in Adolescents

Increased Risk to Mother and Fetus

A. Crisis of pregnancy compounds the crises of adolescence—physical, social, emotional, social development.
B. Patient may be unwed.
C. Physical development may not be complete.
D. High incidence of prematurity and toxemia.
E. Diet may be inadequate.

Nursing Management

A. Encourage early antipartum care.
B. Provide health instruction on pregnancy, nutrition, and hygiene.
C. Observe frequently for complications.
D. Provide emotional support and counseling.

Complications Associated with Pregnancy

Danger Signals

A. Bleeding from vagina.
B. Escape of amniotic fluid denoting premature rupture of membranes.
C. Abdominal pain.
D. Dizziness or blurring of vision.
E. Persistent headache.

F. Edema of face and fingers.

G. Persistent and severe vomiting.

H. Chills and elevated temperature.

Abortion

Definition: Abortion is the expulsion of the fetus before it is viable; abortion may be spontaneous or induced.

Categories of Abortion

A. Threatened—some loss of blood and pain without loss of products of conception.

B. Imminent—bleeding profuse, contractions severe, bearing down sensation; without intervention, products of conception will be lost.

C. Inevitable—bleeding, contractions, ruptured membranes, and cervical dilatation.

D. Incomplete—portion of products of conception remain in uterine cavity.

E. Complete—all products of conception expelled.

F. Habitual—abortion in three or more succeeding pregnancies.

G. Therapeutic—medically terminated for mother's physical or emotional health.

H. Criminal—termination of pregnancy outside medical or approved facilities.

I. Dilatation and curettage—surgical removal of uterine contents.

Etiology

A. Abnormalities of fetus.

B. Abnormalities of reproductive tract.

C. Injuries—physical and emotional shocks.

D. Endocrine disturbances.

E. Acute infectious diseases.

F. Maternal diseases.

G. Psychogenic problems.

Clinical Manifestations

A. Vaginal bleeding.

B. Intermittent contractions and pain—usually beginning in the small of the back; abdominal cramping.

Treatment of Threatened Abortion

A. Notify physician immediately—save all perineal pads.

B. Endocrine therapy—usually progesterone if deficient.

C. Correction of abnormalities or disturbances of reproductive tract.

D. Avoidance of stress and exertion during early pregnancy.

E. Bed rest and sedation—avoid climbing stairs and coitus until at least two weeks after bleeding stops.

F. Oxytoxic drug may be given to hasten process of abortion, if it is inevitable, and to promote contraction of uterus after abortion.

G. Medication for pain if necessary.

H. Blood available for transfusion.

I. Dilatation and curettage may be necessary in an incomplete abortion.

J. Administration of RhoGAM in Rh-negative mothers.

K. Maintain sterile technique in all examinations and treatments.

Nursing Management

A. Offer emotional support and comfort, but do not say, "Everything will be all right," because of the loss of the pregnancy.

B. Save all perineal pads and expelled tissue for examination.

C. Observe for signs of shock and institute emergency measures for treatment if necessary.

D. In criminal abortions, observe for serious complications such as septic shock, thrombophlebitis, and renal failure.

Habitual Abortion

Definition: Habitual abortion is the condition in which the patient has spontaneously aborted three or more consecutive times.

Etiology

A. Endocrine disturbances.

B. Blood incompatibilities.

C. Incompetent cervical os.

D. Chromosomal abnormalities.

E. Abnormalities of reproductive tract.

F. Fibromas of uterus.

G. Psychological.

Treatments Possible

A. Endocrine disturbances—hormone therapy (estrogen and progesterone), thyroid therapy.

B. Incompetent cervical os—Shirodkar procedure: internal os constricted by encircling suture, which is removed when labor begins.

C. Abnormalities and fibromas—surgical correction of abnormalities, if possible, and removal of fibromas.

D. Psychological—psychotherapy for cause.

Extrauterine or Ectopic Pregnancy

Definition: Ectopic pregnancy is one that develops outside the uterus; cannot develop longer than 10 to 12 weeks.

Process of Pregnancy

A. Although the fertilized ovum usually attaches to the uterine lining, it may become implanted at any point between the graafian follicle and the uterus.

B. Tubal pregnancy is the most common form (95 percent) but the ovum may attach to an ovary, the abdomen, or interligaments.

C. Implantation.

 1. Ovum attaches to tube and erodes into mucosa wall, as it would to the endometrial lining of the uterus.

 2. Tube increases in size and stretches.

 3. Pregnancy usually terminates during the first three months by:

 a. Spontaneous tubal abortion.

 b. Tubal rupture.

 c. Death and disintegration of products of conception within the tube.

Etiology

A. Progress of ovum through tube is delayed for some reason.

B. Tubal deformities—congenital, or due to disease such as gonorrhea.

C. Tumors pressing against the tube.

D. Adhesions from previous surgery.

E. Tubal spasms.

F. Migration of ovum to opposite tube.

Clinical Manifestations

A. Woman may or may not know she is pregnant.

B. May have history of missed periods and "spotting."

C. May have slight abdominal pain.

D. Early signs of pregnancy may be present.

E. Uterus enlarges and decidua develops—due to hormonal influence.

F. Often first symptom is a sudden excruciating pain in lower abdomen.

G. May feel faint and have signs of shock as a result of hemorrhage into the peritoneal cavity.

H. May have little external bleeding.

Treatment

A. Immediate removal of the affected tube.

B. Blood transfusions may be necessary.

Nursing Management

A. Observe for signs of shock and give treatment for shock as necessary.

B. Protect patient against exertion.

C. Provide emotional support—patient may be frightened and feel the loss of the pregnancy.

Hydatidiform Mole

Definition: Hydatidiform mole is a benign neoplasm of the chorion, in which chorionic villi degenerate, become filled with a clear viscid fluid, and assume the appearance of grapelike clusters involving all or parts of the decidual lining of the uterus.

Incidence

A. Rare—occurs once in every two thousand pregnancies, except in the Orient where it is more common.

B. Usually there is no fetus found.

Etiology

A. May be pathological ova.

B. High incidence in the Orient may be due to dietary protein deficiency.

Clinical Manifestations

A. Pregnancy appears normal at first.

B. Bleeding varies from spotting to profuse.

C. May be intermittent brownish discharge after the twelfth week.

D. Rapid enlargement of the uterus.

E. Nausea and vomiting appear earlier and are usually more severe and last longer.

F. Severe preeclampsia may develop in the early part of the second trimester.

G. Hypertension may occur with the rapid expansion of the uterus.

H. Characteristic vesicles may be passed.

I. No fetal heart tones heard on fetal parts discerned.

Diagnosis

A. Test for increased titer of chorionic gonadotrophin. It is best to collect a 24-hour specimen for the total daily output.

B. Sonography—gives positive diagnosis in the first trimester.

C. Amniography—X-ray following injection with contrast dye.

Treatment

A. Evacuation of uterus as soon as positive diagnosis is made—by dilatation and curettage or vacuum curettage suction.

B. Follow-up visits to physician for examination, because hydatidiform mole may lead to carcinoma.

C. HCG levels measured at one week and 60 days. Continued elevations of HCG pathological.

Nursing Management

A. Observe for hemorrhage.

B. Provide emotional support—there may be a fear of malignancy or patient may feel the loss of the baby.

C. Encourage follow-up treatment.

Placenta Previa

Definition: Placenta previa occurs when the ovum implants low in the uterus, toward the cervix, and the placenta develops so that it partially or completely covers the internal os. Occurs once in every 150 deliveries.

Types

A. Complete—os entirely covered.

B. Partial—only part of os covered.

C. Marginal—margin overlaps os.

Etiology

A. Occurs more often in multiparas.

B. Occurs more often with increased age of mother.

C. Scarring or tumor of uterus.

Clinical Manifestations

A. Painless vaginal bleeding after the seventh month without precipitating cause.

B. Bleeding may be intermittent or in gushes.

C. As internal os begins to dilate, the part of placenta that overlies the os separates and leaves gaping vessels, so bleeding occurs.

D. Uterus usually remains soft and flaccid.

Diagnosis

A. History of painless bleeding begins late in pregnancy.

B. Localization of placenta by ultrasound or radioisotope.

C. Sterile vagina or pelvic examinations are usually not done as part of diagnosis until adequate preparation has been made.

   1. Have blood available for transfusion.

   2. Set up for possible emergency cesarean delivery.

   3. Determine whether fetal age is adequate for survival.

Treatment

A. Hospitalized immediately.

B. Usually placed on bed rest.

C. Blood typed and crossmatched for possible transfusion.

D. Treatment depends upon type of placenta previa, condition of mother, and viability of baby.

   1. Mechanical pressure applied to placental site by bringing down baby's head and occluding blood vessels—usually accomplished by the rupture of membranes; vaginal delivery is possible if bleeding is checked.

   2. Delivery by cesarean method if bleeding is excessive.

E. If baby is small and bleeding stops, delivery is usually postponed.

Nursing Management

A. Maintain patient on bed rest and provide quiet restful atmosphere.

B. Count perineal pads.

C. Observe for hemorrhage.

D. Give emotional support, explain procedures, and help allay fears.

E. *Do not* perform vaginal examinations.

F. Have emergency setup for cesarean delivery available.

G. Carefully monitor fetal heart tones.

Abruptio Placentae

Definition: Abruptio placentae occurs when the placenta separates from the normal implantation site in upper segment of uterus before birth of baby—occurs once in five hundred deliveries.

Types

A. Complete separation—placenta becomes completely detached from uterine wall.

B. Partial separation—portion of placenta adheres to uterine wall.

C. External—blood escapes from the vagina.

D. Concealed—blood is retained in uterine cavity.

Etiology

A. Trauma.

B. Chronic vascular renal disease.

C. High parity.

D. History of reproductive wastage.

Clinical Manifestations

A. External—chief symptom is vaginal bleeding accompanied by abdominal pain.

B. Concealed.
1. Intense, cramplike uterine pain.
2. Uterine tenderness and rigidity.
3. Lack of alternate contraction-relaxation of uterus.
4. Fetal heart tones—bradycardia or absent.

Treatment

A. Depends upon severity and extent of labor.

B. Moderate bleeding—rupture membranes to hasten delivery and help control bleeding.

C. Severe—immediate cesarean delivery.

D. Treatment for blood loss and shock.

E. Blood drawn for coagulation studies.

F. Narcotics may be given for severe pain.

G. Oxygen may be given.

Nursing Management

A. Keep patient on bed rest.

B. Observe for signs of shock.

C. Carefully monitor contractions, fetal heart tones, and vital signs.

D. If bleeding is severe, begin administration of intravenous solution—5 percent dextrose in Ringer's lactate.

E. Type and crossmatch blood for possible transfusion.

F. Maintain record of intake and output.

G. Nursing interventions after delivery.
1. Observe for hemorrhage.
2. Record intake and output and observe for anuria or oliguria. (Anuria may develop as a result of acute tubular necrosis.)

H. Provide emotional support—fetal prognosis poor.

Disseminated Intravascular Coagulation

A. Possible complication of abruptio placenta, missed abortion, fetal death, amniotic fluid embolism.

B. Results in uncontrolled bleeding.
1. Thromboplastin from placental tissue and clots enters the bloodstream through open vessels at the placental site and initiates an exaggeration of the normal clotting process.
2. As more thromboplastin is introduced into circulation, more fibrinogen and clotting factors are used up.
3. In addition, the fibrinolytic process that disintegrates fibrin is initiated, resulting in fibrin degradation products which in turn further interfere with the clotting process.

C. Treatment.
1. Treatment of hypovolemic shock.

2. Heparin solution prevents clot formation and increases available fibrinogen, coagulation factors, and platelets.
3. Fresh-frozen plasma and/or platelets may be ordered.
4. Source of triggering mechanism removed.
5. Circulatory and renal functions monitored.

Hyperemesis Gravidarum

Definition: Hyperemesis gravidarum is pernicious vomiting during pregnancy. Usually develops during first three months of pregnancy.

Etiology

A. May be caused by the addition of new substances to the body system—a toxicity or maladjustment of the maternal metabolism.
B. Psychological disturbances may be the underlying cause, or a combination of psychological and toxic factors.

Clinical Manifestations

A. Persistent nausea and vomiting.
B. May have abdominal pain and hiccups.
C. Considerable weight loss.
D. May become severely dehydrated.
E. Possible depletion of essential electrolytes because of unreplaced loss of sodium chloride and potassium.
F. May develop metabolic acidosis.
G. Blood urea nitrogen increases.
H. May develop hypoproteinemia and hypovitaminosis.

Treatment

A. Aimed at reducing the severity of symptoms.
B. Frequent small feedings—small amounts every two hours, dry foods preferred.
C. Spicy, fried foods avoided.
D. Antiemetics may be prescribed along with a tranquilizer or a sedative.
E. If vomiting is persistent:
  1. Patient is usually hospitalized.
  2. Dehydration and starvation is treated by administration of parenteral fluids.
  3. Rest and sedatives are prescribed.
F. Psychotherapy, if necessary.

Nursing Management

A. Use tact and understanding of the patient's problem.
B. Carefully record intake and output; maintain I.V.'s.
C. Observe for acetone odor to breath.
D. Provide attractive small meals and remove dishes as soon as the patient finishes eating.
E. Provide rest, reduce stimuli, and restrict visitors.

Toxemias of Pregnancy

Definition: Toxemia is not a specific term, but it relates to a group of conditions with similar symptoms. Incidence is 7 to 10 percent of all pregnancies. Toxemia most frequently occurs in young or elderly primigravidas, women with deficient diets, multiple pregnancies, polyhydramnios, and long-standing diabetes.

Preeclampsia

Definition: Preeclampsia is an acute, hypertensive disease peculiar to pregnancy that may be mild or severe.

Clinical Manifestations

A. Usually appears after the twenty-fourth week.
B. Major symptoms are hypertension, proteinuria, and edema, and they may appear separately or together. Two of these three symptoms are usually needed for diagnosis.
C. Mild.
  1. Blood pressure elevation 15 mm. Hg (systolic or diastolic) above normal.
  2. Generalized edema.
  3. Proteinuria—0.3 g./liter-random specimen.
  4. Weight gain—more than 3 pounds per week in second trimester and 1 pound per week in third trimester.
D. Severe.
  1. Blood pressure 160/110 or above, or systolic 50 mm. Hg above normal.
  2. Massive edema—excessive weight gain.
  3. Proteinuria—5 g. or more in twenty-four hours.
  4. Oliguria—400 cc. or less in twenty-four hours.
  5. Visual disturbances.
  6. Headache.

7. Vasospasms.
8. Hemoconcentration.
9. Epigastric pain (usually a late sign).
10. Irritability.

Treatment

A. Mild.
1. Treatment aimed at preventing further increase in disease.
2. Patient usually remains at home.
3. Extra rest is prescribed.
4. Adequate fluid intake.
5. Diet—increased protein and carbohydrate, reduced fat, moderate salt.
6. Daily weight.
7. Physician may order antihypertensive drugs.
B. Severe.
1. Antihypertensives, sedatives.
2. Diet—increased protein, moderate salt.
3. Bed rest.
4. Efforts to increase diuresis—diuretics may or may not be given.
5. Observe for signs of central nervous system irritability and hyperactivity.

Nursing Management

A. Maintain patient on bed rest and plan care to promote rest.
B. Provide adequate diet.
C. Monitor fetal heart tones and observe for signs of labor.
D. Carefully monitor vital signs and lab values.
E. Record intake and output; examine urine for protein.
F. Immediately report increases in signs and symptoms.
G. Check daily weight at the same time each day.
H. Examine retina daily for arteriole changes or edema.
I. Limit visitors in severe cases.
J. Maintain seizure precautions.
K. Provide diversionary activities.

Eclampsia

Definition: Eclampsia is a more severe form of toxemia, usually accompanied by convulsions and even coma.

Clinical Manifestations

A. Severe edema—tremendous weight gain.
B. Scanty urine.
C. Urine may contain red blood cells, varied casts, and protein.
D. Blood pressure may rise to 200/110.
E. There may be visual disturbances, blurring, or even blindness caused by edema of the retina.
F. Severe epigastric pain.
G. Convulsions—both tonic and clonic.
H. Labor may begin and fetus may be born prematurely or die.

Treatment

A. Control convulsions.
B. Promote vasodilation to combat vasospasms.
C. Promote diuresis.
D. Control blood pressure.
E. Physician may terminate pregnancy at a carefully chosen time.

Nursing Management

A. Provide a quiet, darkened room with a constant attendant.
B. Check patient frequently for edema.
C. Prepare a mouth gag and have it available.
D. Suction if necessary.
E. Provide oxygen as necessary.
F. Keep record of vital signs and lab values.
G. Check BP frequently.
H. Keep patient NPO.
I. Maintain I.V. and give medications.
J. Monitor fetal heart tones.
K. Observe carefully after delivery for anuria, convulsions, headache, and blurred vision.
L. See Appendix 1 for drugs normally used during toxemia.

Hypertensive Vascular Disease

Definition: Hypertensive vascular disease is not true toxemia. Characteristic hypertension is already present and is aggravated by pregnancy, or it may first manifest itself with pregnancy.

Clinical Manifestations

A. Hypertension evident before the twenty-fourth week—BP 140/80 at rest.

B. May manifest itself only by persistent elevated blood pressure and slight retinal changes.

C. Headache may be present; patient may otherwise feel well.

D. Edema—proteinuria is usually *not* present.

Treatment

A. Observe for elevated blood pressure, weight gain, or proteinuria.

B. Mild.
1. Rest and limitation of activity.
2. Curtailment of excessive weight gain.
3. Prevention of edema.

C. Severe.
1. Hospitalization.
2. Bed rest.
3. Increase protein diet.
4. Adequate fluids.
5. Close observation of general condition.
6. Daily weight.
7. Accurate record of intake and output.
8. Check urine for protein.
9. Frequent check of vital signs.
10. Antihypertensives.
11. Serial check of estriol levels to determine well-being of fetus.

Nursing Management

A. Maintain bed rest and create an environment conducive to rest.

B. Provide supportive atmosphere.

C. Accurately record vital signs, check urine for protein, and check weight daily.

D. Monitor fetal heart tones.

E. Keep careful record of I and O.

F. Provide adequate diet and fluids.

G. Report any unusual symptoms.

H. Observe for signs of heart failure or cardiac disease.

Polyhydramnios

Definition: Polyhydramnios is an excessive amount of amniotic fluid. Usual normal amount is 500 to 1000 ml.

In polyhydramnios there is over 2000 ml., which is excessive.

Etiology

A. Actual cause is unknown. Occurs frequently in:
1. Fetal malformations.
2. Diabetes.
3. Erythroblastosis.
4. Multiple pregnancies.
5. Toxemias.

B. Diagnosis—usually made through clinical observation of the greatly enlarged uterus.

Clinical Manifestations

A. Related to pressure of the enlarged uterus or adjacent organs.

B. Edema of the lower extremities.

C. General abdominal discomfort.

D. Occasional shortness of breath.

Treatment

A. Delivery.

B. Amniocentesis offers only temporary relief.

Fetal Demise

Clinical Manifestations

A. Cessation of fetal movement.

B. Absence of fetal heart tones.

C. Failure of uterine growth.

D. Low urinary estriol.

E. Negative pregnancy test—may remain positive for a few weeks due to elevated human chorionic gonadotrophin.

Treatment

A. Labor usually begins spontaneously a few weeks after death of fetus.

B. Labor may be induced if it doesn't occur spontaneously.

C. Patient must be watched closely for signs of disseminated intravascular disease from prolonged retention of the dead fetus.

Nursing Management

A. Provide emotional support to parents—may feel unfulfilled, incomplete.
B. Guide parents in planning future pregnancies.
C. Observe for hemorrhage.
D. Observe for psychological disturbances.
E. Parents may go through mourning process—encourage them to express feelings; may be angry at staff.

Associated Medical Disorders— High Risk

Cardiovascular Disease

Classification

A. Class I—no alteration of activity.
B. Class II—slight limitation of activity.
C. Class III—marked limitation of activity.
D. Class IV—symptoms present at rest.

Considerations

A. Pregnancy expands plasma volume, increasing cardiac output and load on heart.
B. Most deaths are caused by cardiac failure, when blood volume is at a maximum in the last weeks of the second trimester.
C. Heart failure occurs infrequently in labor.
D. Over age thirty-five, there is an increase in the incidence of heart failure and death.

Management During Pregnancy

A. With proper management, mortality is minimal.
B. Patient should avoid acute infections, especially respiratory infections.
C. Patient should rest frequently.
D. Strenuous activities such as stair climbing, heavy cleaning, and straining should be avoided.
E. Patients in Class III and over may be hospitalized before labor for controlled rest and diet.
F. If patient decompensates or has distress symptoms with exertion, she should remain on bed rest or in a chair.
G. Salt intake may or may not be restricted. Diuretics may be prescribed if signs of heart failure occur. The use of highly salted foods is discouraged.
H. Iron supplement is important.
I. Digitalis treatment when indicated.
J. Emotional stress should be avoided.

Management During Labor

A. Observe for signs that cardiac function is deteriorating such as pulse rate over 110 or respiratory rate over 24.
B. Relieve pain and anxiety.
C. Vaginal delivery usually preferred.
D. Patient may decompensate in early postpartum phase.

Nursing Management

A. Educate about classifications and effects of pregnancy before conception.
B. Educate about special needs and danger signals during pregnancy and postpartum.
C. Be alert for signs of decompensation during pregnancy, especially in the second trimester.
D. During labor:
    1. Check vital signs every fifteen minutes or more often as needed.
    2. Keep patient in bed and preferably lying on one side or in semirecumbent position.
    3. Administer oxygen as necessary.
    4. Provide calm atmosphere and emotional support to alleviate fears.
    5. Administer pain medications as ordered to reduce discomfort during labor.
    6. Be alert for signs of impending heart failure.
    7. Monitor fetal heart tones.
E. Careful observation during postpartum period.
F. Counsel during postpartum to have help at home and planned rest periods.

Diabetes

Definition: Diabetes is a chronic metabolic disease due to a disturbance in normal insulin production.

White's Classifications

A. Class A—abnormal glucose tolerance test, indicative of latent or gestational diabetes.

B. Class B—diabetes beginning after age twenty.

C. Class C—diabetes at ages ten to nineteen years, or beginning in adolescence after age ten.

D. Class D—diabetes of long duration, or onset in childhood before the age of ten.

E. Class E—evidence of pelvic vascular disease.

F. Class F—nephropathy, including capillary glomerulosclerosis.

Implications of Diabetes in Pregnancy

A. Diabetes is more difficult to control.

B. There is a tendency to develop acidosis.

C. Patient is prone to infection.

D. Toxemia, hemorrhage, and polyhydramnios are more likely to develop.

E. Latent diabetes may develop into full-blown diabetes.

F. Insulin requirements are increased.

G. Premature delivery is more frequent.

H. Infant may be overgrown but have functions related to gestational age rather than size.

I. Infant is subject to hypoglycemia, hyperbilirubinemia, respiratory distress syndrome, and congenital anomalies.

J. Stillborn and neonatal mortality rates are high, but may be reduced by proper management and control of diabetes.

Medical Management

A. Keep blood sugar near normal through diet and use insulin to avoid complications such as acidosis.

B. Observe for signs of hyperglycemia or hypoglycemia.

C. Instruct patient in nutrition and regulation of diabetes.

D. Be alert for signs of infection, toxemia.

E. Check urine frequently for sugar and acetone.

F. Patient may be hospitalized at thirty-six to thirty-seven weeks gestation for evaluation and possible early termination of pregnancy.
   1. Placental function may be evaluated—placental insufficiency (pathological process in placenta resulting in inefficient exchange of waste and gases between mother and fetus) is common in diabetics due to vascular changes.
   2. Assessment of fetal growth and maturity should early delivery be indicated.

3. Strict control of diabetes.

G. Oral diabetic agents are contraindicated as they may cause congenital malformation.

Nursing Management

A. Teaching the effects of diabetes on the mother and fetus during pregnancy and the reasons for frequent testing of blood sugar and urine for sugar and acetone.

B. Teaching good nutrition and health practices.

C. If hospitalized:
   1. Maintain insulin on regular schedule.
   2. Test urine for sugar and acetone as ordered.
   3. Provide adequate diabetic diet as prescribed by physician.
   4. Provide for diversion.
   5. Monitor fetal heart tone.
   6. Check vital signs, especially blood pressure q.i.d. and p.r.n.
   7. Weigh daily at the same time.
   8. Keep accurate records of intake and output.
   9. Provide support and explanations to help allay fears and reduce anxiety.
   10. Watch for symptoms of hyperglycemia or hypoglycemia.

D. In labor:
   1. Same as above.
   2. Carefully regulate insulin and provide I.V. glucose as labor depletes glycogen.

E. Postpartum.
   1. Close observation for insulin reaction—precipitous drop in insulin requirements usual—hypoglycemic shock may occur.
   2. Close observation for early signs of infection.
   3. Close observation for postpartum hemorrhage.

Anemia

A. Usually caused by iron deficiency.

B. Symptoms.
   1. Patient tires easily and looks pale.
   2. Hemoglobin values are usually checked routinely in antipartum care.
   3. Usually treated by diet and an iron supplement.

Urinary Tract Infection

A. Usually occurs after the fourth month or in early

postpartum—affects 10 percent of maternity patients.

B. Causes.
1. Pressure on ureters and bladder.
2. Hormonal effects on tone of ureters and bladder.
3. Displacement of bladder.
C. Kidneys as well as ureters may be involved.
D. Symptoms.
1. Frequent micturition.
2. Paroxysms—pain in kidney.
3. Fever and chills.
4. Catheterized urine specimen contains bacteria and pus.
E. Treatment.
1. Bed rest.
2. High fluid intake.
3. Antibiotic treatments.
4. Urinary antispasmodics and analgesics.

Infectious Diseases

Rubella

A. In first trimester rubella may cause congenital anomalies.
B. Vaccine is available and should be given to children from age one to puberty or to the mother in early postpartum, while she is still hospitalized. (Vaccine should not be given if pregnancy is suspected.)
C. Titer is usually checked on first prenatal visit.

Acute Infectious Diseases

A. Diseases such as influenza, scarlet fever, toxoplasmosis, and cytomegalovirus may be transmitted to the fetus.
B. Diseases may cause abortions or malformations in early pregnancy or premature labor or infant death in later pregnancy.

Venereal Disease

A. Syphilis.
1. May cause abortion or premature labor.
2. Infection is passed to the fetus after the fourth month of pregnancy as congenital syphilis.
3. Serum test for syphilis on first prenatal visit. (May repeat at a later date as disease may be acquired after initial visit.)
4. Treatment—during pregnancy, procaine penicillin G with 2 percent aluminum monostearate, I.M. normally in divided doses.
5. All cases of syphilis must be reported to health authorities for treatment of contacts.
B. Gonorrhea.
1. Common contagious bacterial disease.
2. Incidence has been steadily rising as a result of increase in premarital sex.
3. May be mildly symptomatic in women and may persist unsuspected.
4. May cause salpingitis after third month if left untreated.
5. Slide for gonorrhea usually done on first prenatal visit.
6. Important to treat sexual partner, as patient may become reinfected.
7. Infection may be transmitted to baby's eyes during delivery, causing blindness.
8. Soon after birth all newborns have prophylactic treatment of one percent silver nitrate or an antibiotic preparation.
9. Treatment—same as for syphilis. Other antibiotics may be used for sensitivity to penicillin.
C. Herpes simplex type 2—genital herpes.
1. Involves external genitalia, vagina, cervix.
2. Development and draining of painful vesicles.
3. Treatment—symptomatic—no specific cure identified.
4. Virus is lethal to fetus if innoculated during vaginal delivery. Usual mode of delivery is C-section.

Assessment of Fetal Maturity and Placental Function

Studies for Delivery Capability

A. Estriol excretion—estrogen metabolism in pregnancy is dependent upon a healthy mother, a healthy fetus, and an intact placenta.
1. Estriol level increases as the fetus grows and decreases when growth ceases.
2. Measured by 24-hour urine specimen or serum estriol levels.
3. Provides guide to:
    a. Placental functioning.

b. Fetal well-being.

4. Excretion of 12 mg. in 24 hours indicates good function; below 12 mg. may indicate fetal jeopardy.

5. Serial assays are usually done, starting at about 32 weeks, to assess the fetal condition.

B. Amniotic fluid studies.

1. Amniocentesis is the introduction of a needle through the abdominal and uterine walls and into the amniotic cavity to withdraw fluid for examination.

a. Preparation of patient.
(1) Have patient empty bladder.
(2) Auscultate fetal heart rate.
(3) Make patient comfortable.
(4) Explain procedure and give assurance that all precautions will be taken to minimize risk.
(5) Prepare abdomen with antiseptic solution.
(6) Have necessary equipment available.

b. Amniocentesis indicates:
(1) Sex of baby.
(2) Certain congenital defects such as mongolism.
(3) State of fetus affected by Rh isoimmunization.
(4) Fetal maturity.

2. Lecithin/sphingomyelin ratio (L/S Ratio).

a. Test for fetal maturity by examining for presence of surfactant.
b. Lecithin major constituent of surfactant.
c. At thirteenth week, the concentration of sphingomyelin is higher than lecithin.
d. Thereafter, lecithin increases slowly until the thirty-fifth week when it is two or more times greater than sphingomyelin. At this time, fetal lungs are said to be mature, and the infant is unlikely to develop respiratory distress syndrome.

3. Creatinine level.

a. Progressive rise as fetus approaches term.
b. Excreted in fetal urine, measures increasing muscle mass.
c. Values of 2 mg./100 ml. amniotic fluid correlates with gestation of about thirty-six weeks.

4. Bilirubin level.

a. Amount of bilirubin in amniotic fluid decreases near term of normal fetus. Usually disappears during the last month of gestation.
b. Exposure of blood sample to light for a period greater than a few seconds invalidates the test.

5. Cytological studies—sebaceous glands of fetus begin to function and shed near term. Percentage of lipid globules present gives indication of fetal age.

C. Sonography.

1. Measures biparietal diameter of the fetal skull after sixteen weeks.

2. Should be measured weekly when growth retardation is suspected.

D. X-ray measure.

1. Total fetal length.
2. Appearance of ossification in epiphyseal centers.
3. Size of fetal skull.

E. Amnioscopy.

1. Transcervical visualization of amniotic fluid through intact membranes.
2. Greenish amniotic fluid indicates fetal distress.
3. Cervix must be dilated to more than 1 cm.

Oxytocin Challenge Test or Stress Test

A. Test designed to measure placental insufficiency and fetus' reaction to uterine contractions.

B. If placental flow is normal, fetus remains oxygenated during uterine contractions.

C. Placental insufficiency produces characteristic late deceleration pattern during contraction. Fetal bradycardia is less than 120 beats/min. or persistent drop of 20 beats below baseline.

D. Procedure.

1. Patient usually not admitted.
2. Place patient in semi-Fowler's or lateral recumbent position to prevent supine hypotensive syndrome.
3. Liquid nourishment may or may not be ordered.
4. Explain procedure to patient.
5. Apply external fetal monitor.
6. Observe for uterine activity and F.H.T.—usually for 10 to 20 minutes to obtain baseline.

7. I.V. solution with oxytocic drug is started—infusion pump usually used to administer more accurate dosage.
8. Dosage is increased q. 15 to 20 minutes until patient has three good contractions in a 10-minute period (oxytocin is discontinued once pattern is established).
9. Observe patient for signs of sensitivity to drug.
10. Record vital signs and oxytocic infusion q. 15 minutes on strip.
11. Monitor contractions and F.H.T. until patient returns to pre-oxytocic state.
12. Discontinue I.V. and prepare patient for discharge.
13. Record all information on chart—monitor strip is considered legal document and becomes part of chart.
14. Observe for complications.
    a. F.H.T. below 120.
    b. Sustained uterine contractions.
    c. Supine hypotensive syndrome—check maternal blood pressure.

E. Test results.
   1. Positive test—persistent late decelerations occurring with at least three contractions.
   2. Negative test—three consecutive contractions in a 10-minute period without decelerations—test may be repeated each week until delivery.
   3. Suspicious—occasional or several nonpersistent decelerations.

Labor and Delivery

Definition: Labor is the process by which the products of conception are expelled from the body. Delivery refers to the actual birth.

Adaptive Processes

Definition: During latter months of pregnancy, the fetus adapts to the maternal uterus enabling it to occupy the smallest space possible. The term *attitude* refers to the posture the fetus assumes in utero; *fetal lie* is the relationship of the long axis of the baby to the long axis of the mother.

Presentation

Definition: The part of the fetus which lies closest to the true pelvis.

A. Cephalic—head is presenting part.
   1. May be vertex, face, or brow.
   2. Vertex most common and most favorable for delivery. Head is sharply flexed in the pelvis with chin near chest.
B. Breech—buttocks or lower extremities are the presenting part.
   1. Types.
      a. Complete or full—buttocks and feet present (baby in squatting position).
      b. Frank—buttocks only present, or legs are extended against anterior trunk with feet touching face.
      c. Incomplete—one or both feet or knees presenting, footling single or double, or knee presentation.
   2. May rotate to cephalic during pregnancy but possibility lessens as gestation nears term.
   3. May be rotated by physician but usually returns to breech position.
C. Transverse lie—long axis of infant lies at right angles to longitudinal axis of mother (necessitates delivery by C-section).

Position

Definition: Relationship of the fetal presenting part to the maternal bony pelvis.

A. Position is determined by locating the presenting part in relationship to the pelvis.
B. Mother's pelvis is divided into four imaginary quadrants: right anterior, right posterior, left anterior, and left posterior.
C. Most common positions (abbreviations usually used).
   1. L.O.A.—left occiput anterior—occiput on left side of maternal pelvis and toward front, face down, favorable for delivery.
   2. L.O.P.—left occiput posterior—occiput on left side of maternal pelvis and toward rear or face up.
      a. Usually causes back pain during labor.
      b. May slow the progress of labor.
      c. Usually rotates before delivery to anterior position.

d.   May be rotated in delivery room by physician.

3.   R.O.A.—right occiput anterior—occiput on right of maternal pelvis, toward front, face down, favorable for delivery.

4.   R.O.P.—right occiput posterior—occiput on right side of maternal pelvis, face up. Same problems as L.O.P.

D.   Means of assessing fetal position during labor.

1.   Leopold's maneuver—method of palpating the maternal abdomen to determine information about the fetus such as presentation, engagement, and rough estimate of fetal size.

2.   Vaginal examination.

3.   Rectal examination.

Engagement

A.   Largest diameter of presenting part has passed into the inlet of the maternal pelvis. Usually takes place two weeks before labor in primiparas, but not until labor in multiparas.

B.   May be assessed by Leopold's maneuver or vaginal or rectal examination.

Station

A.   Degree to which presenting part has descended into pelvis is determined by the station—the relationship between the presenting part and the ischial spines.

B.   Assessed by vaginal or rectal examination.

C.   Measured in numerical terms.

1.   At level of spines, 0 station.

2.   Above level of spines, -1, -2, -3.

3.   Below level of spines, +1, +2, +3.

D.   Other terms used to denote station.

1.   High—presenting part not engaged.

2.   Floating—presenting part freely movable in inlet of pelvis, may be movable in inlets of pelvis.

3.   Dipping—entering pelvis.

4.   Fixed—no longer movable in inlet but not engaged.

5.   Engaged—biparietal plane passed through pelvic inlet.

Fetal Skull

A.   Largest anatomical part of the fetus to pass through the birth canal; usually if the head can pass, the rest of the body can be delivered.

B.   Made up of seven bones: 2 frontal, 2 parietal, 2 temporal, and 1 occipital.

C.   Sutures—membranous interspaces between bones.

1.   Sagittal—between 2 parietal.

2.   Frontal—between 2 front bones.

3.   Coronal—between frontal and parietal.

4.   Lambdoidals—between posterior margin of parietal and occipital.

D.   Fontanels—points where sutures intersect.

1.   Anterior—diamond shaped. Found at the junction of the sagittal and coronal sutures. Becomes ossified sometime after the first year.

2.   Posterior—smaller diamond shaped. Found at the junction of the sagittal and lambdoid sutures. Becomes ossified by the end of the second month after birth.

3.   Other smaller fontanels are also present.

4.   Fontanels allow for fetal skull bones to override as they adapt to the pelvis.

5.   Important points in vaginal or rectal examination to determine position of fetus—posterior or anterior.

Premonitory Signs of Labor

Physical Signs of Impending Labor

A.   Premonitory signs—physiologic changes that take place the last several weeks of pregnancy, indicating that labor is near.

B.   Lightening—descent of the uterus downward and forward, which takes place as the presenting part descends into the pelvis.

1.   Time in which it takes place varies from a few weeks to a few days before labor. In multigravida, it may occur during labor.

2.   Sensations.

a.   Relief of pressure on diaphragm and breathing is easier.

b.   Increased pelvic pressure leading to leg cramps, frequent micturition, and pressure on rectum.

C.   Braxton-Hicks contractions.

1.   May become quite regular but do not effectively dilate cervix.

2.   Usually are more pronounced at night.

3.   May play a part in ripening the cervix.

D. Decrease in weight—there is usually a decrease in water retention due to hormonal influences.

E. Cervical changes—cervix usually becomes softer, shorter, and somewhat dilated. May be dilated 1 to 2 cm. by the time labor begins.

F. Bloody show.

1. Tenacious mucus vaginal discharge, usually pinkish or streaked with blood, is expelled from the cervix as it shortens and begins to dilate.

2. Labor usually begins within twenty-four to forty-eight hours.

G. Rupture of membranes.

1. May break any time before labor or during labor. Occasionally, they remain intact and are ruptured by the physician during labor (amniotomy).

2. May gush or trickle.

3. Patient usually advised to come to the hospital as labor may begin within twenty-four hours.

4. If labor does not begin spontaneously, it is induced to avoid intrauterine infections.

Premature Rupture of the Membranes

A. Nursing management in premature rupture.

1. Test vaginal secretions for alkalinity with Nitrozine paper—normal vaginal pH is acidic.

2. Keep patient on bed rest.

3. Observe for signs of infection.

4. Observe for signs of labor.

5. Observe for prolapse of cord.

6. Monitor fetal heart rate rhythm.

7. Alleviate patient's fears of "dry birth."

8. Observe amniotic fluid for foul odor or signs of fetal distress (meconium staining).

B. Record time, amount, color, and odor of ruptured membranes.

False Labor

A. Signs.

1. Irregular contractions.

2. Contractions may cause discomfort.

3. Usually discomfort is located in abdomen.

4. Labor usually does not intensify.

5. Discomfort may be relieved by walking.

6. Contractions do not bring about appreciable changes in cervix.

B. Sometimes difficult to differentiate false labor from true labor, and patient is observed for several hours in the hospital.

Process of Labor and Delivery

Cause of Labor

A. Alterations in hormonal balance of estrogen and progesterone increases uterine contractibility.

B. Degeneration of the placenta—it no longer provides necessary elements to fetus.

C. Overdistention of uterus creates stimulus triggering release of oxytocin, which initiates contractions.

D. High levels of prostaglandins near term may stimulate uterine contractions.

E. Hormones secreted by fetus.

F. It may be a combination of several of these physiological occurrences that produces the type of contraction necessary for true labor. The actual cause is unknown.

Forces of Labor

A. Muscular contractions primarily of muscles of uterus and secondarily of abdominal muscles.

B. Uterine muscles contract during first stages and bring about effacement and dilatation of the cervix.

C. Abdominal muscles come into play after complete cervical dilatation and help expel the baby—voluntary bearing down effort, urge to push.

D. Contraction of levator ani muscles.

Duration of Labor

A. Varies depending upon individual.

B. Average.

1. Primipara—up to eighteen hours; some may be shorter, others longer.

2. Multipara—up to eight hours; some may be shorter, others longer.

C. Length of labor depends on:

1. Effectiveness of consistent contractions—contractions must overcome resistance of cervix.

2. Amount of resistance baby must overcome to adapt to the pelvis.

3. Stretching ability of soft tissue.

4. Preparation and relaxation of mother. Fear and anxiety can retard progress.

D. Important to judge rate of progress.

Uterine Contractions

A. Characteristics.
   1. Involuntary—cannot be controlled by will of mother.
   2. Intermittent—periods of relaxation between contractions. Intervals allow mother to rest and also allow adequate circulation of uterine blood vessels and oxygenation of fetus.
   3. Regular—once true labor is established.
   4. Discomfort usually starts low in back and radiates around to abdomen.
   5. As labor progresses, increase in discomfort, intensity, frequency, and duration.

B. Contractions are usually divided into three periods.
   1. Increment—increasing intensity.
   2. Acme—peak, or full intensity.
   3. Decrement—decreasing intensity.

C. Contractions are monitored by.
   1. Placing the finger lightly on the fundus of the uterus (the most contractile portion) and relating what you feel in your fingers to seconds and minutes on a clock. Uterus becomes firm, then it hardens, and then it decreases in hardness.
   2. Electronic monitoring device—external (less accurate) or internal (catheter inserted into uterine cavity which measures internal pressures and relays information to a graph).

D. Contractions are monitored for frequency, duration, and intensity.
   1. Frequency—measured by timing contractions from the beginning of one contraction to the beginning of next.
   2. Duration—beginning of contraction to beginning of period of decreasing intensity. Cannot be measured exactly by feeling with the hand.
   3. Intensity—cannot be measured by feeling; must be measured by internal fetal monitoring device. Usually refers to contraction at the beginning of labor. Peaks at about 25 mm. Hg. At the end of labor, it may reach 50 to 75 mm. Hg.
   4. Contractions may be described as mild, moderate, or intense.

E. Purpose of contractions.
   1. To propel presenting part forward.

2. To bring about effacement and dilatation of the cervix.

Effacement and Dilatation

A. Effacement—process by which cervical canal is progressively shortened to a stage of complete obliteration. Progresses from a structure of 1 to 2 cm. long to almost complete obliteration.

B. Dilatation—process by which external os enlarges from a few millimeters to approximately 10 cm.

C. All that remains of the cervix after effacement and dilatation is a paper thin circular opening about 10 cm. in diameter.

D. Effacement and dilatation may be measured by vaginal or rectal examination.

Changes in the Uterus

A. Uterus usually becomes differentiated in two distinct portions as labor progresses.
   1. Upper portion—contractile, becomes thicker.
   2. Lower portion—passive, becomes thinner and more expanded.

B. Boundary between the two segments is termed the *physiologic retraction ring*.

Signs of Imminent Delivery

A. Increase in bloody show.

B. Nausea, vomiting, and shaking.

C. Pressure on rectum and patient feels the urge to push—involuntary bearing down.

D. Deep grunting sound from mother.

E. Mother states she is ready to deliver.

F. Bulging of the perineum.

Stages and Phases of Labor

Definition: Labor is divided into four stages: Stage 1—beginning of true labor to complete cervical dilatation; stage 2—complete dilatation to birth of baby; stage 3—birth to delivery of placenta; and stage 4—first hour after delivery of placenta.

Stage 1

A. Latent phase or period of effacement.
   1. Phase begins with onset of regular contraction pattern.

2. Dilatation 0 to 1 to 4.
3. Contractions are mild and become well established.
4. Contractions are 5 to 15 minutes apart, last about 30 to 45 seconds.
5. Cervix thins.
6. Usually some bloody show.
7. Station is anywhere from −2 to +1 in multipara and 0 in primigravida.
8. Mother may be quite comfortable and talkative, alert and cheerful.
9. Mother has lots of energy and feels she can cope with labor.
10. Membranes usually intact.

B. Active phase or dilatation phase.
   1. Dilatation 4 to 7.
   2. Dilatation is more rapid.
   3. Contractions are 3 to 5 minutes apart, last 30 to 45 seconds.
   4. Increase in bloody show.
   5. Station varies −1 to 0.
   6. Mother becomes tired, less talkative, and shows lack of energy.
   7. Mother may need coaching on breathing techniques or analgesia or anesthesia.

C. Transitional stage.
   1. Dilatation 7 to 10.
   2. Contractions are intense and close—every 2 to 3 minutes, and last 50 to 90 seconds.
   3. Station +3 or +4.
   4. Increased amount of bloody show.
   5. Desire to bear down or defecate.
   6. Membranes may rupture if they have not done so previously.
   7. Mother's attention and feelings are inner-directed; she feels exhausted and no longer able to cope.
   8. Mother may show sign of restlessness, shaking, nausea, vomiting, trembling, burping, and crying.

Stage 2

A. Stage of expulsion.
B. Expulsion brought about by contractions of uterine and abdominal muscles.
C. Contractions are every 2 to 3 minutes, last 60 to 90 seconds.
D. Vagina and perineum stretch and thin to allow for passage of baby.
E. Perineum begins to bulge.
F. Vaginal opening distends from small, narrow opening to wide, round opening.
G. With each contraction, presenting part becomes more visible.
H. Crowning occurs—widest diameter of baby's head is visible and encircled by vaginal opening.
I. Birth of presenting part.
J. Rest of body delivered usually with a gush of fluid.

Mechanism of Labor and Delivery

A. Sequence of movements of presenting part through birth canal. Head usually enters transverse and must rotate L.O.A. or R.O.A. for birth.
B. Engagement—head enters pelvis.
C. Descent—movement which occurs simultaneously with passage of head through pelvis.
D. Flexion—occurs as head descends and meets with resistance. In extreme flexion, the smallest diameter of the head presents.
E. Internal rotation—head usually enters with long diameter conforming to long diameter of inlet (usually transverse position) and must rotate before it can emerge from outlet—head rotates so that smallest diameter presents to conform to pelvis.
F. Extension—follows internal rotation. The head, which is flexed as it passes through birth canal, must extend for birth.
G. External rotation—soon after birth, the head rotates to either mother's right or left side, the fetal position before birth.
H. Expulsion—with delivery of shoulders, rest of body is expelled spontaneously.

Stage 3

A. Placental stage.
B. Phase of placental separation.
   1. Usually takes place with next few contractions after birth.
   2. Usually begins center but may begin at edges.
   3. Some bleeding usually accompanies separation.
C. Phase of expulsion.
   1. May be expelled spontaneously by mother, but is usually expressed manually by the physician after separation is complete.

2. Mechanisms.
   a. Schultze (most common)—placenta is inverted on itself, and the shiny fetal surface appears; 80 percent separate in center.
   b. Duncan—descends sideways, and the maternal surface appears. Separates at edges rather than center.

Stage 4

First critical hour after birth.

Nursing Management in Labor and Delivery

Stage 1

Latent Phase

A. Admission procedures (specific details may vary from one hospital to another).
   1. Check vital signs—temperature, pulse, respirations, and blood pressure.
   2. Check F.H.T. (fetal heart tones).
   3. Determine state of intact or rhythm membranes.
   4. Give prep (perineal shave) and enema (if ordered by physician).
   5. See that appropriate forms are completed.
   6. Determine mother's psychological state and readiness for labor—some patients may complain of intense pain in very early labor.
   7. Encourage mother to void, and check urine for sugar and acetone.
   8. Apply external fetal monitor if ordered.
   9. Determine frequency, intensity (mild, moderate, severe), and duration of contractions.
   10. Determine amount and character of bloody show.
   11. Determine amount of cervical dilatation and effacement.
   12. Keep bell cord within easy reach.
B. Care of patient after admission; latent phase dilatation—3 cm.
   1. Maintain bed rest if membranes have ruptured. (In some hospitals the patient may be allowed out of bed with ruptured membranes if the baby's head is well engaged and the patient is otherwise all right.)
   2. Note frequency, duration, and strength of contraction q. 30 minutes or p.r.n.
   3. Auscultate F.H.T. q. 15 minutes or p.r.n.
   4. Check blood pressure q. 30 minutes or p.r.n.
   5. Check vital signs once per shift or more often if needed.
   6. Give periodic vaginal examination to determine progress.
   7. Observe for ruptured membranes and take F.H.T. immediately if membranes rupture.
   8. Reinforce breathing techniques or teach breathing techniques if mother has had no classes.
   9. Keep family informed of progress.
   10. Encourage the presence of patient's husband or a significant other person.
   11. Allow patient to walk about, if membranes have not ruptured, or provide reading material for patient.
   12. Provide support based upon mother's knowledge of the labor process.
   13. Reduce stimuli if mother wants to rest.
   14. Start I.V. if ordered. Mother usually NPO.
   15. Check for bladder distention.
   16. Observe amount and character of show.

Active Phase, 4 to 7 cm. Dilatation

A. Continue with care listed above.
B. Encourage use of breathing techniques.
C. Maintain I.V. fluids.
D. Apply pressure to sacrum during contraction or encourage baby's father to do so.
E. Urge mother to stay off back, to avoid supine hypertensive syndrome, and to lie on side.
F. Administer medications as ordered. Tranquilizing drugs may be given in early labor, but analgesics are usually not given until labor is well established—4-6 cm. dilatation.
G. Assist with anesthesia, if given, and monitor blood pressure and F.H.T.
H. Continue support and keep the patient informed.
I. Once membranes have ruptured (2-3 cm. dilatation) internal fetal monitor may be applied.

Transitional Stage, 7 to 10 cm. Dilatation

A. Continue with care listed above.

B. Explain progress to patient and encourage her to continue with breathing and relaxing techniques.

C. Discourage bearing down efforts until dilatation is complete.

D. Encourage deep ventilation prior to and after each contraction to avoid hyperventilation.

E. Monitor contractions lightly with fingers as abdomen is sensitive.

F. Accept irritable behavior and aggression and continue supportive care.

G. Help patient to push when ready.

H. Observe for signs of imminent delivery and transfer patient to delivery room when ready.

Assessment of the Fetus During Labor

Observations of Fetal Heart Rate

A. Fetal heart rate normal—120 to 160 beats/minute determine baseline (fetal monitor).
1. Early deceleration—10 to 20 beat drop in rate usually within normal range of 120 to 160.
   a. Occurs before peak or early contracting phase. Recovery as soon as acme of contraction has passed.
   b. Uniform shape.
   c. Indicate head compression—vagal stimulation results in decreased heart rate.
   d. V-shaped appearance.
   e. Not considered ominous.
2. Late deceleration.
   a. Decrease in F.H.T. 10 to 20 beats/minute.
   b. Occurs after peak or late contracting phase.
   c. Uniform shape.
   d. Usually indicates fetal distress.
   e. Likely to appear in any situation where fetal-maternal exchange in placenta is reduced, resulting in hypoxia.
3. Variable deceleration—no uniformity in pattern.
   a. Decrease in F.H.T. occurring any time during contraction phase.
   b. Usually below 120 beats/minute.
   c. May indicate cord compression.
   d. May occur when mother pushes.
   e. Must be evaluated carefully—may or may not indicate fetal difficulty.

B. Any persistent drop of 20 beats below baseline may indicate distress.

C. Loss of beat-to-beat variation in fetal heart rate—may be serious sign of fetal anoxia.

D. Continuous fetal monitoring most accurate means of appraising fetal well-being.

E. Other methods of auscultating F.H.T.
1. Fetascope.
2. Portable Doppler apparatus.
3. Listen in area of maximum density.
4. Listen before, during, and after contraction.
5. Fetal distress may occur between examinations.

Fetal Distress

A. Signs.
1. F.H.T. above 160 or below 120 beats per minute.
2. Meconium-stained fluid. During hypoxia, bowel peristalsis increases, and meconium is likely to be passed.
3. Fetal hyperactivity.
4. If labor is monitored:
   a. Variable deceleration pattern.
   b. Late deceleration pattern.
   c. Fetal pH below 7.2.

B. Immediate nursing interventions.
1. Turn patient to left side; if no improvement, turn to right side. This procedure relieves pressure on umbilical cord during contractions and pressure of uterus on the inferior vena cava.
2. Administer oxygen via mask at 6 to 7 L./minute.
3. Discontinue oxytoxin if infusing.
4. Correction of hypotension—elevate legs and increase perfusion of I.V. fluids.
5. Prepare for delivery and notify physician.

Stages 2 and 3

Delivery Room

A. Transfer patient carefully from bed to delivery table in lithotomy position.

B. Pad stirrups to avoid pressure to popliteal veins and pressure areas. Gently raise both legs simultaneously into stirrups to avoid ligament strain. Adjust stirrups and drape patient.

C. Provide patient with handles to pull on as she pushes.

D. Cleanse vulva and perineum using sterile technique, commonly referred to as perineal "wash down."

E. Auscultate F.H.T. q. 5 minutes or after each push—transient fetal bradycardia not unusual due to head compression.

F. Check blood pressure and pulse q. 15 minutes p.r.n.

G. Administer oxygen if F.H.T. decrease.

H. Allow baby's father in room, and position him at the head of the delivery table.

I. Catheterize if bladder is distended and prevents descent.

J. Encourage patient and keep her informed of advancement of baby.

K. Encourage patient to take a deep breath before beginning to push with each contraction and to sustain push as long as possible—long pushes are preferable to frequent short pushes.

Stage 4

First Hour After Birth
A. Palpate fundus q. 15 minutes and p.r.n.
B. Massage fundus gently if not firm.
C. Check T.P.R. and blood pressure q. 15 minutes.
D. Encourage voiding and measure amounts.
  1. Check for bladder distention.
  2. Maintain I & O first twenty-four hours or until voiding is sufficient.
E. Check lochia for color, consistency, and amount.
F. Inspect perineum and episiotomy for signs of bleeding, unusual redness, or swelling.
G. Weigh perineal pads if unusual bleeding noted.
H. Apply ice packs to perineum if ordered.
I. Provide warm blanket if mother chilled.
J. Offer fluids in small amounts if mother is alert (excessive amounts of fluids may cause nausea).
K. Change mother's gown—gown worn during labor is usually soiled and wet from perspiration.
L. I.V. is usually completed and discontinued unless complications arise.
M. Allow mother privacy to talk to visitors.
N. Encourage mother to rest.
O. Provide medications for pain as ordered and needed.

Induction of Labor

Definition: Induction of labor is bringing about labor through the use of stimulants such as oxytocin.

Oxytocin Infusion
A. Indications for use.
  1. Patient overdue—two weeks or more—placental functions reduced.
  2. Toxemia.
  3. Diabetes.
  4. Premature rupture of membranes (should deliver within twenty-four hours).
  5. Uncontrolled bleeding.
  6. Rh sensitization—rising titer.
  7. Excessive size of fetus.
B. Prerequisites for successful induction.
  1. Fetal maturity.
  2. Cervix amenable for induction (at times, patient may be induced for several days consecutively with rest at night to ripen cervix, if it is desirable to deliver fetus due to complications).
  3. Normal cephalopelvic proportions.
  4. Fetal head engaged.
C. Danger signals.
  1. Prolonged uterine contractions—over 90 seconds with less than 30 seconds rest period between.
  2. Sustained uterine contractions.
  3. Fetal heart tones above 160 or below 120 or change in rhythm.
  4. Hemorrhage and shock.
  5. Elevated blood pressure.
  6. Abruptio placentae.
D. Continuous assessment necessary throughout induction.

Nursing Management
A. Nursing procedures.
  1. Maintain patient on bed rest.
  2. Provide normal care of patient in labor.
  3. Start I.V. fluids.
  4. Piggyback oxytocin solution into main line, 5 to 10 IU in 1000 cc. solution or less if infusion pump such as Harvard pump is used (may have 2.5 IU in 50 cc. I.V. fluid). (Physician usually starts flow and remains present on floor.)
  5. Monitor I.V. drip q. 15 minutes; infusion pump

may be used for more accurate and controlled drip.

6. Start infusion slowly to test uterine sensitivity to drug; then increase flow gradually per doctor's order q. 15 to 30 until regular pattern of contractions is established—three to four good contractions in a ten-minute period.

7. Uterus is usually palpated and contractions monitored continuously by physician and nurse until regular contractions are established.

8. Auscultate fetal heart tones.

9. Explain procedure to patient.

10. Monitor labor with electronic fetal monitor, if available.

B. Emergency measures—check patient frequently and discontinue infusion if abnormalities in contractions or fetal heart tones are noticed and notify physician immediately.

Operative Obstetrics

Obstetrical Procedures

Episiotomy

Definition: Episiotomy is an incision made into the perineum during delivery to facilitate the birth process.

A. Types of episiotomy.
1. Midline—incision from the posterior margin of the vaginal opening directly back to the anal sphincter.
   a. Healing is less painful.
   b. Incision is easy to repair.
2. Mediolateral—incision made at 45-degree angle to either side of the vaginal opening.
   a. Healing process is quite painful.
   b. Incision is harder to repair.
   c. Blood loss greater.

B. Purposes.
1. Spare the muscles of perineal floor from undue stretching and tearing (lacerations).
2. Prevent the prolonged pressure of the baby's head on perineum.
3. Reduce duration of second stage of labor.
4. Enlarge vagina for manipulation.

C. Method.
1. Generally done during contraction, as the baby's head pushes against perineum and stretches it.
2. Blunt scissors are used.
3. Mother is usually given an anesthetic—regional, local, or inhalation.

Forceps Delivery

Definition: In a forceps delivery the baby is extracted from the birth canal by the physician with the use of a specially designed instrument.

A. Types.
1. Low forceps—presenting part on perineal floor.
2. Midforceps—presenting part below or at the level of the eschial spine.
3. High forceps—presenting part not engaged (rarely if ever used today).

B. Indications.
1. Fetal distress.
2. Poor progress of fetus through the birth canal.
3. Failure of the head to rotate.
4. Maternal disease or exhaustion.
5. Mother unable to push (as with regional anesthesia).

C. Complications.
1. Lacerations of the vagina or the cervix; there may be oozing or hemorrhage.
2. Rupture of the uterus.
3. Intracranial hemorrhage and brain damage to the fetus.
4. Facial paralysis of the fetus.

Cesarean Delivery

Definition: A cesarean delivery is an operation to enable the delivery of an infant through an incision cut into the abdominal wall and the uterus.

A. Types.
1. Classical—vertical incision through the abdominal wall and into the anterior wall of the uterus.
2. Low segment transverse—transverse incision made into lower uterine segment after abdomen has been opened.
   a. Incision made into part of uterus where there is less uterine activity and blood loss is minimal.

  b. Less incidence of adhesions and intestinal obstruction.

 3. Cesarean hysterectomy—abdomen and uterus are opened, baby and placenta are removed, and then the hysterectomy is performed. The hysterectomy is performed if:

  a. Diseased tissue or fibroids are present.

  b. There is an abnormal pap smear.

  c. The uterus ruptures.

  d. There is uncontrolled hemorrhage or placenta abruptio or uterine atony, etc.

B. Indications.

 1. Fetal distress unrelieved by other measures.

 2. Uterine dysfunction.

 3. Certain cases of placenta previa and premature separation of placenta.

 4. Prolapsed cord.

 5. Diabetes or certain cases of toxemia.

 6. Cephalopelvic disproportion.

 7. Malpresentations such as transverse lie.

Nursing Management

Postoperative Care

A. Take vital signs (blood pressure, pulse and respiration) every fifteen minutes for two to three hours.

B. Observe site of incision for bleeding every fifteen minutes for two to three hours.

C. Palpate fundus for location and tone every fifteen minutes for two to three hours.

D. Check lochia for amount and color every fifteen minutes for two to three hours.

E. Reinforce abdominal dressing as necessary.

F. Observe drainage from Foley catheter—amount, color, pressure of blood, etc.

G. Check level of consciousness.

H. Measure intake and output.

I. Assist patient to deep breathe, cough, and turn.

J. Change perineal pads as needed.

K. Reassure the patient that the delivery is over and give her information regarding the condition of the baby. (If something is wrong with the baby, the physician usually discusses this first with parents.)

L. Show mother the baby and let her hold it if she is able.

Later Care

A. Help ambulate patient (usually the first postpartum day).

B. Give stool softener as ordered and needed.

C. Encourage patient to talk about delivery and baby.

D. Reinforce physician's teaching about care at home.

 1. Planned rest periods.

 2. Avoid heavy lifting for four to six weeks.

 3. Signs of infection.

 4. Care of the breast.

 5. Avoidance of constipation.

 6. Nutritious diet.

E. Provide regular postpartum care.

Complications of Labor and Delivery

Dystocia

Definition: Dystocia occurs with prolonged and difficult labor and delivery. Labor is considered prolonged when it extends for twenty-four hours or more after the onset of regular contractions.

Classification

A. Dystocia may be classified in several ways, and although the divisions are artificial, they are useful in looking at the processes involved.

 1. Dysfunction of powers or forces with respect to the uterus and abdominal muscles.

 2. Abnormalities of the passengers—fetus and placenta.

 3. Abnormalities of the passages—bony and soft tissue.

 4. May be a combination of two or more **dys**functions and abnormalities.

B. Characteristics.

 1. True labor begins but fails to progress.

 2. Dystocia may occur during latent or active phase of labor.

 3. It is important to look at the rate of progress as well as the overall length of labor; that is, is the patient slowly progressing or is she arrested at one point?

Table 3. Complications and Signs of Distress in the Mother

Complication	Signs of Distress	Possible Nursing Interventions
Infection	Elevated temperature and pulse	1. Maintain sterile technique while doing vaginals 2. Keep vaginals to a minimum 3. Administer antibiotics as ordered
Exhaustion	Loss of emotional stability Lack of cooperation	1. Provide supportive therapy and comfort measures to promote relaxation and relieve tension 2. Encourage rest 3. Administer sedation as ordered
Dehydration	Dry tongue, skin Concentrated urine Acetonuria	1. Administer I.V. fluids as ordered 2. Place a wet cloth to the patient's mouth 3. Make a frequent check of bladder elimination

Dysfunctional Uterine Contractions

A. Uterine contractions inefficient; hence, cervical dilatation, effacement, and descent fail to occur.

B. Prolonged latent phase.

1. Primipara over 2 hours; multipara 14 hours; time required to dilate cervix to 4 cm. is prolonged.
2. Causes or contributing factors.
   a. False labor.
   b. Oversedation.
   c. "Unripe" cervix.
   d. Hypertonic or hypotonic uterine contractions.
   e. Uterine abnormalities such as fibroids.

C. Prolonged active phase or arrested active phase.

1. Primigravida, dilatation slower than 1.2 cm. per hour; and multigravida dilatation slower than 1.5 cm. per hour.
2. Arrested labor—labor fails to progress beyond a certain point.
3. Causes.
   a. Cephalopelvic disproportion (C.P.D.).
   b. Malpositions.
   c. Excessive sedation or anesthesia.
   d. Uterine abnormalities.
   e. Unknown causes.

D. Medical treatment.

1. Usually no active treatment is given if dilatation is regular unless labor will be prolonged over twenty-four hours.
2. Vaginal examination to determine position and station of fetus.
3. X-ray pelvimetry to determine C.P.D.
4. Rest for exhausted patient.
5. Cautious use of oxytocic stimulation if malposition, C.P.D., and other abnormalities are ruled out.
6. Cesarean delivery if appropriate.

E. Complications of prolonged labor (see Tables 3 and 4).

Other Causes of Dysfunctional Labor

A. Tetanic uterine contractions—contraction lasting over ninety seconds. May lead to fetal asphyxia or uterine rupture.

B. Precipitate delivery—labor of three hours or less duration. May lead to injury of mother and fetus due to trauma.

C. Rupture of the uterus—splitting of the uterine wall accompanied by extrusion of all or part of uterine contents into the abdominal cavity. Baby usually dies and mortality rate in mothers is high due to blood loss.

1. Signs of rupture.
   a. Acute abdominal pain and tenderness.
   b. Presenting part no longer felt through cervix.

c. Feeling in patient that something has happened inside her.

d. Cessation of labor pains—no contractions.

e. Bleeding usually internal; may be some external bleeding.

f. Signs of shock—pale appearance, pulse weak and rapid, air hunger, and exhaustion.

2. Treatment.

   a. Laparotomy to remove fetus.

   b. Hysterectomy, although uterus may be sutured and left in.

   c. Blood transfusions.

   d. Antibiotics to prevent infection from traumatized tissues.

Nursing Management of Dysfunctional Labor

A. Promote rest—darken room, reduce noise level.

B. Position patient for comfort.

C. Give patient a back rub.

D. Provide clean linen and gown and allow patient to bathe or shower if permissible.

E. Promote oral hygiene.

F. Give patient reassurance and support.

G. Explain procedures to the patient.

H. Let mother express feelings and emotions freely.

I. Watch for signs of exhaustion, dehydration, and acidosis.

J. Monitor vital signs.

K. Monitor F.H.T.

L. Monitor contractions for frequency, intensity, and duration.

M. Watch for signs of excessive bleeding and fetal distress.

N. Administer medications as ordered.

Abnormalities of the Passenger

Abnormal Presentations and Positions

A. Occiput posterior position.

   1. Usually prolongs labor because baby must rotate a longer distance (35 degrees or more) to reach symphysis pubis.

2. May lead to:

   a. Persistent occiput posterior—head does not rotate.

   b. Deep transverse arrest—head arrested in transverse position.

3. Treatment.

   a. Head usually rotates itself with contraction.

   b. Rotation may be done by physician manually or with forceps.

B. Breech—prolongs labor because soft tissue does not aid cervical dilatation as well as the fetal skull.

C. Face presentation—rare. Results in increased prenatal mortality.

   1. Chin must rotate so it lies under symphysis pubis for delivery.

   2. If baby is delivered vaginally, the face is usually edematous and bruised, with marked molding.

   3. Cesarean delivery is indicated if face does not rotate.

D. Transverse lie.

   1. Long axis of fetus at right angles to long axis of mother.

   2. Spontaneous version may occur. Cesarean delivery is the usual treatment.

Excessive Size of Fetus

A. Disproportion between the size of the fetus and the size of the pelvis when fetus is ten pounds or over.

B. Head is usually large and less moldable.

C. Size of shoulders may also complicate delivery.

D. Causes.

   1. Multiparity—birth weight may progress with each pregnancy.

   2. Maternal diabetes.

E. Size may be determined by sonography and X-ray.

F. Treatment.

   1. Vaginal delivery if disproportion is not too great. Usually there are fetal injuries—brachial plexus, dislocated shoulder.

   2. Cesarean delivery indicated if proportion too great.

G. Fetal abnormalities.

   1. Hydrocephalus.

   2. Tumors.

   3. Abnormal development.

Table 4. Complications and Signs of Distress in the Fetus

Complication	Signs of Distress	Possible Nursing Interventions
Asphyxia	Irregular heart rate Heart rate above 160 or below 120 Passage of meconium in the vertex position	1. Administer oxygen to the mother—turn on left side 2. Constantly observe and monitor F.H.T. 3. Check for prolapse of the cord 4. Prepare delivery room equipment for possible resuscitation of the baby at birth
Generalized infection	Irregular heart rate Heart rate above 160 or below 120	1. Administer antibiotics to the mother 2. Keep vaginals to a minimum 3. Follow same interventions as 1, 2, 4 in asphyxia

Abnormalities of Passage

Cephalopelvic Disproportion

A. Disproportion may be in inlet, mid-pelvis, or outlet—engagement or descent may fail to occur.

B. Pelvis is considered contracted if it is reduced enough in size to interfere with normal delivery.

C. Trial labor may be done in borderline cases—important to evaluate rate of progress, fetal descent, and fetal well-being.

D. Determined by X-ray of pelvis—pelvimetry.

E. Cesarean delivery is the usual treatment.

Other Complications of Labor

Premature Labor and Delivery

Definition: Premature labor and delivery occur when the pregnancy terminates after the period of viability and usually before the end of the thirty-sixth week.

A. Treatment.
   1. Bed rest with mild sedation (cautious use).
   2. Progesterone may be given.
   3. Vasodilan is a common drug given for inhibitory effects on vascular and uterine smooth muscle. A new drug class, beta-adrenergic blocking agents, may soon be approved for use. These drugs produce significant uterine relaxation and may diminish or abolish contractions and allow for fetal maturity.
   4. Alcohol drip is given to inhibit uterine activity. It probably acts by inhibiting pituitary oxytocin secretion.
   5. Narcotics are not usually given to the mother because of their depressive effect on the infant.

B. Attempts to arrest premature labor are contraindicated when:
   1. Pregnancy is thirty-seven weeks or over.
   2. Ruptured membranes exist.
   3. Cervix is dilated 4 to 5 cm.
   4. Maternal disease exists—toxemia, abruptio placenta, etc.
   5. Fetal problems such as Rh isoimmunization become threatening.

C. A drug such as betamethazone may be given to the mother to hasten fetal maturity by stimulating development of lecithin when membranes are ruptured and premature labor cannot be arrested.

Prolonged Pregnancy

Definition: Prolonged pregnancy refers to pregnancy over forty-two weeks gestation.

A. Complications.
   1. Amniotic fluid decreases and vernix caseosa disappears; infant's skin appears dry and cracked.
   2. Infant may lose weight.
   3. Chronic hypoxia may occur due to placental dysfunction.

B. Determination of gestational age usually made to ascertain actual duration of pregnancy—estriol studies, sonography.

C. Oxytocin challenge test to determine fetus' ability to tolerate labor.

D. Labor stimulated with oxytocin.

E. Cesarean delivery if induction contraindicated.

Prolapsed Umbilical Cord

Definition: Prolapsed cord descends through cervical canal along side of the presenting part. It may even protrude from the vagina.

A. Causes.
1. Ruptured membranes before engagement.
1. Abnormal presentations.
3. Premature infant—presenting part does not fill the birth canal and allow for more space.
4. Polyhydramnios.

B. Symptoms.
1. Abnormal fetal heart pattern.
2. Cord may be palpated or seen on vaginal examination.

C. Complications—fetal asphyxia—cord is compressed between presenting part and pelvis.

D. Immediate treatment.
1. Place patient in knee-chest position or exaggerated Trendelenburg.
2. Elevate presenting part of umbilical cord with sterile gloved hand.
3. Administer oxygen (5 liters) to mother by mask.
4. Maintain patient on absolute bed rest.
5. Cover exposed cord with sterile dressing, if available.
6. Auscultate F.H.T. every two minutes.
7. Stay with patient and offer support.
8. Cesarean delivery is prescribed if cervix is not dilated enough to allow the baby to pass. Haste is important.
9. Do not attempt to push cord in.

Amniotic Fluid Embolism

Definition: Amniotic fluid embolism is the escape of amniotic fluid into the maternal circulation. It is usually fatal to the mother.

A. Amniotic fluid contains debris such as lanugo, vernix, and meconium, which may become deposited in pulmonary arterioles.

B. Usually enters maternal circulation through open venous sinus at placental site.

C. Predisposing factors.
1. Premature rupture of membranes.
2. Tumultuous labor.

D. Signs and symptoms.
1. Acute dyspnea.
2. Sudden chest pain.
3. Cyanosis.
4. Pulmonary edema.
5. Shock.
6. Uncontrolled hemorrhage.

E. Treatment.
1. Oxygen under pressure.
2. Digitalis—failing cardiac function.
3. Fibrinogen to replace depleted reserves.
4. Use of heparin to combat fibrinogenemia.
5. Patient may be given whole blood.
6. Forceps delivery if cervix dilated enough to allow for delivery.

Inverted Uterus

Definition: Inverted uterus occurs when uterus turns inside out, usually during delivery of the placenta.

A. Signs—shock, hemorrhage, severe pain; or there may be mild symptoms with incomplete uterine inversion.

B. Treatment—same as for shock, and the manual or surgical replacement of the uterus.

Emergency Delivery by the Nurse

Nursing Responsibilities

A. Care of the mother during labor.
1. Labor may progress with unexpected rapidity.
2. Never leave the mother unattended during this time and never hold baby back. Have another employee notify the physician and bring the emergency delivery pack to room.
3. Reassure the patient that you will remain with her and provide care until the physician arrives.
4. Put on sterile gloves, if they are available and if there is time.

5. With a clean or sterile towel (if available), support baby's head with one hand applying gentle pressure to the head to prevent sudden expulsion and undue stretching of the perineum or brain damage to the infant.

6. If cord is draped around baby's neck, with free hand gently slip it over head.

7. Break membranes immediately if they have not done so spontaneously.

8. Have the mother pant rather than push to avoid rapid delivery of the head.

9. If bulb syringe is available, gently suction baby's mouth and wipe blood and mucus from mouth and nose with towel, if available.

10. Shoulders are usually born spontaneously after external rotation. If shoulders do not deliver spontaneously, ask mother to bear down to deliver them.

11. Support the baby's body as it is delivered.

12. All manipulation should be gentle to avoid injury to mother and baby.

B. After delivery.

1. After delivery, hold baby securely over hand and arm with the head in a dependent position, to allow fluid and mucus to drain.

2. If baby does not cry spontaneously, gently rub its back or the soles of its feet.

3. Dry baby to prevent heat loss.

4. Place the baby on the mother's abdomen to provide warmth. The weight on the uterus will help it to contract.

5. Palpate mother's abdomen to make sure uterus is contracting.

6. Watch for signs of placental separation.

7. Support placenta in your hand after it is expelled.

8. Clamp the cord after it stops pulsating if clamp or ties are available. Cord need not be cut; there will be no bleeding from the placental surface.

9. Wrap the baby in a blanket.

10. Put the baby to the mother's breast. This reassures the mother that the baby is all right and helps contract the uterus.

11. Check the uterus after delivery of the placenta. Make sure the uterus is contracting.

12. Keep an accurate record of the time of birth and other pertinent data.

13. If baby is delivered in bed, unassisted, before the nurse arrives (precipitate delivery), the nurse should immediately:

a. Check the baby to make sure breathing is established.

b. Check the mother for excessive bleeding.

14. Comfort mother.

Obstetric Analgesia and Anesthesia

Analgesia During Labor

A. Narcotics given to the mother in labor cross placental barrier and affect infant; therefore, drugs should be used judiciously.

B. Precautions.

1. Never give narcotics until labor is well established or it may retard progress—drugs usually administered between 4 to 6 cm.

2. Do not administer narcotics within two hours of delivery. Drug will be at level of maximum effect and the infant may be born depressed.

a. In the uterus, gas exchange takes place through placenta; therefore, analgesia given in labor does not pose a threat to infant.

b. After birth, the infant must breathe on his own. Analgesics depress the C.N.S. and affect the respiratory and other centers.

c. Some infants do not become fully alert for two to three days after delivery.

3. Check with the mother before administering drug to determine if mother is allergic to the preparation.

4. Observe patient constantly and keep side rails up.

5. Nurses should be familiar with normal dosages and physiologic effect of preparations used.

6. Monitor mother's vital signs and fetal heart tones regularly.

C. Sedatives may be given early in labor to reduce anxiety and relax mother. Use precautions listed above.

D. For specific drugs—see appendix (pp. 333-336).

Anesthesia During Labor

General Characteristics

A. No optimum anesthesia exists.

B. Ranks fourth as the cause of maternal death; other three—hemorrhage, infection, and toxemia.

C. History and physical should be obtained before administering anesthesia.

D. Should be NPO before use.

E. Should be administered by trained personnel.

F. Choice of the type of anesthesia in obstetrics is determined by the specific patient situation and condition.

General Inhalation Anesthetics

A. Advantages.
1. May anesthetize patient rapidly.
2. Depth—duration can be controlled.
3. Effects are rapidly dissipated in both infant and mother.
4. These anesthetics cause uterine relaxation—when necessary for manipulation.
5. Inhalation anesthetics are preferred in hypovolemic patient and when the condition of the mother prohibits the use of regional anesthetics.

B. Disadvantages.
1. Mother is not awake for delivery.
2. Brings about respiratory depression of the infant.
3. May cause emesis and aspiration in the mother.
4. May be flammatory.

C. Common types.
1. Ether—seldom used.
2. Halothane patent—used in selected cases only.
3. Penthrane—analgesia and light anesthesia; it may be used as a self-administered analgesic.
4. Thiopental (Pentothal)—I.V. anesthesia usually used as an adjunct in induction of anesthesia.
5. Trichloroethylene—Trilene—is often used in self-administration by mask during labor and delivery. Never leave patient alone when she is using self-administered anesthesia.

Regional Analgesia and Anesthesia

Definition: Regional analgesia and anesthesia refer to the drugs given to block the nerves carrying sensation from the uterus to the pelvic region.

A. Some common agents used.
1. Novocaine.
2. Xylocaine.
3. Pontocaine.
4. Carbocaine.

B. Vasoconstrictor agents such as epinephrine commonly used in conjunction with regional anesthetics to:
1. Slow absorption and prolong the effect of the anesthetic.
2. Prevent secondary hypotension.

C. Two principle types of regional anesthesia—nerve root block and peripheral nerve block.

D. Nerve root block.
1. General considerations.
   a. Usually relieves pain completely, if administered properly.
   b. Vasodilation below the anesthetic level, which may be responsible for a decrease in blood pressure—blood pools in legs.
   c. Does not depress the respiratory center, and therefore does not harm the patient—unless hypotension in the mother is severe enough to interfere with uterine flow.
   d. May cause postspinal headache.
   e. Contraindicated in a hypovolemic patient or in the case of central nervous system disease.
   f. Drug may impede labor if given too early—before 5 to 6 cm. dilatation.
   g. Special skill of anesthesiologist required to administer drug.
   h. Infant may need forceps delivery, because the mother usually cannot push effectively due to level of anesthesia.
2. Types.
   a. Caudal—may be continuous.
   b. Lumbar epidural—may be continuous
   c. Saddle block.
   d. Spinal.
3. Nursing management
   a. Have patient void.
   b. Assist patient to a knee-chest position over a bolster or on her left side, with head flexed and knees drawn up.
   c. Monitor blood pressure q. 3 to 5 minutes

until stabilized; then q. 30 minutes or p.r.n.

   d. Auscultate F.H.T.

   e. If hypotension does occur:

     (1) Turn mother to left side, off the inferior vena cava.

     (2) Give oxygen by mask.

     (3) Notify physician.

   f. Watch for signs of dizziness, nausea, faintness, and palpitations.

E. Peripheral nerve block.

  1. General considerations.

    a. May be done by attending physician—does not require an anesthesiologist.

    b. Local injection of anesthetic to block peripheral nerve endings.

    c. Less effective in relieving pain than nerve root block.

    d. May cause transient bradycardia in fetus, possibly due to rapid absorption of the drug into fetal circulation.

    e. Usually there are no maternal side effects.

    f. Needle guide such as Iowa trumpet usually used.

  2. Types.

    a. Paracervical.

    b. Pudendal block.

  3. Nursing management.

    a. Take vital signs before and after.

    b. Auscultate F.H.T. before and after.

    c. Assist patient to a dorsal recumbent position.

    d. Offer reassurance and support during the procedure.

    e. Auscultate F.H.T. q. 5 minutes for 15 to 30 minutes and q. 30 minutes thereafter.

    f. After delivery, check patient for return of sensation and warmth in toes.

Postpartum Period

Physiology of the Puerperium

Definition: Puerperium is the period of four to six weeks following delivery in which the reproductive organs return to the normal, nonpregnant state.

Uterus

A. Involution—rapid diminution in the size of the uterus as it returns to the nonpregnant state.

B. Lochia—discharge from the uterus, consisting of blood from vessels of the placental site and debris from the decidua.

C. Placental site—blood vessels of the placenta become thrombosed or compressed.

Cervix and Vagina

A. Cervix—remains soft and flabby the first few days, and the internal os closes.

B. Vagina—usually smooth walled after delivery. Rugae begin to appear when ovarian function returns and estrogen is produced.

Ovarian Function and Menstruation

A. Ovarian function depends upon the rapidity in which the pituitary function is restored.

B. Menstruation—usually returns in four to six weeks in a nonlactating mother.

Urinary Tract

A. May be edematous and contain areas of submucosal hemorrhage due to trauma.

B. May have urine retention due to loss of elasticity and tone and loss of sensation from trauma, drugs, anesthesia, loss of privacy.

C. Diuresis—mechanism by which excess body fluid is excreted after delivery. Usually begins within the first twelve hours after delivery.

Breasts

A. Proliferation of glandular tissue during pregnancy due to hormonal stimulation. Estrogen—ducts; progesterone—alveoli.

B. Usually secrete colostrum the first two to three days postpartum.

C. Pituitary stimulates secretion of prolactin after placental hormones inhibiting the pituitary are no longer present.

D. In three to four days breasts become firm, distended, tender, and warm (engorged), indicating production of milk.

E. Milk usually produced in response to sucking of infant.

Blood

A. White blood cells increase during labor and early postpartum period and then return to normal in a few days.

B. Decrease in hemoglobin, red blood cells, and hematocrit usually returns to normal in one week.

C. Elevated fibrinogen levels usually return to normal within one week.

Gastrointestinal Tract

A. Constipation due to stretching, soreness, lack of food, and loss of privacy.

B. Postpartum mothers are usually ravenously hungry.

Danger Signals

A. Bright-red bleeding beyond fourth day.

B. Foul odor—lochia.

C. Clots of tissue passed.

D. Pain in lower abdominal area.

E. Bright-red bleeding after lochia alba.

F. Elevated temperature—100.4° or more after first twenty-four hours.

Nursing Management of the Postpartum Patient

Principles of Care

Goals of Postpartum Care

A. To promote involution and healing.

B. To prevent infection.

C. To establish successful lactation.

D. To establish mother-infant relationship

Assessment

A. Check vital signs q. 8 hours and p.r.n.—decreased blood pressure, increased pulse, or temperature over 100.4° F.

B. Check fundus for consistency and level. Massage fundus lightly with fingers if it is relaxed.

C. Check lochia for amount, color, consistency, and odor. Watch for hemorrhage.

D. Check perineum for redness, discoloration, or swelling.

E. Check episiotomy for healing; check for drainage.

F. Check breasts for engorgement and cracking of nipples.

G. Check emotional status of new mother for depression or withdrawal.

H. Check for problems with flatus or elimination and bladder or bowel retention.

Other Nursing Considerations

A. Administer drug to inhibit lactation (if it has not been given immediately postpartum).

B. Administer RhoGAM as ordered within seventy-two hours postpartum to Rh-negative mother who is not sensitized.

C. Maintain intake and output until patient is voiding a sufficient quantity without difficulty.
1. Usually the first two voids are measured.
2. If patient fails to void sufficient quantity within 12 to 24 hours she is usually catheterized.

D. Teach mother perineal care and give perineal care until mother is able to do so.

E. Encourage ambulation as soon as ordered and as patient is able to tolerate it, giving assistance the first time.

F. Encourage verbalization of mother's feelings about labor, delivery, and baby.

G. Give perineal light as ordered.

H. Give warm sitz baths as ordered.

I. Remind mother to return for postpartum checkup.

J. Instruct that sexual relations may be resumed as soon as healing takes place and bleeding stops—3 to 4 weeks.

K. Discuss contraception, if mother so desires.

L. Provide opportunities to enhance mother-infant relationship—rooming-in, early contact, successful feedings, etc.

Emotional Aspects of Postpartum Care— Parenting

Factors Influencing Postpartum Care

A. Begins with parents' own birth—parenting and nurturing.

B. Cultural background.

C. Readiness for parenthood—emotional maturity, pregnancy planned or unplanned, financial status, job status.

D. Physical conditions of mother prior to pregnancy, during labor and delivery, and during puerperium.

E. Physical conditions of infant at birth, prematurity, congenital defects, etc. (parents may feel guilty, angry, cheated, and so forth).

F. Parental career plans.

G. Opportunities for early parental-infant interaction.

H. Parental knowledge of normal growth and development.

Postpartum Phases as Outlined by Rubin

A. Taking-in phase—first 2 to 3 days.
1. Mother's primary needs are her own—sleep, food.
2. Mother is usually quite talkative—focus on labor and delivery experience.
3. Important for nurse to listen and help mother interpret events to make them more meaningful.

B. Taking-hold phase—third postpartum day to 2 weeks —varies with each individul.
1. Emphasis on present, impatient and wants to reorganize self.
2. More in control. Begins to take hold of task of "mothering."
3. Important time for teaching without making mother feel inadequate—success at this time important in future mother-child relationship.

C. Letting-go phase.
1. Mother may feel a deep loss over the separation of the baby from part of her body and may grieve over this loss.
2. Mother may be caught in a dependent-independent role—wanting to feel safe and secure yet wanting to make decisions. Teenage mother needs special consideration because of the conflicts taking place within her as part of adolescence.
3. Mother may in turn feel resentful and guilty about the baby causing so much work.
4. May have difficulty adjusting to mothering role.
5. May feel conflict between the roles of mother and wife.
6. May feel upset and depressed at times—postpartum blues.
7. May be concerned about other children.
8. Important for nurse to encourage vocalization of these feelings and give positive reassurance for task well done.

Nursing Measures to Promote Optimum Parent-Infant Interactions

A. Early postpartum crucial period in beginning parent-infant bonding.
1. Bonding process important to later parent-child relationship.
2. Allow periods of time for both mother and father to be alone with infant.
3. Allow parents to hold infant in delivery and recovery rooms, and provide rooming-in and privacy.

B. Assess maternal and paternal physical and emotional status and readiness to take on parenting role. Determine what parents know about infant care.

C. Based upon assessment, plan nursing care—*important* to begin at same level as parents.

D. Be alert to parental cues but be careful not to label.

E. Support mother in infant care activities and use these opportunities to promote her self-esteem.

F. Provide a role model for parents.

G. Plan nursing care to reduce maternal fatigue and anxiety so that time with her infant is pleasurable.

H. Explain to parents that it is normal at this time to feel fatigued, tense, insecure, and sometimes depressed.

I. At home, counsel mother to:
1. Plan rest periods to avoid over-fatigue.
2. Arrange for time away from baby—to be alone, to spend with other children, and to resume contact with people.
3. Plan time for husband and wife together.

Breast Feeding

Nursing Management

A. Conditions of breast when breast feeding should be postponed.
1. Tenderness and hardness.
2. Pain and redness.
3. Cracking of nipples.

B. Feeding procedure.
1. Wash mother's hands.
2. Put baby to breast as soon as mother's and baby's condition is stable—on the delivery table in some hospitals, or in six to twelve hours in others.

3. Have mother assume comfortable position sitting or lying down.
4. Guide baby to breast; stimulate rooting reflex if necessary—place entire areola in baby's mouth.
5. Gently press breast away from baby's nose.
6. Usually the baby is nursed two to three minutes at each breast the first time, gradually building to ten minutes or so on each side in later feedings.
7. Release suction by inserting a finger into the baby's mouth. The breast will become sore if baby is pulled off it.
8. Burp baby after each breast.
9. Stay with mother each time she nurses until she feels secure or confident with the baby and feedings.
10. Baby should not nurse more than every two hours.

C. Teaching.
1. Explain to the mother that the baby's stool will be yellow and watery, and it is not uncommon for nursing infants to have three to four stools each day or even one for each feeding.
2. Dry the breast after feeding and allow it to air occasionally, especially if it is sore.
3. Use general hygiene and wash the breast once daily.
4. Encourage the mother to eat a well-balanced diet and drink 3000 cc. of fluid daily.
5. Explain to the mother that she may offer sterile water to the baby between feedings, but not formula. (The baby will not be hungry if given formula then and will not nurse well.)
6. Formula may be given at feeding time, or the mother may express milk manually and put it in a bottle if she plans to be away during feeding time.
7. Breasts may leak between feedings or during coitus. Place a washcloth or pad in brassiere.
8. Uterine cramping may occur the first few days after delivery while nursing when oxytocin stimulation causes the uterus to contract.
9. Medications or drugs should be avoided unless specified by the physician—drugs are passed to infant through breast milk.
10. Some foods such as cabbage or onions may alter the taste of milk or cause gas in the infant.
11. Birth control pills are usually avoided while nursing as they decrease milk production and are passed to the infant in the milk.
12. Mother should wear well-fitted brassiere.

Clinical Problems in Puerperium

Postpartum Hemorrhage

Definition: Postpartum hemorrhage occurs when 500 ml. or more of blood is lost during or after delivery.

Causes

A. Uterine atony—exhaustion of muscle is the *first cause.* Uterine atony may be due to:
1. Prolonged labor.
2. Overdistention—multiple pregnancies, polyhydramnios.
3. Sluggish muscle.
4. Overmassage of fundus.
5. Presence of fibroid tumors.
6. Deep inhalation anesthesia—may inhibit uterine activity.
B. Lacerations of the reproductive tract is the *second cause.*
1. Lacerations of the cervix or of the high vaginal walls.
2. Oozing from blood vessels.
C. Retained placental tissue or incomplete separation of the placenta is the *third cause.* (This is the most frequent cause of *late* postpartum hemorrhage.)
D. Late postpartum hemorrhage—twelve to twenty-one days.
E. Hematoma.

Clinical Manifestations

A. Uterine atony.
1. Boggy, relaxed uterus.
2. Dark bleeding.
3. Passage of clots.
B. Lacerations.
1. Firm fundus.
2. Oozing of bright red blood.
C. Retained placental tissue.
1. Boggy, relaxed uterus.

2. Dark bleeding.

D. Signs and symptoms of shock.
    1. Air hunger—difficulty in breathing.
    2. Restlessness.
    3. Weak rapid pulse.
    4. Rapid respirations.
    5. Decrease in blood pressure.

Treatment

A. Recognize abnormal bleeding and determine source.

B. Administer intravenous solutions, blood, or volume expanders.

C. Administer oxytocin if uterus is boggy.

D. Repair laceration.

E. Remove retained placental tissue.

F. Treat for shock.

G. Prevent infection.

H. Hysterectomy may be indicated if bleeding cannot be controlled.

I. Check for clotting defect.

Nursing Management

A. Remain with the patient.

B. Monitor vital signs q. 15 minutes or p.r.n. until stable.

C. Palpate fundus q. 15 minutes or p.r.n. while bleeding continues; then q. 2 to 4 hours.

D. Gently massage fundus until firm. Be careful not to overmassage.

E. Have physician notified.

F. Weigh pads and linen.

G. Provide for warmth.

H. Measure intake and output.

I. Administer fluids and blood as ordered.

J. Explain carefully to patient and family to help allay anxiety.

K. Observe for blood reactions.

L. Return patient to delivery room or to surgery for removal of placental tissue or repair of laceration.

Retained Placenta

Placenta Accreta

Definition: Placenta accreta is a condition that occurs when all or part of the decidua basalis is absent and placenta grows directly onto muscle.

A. May be partial—portion abnormally adherent.

B. Complete—all adheres.

C. Bleeding may be excessive.

D. Treatment.
    1. Removal of placenta by hand.
    2. Hysterectomy if bleeding persists.

Puerperal Infection

Definition: Puerperal infection is an infection in genitalia within 28 days as a consequence of abortion or labor and delivery.

General Considerations

A. Cause.
    1. Organisms which were introduced during labor and delivery.
    2. Bacteria normally present in vaginal tract.

B. Predisposing factors.
    1. Weakened resistance due to prolonged labor and dehydration.
    2. Traumatic delivery.
    3. Excessive vaginal examinations during labor.
    4. Premature rupture of membranes.
    5. Excessive blood loss.
    6. Anemia.
    7. Intrauterine manipulation.
    8. Retained placental fragments.

Clinical Manifestations

A. Elevated temperature of 100.4° F. or more for two consecutive days not counting first 24 hours.

B. Discomfort in the abdomen and perineum.

C. Burning on urination.

D. Foul-smelling lochia or discharge.

E. Pelvic pain.

F. Chills.

G. Rapid pulse.

H. Malaise, anorexia.

Endometritis

Definition: Endometritis is an inflammation of the lining of the uterus.

General Considerations

A. Most frequent site of infection.

B. Uterus may be boggy, relaxed, and tender.

C. If untreated, may spread through lymphatic system to whole body causing septicemia.

Treatment

A. Antibiotics.

B. May have pelvic examination.

C. Laboratory studies—blood and urine.

D. Establish adequate drainage of uterus.

E. Blood transfusion if anemic.

F. Fluids 3000 to 4000 cc. daily, oral or parenteral.

Nursing Management

A. Administer I.V. fluids or blood as ordered.

B. Encourage fluid intake—3000 to 4000 cc. if not contraindicated.

C. Administer medications as ordered.

D. Provide high-calorie nutritious diet.

E. Place patient in Fowler's or semi-Fowler's position as ordered. Position of patient may impede extension of infection from moving upward in pelvis.

F. Provide emotional support to mother, who is usually in isolation and unable to see baby.

Thrombophlebitis

Definition: Thrombophlebitis occurs when the thrombis at placental site becomes infected, causing inflammation of the deep pelvic veins. Thrombophlebitis may be confined to blood vessels in uterine wall, or it may extend to ovarian, hypogastric, or femoral veins. Femoral thrombophlebitis, commonly called "milk leg," may originate in a leg vein.

Clinical Manifestations

A. Discomfort in abdomen and pelvis.

B. Tenderness localized on one side of the pelvis.

C. Femoral symptoms usually don't appear until the second week or later.
   1. Edema and pain in affected leg.
   2. Chills and fever.

Treatment

A. Antibiotics, until temperature is stable.

B. Anticoagulants.

C. Bed rest.

D. Warm compresses and heat.

E. Bed cradle—keep bed clothes off leg.

F. Antiembolic stockings.

Nursing Management

A. Maintain bed rest.

B. Provide diversion.

C. Administer medications as ordered.

D. Teach mother to give heparin.

E. Apply warm compresses as ordered—for fifteen to twenty minutes.

F. Elevate affected leg.

G. Apply bed cradle.

H. Never massage leg and teach mother not to do so.

I. Teach mother to watch for signs of excessive bleeding.

J. Allow mother to express fears and concerns.

K. Watch for signs of pulmonary embolism.

L. Apply antiembolic stocking—teach mother its proper use.

Cystitis and Pyelitis

Causes

A. Slight lesions, edema, hyperemia of bladder due to stretching and trauma in labor and delivery.

B. Temporary loss of bladder tone—pressure and injury.
   1. Less sensitive to fullness.
   2. Increased bladder capacity.

C. May lead to overdistention and residual urine or inability to void.

D. Trauma to urethra may cause difficulty in voiding.

Clinical Manifestations

A. Usually begin several days into the postpartum.

B. Suprapubic or perineal discomfort.

C. Frequent urination.

D. Burning sensation on urination.

E. Elevated temperature.

F. Urine contains pus, bacteria, and red cells on microscopic examination.

G. Pyelitis—pain in flank.

Treatment

A. Antibacterial drugs and antispasmodic specific to urinary tract.

B. Force fluids.

C. Complete emptying of bladder; may require indwelling catheter.

D. Laboratory work on urine specimen to determine the exact infectious organism.

Nursing Management

A. Observe mother closely postpartum for full bladder or residual urine.
1. Palpate bladder for distention.
2. Palpate fundus—full bladder displaces fundus upward and to the sides.

B. Institute measures to help patient void.

C. Insert catheter, as ordered, using sterile technique.

D. Force fluids.

E. Administer drugs as ordered.

F. Obtain urine specimens for microscopic examination.

G. Provide emotional support to patient—allow her to express feelings about her illness and the baby.

Mastitis

Definition: Mastitis is an infection in breast tissue due to invading organisms, usually staphylococcus.

Causes

A. Infected hands of mother or attendants.

B. Bacteria normally present in lactiferous glands.

C. Fissure in nipples.

D. Bruising of breast tissue.

E. Stasis of milk or overdistention may injure tissue, but does not cause infection in itself.

F. Infected baby.

Clinical Manifestations

A. Chills.

B. Fever 103° F. or above.

C. Elevated pulse rate.

D. Lobe may become hard to touch, red, and painful.

E. May progress to abscess if untreated.

Treatment

A. Provide support for breast.

B. Antibiotics.

C. Apply ice to breast.

D. May require incision and drainage if abscess develops.

E. Some physicians recommend breast feeding be stopped, or they favor temporary discontinuance with artificial removal of milk for a few days.

Nursing Management

A. Administer medications as ordered.

B. Apply ice pack as ordered.

C. Make sure mother is wearing snug-fitting, supportive brassiere.

D. Teach mother to empty breast if nursing is to be continued.

E. Wash hands before touching patient's breast.

F. Teach mother careful handwashing and care of the breast.

Subinvolution

Definition: Subinvolution occurs when uterus does not return to usual size as rapidly as normal following delivery.

Causes

A. Retained placental tissue or fetal membranes.

B. Endometritis.

Clinical Manifestations

A. Uterus enlarged and boggy.

B. Profuse red lochia.

Treatment

A. Ergonovine to cause contractions.

B. Antibiotics to prevent infection.

C. Dilatation and curettage if indicated.

D. Manual replacement in malposition.

Nursing Management

A. Administer medications.

B. Explain condition and treatment to patient.

Newborn

Immediate Care of the Newborn

Principles of Maintenance

A. Maintain body temperature.
1. Place infant in heated incubator or crib with radiant heat.
2. Wipe off fluid, mucus, and excessive vernix.
3. Avoid excessive exposure.
4. Wrap infant in warm blankets.
5. Transfer to the nursery after parents have seen and held infant.

B. Maintain respiration.
1. Place infant on side, in modified Trendelenburg position, to prevent cerebral edema and to facilitate drainage of mucus and blood.
2. Suction mucus as needed with bulb or suction catheter attached to mucus trap.
3. Provide oxygen as needed.

C. Prevent infection and injury.
1. Eye care.
    a. To prevent eye infection from gonorrhea.
    b. Usually one percent silver nitrate—two drops in conjunctival sacs. Flush eyes with water in about two minutes.
    c. Alternate treatment—antibiotic ointment is applied to eyes.

2. Cord care—use sterile scissors and clamp.
3. Carry out proper hand washing before receiving baby or wear sterile gloves.

General Observations

A. Apgar scoring, one and five minutes (see Table 5); based on the scoring method developed by Virginia Apgar.

B. Obvious congenital malformations.

C. Umbilical cord—two arteries and one vein.

D. Meconium staining—skin, nails.

E. Abnormal cry or no cry.

F. Injuries caused by birth trauma—dislocated shoulder, edema of scalp, lacerations.

G. Respiratory—nasal flaring, retractions, expiratory grunt.

H. Neurological status—reflexes, tremors, and twitching.

I. Anal patency—nasal patency.

Nursing Management

A. Clamp the cord if the physician does not do so; should be clamped one inch from the base, or left longer if the mother is Rh negative (in case of possible blood exchange).

B. Identify the baby with bands.

C. Show the baby to the parents and allow them to hold the infant with help (if not contraindicated).

D. Observe the mother's reactions to baby.

E. Transfer the baby to the admitting nursery with appropriate data.

Table 5. Apgar Scoring

Sign	0	1	2
Heart tone	Absent	Slow (less than 100)	Over 100
Respiratory effort	Absent	Slow, irregular	Good crying
Muscle tone	Flaccid	Some flexion of extremities	Active motion
Reflex irritability	No response	Cry	Vigorous cry
Color	Blue, pale	Body pink, extremities blue	Completely pink

Care in the Nursery

A. Steps at admission and during the first twelve hours.
1. Check rectal or axillary temperature.
2. Weigh and measure—total length and head circumference.
3. Place in heated crib.
4. Check respiratory rates every hour for two to three hours and p.r.n.
5. Check for nasal flaring, retractions, expiratory grunt, breath sounds.
6. Check apical pulse every hour for two to three hours; watch for above 180 or below 100.
7. Keep bulb syringe available and suction as needed.
8. Administer vitamin K as ordered.
9. Bathe and dress baby when his temperature is stable.
10. Place in an open crib when his temperature is stable.
11. Administer feeding as ordered; usually sterile water or glucose water is given within four to six hours.
12. Assess baby for congenital defects, tremors, color, acrocyanosis. (Acrocyanosis is normal for one to two hours after birth and when infant is cold, because of sluggish peripheral circulation.)

B. Routine nursing management.
1. Assessment.
   a. Observe for jaundice—check general skin color, blanching, sclera of the eyes.
   b. Check for respiratory difficulty—mucus, flaring of nostrils, grunting, etc.
   c. Note tremors, twitching, muscle tone, and reflexes.
   d. Take baby's temperature each shift.
   e. Check baby's weight daily.
   f. Note amount voided and number of stools.
   g. Check for signs of infection on the skin and cord—redness, drainage, odor and bleeding.
2. Apply alcohol to cord daily p.r.n.
3. Circumcision care.
   a. Observe for bleeding.
   b. Change petroleum gauze as necessary.
   c. Keep area clean to prevent infection.
4. Order phenylketonuria (PKU) test third day before discharge.
5. Provide for nutrition and hydration.
6. Teach mother how to hold and burp the baby.
7. Use proper hand washing between babies to prevent spreading infection.
8. Isolate babies with known or suspected infections.
9. Be sure that the mother understands the doctor's orders regarding care of the infant before she goes home, and plans follow-up visits to the physician.
10. Assess mother-infant relationship.

Physical Characteristics

Respiratory Status

A. Infant's respiratory system must function immediately after loss of placental function; adequate maturation at birth is necessary.

B. From 80-100 ml. of fluid are present in the lungs at birth. Approximately one-third is removed as a result of compression of the chest during delivery. The remainder is carried off through pulmonary circulation and by the lymph system.

C. Surfactant (a phospholipid found in the lungs) reduces surface tension in alveoli and keeps them from collapsing. Surfactant is necessary to maintain lung expansion and to prevent respiratory distress syndrome.

D. Normal respiration is about 30-40; over 60 or below 30 may indicate a problem. Respiration may be slightly elevated during crying episodes or shortly afterward. (Always count for one full minute.)

Circulatory Status

A. Ductus arteriosus, ductus venosus, and foramen ovale should close—may not be complete for one or two days.

B. Peripheral circulation may be sluggish—there may be mottling, acrocyanosis.

C. Pulse may be variable—normal 120-160; it may be as high as 170 with crying or below 120 when resting. Always take apical pulse for one full minute.

D. Anemia is common in early months because of the decrease in erythropoiesis and breakdown of red blood cells. Baby may need an iron-supplemented formula.

E. Plethora—red coloring to skin especially visible when baby cries—may be present due to increase in red blood cells.

F. Physiologic jaundice—normal level less than 1 mg. per 100 ml. blood.
   1. Jaundice visible in the skin, sclera.
   2. Does not become visible until the second or third day after birth.
   3. Caused by impairment in the removal of bilirubin—deficiency in the production of glucuronide transferase, which is needed to convert indirect insoluble bilirubin to direct water soluble bilirubin which is excreted.
   4. Jaundice begins to decrease by the sixth or seventh day.
   5. Should be watched carefully although usually does not require treatment.
   6. Usual treatment is phototherapy (13 mg./100 ml. blood —lower in premature infant). If the indirect bilirubin continues to go up, a cause other than physiologic jaundice is searched for.
   7. Infant may be on force fluids between feeding to aid in excretion of bilirubin as it is broken down.
G. Transitory deficiency in the ability of the blood to clot. Bacteria in the intestines are necessary for the production of vitamin K. Bacteria are not present in the intestines during the first few days after birth. Vitamin K I.M. usually given after birth to aid in blood coagulation.

Ability to Maintain Body Heat

A. The baby suffers a large loss of heat because he is wet at birth and because of the coolness of the delivery room. The infant should be placed immediately in a warmer and dried off.
B. Means of heat production in the newborn.
   1. Increasing metabolism.
   2. Shivering—poor in newborn.
   3. Metabolism of brown fat—less mature infants have less brown fat.
C. Effects of chilling—cold stress.
   1. Increased consumption of oxygen.
   2. Use of glucose stored as glycogen.
   3. May become hypoglycemic.
   4. May develop metabolic acidosis—products of incomplete metabolism accumulate along with fatty acids from breakdown of brown fat.
D. The baby may have a decrease in the production of surfactant.
   1. Glucose, pO_2, and proper pulmonary circulation

are necessary for the production of surfactant.
   2. Decrease in surfactant may lead to respiratory distress.
E. Temperature may be taken by rectum or axilla (usually taken by rectum the first time to check for patent anus).

Weight

A. Infants usually lose between 5 to 10 percent of their body weight the first few days, because of low fluid intake and loss of excess fluid from tissue.
B. Usually regain weight lost within seven to fourteen days.

Head

A. Head or face may be asymmetrical due to birth trauma.
B. Molding of head may be present (elongation of head as it passes through birth canal to accommodate pelvis); usually disappears in about a week.
C. Caput succedaneum—diffuse swelling of soft tissues of scalp, caused by an arrest in circulation in those tissues present over the cervix as it dilates.
D. Cephalohematoma—extravasation of blood beneath periosteum of one of the cranial bones because of a ruptured blood vessel during the trauma of labor and delivery.
E. Anterior and posterior fontanel.
   1. Should be open.
   2. Should neither bulge (may indicate intracranial pressure) nor be depressed (may indicate dehydration).
F. Ears well formed and cartilage present.

Gastrointestinal System

A. Salivary glands immature.
B. May have Epstein's pearls—white raised areas on palate caused by an accumulation of epithelial cells.
C. May have transient circumoral cyanosis.
D. Sucking pads—fatty tissue deposits in each cheek that aid in sucking. They usually disappear when no longer needed.
E. Infant stools.
   1. Meconium plug—thick gray-white mucus passed before meconium.
   2. Meconium—sticky, black, tarry looking stools,

consisting of mucus, digestive secretions, vernix caseosa, and lanugo; usually passed during the first twenty-four hours after birth.

3. Transitional stool—second to fifth day—greenish-yellow color, and loose (partly meconium and partly milk).
4. Number of stools varies. Breast-fed infants usually have more bowel movements.
5. Stools should be observed for color, frequency, and consistency.

F. Regurgitation following feeding is common. It may be reduced by frequent burping during feedings.

Genitourinary System

A. Urinary functions.
   1. Observe ability to concentrate urine and check to see if specific gravity elevated.
   2. Uric acid crystals (pink or reddish spots) may appear on diaper due to high uric acid secretion.
G. Genitalia.
   1. Female.
      a. May have heavy coating of vernix between labia.
      b. Usually has mucus discharge. Mucus may be blood-tinged due to elevated hormonal levels in mother.
   2. Male.
      a. Size of penis and scrotum vary.
      b. Testicles should be descended or in inguinal canal.
      c. Circumcision—surgical removal of foreskin of penis by physician.
         (1) Usually performed by the second or third day.
         (2) Observe for bleeding from postoperative site.

Skin

A. Should be pinkish color.
B. Acrocyanosis (cyanosis of extremities) may be present for the first hour or two after birth. Persistent blueness may indicate complications such as heart disease.
C. Lanugo and vernix caseosa may be present.
D. Petechiae may be present because of the trauma of birth.

E. Milia—secretions of sebaceous materials in obstructed sebaceous glands—may be present and will disappear.
F. Erythema toxicum neonatorum—small harmless eruptions on the skin—transient in nature.
G. Hemangiomas may be present on nape of neck or upper eyelids.
H. Skin may appear dry or cracked.
I. Mongolian spots—bluish pigmented areas present on the buttocks of babies of Oriental, Negro, or Mediterranean heritage.
J. Mottling may occur if the infant is chilled.

Effects of Maternal Hormones

A. Maternal hormones may cause enlargement of breast in both male and female infants, and "witches" milk, a milk-like substance, may be excreted from the breasts.
B. Vaginal bleeding in female infant.
C. Hypertrophy of labia or scrotum.

Neurological System

A. Reflexes present at birth (see Appendix 2 in Pediatric Nursing, p. 411).
B. Muscle tone.
   1. Fist usually kept clenched.
   2. Baby should offer resistance when change in position is attempted.
   3. Head should be supported when baby is lifted.
   4. Muscles should not be limp.
C. Cry.
   1. Cry should be loud and vigorous.
   2. Baby should cry when hungry or uncomfortable.
D. Hunger.
   1. Usually becomes fretful and restless at three- to four-hour intervals.
   2. May suck fingers or anything placed near mouth.
E. Sleep.
   1. Sleeps about twenty out of twenty-four hours.
   2. Often stirs and stretches while sleeping.
F. Senses.
   1. Eyes.
      a. Eyelids may be edematous or have purulent discharge from the chemical irritation of silver nitrate.

     b. Light perception is present.

     c. Eye movement is uncoordinated.

     d. Usual color of eyes is blue-gray.

     e. May have subconjunctival hemorrhages, which disappear in a week or two.

     f. May gaze at or follow bright objects.

  2. Nose.

     a. Newborn breathes through nose.

     b. Sense of smell is present.

  3. Ears—hearing is present at birth.

  4. Taste is present at birth.

  5. Touch is present at birth. Responds to stimuli and discomfort.

G. Immunity.

  1. May receive from the mother some passive immunity to infectious diseases, such as measles, mumps, and diphtheria.

  2. Capacity to develop own antibodies is slow during first few months.

  3. Has little resistance to infection.

Feeding the Newborn

Schedules of Feeding

A. First feeding.

  1. May be breast fed on the delivery table.

  2. First feeding is usually within four to twelve hours after birth.

  3. First feeding of glucose or sterile water is made to determine the baby's ability to swallow.

B. Subsequent feeding.

  1. Routine schedule—three- to four-hour feedings.

  2. Self-demand—baby is fed according to his needs, when he is hungry, usually every three to six hours.

Calories and Fluid Needs

A. Fluid—150–200 ml./kilogram of body weight in twenty-four hours. More fluids should be given in hot weather or when the baby has an elevated temperature.

B. Caloric needs—approximately 10 calories/kilogram of body weight or 50 calories/pound of body weight.

High Risk Infants

Premature Infant

Definition: An infant born before the end of the 37th week regardless or birth weight.

Etiology

A. Maternal factors—diabetes, toxemia, chronic disease, chronic poor nutrition, premature rupture of membranes, placenta previa, abruptio placenta, incompetent cervix, other premature births, age, multiple pregnancies, etc.

B. Fetal factors—congenital anomalies, infection, other diseases.

C. Socioeconomic factors—low socioeconomic status, poor nutrition, unmarried, under seventeen years of age.

D. Other—cause unknown; accounts for large percentage of premature births.

E. Incidence—8 percent of all live births.

  1. Factors associated with prematurity make it the leading cause of death in neonates.

  2. Primarily due to respiratory distress syndrome, infection, and intracranial hemorrhage.

Characteristics

A. Digestive system.

  1. Gag and suck reflexes may be weak and poorly developed.

  2. Suck and swallow reflexes may be uncoordinated.

  3. Small stomach capacity.

  4. Poor ability to tolerate fats.

  5. Immature enzyme system.

B. Central nervous system and muscle tone.

  1. Poor muscle tone—muscles appear limp; baby assumes frog-like position when placed on abdomen.

  2. Weak, feeble cry.

  3. Weak reflexes.

  4. Heat regulation unstable.

     a. Body temperature may be below normal; small muscle mass; absent sweat or shiver responses.

Table 6. Nursing Care of Premature Infants

Need	Nursing Management
Needs of Family	
Keep separation to a minimum	Allow parents to visit baby frequently; as soon as possible, allow parents to help care for infant to promote parent-to-infant attachment.
Information on baby's progress	Answer questions openly, provide up-to-date information on baby's progress.
Express feelings and concerns	Allow parents to talk freely about infant, give support as needed and help parents to accept reality of situation.
Teaching	Explain specialized care to parents. Have them report to pediatrician any of the following symptoms: diarrhea, vomiting, lack of appetite, or elevated temperature.
	Allow mother to feel confident in care of infant before discharge. Explain to mother infant's special needs.
Needs of Infant	
Warmth	Immediate attention in delivery room and transporting to nursery to maintain heat. Maintain skin temperature at about 36°C or 97.6°F in isolette or heated crib.
	Gradually wean infant from heated environment and watch temperature closely until stable. Warming infant too quickly may cause apneic spells.
Oxygen and humidity	Administer oxygen (should be warmed and humidified). Administer humidity (distilled water) usually between 40 to 70 percent as ordered.
	Check respiratory rate—1 hour and p.r.n.
	Observe for signs of respiratory distress, color, flaring, grunting retractions, skin color, auscultate breath sounds with stethoscope. Analyze oxygen concentration 2 to 4 hours or as necessary to prevent retrolental fibroplasia and to ensure adequate oxygenation. Observe for periods of apnea and stimulate by gently rubbing chest or tapping foot; percuss, vibrate and suction as ordered to remove mucus.
	Reposition q. 2 hours to promote aeration of all lobes of lung and facilitate drainage.
	Monitor blood gases and electrolytes frequently. (Oxygen administration is determined by blood gases.) Toxic levels of oxygen may lead to bronchopulmonary dysplasia and retrolental fibroplasia.
Nutrition and hydration	May require I.V. feedings through umbilical catheter until stabilized. I.V. regulated by infusion pump to prevent circulatory overload. Initiate feedings as ordered (usually begin with sterile water or glucose water). Progress to dilute formula or breast milk to full strength formula as tolerated.
	Usually gavage feeding if respirations are about 60 breaths per minute. Use premie nipple if bottle feeding. Infants often require alternate feedings of gavage and bottle feeding.
	Maintain I&O including stool, weigh daily and organize care to conserve energy with rest periods after each feeding. Measure head circumference and length at least 1 time a week.
Prevention of infection	Maintain aseptic technique.
	Strict isolation techniques with infected babies.
	Prevent skin breakdown—change position, careful cleansing and handling.
	Observe for signs of infection—vomiting, jaundice, lack of appetite, lethargy; cover I.V. sites.

Need	Nursing Management
Maintain circulatory functioning	Check heart rate by apical pulse for a full minute q. 1 to 2 hours.
	Frequently check for bleeding from umbilical catheter. Apply pressure to puncture site as necessary to prevent bleeding. Administer vitamin K as ordered after birth to prevent hemorrhage.
Mothering and physical stimulation	Gently stroke and talk to baby when giving care.
	Hang colorful mobiles or other nonharmful objects in crib.
	Hold baby during feeding as soon as condition permits.
	Encourage parents to hold, cuddle, feed and diaper baby as soon as baby's condition permits.

    b.   Large body surface in proportion to body weight.

    c.   Lack of subcutaneous fat.

    d.   Poor capillary response to environmental changes.

  5. Susceptibility to brain damage from lower levels of bilirubin.

C. Respiratory system.

  1. Insufficient production of surfactant.

  2. Immaturity of alveolary system.

  3. Immaturity of musculature and rib cage.

  4. Prone to respiratory disease.

D. Integumentary system.

  1. Skin thin and capillaries easily seen.

  2. Little subcutaneous fat.

  3. Lanugo prominent—hair on head is fine and fuzzy.

  4. Vernix may cover body if born between 31 and 33 weeks.

E. Immune system—resistance to infection decreased.

  1. Lack of passive immunity from mother (occurs late pregnancy).

  2. Inability to produce own antibodies—immature system.

  3. Skin is thin and offers little protection from disease-causing organisms.

F. Hepatic system—liver immature.

  1. Poor glycogen stores—increased susceptibility to hypoglycemia.

  2. Inability to conjugate bilirubin—susceptible to hyperbilirubinemia.

  3. Decreased ability to produce clotting factors.

  4. Decreased ability to produce immune factors.

G. Circulatory system.

  1. Capillary fragility increases susceptibility to hemorrhage, especially intracranial.

  2. Prone to anemia—poor iron stores.

H. Renal system.

  1. Renal function immature—poor ability to concentrate urine.

  2. Fluid and electrolyte balance precarious.

  3. Easily dehydrated.

Dysmature Infants

Definition: Refers to infants who are significantly undersize for gestational age. Also called small for gestational age (S.G.A.) and intrauterine growth retardation (IUGR).

Etiology

A. Postmature infants.

B. Defective embryonic development.

C. Placental insufficiency.

D. Associated factors—diabetes, toxemia, maternal infection, maternal malnutrition, cigarette smoking, multiple gestation.

Nursing Management

A. Similar to care given to premature infant until the infant is stabilized.

B. Protect from cold stress—keep warm, usually in isolette.

C. Watch for signs of hypoglycemia (poor glucose stores), twitching, lethargy, irregular respirations, convulsions.

D.   Lab tests for glucose levels.

E.   Weigh daily and maintain intake and output.

Postmature Infants

Definition: Refers to infants of over 42 weeks' gestation.

Etiology

A.   Placental function decreased.

B.   Nutritional and oxygen needs are not met.

C.   Infants exposed to chronic hypoxia.

Clinical Manifestations

A.   Vernix and lanugo no longer present.

B.   Skin appears dry and wrinkled.

C.   Fingernails and toenails long—may be meconium-stained.

D.   May be S.G.A. due to nutritional deficiency and chronic hypoxia.

E.   Easily stressed during labor.

F.   Increased morbidity and mortality due to above factors.

Nursing Management

A.   Similar to care given to premature infant if premature characteristics are observed.

B.   Observe for hypoglycemia.

C.   Observe for signs of birth injury—dislocated shoulder, fractured pelvis, facial paralysis, and CNS injury.

D.   Symptomatic depending upon condition at birth. Care for as S.G.A. in those infants who are underweight for gestational age.

Diseases Affecting the Newborn

Respiratory Distress Syndrome

Definition: Respiratory distress syndrome refers to a group of clinical symptoms signifying that the infant is experiencing problems with the respiratory system.

Etiology

A.   Symptoms are the result of a decrease in the amount of surfactant in the infant's lungs as a result of one of the following conditions.
   1.   Prematurity—immaturity of lungs and inability to produce surfactant.
   2.   Hypoxia and acidosis.
   3.   Hypothermia.
   4.   High concentration of oxygen.

B.   Respiratory distress syndrome is the most common cause of death in infants.

Clinical Manifestations

A.   Increased respirations—greater than 60/min.

B.   Retractions—subcostal followed by intercostal.

C.   Cyanosis.

D.   Expiratory grunting.

E.   Increased apical pulse.

F.   Nasal flaring.

G.   Chin lag.

H.   Lack of activity.

I.   Inability to take in sufficient oxygen leading to low oxygen and hypoxemia.

J.   Hypercarbia due to elevated levels of carbon dioxide.

K.   Respiratory acidosis due to retention of carbon dioxide owing to inadequate pulmonary ventilation.

L.   May show decreased body temperature.

M.   Metabolic acidosis due to increased production of lactic acid.

N.   X-ray examination reveals:
   1.   Atelectasis—collapsed portions of lung.
   2.   Fibrinous membrane that lines alveolar ducts and terminal bronchioles; membrane is formed by transudation of fluid from pulmonary tissue.

Nursing Management

A.   Primarily supportive.

B.   Prevent cold stress—infant usually placed in isolette or open crib with overhead radiant warmer. Skin temperature is maintained with probe at 97.6°F.

C.   Provide for nutrition and hydration—usually give I.V. glucose fluids during acute periods, then gradually increase feedings as tolerated.

D.   Careful monitoring of blood gases and electrolytes.

E.   Administration of oxygen, warmed and humidified

in lowest concentration possible via hood, nasal prongs, endotracheal tubes or bag and mask. Oxygen may be given at atmospheric or increased airway pressure.

F. Continuous positive pressure applied to lungs during spontaneous breathing.

G. Positive pressure applied to lungs during expiratory cycle when using the mechanical ventilator.

H. When nasal prongs are being used they should be checked and changed frequently.

I. When endotracheal tube is being used, it should be loosely taped and checked frequently for correct placement and connection at adaptor site.

J. Suctioning infant with endotracheal tube.
   1. Disconnect from respirator at site of adaptor.
   2. Instill few minims to 0.5 ml. of sterile normal saline into tube to loosen secretions.
   3. Suction no longer than five seconds using sterile catheter.
   4. Ventilate infant as needed during procedure.
   5. Reconnect tube to respirator, being sure it is in place and adaptor is secure.
   6. Auscultate chest for breath sounds.

K. Postural drainage, percussion, and suction as ordered.

L. Analyze oxygen concentration.

M. Keep parents informed of infant's progress.

N. Allow parents to visit child as much as possible and express their feelings about child's illness.

O. Gently stroke and talk with child while giving care.

Hyperbilirubinemia

Definition: Hyperbilirubinemia is an abnormal elevation of bilirubin in the newborn (above 13-15 mg./100 ml.) in full term infant.

Etiology

A. Functional immaturity of the liver—usually appears after twenty-four hours and disappears after ten days—physiologic jaundice.

B. Bacterial infections.

C. ABO and Rh incompatibilities—usually show up in the first twenty-four hours and may be severe.

D. Enclosed bleeding, such as hematoma, from trauma of delivery.

E. Pregnanediol hormone present in mother's breast milk may contribute to jaundice. (It inhibits conjugation of bilirubin by glucuronyl transferase.)

Clinical Manifestations

A. Jaundice appears, progressing from head to extremities.

B. Pallor appears.

C. Infant is lethargic and feeds poorly.

D. Urine is concentrated and stools are light in color.

E. If untreated, infant may progress to muscular rigidity or flaccidity, increased lethargy, high-pitched cry, respiratory distress, decreased Moro's reflex, and spasms.

F. Blood tests.
   1. Hemoglobin.
   2. Bilirubin—important to measure amount of indirect bilirubin in blood, since unbound bilirubin is free to deposit in body tissues, such as skin, cardiac muscle, brain, and kidney. Unconjugated bilirubin deposited in the brain determines the extent of kernicterus.

Nursing Management

A. Careful observation of infant for signs of increased jaundice.

B. Careful observations for and prevention of acidosis/hypoxia and hypoglycemia, which decrease binding of bilirubin to albumin and contribute to jaundice.

C. Maintain adequate hydration and offer fluids between feedings as ordered.

D. Maintain skin temperature at 97.6°F; avoid cold stress.

E. Careful avoidance of infection.

F. Phototherapy—fluorescent light breaks down bilirubin into water soluble products.
   1. Do not clothe infant.
   2. Cover infant's eyes to prevent retinal damage.
   3. Change baby's position every two hours to ensure adequate exposure.
   4. Remove infant from light and remove eye patches during feedings—dress to keep warm.
   5. Carefully examine eyes for signs of irritation from eye patches.
   6. Keep an accurate record of hours spent under fluorescent lights.

G. Meet emotional needs—cuddle, talk to infant, etc.

H. Reinforce physician's teaching to parents and allow parents to express concerns and feelings.

I. Exchange transfusion—considered when bilirubin reaches high levels (20 mg./ml. in full term infant; lower levels in premature infants).

1. Usually performed in operating or delivery room.

2. Infant usually placed in radiant warmer and restrained.

3. Resuscitative equipment and oxygen should be available.

4. Blood should be no more than twenty-four hours old and warmed.

5. Stomach contents are aspirated to prevent vomiting.

6. Baseline vital signs are obtained and checked every fifteen to thirty minutes.

7. Transfusion is usually given via umbilical catheter.

8. Exchange usually done by alternately withdrawing and adding—maximum 500 ml. Rh-negative blood is given.

9. Usually takes forty-five to sixty minutes.

10. After transfusion:

a. Observe for bleeding from the umbilical cord.

b. Observe vital signs frequently.

c. Maintain warmth.

d. Administer oxygen if needed.

e. Observe for signs of hypoglycemia, sepsis, cardiac arrest, or irregularities.

f. Careful handling.

g. Resume feedings after four to six hours.

h. Keep umbilical cord moist in case other transfusions are indicated.

Hemolytic Disease (Erythroblastosis Fetalis)

Definition: Hemolysis is the destruction of red blood cells that results from an antigen-antibody reaction.

Etiology

A. Rh incompatibility—Rh antigens from the baby's blood enter the maternal bloodstream through the placenta. The mother's blood does not contain Rh factor, so she produces anti-Rh antibodies. These antibodies are harmless to the mother but attach to the erythrocytes in the fetus and cause hemolysis.

1. RhoGam, human Rh$_O$ (D) immune globulin, should be given during first 72 hours after delivery if Rh-negative mother delivers Rh-positive fetus but remains unsensitized.

2. Sensitization rare with first pregnancy.

3. Diagnosis of Rh incompatibility.

a. Begins in pregnancy, with discoveries of antibodies in an Rh-negative mother's blood by means of indirect Coombs' test.

b. Titration is used to determine the extent to which antibodies are present.

c. Spectrophotometric analysis of amniotic fluid for bilirubin determines the severity of the disease—the higher the bilirubin content, the more severe the disease.

d. Testing of cord blood—direct Coombs' test—determines the presence of maternal antibodies attached to baby's cells.

B. ABO incompatibility—usually less severe.

Clinical Manifestations

A. Anemia—caused by destruction of red blood cells.

B. Jaundice—develops rapidly after birth, before 24 hours.

C. Edema—usually seen in stillborn infants or those who die shortly after birth, most likely due to cardiac failure.

Treatment

A. Immunization against hemolytic disease with Rho-Gam.

B. Severe—exchange transfusion after birth or intra-uterine transfusion.

Sepsis in the Neonate

Predisposing Factors

A. Prolonged rupture of membranes—over twenty-four hours.

B. Long difficult labor or prolonged resuscitation after birth.

C. Maternal infection.

D. Aspiration of amniotic fluids or vaginal secretions during birth.

E. Aspiration of formula after birth.

F. Infection within nursery or among nursery personnel—nosocomial.

G. Usually appears within the first forty-eight hours after birth.

H. May quickly lead to septicemia or meningitis if not treated promptly.

Clinical Manifestations

A. May be vague.

B. May feed poorly and have poor sucking reflex.

C. May regurgitate feedings.

D. May have diarrhea.

E. Periods of apnea or irregular respirations.

F. Jaundice may appear.

G. May have a low-grade fever or subnormal temperature.

H. Lethargy.

I. Irritability.

Diagnosis

A. Aspiration of gastric contents—examined for polymorphonuclear cells.

B. Cultures taken of blood, urine, spinal fluids, throat, skin lesions, and the umbilical area.

Nursing Management

A. Antibiotics—observe carefully for toxicity because of liver and kidney immaturity.

B. Maintain warmth—usually in an isolette.

C. Administer oxygen as necessary.

D. I.V. fluids may be ordered; otherwise, give fluids as ordered to maintain hydration, electrolytes, and calories.

E. Maintain isolation and proper hand washing techniques.

F. Check respiratory apical pulse frequently.

G. Stimulate if apnea is present by gently rubbing chest or foot.

H. Maintain intake and output.

I. Check temperature.

J. Weigh daily.

K. Observe for signs of jaundice.

L. Keep parents informed of infant's progress.

M. Allow parents to visit child as much as possible.

N. Talk to infant and gently stroke him while giving care.

Infants of Diabetic Mothers

General Considerations

A. May be delivered early to prevent intrauterine death—usually delivered after thirty-six weeks.

B. Often delivered by cesarean section.

C. Children with diabetic mothers have a higher incidence of congenital anomalies than the general population.

D. High incidence of hypoglycemia, respiratory distress, hypocalcemia, and hyperbilirubinemia.

Clinical Manifestations

A. Baby is usually excessive in size and weight due to excess fat and glycogen in tissues.
   1. High blood sugar levels in mother cross the placenta and enter the baby's bloodstream, elevating blood sugar levels.
   2. High blood sugar stimulates infant's metabolic system to store glycogen and fat and increase the production of insulin.

B. May have puffy appearance in face and cheeks.

C. Enlarged heart, liver, and spleen.

D. Lethargy.

E. Irregular respiration.

Nursing Management

A. Observe for signs of hypoglycemia—twitching, difficulty feeding, lethargy, apnea, seizures, and cyanosis.

B. Observe for signs of respiratory distress—tachypnea, cyanosis, retractions, grunting, nasal flaring.

C. Care is the same as for a premature infant.

D. Initiate feedings with sterile water or glucose water within two to four hours after birth, as ordered by physician.

Hypoglycemia

Predisposing Factors

A. Placental dysfunction.

B. Diabetes in mother.

C. Cold stress.

D. Renal disease, cardiac disease, preeclampsia or chronic infection in the mother.

E. Small for gestational age infants.

F. Postterm infant.

G. Asphyxia at birth.

H. Infection in infant or any condition that stresses the metabolic rate and increases the need for glucose.

Clinical Manifestations

A. Cyanosis.

B. Increased respiratory rate.

C. Twitching or jitteriness, convulsions.

D. Lethargy and poor muscle tone.

E. Unstable temperature.

F. Shrill cry.

G. Hunger, but has feeding problems.

H. Apneic periods.

Diagnosis

A. Blood sugar values—normal 45-100/100 ml. of blood. Usually around 60-75/100 ml.
   1. Term infant—30/40 mg./100 ml. blood.
   2. Preterm—20 mg./100 ml. blood.

B. Screening may be done with special testing sticks, with laboratory studies done as a follow-up.

Nursing Management

A. Prevention through early feedings.

B. Administration of glucose orally or I.V., depending upon baby's condition.

C. Close monitoring of blood sugar values every one to two hours.

D. Care as for other high risk infants.

Infant Born to Mother with Drug Addiction

General Considerations

A. There is a direct relationship between the duration of the maternal addiction and dosage and the severity of symptoms in the infant.

B. Heroin and morphine addiction common offenders.

C. Infants are usually of low birth weight.

D. Withdrawal symptoms usually occur in infants within forty-eight to seventy-two hours.

Clinical Manifestations

A. Irritability, tremors, hyperactivity and hypertonicity.

B. Vomiting.

C. High-pitched cry.

D. Sneezing—nasal stuffiness.

E. Respiratory distress.

F. Fever.

G. Diarrhea.

H. Excess sweating.

I. Feeding problems—hungry but poor feeder, regurgitation.

J. Sucking of fist.

K. Convulsions—rare.

Nursing Management

A. Monitor respiratory and cardiac rates every thirty minutes and p.r.n.

B. Take temperature every four to eight hours and p.r.n.

C. Maintain warmth and swaddle infant in blanket.

D. Reduce external stimuli and handle infant infrequently.

E. Hold firmly and close to body during feedings and when giving care.

F. Pad sides of crib to protect infant from injury.

G. Administer small, frequent feedings as ordered.

H. Suction if necessary.

I. Careful skin care—cleanse buttocks and anal area carefully.

J. Measure intake and output.

K. Keep mother informed of infant's progress.

L. Promote mother's interest in infant.

M. Administer medications as ordered—usually paragoric or phenobarbital.

Conditions of the Female Reproductive Tract

Menstruation

Definition: Menstruation is the sloughing off of the endometrium, which occurs at regular monthly intervals if conception fails to take place. The discharge consists of blood, mucus, and cells, and it usually lasts for four to five days.

A. Menarche—onset of menstruation—usually occurs between the ages of eleven and fourteen.

B. Discomforts associated with menstruation.
   1. Breast tenderness and feeling of fullness.
   2. Tendency toward fatigue.
   3. Temperament and mood changes—because of hormonal influence, levels of estrogen and progesterone drop sharply.
   4. Discomfort in pelvic area, lower back, and legs.
   5. Retained fluids and weight gain.

C. Abnormalities of menstruation.

   1. Dysmenorrhea—painful menstruation.
      a. May be caused by psychological factors: tension, anxiety, preconditioning (menstruation is a "curse" or should be painful).
      b. Physical examination is usually done to rule out organic causes.
      c. Treatment.
         (1) Oral contraceptives—produce anovulatory cycle.
         (2) Mild analgesics such as aspirin.
         (3) Urge patient to carry on normal activities, to occupy her mind.
         (4) Dysmenorrhea may subside after childbearing.

   2. Amenorrhea—absence of menstrual flow.
      a. Primary—over the age of seventeen and menstruation has not begun.
         (1) Complete physical necessary to rule out abnormalities.
         (2) Treatment aimed at correction of underlying condition.
      b. Secondary—occurs after menarche—does not include pregnancy and lactation.
         (1) Causes include psychological upsets or endocrine conditions.
         (2) Evaluation and treatment by physician is necessary.

   3. Menorrhagia—excessive menstrual bleeding. May be due to endocrine disturbance, tumors, or inflammatory conditions of the uterus.

   4. Metrorrhagia—the bleeding between periods. Symptom of disease process, benign tumors, or cancer.

D. Role of the nurse.
   1. Education about the physiology of normal menstruation—there are many myths and cultural beliefs associated with menstruation.
   2. Education about abnormal conditions associated with menstruation—absence of, bleeding between, etc.
   3. Education related to normal hygiene during menstruation.
      a. Importance of cleanliness.
      b. Use of perineal pads and tampons.
      c. Normal activities may be continued.

Menopause

Definition: Menopause is the cessation of menstruation caused by physiologic factors; ovulation no longer occurs. Menopause usually occurs between the ages of forty to fifty.

A. Mechanisms in menopause.
   1. Ovaries lose the ability to respond to pituitary stimulation and normal ovarian function ceases.
      a. Gradual change due to alteration in hormone production.
         (1) Failure to ovulate.
         (2) Monthly flow becomes smaller, irregular, and gradually ceases.
      b. Menopause is accompanied by changes in reproductive organs—the vagina gradually becomes smaller; uterus, bladder, rectum, and supporting structures lose tone, leading to uterine prolapse, rectocele, and cystocele.
   2. Atherosclerosis and osteoporosis are more likely to develop at this time.

B. Signs and symptoms.
   1. Varies with individual—mild to severe.
   2. May be accompanied by psychological symptoms—feelings of loss, children grown, aging process occurring.
   3. May be accompanied by hot flashes and nervous symptoms, such as headache, depression, insomnia, weakness, and dizziness.

C. Treatment.
   1. Estrogen therapy—usually given on cyclic basis: one pill daily except for five days during the month when medication is not taken.

2. Treatment for psychological problems, if present.

Gynecological Examination

A. Pelvic exam.
   1. Inspection of external genitalia for signs of inflammation, bleeding, discharge, and epithelial cell changes.
   2. Speculum may be inserted for visualization of vagina and cervix.
   3. Bimanual examination is done—gloved fingers of one hand inserted into vagina while abdomen palpated with other hand.
   4. Rectal exam.
B. Breast exam may also be done when woman comes in for pelvic examination.
C. Papanicolaou smear.
   1. Diagnosis for cervical cancer.
   2. Vaginal secretions and secretions from posterior fornix are swabbed and smeared on a glass slide.
   3. Pathological classifications.
      a. Class I—no abnormal or atypical cells present.
      b. Class II—atypical or abnormal cells present but no malignancy found; repeat pap smear and follow-up if necessary.
      c. Class III—cytology, suggestive of malignancy; additional procedures indicated (biopsy, D and C).
      d. Class IV—cytology, strongly suggestive of malignancy; additional procedures indicated (biopsy, D and C).
      e. Class V—cytology conclusive of malignancy.

Conditions of the Vulva

Vulvitis

Definition: Vulvitis is an inflammation of the vulva, which usually occurs in conjunction with other conditions such as vaginal infections and venereal disease

A. Clinical manifestations.
   1. Burning pain during urination.
   2. Itching.
   3. Red and inflamed genitalia.
   4. Discharge.
B. Treatment.

1. Careful evaluation for related conditions, psychological factors, endocrine disorders, and reactions to chemical substances that the patient may be using.
2. Soothing compresses, colloidal baths.
3. Medicated creams.
4. Sedation with antihistamines.

Vaginal Conditions

Vaginal Infections

A. Vagina normally protected from infection by acidic environment.
B. Leukorrhea—whitish vaginal discharge—normal in small amounts at ovulation and prior to menstruation.
C. Trichomoniasis vaginalis—overgrowth of protozoan normally present in vaginal tract—normal pH altered and overgrowth occurs.
D. Monoliasis—fungal infection caused by Candida albicans.
   1. Thrives in carbohydrate-rich environment—common in poorly controlled diabetes.
   2. Found in patients on antibiotic or steroid therapy, which reduces protective organisms normally present.
E. Treatment—medications and vaginal inserts as prescribed.

Conditions of Ovaries and Pelvic Cavity

Endometriosis

Definition: Endometriosis is the abnormal growth of endometrial tissue outside the uterine cavity and is a common cause of infertility.

A. Etiology—several theories.
   1. Embryonic tissue that remains dormant until ovarian stimulation after menarche.
   2. Endometrial tissue transported from the uterine cavity through the fallopian tubes during menstruation.
   3. Endometrial tissue transported by lymphatic tissue during menstruation.
   4. Accidental transfer of endometrial tissue to pelvic cavity during surgery.
B. Clinical manifestations.
   1. Lower abdominal and pelvic pain during menstruation due to distention of involved tissue and surrounding area by blood—symptoms are acute during menstruation.

2. Dysmenorrhea—usually steady and severe.
3. Abnormal uterine bleeding.
4. Pain during intercourse.
5. Back and rectal pain.

C. Treatment.
1. Pregnancy—may delay growth of lesions—symptoms usually recur after pregnancy.
2. Hormone therapy with oral contraceptives—usually eliminates menstrual pain and controls endometrial growth.
3. Surgical intervention; total hysterectomy may be indicated.

Pelvic Inflammatory Disease (P.I.D.)

Definition: Pelvic inflammatory disease is an inflammatory condition of the pelvic cavity that may involve ovaries, fallopian tubes, vascular system, or pelvic peritoneum.

A. Etiology.
1. Staphylococcus or streptococcus.
2. Venereal disease.
3. Tubercle bacilli.

B. Clinical manifestations.
1. Elevated temperature.
2. Nausea and vomiting.
3. Abdominal and low back pain.
4. Purulent, foul-smelling vaginal discharge.
5. Leukocytosis.

C. Treatment.
1. Control the spread of infection.
2. Antibiotic therapy.
3. Semi-Fowler's position—dependent drainage.
4. Heat to abdomen for comfort.
5. Warm douches to improve circulation.

D. Nursing management.
1. Take vital signs every four hours and record.
2. Administer antibiotics, douches, and abdominal heat as ordered.
3. Note nature and amount of vaginal discharge.
4. Avoid use of tampons and urinary catheterization to prevent the spread of infection.
5. Promote good nutrition and fluid intake.

Conditions of the Uterus

Displacements

A. Retroversion and retroflexion: backward displacement of the uterus.
1. May cause difficulty in becoming pregnant.
2. Treatment—moving the uterus to the normal position by shortening its ligaments.

B. Prolapse.
1. Weakening of uterine supports causes the uterus to slip down into the vaginal canal; the uterus may even appear outside the vaginal orifice.
2. Prolapse may cause urinary incontinence or retention.
3. Treatment.
   a. Pessary: instrument that keeps the uterus in place by exerting pressure on ligaments—usually used in patients of advanced age.
   b. Surgery to reposition uterus and shorten ligaments; or hysterectomy.

Fibroid Tumors

A. Fibroid tumors are benign.
B. Occur in 20 to 30 percent of all women between the ages of twenty-five to forty.
C. Symptoms include menorrhagia, back pain, urinary difficulty, and constipation.
D. Fibroid tumors may cause sterility.
E. Treatment.
1. Removal of tumors, if they are small.
2. Hysterectomy is performed when there are large tumors.

Therapeutic Abortion

General Considerations

A. Legality.
1. Abortion is now legal in all states, as the result of a Supreme Court decision in January 1973.
2. It is regulated in the following manner. First trimester—decision between patient and physician; second trimester—decision between patient and physician (state may regulate who performs the abortion and where it can be done); third trimester—states may regulate and prohibit abortion except to preserve the health or life of the mother.

B. Indications.
   1. Medical—psychiatric conditions or diseases such as chronic hypertension, nephritis, severe diabetes, cancer, or acute infection such as rubella; possible genetic defects in the infant or severe erythroblastosis fetalis.
   2. Nonmedical—socio-economic reasons, unmarried, financial burden, too young to care for infant.
C. Preparation of the individual.
   1. Advise patient of available sources of abortion.
   2. Inform patient as to what to expect from the abortion procedure.
   3. Provide emotional support during decision-making period.
   4. Maintain an open, nonjudgmental atmosphere, in which the individual may express concerns or guilt.
   5. Encourage and support the individual once the decision is made and after surgery.
   6. Give information about contraceptives.
D. Complications and effects.
   1. Abortion should be performed before the twelfth week, if possible, because complications and risks are lower during this time.
   2. Complications.
      a. Infection.
      b. Bleeding.
      c. Sterility.
      d. Uterine perforation.

Techniques

A. First trimester.
   1. Dilatation and curettage (D & C).
      a. Cervical canal is dilated with instruments of increasingly large diameter.
      b. Fetus and accessory structure is removed with forceps.
      c. Endometrium is scraped with curette to assure that all products of conception are removed.
      d. Process usually takes fifteen to twenty minutes.
   2. Vacuum aspirator.
      a. Hose-linked curette is inserted into dilated cervix.
      b. Hose is attached to suction.
      c. The vacuum aspirator lessens the chance of uterine perforation, reduces blood loss, and reduces the time of the procedure.
B. Second trimester abortion.
   1. Hysterotomy.
      a. Incision is made through abdominal wall into uterus.
      b. Procedure is usually performed between the fourteenth and sixteenth week in pregnancy.
      c. Products of conception are removed with forceps.
      d. Uterine cavity is curetted.
      e. Tubal ligation may be done at same time.
      f. Patient usually requires several days of hospitalization.
      g. Operation requires general or spinal anesthesia.
   2. Intraamniotic injection or amniocentesis abortion.
      a. Performed after the fourteenth to sixteenth week of pregnancy.
      b. From 50–200 ml. of amniotic fluid are removed from the amniotic cavity and replaced with hypertonic of 20–50 percent saline installed through gravity drip over a period of forty-five to sixty minutes.
      c. Increased osmotic pressure of the amniotic fluid causes the death of the fetus.
      d. Uterine contractions usually begin in about twelve hours and the products of conception are expelled in twenty-four to thirty hours.
      e. Oxytocic drugs may be given if contractions do not begin.
      f. Complications.
         (1) Infusion of hypertonic saline solution into uterus.
         (2) Infection.
         (3) Disseminated intravascular coagulation disease may develop during procedure.
         (4) Hemorrhage.
   3. Prostaglandins.
      a. These hormone-like acids cause abortion by stimulating the uterus to contract.
      b. They may be administered I.V. into the uterine cavity through the cervical canal, into the posterior fornix of the vagina, or

after twelve weeks into the amniotic cavity. The I.V. method is least effective and has many possible side effects.

C. Nursing management.
1. Administration of preoperative medications.
2. Ensure that patient understands the procedure.
3. Offer emotional support and let patient express feelings.
4. Monitor I.V.
5. Check vital signs postoperatively.
6. Check for excessive bleeding.
7. Administer pain medications as ordered.
8. Instruct patient to watch for signs of excessive bleeding (more than a normal menstrual period) and infection (elevated temperature, foul-smelling discharge, persistent abdominal pain).
9. Administer oxytocic drug as ordered.
10. Administer RhoGAM as ordered for an Rh-negative patient.
11. Offer fluids as tolerated, after vital signs are stable and patient is alert and responsive.

Control of Parenthood

Influences on Parenthood

A. Tendency toward smaller families.
B. Career-oriented women who limit family size or who do not want children.
C. Early sexual experimentation, necessitating sexual education, contraceptive information.
D. Tendency toward postponement of children.
1. To complete education.
2. Economic factors.
E. High divorce rates.
F. Alternate family designs.
1. Single parenthood.
2. Communal family.

General Concepts Related to Family Planning

A. General concepts.
1. Dealing with individuals with particular ideas regarding contraception.
2. No perfect method of birth control.
3. Method must be suited to individual.

4. Individuals involved must be thoroughly counseled on all available methods and how they work—including advantages and disadvantages. This includes not only female but also sexual partner (if available).
5. Once a method is chosen both parties should be thoroughly instructed in its use and how it works.
6. Individuals involved must be motivated to succeed.

B. Effectiveness depends upon:
1. Method chosen.
2. Degree to which couple follow prescribed regime.
3. Thorough understanding of method.
4. Motivation on part of individuals concerned.

Methods

A. Rhythm.
1. Based upon three principles:
   a. Ovulation usually occurs fourteen days before period begins.
   b. An ovum may be fertilized twelve to twenty-four hours after release from ovary.
   c. Sperm usually survives no longer than twenty-four hours in the uterine environment.
2. Based on these principles, if coitus is avoided during the fertile period, pregnancy should not occur.

B. Chemical agent.
1. Agent acts by killing or paralyzing the sperm.
2. Combined with a compound which coats the vagina, agent acts as a vehicle for spermicide as well as a mechanical barrier through which sperm cannot swim.
3. Available forms are foams, creams or jellies.

C. Diaphragm.
1. Functions by blocking external os and closing access to cervical canal by sperm. It is a mechanical barrier.
2. Must be used in conjunction with vaginal cream or jelly to be effective.

D. Condom.
1. Acts as a mechanical barrier by collecting sperm and not allowing contact with vaginal area.
2. It is relatively inexpensive and may be easily purchased in a drugstore.

E. Coitus interruptus.
   1. Early form of contraception.
   2. Requires withdrawal of penis before ejaculation.
F. Oral contraceptives.
   1. Contraceptive effect occurs by:
      a. Artificially raising the blood levels of estrogen and progesterone, thereby preventing the release of F.S.H. from the anterior pituitary. Without F.S.H. the follicle does not mature and ovulation fails to take place.
      b. Endometrial changes.
      c. Alteration in cervical mucus making it hostile to sperm.
      d. Altered tubal function.
   2. Types of birth control "pills."
      a. Combined—contain both estrogen and progesterone.
      b. Sequential (mimics normal hormonal cycle)—estrogen given alone 15-16 days, followed by combination of estrogen and progestin for the next five days.
   3. Minor side effects—usually diminish within a few months.
      a. Breast fullness and tenderness.
      b. Edema, weight gain.
      c. Nausea and vomiting.
      d. Chloasma.
      e. Breakthrough bleeding.
   4. More serious side effects.
      a. Thrombophlebitis.
      b. Pulmonary embolism.
      c. Hypertension.
G. Intrauterine devices.
   1. Methods of action—not completely clear.
      a. More rapid transport of ovum through tube reaching endometrium before it is "ready" for implantation.
      b. IUD may cause substances to accumulate in uterus and interfere with implantation.
      c. IUD may stimulate production of cellular exudate which interferes with the ability of sperm to migrate to fallopian tubes.
   2. Usually made of soft plastic or nickel-chromium alloy.
   3. There are many types of devices available on market.
   4. Complications.
      a. Perforation of uterus.
      b. Infection.
      c. Spotting between periods.
      d. Heavy menstrual flow or prolonged flow.
      e. Cramping during menstruation.

Sterilization

A. General considerations.
   1. Should be considered permanent—no guarantee fertility can be restored.
   2. Requires written consent of responsible, fully-informed individual.
B. Male sterilization—vasectomy—severing of sperm duct from each testicle making it impossible for sperm to pass from testes.
C. Female sterilization—may be accomplished by the removal of the uterus and the ovaries, or the destruction of ovum-conducting ability of fallopian tubes.

Role of Nurse in Family Planning

A. Education of client in various methods available, their effectiveness and side effects.
B. Help clients explore their feelings regarding birth control and what they find acceptable and not acceptable.
C. Create open relaxed atmosphere allowing clients to express concerns and feelings about birth control.
D. Thorough explanation of how method works and client's role such as insertion or checking, etc.
E. Instruction of client in possible complications and side effects.

Appendix 1. Common Drugs in Obstetrics and Gynecology

Name of Drug and Action	Uses and Side Effects	Nursing Implications
Oxytocin, Syntocinon Pitocin Classification—oxytocic Produces rhythmic contractions of uterine musculature Dosage: varies with method and purpose of administration. I.V.—5-10 USP units in 500 or 1,000 ml. 5% dextrose in VS infused at rate 0.5-0.75 ml./min. Calibrated pump 2.5 USP units in 50 ml. 5% D/W. Start at 1 mic/min. and increase as necessary	Used to induce labor, constrict uterus, and decrease hemorrhage after delivery and postabortion Stimulates contractile tissue in lactating breast to eject milk Side effects: water intoxication; allergic reactions; death due to uterine rupture; pelvic hematomas; bradycardia	Observe for signs of sensitivity and overdose Monitor strength and duration of uterine contractions Check FHT every 15 minutes and p.r.n. Take P & BP every hour
Methergine Classification—oxytocic Produces constrictive effects on smooth muscle of uterus (more prolonged constrictive effects as compared to rhythmic effects of oxytocin or ergotrate); also has generalized vasoconstrictive effect Usual I.M. dose 0.2 mg. may be repeated in 2-4 hrs; usual oral dose 0.2 mg. 3-4 x a day for 2 days	Used primarily after delivery to produce firm uterine contractions and decrease uterine bleeding May be used to prevent postabortal hemorrhage Side effects include nausea, vomiting, dizziness, increased BP, dyspnea, and chest pain	Check BP and pulse before administration of medication and check vital signs frequently after administration Injectable form deteriorates rapidly when exposed to lights and heat—do not use if discoloration occurs
Vasodilan (isoxsuprine) Classification—vasodilator—pure beta drug Relaxing effects on circulatory and uterine smooth muscle Usual oral maintenance dose 10-20 mg.; tablets 3-4 times daily. I.M. dosage 10-20 mg. q. 2-3 hrs. Continue for 24 hrs.	Treatment of premature labor or during labor when contractions are unusually frequent and not coordinated. Most effective when given in early latent phase of labor; rarely stops active labor Side effects include nausea, vomiting, dizziness, transient hypotension and tachycardia	Take BP & P frequently Observe for signs of tachycardia and hypotension

Name of Drug and Action	Uses and Side Effects	Nursing Implications
Ethyl alcohol Relaxing effects on smooth muscles of uterus. Contractions decrease or cease Usual I.V. dose—initial dose 15 ml./kg./hr; maintenance dose 1.5 ml./kg./hr. 6-10 hrs.	Treatment of premature labor Side effects include signs of intoxication and loss of insight, discrimination, and judgment	Observe for vomiting and aspiration Check vital signs frequently
Deozoxide Classification—antihypertensive Produces dilatation of peripheral arterioles reducing systolic and diastolic pressures Usual dosage: 300 mg. I.V. in 10 seconds	Treatment of hypertension associated with toxemia of pregnancy Side effects include hypoglycemia	Observe for signs of hypoglycemia because medication has hyperglycemic effects Monitor BP & P closely in order to assess effects of drug
Magnesium sulfate Depressive effects on central nervous system, and smooth, skeletal, and cardiac muscle Produces peripheral vasodilation Given I.V. in preeclampsia and eclampsia; dosage varies Usual dosage: initial dosage 4 gm. in 250 ml. 5% D/W followed by 4-5 gm. I.M. in each buttock at 4 hr. intervals; usual range 1-10 gm. daily	Used in treatments of hypertension associated with toxemia of pregnancy; also has anticonvulsive effects; also effective to counteract uterine tetany after large doses of oxytocin Side effects include extreme thirst, hypotension, flaccidity, circulatory collapse, depression of CNS and cardiac system	Observe carefully for signs of magnesium toxicity: extreme thirst, feeling hot all over; loss of patellar reflex Monitor BP & P closely in order to assess effect of drug. Never leave patient alone Patellar reflex should be checked before each dose Check respiration (16 per min) and urine output before each dose
Pergonal Classification—hormone, purified preparation of gonadotrophic hormones Promotes follicular growth and maturation in women with secondary anovulation; must be given with human chorionic gonadotrophin to induce ovulation Usual dosage: 75 IU of FSH and 75 IU of LH I.M. daily for 9-12 days, followed by 10,000 U of HCG I.M. one day after last dose	Treatment of sterility due to defective luteal function Side effects include nausea, vomiting, diarrhea, fever, possible multiple births	Inform patient of complications and hazards of multiple births

Name of Drug and Action	Uses and Side Effects	Nursing Implications
Estrogen preparations Classification—hormones Development and maintenance of sexual characteristics through-out adult life Common preparations Estradiol, Diethylstilbestrol, Tace, Premarin Dosage varies, depends upon purpose for giving	Given to replace deficiencies, to control conception, relieve breast engorgement when lactation is to be suppressed Side effects include nausea, vomiting, diarrhea, skin rash, edema	Encourage follow-up visits to physician
Progesterone preparations Classification—hormones Normal functions—preparation and maintenance of edometrium for pregnancy. Suppresses ovulation and pregnancy and decreases uterine irritability Dosage varies	Given to control conception, amenorrhea, abnormal uterine bleeding, threatened abortion Side effects include GI symptoms, dizziness, headache, allergic reactions	Encourage follow-up visits to physician
Demerol Classification—synthetic narcotic analgesic Onset of action 15 min. peaks 1 hr. depresses CNS probably at both cortical and subcortical levels Dosage: 25–50 mg. I.M. every 3–4 hr. p.r.n. relief of postdelivery pain	Produces analgesia in labor, postoperative relief of pain Side effects include dizziness, nausea, vomiting, dry mouth, sweating, decrease in BP	Evaluate carefully progress of labor; if given too late in labor, infant may be depressed Check for level of consciousness before administration Observe for nausea and vomiting
Morphine Classification—analgesic Combination of depressive and stimulative effects on CNS and smooth muscles of gut Raises pain threshold and produces euphoria and sedation Usual dose: 3–10 mg. I.M. during labor; postoperative—10 mg.	Produces analgesia during labor, relief of postoperative pain. Side effects include nausea, vomiting, constipation, depression of respiratory center and cough, allergic reactions such as urticaria	Check level of consciousness and respiratory rate before administration Careful evaluation of progress of labor; if given too late, infant may be depressed

Name of Drug and Action	Uses and Side Effects	Nursing Implications
Nisentil Classification—synthetic analgesic Action similar to Demerol and morphine, but acts more quickly than Demerol and over a shorter period of time Dosage: 20-40-60 subcutaneous or I.M. every 2-4 hrs.	Analgesia during labor; relief of pain after abortion Side effects include nausea, vomiting, depression of respiratory center	Monitor progress of labor carefully; if given too late in labor, infant may be depressed Check respiratory rate before administration
Nalline Hydrochloride, Narcan, Lorfan Classification—narcotic antagonists Acts as an antagonist to morphine and Demerol and related analgesics	Treatment of respiratory depression in newborn when narcotic effect has not worn off in the mother prior to delivery Nalline may be given to the mother shortly prior to delivery to prevent respiratory depression due to analgesic side effects Side effects include drowsiness, lethargy, sweating	Check respiratory rate and color and cardiac rate of infant to see if medication is having desired effect
Diuril Classification—diuretic Brings about diminished reabsorption of sodium and chlorides Results in increased urinary output; potassium may also be excreted Usual dosage: 500 mg. IGM one or two times daily	Diminish fluid retention in toxemia of pregnancy Side effects include allergic reactions, nausea, weakness, dizziness, and muscle cramps	Give drug early in day to avoid disturbing sleep Encourage addition of potassium foods in diet (orange juice) to avoid depletion
Phenobarbital Classification—barbiturate Slow acting in low doses—depression of sensory functions. In higher doses depression of motor functions Usual dosage for sedative effect: range 15-50 mg. 3-4 times daily	Sedative and anticonvulsive effects in toxemia of pregnancy Side effects include listlessness, depression, nausea, skin rash, restlessness, emotional disturbances	Check level of consciousness and responsiveness before administration

Appendix 2. Drugs Adversely Affecting the Human Fetus

Drugs	Adverse Effect	Comments
Analgesics		
Heroin and morphine	Respiratory depression; neonatal death; addiction	Near term Fairly well documented
Salicylates	Neonatal bleeding; coagulation defects	Near term
Anesthetics		
Mepivacaine	Fetal bradycardia; neonatal depression	Near term More studies needed
Antibacterials		
Chloramphenicol	"Gray syndrome" and death	Near term Fairly well documented
Nitrofurantoin	Hemolysis	Near term More studies needed
Novobiocin	Hyperbilirubinemia	Near term More studies needed
Streptomycin	8th nerve damage; hearing loss; multiple skeletal anomalies	Throughout pregnancy Debatable, more studies needed
Sulfonamides (long acting)	Hyperbilirubinemia and kernicterus	Near term Fairly well documented
Tetracyclines	Inhibition of bone growth; discoloration of teeth	2nd and 3rd trimesters Fairly well documented
Anticarcinogens		
Amethopterin	Cleft palate; abortion	1st trimester Fairly well documented
Aminopterin	Cleft palate; abortion	1st trimester Known teratogen
Cyclophosphamide	Severe stunting; fetal death; extremity defects	1st trimester More studies needed
Anticoagulants		
Warfarin	Fetal death; hemorrhage	Throughout pregnancy More studies needed
Antidiabetics		
Chlorpropamide	Prolonged neonatal hypoglycemia	Throughout pregnancy More evidence needed before implication

Drugs	Adverse Effect	Comments
Tolbutamide	Congenital anomalies	Throughout pregnancy One reported case only; evidence lacking
Antimalarials Quinine	Deafness	More studies needed
Anti-Mitotic Agents Podophyllum	Fetal resorption; multiple deformities	More studies needed
Anti-Thyroid Agents Methimazole	Goiter and mental retardation	From 14th week on Fairly well documented
Potassium Iodide	Goiter and mental retardation	From 14th week on Fairly well documented
Prophylthiouracil	Goiter and mental retardation	From 14th week on Fairly well documented
Radioactive Iodine	Congenital hypothyroidism	From 14th week on Fairly well documented
Depressants Phenobarbital	Neonatal bleeding; increased rate of neonatal drug metabolism	In excessive amounts
Reserpine	Nasal block	Near term One report only More studies needed
Thalidomide	Phocomelia; hearing defect	28th–42nd day Known teratogen
Diuretics Ammonium chloride	Acidosis	
Thiazides (Hydrochlorothiazide) (Chlorothiazide) (Methyclothiazide)	Thrombocytopenia; neonatal death	Latter part of pregnancy One report only; evidence lacking
Stimulants Dextroamphetamine	Transposition of great vessels	One report only More evidence needed
Phenmetrazine	Skeletal and visceral anomalies	4th–12th week One report only More evidence needed

Drugs	Adverse Effect	Comments
Sex Steroids		
Androgens, estrogens and oral progestogens	Masculinization and labial fusion (early in pregnancy); clitoris enlargement (later in pregnancy)	Fairly well documented
Miscellaneous		
Acetophenetidin	Methemoglobinemia	More studies needed
Cholinesterase Inhibitors	Transient muscular weakness	Throughout pregnancy More studies needed
Hexamethonium Bromide	Neonatal ileus and death	Throughout pregnancy More studies needed
Iophenoxic Acid	Elevation of serum protein-bound iodine	
Isonicotinic Acid Hydrazide (INH)	Retarded psychomotor activity	More studies needed
Lysergic Acid Diethylamide (LSD)	Chromosomal damage; stunted offspring	1st trimester More studies needed
Nicotine and Smoking	Small babies	Throughout pregnancy More studies needed
Vitamin A	Congenital anomalies; cleft palate; eye damage, syndactyly	Throughout pregnancy In large doses only
Vitamin D	Excessive blood calcium; mental retardation	Throughout pregnancy In large doses only
Vitamin K analogues	Hyperbilirubinemia; kernicterus	Near term In large doses

Excerpted from "Drugs Adversely Affecting the Human Fetus," 1971, Ross Laboratories, Columbus, Ohio.

Appendix 3. Recommended Daily Dietary Allowances for Pregnancy and Lactation

	Pregnancy		Lactation		Function	Sources
	14 to 18	Adult	14 to 18	Adult		
Calories	2400	2300	2600	2500	Meet increased nutritional needs as well as body maintenance.	All foods. Important to emphasize food values of foods and avoid empty calories.
Protein	78	76	68	66	Augment maternal tissues—bust, uterus, blood. Growth and development of placenta and fetal tissue. Constant repair and maintenance of maternal tissue.	All essential amino acids may be found in milk, meat, eggs, and cheeses. Other sources, though not complete protein by themselves: tofu, whole grains, legumes, nuts, peanut butter.
Iron	+ 18 mg	+ 18 mg	18 mg	18 mg	Essential constituent of hemoglobin. Part of various enzymes. Fetal development and storage, especially later part of pregnancy.	Good sources: liver, kidney, heart, cooked dry beans, lean pork and beef, dried fruits such as apricots, peaches, prunes, and raisins. Fair sources: spinach, mustard greens, eggs.
Calcium	1200 mg	1200 mg	1200 mg	1200 mg	Skeletal tissue. Bones; teeth. Blood coagulation. Neuromuscular irritability. Myocardial function. Fetal stores, especially last months.	Good sources: milk, cheese, ice cream, yogurt. Fair sources: broccoli, canned salmon with bones, dried beans, dark leafy vegetables.
Phosphorus	1200 mg	1200 mg	1200 mg	1200 mg	90 percent compounded with calcium. Rest distributed throughout cells—involved in energy production, building and repairing tissue, buffering.	Whole grain items: cereals, whole wheat bread, brown rice; milk.
Sodium	0.5 g	0.5 g	0.5 g	0.5 g	Metabolic activities. Fluid balance and acid-base balance. Cell permeability. Muscle irritability.	Table salt, meat, eggs, carrots, celery, beets, spinach, salted nuts, carbonated beverages.

	Pregnancy		Lactation		Function	Sources
	14 to 18	Adult	14 to 18	Adult		
Iodine	125 ug	125 ug	125 ug	125 ug	Necessary for health: mother and fetus; prevents goiter in mother; decreases chance of cretinism in infants.	Iodized table salt, cod liver oil.
Vita-min A	5000 Iu	5000 Iu	6000 Iu	6000 Iu	Tooth formation and skeletal growth. Cell growth and development. Integrity of epithelial tissue. Vision—light/dark adaptation. Fat metabolism.	Good sources: butter, egg yolk, fortified margarine, whole milk, cream, kidney, and liver. Fair sources: dark green and yellow vegetables such as sweet potatoes, pumpkins, mustard greens, collards, kale, bok choy, carrots, cantaloupe, apricots.
Ribo-flavin	1.7 mg	1.5 mg	1.9 mg	1.7 mg	Enzyme systems. Tissue functioning. Tissue oxygenation and respiration. Energy metabolism. Excreted in breast milk.	Good sources: kidney, liver, heart, milk. Fair sources: cheese, ice cream, dark leafy vegetables, lean meat, poultry.
Thia-mine	1.4 mg	1.3 mg	1.4 mg	1.3 mg	Carbohydrate metabolism. Normal appetite and digestion. Health of nervous system.	Good sources: enriched and whole grain products—bread and cereals, dried peas, beans, liver, heart, kidney, nuts, potatoes, lean pork. Fair sources: eggs, milk, poultry, fish, vegetables.
Niacin	16 mg	15 mg	18 mg	17 mg	Cell metabolism.	Good sources: fish, lean meat, poultry, liver, heart, peanuts, peanut butter. Fair sources: enriched and whole grain cereals and bread, milk, potatoes.
Folic acid B_{12}	4.0 mg	4.0 mg	4.0 mg	4.0 mg	Cell growth. Reproduction and formation of heme. Enzyme activities in production of protein. Deficiency results in megaloblastic anemia.	Dark green and leafy vegetables.

	Pregnancy		Lactation		Function	Sources
	14 to 18	Adult	14 to 18	Adult		
Pyri-doxine B₆	2.5 mg	2.5 mg	2.5 mg	2.5 mg	Essential coenzyme with amino acids. Deficiency may lead to hypochromic micro-cytic anemia.	Animal and vegetable protein such as meat, fish, beans, nuts and seeds, milk and milk products.
Vita-min D	400 Iu	400 Iu	400 Iu	400 Iu	Influences absorption, retention and utilization of calcium and phos-phorus. Formation of bones, teeth and other tissue.	Good sources: fortified milk, butter, egg yolk, liver, fish oils.
Vita-min C Ascorbic acid	60 mg	60 mg	80 mg	80 mg	Production of intracellular substances necessary for development and main-tenance of normal con-nective tissue in bones, cartilage and muscles. Role in metabolic processes involving protein and tissues. Increases absorption of iron.	Good sources: citrus fruits and juice, broccoli, cantaloupe, collards, mustard and turnip greens, peppers. Fair sources: asparagus, raw cabbage, other melons, spinach, prunes, tomatoes, canned or fresh chilis.

Source of daily requirements: *Nutrition During Pregnancy and Lactation.* California Department of Health, 1975.

Appendix 4. Nutritional Guidelines

A. Influences upon dietary habits and nutrition.
1. Food—many emotional connotations originating in infancy.
2. Eating habits influenced by:
   a. Emotional factors.
   b. Cultural factors.
   c. Religious beliefs.
   d. Nutritional information.
   e. Age—especially adolescent and aged.
   f. Physical health.
   g. Personal preferences.

B. Nutritional needs in pregnancy.
1. Influenced by above factors.
2. Must supply caloric and nutritional needs of mother as well as promote optimum fetal growth.
3. May be complicated by:
   a. Poor maternal nutrition before pregnancy.
   b. Medical complications prior to pregnancy (diabetes, anemia).
   c. Complications resulting from pregnancy (toxemia, anemia).
   d. Pica (cravings).

C. Weight gain in pregnancy.
1. Average weight gain recommended (even for obese patients)—24 pounds.
   a. 1st trimester—3 to 4 pounds.
   b. 2nd trimester—10 pounds.
   c. 3rd trimester—10 pounds.
2. Weight gain accounted by:
   a. Product of conception.

Fetus—average size	7.5 pounds
Placenta	1.5
Amniotic fluid	2
Uterus	2.5
Breast	1
Extracellular fluid	3
Blood volume	3
	20.5 pounds

   b. Rest of weight gain deposited as fat stores or fluid representing energy stored for lactation.

D. Revised daily food guide.
1. This revised daily guide meets R.D.A. standards for daily nutrients except for:
   a. Iron and folacin—cannot be ingested in sufficient quantities by dietary means. Must be supplemented during pregnancy.
   b. 400 additional calories needed to meet recommended allowances.
2. Protein intake includes both animal and vegetable protein.
   a. Vegetable protein may be omitted in those whose income will allow by increasing animal servings to three 3-oz. servings.
   b. One serving at least should be red meats.
3. Whole grain items are better choices than enriched breads and cereals. They contain more magnesium, zinc, folacin, and vitamin B_6.
4. At least two tablespoons of fat or oils should be consumed daily for vitamin E and essential fatty acids.

E. Special diets.
1. Adolescents.
   a. Have high proportion of low-birth-weight infants.
   b. Dietary habits often poor.
   c. Plan menu to include necessary items around foods they like.
   d. Stress balanced diet—avoid empty calories.
2. Low sodium.
   a. Presently sodium restriction is *deemphasized*.
   b. Sodium essential in maintaining increased body fluids needed for adequate placental flow, increased tissue requirements, and renal blood flow.
   c. If moderate salt intake is necessitated, avoid highly salted foods such as canned soups, potato chips, soda pop.
3. Weight control.
   a. Presently, weight loss in pregnancy is discouraged.
   b. Even obese patient should gain 24 pounds to insure adequate nutrition for fetal growth.

   c. Strict dieting may lead to ketosis which has proven harmful to fetal brain development.

   d. Stress careful dietary planning to include essential nutrients and avoid empty calories.

   e. Weight reduction program should begin *after* lactation only.

4. Vegetarians.

   a. Sound nutritional planning to include those combinations of foods which, when combined, include all essential amino acids.

5. Ethnic groups—counseling includes careful assessment of food preferences and economic status.

   a. Mexican-American—includes variety of meats, poultry, legumes, eggs. Meat and poultry boiled or fried. Also includes tortillas, tomatoes, green chili, cheese. Most popular fruits: oranges, apples, bananas. Inadequate intake of milk, green and yellow vegetables. May be excessive intake of empty calories.

   b. Blacks—includes protein sources, beef, pork, and chicken. Meat is usually fried. Also includes whole milk, ice cream and cheddar cheese, biscuits, cornbread, rice, greens, and sweet potatoes. Vegetables are boiled excessively. Inadequate intake of milk, vegetables, fruit, especially those high in vitamin C. Obesity is a common problem due to high intake of breads, rice, potatoes, fried foods, and empty calories.

   c. Chinese—includes many varieties of seafood, pork, poultry, legumes, eggs, and nuts. Rice is predominant grain product. Wide variety of vegetables are eaten. Fresh fruits are eaten. Major problem is inadequate intake of milk and milk products. Diet may be low in protein.

   d. Japanese—protein intake includes meat, fish, eggs, legumes, nuts, tofu, and eggs. Rice is major grain product. Fresh and canned fruit included in diet. Variety of vegetables are eaten. Major problem is inadequate milk consumption. Discourage use of refined rice or of washing rice before cooking.

   e. American Indian—favorite foods include acorn bread, salmon, deer meat, fried breads, berries. Diet mainly "Americanized." Major health problems: iron deficiency anemia, obesity, diabetes, alcoholism, and dental caries. Stress protein foods, milk products, vegetables, and fruits. Restrict use of sugar.

Review Questions

1. Baby Guthrie, an 8 lb. 6 oz. baby girl, was born at 8:15 A.M. in a normal, spontaneous birth. Apgar score was 9/9 and no abnormalities were noted. The cord was clamped and the baby was placed in a heated crib in the Trendelenburg position. The infant was dried thoroughly, banded, and silver nitrate one percent placed in both eyes and flushed. Baby Guthrie was then rewrapped and held by her parents before being brought to the nursery. The Apgar scoring is done on this infant

   A. To determine the sex of the baby.
   B. To appraise the infant for congenital anomalies.
   C. As an immediate appraisal of the infant's cardiac and respiratory status.
   D. As an immediate assessment of the infant's Rh status.

2. Baby Guthrie was given an Apgar score of 9 at sixty seconds after delivery because

   A. Her heart rate was over 100.
   B. She gave a good strong cry.
   C. She had active movement of her arms and legs.
   D. She demonstrated acrocyanosis of the hands and feet.

3. The infant is usually placed in a heated crib in the Trendelenburg position immediately after birth to

   A. Prevent loss of heat and facilitate drainage of mucus.
   B. Increase oxygen intake.
   C. Allow the parents to view the infant more closely.
   D. Place the infant in an environment similar to the uterus.

4. Silver nitrate one percent is inserted into the newborn's eyes to prevent

   A. Spirochete infection.
   B. Gonococcal infection.
   C. Toxaplasmosis.
   D. Thrush.

5. An injection of vitamin K was given to Baby Guthrie in the nursery. Vitamin K is given to

   A. Help conjugate bilirubin.
   B. Prevent Rh sensitization in the infant.
   C. Reduce the possibility of hemorrhage in the infant.
   D. Increase the infant's resistance to infection.

6. Baby Guthrie had a large caput succedaneum on her head. The mother is concerned and asks what the swelling is. You would tell her

   A. It is extravasion of blood into the tissue caused by trauma from delivery.
   B. It will take a couple of weeks to disappear on its own.
   C. The infant may suffer brain damage as a result of the caput.
   D. It is a swelling of the soft tissues of the scalp due to pressure on the cervix during dilatation.

7. The normal respiratory rate in the newborn is between

   A. 16 and 20.
   B. 60 and 80.
   C. 80 and 100.
   D. 30 and 50.

8. The normal apical pulse rate on the newborn is between

   A. 120 and 160.
   B. 60 and 80.
   C. 80 and 100.
   D. 180 and 200.

9. Baby Guthrie showed signs of jaundice and her lab value for bilirubin showed a total bilirubin of 15.0, direct bilirubin 1.7, and indirect bilirubin 13.3. The physician ordered continuous bile light and force fluids between feedings. Physiologic jaundice is due to

   A. Rh incompatibility with the mother.
   B. Presence of staphylococcus infection within the newborn.
   C. ABO incompatibility.
   D. Inability of the newborn to conjugate bilirubin.

10. An important principle to consider with an infant receiving phototherapy would be to

    A. Cover the eyes with eye patches to prevent retinal damage.
    B. Dress the infant to prevent chilling.
    C. Isolate the infant to prevent cross-contamination.
    D. Avoid handling the infant, because it interferes with the treatment.

11. Baby Guthrie's lab tests showed a steady decline in the level of indirect bilirubin after two days' treatment with phototherapy. She was discharged by the physician on a formula of Similac 20 on a demand feeding schedule. Physiologic jaundice usually appears

    A. Within the first twenty-four hours and disappears after three days.
    B. Within the first twenty-four hours and lasts six to seven days.
    C. On the second or third day and lasts forty-eight hours.
    D. On the second or third day and begins to decrease on the sixth or seventh day.

12. Which of the following is true regarding the new-born's weight after birth?

    A. Weight usually remains constant the first few days, then drops when infant goes home.
    B. Infant usually loses between 5 to 10 percent of body weight during the first few days after birth, and then begins to increase in weight after the fourth day.
    C. Infant usually begins to gain weight the first day after birth, when put on bottle or breast.
    D. Infant normally loses between 15 to 20 percent of body weight after birth but regains it rapidly.

13. Of the following conditions which one is not a result of metabolic error in the fetus?

    A. Phenylketonuria.
    B. Maple syrup urine disease.
    C. Galactosemia.
    D. Pyloric stenosis.

14. Considering the conditions above (inborn errors of metabolism), the most frequent traumatic result in the baby of such a condition is

    A. Mental retardation.
    B. Fetal death.
    C. Retrolental fibroplasia.
    D. Hypoxia.

15. Mrs. Jackson is a Rh-negative woman with a Rh-positive husband. Mrs. Jackson had two abortions before she was married. She is now twenty-four and anxiously expecting a child at any moment. Mrs. Jackson was watched carefully during her pregnancy. Her Rh-antibody titer and indirect Coombs' test showed signs of slight elevation during her pregnancy. During her last trimester, an amniocentesis was done and the spectrophotometric analysis showed a relatively low titer and was not repeated. Mrs. Jackson delivered at forty weeks a 7 lb. 6 oz. baby boy. Lab tests on cord blood indicated the infant was Rh positive. The Coombs' test was positive and the serum bilirubin was 5.9. Nursing observation of the infant for hyperbilirubinemia would include all the following *except*

    A. Pallor.
    B. Flushing.
    C. Progressive jaundice.
    D. Lethargy.

16. Hyperbilirubinemia occurs in Rh incompatibility between mother and fetus because

    A. The mother's blood does not contain the Rh factor, and so she produces anti-Rh antibodies that cross the placental barrier and cause hemolysis of red blood cells in infants.
    B. The mother's blood contains the Rh factor and the infant's does not, and antibodies are formed in the fetus that destroy red blood cells.

    C. The mother has a history of previous yellow jaundice caused by a blood transfusion, which was passed to the fetus through the placenta.
    D. The infant develops a congenital defect shortly after birth that causes the destruction of red blood cells.

17. Baby Jackson's condition continues to worsen and he is given an exchange transfusion. Nursing care of the infant following the transfusion would include all the following *except*

    A. Observe for bleeding from the umbilical cord.
    B. Take vital signs frequently.
    C. Give IPPB therapy.
    D. Observe for signs of hypoglycemia and sepsis.

18. The development of anti-Rh antibodies within the mother could have been prevented with the administration of RhoGAM postabortions. Which of the following is true about RhoGAM?

    A. It must be given on the sixth day post delivery.
    B. It should be given after each pregnancy or abortion.
    C. It may be given even after sensitization occurs.
    D. It may be given to the infant.

19. Signs of sepsis in the newborn would include all the following *except*

    A. Periods of apnea or irregular respiration.
    B. Poor sucking reflex and feeding.
    C. Constipation.
    D. Irritability.

20. Mrs. Jones, who delivered a baby boy the previous evening, is crying when you enter her room. When you ask her what is wrong, she tells you that the doctor told her that her baby has a functional heart murmur. The best nursing response in this situation would be to

    A. Tell her to ask the doctor what it means.
    B. Tell her everything will work out all right.
    C. Tell her that a functional murmur is normal and will last a few weeks.
    D. Tell her that this type of murmur may indicate heart damage but the baby will certainly survive.

21. Baby Loya, an 11 lb. 6 oz. baby girl, was delivered by cesarean section to a diabetic mother. Apgar score: 7/9. The infant was suctioned and placed in the intermediate nursery for observation. Observations of the infant of a diabetic mother would include all the following except

    A. Hypoglycemia.
    B. Sepsis.
    C. Respiratory distress.
    D. Hypocalcemia.

22. Infants of diabetic mothers are often of excessive weight because

A. High blood sugar levels in the mother stimulate infant's metabolic system to store glycogen and fat.
B. The infant also is diabetic and stores fat.
C. The infant is suffering from excessive edema.
D. Inactivity in infant caused by elevated blood sugar results in fetal inactivity and weight gain.

23. Signs of hypoglycemia in the infant include all the following except

A. Twitching or jitteriness.
B. Increased respiratory rate.
C. Apathy and poor muscle tone.
D. Weak, soft cry.

24. Nursing care of the infant with hypoglycemia would include which of the following?

A. Administer whole blood.
B. Administer glucose I.V. or orally if infant is able to suck and swallow.
C. Place infant on respirator.
D. Administer tranquilizers.

25. Nursing care of the "addicted" infant includes all of the following except

A. Frequent handling of infant.
B. Frequent monitoring of cardiac and respiratory rates.
C. Padding side of crib to protect from injury.
D. Cleansing buttocks carefully to avoid skin breakdown from diarrhea.

26. RhoGAM is given to Mrs. Bates, who delivered a healthy baby twenty-four hours ago. In order for it to be effective, which of the following conditions should *not* be present?

A. Mrs. Bates is Rh^o.
B. The baby is Rh^+.
C. Mrs. Bates has no titer in her blood.
D. Mrs. Bates has some titer in her blood.

27. On April 16 at 3:45 P.M., Baby Han, a thirty-four-week 1550 gm. female infant, was delivered to a seventeen-year-old unmarried primigravida. The infant demonstrated nasal flaring, intercostal retractions, expiratory grunt, and slight cyanosis. An umbilical catheter was inserted with I.V. infusion of 5 percent dextrose and water 30 cc. to run over a ten-hour period. Blood gases and electrolyte studies were ordered immediately. All the statements below are criteria for diagnosis of prematurity except

A. Birth weight.
B. Length of gestation.
C. Skin color.
D. Body length.

28. Baby Han was placed in a heated isolette because

A. The premature infant has a small body surface for her weight.

B. Heat increases flow of oxygen to extremities.
C. Temperature control mechanism is immature.
D. Heat within the isolette facilitates drainage of mucus.

29. The temperature of the infant in the heated isolette should be taken regularly to prevent

A. Bradycardia.
B. Cold stress.
C. Decreased need for oxygen.
D. Elevated glucose levels.

30. Immediate assessment of the premature infant in the nursery by the nurse would include all the following except

A. Hunger status.
B. Cardiac status.
C. Respiratory status.
D. Congenital abnormalities.

31. An infant with respiratory distress will show all the following except

A. Respiration between 30-40.
B. Cyanosis.
C. Expiratory grunt.
D. Carbon dioxide between 35-45.

32. Blood gases and electrolyte studies were ordered immediately on Baby Han to assess

A. The infant's leukocyte count.
B. The infant's oxygen and carbon dioxide and pH levels.
C. The infant's antibody titer for Rh.
D. The infant's blood glucose level.

33. Baby Han was diagnosed as having respiratory distress syndrome. Premature infants are likely to develop respiratory distress. Which one of the following conditions is *not* considered a possible cause?

A. Alveoli are immature and produce inadequate amounts of surfactant.
B. The premature infant has not received adequate numbers of antibodies from her mother before birth.
C. Nerves and respiratory center are immature.
D. The premature infant's thoracic cage and respiratory muscles are weak.

34. The air in Baby Han's isolette is humidified to

A. Improve cardiac rhythm.
B. Prevent hyperbilirubinemia.
C. Increase the infant's temperature.
D. Prevent drying of bronchial secretions.

35. The physician will carefully regulate the concentration of oxygen Baby Han receives, based upon the infant's pO_2 and pCO_2 levels, because high blood levels of oxygen

A. May produce kernicterus.
B. May cause retinal spasms leading to the development of retrolental fibroplasia.
C. Cause peripheral circulatory collapse.
D. Cause cardiac damage, but it is not permanent.

36. The nurses caring for Baby Han use careful handwashing techniques while caring for her, because they know premature infants are more susceptible to infection than full-term infants. Which of the following does not explain why premature infants are more likely to develop infection?

A. Liver enzymes are immature.
B. Antibody formation is immature.
C. Premature infants receive few antibodies from the mother, because antibodies pass across the placenta during the last month of pregnancy.
D. Cellular and white blood cell defense may be ineffective.

37. Nursing care of the premature infant in preventing infection includes all the following interventions except

A. Cover I.V. sites and keep dressings clean.
B. Avoid caring for the infant if you have an infection.
C. Use tap water for suctioning.
D. Prevent skin breakdown with careful skin cleansing and little use of tape.

38. The premature infant has a tendency toward hemorrhage and anemia. Nursing care of Baby Han would include all the following except

A. Administer vitamin C shortly after birth.
B. Record all blood loss including blood tests.
C. Use care in handling the infant.
D. Secure all I.V. connections and look for backflow of blood in tubing.

39. One of the most important principles in providing nutrition to Baby Han would involve

A. Using a regular nipple for bottle feeding.
B. Feeding every 6–8 hours.
C. Using premie nipple for bottle feeding.
D. Using milk high in fat.

40. The premature infant has difficulty concentrating urine and may have large amounts of fluid lost. The nurse caring for Baby Han would

A. Force fluids every half hour.
B. Observe color and amounts of urine and check its specific gravity.
C. Administer only high protein fluids.
D. Warm fluids before administering them.

41. Which of the following statements is most correct about diabetes and pregnancy?

A. The mortality rate of well-controlled pregnant diabetics is about the same as nondiabetics.
B. The fertility rate of poorly-controlled diabetics is higher than those who are well controlled.
C. Well-controlled diabetics are as able to have large, healthy families as nondiabetics.
D. Because of the complexities of diabetes, pregnancy should be discouraged.

42. Pregnant diabetic women are more prone to bladder infection. All of the following are causes of this except

A. Uterine pressure.
B. Effects of progesterone.
C. Fetal hypoinsulinemia.
D. Increased urinary glucose.

43. Estelle comes to your prenatal clinic. She has a history of mild diabetes and has had numerous female cousins and aunts who were diabetic who have had pregnancies. Estelle has, to date, been controlled by insulin. She asks you what will happen to her insulin requirements during her pregnancy. Your best response is

A. "Because your case is so mild, you are likely not to need much insulin during your pregnancy."
B. "It's likely that as the pregnancy progresses to term you will need increased insulin."
C. "Every case is individual so there's really no way to say."
D. "If you follow the diet well and don't gain too much weight, your insulin needs should stay about the same."

44. Estelle seems to be concerned about something. On further inquiry she asks you what her pregnancy will be like. Your best response is

A. "Since you are well controlled in the diabetes, it should be like any other normal pregnancy."
B. "It should go well and toward the end we will do tests to see if you need to have an early delivery."
C. "It's hard to say for sure; everything should go well and your regular attendance at clinic will help to make sure it will."
D. "It should be fairly normal. Tell me what you expect and know about pregnancy in diabetics."

45. Which of the following statements is most accurate regarding breast feeding by diabetic mothers?

A. It is contraindicated because insulin is passed to the infant through the milk.
B. It is contraindicated because the diabetic's milk production mechanism is faulty.
C. It is contraindicated because it puts too much stress on the mother's body.
D. It is not contraindicated.

46. Which of the following is the least important information for providing good nursing care of the infant of a diabetic woman?

 A. Mother's age.
 B. Apgar score.
 C. Mother's diabetic classification
 D. Baby's gestational age.

47. Barbara, a twenty-one-year-old female patient, who is eighteen weeks pregnant, is admitted to the hospital for a saline abortion. Care of the patient during the saline infusion would include which of the following?

 A. Check urine for sugar and acetone.
 B. Ask the patient to deep breathe at appropriate times.
 C. Observe for signs of saline leakage within the mother's circulatory system.
 D. Massage the fundus of the uterus.

48. Nursing management of the patient after a saline abortion would include all the following except

 A. Administration of RhoGAM to Rh-negative mothers.
 B. Check vital signs frequently.
 C. Administer pain medication.
 D. Explain to the patient she will probably have bright red bleeding for about three weeks.

49. After her abortion, Barbara begins to cry and says, "I feel so guilty. I should never have killed my baby." You could be most supportive to Barbara by saying,

 A. "You should be more careful in the future and use a method of birth control."
 B. "It's natural to feel sad, but you'll be back to normal in a short time."
 C. "You are feeling very sad right now, Barbara. I'll sit with you for a while; it may help to talk about it."
 D. "Your friend will be here soon to pick you up. Why don't you tell her about it when she comes."

50. Of the following conditions which one is a known teratogen?

 A. Scarlet fever.
 B. Rubella.
 C. Coronary heart disease.
 D. Dental X-rays.

51. Which of the following conditions might precipitate acidosis in a pregnant diabetic woman?

 A. Decreased salt diet.
 B. Decreased activity.
 C. Diarrhea.
 D. High protein diet.

52. In an emergency delivery which of the following principles best explains why the nurse would not cut the cord?

 A. It is the physician's responsibility to cut the cord.
 B. Cutting the cord under emergency conditions might lead to hemorrhage.
 C. Cutting the cord under emergency conditions might lead to infection.
 D. The nurse was never trained in the proper procedure.

53. Nancy is a primip Rh-negative and has just given birth to a healthy child. Her RhoGAM studies indicate she is a candidate for RhoGAM. On discussing it with her she tells you it is against her religion to have blood. As the nurse your best reply is

 A. "This is different, it's not whole blood."
 B. "That choice is yours to make. I would like you to discuss it further with the doctor."
 C. "I can understand your feelings, but this affects future pregnancies."
 D. "If you're sure you don't want it, I'll send it back."

54. Janice is a nineteen-year-old primip. She is three months pregnant and you have just received the results of her serology test which indicates she has syphilis. When discussing this with her she says, "That's not possible. I've only slept with my boyfriend." As the R.N., your best response would be

 A. "Well then, he has probably slept with someone else which would get him infected."
 B. "It's all right to tell me the truth, our conversation is confidential."
 C. "Can you tell me what you know about syphilis?"
 D. "How you got it doesn't really matter. What's important is that we treat it now."

55. Janice is being treated for syphilis with penicillin. Which statement regarding this treatment is most accurate?

 A. Unless she is reinfected later, the infant will not be affected by the syphilis.
 B. She is likely to become reinfected based on her social history.
 C. Although treatment will cure the mother, the infant has still been affected.
 D. Treatment of the mother is assured but the infant will have to be checked for six months.

56. Sharon comes to the clinic and says she is sexually active and would like some form of birth control. After discussing the various methods of contraception, she decides she would like to use the pill. You tell Sharon that the physician will need to know

A. A list of her contacts.

B. A complete history of her sexual experiences.

C. If she has a history of thrombophlebitis or migraine headaches.

D. If her parents approve and will sign a written consent.

57. In explaining the side effects of the pill to Sharon, you would tell her that

A. There are no known side effects of the pill.

B. The pill is so effective that Sharon need not be concerned with the side effects.

C. If side effects show up, she should skip the pill for a few days.

D. Side effects such as weight gain, nausea and vomiting may appear but these usually clear up within the first to third cycle.

58. In preparing a patient for an IUD, you would

A. Explain how an IUD functions and where it is placed.

B. Tell the patient that the IUD will probably interfere with coitus.

C. Tell the patient she will no longer be able to wear tampons.

D. Explain that it is impossible to expel the IUD once it is in place.

59. When discussing family planning methods with a couple, the nurse should

A. Include only the female in the discussion.

B. Help the couple to have a thorough understanding of the method they choose.

C. Choose the method she feels would best suit the couple.

D. Point out that all methods are 99.9 percent effective so it makes no difference which method they choose.

60. Genetic counseling is highly recommended for which of the following groups?

A. A couple who is just planning to start their family.

B. Parents who have had one abnormal child.

C. Two people who are not married but planning to have a child.

D. All parents or potential parents.

61. The follicle-stimulating hormone FSH, which stimulates the development of the ovarian follicle, is produced by

A. The adrenal cortex.

B. Graafian follicle.

C. Anterior pituitary.

D. Cerebral cortex.

62. Which of the following is not a physiologic function of estrogen?

A. Acts as nourishment for the embryo.

B. Stimulates hypertrophy of the endometrium.

C. Suppresses secretion of the follicle-stimulating hormone.

D. Is responsible for growth of myometrium after implantation.

63. The hormone progesterone has all the following physiologic effects except

A. Acts upon endometrium to prepare it for pregnancy.

B. Facilitates transport of the fertilized ovum through the Fallopian tubes.

C. Inhibits implantation.

D. Inhibits uterine motility during pregnancy.

64. Fertilization usually takes place in

A. The corpus luteum.

B. The outer third of the Fallopian tube.

C. The corpus of the uterus.

D. The cervix of the uterus.

65. Each reproductive cell (gamete) carries how many chromosomes?

A. 24.

B. 46.

C. 23.

D. 21.

66. Implantation occurs on the

A. Fifth day after fertilization.

B. Eleventh day after fertilization.

C. Third day after fertilization.

D. Seventh day after fertilization.

67. Which of the following is not a characteristic of amniotic fluid?

A. Is normally yellow-greenish in color.

B. Contains fetal urine, fetal lanugo, and epithelial cells.

C. Provides a cushion against injury to the fetus.

D. Provides optimum temperature to the fetus.

68. The placenta produces which one of the following hormones?

A. Follicle-stimulating hormone.

B. Adrenalin.

C. Human chorionic gonadotrophin.

D. Testosterone.

69. Which of the following is *not* a characteristic of the placenta?

A. Is formed by a union of the chorionic villi and decidua basalis.

B. Allows bacteria to pass to the fetus.

C. Is an organ of nutrition, respiration, and elimination of waste of the fetus.

D. Allows exchange between mother and fetus to take place through diffusion.

70. Single ovum twins are characterized by

    A. The same or different sex.
    B. Brother and sister resemblance.
    C. Two chorions and two amnions.
    D. The union of a single ovum and a single sperm.

71. Sarah, a twenty-four-year-old married female, comes to the maternity clinic of a local hospital because she suspects that she is pregnant. She gives her last menstrual period as 8/9/76, which was two months ago. On talking to Sarah, you learn her menarche began at thirteen and she has had no major illnesses during her childhood or adult years. Sarah says, "If I am pregnant, when will my baby be due?" According to Naegele's rule, you would tell her

    A. 5/16/77.
    B. 4/13/77.
    C. 1/12/77.
    D. 6/6/77.

72. Upon examining Sarah, the physician finds Chadwick's sign. Chadwick's sign is

    A. Wavy streaks which appear on the abdomen, breast, and thighs during pregnancy.
    B. Thin yellowish fluid present in the breasts during pregnancy.
    C. Separation of the muscles due to abdominal distention during pregnancy.
    D. Deep reddish or purplish discoloration of the vagina due to increased vascularity.

73. Changes in the uterus during pregnancy include all the following except

    A. Increase in size and number of blood vessels.
    B. Atrophy of muscle cells.
    C. Hypertrophy of lymphatic system.
    D. Development of elastic tissue increasing contractility.

74. Changes in the breast during pregnancy include all the following except

    A. Increase in size and firmness.
    B. Superficial veins grow more prominent.
    C. Montgomery's glands decrease in size.
    D. Nipples become more prominent and areola deepens in color.

75. Sarah was instructed by the nurse to immediately report any visual disturbances she was experiencing. The best rationale for this instruction is that the symptom

    A. Is a forerunner to preeclampsia.
    B. Indicates increased intracranial pressure.
    C. Is indicative of malnutrition.
    D. Is indicative of renal failure.

76. Sarah says, "I feel so different since I am pregnant." Which of the following is an expected characteristic of the altered emotional changes that take place during pregnancy?

    A. Quick mood changes.
    B. Violent outburst.
    C. Complete rejection of pregnancy.
    D. Emotionally insecure.

77. Presumptive signs of pregnancy include all the following except

    A. Periods of drowsiness and lassitude.
    B. Increased pigmentation of skin.
    C. Increased levels of the follicle-stimulating hormone.
    D. Frequency.

78. Probable signs of pregnancy include all the following except

    A. Increased gastric motility.
    B. Enlargement of abdomen.
    C. Changes in internal organs.
    D. Positive pregnancy tests.

79. Which of the following would be a positive sign of pregnancy?

    A. Hegar's sign.
    B. Nausea.
    C. Auscultation of fetal heart tones.
    D. Outline of fetus by abdominal palpation.

80. In instructing Sarah about her nutritional needs during pregnancy, you would tell her that she has an increased need for all the following except

    A. Calories.
    B. Protein.
    C. High fat, high carbohydrate foods.
    D. Iron.

81. In giving prenatal instructions to Sarah, you would tell her that

    A. It is all right to take drugs during pregnancy because they do not cross the placenta.
    B. Smoking has little effect on the developing fetus.
    C. Sports should always be avoided during pregnancy.
    D. Frequent rest periods should be planned to avoid needless fatigue.

82. Danger signals in pregnancy would include all the following except

    A. Vaginal bleeding.
    B. Persistent headache.
    C. Edema of hands and face.
    D. Constipation.

83. During which stage of a woman's pregnancy is it most difficult to control diabetes?

    A. When she first discovers she is pregnant.
    B. Early postpartum period.

C. During the delivery process.
D. During labor.

84. During which stage of labor would the nurse expect a mucous plug to be expelled?

A. Braxton-Hicks' contractions.
B. Effacement of the cervix.
C. Transitional stage.
D. Before delivery of the placenta.

85. Characteristics of the patient during the active stage of labor would normally include all the following except

A. Contractions 1/2 to 1 minute apart and lasting 90 seconds.
B. Dilatation of 4–7 centimeters.
C. Mother less talkative.
D. Increase in bloody show.

86. In the delivery room Sarah has just delivered a healthy seven-pound baby boy. The physician instructs you to suction the baby. The procedure you will follow will be to

A. Suction the nose first.
B. Suction the mouth first.
C. Suction neither nose nor mouth until doctor assesses respiratory status of the baby.
D. Turn the baby on his side before starting the suctioning procedure.

87. Sarah is transferred from the recovery room to the postpartum unit. Routine care of the postpartum patient would include all the following except

A. Maintain intake and output until patient is voiding in sufficient quantities.
B. Massage fundus firmly every fifteen minutes.
C. Assess emotional status of new mother.
D. Check breast for engorgement and cracking of nipples.

88. Mrs. Lambert is admitted to the maternity unit in her 36th week of pregnancy in an effort to control the further development of eclampsia. She is placed in a private room. The best rationale for this room assignment is

A. Mrs. Lambert is financially able to afford it.
B. Mrs. Lambert would be disturbed to be placed in a room where another mother was in active labor.
C. A quiet, darkened room is important to reduce external stimuli.
D. A rigid regimen is an important aspect of eclamptic care.

89. You are caring for a mother who has delivered an infant with a congenital defect. You recognize that a crisis now exists, and from your knowledge of crisis intervention you will

A. Continue to support and comfort the mother.
B. Implement specific nursing care.
C. Help the family acknowledge that a crisis does exist.
D. Act as if everything is fine so the family won't worry.

90. An expected symptom of a ruptured ectopic pregnancy would be

A. Elevated blood glucose levels.
B. Sudden excruciating pain in lower abdomen.
C. No signs of shock.
D. Extensive external bleeding.

91. Signs and symptoms of placenta previa would include all the following except

A. Uterus remains soft and flaccid.
B. Bleeding may be intermittent.
C. Bleeding occurs as internal os begins to dilate.
D. Bleeding is accompanied by intense pain.

92. Of the following conditions which one does not necessarily indicate the need for a cesarean delivery?

A. Breech baby.
B. Baby with absence of flexion of the head.
C. Abnormally large sized baby.
D. Abnormally small sized baby.

93. One of the known complications in infants delivered by cesarean section is

A. Respiratory distress.
B. Renal impairment.
C. ABO incompatibility.
D. Kernicterus.

94. Treatment of the patient with mild preeclampsia would include all the following except

A. High sodium diet.
B. Adequate fluid intake.
C. Daily weight.
D. Planned rest periods.

95. Of the following conditions which one is a cardinal symptom of toxemia of pregnancy?

A. Weight gain of one pound a week.
B. Concentrated urine.
C. Hypertension.
D. Feeling of lassitude and fatigue.

96. Nursing care of the patient during pregnancy with cardiac problems would include all the following except

A. Alert patient to special needs during pregnancy, such as avoiding overexertion, sore throats, colds.
B. Alert patient to signs of decompensation, especially during second trimester.

C. Stress importance of taking prescribed medication, such as digitalis, and of observing for side effects.
D. Maintain patient on complete bedrest.

97. To promote optimal parent-to-infant attachment the most important nursing intervention would be to

A. Encourage both parents to hold the infant after delivery unless condition of infant or mother does not permit this.
B. Encourage rooming-in so the mother can spend time with her baby.
C. Encourage parents of premature infants to visit but not touch or hold infant.
D. Provide a role model for the parents.

98. The highest priority nursing intervention for a patient with a prolapsed cord would be to

A. Cover exposed cord with sterile dressing.
B. Leave the room momentarily to obtain assistance.
C. Place patient in knee-chest or exaggerated Trendelenburg's position.
D. Monitor fetal heartbeats.

99. Nursing care of the mother receiving regional anesthesia would include

A. Walking the patient to ensure medication is evenly distributed.
B. Asking the mother to turn from side to side every fifteen minutes.
C. Monitor blood pressure every three to five minutes until stabilized.
D. Give patient sips of water to swallow during procedure.

100. Signs and symptoms of infection as a complication of the postpartum period would include all the following except

A. Foul-smelling lochia or discharge.
B. Rapid pulse.
C. Discomfort and tenderness of the abdomen.
D. Generalized rash.

Answers and Rationale

1. (C) Apgar scoring indicates whether or not resuscitative measures are required. A score of 7–10 is vigorous, and these babies usually cry soon after birth; a score of 4–6 is depressed, some resuscitative measures required; 0–3, severely depressed, resuscitation required.

2. (D) Apgar scoring is the evaluation of five vital signs: heart rate, respiratory rate, muscle tone, reflex irritability, and color. Scores of 0, 1, or 2 are given to each vital sign for a total of 10. Since the infant showed acrocyanosis, a score of 1 was given for color, for a total score of 9.

3. (A) The infant is wet and delivery rooms are usually cool, resulting in heat loss in the infant through conduction, convection, and radiation. Placing her in a heated crib decreases heat loss and the Trendelenburg position is used to facilitate drainage.

4. (B) Silver nitrate is an antiinfective agent and is used to prevent development of gonorrheal conjunctivitis in the newborn.

5. (C) Vitamin K is necessary for blood coagulation. The newborn has a transitory deficiency in the ability of the blood to clot. Bacteria are necessary for the production of vitamin K in the intestines and bacteria are not present in sufficient numbers in the newborn until several days after birth.

6. (D) Caput succedaneum is edema of the soft tissues of the scalp due to the difference in pressure on the scalp between those tissues directly against cervix and those which lie on the dilated portion of cervix.

7. (D) Normal respiratory rate in infants is between 30–50. Above or below that indicates respiratory distress.

8. (A) Normal cardiac rate in an infant is between 120–160. It may drop down to 100 when the child is resting and up to 180 when he is crying. Above or below that indicates a cardiac or circulatory problem.

9. (D) The newborn's liver is immature; consequently, it cannot conjugate bilirubin (bind it to glucuronic acid), in order to excrete it from the body.

10. (A) The eyes of the infant are covered with patches during treatment because of the possibility of damage to the retina.

11. (D) Physiologic jaundice shows up as the bilirubin level in the blood rises. As liver function increases, bilirubin is excreted and blood levels of bilirubin go down. Rh incompatibility usually shows up within the first 24 hours.

12. (B) The infant usually loses 5 to 10 percent of his weight after birth due to excess loss of fluids from body tissues and relatively low fluid intake. Infant usually regains weight in ten to fourteen days.

13. (D) This is an example of a congenital abnormality and does not fall into the category of a disorder of protein (abnormal or missing enzyme which interferes with metabolism).

14. (A) Metabolic errors are often associated with mental retardation as it is believed that the missing

enzyme causes metabolic changes which lead to retardation.

15. (B) The infant with hyperbilirubinemia usually has an excessive breakdown of red blood cells, resulting in pallor. Flushing is usually not observed as part of this syndrome.

16. (A) Rh antigens from the fetus enter the bloodstream of the mother, inducing the production of anti-Rh antibodies in the mother. These anti-Rh antibodies cross the placenta, enter the fetal circulation, and cause hemolysis. The red blood cells are destroyed and broken down faster than the products of hemolysis, including bilirubin, can be excreted. Serum bilirubin rises quickly.

17. (C) Intermittent positive-pressure breathing (IPPB) therapy is prescribed in respiratory conditions when the infant is having difficulty with oxygen-carbon dioxide exchange.

18. (B) RhoGAM should be given after an abortion, since fetal blood may enter the mother's circulation and set up a sensitization process.

19. (C) Constipation is rarely a problem in the newborn. Diarrhea would more likely be the result of sepsis.

20. (C) Your responsibility is to clarify her understanding of the meaning of the term functional heart murmur and to allay her fears.

21. (B) The infant of a diabetic mother may develop sepsis, but usually from a cause unrelated to the diabetes itself. Infants of diabetic mothers are prone to develop hypoglycemia, respiratory distress, and hypocalcemia. Hyperbilirubinemia is also fairly common in these infants.

22. (A) Glucose of the diabetic mother passes into the baby's bloodstream keeping the infant's blood glucose level high. The elevated blood sugar in the infant exaggerates certain metabolic functions, resulting in increased storage of glycogen and fat.

23. (D) Infants with signs and symptoms of hypoglycemia usually have a high-pitched cry.

24. (B) Administration of glucose usually establishes normal glucose blood levels in the newborn.

25. (A) Infants born to mothers with drug addiction are hyperirritable and care should be planned so as not to constantly stimulate the infant. When held, the infant should be wrapped snugly in blankets and held close to the body.

26. (D) RhoGAM will not work if there is any titer in the blood; thus it is important to administer it within 72 hours after delivery or abortion if the mother shows no evidence of antibody production.

27. (C) Skin color is an indication of respiratory status. Diagnosis of prematurity is based on weight, length, length of gestation, and neurological and physical characteristics.

28. (C) The premature infant has poor body control of temperature and needs immediate attention to keep from losing heat. Reasons for heat loss include little subcutaneous fat and poor insulation, large body surface for weight, immaturity of temperature control, and lack of activity.

29. (D) If temperature in isolette is too hot, the infant may have periods of apnea and have increased need for oxygen or become dehydrated. If temperature in the isolette is too cool, the infant may have periods of apnea, develop cold stress, and increased need for oxygen. Cold stress will increase metabolism and deplete glucose levels, not elevate glucose levels.

30. (A) It is important to provide nutrients to the infant and not deplete glucose stores, but other factors are more important in the immediate assessment—cardiac, respiratory, temperature, neurological status, and the presence of congenital abnormalities.

31. (A) An infant with respiratory distress will have an elevated respiratory rate to try and increase the intake of oxygen in his damaged lungs, which are not functioning properly. A respiratory rate between 30–40 is within the normal range.

32. (B) Blood gases are drawn to determine if the oxygen, carbon dioxide, and pH levels are within normal range. The treatment given to the infant depends to a great extent on these results. For example, if the blood pO_2 level is down and the pCO_2 is elevated, the concentration of oxygen the infant is receiving will be increased and the infant may be placed on a CPAP or PEEP to increase residual capacity and improve oxygenation. Drugs such as sodium bicarbonate may be given to correct acidosis or a low pH. Normal values: pH 735–7.45, pO_2 40–60, pCO_2 35–45.

33. (B) Premature infants are prone to respiratory distress, because they are unable to produce surfactant which leads to atelectasis. The alveolar and the thoracic cage and respiratory muscles are weak, so the infant cannot take in enough air on inspiration.

34. (D) The infant has a weak cough and gag reflex and has difficulty removing mucus. Should the bronchial secretions become dry, they become tenacious and almost impossible for the baby to bring up and difficult to remove by suctioning. Oxygen is very drying to the mucous membranes and should always be humidified while being given (whether to an infant or adult).

35. (B) High blood levels of oxygen cause spasms of the retinal vessels, and the destruction of these vessels can cause retrolental fibroplasia and blindness.

36. (A) Immaturity of the liver is responsible for hyperbilirubinemia but is not directly related to

the infant acquiring an infection.

37. (C) Sterile water should be used for suctioning and changed at least once during each shift.

38. (A) Vitamin K is administered after birth to aid in the clotting process.

39. (C) A regular nipple is too hard and will make it difficult for the infant to suck, causing unnecessary fatigue. A premie soft nipple should be used.

40. (B) It is important for the nurse to note the amount and color of urine excreted and to check its specific gravity when there is any question about the concentration. Fluids are usually administered at room temperature and include glucose (carbohydrate) as well as protein. The premature infant does not absorb fat well. Fluids are usually given routinely, but not on a force fluid basis because it would be too fatiguing.

41. (A) Prior to insulin, few diabetics got pregnant and among those who did the mortality rate was high. Because of the progressiveness of the disease, family size should be limited.

42. (C) In diabetes there is fetal hyperinsulinemia due to increased glucose levels in the mother. This fetal state has little effect on maternal urine. Mechanical pressure of uterus on bladder causes stasis of urine, while progesterone causes smooth muscle of the bladder to relax and increased urinary glucose provides good breeding media for bacteria.

43. (B) Because of normal changes and the diabetes, there is usually an increased insulin need in the 2nd and 3rd trimesters.

44. (D) All statements are fairly accurate but D is the best choice. It gives you baseline information of her knowledge and expectations which, in this case, is extremely important because of the female family members who are diabetic and have had pregnancies.

45. (D) Insulin does not cross into the milk. Mother's calorie intake needs to be adjusted with an increase in protein intake. Insulin must be adjusted and care must be exercised during weaning.

46. (A) The mother's age has less to do with the physical needs of the infant than the others. Apgar gives you clues to infant's behavior at birth. If the mother's diabetic status is progressive, problems will be more acute. Gestational age is important because these babies are big and appear more mature than they are.

47. (C) A major complication of saline abortion is the introduction of the hypertonic saline solution into the patient's bloodstream during the saline infusion causing symptoms of thirst, flushed face, headache, tachycardia, numbness, and tingling in extremities.

48. (D) After an abortion, there should be slight bleeding about the same as for a menstrual period for about seven days. Any bright red bleeding after

this time would indicate that the products of conception were probably not completely expelled.

49. (C) The patient following an abortion may have feelings of remorse and guilt. It is important for the nurse to allow the patient to express these feelings openly. The nurse should be an active listener and not pass judgment.

50. (B) Teratogen is a term denoting monster-former and rubella in the first trimester is known to produce monster babies. X-rays are also considered teratogens, but dental X-rays would not have high roentgens.

51. (C) Diarrhea would cause excessive loss of fixed base from the body which would lead to acidosis.

52. (C) Since the Warton's jelly expands as it hits the air ligating blood vessels, there is no danger to the baby. Cutting the cord under emergency conditions could lead to infection.

53. (B) It is the choice of the client whether or not she wants it, but the physician must be aware so that refusal forms can be signed.

54. (C) This is a good opportunity for patient teaching and the first thing the nurse must do is ascertain the patient's level of knowledge.

55. (A) If treated before the 5th month of pregnancy, the fetus is not affected. The spirochetes are transmitted across the placenta to the fetal blood stream sometime between the 5th month and term.

56. (C) Since one of the suspected side effects of the pill is thrombophlebitis, it is important to know the patient's history. If it indicates a predisposition, the pill would not be the contraceptive method of choice.

57. (D) Side effects may appear during the first few months while taking birth control pills due to the hormonal influence. These side effects usually disappear after the third month as the body adjusts.

58. (A) Since the IUD may cause cramping and heavy bleeding the first few months after insertion, it is important that the client be thoroughly instructed in where the IUD is inserted, how it works, and common discomforts following its insertion. The client should also be instructed in how to feel the strings to determine if it is in place and that these strings will in no way interfere with intercourse.

59. (B) Contraceptive methods must be thoroughly understood if they are to be used properly and prevent pregnancy. Both partners should be instructed.

60. (B) The process of genetic counseling will give the parents with one abnormal child the necessary information (diagnosis of problem and risk figures for future pregnancies) upon which to base a decision about having more children.

61. (C) The basophilic cells of the anterior pituitary

secrete the gonadotrophic hormones, the follicle-stimulating hormone, and the luteotrophic hormone.

62. (A) The embryo receives its nourishment from the egg until implantation, and thereafter from the chorionic villi which later fuse into the placenta. Estrogen is responsible for growth of the myometrium but does not nourish the embryo.

63. (C) Progesterone inhibits uterine motility and favors implantation of the embryo. It also aids in preparing the endometrium to make it suitable for implantation.

64. (B) Fertilization usually takes place in the outer third of the Fallopian tube.

65. (C) Each gamete carries 23 chromosomes, so that after union of the sperm and egg, there is a total of 46 chromosomes.

66. (D) Implantation usually occurs on the seventh day after fertilization.

67. (A) Amniotic fluid should be a clear fluid. Yellow-green amniotic fluid usually indicates that it is meconium stained and the fetus is stressed or has been recently stressed.

68. (C) The placenta takes over ovarian production of hormones and produces estrogen and progesterone as well as human chorionic gonadotrophin (HCG).

69. (B) The placenta acts as the organ of respiration, excretion, and nutrition for the fetus. Drugs and small molecules such as viruses may pass the placental barrier but the bacteria molecule is too large to pass through the placental barrier.

70. (D) Single ovum twins, or identical twins, are formed by the union of a single sperm and single ovum.

71. (A) Naegele's rule is to subtract three months and add seven days. Using this formula, Sarah would deliver on or around 5/16/77.

72. (D) With pregnancy, there is an increased vascularity and blood supply to the vaginal area causing tissue to appear deep red or purplish in color.

73. (B) There is hypertrophy of the uterine muscle during pregnancy to allow for increased size.

74. (C) Montgomery's glands enlarge and become more visible during pregnancy.

75. (A) Visual disturbance is a symptom of pre-eclampsia and the patient must immediately be put under a physician's care to prevent further development of eclampsia.

76. (A) Quick mood changes are expected and are the result of changes in hormonal balance in the body as well as the woman's attempt to adjust to the new life style necessitated by having a child.

77. (C) Follicle stimulating hormone stimulates development of the Graafian follicle which then ruptures

at ovulation releasing a mature ovum. During pregnancy, this cycle is interrupted until after delivery and the menstrual cycle resumes.

78. (A) During pregnancy, gastric motility is decreased, not increased, due to the physiological changes taking place during pregnancy.

79. (C) Auscultation of fetal heart tones, sonography, and X-ray are considered positive signs of pregnancy. Outlining the fetus by palpation is not always indicative of pregnancy as a tumor may feel by abdominal palpation like a baby.

80. (C) During pregnancy, there is an increased need for calories, protein, iron, calcium, and other minerals and vitamins. A high fat, high carbohydrate diet is not recommended because it may cause excessive weight gain and fat deposits which are difficult to lose after pregnancy.

81. (D) Fatigue is common during pregnancy, and rest periods should be planned during the day to maintain optimum health and functioning.

82. (D) Constipation is a discomfort associated with pregnancy but is not usually a complication of pregnancy. Signs of complications of pregnancy are vaginal bleeding, persistent headache, edema of hands and feet, and elevated blood pressure.

83. (B) Early postpartum is a crucial period, for the placenta contains the hormone insulinase which blocks the use of insulin during pregnancy.

84. (B) The mucous plug occludes the pregnant cervix and is expelled as the cervix begins to efface or dilate. It is most often discharged prior to admission to the hospital.

85. (A) Contractions during the active stage of labor (dilatation 4–7 centimeters) are usually 2—3 minutes apart and last thirty-five to forty-five seconds. Contractions every 1/2—1 minute do not allow for uterine resting period between contractions. This resting period is necessary to allow for adequate oxygenation of the uterus and the fetus.

86. (B) It is important to suction the mouth first as the delicate receptors on the nose may be stimulated and cause the infant to inhale the mucus in the mouth.

87. (B) The uterus should be massaged only when it feels boggy, and then it should be massaged very lightly with one hand over the symphysis pubis (to prevent inversion of the uterus) and the other placed lightly on the top of the fundus. To massage a contracted uterus firmly every fifteen minutes could cause it to lose its tone.

88. (C) An important aspect of the treatment for pre-eclampsia is absolute quiet and only a private room could accomplish this objective.

89. (C) Studies in crisis intervention have shown that to survive a crisis an individual must first be aware of and acknowledge that the crisis exists.

90. (B) In a ruptured ectopic pregnancy, there may be signs of shock, excruciating pain, and little bleeding. There should be no effect on blood glucose levels.

91. (D) Bleeding in placenta previa is usually not accompanied by pain. Bleeding accompanied by intense pain usually indicates abruptio placenta.

92. (D) A small baby could easily be delivered naturally if there were no abnormalities of the power or passage, while all the other conditions would require a cesarean delivery.

93. (A) During a normal birth, the fetus passes through the birth canal and pressure on the chest helps rid the fetus of amniotic fluid that has accumulated in the lung. The baby delivered by cesarean section does not go through this process.

94. (A) The patient with mild preeclampsia would more than likely be placed on a limited sodium diet or normal diet avoiding highly salted foods. This is because the preeclamptic patient has a tendency to retain sodium and fluids and become edematous.

95. (C) High blood pressure is one of the cardinal symptoms of toxemia along with excessive weight gain, edema and albumin in the urine.

96. (D) Bed rest is not necessary for those individuals with cardiac disease during pregnancy unless they are suffering from an extreme form of the disease. Bed rest may be advisable at certain times during pregnancy when the workload is especially hard on the heart or if signs of cardiac decompensation occur.

97. (A) Attachment or bonding can begin as soon as the delivery process is completed, and encouraging both parents to hold infant immediately after delivery would promote this attachment.

98. (C) Cord prolapse is a very serious complication. The danger to the fetus is great because compression on the cord leads to deprived oxygenation. Those patients should never be left alone and the highest priority measure should be taken to relieve the pressure of the fetal body or head off the cord. This nursing action should be followed by administration of oxygen.

99. (C) Regional anesthesia such as caudal or epidural may cause vasodilatation in causing blood to pool in the extremities. This may lead to maternal hypotension. Immediate treatment is to elevate both legs for a few minutes in order to return the blood to the central circulation and then turn the patient on her side to reduce pressure on the veins and arteries in the pelvic area.

100. (D) A generalized rash would not be a sign of postpartum infection but rather may indicate a virus infection, such as measles, from another source or an allergic reaction to a medication or food. A rash should never be ignored; rather it should be charted and its cause investigated.

Pediatric
Nursing

*This chapter presents an overview of the
basic principles of pediatric nursing and is
organized by system. In addition to a thorough
exploration of each illness or disease, its clinical
manifestations and treatment, this chapter
describes therapeutic approaches for each
phase of child development.*

*An understanding of these pediatric con-
cepts enables the nurse to deal more effectively
with the psychological aspects of illness and
hospitalization for the child and his family. With
this in mind, the nursing management sections
cover therapeutic interventions, communication techniques, and instruction of parents who
are coping with the ill child in the hospital and at
home.*

*The appendices feature an extensive
growth and development section as well as
useful tables on nutrition, immunization, dental
development and pediatric assessment. These
appendices are an excellent reference source
for the student who is reviewing pediatrics.*

Psychological Effects of Illness

Hospitalization of Infants

Psychological Implications of Hospitalization

A. Separation from the mother.

B. Decrease in sensory stimuli.

C. Breakdown in mother-infant relationship due to:
1. Maternal guilt.
2. Hostile, cold hospital environment.
3. Mother's feelings of inadequacy in the mothering role.
4. Subordination of the parents by the staff.

Separation Anxiety Syndrome

A. Protest is the first stage.
1. Characteristics: crying loudly, throwing tantrums.
2. Nursing behaviors: stay close to the child to provide warmth and support.

B. Despair is the second stage.
1. Characteristics: in periods of longer hospitalization, the child will withdraw—show no interest in eating, playing, etc.
2. Nursing behaviors: recognize the syndrome and establish a relationship with the child—attempt to engage and involve the child in an activity.

C Denial is the final stage.
1. Characteristics: exhibits behavior that is often mistaken for happy adjustment; child ignores mother and may regress.
2. Nursing behaviors: reassure the mother, build a relationship with the child, and provide warmth and support to the child during long hospitalization.

Behavior of Infants as Response to Illness

A. Indication of discomfort or pain.
1. Cries frequently.
2. Displays excessive irritability.
3. Lethargic or prostrate.
4. Has high temperature.
5. Has decreased appetite.

B. Positive reaction behaviors.
1. Cries loudly.
2. Fussy and irritable.
3. Rejects everyone except mother.

C. Negative reaction behaviors.
1. Withdraws from everyone.
2. Cries monotonously.
3. Completely passive.

Nursing Management

A. Nursing actions help prevent the detrimental effects of hospitalization.

B. Hold a prehospitalization nursing interview with the parents and give a tour of the pediatric unit.
1. Parents should meet the staff, have procedures and regulations explained to them, and be told the rationale behind the rules.
2. They should be encouraged to visit frequently and/or to room in, if possible.

C. Counsel the parents regarding the child's illness, and elicit their understanding of the disease and its course of action. Correct any misconceptions and, if appropriate, reassure them that they are not the cause of the illness.

D. Encourage the parents to participate in the child's care if they show an interest in doing so.
1. Teach the parents procedures they are capable of doing.
2. Show respect for their superior knowledge of the infant, his likes and dislikes, and his habits.

E. Nurse's role for the absent mother.
1. Limit the number of people handling the infant in the beginning.
2. Allow one person to become familiar with the child and gradually introduce others.
3. Provide closeness and warmth (cuddling).
4. Avoid isolating the child from sensory stimulation.
5. Provide stimulation for the infant during feeding.
6. Hang brightly colored mobiles within the infant's sight.
7. Encourage play activities.

Hospitalization of Toddlers and Preschoolers

Psychological Implications of Hospitalization

A. Hospitalization is a very threatening experience to the child because of the total number of new experiences involved.

B. Because of the threat involved, hospitalization has the potential for disrupting the toddler's new sense of identity and independence.

C. Separation anxiety—the child mourns the absence of the mother through protest, despair, and denial.

D. The child fears the loss of "body integrity." He also has no realistic perception of how the body functions and may overreact to a simple procedure. Some toddlers believe that drawing blood will leave a hole and that the rest of their blood will leak out.

E. The child resents the disruption of his normal rituals and routines. Toddlers are often very rigid about certain procedures, which allows them a sense of security and control over otherwise frightening circumstances.

F. Loss of mobility is frustrating to the child.

G. Regression—the toddler frequently abandons the most recently acquired behaviors and reverts to safer, less mature patterns.

Behavior of Toddlers-Preschoolers as Response to Illness

A. Indications of discomfort or pain.
   1. Cries frequently.
   2. Displays excessive irritability.
   3. Lethargic.
   4. Has high temperature.
   5. Change in appetite.
   6. Verbalizes discomfort.
B. Positive reaction behaviors.
   1. Aggressive behavior.
   2. Occasionally withdrawn.
   3. Fantasizes about illness and procedures.
   4. Regressive behavior.
C. Negative reaction behaviors.
   1. Completely passive or excessively aggressive.
   2. Displays excessive regressive behavior.
   3. Withdraws from everyone.

Nursing Management

A. Introduce the child to hospital surroundings, preferably prior to hospitalization.

B. Explain in simple terms all the procedures, and allow him to discuss them further if he desires.

C. Encourage rooming-in or frequent visits of parents, once the child is hospitalized.

D. Suggest that the mother leave an object that the child connects closely with her for the child to "care for" until she can return. This procedure assures the child that his mother will return.

E. Encourage the parents to be honest about when they are going and coming—do not tell the child they will stay all night and then leave when the child is asleep.

F. Have the family pictures pasted to the crib.

G. Use puppet play to explain procedures and to gain an understanding of the child's perception of his hospitalization. Use puppets to work out anxiety, anger, and frustration.

H. During developmental history, elicit exact routines and rituals that the child uses; attempt to modify hospital routine to continue these rituals.

I. Provide stretchers, wheelchairs, and carts for immobilized patients.

J. Do not punish the child for regression, and explain the reasons for its occurrence to the parents.

Hospitalization of the School-age Child

Psychological Implications of Hospitalization

A. The school-age child wants to understand why things are happening.

B. There is a heightened concern for privacy.

C. The child is modest and fears disgrace.

D. Hospitalization means an interruption in his busy school life, and he fears that he will be replaced or forgotten by his peer group.

E. Absence from his group means a disruption of close friendships.

Behavior of School-age Children as Response to Illness

A. Indications of discomfort or pain.
   1. Expresses that something is wrong. ("I feel sick.")
   2. Cries easily.
   3. Tells adult he is ill so adult may do something about it.
B. Positive reaction behaviors.
   1. Shows anger.
   2. Feels guilty.
   3. Fantasizes and is fearful.
   4. Displays increased activity as response to anxiety.
   5. Reacts to immobility by becoming depressed or angry or by crying.
   6. Cries or aggressively resists treatment.
   7. Needs parents and authority.
C. Negative reaction behaviors.
   1. Is excessively guilty and angry and is unable to express his feelings.
   2. Experiences night terrors.
   3. Displays excessive hyperactivity.
   4. Will not talk about experience.
   5. Is regressive and completely withdrawn.
   6. Shows excessive dependency.
   7. Has insomnia.

Nursing Management

A. Teach the child about his illness; take the opportunity to explain the functioning of the body.
B. Explain all procedures completely; allow the child to see special rooms (e.g., intensive care, cardiac cath. lab) prior to being sent there for treatments.
C. Provide opportunities for the child to socialize with his peer group at meals and through team tournaments of cards, chess, and checkers.
D. Allow telephone privileges for calls to his home and his friends.
E. Provide outlets, such as a dart board and a boxing bag, for anger and frustration.
F. Give him the opportunity to make choices and use independence.
G. Protect his privacy.
H. Continue his schooling by providing tutors.
I. Provide him the opportunity to master developmental tasks of age group.

Effects of Illness on Adolescents

Psychological Implications of Illness

A. Disruption of social system and peer group.
B. Alteration of body image.
C. Fear of loss of independence.
D. Alteration in plans for future.
E. Interruption in development of heterosexual relationships.
F. Loss of privacy.
G. The degree to which the young adult is affected is dependent on:
   1. Whether the illness is chronic or acute.
   2. Whether the prognosis necessitates a change in the patient's future aspirations.
   3. How many changes must be accepted.

Behavior of Adolescents as Response to Illness

A. Indications of discomfort or pain.
   1. Realizes something is wrong and seeks help.
   2. High anxiety level.
   3. Verbalizes discomfort.
B. Positive reaction behaviors.
   1. Shows resistance to accepting illness.
   2. Rebels against authority.
   3. Demands control and independence.
   4. Is fearful.
   5. Temporarily withdraws from social scene.
   6. Verbalizes how illness has affected him.
C. Negative reaction behaviors.
   1. Holds in feelings about illness.
   2. Tries to manipulate staff.
   3. Becomes completely dependent.
   4. Denies his illness.

Nursing Management

A. Adolescents should be in rooms with their peers.
B. Allow telephone privileges, with some limit setting.
C. Encourage the feeling of self-worth—allow as much independence as possible.
D. Allow heterosexual relationship to develop within reason.
E. Provide for privacy.
F. Assist patient in identifying role models.

G. Realistically discuss problems of the illness with the patient.

H. Always provide information honestly.

I. Encourage the adolescent, if possible, to accept some responsibility on the hospital unit.

Cardiovascular System

Diagnostic Procedures

Cardiac Catheterization

A. A procedure in which a catheter is passed into the heart and its major vessels for examination of blood flow, pressures in all chambers and vessels, and oxygen content and saturation. The catheter may be passed through the arterial system into the left side of the heart, or through the venous system into the right side of the heart.

B. Nursing responsibilities before procedure.
1. Prepare parents and child for procedure by showing equipment, procedures, table.
2. Establish vital sign baseline.
3. Promote good physical condition prior to test.

C. Nursing responsibilities during procedure.
1. Carefully observe vital signs.
2. Observe for cyanosis or pallor, bradycardia, and apnea.
3. Assist in restraining and comforting the child.

D. Nursing responsibilities following procedure.
1. Check for peripheral pulses in the extremity used for entrance of the catheter.
2. Take and record vital signs every fifteen minutes until stable.
3. Observe for thrombosis: weak arterial pulses, coolness, cyanosis, blanching of extremity or mottled skin.
4. Observe for hypotension and signs of infection.
5. Observe for reactions to dye used in procedure.
6. Observe for subnormal temperatures due to prolonged body exposure in chilly room.
7. Check incision site for bleeding.

Echocardiography

A. A non-invasive cardiac procedure which reflects mechanical cardiac activity. Usually used to diagnose valvular and other structural anomalies.

B. Nursing responsibilities.
1. Before procedure, assure child that procedure is painless and prepare child for procedure to help insure cooperation.
2. After procedure, no specific care—general reassurance.

Phonocardiogram

A. A graphic recording of the occurrence, timing and duration of the sounds of the heart.

B. Nursing responsibilities.
1. Before procedure, explain equipment to child and promote quiet to eliminate any extraneous noises during procedure.
2. After procedure, no specific care.

Congenital Heart Disease

Fetal Circulation

Physiology

A. Major structures of fetal circulation.
1. Ductus venosus—a structure that shunts blood past the portal circulation.
2. Foramen ovale—an opening between the right and left atria of the heart that shunts blood past the lungs.
3. Ductus arteriosus—a structure between the aorta and the pulmonary artery that shunts blood past the lungs.

B. Changes in circulation at birth.
1. The umbilical arteries and vein and the ductus venosus become nonfunctional.
2. The lungs expand, reducing resistance, and greater amounts of blood enter the pulmonary circulation.
3. More blood in the pulmonary circulation increases the return of blood to the left atrium, which initiates the closure of the flap of tissue covering the foramen ovale.
4. The ductus arteriosus contracts and the blood

flow decreases; eventually, the duct closes.

C. Two major clues to presence of heart disease.
   1. Congestive heart failure.
      a. Begins before one year of age in majority of infants.
      b. Most infants are less than six months old.
   2. Cyanosis.

Cyanotic Type of Defect

A. Conditions which allow unoxygenated blood into the systemic circulation and conditions which result in obstructive pulmonary blood flow.
B. Signs and symptoms.
   1. Retarded growth and failure to thrive.
   2. Lack of energy.
   3. Frequent infections.
   4. Polycythemia.
   5. Clubbing of fingers and toes.
   6. Squatting.
   7. Cerebral abscess.
C. Diseases that belong in the cyanotic category.
   1. Tetralogy of Fallot.
   2. Complete transposition of the great vessels.
   3. Truncus arteriosus.
   4. Tricuspid atresia.

Tetralogy of Fallot

Definition: A cardiac malformation with anatomic abnormalities caused by the underdevelopment of the right ventricular infundibulum.

Abnormalities

A. Ventricular septal defect.
B. Dextroposition of aorta so that it overrides the defect.
C. Hypertrophy of the right ventricle.
D. Stenosis of the pulmonary artery.
E. Hemodynamics—a right to left shunt arises in this anomaly due to the position of the aorta and the hypertrophied right ventricle; thus, partially unoxygenated blood is sent back to the systemic circulation.

Clinical Manifestations

A. Those already mentioned for cyanotic conditions.
B. Hypoxic episodes with potential for seizure activity.
C. Rapid pulse.
D. Fatigue with exercise.
E. Dyspnea, tachypnea.

Treatment

A. Palliative—Blalock-Taussig or Potts procedure, which increases blood flow to the lungs.
B. Open-heart surgery for corrective treatment of pulmonary stenosis and ventricular defect.

Complete Transposition of the Great Vessels

Definition: In this condition, the aorta arises from the right ventricle, and the pulmonary artery arises from the left ventricle—which is not compatible with survival unless there is a large defect present in ventricular or atrial septum.

Clinical Manifestations

A. Development of subvalvular pulmonic stenosis, decreased pulmonary blood flow, hypoxia, and polycythemia.
B. Profound cyanosis.
C. Heart failure.

Treatment

A. Palliative—creation or enlargement of a large septal defect.
B. Corrective—Mustard Procedure.
   1. Removal of the atrial septum with creation of a new septum.
   2. This directs the systemic venous return into the pulmonary ventricle and the pulmonary venous return into the aortic ventricle.

Truncus Arteriosus

Definition: A single arterial trunk arises from both ventricles that supplies the systemic, pulmonary, and coronary circulations. A ventricular septal defect and a single, defective, semilunar valve also exist.

Clinical Manifestations

A. Mottled skin and ashen color.

B. Other cyanotic symptoms.

C. Systolic murmur.

Treatment

A. Complete open-heart repair is necessary.

B. Prognosis is poor.

Tricuspid Atresia

Definition: Two components of this defect are complete closure of the tricuspid valve and hypoplastic right ventricle, frequently accompanied by ventricular and atrial septal defect.

Clinical Manifestations

A. Hemodynamics—a right-to-left shunt through the atrial septal defect; blood mixes with pulmonary venous blood and enters the left ventricle. From the left ventricle, some blood is shunted to the right ventricle and then to the pulmonary artery. The rest passes into the aorta.

B. Those already mentioned for cyanotic conditions.

C. Cyanosis at birth.

Treatment

A. Palliative surgery designed to increase pulmonary blood flow.

B. Prognosis is poor.

Acyanotic Type of Defect

A. Conditions that interfere with normal blood flow through the heart either by slowing it down, or by shunting back to the right side of the heart.

B. Signs and symptoms.

1. Audible murmur.
2. Discrepancies in pulse pressure in the upper and lower extremities.
3. Tendency to develop respiratory infections.
4. May develop heart failure with little stress.

C. Diseases that belong in the acyanotic category.

1. Patent ductus arteriosus.
2. Atrial septal defect.
3. Ventricular septal defect.
4. Coarctation of the aorta.
5. Pulmonic stenosis.

Patent Ductus Arteriosus

Definition: A patent ductus is present when normal closing at birth fails to occur. The potential for difficulty with this defect is dependent on the amount of blood passing through the defect.

Clinical Manifestations

A. Machinery-type murmur over pulmonary artery.

B. Low diastolic blood pressure.

C. Poor feeding.

D. Respiratory distress and frequent respiratory infections.

E. Visualization of ductus during cardiac catheterization.

Treatment

A. Surgical ligation of ductus is usually done at two or three years of age.

B. In uncomplicated cases, prognosis is good.

Atrial Septal Defect

Definition: Involves two types of defects that occur during the development of the atrioventricular canal.

Types of Defects

A. Patent foramen ovale.

1. In 20 percent of all births, a slit-like opening remains in the atrial septum.
2. This defect is usually functional murmur and requires no surgical intervention.

B. Ostium defects.

1. A high defect, ostium secundum.

   a. Frequently asymptomatic.

   b. Murmur in area of pulmonary artery.

   c. Usually well tolerated in childhood.

2. A low defect, ostium primum—atrial septum allows a flow of blood from the left high pressure chamber to the right atrial chamber.

   a. Usually accompanied by mitral insufficiency.

   b. Frequently asymptomatic if there are no other abnormalities.

Treatment

A. Depends on severity of symptoms.

B. Surgical repair using cardiopulmonary bypass.

Ventricular Septal Defects

Definition: The majority of defects occur in the membranous septum, and severity is related to the size of the defect and amount of pulmonary blood flow.

Types of Defects

A. Lower defect symptoms—small defects in lower portion of the septum.
   1. Loud systolic murmur.
   2. Generally asymptomatic.
   3. Usually no treatment required.
B. Upper defect symptoms—large defects in the upper portion of the septum.
   1. Cardiac enlargement.
   2. Pulmonary engorgement.
   3. Children are small for their age.
   4. Dyspnea.
   5. Frequent respiratory infection.
   6. Loud systolic murmur.
   7. Treatment involves surgical placement of patch over defect.

Coarctation of Aorta

Definition: Coarctation applies to any constriction of the lumen of the aorta.

Clinical Manifestations

A. Leg pains occur under exertion.
B. Symptoms are secondary to systolic and diastolic hypertension.
C. Impaired circulation in the lower extremities.
D. Most children do not develop life-threatening symptoms during the first year of life.
E. Sometimes asymptomatic.

Treatment

A. If the child is asymptomatic, surgical correction can be delayed until child is eight to ten years old.
B. Prognosis is good following surgical intervention.

Pulmonic Stenosis

Definition: Any lesion that obstructs the flow of blood from the right ventricle.

Clinical Manifestations

A. Usually the pulmonary valve is stenotic.
B. Generally asymptomatic.
C. Increase in right ventricular pressure.
D. Sometimes a decrease in exercise tolerance, and dyspnea.
E. Ejection murmur over pulmonic area.

Treatment

A. Peripheral pulmonic stenosis is not correctable at present.
B. Valvular and infundibular stenosis can be surgically corrected with excellent results.

Acquired Cardiac Disease

Rheumatic Fever

Definition: A systemic inflammatory (collagen) disease that usually follows a group A beta-hemalytic streptococcus infection.

Clinical Manifestations

A. Jones criteria are utilized for diagnosis because there is no single clinical pattern.
B. Two major criteria, or one major and two minor criteria, are necessary for a diagnosis.
   1. Major criteria.
      a. Carditis.
      b. Polyarthritis.
      c. Chorea.
      d. Erythema marginatum.
      e. Subcutaneous nodules.
   2. Minor criteria.
      a. Fever.
      b. Arthralgia.
      c. Previous rheumatic fever or rheumatic heart disease.
      d. Elevated erythrocyte sedimentation rate.
      e. Positive C-reaction protein.
      f. P-R interval prolonged.
C. Supporting evidence.
   1. Recent scarlet fever.
   2. Positive throat culture for group A streptococci.

3. Increased streptococcal antibodies.

Treatment

A. Antibiotic therapy against any remaining strep-tococci.
B. Aspirin for joint symptoms.
C. Bed rest.
D. Prevention of further infection.
E. Protection through use of antibacterial prophylaxis.

Subacute Bacterial Endocarditis

Definition: An infectious disease which involves abnormal heart tissue, particularly rheumatic lesions or congenital defects.

Clinical Manifestations

A. Insidious onset of symptoms.
B. Fever.
C. Lethargy.
D. General malaise.
E. Anorexia.
F. Splenomegaly.
G. Retinal hemorrhages.

Treatment

A. Large doses of antibiotic therapy.
B. Bed rest.

Nursing of Cardiac Children

General Principles

A. Encourage normal growth and development.
B. Counsel parents to avoid overprotection.
C. Deal with parents' concerns and anxieties.
D. Educate parents about conditions, tests, planned treatments, medications.
E. Assist parents in developing ability to assess child's physical status.

Congestive Heart Failure

Nursing Management

A. Promote rest.
   1. Provide outlets such as drawing, doll play, and

reading for the child who may be frustrated by restricted activity.
   2. Organize care to limit time spent disturbing child's rest.
B. Diet supervision.
   1. Provide small frequent feedings.
   2. Make the low sodium diet more palatable through imaginative play and an attractive food arrangement.
   3. Educate parents about diet and its purpose.

C. Medication supervision.
   1. Digoxin.
      a. Monitor vital signs every hour during digitalization.
      b. Observe for digoxin toxicity.
         (1) Nausea, vomiting, and diarrhea.
         (2) Anorexia.
         (3) Dizziness and headaches.
         (4) Arrhythmias.
         (5) Muscle weakness.
      c. Always check pulse prior to giving digoxin.
   2. Diuretics.
      a. Observe for electrolyte abnormalities.
      b. Weigh the child daily.

Cardiac Surgery

Preoperative Nursing Care

A. Extensively prepare the child and the parents for the experience—demonstrate tubes and bandages and describe the scar the operation leaves.
B. Teach coughing and deep breathing to the child.
C. Conduct the child and the parents on a tour of the intensive care unit and introduce them to the staff.
D. Observe the child for signs of infection.
E. Make sure all laboratory tests are completed.

Postoperative Nursing Care

A. Maintain adequate pulmonary function.
   1. Keep patent airway.
   2. Patient should deep breathe and cough. Monitor use of IPPB.
   3. Suction if necessary.
   4. Oxygen.
   5. Chest suction for refilling lungs.

6. Check rate and depth of respirations.
7. Check water-seal chest drainage.

B. Maintain adequate circulatory functioning.
   1. Check vital signs.
   2. Replace blood where necessary.
   3. Check intake and output every hour.

C. Provide for rest through organized care.

D. Establish adequate hydration and nutrition.

E. Take measures to prevent postoperative complications.
   1. Antibiotic therapy.
   2. Turn patient frequently.
   3. Skin care.
   4. Check extremities for occlusions of major vessels with blood clots: cyanosis, paleness of extremity, or coldness to the touch.
   5. Passive range of motion.
   6. Check dressing for signs of hemorrhage.

Complications of Cardiac Surgery

A. Pneumothorax.

B. Hemothorax.

C. Shock.

D. Cardiac failure.

E. Heart block.

F. Cardiac tamponade.

G. Hemorrhage.

H. Hemolytic anemia.

I. Postcardiotomy syndrome—sudden fever, carditis, and pleurisy.

J. Postperfusion syndrome (three to twelve weeks after surgery)—fever, malaise, and splenomegaly.

Respiratory System

General Principles

Respiratory Terms

A. Respiratory center—located in pons and medulla portions of the brain. The center is an integrated group of nerve cells that regulate respiratory muscles to take in oxygen and expel carbon dioxide.

B. Hypoxia—decrease in arterial oxygen saturation, causing increased activity in the respiratory center.

C. Hypercapnia—increase in arterial carbon dioxide, causing respiratory center to increase respiratory rate.

D. Ventilation—the exchange of carbon dioxide in alveoli with oxygen in the environment.

Components Required to Avoid Respiratory Distress

A. Functioning respiratory center in the brain.

B. Intact nerve cells to regulate respiratory muscles.

C. Patent airway for exchange of gases.

D. Alveoli that are able to expand and contract.

E. Adequate pulmonary capillary bed to allow exchange of gases.

F. Adequate supply of oxygen.

G. Functioning cardiovascular system.

Indications for Administering Oxygen

A. Gasping and/or irregular respirations

B. Bradycardia.

C. Flaring nostrils.

D. Tachycardia.

E. Cyanosis.

F. Increased blood pressure followed by decreased blood pressure.

Major Nursing Objectives

A. Conservation of patient's energy.

B. Fluid maintenance.

C. Temperature control.

D. Humidified air.

E. Adequate oxygen supply.

F. Isolation.

G. Observation for complications.

Low Obstructive Respiratory Problems

Bronchitis

Clinical Manifestations

A. Inflammation of the bronchial tubes.

B. Preceded by upper respiratory infection—fever,

irritability, restlessness, nasal discharge, and frequent vomiting and diarrhea.

C. Hacking moderately productive cough.

D. Rhonchi and rales.

Nursing Management

A. Postural drainage.

B. Humidified air.

C. Increased fluid intake.

D. Observe for complications—increased heart rate and temperature and difficult respirations.

Bronchiolitis

Definition: Thick production of mucus which causes occlusion of the bronchiole tubes and small bronchi.

Clinical Manifestations

A. Preceded by upper respiratory infection.

B. Abrupt onset of accelerated respiratory rate and intercostal and subcostal retractions with prolonged expiratory phase.

C. Tachycardia.

D. Cyanosis.

E. Harsh cough with expiratory wheeze and grunt.

Nursing Management

A. Conserve patient's energy—child usually sedated.

B. Administer cool, moist O_2.

C. Maintain adequate hydration.

D. Position to increase lung expansion; put on abdomen.

E. Observe for signs of adequate oxygen and carbon dioxide exchange—skin color, quality and rate of respirations.

F. Observe for signs of dehydration.
   1. Sunken fontanel.
   2. Poor skin turgor.
   3. Decreased and concentrated urinary output.

Pneumonia

Definition: Inflammation of the lung caused by either diplococcus or staphylococcal bacteria or a virus.

Pneumococcal Pneumonia

A. Clinical manifestations.

   1. Appears suddenly.
   2. High fever.
   3. Increased respiratory rate with retractions.
   4. Increased pulse.
   5. Cough with expectoration.

B. Nursing management.
   1. Supervise antibiotic therapy.
   2. If cyanosis is present, use oxygen therapy.
   3. Conserve patient's energy.
   4. Place child on abdomen or side to prevent aspiration.
   5. Reduce body temperature with cool-water mattress.
   6. Isolation.

Staphylococcal Pneumonia

A. Clinical manifestations.
   1. Usually, multiple abscesses form throughout lungs.
   2. Possible pneumothorax or empyema.
   3. Abrupt onset of fever, cough, and respiratory distress.
   4. Possible severe dyspnea and cyanosis.

B. Nursing management.
   1. Oxygen tent.
   2. I.V. therapy.
   3. Supervision of medication (frequently methicillin) and side effects (hematuria and proteinuria).
   4. Supervision of chest tubes.
   5. Strict isolation techniques.

Viral Pneumonia

A. Clinical manifestations.
   1. Insidious onset preceded by upper respiratory infection.
   2. Tachypnea, chest wall retractions.
   3. Cough, rales and wheezing.

B. Nursing management.
   1. Therapy similar to that for bacterial pneumonia: humidified oxygen, physiotherapy, IPPB.
   2. Observe for complications: atelectasis, bronchiectasis.

Treatment for Pneumonia

A. In general, antibiotic treatment is instituted.

B. Control of environment is maintained, especially with staphylococcal infection.

C. Humidified oxygen.
D. Pulmonary physiotherapy.
E. Prevention of respiratory acidosis or for adequate oxygenation.
   1. Tracheal intubation.
   2. Mechanical ventilation.
F. Supportive care for symptom manifestation.
   1. Adequate fluid intake.
   2. Bedrest and decreased activity.

Asthma

Definition: A pulmonary disorder in which physical or chemical irritants cause the release of histamine and other substances which cause edema of the bronchial walls, excess secretion of mucus by the bronchial glands, and constriction of the bronchi.

Clinical Manifestations

A. An attack may be provoked by exposure to certain foods, infections, vigorous activity, or emotional excitement.
B. Bronchiolar musculature goes into spasm.
C. Thick tenacious mucus accumulates and causes obstruction of air passages.
D. Trapping of air occurs causing obstructive emphysema.
E. Symptoms include wheezing and rales.
F. Attack may occur slowly or quickly.
G. Child usually coughs continually.
H. Neck veins may distend.
I. Cyanosis may occur.
J. Child appears anxious and upset.
K. Symptoms may become rapidly worse with acute respiratory failure with cyanosis and acidosis.

Nursing Management

A. Identification and removal of suspected allergen.
B. Medication supervision.
   1. Epinephrine—acts to reduce congestion and edema.
   2. Ephedrine sulfate—reduces congestion and edema.
   3. Aminophylline—bronchodilator.
C. Removal and control of secretions.
   1. Large fluid intake to liquefy secretions and maintain electrolyte balance.

2. Mist tent.
3. Chest physical therapy and postural drainage.
D. Emotional support for parents and child to reduce anxiety.
E. Child educated to live optimally with chronic problem.

High Obstructive Respiratory Problems

Laryngotracheobronchitis

Definition: Viral croup is a syndrome caused by a variety of inflammatory conditions of the upper airway. Viral croup is the most common and bacterial croup is the most serious.

Clinical Manifestations

A. Preceded by rhinitis and cough for several days.
B. Gradual onset, then barking cough and inspiratory stridor—usually for 3–7 days.
C. Seen in children less than three years old.
D. Mild elevation in temperature (below 102°F.).
E. Hypoxemia results in anxiety and restlessness.
F. Cyanosis is a late sign; may indicate complete airway obstruction.

Nursing Management

A. Home treatment if no inspiratory stridor.
   1. Instruct parents in signs of airway obstruction.
      a. Tachypnea.
      b. Cyanosis.
      c. Increased anxiety.
   2. Instruct parents in using the shower for warm mist therapy. (Cool mist preferable but not usually available at home.)
B. Hospital care for acute onset of inspiratory stridor.
   1. Provide cool mist therapy.
   2. Monitor I.O. for hydration status.
   3. Watch closely for signs of hypoxia and impending respiratory failure.

Epiglottitis

Definition: Acute viral infection of the epiglottis.

Table 1. Differentiation Between High and Low Obstruction

High Obstruction	Low Obstruction
1. Toxicity	1. Toxicity
2. Fatigue	2. Fatigue
3. Increasing air hunger	3. Decreasing air hunger
4. Increasing dyspnea	4. Increasingly severe dyspnea
5. Severe sternal retractions	5. Intercostal retractions (mild chest wall)
6. Prolonged inspiratory phase	6. Prolonged expiratory phase
7. Respiratory rate 45–50 per minute	7. Respiratory rate 100–110 per minute
8. Cardiac rate 140–160	8. Cardiac rate 180–200 per minute
9. Tracheostomy at cardiac rate over 160	9. No tracheostomy necessary
10. Barking cough	10. Harsh cough
11. Marked inspiratory stridor with hoarseness	11. Expiratory wheeze and grunt
	12. Moist rales
	13. Flaring alae nasi

Clinical Manifestations

A. Preceded by upper respiratory infection.

B. Rapid onset with inspiratory stridor and retractions, cough, muffled voice, high fever.

C. Generally seen in preschool children.

Nursing Management

A. Never use tongue blade in assessment.

B. Moist air.

C. Oxygen.

D. Hydration.

E. Tracheostomy set at bedside.

Otitis Media

Definition: A common complication of an acute respiratory infection that occurs when edema of the upper respiratory structures traps the infection in the middle ear.

Clinical Manifestations

A. Severe pain in the ear.

B. Continued symptoms of infections.

Nursing Management

A. Patient is treated with decongestants and antibiotics if a bacterial cause is present.

B. Supervision of antibiotic and decongestant therapy.

C. Conservation of the child's energy.

D. Maintenance of adequate diet and fluid intake.

Tonsillitis and Adenoiditis

Definition: Infection and inflammation of the palatine tonsils and adenoids.

Causes

A. Group A beta-hemolytic strep.

B. Viruses.

Clinical Manifestations

A. Tonsillitis.
 1. Fever, sore throat, anorexia.
 2. General malaise; difficulty in swallowing.

B. Adenoiditis.
 1. Stertorous breathing.
 2. Pain in ear, recurring otitis media.

Indications for Surgery

A. Repeated episodes of tonsillitis—infection.

B. Difficulty in swallowing—enlargement.

C. Interference with breathing.

D. Blocked eustachian tube—chronic otitis media.

E. Surgery performed only when absolutely necessary—tonsils are thought to have important protective immunologic functions.

Preoperative Nursing Management

A. Take samples for blood tests (CBC, Hgb, Hct, Bleeding and Clotting time), serologic tests, and throat culture.

B. Obtain complete health history, including history of allergies.

C. If patient is a child, provide emotional support.
1. Separation from family.
2. Hospitalization procedure.
3. Physical layout of surgery room.
4. Induction of anesthesia.
5. Recovery room procedure.
6. Postoperative pain.
7. Postoperative activity level (play therapy useful).

D. Provide routine preoperative care.

Postoperative Nursing Management

A. Maintain in prone or Sims' position until fully awake to facilitate drainage of secretions and prevent aspiration. Then change to semi-Fowler's.

B. Avoid suctioning and coughing to prevent hemorrhage.

C. Observe for signs of shock.
1. Restlessness.
2. Alterations in vital signs (increased pulse, decreased blood pressure, increased respiration).
3. Frequent swallowing.
4. Excessive thirst.
5. Vomiting of blood.
6. Pallor.

D. Maintain calm, quiet environment to prevent anxiety (which can lead to shock).

E. Provide ice collar.

F. Force fluids.
1. Encourage cold fluids, popsicles, ice chips.
2. Avoid use of citrus juices, milk, hot liquids.
3. Do not use straws.

G. Administer Tylenol for pain (as ordered).

Cystic Fibrosis

Definition: Cystic fibrosis is a genetic disorder in which the mucus-producing glands—particularly those of the lungs and pancreas—are abnormal, producing thick and viscous mucus; abnormal mucus production in the pancreas leads to pancreatic insufficiency and, in the lungs, to emphysematous changes.

Clinical Manifestations

A. Infants with high caloric intake do not gain weight.

B. Recurrent, severe respiratory infections because of thick mucus and bronchial plugs which can cause atelectasis.

C. Malabsorption of fats and proteins and mild diarrhea with greasy, malodorous stools.

D. Abnormally high levels of sodium chloride in sweat.

E. Diagnostic tests include the sweat test for sodium content, and the trypsin test. (Trypsin is absent in cystic fibrosis.)

Treatment

A. Nutritional.
1. Pancreatic enzymes, Viokase and Cotazym, prior to meals.
2. Water-soluble vitamins.
3. Fat-soluble vitamins A, D, and E in water-miscible form.
4. Diet high in calories and protein and low in fat.
5. Maintain sodium balance.

B. Respiratory.
1. Major objective is to keep lungs clear of mucus.
2. IPPB mucomist.
3. Mist tent at night to liquefy secretions.
4. Postural drainage t.i.d. following IPPB.
5. Child tends to breathe shallowly—thus need to teach child breathing exercises.

C. Prevent infection through antibiotics.

Nursing Management

A. Parental education.
1. Child is usually maintained at home, so the parents require extensive guidance.
2. Offer an explanation of the disease and reasons for the therapeutic regime.
3. Demonstrate respiratory therapy techniques.
4. Explain the care and proper use of equipment in the home.

B. Parental counseling.
1. The nurse needs to assist the family in dealing with this chronic disease and its potentially fatal aspects.
    a. Children are irritable and need much attention, but firm discipline.
    b. Children are insecure and frightened; they need reassurance.

2. Genetic counseling.
3. Refer parents to the National Foundation for Cystic Fibrosis Research as a resource.
4. Encourage normal family routine as much as possible.

Sudden Infant Death Syndrome

Definition: The sudden, unexplained death of an infant during sleep.

Clinical Manifestations

A. Largest single cause of death after neonatal period.
B. Peak incidence 2 to 4 months.
C. Higher incidence in winter months, in low income groups, and in low birth weight infants.
D. On autopsy, inflammation of upper respiratory tract is found.
E. Etiology unknown and controversial. Many theories involving CO_2 sensitivity, massive virus, poor response to stimulus.

Treatment

A. Support of parents—help work through feelings of guilt and loss.
B. Refer to National Foundation for Sudden Infant Death.

Closed Drainage of the Chest

Underlying Principles

A. For respiratory distress or disease (e.g., pneumonia), the purpose of closed drainage is to remove fluid and air from the pleural cavity and to reestablish a negative interpleural pressure.
B. Method—negative pressure is created by submerging the drainage tubes 1 or 2 cm. below the surface of the water, that is, placed at a lower level than the patient.
C. Types (see p. 260 for full explanation).
    1. One-bottle system—useful when cavity is expected to drain air and only a small amount of fluid.
    2. Two-bottle system—used when a large amount of fluid is expected to drain from cavity.

3. Three-bottle system—first bottle from patient is usually empty; thus, a more accurate measurement of color, consistency, and amount of drainage is possible.

Nursing Precautions

A. Keep two hemostats near the patient at all times.
B. Check system frequently to make sure there are no leaks.
C. Check tubes frequently for patency.
D. Keep drainage apparatus at a lower level than the patient at all times.
E. Nonmechanical drainage.
    1. Water level should increase on inspiration and decrease on expiration.
    2. Air vent should be open to the atmosphere.
F. Make sure all connections are reinforced.
G. "Milk" tubes if clotting occurs.
H. Accurately label fluid levels and times on bottles.
I. Clamp tubes as close to chest as possible if there is leakage.
J. Mechanical drainage (see pp. 260-262).

Neurological System

Diagnostic Procedures

Pneumoencephalogram

A. A procedure in which air is injected into subarachnoid space to visualize the ventricular system.
B. Nursing responsibilities prior to procedure.
    1. NPO 6-8 hours prior.
    2. Explain to child and/or parents exactly what is going to be done.
    3. May be premedicated to produce maximum relaxation and cooperation.
    4. Obtain baseline data on level of consciousness.
C. Nursing responsibilities following procedure.
    1. Observe for any changes in level of consciousness.
    2. Observe neurological signs and vital signs every 15 minutes until stable.

3. Encourage fluid intake.
4. Keep flat and promote rest.
5. Observe for signs of headache, nausea, vomiting, and elevated temperature.

Myelogram

A. Visualization of the spinal subarachnoid space to define it and to evaluate lesions involving neural elements.
B. Nursing responsibilities prior to procedure.
   1. NPO 6-8 hours.
   2. Maintain baseline record of vital signs and neurological status.
   3. Administer sedative, as ordered.
C. Nursing responsibilities following procedure.
   1. Frequently observe neurological signs and vital signs and compare to baseline.
   2. Check for adequate voiding.
   3. Keep flat for 24 hours and promote rest.
   4. Watch for signs of infection.
   5. Slightly elevate head if some contrast media is retained.

Angiogram

A. Radiopaque substance is injected into cerebral vasculature or its extracranial sources to evaluate vascular anomalies, lesions, or tumors.
B. Nursing responsibilities prior to procedure.
   1. Shave and prep area where puncture is to be made.
   2. No solid foods for 6-8 hours prior to procedure.
   3. Baseline record of neurological and vital signs.
   4. Frequently, a sedative is administered to relax patient.
C. Nursing responsibilities following procedure.
   1. Observe for changes in level of consciousness, transient hemiplegia, seizures, sensory or motor deterioration, or elevation of blood pressure with widening pulse pressure.
   2. Apply cold compress to injection site.
   3. Keep patient flat, promote rest.
   4. Encourage fluid intake.
   5. Check extremity for adequate peripheral pulses, color, temperature.

Lumbar Puncture

A. Withdrawal of cerebral spinal fluid by insertion of a hollow needle between lumbar vertebrae into sub arachnoid space to identify intracranial pressure, signs of infection, or hemorrhage.
B. Nursing responsibilities prior to procedure.
   1. Maintain baseline record of vital signs.
   2. Explain to the parents and child exactly what will happen.
C. Nursing responsibilities during procedure.
   1. Place child on side in knee-chest position with head flexed on chest.
   2. Help child remain steady in this position and reassure him throughout procedure.
D. Nursing responsibilities following procedure.
   1. Keep patient flat in bed.
   2. Encourage fluid intake.
   3. If headache occurs when sitting up, return patient to flat position and give analgesic
   4. Observe neurological status for signs of det rioration.

Neurological Disorders

Hydrocephalus

Definition: A condition in which the normal circulation of the spinal fluid is interrupted, resulting in pressure on the brain, deformity, and the progressive enlargement of the head.

Clinical Manifestations

A. Gradual enlargement of the head (more than one inch per month).
B. Separation of skull sutures.
C. Sclera visible above the iris ("sunset eyes").
D. Hyperactive reflexes.
E. Irritability, failure to thrive, and high-pitched cry.
F. Projectile vomiting without nausea.

Treatment

A. Depends on the cause of increased pressure.
B. Removal of part of choroid plexus to decrease production of cerebral spinal fluid.
C. Shunting the fluid out of the brain to the heart.
D. Shunting the fluid out of the brain to the peritoneal cavity.

Nursing Management

A. Preoperative care.
1. Prevent pressure sores on the head.
2. Provide good head support when child is sitting.
3. Promote optimal nutritional status.
B. Postoperative care.
1. Observe closely for signs of increasing intracranial pressure.
2. Watch for signs of electrolyte imbalance, especially sodium imbalance (spinal fluid is high in sodium, and if it bypasses the kidney, sodium is lost).
3. Observe for signs of infection (rapid pulse, increased temperature, fussiness).
4. Observe for vomiting and abdominal distention.
5. Observe for symptoms of dehydration.
6. Observe for symptoms of shunt obstruction.

Spina Bifida

Definition: The failure of the posterior portion of the lamina of the bony spine to form, which causes an opening in the spinal column.

Types

A. Spina bifida occulta.
1. Involves a bony defect only and does not involve the spinal cord or the meninges.
2. Requires no treatment.
B. Meningocele.
1. The meninges of the spinal cord extend through the opening in the spine.
2. Usually causes no paralysis—treated by removal of sac.
C. Meningomyelocele.
1. The cord and the meninges extend through the defect in the spine.
2. This defect causes neuromuscular involvement, which can vary from flaccidity and lack of bowel and bladder innervation to weakness of lower extremities.

Complications—Meningomyelocele

A. Hydrocephalus is frequent.
B. Urological involvement.
1. Frequent bladder infections.
2. Potential for progressive renal damage.

3. Ileal conduit surgery is frequently required.
4. Credé method of managing urinary retention involves systematic "milking" of the bladder at periodic intervals.
C. Orthopedic involvement.
1. Braces, crutches, or a wheelchair may frequently be required.
2. Prevention of contractures.
D. Parents frequently have great difficulties handling the child along with their other family responsibilities. They require a great deal of counseling and emotional support.

Nursing Management

A. Dependent on severity of handicap.
B. Hydrocephalus (see p. 374).
1. Measure head circumference daily.
2. Observe for symptoms of increased intracranial pressure.
C. Urological.
1. If patient is catheterized, use strict sterile technique.
2. Keep a careful record of intake and output.
3. If Credé treatment is ordered, teach parents the method.
4. Observe for signs of urinary tract infection.
5. Children are frequently medicated with high doses of vitamin C to increase the acidity of the urinary tract and thus prevent infection.
6. Promote increased fluid intake.
D. Orthopedic.
1. Provide opportunities for the child to exercise and develop unaffected areas.
2. Note the possible range of motion of affected extremities.

Epilepsy

Definition: This recurrent, convulsive disorder has a variable symptomatology, characterized by recurrent attacks of unconsciousness or altered consciousness usually with a series of tonic (stiffening) or clonic (twitching) muscular spasms or other abnormal behavior.

Etiology

A. Idiopathic—the majority of cases do not have an identifiable cause, although a genetic defect in the cerebral metabolism is thought to be responsible.

B. Organic.

1. A group of genetic conditions include epilepsy in their symptomatology, for example, phenylketonuria and hypoglycemia.

2. Epilepsy can result from cerebral damage acquired in the prenatal, natal, or postnatal period.

Types of Seizures

A. Grand mal.

1. Aura—a sensation which frequently precedes the onset of this type of seizure. Sometimes includes twitching or spasm of certain muscle groups, or the sensing of strange odors, visions, or sounds. Children have difficulty describing the experience, although parents or caretakers are able to identify headaches, nausea, and irritability as precursors to seizure.

2. Tonic stage.

   a. Onset is abrupt, and tonic (stiffening) contractions may occur simultaneously with loss of consciousness.

   b. The child usually pales, pupils dilate and eyes roll upward and to one side, head is thrown backward and to one side, the abdominal and chest muscles are held rigidly, and the limbs are contracted irregularly or are rigid.

   c. The tongue may be bitten as the jaw clamps down in contraction.

   d. Urination and defecation sometimes occur from hard contraction of abdominal muscles.

   e. Cyanosis, sometimes severe, may occur with prolonged respiratory cessation.

   f. Tonic phase lasts about twenty to forty seconds; then the clonic stage commences.

3. Clonic stage.

   a. Lasts for variable periods of time.

   b. Clonic movements include a quick, jerking, back-and-forth motion of extremities and spasmodic movements of the face.

4. Recovery stage.

   a. The child usually sleeps following the seizure.

   b. He may awake with a headache or a feeling of drowsiness or stupor.

5. Nighttime seizures may occur as evidenced by swollen, bitten tongue, blood on the pillow, wet bed, or headaches.

6. Status epilepticus occurs when seizures are so frequent that they appear constant and constitute a medical emergency due to possible brain damage from lack of oxygen.

B. Petit mal.

1. Transient loss of consciousness.

2. May be evidenced by eye-rolling, drooping head, and slight quivering of trunk and extremity muscles.

3. Attacks usually last less than thirty seconds.

4. Attacks may occur from once or twice a month to several hundred a day.

C. Psychomotor seizures.

1. Purposeful but inappropriate motor acts which are repetitive.

2. Frequently a slight aura.

3. Frequent vasomotor changes such as circumoral pallor.

4. Usually no tonic or clonic activity.

5. Following a one-to-five-minute period of unconsciousness, the child may resume normal activity or sleep.

D. Focal or Jacksonian seizures.

1. Sensory or motor, depending upon the location of the focal area of abnormal neural discharge.

2. Sometimes preceded by tonic phase.

3. Usually clonic in nature.

4. Muscles used in voluntary movement are most frequently involved, such as face and tongue, hand, and sometimes feet and trunk.

5. Usually begins in one area and spreads in a fixed pattern.

6. If seizure is localized to one area, loss of consciousness may not occur.

7. If spread of seizure is extensive and rapid, consciousness is lost and generalized confusion follows, similar to grand mal.

Nursing Management

A. Counseling of parents and caretakers.

1. Safety factors.

   a. Avoid hazardous play.

   b. During seizure, do not restrain movement of limbs, but protect head with a pillow.

c. Counsel on the use of the tongue depressor.

d. Make the child's environment free of sharp-cornered objects.

e. Keep medication out of the reach of children.

f. Reduce stress.

g. Avoid loud noises and blinking lights.

2. Medication.

a. Observe for side effects.

(1) Dilantin—hypertrophy of gums and stomatitis.

(2) Zarontin—blood dyscrasias.

b. Observe for signs of toxicity.

c. Administer dose accurately.

d. Keep medication out of reach of children.

3. Emotional.

a. Assist family in understanding the disease and helping child to have as normal a life as possible.

b. Prevent overprotection.

B. Care of the child in the hospital.

1. Have suction equipment ready and at bedside.

2. Keep a padded tongue depressor with the child at all times.

3. When seizure occurs, observe its progress and note it accurately to aid in the diagnosis of type of seizure.

4. Place the child near nurses' station.

5. Observe the reaction to medication.

6. Make sure crib or bed has side rails.

Cerebral Palsy

Definition: This term is used to describe a group of neuromuscular disorders caused by malfunctions of the motor centers and pathways of the brain.

Clinical Manifestations

A. Etiology is anoxia to the brain. Infections of the CNS are also a major factor.

B. Abnormal movements.

1. Spasticity.

a. Voluntary muscles lose normal smooth movements and respond with difficulty to both active and passive movement.

b. Increased deep tendon reflexes, scissoring.

c. Contractures of antigravity muscles.

2. Athetosis.

a. Involuntary muscle action with smooth, writhing movement of extremities.

b. Reflexes usually normal.

3. Ataxia—lack of coordination and possibly hypotonia.

C. Seizures occur in 75 percent of cerebral palsy children.

D. Vision disturbances occur in 20 percent.

E. At least 50 percent function mentally at a subnormal level—many cerebral palsy children are diagnosed as mentally retarded due to slow motor skills or aphasia.

Treatment

A. Each child requires an individualized program according to his particular manifestations of the disease and his capacities.

B. Prognosis is guarded.

Nursing Management

A. Child is usually admitted to hospital for orthopedic surgery.

B. Nurse should elicit a complete developmental history, both mental and physical, from the parents.

C. Child should be approached in a manner appropriate to his developmental age, not his chronological age.

D. Remember that physical limitations and unpleasant side effects of the condition (such as drooling) do not necessarily mean that the child is mentally deficient.

E. Parents need support and teaching in order to maintain discipline (security) and to cope with the illness.

Meningitis

Definition: An acute inflammation of the meninges.

Clinical Manifestations

A. May be caused by viral or bacterial agents.

B. Diagnosis based on symptoms and culture of C.S.F.

C. Typically, nuchal-spinal rigidity, headache, irritability, nausea, vomiting, and fever. Kernig's and Brudzinski's signs are positive.

Treatment

A. Administer appropriate I.V. medications.

B. Maintain adequate bed rest.

C. Maintain airway.

D. Provide fluid management.

Nursing Management

A. Observe and care for seizures.

B. Assess neurological signs.

C. Maintain excellent hydration.

D. For comfort, keep body in alignment.

E. Provide quiet activities which are age appropriate.

Gastrointestinal and Urinary Systems

Diagnostic Procedures

Barium Enema

A. A procedure in which a barium mixture is placed in the large intestine via a rectal catheter for X-ray visualization of the entire large intestine.

B. Nursing responsibilities prior to procedure.
   1. Cleanse the bowel through enemas.
   2. Restrict diet (clear fluids for 24 hours).

C. Nursing responsibilities following procedure.
   1. Avoid impaction from barium.
      a. Large fluid intake.
      b. Administer laxative or cleansing enemas.
   2. Advise parents and child that stools will be white for 24-72 hours following procedure.

Cystoscopy

A. A urological procedure usually done under general anesthesia which allows for direct visualization of the bladder and urethra.

B. Nursing responsibilities prior to procedure.
   1. NPO 6-8 hours prior to procedure.
   2. Explain procedure to parents.

C. Nursing responsibilities following procedure.
   1. Carefully check I & O.

   2. Watch for urinary retention.
   3. Check for hematuria.
   4. When permitted, encourage fluids.
   5. Observe for signs of infection.

Intravenous Pyelogram (IVP)

A. A radiographic study of the kidneys, bladder, and associated structures by injection of a contrast medium.

B. Nursing responsibilities prior to procedure.
   1. Clear out bowels—usually by a cathartic.
   2. NPO 6-8 hours.
   3. Have patient void immediately prior to the procedure.
   4. Explain procedure.

C. Nursing responsibilities following procedure.
   1. Watch for any reaction to contrast material.
   2. Evaluate patient's alertness and gag reflex before ingesting fluids.
   3. Evaluate for signs of perforation: intense pain in stomach or chest.

Gastrointestinal Disorders

Pyloric Stenosis

Definition: The pyloric canal, which is at the distal end of the stomach and connects with the duodenum, is greatly narrowed. This narrowing is believed to be caused by a combination of muscular hypertrophy, spasms, and edema of the mucous membrane.

Clinical Manifestations

A. Vomiting in newborn usually begins after two weeks and before two months of age.
   1. Progressively increases in frequency and force.
   2. Projectile vomitus may contain mucus and blood.

B. Constant hunger, fussiness, and frequent crying.

C. Stools usually decrease in size and number, and there may be constipation.

D. Peristaltic waves are frequently observed passing from left to right during, or immediately following, a feeding.

E. Later symptoms may include malnutrition, dehydration, electrolyte imbalance, and alkalosis.

Treatment

A. Correction of metabolic alkalosis from vomiting.

B. Requires surgical intervention—Fredet-Ramstedt procedure.

Nursing Management

A. Preoperative care.
   1. Prevent dehydration by accurate regulation of I.V. and accurately record intake and output.
   2. Observe feeding behavior for definitive diagnosis.
   3. Support mother and infant.

B. Proper insertion and observation of gastric tube.
   1. Length—measure tube externally on patient from nose to ear to stomach.
   2. Check position of the tube—infant should show no sign of respiratory difficulty with external end of tube occluded; gastric contents are siphoned through tube; no gagging, redness, or coughing should be observed.
   3. Place end of tube in a glass of water. If air bubbles emerge in a pattern that is similar to an inspiration-expiration cycle, remove the tube from the glass of water. Frequently, when the tube is first placed in the stomach, there is a release of trapped air, which should stop within a few seconds and not return.

C. Nursing care following surgery. Follow standard postoperative procedures.
   1. Maintain patent airway.
   2. Observe for shock.
   3. Keep a careful record of feeding behavior to assist physician in determining progress of feedings.

Esophageal Atresia

Definition: There are several different types of esophageal atresia. The most simple type involves the narrowing of the esophagus. In the second type, the upper and lower segments of the esophagus are not attached to each other, creating two blind pouches. Other types involve the trachea as well as the esophagus. Some have fistulas between the upper and/or lower segments of the esophagus and the trachea. The fistulas may be present when the esophagus is patent, when it is narrowed, or when it is not joined to its distal portion.

Clinical Manifestations

A. Excessive amounts of mucus.

B. Coughing, choking, and cyanosis when fed.

C. Food may be expelled through the nose immediately following the feeding.

D. Frequent respiratory problems.

E. Gastric distention.

Treatment

A. Depends on the type of esophageal atresia. If the gap between esophagus and stomach is small, surgery is usually performed following the diagnosis.

B. If the gap is large, a segment of the bowel is brought up to connect the esophagus with the stomach.

Nursing Management

A. Prevent the accumulation of oral secretions in the blind pouch through suctioning and positioning. (Prevent aspiration pneumonia.)

B. Observe for signs of respiratory distress—retractions, intermittent cyanosis, fussing, and nasal flaring.

C. Maintain a thirty-degree elevation of head and shoulders.

D. Maintain oral hygiene.

E. Observe for patency of all tubes.

F. Observe for dehydration.

G. Following surgery—follow standard postoperative procedures.

Intussusception

Definition: A segment of the bowel telescopes into the portion of bowel immediately distal to it. Probably results from hyperactive peristalsis in the proximal portion of the bowel, with inactive peristalsis in the distal segment. Usually occurs at the junction of the ileum with the colon.

Clinical Manifestations

A. Sudden onset—occurs most often when the child is between four and six months old.

B. Gastrointestinal symptoms—vomiting, abdominal

pain and distention, and infrequent stools with blood and mucus.

C. Child frequently pulls knees to chest when pain occurs.

D. Dehydration.

Treatment

A. The first choice of treatment is a barium enema, which frequently reduces the bowel.

B. If symptoms recur, surgery is performed for bowel reduction.

Nursing Management

A. Observation and maintenance of I.V. fluid and electrolyte replacement.

B. Nasogastric suction to deflate the stomach to prevent vomiting.

C. Gradual reintroduction of fluids and foods.

D. Care of operative site following surgery.

Diarrhea—Severe

Definition: Diarrhea is seen when there is a disturbance of the intestinal tract that alters motility and absorption and accelerates the excretion of intestinal contents (three to thirty stools per day). Fluids and electrolytes which are normally absorbed are excreted, causing electrolyte imbalances. Most infectious diarrheas in this country are caused by a virus. Diarrhea can be a separate disease, or it may be a symptom of another disease.

Clinical Manifestations

A. Increased rate of peristalsis carrying intestinal contents (including base-bicarbonates) along.
   1. Blood, pus, or mucus in stools, which are often green in color.
   2. Increase in frequency of stools of watery consistency.

B. Signs of dehydration.
   1. Mucous membranes become dried and cracked.
   2. Skin dries and loses its normal elasticity.
   3. Fontanels are depressed and eyes appear sunken.
   4. The urine decreases greatly in amount and becomes dark in color (concentrated).
   5. Acidosis is a common result.

Treatment

A. Correction of electrolyte imbalances and dehydration.

B. Correction of underlying disorder if any.

C. A period of rest for the gastrointestinal tract is usually ordered for twenty-four to forty-eight hours.

D. Diet progresses from water to carbohydrates, proteins, fats, fruits, and vegetables as tolerated.

Nursing Management

A. Strict isolation until causal organism or other factors are determined.

B. Stools and diapers disposed of in proper containers. (Disposable diapers recommended.)

C. Careful ongoing assessment of dehydration level and acidosis.

D. Accurate recording of the number and consistency of stools.

E. Prevention of dehydration and electrolyte imbalance.
   1. Strict observation of intake and output.
   2. Supervision of I.V. therapy.
   3. Monitoring electrolyte laboratory results.

F. Excellent skin care to prevent excoriation caused by alkaline stools.

Hirschsprung's Disease

Definition: A disease caused by the congenital absence of parasympathetic nerve ganglion cells in the distal bowel. As a result, this portion of the bowel is unable to transmit regular peristaltic waves, which are coordinated with the proximal portion of the bowel. When a stool reaches the diseased area, it is not transmitted on down the colon, but accumulates in the segment just proximal to this area, forming a functional obstruction. The bowel above the obstructed portion eventually becomes hypertrophied in its attempts to transmit the stool.

Clinical Manifestations

A. Failure to pass meconium in newborn.

B. Vomiting and reluctance to feed.

C. Signs of intestinal obstruction.

D. Signs of constipation.

E. Abdominal distention.

F. Foul odor of breath and stool.

G. Older child—constipation, offensive and ribbon-like stools.

Treatment

A. The first stage of treatment is usually a transverse or sigmoid colostomy.

B. The child is then brought back to optimal health and nutritional status.

C. The final procedure consists of dissection and removal of the nonfunctional bowel and anastomosis.

D. Closure of temporary colostomy.

Nursing Management

A. Prior to diagnosis, the nurse should observe carefully for all gastrointestinal manifestations of the disease and report them accurately.

B. Prior to the colostomy procedure.

  1. Clean bowel.

    a. Stool softeners.

    b. Liquid diet.

    c. Colonic irrigation—saline.

  2. Prepare parents for the procedure.

    a. Clarify the surgical technique.

    b. Describe stoma.

    c. Prepare for care of the colostomy patient.

    d. Give parents the opportunity to express their feelings about the procedure.

C. Postoperative care.

  1. Maintenance of optimal nutrition.

  2. Close observation of stools for reestablishment of normal elimination pattern.

  3. Skin care of colostomy and anal areas.

Cleft Lip

Definition: A birth defect that involves a fissure resulting from incomplete merging of embryonic processes that normally form the face or jaws.

Etiology

A. Usually considered hereditary; may be familial.

B. Types.

  1. Unilateral.

  2. Bilateral.

  3. Midline (rare).

Treatment

A. Surgical repair and closure of the cleft.

B. Usually done as soon as the child reaches ten pounds.

Nursing Management

A. Preoperative care.

  1. Use soft or regular nipple with crosscut.

  2. Place nipple on opposite side from cleft.

  3. Bubble frequently.

B. Postoperative care.

  1. Observe for respiratory distress and swelling of tongue, nostrils, and mouth.

  2. Avoid circumstances which will cause crying.

  3. Watch for hemorrhage.

  4. Use elbow restraints—with supervised rest periods to exercise arms.

  5. Feed with rubber-tipped medicine dropper on the side opposite the repaired cleft for three weeks.

  6. After feeding, clean suture line with half-strength hydrogen peroxide.

  7. Prevent crust formation on suture line.

  8. Lay infant on side or back with support, to prevent rolling over on the abdomen.

Cleft Palate

Definition: A birth defect in which the palates—opening between the nose and the roof of the mouth—fail to close properly. It is usually considered hereditary. Types include clefted soft palate, clefted hard palate, and a cleft that infrequently involves the nose.

Clinical Manifestations

A. Difficulty in sucking.

B. Increase in upper respiratory infections.

C. Difficult mother-child relationship—mother feels frustrated and baby is fussy.

Treatment

A. Surgical repairs—some surgeons prefer to wait until the palate has had the opportunity to grow; others prefer to operate prior to the onset of speech.

B. Repair in stages—may be required with extensive defects.

C. Surgical repair usually needs to be followed by treatment from an orthodontist, a speech therapist, and a plastic surgeon.

Nursing Management

A. Preoperative care.
1. Infant should be sitting up when fed.
2. Frequent mouth care.
3. Introduce the method of postoperative feeding; for example, have the child drink from a cup.
4. Practice arm restraints on the child, so that he becomes familiar with them.
5. Prepare parents and give them support.

B. Postoperative care.
1. Immediate postoperative period.
   a. Place child on abdomen to prevent aspiration of mucus or blood.
   b. Observe for signs of airway obstruction and have suction apparatus at the bedside.
   c. Observe for shock or hemorrhage.
   d. Elbow restraints should be in place and should be released frequently.
   e. Irrigate suture line frequently.
   f. Provide a mist tent.
2. Second postoperative day prior to discharge.
   a. Start introducing fluids by paper cup; avoid straws and glasses.
   b. Advance diet as tolerated.
   c. Irrigate sutures following feedings.

Celiac Disease

Definition: A chronic disease of intestinal malabsorption precipitated by ingestion of gluten or protein portions of wheat or rye flour.

Clinical Manifestations

A. May occur as early as six months and continue until fifth year.

B. Highest incidence in white race.

C. Symptoms.
1. Diarrhea or loose stools—bulky, foul smelling, pale, and frothy.
2. Abdominal distention.

3. Anorexia.
4. Irritability.

D. Celiac crisis.
1. Vomiting and diarrhea.
2. Acidosis and dehydration.
3. May be precipitated by respiratory infection.
4. Excessive sweat.
5. Cold extremities.

Nursing Management

A. Diet.
1. Wheat and rye gluten eliminated.
2. Low fat.
3. Slow feedings, small amounts at a time.
4. Strict intake and output.
5. Strict calorie control.

B. Parental support.
1. Teach diet.
2. Provide for follow-up of public health nurse for continued teaching and assistance.
3. Explain prognosis—clinical symptoms decrease with increasing age.

C. Prevent infection.

Parasitic Worms

Roundworms

A. Life cycle.
1. Eggs are laid by the worm in the gastrointestinal tract of any host animal and passed out in feces.
2. After the worms have been ingested, egg batches are laid.
3. Larvae in the host invade lymphatics and venules of the mesentery and migrate to the liver, the lungs, and the heart.
4. Larvae from lungs reach the host's epiglottis and are swallowed; once in the gastrointestinal tract, the cycle is repeated—larvae mature and mate, and the female lays eggs.

B. Symptoms.
1. Atypical pneumonia.
2. Gastrointestinal symptoms—nausea, vomiting, anorexia, and weight loss.
3. Insomnia.
4. Irritability.
5. Signs of intestinal obstruction.

C. Treatment—piperazine citrate.

D. Nursing management.

1. Prevention of infection through the use of a sanitary toilet.
2. Hygiene education of the family.
3. Careful disposal of infected stools.

Pinworm (Oxyuriasis)

A. Life cycle.

1. Eggs ingested.
2. Eggs mature in cecum, then migrate to anus.
3. Worms exit at night and lay eggs on host's skin.
4. Itching and reingestion occur.

B. Symptoms.

1. Acute or subacute appendicitis.
2. Eczematous areas of skin.
3. Irritability.
4. Loss of weight and anorexia.
5. Insomnia.
6. Diagnosis by tape test—place transparent adhesive tape over anus and examine tape for evidence of worms.

C. Treatment.

1. Piperazine hexahydrate.
2. All infected persons living communally must be treated simultaneously.

D. Nursing management.

1. During treatment, maintain meticulous cleansing of the skin, particularly in the anal region, and the hands and the nails.
2. Bed linens and clothing must be boiled.
3. Use ointment to relieve itching.
4. Teach careful hygiene as a preventative measure.

Hookworm

A. Life cycle.

1. Eggs of the worm are evacuated from the human bowel in feces and left in the soil.
2. Once the larvae are infective (in five to ten days), they invade the host when in contact with the skin—which occurs either by handling the soil or by walking barefoot.
3. The worms live in the upper gastrointestinal tract of the host or suck blood from the intestinal wall for nourishment.

B. Characteristics.

1. Disturbed digestion.
2. Unformed stools containing undigested food.

3. Tarry stool with decomposed blood.
4. Blood loss.
   a. Pallor.
   b. Dull hair.
   c. Anemia.
   d. Increased pulse.
   e. Mental apathy.

C. Treatment.

1. Drug—tetrachloroethylene.
2. Possibly blood transfusions.

D. Nursing management.

1. NPO the evening preceding the treatment.
2. Avoid fats, oils, and alcohol for twelve hours following medication.
3. Prevention of infection.
   a. Hygiene instruction.
   b. Use of shoes in hookworm areas.
4. Careful disposal of stools.

Obesity

Definition: Accumulation of excess body fat.

Clinical Manifestations

A. The impact of childhood obesity becomes most obvious at adolescence when body image and peer approval become important.

B. Occasionally, obesity is a sign that the child is missing other satisfaction.

C. Sometimes food is the only source of pleasure a child can find.

D. Eating can relieve anxiety for some children.

E. The child is often the victim of nagging and begins to associate overweight with feelings of worthlessness.

Nursing Management

A. Diet—provide a balanced diet with limited calories.

B. Exercise—set up a routine of daily exercise; frequently, groups for after school exercise programs can be organized by school nurses.

C. Counseling and/or therapy—help the young person work through underlying problems causing or caused by obesity.

D. Family counseling.

1. Examine the eating patterns of the family—

some cultures have a high proportion of starches; others associate large meals with prosperity.

2. Suggest the use of positive reinforcement for the adolescent rather than shaming him.

3. Have family support child by removing high calorie food from their meals.

Ulcerative Colitis

Definition: This is an inflammatory disease of the colon and the rectum in which the mucous membrane becomes hyperemic, bleeds easily, and tends to ulcer.

Etiology

A. Unknown, although the increased incidence within families has given rise to the hypothesis suggesting a hereditary predisposition or an emotional and/or environmental causation.

B. Incidence—highest in young adults and middle-age groups.

Clinical Manifestations

A. Symptoms.
   1. Diarrhea.
   2. Weight loss.
   3. Rectal bleeding.
   4. Abdominal pain, nausea, and vomiting.
   5. Anemia.
   6. Fever and dehydration.

B. Children with the disease tend to be passive, pessimistic, fearful, and strongly, though ambivalently, attached to a parent.

Nursing Management

A. Control of inflammation.
   1. Supervision of medication regime.
   2. Adequate hydration with intravenous therapy and oral fluids as indicated.

B. Provide rest of intestinal tract.
   1. Observe for amount of bowel activity and symptoms of bleeding and hyperactive peristalsis.
   2. Administer tranquilizers and observe for side effects.

C. Diet therapy.
   1. Low residue, bland, high protein diet.

2. Vitamin therapy.
3. Avoid cold foods because they increase gastric motility.
4. Arrange for attractive environment with opportunities for socialization at mealtimes.
5. Avoid sharp cheeses, highly spiced foods, smoked or salted meats, fried foods, raw fruits, and vegetables.

D. Counseling.
   1. Educate patient about diet, medication, and symptoms of bleeding.
   2. Observe for signs of psychological problems; initiate referral if necessary.

Renal Disorders

Acute Glomerulonephritis

Definition: Acute glomerulonephritis is believed to be an antigen-antibody reaction secondary to an infection from group A beta-hemolytic streptococci originating elsewhere in the body.

Clinical Manifestations

A. Renal system.
   1. Protein and blood cells present in urine.
   2. Oliguria and occasional anuria.
   3. Edema.

B. Cardiovascular system.
   1. Possibly hypertension and slowed pulse.
   2. Cerebral edema.
   3. Possible congestive heart failure, circulatory congestion.

C. Other symptoms.
   1. Intermittent fever.
   2. Occasionally, anorexia is present.

Treatment

A. Bed rest during acute stage.
B. If there are positive bacterial cultures, child is treated with antibiotics.
C. Protein and potassium-free diet.
D. Antihypertensive drugs, e.g., reserpine, magnesium sulfate.

Nursing Management

A. Prevention of fluid overload.

    1. Daily weights.

    2. Meticulous measurement of intake and output.

B. Prevention of problems secondary to edema.

    1. Observe for signs of cerebral edema.

    2. Observe for respiratory embarrassment.

    3. Monitor blood pressure frequently.

    4. Prevent skin breakdown.

C. Diet low in protein and potassium.

The Nephrotic Syndrome

Definition: A symptom complex with multiple and varied pathological manifestations and causes, the etiology of which is unknown.

Clinical Manifestations

A. Generalized edema.

B. Marked proteinuria.

C. Hematuria.

D. Hypertension.

E. Average age of child at onset is two-and-a-half years.

Treatment

A. Prevention of infection.

B. Symptomatic care.

Nursing Management

A. Prevention and control of infection—antibiotics.

B. Edema.

    1. Meticulous skin care.

    2. Daily weights.

    3. Change body position.

    4. Accurate intake and output.

    5. Diuretics.

C. Steroids—usually prednisone—reduces edema and proteinuria.

    1. Produces diuresis in ten to twelve days.

    2. Tapered dosage.

    3. Prepare child and family for side effects:

        a. Cushing's syndrome.

        b. Weight gain.

        c. Acne.

        d. Hirsutism.

D. Diet.

    1. High protein.

    2. Low sodium—500 mg./day.

    3. High calorie diet.

Blood and Lymph System

Blood Transfusions

A. General type of therapy.

    1. Packed red cells administered slowly.

    2. Dosage not to exceed 10 mL/Kg.

    3. Severely ill child may receive partial exchange transfusion (isovolumetric).

B. Nursing responsibilities during blood transfusion.

    1. Closely observe patient, apparatus, and flow.

    2. Check on type and cross match of blood.

    3. Obtain baseline vital signs.

    4. Never give medications in blood, and never hang blood with dextrose and water.

    5. Observe for transfusion reaction: backache, generalized discomfort, chilly sensations, distention of neck veins, tachycardia, tachypnea, and fall in blood pressure.

    6. Observe for allergic reactions: wheezing, laryngeal edema, hives, itching and rash, and flushed appearance.

    7. If either reaction occurs, close off transfusion and call physician.

    8. Never use blood that is discolored or cloudy or that has been unrefrigerated for more than twenty minutes.

Sickle Cell Anemia

Definition: A recessive hereditary disorder in which red blood cells sickle when under low oxygen tension. Usually confined to Blacks, the abnormal hemoglobin is transmitted as a dominant trait.

Clinical Manifestations

A. Symptoms.

    1. Severe chronic anemia—pallor.

2. Periodic crises with abdominal and joint pain.
3. Lethargy and listlessness.
4. Irritability.
5. High fever.
6. Enlarged spleen from increased activity.
7. Jaundice from excessive blood cell destruction.
8. Widening of the marrow spaces of the bones.
9. Gallstones.

B. Crises—patients characteristically experience episodes with the following symptoms.
1. Thrombotic crises.
  a. Most frequent type.
  b. Caused by occlusion of the small blood vessels producing distal ischemia and infarction.
  c. Beginning of crises may be characterized by the swelling of the hands and feet or decreased appetite, irritability, or fever.
  d. May experience pain and swelling in abdomen.
2. Sequestration crises.
  a. Occurs usually in children under five.
  b. Caused by pooling of blood in spleen.
  c. Enlargement of spleen and circulatory collapse.

Nursing Management

A. Alleviate pain with analgesics.
B. Prevent dehydration with intravenous infusion, if necessary, and increased fluid intake.
C. Keep child warm.
D. Offer parents genetic counseling.
E. Counsel the family on physiology and prognosis of disease.
F. During sequestration crises—supervise blood transfusions.

Hemophilia

Definition: An inborn error of metabolism in which certain factors necessary for coagulation of the blood are missing. Transmission of sex-linked traits are passed from affected father to carrier daughters.

Types

A Hemophilia A—Factor VIII deficiency.
B. Hemophilia B—Factor IX deficiency (Christmas disease).
C. Hemophilia C—Factor XI deficiency.

Clinical Manifestations

A. Type A and B.
1. Possible bleeding tendency in neonatal period because factors are not passed through the placenta.
2. Excessive bruising.
3. Large hematomas from minor trauma.
4. Persistent bleeding from minor injuries.
5. Hemarthrosis with joint pain, swelling, and limited movement.
6. Possible progressive degenerative changes with osteoporosis, muscle atrophy, and fixed joints.
B. Type C.
1. Usually appears as a mild bleeding disorder.
2. Autosomal dominant trait with both sexes affected.

Treatment

A. Type A and B—cryoprecipitate or fresh frozen plasma.
B. Type C—fresh frozen plasma.
C. Fresh frozen plasma preferred as clotting factors are reduced in stored blood plasma.

Nursing Management

A. Prevent bleeding.
1. Protective environment—padded crib and playpen.
2. Careful supervision when child is learning to walk.
B. Observe for signs of blood transfusion reaction.
C. Observe for signs of volume overload with plasma administration.
D. Bleeding.
1. Apply cold compresses and pressure.
2. Hemarthrosis (effusion of blood into joint).
  a. Immobilize joint initially.
  b. Initiate passive range of motion within forty-eight hours to prevent stiffness and fibrosis.
3. Immobilize site of bleeding.
E. Educate family for home administration of transfusions.

Infectious Mononucleosis

Definition: Mononucleosis is an infectious disease, believed to be viral in origin, which causes an increase in the mononuclear elements of the blood.

Clinical Manifestations

A. Incubation period is around eleven days.
B. Symptoms.
 1. Malaise.
 2. Sore throat with pharyngitis.
 3. Prolonged fever.
 4. Enlargement of the lymph nodes.
 5. Splenomegaly.
 6. About 10 to 20 percent of the cases exhibit skin rashes that appear between day four and ten. The rash is usually the macular type, occurring primarily on the trunk.

Nursing Management

A. Symptomatic and supportive.
 1. Initially, bed rest is indicated.
 2. Increase in activity should be gradual.
 3. Salicylates are given for fever, chills, and muscle pain.
B. No isolation procedures are required.

Musculoskeletal Disorders

Legg-Perthes Disease

Definition: This disease is an ideopathic, aseptic necrosis of the capital femoral epiphysis. Vascular disruption of the femoral head causes necrosis and variable deformity of the upper femoral epiphysis.

Clinical Manifestations

A. Usually afflicts males between the ages of four and ten.
B. Usually the disease is unilateral.
C. Stages.
 1. Aseptic necrosis—nine to twelve months.
 2. Revascularization—nine to twelve months.
 3. Reossification—nine to twelve months.
D. Symptoms.
 1. Pain in the hip or knee.
 2. Limp.
 3. Limited movement of the hip joint.
E. Treatment—avoidance of weight on the affected leg until healing is finished.

Nursing Management

A. Case finding and referral.
B. During immobilization.
 1. Provide carts or stretchers for mobility.
 2. Exercise child's upper extremities.
 3. Promote active games in which the child can participate while lying on the cart.
 4. These children usually develop extremely strong muscles in their upper extremities, which gives them the strength to maneuver on the low stretchers.
 5. Assist the parents in arranging a home environment to accommodate the child's needs of mobility.

Congenital Dislocation of Hip

Definition: The malrotation of the hip at birth; cause usually unknown.

Clinical Manifestations

A. Unequal major gluteal folds.
B. Presence of a hip "click" on abduction.
C. Femur appears shortened.

Treatment

A. Splinting of hip in alignment.
B. Hip maintained in flexion and abduction.

Nursing Management

A. Case finding and referral.
B. Teach parents how to apply splint.
C. Protect skin under the splint.
D. Bring environment to child—surround with age appropriate toys.

Osteomyelitis

Definition: Infection usually of the long bones caused most frequently by Staphylococcus aureus.

Clinical Manifestations

A. Abrupt onset.

B. Fever, malaise, and pain.

C. Localized tenderness in the bone at the metaphysis.

D. Swelling and redness over affected bone.

E. Occurs most frequently in boys between five and fourteen years old.

Nursing Management

A. Control of infection.
   1. Supervision of antibacterial therapy.
   2. Careful handling of drainage.

B. Control of pain.
   1. Immobilization of affected limb.
   2. Analgesics.

C. Occupational activities during immobilization.
   1. Painting and crafts.
   2. Passive games.
   3. Interaction with peers.

Juvenile Rheumatoid Arthritis

Definition: This is a systemic disease with multiple manifestations, arthritis being the most characteristic. Etiology is unknown.

Clinical Manifestations

A. Pathology.
   1. Inflammation of joints.
   2. Edema and congestion of synovial tissues.
   3. As the disease progresses, synovial material fills the joint spore, causing narrowing, fibrous ankylosis, and bony fusion.
   4. Growth centers adjacent to affected joints may undergo either premature closure or accelerated epiphyseal growth.

B. Joints.
   1. Arthritis may start slowly with gradual development of joint stiffness, swelling, and loss of motion.
   2. Most frequently affects knees, ankles, feet, wrists, and fingers—although any joint may be involved.
   3. Affected joints are swollen, warm, painful, and stiff.
   4. Young children appear irritable and anxious, guarding their joints.
   5. Weakness and atrophy of muscles appear around affected joints.
   6. Chronically affected joints may become deformed, dislocated, or fused.

C. Systemic involvement.
   1. Frequent.
   2. Irritability, anorexia, and malaise.
   3. Fever.
   4. Intermittent macular rash is occasionally seen.
   5. Hepatosplenomegaly and generalized lymphadenopathy in 20 percent of the patients.
   6. Anemia is common with active cases of the disease.
   7. Inflammation of eye—redness, pain, photophobia, decreased visual acuity, and nonreactive pupil.

Treatment

A. No specific cure.

B. Objectives of treatment.
   1. Prevention of joint destruction.
   2. Emotional support of the chronically ill child and his family.

Nursing Management

A. Supervision of medications.
   1. Salicylates—given in large doses.
   2. Observe for signs of toxicity and side effects.
      a. Ringing in the ear.
      b. Gastric irritation—give drug with milk or antacids.
      c. Headaches.
      d. Disturbances of mental state.
      e. Hyperventilation and drowsiness.
   3. Gold salts.
      a. Usually given in weekly injections.
      b. Observe for side effects.
         (1) Dermatitis.
         (2) Stomatitis.
         (3) Nephritis with hematuria or albuminuria.
         (4) Thrombocytopenia.
         (5) Bone marrow depression.

c. Weekly blood and urine tests.

4. Steroids.

    a. Observe for side effects and toxicity.

       (1) Masked infection.

       (2) Hypertension.

       (3) Vascular disorders.

       (4) Mental disturbances.

       (5) Edema—weight gain.

       (6) Increased appetite.

       (7) Peptic ulcer.

    b. Regular observation of vital signs.

    c. Careful supervision during initiation and tapering off of drug.

B. Maintenance of joint mobility.

1. Exercise joints.

2. Provide night splints.

3. Educate parents in how patient should perform exercises and impress upon them the patient's need for physical therapy and night splints.

C. Prevention of eye damage—encourage parents to report any signs of eye problems in the patient immediately to the physician.

D. Counseling of family.

1. Explain physiology and unpredictable nature of the disease to the parents and the patient.

2. Provide emotional support to the parents for dealing with a chronically ill child or adolescent.

3. Encourage independence in the patient.

4. Encourage mastery of developmental tasks appropriate to the age group of the patient.

Curvature of the Spine

Types

A. Kyphosis—flexion deformity usually at thoracic spine.

B. Lordosis—fixed extension deformity usually occurring to compensate for other abnormalities.

C. Scoliosis—lateral curvature of the spine.

1. Nonstructural—caused by changes outside the spine; treated with exercises.

2. Structural—the spine itself has rotated; treated by bracing, exercise, or insertion of the Harrington rod.

Characteristics of Scoliosis

A. Affects more girls than boys.

B. Usually not noticed until adolescence.

C. Structural scoliosis will continue to worsen with growth unless intervention is initiated.

Clinical Manifestations

A. One shoulder higher than the other.

B. At home, female patients have noticed difficulty in getting even hems on their skirts because of unevenness in the height of hips.

C. One flank area may be different from the other.

D. Occasionally mild pain.

E. When patient touches his toes, one side of the back has a lump.

Nursing Management

A. Milwaukee brace.

1. Teach adolescent to wear the brace correctly and remove it only to bathe or as prescribed by the physician.

2. Provide skin care where brace touches.

3. Assist adolescent to understand the need for the brace, and help the patient deal with the altered body image.

B. Harrington rod insertion.

1. Definition—surgical placement of permanent rod along spine to correct curvature.

2. Preoperative care.

    a. Teach coughing, deep breathing, and log rolling.

    b. Explain operative procedure, and prepare for difficult aspects following surgery—pain and immobility.

3. Postoperative care.

    a. Observe for correct nerve innervation to extremities.

    b. Observe for signs of bleeding—check dressing, blood pressure, and pulse.

    c. Keep a careful record of intake and output—damage of nerves to the bladder can be a hazardous side effect.

    d. Log roll patient.

    e. Have patient progress slowly from bed sitting to standing to walking.

    f. Following casting, observe for movement

of extremities, blood, cyanosis, blanching, or burning.

   g. Protect patient's privacy during examinations.

C. General considerations.

   1. Alterations and confusion in body image require counseling.

   2. Teaching important.

      a. Physical structure of body and purpose of brace/rod insertion.

      b. Correct procedures for wearing brace.

Endocrine System

Endocrine Disorders

Juvenile Diabetes

Definition: Diabetes is thought to be a genetic condition in which varying metabolic derangements exist that interfere in the production, availability, or effectiveness of insulin.

Table 2. Insulin Treatment

Types	Onset (hrs.)	Duration of maximum effect (hrs.)	Total duration (hrs.)
Regular	½	4 to 6	6 to 8
Semilente	½	4 to 6	10 to 12
NPH	2	8 to 12	12 to 18
Lente	2	8 to 12	20 to 26
Protamine zinc (PZI)	4 to 8	14 to 20	24 to 36
Ultralente	6 to 8	16 to 18	24 to 36

Clinical Manifestations

A. Pathology.

   1. Interference with the utilization of sugar.

   2. Impaired transportation of glucose across cellu-

lar membranes and impaired utilization within the cell.

   3. Increased glycogenesis.

   4. Diuresis from hyperglycemia, resulting in glucosuria and excessive losses of electrolytes and water.

   5. Increased oxidation of fats and proteins, leading to proteinuria and acidosis.

B. Specific symptoms.

   1. Rapid onset.

   2. Loss of weight.

   3. Increased thirst and appetite, polydypsia, and polyphagia.

   4. Polyuria and nocturia.

   5. Onset is frequently associated with ketoacidosis—an acute, life-threatening condition.

      a. Drowsiness.

      b. Dryness of skin.

      c. Flushed cheeks.

      d. Acetone breath.

      e. Hyperpnea.

      f. Nausea, vomiting, and abdominal pains.

C. Prognosis—degenerative changes associated with diabetes mellitus begin in young adults who have had the disease for ten to twenty years.

   1. Arteriosclerosis with hypertension.

   2. Retinal changes and cataracts.

   3. Nephropathy.

Treatment

A. Insulin. (Oral hypoglycemic agents generally do not produce satisfactory results because they require some pancreatic function to be effective.)

   1. Side effects: hypoglycemia with hunger, irritability, nervousness, headaches, and slurred speech.

   2. Types of treatment (see Table 2).

B. Diet should be adequate for normal growth and development and regulated according to diabetic needs. The type of diet prescribed is influenced by the philosophy of the physician—diets vary from free diets to strict dietary control.

Nursing Management

A. Family and patient education.

   1. Signs and symptoms of disease, including acidosis and hypoglycemia.

2. Instruction in insulin injection, sterile technique, and urine testing.
3. Diet control as prescribed by the physician.
4. Prevention of infections through adequate skin and foot care.
5. Patient should be aware of the effects of increased physical activity and stress on food needs.
6. The patient should accept responsibility for administering insulin and managing his diet.
7. Encourage normal activity and life style appropriate to age of patient.

B. Adolescent patients frequently need special counseling because of their heightened sensitivity to being different and their frequently unusual dietary habits.

Skin Disorders

Impetigo

Definition: A skin infection caused by streptococcus, staphylococcus, or pneumococcus.

Clinical Manifestations

A. Multiple macular-papular rash seen at various stages of healing.
B. Rupture of papules produces serous exudate which forms a crust.
C. Usually found on head and neck.

Treatment

A. In newborn, immediate local and systemic antibiotic therapy and isolation.
B. In older child and adult, frequent cleansing with soap and removal of crusts.
C. Nails are cut to avoid scratching.

Eczema

Definition: An atopic dermatitis which is generally seen in children with allergic tendencies.

Clinical Manifestations

A. Erythema, papules, vesicules.
B. Drainage and crusting.
C. Intense itching.
D. Seen in children 4 months to 4 years.
E. Often commences with the introduction of new foods—particularly eggs and cow's milk and the cessation of breast feeding.

Treatment

A. Elimination of foods which exacerbate problem.
B. Removal of dust-carrying objects in environment (stuffed animals).
C. Elimination of all strong soaps.
D. Symptomatic treatment of lesions—frequent soaks with Burow's solution or normal saline.
E. Prevention of scratching.

Burns

Classifications or Assessment of Burn Injury

A. First-degree or superficial—involves only reddening of the skin.
B. Second-degree or partial thickness—skin blisters, regeneration of epithelium without grafting.
C. Third-degree or full thickness—destruction of most of the epidermal tissue; unable to regenerate without graft.

Treatment of Wound

A. First aid.
  1. Provide comfort and prevent chilling.
  2. Wash area with cool, sterile solution or water if no sterile solution is available.
  3. Cover with a sterile cloth—prevent liquid contamination.
  4. Do not apply greasy substances until burn is evaluated.
  5. Wash surrounding area thoroughly with mild detergent.
B. Exposed method—no dressing is used so that hard eschar forms, protecting wound from infection. This method is excellent for areas difficult to bandage effectively. Requires reverse isolation and is difficult for a child.

C. Closed method—sterile occlusive dressing is applied frequently, usually with topical medications. Debridement occurs every time the dressing is changed, preventing a large loss of blood at one time, as when eschar is removed.

D. Silver nitrate therapy in closed method—a popular treatment because of its effectiveness against most organisms found in burns, but it may cause loss of electrolytes.

E. Sulfamylon therapy—effective against many gram negative and positive organisms, but may cause acid-base derangements and is painful when applied.

Problems Associated with Burns

A. Fluid and electrolyte imbalances.
   1. In deeper wounds, edema appears around the wound from damage to capillaries.
   2. There is a loss of fluid at the burn area.
   3. On the second day, there is a large loss of potassium.
   4. Objective of fluid therapy is to maintain adequate tissue perfusion.

B. Circulatory changes.
   1. Drop in cardiac output, initially.
   2. Decrease in blood volume from loss of plasma protein into extravascular and extracellular spaces.
   3. Moderate amount of hemolysis of red blood cells.

C. Pulmonary changes—inhalation injury.
   1. Pulmonary edema.
   2. Obstruction of the air passages from edema of the face, neck, trachea, and larynx.
   3. Restriction of lung mobility from eschar on chest wall.

D. Renal changes.
   1. Renal insufficiency caused by reaction to hypovolemic shock.
   2. Decreased blood supply to kidneys results in decreased renal perfusion.
   3. In burns of 15 to 20 percent of the body surface, there is a decreased urinary output that must be avoided or reversed.
   4. Urinary tract infections are frequent.

E. Gastrointestinal changes.
   1. Acute gastric dilation.
   2. Paralytic ileus.

   3. Curling's ulcer—producing "coffee ground" aspirant.
   4. Hemorrhagic gastritis—bleeding from congested capillaries in gastric mucosa.

F. Lifelong sequelae of disfigurement.
   1. Psychological problems associated with disfigurement.
   2. Problems encountered with long-term plastic surgery.

Nursing Management

A. Prevention of infection.
   1. Sterile technique and environment.
   2. Observe for signs of infection, increased temperature and pulse.
   3. Prophylactic—tetanus and antibiotics.

B. Prevention of pulmonary complications.
   1. Establishment and observation of adequate airway.
   2. Suction p.r.n.
   3. Humidified oxygen p.r.n.
   4. Cough and deep breathing.
   5. Frequent position changes.

C. Establishment of adequate circulatory volume.
   1. Observe for signs of hypovolemia—thirst, vomiting, increased pulse, decreased blood pressure, and decreased urinary output.
   2. Observe for signs of circulatory overload, particularly around the second to fifth day, when fluid in extracellular tissues returns to circulation—there is danger of congestive heart failure.
   3. Supervise intravenous therapy.
   4. Monitor intake and output.

D. Prevention of contractures.
   1. Keep body parts in alignment.
   2. Elevate burned extremities.
   3. Provide active and/or passive range of motion to all joints.

E. Adequate nutrition.
   1. Calories should be twice the normal amount.
   2. Protein should be three to four times the normal requirements.
   3. There should be small, frequent meals that look attractive.
   4. Frequently patient anorexic—needs encouragement to eat.
   5. Meals should not immediately follow dressing

change or other painful or malodorous procedures.

F. Design activities for the burned child while he is hospitalized.
   1. Actively involve the child (e.g., acting out part of a story verbally).
   2. Provide television, books, and games.
   3. Allow the child to associate with other children.
G. Counseling.
   1. Parents and patient have difficulty dealing with disfigurement and need assistance.
   2. Parents frequently feel guilty, although they are usually not at fault, and need assistance working out these feelings.

Pediatric Oncology

Malignant Diseases

Wilms's Tumor (Nephroblastoma)

Definition: Wilms's tumor is a cancerous abdominal tumor seen in children.

Clinical Manifestations

A. Usually, presence of the mass itself initiates diagnostic workup; however, the child may have a fever and abdominal pains.
B. Once the presence of a functioning, nonaffected kidney is ascertained, an immediate nephrectomy is done.

Nursing Management

A. Avoid palpation of the tumor—it may spread.
B. Provide support for the family.
C. Observe carefully intake and output.
D. Observe for toxic reactions to chemotherapy, such as mouth lesions.
E. If X-ray therapy is given, provide good skin care.

Leukemia

Definition: Leukemia is a fatal, malignant disease caused by the proliferation of leukocytes and their precursors. Average life expectancy is three to four years.

Major Types

A. Acute lymphocytic leukemia—responsible for about 80 percent of all childhood cases.
B. Chronic myelocytic leukemia—primarily a disease of young adults.

Clinical Manifestations

A. Early.
   1. Bone and abdominal pain.
   2. Fever.
   3. Bruising.
   4. Lethargy and pallor.
   5. Lymph node enlargement.
B. Later.
   1. Oral and rectal ulcers.
   2. Hemorrhage.
   3. Infection.
C. Clinical course.
   1. Untreated—rapid deterioration and death.
   2. Treated—with chemotherapy, 90 percent of those treated experience at least an initial remission.

Treatment

A. Initial remission usually occurs following the commencement of chemotherapy.
B. Chemotherapy is usually continual for three years of remission and then stopped.
C. Drugs most commonly used for initiations and maintenance of remissions are:
   1. Prednisone.
   2. Mercaptopurine.
   3. Methotrexate.
   4. Cytoxan.
   5. Vincristine.
D. Methotrexate usually administered soon after start of remission to prevent central nervous system involvement.

Nursing Management

A. Prevent infection.
  1. Avoid contact with communicable diseases.
  2. Do not give regular immunizations.
  3. Provide oral hygiene.
  4. Change intravenous tubing daily.
  5. If resistance very low, reverse isolation.
B. Prevent hemorrhage.
  1. Watch platelet count.
  2. Avoid all unnecessary intramuscular and intravenous injections.
  3. Avoid aspirin, alcohol, spicy foods.
  4. Use electric razor to shave legs and face.
C. Treat hyperuricemia (due to increased cellular proliferation and the breakdown of leukemia cells).
  1. Increase fluid intake.
  2. Observe pH of urine.
  3. If ordered, administer allopurinol.
D. Promote healthy nutrition.
  1. Administer antiemetic ½ hour before meals.
  2. Use anesthetic mouth wash before meals.
  3. Avoid toothbrushes.
  4. Offer cold liquids high in calories.
E. Observe for side effects and signs of the toxicity of chemotherapy.
F. Counsel parents and siblings.
  1. During periods of remission, encourage normal activity.
  2. Assist in psychological preparation for death.
  3. Refer to parents' group.
  4. Provide for continuing follow-up of family following death.

Hodgkin's Disease

Definition: This malignancy of the lymph system is characterized by a large, primitive, reticulum-like, malignant cell.

Clinical Manifestations

A. Incidence—peak occurrence is between fifteen to twenty-nine years of age.
B. Enlarged painless lymph nodes—nodes are firm and movable.
C. Anergy—lessened sensitivity to specified antigens.
D. Frequent infections.
E. Prognosis is guarded.

Types

A. Stage I—disease is restricted to single anatomic site, or is localized in a group of lymph nodes; asymptomatic.
B. Stage II(a)—two or three adjacent lymph nodes in the area on the same side of the diaphragm are affected.
C. Stage II(b)—symptoms appear.
D. Stage III—disease is widely disseminated into the lymph areas and organs.
E. Radiation is used for Stages I, II and III in an effort to eradicate the disease.

Nursing Management

A. Symptomatic relief of the side effects of radiation and chemotherapy (used in combination is treatment of choice).
B. Counseling.
  1. Assist the family and the adolescent patient to accept the process of treatment.
  2. Encourage independence where possible.
C. Observation for pressure from enlargement of the lymph glands on vital organs, particularly for respiratory problems from the compression of the airway.

Brain Tumors

Characteristics

A. Seventy-five percent of childhood brain tumors are impossible to remove or are so situated as to cause damage if completely removed.
B. Incidence—occur most frequently in the five-to-seven age group.
C. Location—most occur in the posterior fossa.
D. Types most frequently seen in children.
  1. Astrocytoma.
    a. Located in the cerebellum.
    b. Insidious onset and slowly progressive course.
    c. Surgical removal usually possible.
  2. Medulloblastoma.
    a. Located in the cerebellum.
    b. Highly malignant.
    c. Prognosis poor.

3. Ependymoma.
   a. Usually there is ventricular blockage, leading to signs of increased intracranial pressure.
   b. Treated with incomplete internal compression and radiation therapy.
4. Brain stem gliomas.
   a. Seventy-five percent of childhood brain tumors.
   b. Develops slowly with initial symptoms of cranial nerve palsies.

Clinical Manifestations

A. Variety of symptoms depending on location of tumor.
B. Increased intracranial pressure.
   1. Vomiting without nausea.
   2. Headache.
   3. Diplopia.
C. Enlargement of the head in children under four years old.
D. Mental change: lethargy, irritability, drowsiness, and stupor.

Nursing Management

A. Control and relief of symptoms.
B. Seizure precautions.
C. Postoperative care.
   1. Maintain patient flat in bed on unaffected side.
   2. Log roll for change of position.
   3. Control fever with hypothermia mattress.
   4. Frequently observe vital signs until stable.
   5. Reinforce dressing, if wet, with sterile gauze.
   6. Notify physician of increased wetness of dressing—possible cerebral spinal fluid leakage.
D. Education and counseling for the family.
   1. Counsel family and patient through the stages of acceptance of the disease.
   2. Instruct on the use of medications and dosage.
   3. Alert them to signs of increased intracranial pressure.
   4. Suggest the use of a wig, a hat, or a scarf to cover the child's shaved head.
   5. Encourage return of the independence of the child.
E. Radiation therapy.
   1. Prepare parents for toxic effects of treatment

(see section on radiation side effects, p. 397).
   2. Treat side effects as they arise.

Bone Tumors

Osteogenic Sarcoma

Definition: A malignant tumor originating from osteoblasts (bone-forming cells).

Clinical Manifestations

A. Tumor usually located at the end of the long bones (metaphysis).
B. Most frequently seen at the distal end of the femur or the proximal end of the tibia.
C. Primary symptoms are pain at site, swelling, and limitation of movement.
D. Lungs most common site of metastasis.
E. Occurs twice as frequently in boys as in girls.

Treatment

A. Usually amputation followed by chemotherapy.
B. Frequently used drugs.
   1. Vincristine.
   2. Cytoxan.
   3. Actinomycin D.

Ewing's Sarcoma

Definition: A malignant tumor of the bone originating from myeloblasts.

Clinical Manifestations

A. Tumor usually located on the shaft of the long bones.
B. Femur, tibia, and humerus common sites.
C. Primary symptoms.
   1. Pain at site.
   2. Swollen area with tenderness.
   3. Fever.
D. Early metastases to lung, lymph nodes, and other bones.
E. Occurs twice as frequently in boys as in girls.

Treatment

A. Usually radiation, sometimes followed by amputation.

B. Chemotherapy to treat tumor and prevent metastases.

C. Frequently used drugs.
   1. Vincristine.
   2. Cytoxan.
   3. Actinomycin D.

Nursing Management

A. Encourage inclusion of patient in discussions of treatment, options, risks and prognosis.

B. Listen to parents, child, and siblings as they work through denial, anger, acceptance—allow them their grieving process.

C. Promote age appropriate activities and group discussions with peers.

D. Assist parents in avoiding overprotection.

E. Treat the side effects of chemotherapy and radiation.

Chemotherapy

Basic Principles

A. Chemotherapeutic agents work on dividing cells.

B. Tumor's location and cell type affect choice of drugs.

C. Most antineoplastic drugs are metabolized in the liver and excreted by the kidneys so they must be in functioning order to prevent toxicity.

Nursing Management

A. Establish baseline data.
   1. Nutritional status.
   2. Oral condition.
   3. Skin condition.
   4. Degree of mobility.
   5. Psychological status.
   6. Neurological condition.

B. Observe for side effects of cell breakdown
   1. BUN on rise.
   2. Stone formation in urinary tract.

C. Observe for side effects on rapidly dividing cells.

1. Gastrointestinal mucosa—diarrhea, nausea, vomiting.
   a. Administer antiemetics.
   b. Provide mouth care with hydrogen peroxide every 4 hours. No toothbrush or glycerin.
   c. Administer anesthetic spray to mouth prior to meals.
   d. Provide frequent cold, high calorie beverages.

2. Hair follicles—loss of hair.
   a. Prepare patient for loss—suggest wig, scarf.
   b. Reassure that it will return in 6 weeks.
   c. Apply tourniquet around scalp during chemotherapy plus 2-3 hours following to lessen amount of hair lost.

Common Drugs

A. Prednisone.
   1. Side effects.
      a. Ravenous appetite.
      b. Change in fat distribution.
      c. Retention of fluid.
      d. Hirsutism.
      e. Occasional hypertension.
      f. Psychological disturbance.
   2. Nursing management—watch blood sugar and tapering of medication.

B. 6-Mercaptopurine.
   1. Interrupts the synthesis of purines essential to the structure and function of nucleic acids.
   2. Side effects.
      a. Produces very little toxicity in children.
      b. Increases amount of uric acid that the kidneys must excrete.
   3. Nursing management.
      a. Observe kidney function.
      b. Increase fluid intake.

C. Methotrexate.
   1. A folic acid antagonist that suppresses the growth of abnormal cells enough to permit regeneration of normal cells.
   2. Side effects.
      a. Ulceration of oral mucosa.
      b. Nausea, vomiting, diarrhea, and abdominal pain.

3. Nursing management.
   a. Observe for ulcerations—drug must be temporarily discontinued at the appearance of ulcers.
   b. Observe renal function—drug is excreted.
D. Cytoxan.
   1. Alkylating agent that suppresses cellular proliferation; it has greater effect on abnormal than normal cells.
   2. Side effects—hemorrhagic cystitis.
   3. Nursing management—provide large quantities of fluids preceding and immediately following drug administration to prevent side effects.
E. Vincristine.
   1. Alkylating agent.
   2. Side effects.
      a. Insomnia.
      b. Severe constipation.
      c. Peripheral neuritis or palsies.
   3. Frequently used to induce remissions rapidly, after which the patient is maintained on another, less toxic drug.

Radiation

Basic Principles

A. Radiation affects all cells but is particularly lethal to rapidly developing cells.
B. Radiation can be utilized in conjunction with chemotherapy.
C. Radiation may be used to eradicate the tumor or to relieve pressure.

Nursing Management

A. Treatment of radiation sickness.
   1. Symptoms—nausea, vomiting, malaise.
   2. Offer frequent high caloric feedings (milkshakes with extra protein and vitamins).
   3. Make food trays attractive, palatable.
B. Observe side effects of cell breakdown.
   1. BUN on rise.
   2. Accumulation of uric acid.
   3. Stone formation in urinary tract.
C. Treat side effects of cell breakdown.
   1. Increase fluid intake.

2. Monitor intake and output.
D. Treat skin breakdown.
   1. Check patient regularly for any redness or irritation at radiation site.
   2. Immediately notify physician.
   3. Usual treatment—apply lotion to area, cover loosely with sterile gauze.
   4. Avoid any irritation to area from clothing, soap or weather extremes.
E. Treat bone marrow depression.
   1. Carefully watch lab values.
   2. Isolate (low leukocytes).
   3. Avoid injections (low platelets).
   4. Antibiotics.

Special Topics in Pediatric Nursing

Venereal Diseases

Syphilis

Definition: A chronic infectious disease caused by *Treponema pallidum.*

A. Characteristics.
   1. Transmission—by intimate physical contact with syphilitic lesions, which are usually found on the skin or the mucous membranes of the mouth and the genitals.
   2. Incubation period—two to six weeks following exposure.
   3. Primary stage.
      a. Most infectious stage.
      b. Appearance of chancres, ulcerative lesions.
      c. Usually painless, produced by spirochetes at the point of entry into the body.
   4. Secondary stage.
      a. Lesions appear about three weeks after the primary stage and may occur anywhere on the skin and the mucous membranes.
      b. Highly infectious.
      c. Generalized lymphadenopathy.

5. Tertiary stage.
   a. The spirochetes enter the internal organs and cause permanent damage.
   b. Symptoms may occur ten to thirty years following the occurrence of an untreated primary lesion.
   c. Invasion of the central nervous system.
      (1) Meningitis.
      (2) Locomotor ataxia—foot slapping and broad-based gait.
      (3) General paresis.
      (4) Progressive mental deterioration leading to insanity.
   d. Cardiovascular—most common site of damage is at the aortic valve and the aorta itself.
B. Treatment—intramuscular penicillin.

Gonorrhea

Definition: An infection caused by *Neisseria gonorrhoeae,* which causes inflammation of the mucous membrane of the genitourinary tract.

A. Characteristics.
   1. Transmission—almost completely by sexual intercourse.
   2. Incidence of epidemic proportions in the United States.
   3. Signs and symptoms.
      a. Male.
         (1) Painful urination.
         (2) Pelvic pain and fever.
         (3) Epididymitis with pain, tenderness, and swelling.
      b. Female—usually asymptomatic.
         (1) Vaginal discharge.
         (2) Urinary frequency and pain.
   4. Complications.
      a. Female—pelvic inflammatory disease (PID) with abdominal pain, fever, nausea, and vomiting.
      b. Male—postgonococcal urethritis and spread of infection to posterior urethra, prostate, and seminal vesicles.
      c. PID can lead to sterility.
      d. A secondary infection can develop in any organ.

B. Treatment—of choice.
   1. Procaine penicillin G, 4.8 million units.
   2. Preceded by (½ hour) 1 gram probenecid by mouth.

Nursing Management

A. Aimed at control of the disease.
B. Education of public about signs and symptoms of the disease and the need for regular testing.
C. Contacts of known cases should be found and treated.
D. Regular testing and physical examination of target population (sexually active with more than one partner).

The Mentally Retarded Child

General Concepts of Mental Retardation

Nursing Management

A. The child is treated according to his developmental age rather than chronological age.
B. The child needs as much stimulation and love as a normal child.
C. Retarded children are frequently more susceptible to infections and disease.
D. Behavioral modification frequently works well with these children.
E. Help support parents' reaction to the birth of a mentally retarded child.
   1. Birth presents a threat to the parents' marital relationship and family dynamics.
   2. Stages of reactions.
      a. Denial—initial reaction of defense which protects the parents from admitting that this child, this extension of themselves, is not normal.
      b. Self-awareness—recognition of difference between their child and other children.
      c. Recognition of problem—in this stage the parents begin to search for information on their child's problem and are ready to seek professional advice.

Down's Syndrome

Etiology

A. Down's syndrome is caused by the presence of an extra chromosome or the translocation of a chromosome in the genetic chain.
B. The chromosome is usually number 21.

Clinical Manifestations

A. Facial characteristics—almond-shaped eyes, round face, protruding tongue, flattened posterior and anterior surfaces of the skull, epicanthus, and flat nose.
B. Musculoskeletal—muscles are flaccid and the joints are loose.
C. Extremities—broad hands, abnormal palmar crease, and incurved fifth finger; first and second toe are widely spaced.
D. Mental capacity ranges from slightly incapacitated (educable) to severely retarded.

Nursing Management

A. Refer for genetic counseling.
B. Following discharge from hospital, provide follow-up for the family for counseling and child guidance.
C. Refer to the community health agency for follow-up.
D. Alert the parents to the child's increased susceptibility to infections and the need for extra precautions to prevent illness.
E. Assist the parents in developing a program for the child by identifying for them signs of neurological development in the child which will indicate readiness for developmental tasks such as sitting, self-feeding, and crawling.

Cretinism (Congenital Hypothyroidism)

Definition: The term cretinism is usually used to describe a condition in which there are rudiments of a thyroid gland that is hypoactive, or in which there is no thyroid tissue at all.

Clinical Manifestations

A. The condition is recognizable when the child is two to three months old.
B. Body growth is retarded.
C. Eyes are puffy.
D. The tongue is thick and large, and protruding.
E. Hands and feet are short and square.
F. The skin is very dry, pale, and coarse.
G. Hair is very dry and coarse.
H. Frequently, there is an umbilical hernia.
I. Feeding difficulties include choking, lack of interest in food, and sluggishness.
J. Respiratory difficulties—apneic episodes, noisy respirations, and nasal obstructions.

Treatment

A. Infants are given thyroid hormone.
B. Prognosis—fifty percent of the children treated before the age of six months will achieve an IQ of 90 or more.

Table 3. Levels of Mental Retardation

Type I	Type II	IQ	Description
Mild	Educable	50 to 75	Can develop social and sensorimotor skills. Self-supportable.
Moderate	Trainable	35 to 50	Can communicate. Minimal learning ability, poor social interaction skills, but can be independent with supervision.
Severe	Trainable	20 to 35	Poor communicative, social, and sensorimotor skills. Needs supervision and can benefit from habit training.
Profound	Custodial	Below 20	Minimal capacity to function. Needs constant supervision.

Phenylketonuria

Definition: PKU, or phenylketonuria, is a genetically transmitted condition in which an infant fails to metabolize the amino acid phenylalanine normally. High levels of this amino acid in the blood can cause mental retardation.

Clinical Manifestations

A. Diagnosis—most states have mandatory PKU testing before discharging the infant from the hospital.

B. Clinical manifestations if untreated.
1. Arrested brain development by four months of age.
2. By one year the child is moderately to severely retarded. Retardation level correlates with high PKU levels and is irreversible.

Treatment

A. Restrict phenylalanine in the diet—Lofenaloc formula.
B. Restrict foods high in protein, e.g., meat, poultry, fish, eggs, nuts, legumes, and milk products.

Nursing Management

A. Provide nutrition referrals and follow-up.
B. Educate the parents about the disease.
C. Observe for signs of phenylalanine deficiency—lethargy, anorexia, anemia, skin rashes, and diarrhea.
D. Provide continued counseling throughout childhood for the prevention of emotional problems that can arise from diet restriction.
E. Screen future children born to the same parents.
F. Provide genetic counseling.

Accidents

Definition: Unexpected events that lead to recognizable injury or metabolic changes.

General Categories of Accidents

A. Incidence: accidents are the leading cause of death from the age of one year through twenty-four years.

B. Most common types of fatal accidents by age.
1. Infant—under twelve months.
   a. Aspiration.
   b. Motor vehicle.
2. From one to four years.
   a. Motor vehicle.
   b. Fires or burns.
3. From five to nineteen years.
   a. Motor vehicle.
   b. Drowning.

Prevention of Accidents

A. Control of agent when possible.
1. Education of parents as to what substances are hazardous and how to "safety-proof" a home.
2. Safe storage of poisons.
3. Safety caps on prescriptions.
4. Use of special car seats and seat belts.
B. Recognition of risk.
1. Provide accident prevention education appropriate to the age of the child.
2. For children with a history of accidents, take special care to make the environment safe.
C. Control of the environment—during crisis periods in families, suggest help for child care and supervision.

Treatment of Poisoning at Home

A. At a well-child visit, give the mother the telephone number of the local poison control center.
B. Suggest keeping ipecac syrup with the poison control telephone number wrapped around it.
C. Instructions to the family.
1. When poisoning occurs, telephone the control number. Be sure to know the brand name of the poison and the approximate amount ingested.
2. Institute the program suggested by poison control.
3. If no telephone number is available, call a physician and take the child to the emergency room; bring the bottle of poison and have a neighbor or a friend drive.
D. Diagnostic information the physician will need

1. What infant ingested.
2. The amount ingested.
3. Odor on breath.
4. Pupil changes.
5. Presence of abdominal pain, nausea, or vomiting.
6. Convulsions.

Lead Poisoning

Definition: An environmental disease caused by the ingestion of lead-based materials, such as paint. Death results in 25 percent of the cases of lead encephalopathy, and there are many neurologic residual problems in survivors.

Clinical Manifestations

A. Child is usually twelve months to thirty-six months old.
B. Gastrointestinal symptoms.
 1. Unexplained, repeated vomiting.
 2. Vague chronic abdominal pain.
C. Central nervous system symptoms
 1. Irritability.
 2. Drowsiness.
 3. Ataxia.
 4. Convulsive seizures.
D. Prevention.
 1. Inspection of buildings twenty-five years old or older.
 2. Areas painted with lead paint should be covered with plywood or linoleum.
 3. Education of parents.
E. Treatment.
 1. Acute—gastric lavage followed by magnesium sulfate.
 2. Chronic—administer medications which aid in removal of lead calcium disodium edetate (EDTA) dimercaprol (BAL).

Battered Child Syndrome

Definition: Any nonaccidental physical abuse resulting from an absence of reasonable standards of care by the parents or the child's caretaker.

Epidemiology

A. Incidence.
 1. Six out of 1,000 children born become battered children.
 2. In the hospital emergency room, it is estimated that ten percent of the injuries seen in children under five are actually caused by parents or are the result of negligence.
B. Victims.
 1. One-third of the victims are less than six months old.
 2. One-third are six months to three years old.
 3. One-third are over three years old.
 4. Premature infants have a three times greater risk of becoming battered children than full-term infants.
 5. Stepchildren have an increased risk.
C. Environment.
 1. The abused child usually has characteristics that make him demanding.
 2. The abuse usually occurs on the same day as a crisis or stressful event.
 3. The abuse usually occurs in anger, after the parent is provoked.

Clinical Indications of Abuse

A. History of the problem.
 1. The cause given for the condition is implausible —punishment is inappropriate for the age of the child.
 2. There are discrepancies in the history from neighbors or various members of the family.
 3. There is a delay in seeking medical help for the child.
B. Physical examination and indications for diagnosis.
 1. Bruises, welts, and scars in multiple stages of healing.
 2. Fingermark pattern of bruises.
 3. Bite, rope, or choke marks.
 4. Cigarette and/or hot water burns.
 5. Eye damage, subdural hematoma, failure to thrive, and/or intraabdominal injuries.
 6. Radiographic findings of multiple bone injuries at different stages of healing.
 7. Passive, noncommunicative, and/or withdrawn child.

Characteristics of Abusive Parents

A. Parents were usually abused as children.

B. Abusers are unable to utilize outside help (neighbors, friends, or professionals) when angry at their child.

C. Abusers usually are isolated people.

D. Spouse of abuser frequently does not know how to prevent the occurrence or recurrence of the abuse.

E. Abusive parents frequently have unreasonable expectations of their children—they expect a baby to meet their needs.

F. Personality characteristics.
   1. Dependent personality.
   2. Low self-esteem and poor self-image.
   3. Immature personality.
   4. Low impulse control and inability to handle feelings.

Legal Responsibility

A. Both nurse and doctor are legally responsible to report a suspected battered child to the proper authorities.

B. The designated community authorities are responsible to determine placement of the abused child.

Death and Children

A. Understanding of death.
   1. Young child's concerns.
      a. Views death as temporary separation from parents, sometimes viewed synonymously with sleep.
      b. May express fear of pain and wish to avoid it.
      c. Child's awareness is lessened by physical symptoms if death comes acutely.
      d. Gradual terminal illness may simulate the adult process: depression, withdrawal, fearfulness and anxiety.
   2. Older children's concerns.
      a. May identify death as a "person" to be avoided.
      b. May ask directly if they are going to die.
      c. Concerns center around fear of pain, fear of being left alone and leaving parents and friends.
   3. Adolescent concerns.
      a. Recognize death as irreversible and inevitable.
      b. Often avoids talking about impending death and staff may enter into this "conspiracy of silence."
      c. Adolescents have more understanding of death than adults tend to realize.

B. Nursing management.
   1. Always elicit a child's understanding of death before discussing it with him.
   2. Before discussing death with child, discuss it with his parents.
   3. Parental reactions include the continuum of grief process and stages of dying.
      a. Reactions depend on previous experience with loss.
      b. Reactions also depend on relationship with the child and circumstances of illness or injury.
      c. Reactions depend on degree of guilt felt by parents.
   4. Assist parents in expressing their fears, concerns and grief so that they may be more supportive to the child.
   5. Assist parents in understanding siblings' possible reactions to a terminally ill child.
      a. Guilt—believing they caused the problem or illness.
      b. Jealousy—wanting equal attention from the parents.
      c. Anger—feelings of being left behind.

Appendix 1. Growth and Development of Children

Table 1. Erikson's Stages of Personality Development

Stage	Approximate Age	Psychological Crises	Significant Persons	Accomplishments
Infant	0–1	Basic trust vs. mistrust	Mother or maternal figure	Tolerates frustration in small doses Recognizes mother as separate from others and self
Toddler	1–3	Autonomy vs. shame and doubt	Parents	Begins verbal skills Begins acceptance of reality vs. pleasure principle
Preschool	3–6	Initiative vs. guilt	Basic family	Asks many questions Explores own body and environment Differentiates between sexes
School	6–12	Industry vs. inferiority	Neighborhood school	Gains attention by accomplishments Explores things Learns to relate to own sex
Puberty and adolescence	12–?	Identity vs. role diffusion	Peer groups External groups	Moves toward hetero-sexuality Begins separation from family Integrates personality (altruism, etc.)
Adolescence and young adult	—	Intimacy and solidarity vs. isolation	Partners in friendship, sex	Is able to form lasting relationships with others Learns to be creative and productive

Based on Erikson: *Childhood and Society*

Table 2. Piaget's Cognitive Development

Age	Developmental Level

Infancy to two years	Sensorimotor
	    Development of intellect through sensory-motor apparatus
	    Simple problem-solving

Two to seven years	Preoperational Thought

Two to four years	Preconceptual Phase
	        Use of symbols – language
	        Imitative play to understand the world

Four to seven years	Intuitive Phase
	        Egocentric and stage of "moral realism"
	        Beginning use of symbols for cognition
	        Asks questions

Seven to twelve years	Concrete Operational Thought
	    Wide use of symbols
	    Observes relationships between objects
	    Understands cause and effect
	    Visualizes conclusions

Twelve-plus years	Formal Operational Thought
	    Abstract thinking processes
	    Conceptualization
	    Ability to test hypotheses

Table 3. Growth, Development, and Play Guide

Age	Physical and Motor Development	Language and Social Development	Play and Counseling Guide
One Month	Follows with eyes to midline Eyes follow bright, moving objects Lifts head slightly from prone Lies awake on back with head averted Keeps fists clenched Responds to sharp sounds (bell, etc.) Does not grasp objects	Regards face, may smile Responds to voice Makes throaty noises Alert about one out of every ten hours	Smile and talk to infant Touch, stroke, cuddle Talk, sing to infant Play soft music Play with infant Hold infant while feeding *Toys:* colorful hanging mobiles
Two Months	Ceases activity to listen for a bell Eyes follow better vertically and horizontally with jerky eye movements Moves arms and legs vigorously Lifts head to 45 degrees when prone on abdomen	Vocalizes, smiles responsively Visually follows moving person Makes single vowel sounds ("ah," "eh," "uh") Crying becomes differentiated Begins social smile Stimulation still tactile and oral, not social	Smile and talk to infant Use cradle gym, infant seat Allow infant the freedom of kicking with clothes off Place infant in prone position on floor or in bed Expose infant to different textures

Age	Physical and Motor Development	Language and Social Development	Play and Counseling Guide
	Advances from creeping to crawling Can pull self to feet with assistance Feeds self a cracker Develops eye-to-eye contact while talking Engages in social games	Listens to conversations	Give child soft finger-foods Use safety precaution as child puts everything into mouth Show excitement at child's achievements *Toys:* squeeze toys in bath; toys that make noise, large nesting toys, crumpled paper
Ten to Eleven Months	Sits without support indefinitely Pulls self to feet Stands on toes with support Creeps and cruises very well Can pick up objects fairly well Uses index finger and thumb to grasp Can hold own bottle or cup Shows interest in tiny objects	Vocabulary of one to two words ("Mama," "Dada") Recognizes meaning of "no-no" Shows moods; looks hurt, sad Very aware of environment Responds to own name Imitates gestures, facial expressions, sounds Begins to test parental reaction during feeding and at bedtime Entertains self for long periods of time	Use plastic bottle Protect child from dangerous objects Have child with family at mealtime Allow exploration outdoors *Toys:* new objects (blocks); toys that stimulate; containers (milk cartons); toys that can be filled, emptied, knocked down, and stacked up; fabric books
Twelve to Eighteen Months	Stands and walks alone Explores environment and pokes fingers in holes Puts objects in and out of containers Can release objects at will Points to indicate wants Climbs stairs with help Holds a cup with both hands Throws a ball Looks at pictures with interest Weight triples from birth at 12 months; anterior fontanel closes Fine muscle coordination begins to develop Abdomen protrudes	Uses jargon, imitates sounds Understands simple commands Aware of expressive function of language Cooperates in dressing; removes socks Likes an audience and will repeat performance Shows anxiety about strangers Distinguishes self from others Has a vocabulary of 10 words that have meaning Finds security in a blanket, favorite toy, or thumb sucking Plays alone but near others (parallel play) Is dependent upon parents but shows first signs of desire for autonomy Develops new awareness of strangers	Make no attempt to change from use of left to right hand Provide frequent changes of environment Allow self-directed play rather than adult-directed play Continue to expose child to different foods Show affection and encourage child to reciprocate Create safe environment (medications locked up and harmful items out of reach) *Toys:* pull and push toys; Teddy bears; pots and pans; musical toys, and telephone; sand box and fill toys; cloth picture books with colorful, large pictures

Age	Physical and Motor Development	Language and Social Development	Play and Counseling Gui...
	Turns from side to back Grasp becomes voluntary Crossed extensor reflex disappears		Exercise infant's arms ar... *Toys:* bright pictures an... hanging objects that r...
Three Months	Lifts head and chest when prone Brings objects to mouth Fingers nimble and busy Rotates head from side to side Convergence improves Discovers and stares at hands Briefly holds toy in hand	Babbles, pronounces initial vowels, coos Smiles more readily Ceases to cry when mother enters room or caresses him Enjoys playing during feeding Stays awake longer without crying Turns head to follow familiar person	While infant prone on ab... move bright object up... encourage head move... Bounce infant on bed Continue to introduce n... sounds Social stimulation impor... Play with infant during f... *Toys:* rattles, large soft a...
Four Months	Lifts head and shoulders to a 90-degree angle Looks ahead while in prone position on abdomen Can follow object 180 degrees Tries to roll over Can move from side to side Grasps for toy with whole hand Brings hands or toys to mouth Sucks thumb or fist Teething begins Weight doubles from birth	Coos, gurgles, and laughs aloud Begins babbling Knows mother Imitates mother Demands attention by fussing Begins to respond to "no" Enjoys being placed in sitting position with support Responds to and enjoys being handled	Show child his reflection... mirror Increase sensory stimula... Child enjoys splashing in... Child still enjoys holding... and rattles Quieted by music Move mobile out of reac... may grab it and injure... Repeat child's sounds to... *Toys:* soft, colorful sque... toys; mirror; toys who... cannot be removed
Five to Six Months	Visually pursues lost object Holds block in each hand Hand-eye coordination begins to appear Sits for short periods in leaning position Creeps and rocks Reaches for objects beyond grasp Turns completely from stomach to stomach	Begins to recognize strangers Shows fear and anger Vocalizes vowel sounds and well-defined syllables Shows anticipation, waves and raises arms to be picked up Expresses protest Understands name	Play sitting-up games Encourage reaching for o... *Toys:* teething toys, soft... and squeeze toys, met... and wooden spoon fo... banging
Seven to Nine Months	Reaches for objects unilaterally Can transfer a toy Complete thumb opposition Sits alone steadily with good coordination	Begins imitative expressions Shows fear of strangers Makes polysyllabic vowel sounds Play is self-contained Laughs out loud	Play social games such as... a-boo and pat-a-cake Likes to drop and retrieve... Allow child to play with s... at feeding

Age	Physical and Motor Development	Language and Social Development	Play and Counseling Guide
Eighteen Months to Two Years	Eye accommodation well developed Walks up and down stairs one at a time with pauses Turns door knobs Climbs on furniture Chews more effectively Scribbles Walks and runs with a stiff gait and wide stance Uses a spoon without spilling Builds tower of six cubes Kicks a ball in front of him without support Daytime bladder and bowel control; occasional accident and nighttime control not complete	Speaks vowels correctly Receptive vocabulary of 200 to 300 words Begins to use short sentences Uses words "mine" and "no" constantly Has fear of parents leaving Helps to undress; tries to button "Snatch and grab" stage: wants to hoard and not share Violently resists having toys taken away from him Begins to have feelings of autonomy Process of identification is beginning; uses "no" as assertion of self Begins cooperation in toilet training	In toilet training, allow child to follow own pattern Child needs peer companionship Begin to have child eat his meal with the family Role-modeling for positive behavior is important for child *Toys:* building blocks, wagons, pull toys, pounding toys like a drum, books with pictures
Two and One-half Years	Pushes and pulls large toys Jumps Squats to play Kicks ball Builds tower of eight blocks Copies horizontal and vertical strokes Feeds self; uses fork Pours from pitcher Can undress Walks backward Begins to use scissors Has full set (20) of baby teeth	Knows full name Refers to self by pronoun "I" Still in "snatch and grab" stage Negativism, temper tantrums Is ritualistic Learns power of "yes" and "no" Poorly developed judgment Can tolerate short periods of separation from parents Begins to identify sex (gender) roles Explores environment outside the home Engages in associative play	Allow child his/her preferences Control temper tantrums Allow ritualism, especially at night Be aware that negativism and ritualism is normal behavior at this age Discipline as a way of socializing and educating child is important Discipline simply for the sake of establishing authority is counterproductive Firmness and consistency are necessary Read simple book to child to help develop language and memory skills *Toys:* manipulative toys for muscle coordination; crayons and paper; simple games
Three Years	Goes up and down stairs, alternating feet Rides tricycle Stands momentarily on one foot Swings, climbs	Beginning to cooperate but self-centered Begins imaginative and make-believe play Wants to please Knows own age and sex, and the	Encourage and promote social contacts, imaginative outlets Group activity must be alternated with solitary play Listen to child's conversations and narratives

Age	Physical and Motor Development	Language and Social Development	Play and Counseling Guide
	While running, can stop suddenly or turn corners	concept of *one* Verbalizes toilet needs and goes to toilet by self (needs help wiping) Uses "I," "me," "you" speech Has vocabulary of 900 words Begins to understand what it means to take turns Can remember and repeat three numbers	Base expectations within child's limitations *Toys:* climbing apparatus, keys, tricycle, wagons, dump trucks, simple puzzles, music, record player
Three to Four Years	Vision now 20/20 Races up and down steps Has good balance Skips, hops, performs stunts Draws man with 2 to 4 parts besides the head Cuts on line with scissors Can button buttons Feeds self Dresses self; laces shoes but cannot tie Brushes teeth	Abundant questions: What? Why? How? Recites nursery rhyme, poem, or sings a song Gives full name Interested in world about him— nurses, firemen, police, doctors Begins to share; seeks peer relationships Imaginative and make-believe play is rampant Less negativistic Can tolerate separation from mother longer	Encourage widening horizon and exploration of environ- ment, imagination, peer relationships Encourage pretending, story telling, expressing Child can be given simple explanation as to cause and effect *Play:* alternate periods of active and quiet play; books, puzzles, drawing, utensils, puppets
Four to Five Years	More agile and graceful Jumps, hops, skips on alternate feet Draws recognizable pictures Quieter; less restless; greater concentration Draws triangle and square from copy Names four colors, the heavier of two weights, and the longer of two lines Builds steps Posture good, arms carried near body, stance narrow Transports objects in trucks and cars Dresses and undresses with skill but still needs some supervision	Concept and language develop- ment improving Asks questions about the meaning of words Prints simple words Cooperative, poised, and controlled Creative Capable of longer attention span, completing activities, imagina- tive, dramatic play Drawing shows planning, space, depth, expression, and creativity Begins to develop an elementary conscience	Needs kind but unmistakable discipline Build self-confidence Consistent control Encourage responsibility for putting things away Widen and vary experiences in reading and music Encourage group play and cooperation in projects May begin kindergarten *Play:* child learns to share, participate in group play, wait turn; develops strength and coordination; high energy dispersed through play

Age	Physical and Motor Development	Language and Social Development	Play and Counseling Guide
Five to Six Years	Balance improves Begins to ride two-wheel bicycle Runs skillfully and plays games at the same time Able to wash without wetting clothing Begins to lose baby teeth Small motor movements well controlled Can catch a ball Little awareness of dangers, but has good motor development Uses hands as manipulative tools in cutting, pasting, hammering	Has well-developed vocabulary Repeats sentence of 10 syllables or more Talks constantly Cooperative Does simple chores at home Begins to take responsibility for his actions Understands units such as a week or month Knows right and left hand Still requires parental support but pulls away from overt signs of affection	Family atmosphere important for child's emotional development Needs guidance and limits, but humiliating punishment is destructive Exercise is important to stimulate motor and psychosocial development *Play:* other children for stimulation, books, games, bicycle
Six to Seven Years	Growth spurt begins Very active, impulsive Dresses self	Defines words by use More independent in play Enjoys group play in small groups Begins to accept authority outside home Considers ideas of teachers important Learns to read Knows number combinations to 10	Enjoys collecting various items *Play:* imaginary dramatic play: girls—"dress up," school; boys—firemen, soldiers, etc.; table games (tiddlywinks, marbles); dolls
Seven to Eight Years	Eyes become fully developed Less impulsive and boisterous in activities Frequently develops nervous habits such as nail-biting More coordinated Capable of fine hand movements	More competitive Recognizes differences between his home and others Wishes to be like his friends Tells time, knows days of the week Curious about sex differences May have periods of shyness	Recognize child's periods of shyness as normal behavior Give reassurance and understanding if and when nightmares occur *Play:* table games and card games; magic tricks; games that develop physical and mental skill
Eight to Nine Years	Arms grow longer in proportion to body Good coordination of fine muscles Engages in active play Females may begin secondary sex characteristics Learns to use script	More self-assured in environment Likes group projects, clubs Increased modesty Recognizes property rights Needs help accepting defeat in games Begins to have sense of humor Through play, child learns new ideas and independence: competition, compromise, cooperation, and beginning collaboration	Needs to be considered important by adults Can be given small household responsibilities Answer child's questions regarding sex in simple, honest answers Do not become overly concerned with common problems such as teasing and quarreling, as they are usually temporary

Age	Physical and Motor Development	Language and Social Development	Play and Counseling Guide
			Play: sports, books (geography and adventure), erector sets, comics and funny papers
Nine to Ten Years	Skillful in manual activities because hand-eye coordination is developed Growth in height decreases Very active physically Cares completely for own physical needs	Sex differences in play Likes to have secrets Often antagonism develops between the sexes Grasps easy multiplication and division "Chum" stage occurs; has special friend in whom child confides	Lying and stealing may be problems; the causes must be determined Understanding from parents is very important Enjoys clubs and organizations *Play:* books, musical instruments, TV, records, practical projects
Ten to Eleven Years	Onset of major secondary sex characteristics appears in some males Perfection of physical skills is important to child	Enjoys companionship more than play Needs privacy occasionally Increased ability to discuss problems Has growing capacity for thought and conceptual organization Sees physical qualities as constant despite changes in size, shape, weight, volume Period of group conformity	Important to continue sex education and preparation for adolescent body changes Encourage participation in organized clubs, youth groups
Eleven to Twelve Years	Onset of puberty; physical changes appear in both males and females Females may begin menstruation Separation of males and females in physical competition May require more sleep due to body changes	Participates in community and and school affairs Tends toward segregation of the sexes Likes to be alone occasionally Interested in world affairs Comprehends world of possibility and abstraction Begins to question parental values	Adolescent needs help in channeling energy in proper direction—school and sports Adolescent needs democratic guidance as he works through dependence/independence conflict Needs realistic limits Requires adequate explanation of body changes Special consideration is needed for child who lags behind in physical development

Early Adolescence

Age	Physical and Motor Development	Language and Social Development	Play and Counseling Guide
Twelve to Thirteen Years	Further development of secondary sex characteristics Poor posture Rapid growth makes adolescent awkward and uncoordinated Changes in body size and development	Social priority of peer group Strives for independence from family One or two very close friends in peer group Becomes more interested in opposite sex	Needs understanding as he attempts to deal with social, intellectual, and moral issues Allow some financial independence Still needs limits to assure security

Age	Physical and Motor Development	Language and Social Development	Play and Counseling Guide
		Period of upheaval; confusion about body image may be present Must again learn to control strong feelings (love, aggression)	Assurance necessary to help adolescent accept changing body image Flexibility in "hanging out" with emotional and erratic mood swings Calmness and stability are important to adolescent

Late Adolescence

Age	Physical and Motor Development	Language and Social Development	Play and Counseling Guide
Thir- teen to Eight- een Years	Completes sexual development Body growth slowed down Capable of reproduction More energy after growth spurt tapers off Increased muscular ability and coordination	Less attached to peers Increased maturity More interdependence with family Begins romantic love affairs Mastery over biologic drives increases Relationships to parents more mature Values include fidelity, friendship, cooperation Ability to begin vocation is the culmination of development	Assist adolescent in vocational choice Safety education important, especially regarding driving Encourage good attitudes toward health in issues of nutrition, drugs, smoking, and drinking Attempt to understand own (parental) difficulties in accepting transition of adolescent to independence and adulthood

Appendix 2. Reflexes in the Newborn

Palmar Grasp

A. Automatic reflex of full-term newborns; elicited by placing finger in infant's palm.

B. Present at birth.

C. Disappears at four months.

Asymmetrical Tonic Neck Reflex

A. Infant assumes fencer's position—when head is turned to one side, arm on that side is extended, and opposite arm is flexed.

B. Present at birth.

C. Disappears at four months.

Moro's Reflex (Startle Reflex)

A. When infant is suddenly jarred or hears a loud noise, his body stiffens, the legs are drawn up, and the arms are brought up, out, and then in front in an embracing position.

B. Present at birth.

C. Disappears at four months.

Reciprocal Kicking

A. Movements of newborns are jerky and usually alternate in the legs.

B. Evolving at birth.

C. Disappears at nine months.

Rooting

A. When infant's cheek is brushed, he will turn his head to that side.

B. Present at birth.

C. Rooting while awake disappears at three to four months.

D. Rooting while asleep disappears at seven to eight months.

Sucking

A. Infants make sucking movements when anything touches their lips.

B. Present at birth.

C. Involuntary sucking disappears at nine months.

Neck Righting Reflex

A. When the head is turned to one side, the opposite shoulder and trunk will follow.

B. Evolving at four months.

C. Involuntary movement disappears at nine to twelve months.

Babinski's Sign

A. Extension of the great toe on stroking the sole of the foot.

B. Present at birth.

C. Disappears between twelve to eighteen months.

Appendix 3. Nutrition

Nutrition for the Infant

A. Calories.
1. Birth to three months—give 50 to 55 calories per pound per day.
2. Three months to one year—give 45 calories per pound per day.

B. Fluids.
1. First six months—two to three ounces per pound per day.
2. Requirements increase in hot weather.

C. Number of feedings.
1. First week—six to ten per day.
2. One week to one month—six to eight per day.
3. One to three months—five to six per day.
4. Three to seven months—four to five per day.
5. Four to nine months—three to four per day.
6. Eight to twelve months—three per day.

D. Vitamins.
1. Breast-fed infants—if mother's source adequate, infant adequate.
2. Formula-fed infants—vitamin supplements depend on type of formula and what vitamins are already included in it.

E. Solid foods—recent trends suggest introducing solid foods at four to six months of age.
1. Cereal—infants are least allergic to rice.
2. Fruits and vegetables.
   a. New foods should be introduced once a day in small amounts until the child becomes accustomed to them.
   b. Introduce only one new food per week.
   c. Bananas and applesauce are well tolerated.
   d. Orange juice is usually not well tolerated, initially. It can be introduced, diluted with water, when the child is six months old.
   e. Green and yellow vegetables can be introduced at about four months of age.
3. Eggs.
   a. Introduce yolks after child is six months old.
   b. Usually yolks are well tolerated, but sometimes there are allergic reactions to egg whites.
4. Meat.
   a. May be introduced at six months.
   b. Usually more palatable if mixed with fruits or vegetables.
5. Starchy foods.
   a. May be introduced during the second six months.
   b. Should not be given in place of green vegetables or fruit.
   c. Chief value is caloric.
   d. Zweiback and other crackers are good for the gumming infant.
6. Avoid 2% milk, skim milk, whole milk.

F. Diarrhea—temporary.
1. Usually caused by incorrect formula preparation, contaminated food, or viral infection.
2. Review feeding preparation and storage of formula with caretaker.
3. Usually corrected by withholding all solids and milk for two or three feedings and giving boiled, cooled, sugar water or balanced electrolyte solution.

G. Constipation.
1. Increase fluid and sugar intake.
2. In child three months old or older, increase cereal, fruit, and vegetable intake.
3. On occasion, prune juice (half an ounce) may be given.

Nutrition for the Second Year

A. Rate of growth is slowing down; thus there is a decreased caloric need.

B. Self-selection—children usually select over a period of several days a diet that is balanced.
    1. Serve small amount of food so child can finish it.
    2. Don't mix food on plate.

C. Child should be feeding himself, with some assistance.

D. Assess food intake by associated findings.
    1. Weight, growth normal for age.
    2. Level of activity.
    3. Assess condition of skin, eyes, hair.
    4. Assess elimination problems.
    5. Assess emotional state: is child happy and content, fussy or unhappy.

E. Avoid baby bottle syndrome: sweet formula or milk bottle at night leads to destruction of teeth.

Nutrition for the Preschooler

A. Child begins to imitate his family's likes and dislikes.

B. Finger foods are popular.

C. Single foods are preferable to a combination.

D. Counsel mothers—they express concerns about poor eating habits which are common at this age.

Nutrition for the School-Age Child

A. Patterns of good eating habits are established at this time.

B. Avoid snacks—except fruits.

C. Appetite increases due to increased calorie needs for growth.

D. Child's appetite at a meal is influenced by the day's activity level.

E. Boys require more calories than girls.

F. Both boys and girls need more iron in pre-puberty than in 7 to 10 age group.

G. Tendency toward obesity at this age.

H. Every child needs daily exercise.

Adolescent Eating Patterns

A. Period of rapid growth and appetite increases

B. Adolescents frequently gain weight easily and use fad diets.

C. Girls adapt themselves to fashionable weight goals, which may be unhealthy.

D. There is social eating of nonnutritious foods.

E. One form of rebellion against parents is to refuse to eat "healthy" foods.

F. Adolescent girls are often deficient in iron, calcium, vitamins C and A.

G. Important teaching for adolescents is that they must not just fill stomachs with food, but nutritious food necessary for growth.

Malnutrition Disorders

A. Kwashiorkor—caused by a lack of protein; frequently seen in ages 1 to 3, when high protein intake is necessary.

B. Nutritional marasmus—a disease caused by a deficiency of food intake. It is a form of starvation.

C. Vitamin A deficiency—night blindness may progress to xerophthalmia and finally, keratomalacia.

D. Vitamin C deficiency: *scurvy*—symptoms begin with muscle tenderness, for walls of capillaries become fragile. Hemorrhage of vessels results.

E. Vitamin D deficiency: *rickets*—caused because vitamin D is necessary for adequate calcium absorption by the bones.

F. Thiamine deficiency: *beriberi*—primarily a disease of rice-eating people; symptoms include numbness in extremities and exhaustion.

G. Niacin deficiency: *pellagra*—symptoms include dermatitis, diarrhea, dementia, and finally, death.

H. Iodine deficiency—leads to hyperplasia of the thyroid gland, or goiter.

Appendix 4. Dental Development

Deciduous

	Age at Eruption		Age at Shedding	
	Maxillary	Mandibular	Maxillary	Mandibular
Central incisors	6 to 8 months	5 to 7 months	7 to 8 years	6 to 7 years
Lateral incisors	8 to 11	7 to 10	8 to 9	7 to 8
Cuspids	16 to 20	16 to 20	11 to 12	9 to 11
First molars	10 to 16	10 to 16	10 to 11	10 to 12
Second molars	20 to 30	20 to 30	10 to 12	11 to 13

Permanent Eruption

	Maxillary	Mandibular
Central incisors	7 to 8 years	6 to 7 years
Lateral incisors	8 to 9	7 to 8
Cuspids	11 to 12	9 to 11
First molars	6 to 7	6 to 7
Second molars	12 to 13	12 to 13
First premolars	10 to 11	10 to 11
Second premolars	10 to 12	11 to 13
Third molars	17 to 22	17 to 22

Appendix 5. General Assessment of the Child

General Principles

A. Maturational ability of the child to cooperate with the examiner is of major importance to adequate physical assessment.

B. When planning physical assessment of the child, the following points should be considered:

   1. Establish a relationship with the child prior to the examination.

      a. Determine child's maturational level.
      b. Allow the child an opportunity to become more accustomed to the examiner.

   2. Explain in terms appropriate to the child's level of understanding the extent and purpose of the examination.
   3. Realize that the physical examination may be a stressful experience for the child, who is helpless and depends on others for protection.
   4. Limit the physical examination to what is essential in determining an adequate nursing diagnosis.
   5. Proceed from the least to the most intrusive procedures.
   6. Allow active participation of the child whenever possible.

Special Considerations for Each Age Group

The Infant

A. Accomplish as much of the examination as possible while the infant is sleeping or resting undisturbed.

B. Assess general condition.

   1. Symmetry and location of body parts.
   2. Color and condition of the skin.
   3. State of restlessness and sleeplessness.
   4. Adjustment to feeding regimen.
   5. Quality of cry.

C. Congenital anomaly appraisal.

   1. Neurological system.

      a. Reflexes: absent or asymmetrical (*see* Appendix 2).
      b. Head circumference: microcephaly, hydrocephaly.

         (1) 35 cm. at birth.
         (2) 40 cm. at 3 months.
         (3) 45 cm. at 9 months.
         (4) At birth, the head size is 2 cm. larger than the chest. Equals or exceeds chest until 2 years of age.

      c. Fontanels: closed, bulging.

         (1) Anterior measures 3.5 cm. by 3.5 cm. and closes by 18 months.
         (2) Posterior measures 1 cm. by 1 cm. and closes at 2 months.

      d. Eyes: cataracts, lid folds, spots on iris.

   2. Respiratory system.

      a. Breath sounds: signs of aspiration, asymmetry of lung expansion, retractions, grunting.
      b. Apnea.

   3. Cardiovascular system.

      a. Color: cyanosis.
      b. Rate and rhythm: murmurs, tachycardia, bradycardia.
      c. Energy level: cannot suck for fifteen minutes without exhaustion or cyanosis.

4. Gastrointestinal tract.
   a. History of polyhydramnios.
   b. Patency: mucus, spitting, cyanosis, cannot pass nasogastric tube to stomach.
   c. Mouth: palate or lip not intact.
   d. Anus: not patent.
5. Genitourinary.
   a. Umbilical vessels: missing normal two arteries and one vein.
   b. Urine: abnormal stream.
   c. Masses: abdominal (Wilms' tumor).
   d. Boys: undescended testicles, hernia, urethra not opening at the end of the penis.
   e. Girls: labial adhesions.
6. Skeletal system.
   a. Fractured clavicle.
   b. Dislocated hip: asymmetric major gluteal folds, hip click.
   c. Legs and feet: clubbing, without straight tibial line.
   d. Spine: curved, inflexible, open.

D. Common Problems — Appropriate Nursing History and Observations

Common Problems	Appropriate Nursing History and Observations
1. Ear infections	Increased temperature, irritability, rubbing or pulling ear, change in eating habits.
2. Upper respiratory infections	Duration of symptoms, severity; wheezing, barking cough, anxiety, restlessness, use of accessory muscles. If throat is sore, check white patches on tonsils.
3. Rashes	Onset, duration, description, location, or any event such as new food, exposure to animals.
4. Contact dermatitis	Allergic problems. Diaper area rash: use of soap, lotions, powders. Method of cleaning cloth diapers.
5. Hernias	Inguinal: lump in groin, with or without pain. Umbilical: can it be pushed back without difficulty or pain.
6. Scalp-cradle cap	Scalp scaling, crusted. Method of washing hair. Application of any lotions or balms to hair.
7. Birth marks	Change in size, color, shape. Any bleeding or irritation.
8. Eye symmetry	Frequency of a problem with eye alignment: (time of day eyes wander). Light reflex symmetrical in both eyes.

E. Screening procedures.
   1. Developmental landmarks—DDST (Denver Developmental Screening Test).
   2. Vision.
   3. Hearing.
   4. Growth charts: head circumference, weight, length.
F. Nursing guidance areas.
   1. Growth and development changes.
   2. Stranger anxiety.
   3. Separation anxiety.
   4. Transitional objects.
   5. Accident prevention.

The Toddler and the Preschool Child

A. General considerations.
   1. Remember that separation anxiety is most acute at toddler age and body integrity fears most acute at preschool age.
   2. Involve the parent in examination as much as possible.
   3. Restrain child as much as necessary to protect the child from injury.
   4. Give careful explanation of each portion of the exam.
   5. Allow the child to handle the equipment and try out on doll.

B. Common Problems — Appropriate Nursing History and Observations
   1. Feeding and eating — Review food in last 48 hours, types of foods, adequate source of vitamins, minerals.
   2. Temper tantrums — Frequency, duration, precipitating event, response of caretaker.
   3. Toilet training — Check ability to ambulate (indicating neuromuscular maturity). Bothered by wet diapers. Interested in toileting.
   4. Respiratory infections — See Infant section.
   5. Communicable diseases — Onset of symptoms, progression of disease, treatment of symptoms, observation of complications.
   6. Gastrointestinal — Onset, duration, intake and output, signs of dehydration.

C. Screening procedures (same as Infant).

School Age Child

A. General considerations.
   1. Modesty important.
   2. Explain all procedures.
   3. Direct questions to child.

B. Common Problems — Appropriate Nursing History and Observations
   1. School — Signs of school phobias, vomits before school, delays going.
   2. Nervous habits (stuttering, twitching, etc.) — Onset, duration, precipitating event, anxiety of child and parent over problem.
   3. Accidental trauma — Understanding of accident, prevention, physical limitations.
   4. Respiratory infections — See Infant section.
   5. Gastrointestinal infections — See Preschooler section.

C. Screening procedures.
   1. Snellen vision testing.
   2. Sweep check audiometry.
   3. Height and weight measurement.
   4. Inspection of skin and teeth.

D. Nursing guidance areas.
   1. Need for autonomy.
   2. Toilet training.
   3. Imaginary friends.
   4. Fear of dark.
   5. Rituals and routines.

Adolescent

A. General considerations.
    1. Examine child alone if he wishes (privacy important).
    2. Note signs of puberty.
    3. Ascertain feelings about body image.
B. Common Problems   Appropriate Nursing History and Observations
    1. Acne   Existing skin care program. Personal hygiene.
    2. Dysmenorrhea   Degree of pain, missed school, use of analgesics, amount of exercise.
    3. Obesity   Eating patterns, family concern, amount of exercise.
C. Screening procedures (same as School Age).
D. Nursing guidance areas.
    1. Hazards of cigarette smoking and alcohol.
    2. Transmission and symptoms of venereal disease.
    3. Review sex education.
    4. Accident prevention—particularly automobile.
    5. Principles of nutrition.

Vital Signs for Children at Different Ages

Vital Sign Chart

Age	Range of Normal Pulse	(average)	Average Blood Pressure	Average Respiration
Newborn	70 - 170	120	80/45	40 - 90
1 year	80 - 160	115	96/65	20 - 40
2 years	80 - 130	110	99/65	20 - 30
4 years	80 - 120	100	99/65	20 - 25
6 years	75 - 115	100	100/56	20 - 25
8 years	70 - 110	90	105/56	15 - 20
10 years	70 - 110	90	110/58	15 - 20

Pulse

A. Increased rate is significant if maintained during sleep.
B. Body temperature elevation causes an increase of 8 to 10 pulse beats for each degree of elevation.

Appendix 6. Pediatric Communicable Diseases

Disease	Characteristics	Transmission	Nursing Care
Chickenpox (varicella)	Acute viral disease; onset is sudden with high fever; maculopapular rash and vesicular scabs in multiple stages of healing. Incubation is 10 to 21 days.	Spread by droplet or airborne secretions; scabs not infectious.	Isolate. Treat symptoms: ASA fluids for fever. Prevent scratching.
Mumps	Acute viral disease, characterized by fever, swelling, and tenderness of one or more salivary glands. Potential complications, including meningoencephalitis.	Spread by droplet and direct and indirect contact with saliva of infected person. Most infectious 48 hours prior to swelling.	Prevent by vaccination. Isolate. Treat symptoms: ice pack to neck and force fluids. Watch for symptoms of neurological involvement: fever, headache, vomiting, stiff neck.
Measles (rubeola)	Acute viral disease, characterized by conjunctivitis, bronchitis, Koplik's spots on buccal mucosa. Dusky red and splotchy rash 3 to 4 days. Usually photophobia. Complications can be severe in respiratory tract, eye, ear, and nervous system. Incubation is 10 to 12 days.	Spread by droplet or direct contact.	Symptomatic: bedrest until cough and fever subside; force fluids, dim lights in room; tepid baths and lotion to relieve itching.
German Measles (rubella)	Viral infection. Slight fever, mild coryza and headache. Discrete pink-red maculopapules that last about 3 days. Incubation is 14 to 21 days.	Spread by direct and indirect contact with droplets. Fetus may contract measles in utero if mother has the disease.	Basically a benign disease. Symptomatic: Bedrest until fever subsides.
Diphtheria	Local and systemic manifestations. Malaise, fever, cough with stridor. Toxin has affinity for renal, nervous and cardiac tissue. Incubation 2 to 6 days or longer.	Spread by droplets from respiratory tract or carrier.	Antitoxin and antibiotic therapy to kill toxin. Strict bedrest; prevent exertion. Liquid or soft diet. Observe for respiratory obstruction. Suctioning, oxygen, and emergency tracheotomy may be necessary.

Disease	Characteristics	Transmission	Nursing Care
Tetanus (lockjaw)	Acute or gradual onset. Muscle rigidity and spasms, headache, fever and convulsions. Death may result from aspiration, pneumonia or exhaustion. Incubation is 3 to 21 days.	Organisms in soil. Enter body through wound. Not communicable man to man.	Toxins must be neutralized. Bedrest during illness in quiet, darkened room. Avoid stimulation which can cause spasms. Observe for complications of laryngospasm and respiratory failure.
Pertussis (whooping cough)	Dry cough occurring in paroxysms. Dyspnea and fever may be present. Lymphocytosis. Incubation is 5 to 21 days.	Direct contact or droplet from infected person.	Symptomatic: rest, warm, humid air. Maintain nutritional status. Need to protect from secondary infections.

Appendix 7. Immunizations

Age	Prevention
2 months	DPT*, TOPV†
4 months	DPT, TOPV
6 months	DPT, TOPV
1 year	MMR‡, Tuberculin test
1½ years	DPT, TOPV
4 to 6 years	DPT, TOPV
14 to 16 years	TD§, and thereafter every ten years

*DPT—diphtheria and tetanus toxoids and pertussis vaccine

†TOPV—trivalent oral polio virus vaccine

‡MMR—measles, mumps, and rubella vaccines—may be combined or separate

§TD—combined tetanus and diphtheria toxoids

Appendix 8. Drug Conversion for Children

A. Clark's weight rule: Child's dose
$$= \frac{\text{Child's weight in pounds}}{150} \times \text{Adult dose}$$

B. Intravenous microdrip usually has 60 drops/cc.

C. Conversion of administration units:

    1 tsp. = 5 ml.

    1 tbl. = 15 ml.

    1 ml. = 16 minims.

    1 grain = 60 mg.

    1 gm. = 1,000 mg.

    1 oz. = 30 ml.

    1 dram = 4 ml.

Review Questions

1. A three-day-old infant, Timmy Brown, is admitted to the pediatric floor from the nursery. The mother seems distant with the child when she comes to visit him. A reason for this is that a breakdown in mother-infant relationship has occurred due to

   A. Feelings of inadequacy as a mother.
   B. Maternal guilt.
   C. Hostile hospital environment.
   D. All of the above.

2 Timmy is diagnosed as having esophageal atresia type III. The mother says to the nurse, "I feel as though I've done something wrong to make my child sick." The most appropriate response would be

   A. "Don't be silly, your child was born with this. You've done the best you can."
   B. "It does no good to feel that way. Your child is sick and needs you. You should spend your time caring for him."
   C. "A lot of mothers feel guilty when their child is sick."
   D. "I can understand your feelings, but remember that this is a congenital defect, which you did not cause."

3 A premature infant is visited by his mother. The nurse asks the mother if she would like to feed it. The mother says, "Oh, no, you do it so well. I want my child to be well cared for." The nurse should interpret this as

   A. A compliment to the nurse's ability.
   B. A sign that the mother is still tired from the delivery and is not yet ready to care for the child.
   C. An expression of her sense of inadequacy in caring for her own child.
   D. An admission of her inexperience in dealing with premature infants.

4. The most appropriate response by the nurse to the mother of the premature infant would be

   A. "I'll feed him today. Maybe tomorrow you can try it."
   B. "It's not difficult at all. He is just like a normal baby, only smaller."
   C. "You can learn to feed him as well as I can; I wasn't good when I first fed a premature infant either."
   D. "It's frightening sometimes to feed an infant this small, but I'll stay with you to help."

5. A seventh-month-old child is admitted to the pediatric unit for a cardiac catheterization. The mother sees the nurse having difficulty feeding the child cereal and says, "She won't take cereal before her bottle, only after." The most appropriate response by the nurse would be

   A. "It's not good to give a bottle first because the infant becomes full and has no desire to eat anything else."
   B. "I think it is time that she became used to having her cereal first because that is what she will have to do here."
   C. "Thank you. I'll try it that way and tell the other nurses."
   D. "That's unusual. Most babies like it this way."

6. The surgical procedure used to correct pyloric stenosis is

   A. Mustard.
   B. Fredet-Ramstedt.
   C. Gastrostomy.
   D. Blalock-Taussig.

7. The most important nursing goal prior to surgery for correction of pyloric stenosis is

   A. Prevention of dehydration.
   B. Education of the parents about the procedure.
   C. Provide sensory stimuli for the infant.
   D. Prevention of the development by the infant of a negative attitude toward feeding.

8. A nurse must insert a nasogastric tube in an infant. Which of the following signs would best indicate that it is in the appropriate place?

   A. Regular intermittent bubbling when the tube is submerged in water.
   B. A rush of bubbles immediately following submersion of the tube in water that stops after two to three seconds.
   C. Aspiration of mucus through the tube.
   D. No coughing or choking when the tube is inserted.

9. Esophageal atresia exists when

   A. There is a fistula between the esophagus and the trachea.
   B. The esophagus ends in a blind pouch.
   C. There is narrowing of the esophagus.
   D. All the above.

10. The primary problem with esophageal atresia that a nurse should be concerned about is

    A. Aspiration.
    B. Gastric distention.
    C. Poor feeding habits.
    D. Esophageal irritation.

11. The first choice of treatment for intussusception is

    A. Gastric lavage.
    B. Barium enema.
    C. Bowel reduction
    D. Colostomy

12. Frequent, watery stools with blood, pus, and mucus are usually found in

    A. Intussusception.
    B. Diarrhea.
    C. Hirschsprung's disease.
    D. Late appendicitis.

13. A child diagnosed as being profoundly retarded would have an IQ that is

    A. Below 20.
    B. Unmeasurable.
    C. Below 10.
    D. Below 30.

14. The type of training that has been found to be very successful with mentally retarded children is

    A. Structured.
    B. Self-pacing.
    C. Behavior modification.
    D. Unstructured.

15. When parents learn they have a mentally retarded child, they go through stages of acceptance. During which of the following stages would it be most appropriate for the nurse to ask the parents if the child is developing the way they expected?

    A. Disorganization.
    B. Denial.
    C. Self-awareness.
    D. Recognition of the problem.

16. Trisomy 21 usually results in

    A. Turner's syndrome.
    B. Down's syndrome.
    C. Klinefelter's syndrome.
    D. Phenylketonuria.

17. Which of the following is *not* a characteristic of a a child with Down's syndrome?

    A. Abnormal palmar creases.
    B. Protruding tongue.
    C. Low-set ears.
    D. Loose joints.

18. Cretinism is caused by

    A. A malfunctioning pituitary gland.
    B. A hyperactive pancreas.
    C. An inactive or absent thyroid gland.
    D. Amino acid deficiency.

19. While bathing a one-year-old, a nurse feels a large mass in the abdominal area. She thinks it may be a Wilms's tumor. She should

    A. Palpate it to ascertain its exact size and position.
    B. Immediately notify the doctor.
    C. Ask the child if it hurts.
    D. Tell the mother that she should tell the pediatrician about it at the child's next visit.

20. Greg was admitted for a shunting procedure for hydrocephalus. Following this procedure, a nurse should be watching for signs of

    A. Infection.
    B. Increased intracranial pressure.
    C. Dislodgement.
    D. All of the above.

21. A twenty-two-month-old infant is brought to the hospital for treatment of an acute illness. The child's initial adjustment to the hospital will be facilitated if the nurse understands that

    A. It will be beneficial to the child if his mother leaves as soon as the nurse begins the admission procedure.
    B. Participation by the mother in the admission procedure is likely to be beneficial both to her and to the child.
    C. The child's cooperation during the admission procedure will be assured if the mother is allowed to hold the child for a while prior to the procedure.
    D. The mother should be seated at the foot of the crib where the child can see her throughout the admission process.

22. A toddler is hospitalized for surgery. His parents are unable to room in because of other responsibilities at home. The child becomes very quiet and never cries during painful hospital procedures. The nurse should interpret this behavior as evidence that the child

    A. Has given up fighting and has become despondent and hopeless.
    B. Was well prepared by his parents for the separation and hospitalization.
    C. Has been taught not to misbehave in front of strangers.
    D. Does not feel well.

23. A mother of a toilet trained fourteen-month-old expresses concern over her child's bedwetting while hospitalized. The most appropriate response by the nurse would be

    A. "He was a little young to be toilet trained. In a few more months he will be old enough."
    B. "Children get scared in the hospital and frequently wet their beds."
    C. "Hospitalization is so frightening to children that they frequently abandon behaviors that they have recently acquired."
    D. "I'll tell the night nurse to wake him up and take him to the toilet."

24. Which of the following is a cyanotic heart defect?

    A. Ventricular septal defect.
    B. Aortic stenosis.
    C. Tetralogy of Fallot.
    D. Pulmonic stenosis.

25. Which of the following organs has some blood shunted past it in fetal circulation?

   A. Heart.
   B. Lungs.
   C. Brain.
   D. Kidney.

26. What must be present in order for an infant with complete transposition of the great vessels to survive at birth?

   A. Coarctation of the aorta.
   B. Large septal defect.
   C. Pulmonic stenosis.
   D. Mitral stenosis.

27. A twelve-month-old with tetralogy of Fallot develops circumoral pallor during feeding. The most appropriate nursing action would be to

   A. Immediately notify the doctor.
   B. Stop the feeding and return the child to bed.
   C. Finish the feeding as quickly as possible and then put the child to bed.
   D. Continue the feeding, allowing the child periods of rest.

28. Which of the following is *not* a frequent problem of children with acyanotic heart defects?

   A. Frequent respiratory infections.
   B. Development of heart failure.
   C. Enlargement of the heart.
   D. Polycythemia.

29. When a child returns to the pediatric unit following a cardiac catheterization, what nursing activity should immediately follow the taking of vital signs?

   A. Place the child in a warm bed and encourage sleep.
   B. Provide the child with fluids.
   C. Check the peripheral pulses.
   D. Reapply the dressing where the dye was injected.

30. Which of the following activities should a nurse always do prior to administering Digoxin?

   A. Obtain an EKG.
   B. Take the blood pressure.
   C. Take the temperature.
   D. Take the pulse.

31. A four-year-old with congestive heart failure is being digitalized. The nurse who is giving the third dose of Digoxin observes that the child's temperature is 99.8 and his pulse is 100. She should

   A. Call the physician.
   B. Recognize that these are signs of Digoxin toxicity and withhold the dose.
   C. Give the medication.
   D. Give the medication but make a note that the pulse is lower than normal.

32. The best method of feeding an infant with a cleft lip is with a

   A. Gavage tube.
   B. Nipple on the side with the cleft.
   C. Nipple on the side without the cleft.
   D. Rubber tipped medicine dropper placed on the side without the cleft.

33. The best method of feeding an infant in the first week following the repair of a cleft lip is with a

   A. Gavage tube.
   B. Nipple on the side with the suture.
   C. Nipple on the side without the suture.
   D. Rubber tipped medicine dropper placed on the side without the suture.

34. What is the most important developmental task you would encourage a mother to teach her child prior to surgery for the repair of cleft palate?

   A. Socialization with peers.
   B. To be comfortable with strangers.
   C. Toilet trained.
   D. Drink from a cup.

35. Over 50 percent of the children who are abused are

   A. Under one year of age.
   B. Under three years of age.
   C. From three to six years of age.
   D. From six to ten years of age.

36. Which of the following characteristics is least often seen in parents who abuse their children?

   A. They do not want their child.
   B. They are loners.
   C. They expect the child to act older than he is.
   D. They were abused as children.

37. Of the following disorders the condition that would indicate use of the drug Dilantin would be

   A. Grand mal seizures.
   B. Psychomotor seizures.
   C. Vascular headache.
   D. All the above.

38. A child in the hospital starts to have a grand mal seizure while the nurse is in the room. The child's jaws are clamped, and he is in his crib. What is the most important nursing activity at this time?

   A. Place a padded tongue blade over the child's tongue.
   B. Prepare the suction equipment.
   C. Protect the child from harm from the environment.
   D. Restrain the child to prevent injury.

39. A mother of a five-year-old boy who was recently diagnosed to have Legg-Perthes disease says to the nurse, "It is going to be very difficult to take care

of him at home with the other children." The most appropriate response would be

A. "At least it's a temporary disease. If cared for correctly, these children have no disability when they recover."
B. "How many other children do you have?"
C. "It is going to make your home life more complicated. Maybe we can talk over ways to work out some of the problems."
D. "Have you considered putting him in a residential facility?"

40. During a well-child conference the nurse instructs the mother on the best procedure to follow if her child swallows poison. Which of the following should the mother do first?

A. Telephone the local poison control center.
B. Bring the child to the emergency room.
C. Give the child some alcohol to drink to induce vomiting.
D. Ascertain what substance the child drank

41. The leading cause of accidental deaths in children from one to four years of age is

A. Motor vehicle.
B. Fires or burns.
C. Poisoning.
D. Drowning.

42. Which of the following are early symptoms of leukemia?

A. Low grade fever and lethargy.
B. Rectal ulcers.
C. Bruising.
D. All the above.

43. Which of the following nursing activities is particularly important when caring for a child receiving Cytoxan?

A. Observe for ulceration of the oral mucosa.
B. Give large quantities of fluids prior to and following drug administration.
C. Observe for signs of gastrointestinal disturbance.
D. Observe for changes in mental alertness.

44. The test used in the diagnosis of cystic fibrosis is

A. Sweat chloride.
B. Blood glucose.
C. Sputum culture.
D. Examination of stools for fat content.

45. A child with cystic fibrosis is being discharged from the hospital. The nurse is instructing the mother on the administration of pancreatic enzymes, which the child should take three times a day. Which of the following instructions would be correct?

A. The child should take them at intervals of eight hours with a large glass of milk.

B. The medication should be given following breakfast, lunch, and dinner.
C. The child can take them at any time from six to eight hours apart. The timing should depend on what is most convenient for the family schedule.
D. The medication should be taken prior to meals.

46. The diet regime usually prescribed for a child with acute glomerulonephritis is

A. Low sodium, low calorie.
B. Low potassium, protein free.
C. Fluid intake of 1000 cc./24 hours.
D. Low calcium, low potassium.

47. Hookworms are most frequently transmitted by

A. Contact with contaminated feces.
B. Ingestion of poorly cooked food.
C. Walking barefoot in soil.
D. Poor housekeeping.

48. The treatment of choice for patients with roundworm is

A. Flagyl.
B. Gastric lavage.
C. Cathartics.
D. Piperazine citrate.

49. The major objective of nursing a child with meningomyelocele prior to surgery is

A. Observation of muscle movement below the level of the lesion.
B. Prevention of infection.
C. Prevention of contractures.
D. Maintenance of fluid and electrolyte balance.

50. Credé is a term used for

A. A type of french catheter.
B. A surgical procedure for urinary diversion.
C. A manual method of expelling urine from the bladder.
D. A method of early toilet training.

51. A controlled diet instituted relatively early after birth may prevent or limit mental retardation in which of these conditions?

A. Cretinism.
B. Down's syndrome
C. Phenylketonuria.
D. Tay-Sachs disease.

52. Which of the following reactions would you be most likely to find in a school-age child who is hospitalized?

A. Fear of abandonment.
B. Fear of displacement at school.
C. Concern about body image.
C. Disruption in identity formation.

53. In preparing a child who is five for a procedure, the nurse should give consideration to the fact that the normal five-year-old

    A. Is beyond the stage of fearing intrusive procedures.
    B. Responds poorly to verbal directions.
    C. Understands simple directions.
    D. Is quiet and shy.

54. The treatment for a child with Legg-Perthes disease is aimed at

    A. Preventing deformity in the shaft of the femur.
    B. Preventing degenerative changes in the knee joint.
    C. Reducing muscle spasm.
    D. Preventing pressure on the head of the femur.

55. When planning activities for school-age children who are in the hospital, it would be appropriate to consider that school-age children

    A. Work well in groups.
    B. Like immediate gratification from projects.
    C. Have a short attention span.
    D. Prefer games that are noncompetitive.

56. A school-age child with a cardiac condition is placed on a low sodium diet. The most appropriate method of ordering meals would be to

    A. Have the child fill out the menu with the nurse's assistance.
    B. Have the child's mother fill out the menus after the nurse teaches her the diet.
    C. Have the nurse fill out the menu.
    D. Ask the dietician to order the meals.

57. Jon Stevens is eleven years old and has type A hemophilia. He is brought to the emergency room after being knocked down in a touch football game. In type A hemophilia a child is deficient in what clotting factor?

    A. VIII.
    B. IX.
    C. XI.
    D. XII.

58. Jon's mother is in the emergency room with him. She says to the nurse, "This never would have happened if I had watched him more closely." The most appropriate response by the nurse would be

    A. "Hemophiliac children should not be allowed to play contact sports."
    B. "I understand how you feel, but at some point Jon is going to have to accept responsibility for monitoring his own activities."
    C. "All mothers of chronically ill children feel this way, but it doesn't accomplish anything."
    D. "It is difficult not to feel guilty, particularly when you could have watched him more closely."

59. Jon is found to be bleeding into his knee joint. The most likely treatment if all materials are available is

    A. Vitamin K.
    B. Fresh, whole blood.
    C. Cryoprecipitate.
    D. Exchange transfusion.

60. Jon has been transferred to the pediatric ward. Immediate nursing care would include

    A. Immobilization of the joint.
    B. Passive exercises to the affected limb.
    C. Traction of the affected limb.
    D. Active exercises to the affected limb.

61. Sharon is diagnosed as having sickle cell anemia. The most accurate description of this disease is

    A. Chronic anemia due to the inability to utilize iron.
    B. Sickle shaped red blood cells.
    C. Red blood cells that sickle under low oxygen tension.
    D. Anemia due to sickle cells in the blood that combine with the red blood cells and make them less available to the tissues.

62. Sharon experiences her first thrombic crisis. Which of the following symptoms would you be likely to see?

    A. Abdominal pain.
    B. Swelling of the large joints, hands, and feet.
    C. Pain in joints.
    D. All the above.

63. Thrombic crises are the result of

    A. Pooling of the blood in the spleen.
    B. Occlusion of small blood vessels.
    C. Hemarthroses.
    D. Injury to the joints.

64. Sharon is given a blood transfusion. Which of the following signs and symptoms are most characteristic of an allergic reaction to blood?

    A. Fall in blood pressure, distention of neck veins, and rash.
    B. Backache, laryngeal edema, and generalized discomfort.
    C. Wheezing, flushing, and laryngeal edema.
    D. Tachycardia, hives, and flushed skin.

65. If an allergic reaction occurs the nurse should

    A. Relieve the symptoms and make the patient comfortable.
    B. Call the physician.
    C. Slow the rate of infusion.
    D. Shut off the transfusion.

66. Which of the following would not be an appropriate first-aid method for treating burns?

A. Cover the area with a sterile cloth.
B. Wash with cool, sterile water.
C. Apply oil-based ointment.
D. Wash surrounding area with mild detergent.

67. One of the disadvantages of treating burns with sulfamylon cream is

A. It causes a large loss of blood during debridement.
B. It results in an acid-base imbalance.
C. It is difficult to apply correctly.
D. It can cause skin discoloration.

68. Which of the following statements about cerebral palsy is not true?

A. Seventy percent of the children function mentally at a subnormal level.
B. Cerebral palsy can be the result of difficult labor.
C. Seventy-five percent of cerebral palsy children have a seizure disorder.
D. Children with cerebral palsy can exhibit spastic, athetoid, or ataxic movements.

69. Brain tumors are

A. Rare in children.
B. Seen primarily in the five to seven age range.
C. Seen primarily in adolescents.
D. Seen primarily in infants.

70. The main reason that a high percentage of brain tumors in children cannot be successfully treated is that

A. By the time the symptoms appear metastasis has occurred.
B. Most parents refuse to permit brain surgery.
C. Most tumors are highly malignant.
D. A large number of tumors are impossible to remove because of their position in the brain.

71. Susan Medieras, fourteen years old, is admitted to the adolescent ward with a tentative diagnosis of juvenile diabetes mellitus. Which of the following fears would you most likely find in Susan?

A. Fear of being displaced.
B. Fear of separation.
C. Fear of loss of independence.
D. Fear of the unknown.

72. Which of the following symptoms would you expect Susan to exhibit when her insulin injection is delayed?

A. Thirst, polyuria, and decreased appetite.
B. Flushed cheeks, acetone breath, and increased thirst.
C. Nausea, vomiting, and diarrhea.
D. Gain of weight, acetone breath, and thirst.

73. Her mother is concerned about Susan's future

health and her ability to lead a normal life. The most appropriate comment by the nurse would be

A. "Susan will be able to lead a normal life."
B. "If Susan follows the correct regime she will have no problems."
C. "Juvenile diabetes does not cause a shortened life span."
D. "Diabetes can have some long term effects on an individual's health; however, how much Susan will be affected is impossible to tell at this time."

74. Susan has been regulated on semilente insulin. When teaching her about its effects, the nurse would tell her that this type of insulin has an onset of

A. One half hour.
B. One hour.
C. Two hours.
D. Two and one-half hours.

75. When teaching Susan about regulation of her diabetes at home, which of the following would not be included?

A. Limitation of vigorous exercise.
B. Elimination of sugar from diet.
C. Urine testing for sugar.
D. Test for acetone.

76. Adolescent diabetics frequently have more difficulty than diabetics in other age groups because

A. The disease is usually more severe in adolescents than in younger children.
B. Adolescents as a group have poor eating habits.
C. Adolescents have a difficult time with long-acting insulin.
D. Adolescents need table sugar for growth.

77. Which of the following facts about obese adolescents is not true?

A. They usually have an overweight parent.
B. They were fat as infants and children.
C. They frequently have a thyroid disorder.
D. They are very aware of their excess weight.

78. Karen is fifteen years old and has been admitted to the adolescent ward for scoliosis and insertion of a Harrington rod. Considering the course of therapy with a Harrington rod insertion, which of the following problems would Karen be most likely to exhibit?

A. Identity crisis.
B. Body image changes.
C. Feeling of displacement.
D. Loss of privacy.

79. The organism responsible for syphilis is

A. Herpes virus type II.

B. *Neisseria gonorrhoeae.*
C. *Treponema pallidum.*
D. Trichomonas.

80. During a routine physical examination the following reflexes are noted in a nine-month-old child. Which of the following is an abnormal finding?

   A. Parachute reflex.
   B. Neck righting reflex.
   C. Rooting and sucking reflex.
   D. Moro's reflex.

81. Which of the following toys would be most suitable for a ten-month-old?

   A. Play dough.
   B. A baseball-sized ball.
   C. A box of jacks.
   D. A mobile.

82. At which of the following ages would finger foods be appropriate for an infant.

   A. Four months.
   B. Six months.
   C. Nine months.
   D. None of the above.

83. In separation anxiety the child may go through all of the following phases except

   A. Protest.
   B. Despair.
   C. Denial.
   D. Adjustment.

84. Following Clark's rule, a child's dosage of a medication would be calculated by which of the procedures listed below?

   A. Adult dose minus child's weight in pounds divided by 150.
   B. Adult dose times child's weight in kilograms divided by 150.
   C. Adult dose times child's weight in pounds divided by 150.
   D. Adult dose times child's weight divided by 100.

85. A child weighs 10 kilograms and the adult dose of a medication is 10 mg. What would be the closest correct dosage to give the child?

   A. 1.0 mg.
   B. 1.5 mg.
   C. 2.0 mg.
   D. None of the above.

86. In administering medications to children, all the following considerations would be important except

   A. Explanation about the medication should be on the child's level of understanding.
   B. It may be necessary to mix a distasteful medication with a small amount of appetizing food or syrup.

C. If a child refuses an oral medication tell him he will have to have an injection.
D. The nurse's approach should indicate that she expects the child to take the medication.

87. When administering an intramuscular injection to an infant, the appropriate actions by the nurse would include all of the following except

   A. Place the infant in a secure position to prevent movement.
   B. Do not use a needle longer than 2.5 cm.
   C. Use the upper inner quadrant of the thigh.
   D. Hold and cuddle the infant following the injection.

88. When an infant who is nursing is hospitalized it is the nurse's responsibility to encourage the mother to

   A. Accept the fact the baby will need formula while in the hospital.
   B. Continue breast feeding if the baby's condition does not contraindicate it.
   C. Pump her breasts and bring the milk to the hospital.
   D. Breast feed once a day to relieve pressure of milk in the breasts.

89. Six-month-old Brian is admitted to the hospital with severe diarrhea. Which of the following nursing objectives would be *most* important on admission?

   A. Weight.
   B. Apical-radial heart rate.
   C. Skin care.
   D. Diet preferences.

90. Brian continues to have diarrhea in the hospital so it has been decided to feed him via hyperalimentation. The best explanation for this procedure is

   A. A method of providing the necessary fluids and electrolytes to the body.
   B. A method of providing complete nutrition by the intravenous route.
   C. A method of tube feeding that provides necessary nutrients to the body.
   D. A method of blood transfusion.

91. The nurse assigned to Brian knows that she must observe for signs of complications resulting from the therapy. Which of the following signs is *not* considered a possible complication related to the implanted catheter?

   A. Plugging or dislodging of the catheter.
   B. Cardiac arrhythmia.
   C. Catheter is in the superior vena cava.
   D. Local skin infection.

92. Which of the following symptoms would not be an indication of the need for oxygen?

   A. Flaring nostrils.

B. Cyanosis.
C. Brachycardia.
D. Deep, regular breathing.

93. In sickle cell anemia let us say that one parent has the trait. How many of the children will get the disease?

A. None.
B. All of the children.
C. Half of the children.
D. Can't tell from the information given.

94. You are assigned to care for Tommy, a nine-year-old boy who has been hospitalized for a week with cystic fibrosis. He has greatly improved and is about to be discharged. Knowing that cystic fibrosis children often develop pneumonia secondary to colds, what self-care principles would it be important to teach Tommy before discharge?

A. Need for protein enzymes in his diet to protect him from colds.
B. Exercise restrictions he must adhere to after discharge to prevent sweating and catching a chill.
C. Breathing exercises to develop lung potential.
D. Need for high protein, high fat diet to improve nutritional status.

95. A high protein diet would be prescribed for all of the following childhood conditions except

A. Malabsorption syndrome.
B. Malnutrition.
C. Acute leukemia.
D. Chronic glomerulonephritis.

96. Mrs. Saviana is about to take her one-year-old child home from the hospital. The child was admitted one week previously with a diagnosis of croup. One of the home care techniques you might teach Mrs. Saviana if her child begins to cough and cannot stop is to

A. Take the child into the bathroom and turn on the shower.
B. Give the child frequent doses of prescribed cough medicine.
C. Do not allow the child outside for the cold air will just prolong the coughing.
D. Call the doctor immediately.

97. Besides hemorrhage, the most important objective in patient care following a tonsillectomy is

A. Prevention of coughing.
B. Prevention of swallowing of blood.
C. Prevention of aspiration of mucus.
D. Prevention of airway constriction.

98. Baby Bowden has a diagnosis of T.E. fistula and the doctor has decided to operate. From your knowledge of pediatrics, when is the newborn the best operative risk?

A. First twenty-four hours.
B. Forty-eight to seventy-two hours.
C. Three weeks old.
D. One week old.

99. The doctor has ordered a blood transfusion following a tonsillectomy after which the child hemorrhaged. Before the blood transfusion, one important action by the nurse would be to

A. Check for skin rash or a change in skin color.
B. Check for restlessness or irritability.
C. Take the child's temperature.
D. Check the child for chills or cold sweats.

100. You are assigned to care for a child suffering from third-degree burns on his hands and arms. Of the following which would be an appropriate activity for an eight-year-old child?

A. Read a story and act out the parts verbally.
B. Watch a puppet show.
C. Watch TV.
D. Listen to the radio.

Answers and Rationale

1. (D) All of these reactions are commonly found in mothers whose children have been hospitalized.

2. (D) The nurse recognizes the mother's feelings, but tries to show that they are not based on fact.

3. (C) This mother is implying that she is not capable of caring for her own child.

4. (D) The nurse, while recognizing and accepting this mother's apprehension, assures her that she will have assistance.

5. (C) The nurse recognizes that the mother knows the child's habits better than anyone else.

6. (B) The Fredet-Ramstedt procedure is used to correct pyloric stenosis.

7. (A) Dehydration from persistent vomiting is the most frequent complication of pyloric stenosis.

8. (B) An immediate rush of bubbles is caused by air in the stomach. The bubbling should last only a few seconds and then stop. Though D is partially correct, it does not definitively indicate that the tube is in the correct position.

9. (D) Esophageal atresia can include all these malformations.

10. (A) Aspiration is the most potentially harmful complication of this deformity.

11. (B) Most physicians will attempt to reduce the bowel with a barium enema. If this is not successful, a bowel reduction is done.

12. (B) Usually the latter two problems cause constipation. Intussusception can cause stools with blood, pus, and mucus, but the stools are usually infrequent.

13. (A) Profound is the most severe category of mental retardation.

14. (C) Behavior modification with its immediate reward system is best understood by slow children.

15. (C) During this stage the parents are beginning to recognize the problem.

16. (B) This is a tricky question because A and C are caused by chromosomal defects and D is a genetic disorder.

17. (C) Although low-set ears are a sign of congenital defects, they are usually associated with some kidney problem.

18. (C) The first two answers are glandular disorders.

19. (B) A suspected Wilms's tumor should never be palpated more than necessary because of the potential for metastasis and should be treated immediately following discovery.

20. (D) The nurse should be watching for all of these conditions, as all are potential complications of a shunting procedure.

21. (B) The mother is accepted as an important participant in the child's care, and the child does not feel as though he is being deserted by his mother to face hospitalization alone.

22. (A) A toddler who passively accepts aggressive painful intrusions into his life has usually given up any sense of hope.

23. (C) Here the nurse explains the principle of regression.

24. (C) In cyanotic heart defects there is a right-to-left shunt which permits unoxygenated blood to move into the systemic circulation.

25. (B) The ductus arteriosus and foramen ovale permit the shunting of blood past the lungs in the fetus.

26. (B) Since complete transposition results in two closed blood systems, the child can survive only if

there is an opening between the two, such as a ventricular or atrial septal defect.

27. (D) It is not uncommon for these children to be somewhat cyanotic, but it is important to allow for frequent rest periods when feeding.

28. (D) Polycythemia develops most often in children with cyanotic heart defects.

29. (C) The nurse must ensure that the peripheral circulation is intact. The nurse should not have to touch the dressing except to make sure that no hemorrhaging is occurring.

30. (D) The nurse should always check the patient's pulse prior to administering Digoxin because of its slowing effect on the heart.

31. (C) A normal pulse for a four-year-old is 100, and elevated temperature is not a sign of Digoxin toxicity.

32. (C) A nurse should use a soft or regular nipple with a slightly enlarged hole and feed on the side opposite the cleft.

33. (D) Following surgery the nurse must prevent any pressure on or trauma to the suture line.

34. (D) It is imperative that a child know how to drink from a cup prior to surgery, since this is the least traumatic method of drinking following surgery.

35. (B) The highest number of abused children are under three years old.

36. (A) Abused children are usually wanted by the parents. It is after the arrival of the child that the parents experience anger and frustration that leads to abuse.

37. (D) Dilantin is used not only for relief of seizures but also for vascular conditions such as migraine headache.

38. (C) The best way to protect a child from injury during a seizure is to remove all toys and other objects from his vicinity and to place padding under his head if he is on a hard surface. The child should never be restrained, and once his jaws are clamped, you should not try to open them.

39. (C) The nurse is picking up on the mother's concern of managing at home and is suggesting a method of dealing with it.

40. (D) It is important that the mother know what the child drank since the course of emergency treatment will depend on the type of substance consumed.

41. (A) It is important for the nurse to know the leading causes of accidents and deaths in children so that she can teach appropriate preventive measures for different age groups.

42. (D) All the above can be early signs of leukemia.

43. (B) A serious side effect of Cytoxan is hemorrhagic cystitis, and fluids would help prevent this from occurring.

44. (A) Cystic fibrosis children produce abnormally high levels of sodium chloride in their sweat. Though C and D might be used during the diagnostic workup, they do not definitively diagnose the disease.

45. (D) The purpose of the pancreatic enzymes is to replace the enzymes unavailable in the child's system that assist with the digestion of fats. Therefore, they should be taken prior to the ingestion of food.

46. (B) A diet restricted from potassium and protein is necessary for all children who demonstrate some degree of renal failure.

47. (C) Hookworm is usually transmitted through soil contaminated with feces. Poor housekeeping and hygiene may contribute to the spread of roundworms.

48. (D) This is also the treatment of choice for pinworm.

49. (B) Though the other objectives are important, infection represents the greatest threat to this child prior to surgery and should receive first priority of care.

50. (C) Credé is never used on a child with normal nerve functioning.

51. (C) A strictly controlled diet for PKU children will prevent or limit mental retardation.

52. (B) A school-age child's concern is primarily present oriented.

53. (C) A preschooler can understand simple directions. Although he may be quiet and shy, these qualities are not applicable to the situation described in the question.

54. (D) Legg-Perthes disease affects the femoral epiphysis in which aseptic necrosis occurs. Pressure on the necrotic femur can cause permanent damage.

55. (A) This age group benefits from association and interaction with peers in a group setting.

56. (A) Ordering meals in this manner allows the child some independence and control and at the same time provides an excellent teaching opportunity.

57. (A) Type A is a factor VIII deficiency; type B, a IX deficiency; and type C, a factor XI deficiency.

58. (B) The nurse acknowledges the mother's feelings, but at the same time identifies a factor that must be dealt with as the child grows older and demands more independence.

59. (C) Cryoprecipitate is the treatment of choice. Whole blood has the potential risk of causing a volume overload in the circulatory system.

60. (A) Passive range of motion exercises should be started forty-eight hours following immobilization.

61. (C) The patient's red blood cells are not always sickled but become this way under certain conditions.

62. (D) All these are symptoms of a thrombic crisis in sickle cell anemia.

63. (B) Thrombic crises are the result of occlusion of small blood vessels. Sequestration crises are the result of pooling of blood in the spleen.

64. (C) All other symptoms listed are a combination of allergic reactions and transfusion reactions.

65. (D) If the nurse suspects an allergic reaction, the blood should be shut off immediately, and then the physician should be notified.

66. (C) Never apply any greasy substances on a burn until it has been evaluated.

67. (B) Careful monitoring of the patient's acid-base balance is necessary.

68. (A) Approximately 50 percent of cerebral palsy children function mentally at a subnormal level.

69. (B) School-age children have the highest incidence of brain tumors in children.

70. (D) Many tumors are so placed that to remove them would involve brain damage.

71. (C) Adolescents, having recently achieved some measure of independence, have a fear of losing it.

72. (B) All the other choices have one wrong answer, which makes this answer tricky.

73. (D) The best response is to be honest with Susan's mother.

74. (A) Semilente insulin has an onset of one-half hour, peaks at two to four hours, and has a duration of ten to twelve hours.

75. (A) If a patient is in good health and understands the increased glucose needs of the body following exercise, there is no reason to restrict her activity.

76. (B) As young adults start spending more time with their peer groups, they frequently adopt eating habits of this group which are often not appropriate for diabetics.

77. (C) The great majority of obese adolescents are overweight due to a poor eating pattern.

78. (B) This question is difficult. The body casting that follows Harrington rod insertion does create some privacy problems; however, Karen's changed body image is likely to cause more difficulty.

79. (C) All of the answers are the cause of venereal disease; however, syphilis is specifically caused by *Treponema pallidum.*

80. (D) Moro's reflex begins to fade at the third or fourth month.

81. (B) Play dough is more appropriate for a toddler and older children. Jacks will go right into the infant's mouth.

82. (C) Nine months is an appropriate age to introduce finger foods.

83. (D) Denial may be mistaken for a happy adjustment.

84. (C) The adult dose is multiplied by the child's weight in *pounds* and then is divided by 150.

85. (B) To calculate this problem translate the child's weight into pounds and then apply Clark's rule.

86. (C) Never threaten a child with an injection if he refuses an oral medication.

87. (C) The upper outer quadrant of the thigh is the appropriate site for I.M. injections.

88. (B) If possible, it is more therapeutic for both mother and baby to continue breast feeding.

89. (A) While all the objectives listed in the answers are important, assessment of a baseline weight is one of the best indications of change in hydrational status.

90. (B) This is a method that involves infusion of a solution of protein, glucose, electrolytes, vitamins, and minerals—complete nutrition by the intravenous route.

91. (C) This is not a complication, but the actual site that the indwelling catheter is inserted.

92. (D) Shallow and irregular breathing indicate the need for oxygen.

93. (A) No children will get sickle cell anemia if both parents do not have at least recessive genes, but one parent can pass the gene on so that the children may be carriers.

94. (C) Cystic fibrosis children typically evidence shallow breathing, which does not utilize lung potential and may contribute to frequent infections.

95. (D) In renal disease, a demonstrated degree of renal failure protein would be restricted.

96. (A) Warm, moist air reduces epiglotic edema and helps to relieve coughing.

97. (D) Trauma to the airway may cause a severe inflammatory response resulting in blockage.

98. (A) During the first twenty-four hours the newborn is the best risk as he still has the extra blood volume, placenta hormones, and nourishment from the mother.

99. (C) It is important to take the child's temperature before administration of blood. If it rises after the transfusion has begun, it would be an indication of a reaction to the blood. All the other actions would be carried out after the transfusion had begun to check for an untoward reaction.

100. (A) This activity involves the child so that he is actively, if not physically, participating in play.

Psychiatric
Nursing

This chapter emphasizes principles of the nurse-client relationship, the foundation of psychiatric nursing. The material covers many important and recent developments in the field of psychiatric nursing. Effective communication techniques, including interviewing and counseling skills, vital to psychiatric nursing are fully explained to help students distinguish between therapeutic and nontherapeutic nursing approaches. Signs and symptoms of major psychiatric disorders are described along with the appropriate nursing interventions.

An overall review of psychotherapeutic techniques is provided, including how these techniques are applied in environmental, group, and family therapy. This chapter also contains special sections on child psychiatry, death and dying, the grief process, and basic treatment modalities, such as behavior modification and crisis intervention. Psychotropic drugs are covered extensively. A unique section addresses the legal issues relating to psychiatric nursing, because an important concern today is the civil rights of psychiatric clients as well as the legal implications for institutions, physicians, and nurses.

The Nurse-Client Relationship

Definition: The nurse-client relationship is a therapeutic, professional relationship in which interaction occurs between two persons—the nurse, who possesses the skills, abilities, and resources to relieve another's discomfort, and the client, who is seeking assistance for alleviation of some existing problem.

Principles of Relationship Therapy

A. Goal is to assist client to meet own needs.
   1. Give the client the feeling of being accepted.
   2. Develop mutual trust through consistent, congruent behavior.
   3. Promote increased self-esteem of the client.
   4. Provide a supportive environment.
B. Empathic understanding is therapeutic; sympathy is nontherapeutic.
C. Some degree of emotional involvement is required, but objectivity must be maintained.
D. Appropriate limits must be set, and consistency must be maintained.
E. Honest and open communication is basic to therapeutic process.
F. Expression of feelings, within safe limits, should be encouraged.
G. The client's value as an individual must be acknowledged.
H. Awareness of the total client, including his/her physical needs, is important.
I. Nurse's understanding of herself, her own motives and needs, is important in the therapeutic process.

Phases in Nurse-Client Relationship Therapy

A. Initiation or orientation phase.
   1. Establish boundaries of relationship.
   2. Identify problems.
   3. Assess anxiety levels of self and client.
   4. Identify expectations.
B. Continuation or active working phase.
   1. Promote attitude of acceptance of each other, which decreases anxiety.
   2. Use specific therapeutic and problem-solving techniques to develop working relationship.
   3. Continually assess and evaluate problems.
   4. Focus on increasing the client's independence, and decreasing client's reliance on the nurse.

5. Maintain the goal of client's confronting and working through identified problems.
C. Termination phase.
   1. Plan for the conclusion of therapy early in the development of relationship.
   2. Maintain initially defined boundaries.
   3. Anticipate problems of termination.
      a. Client may become too dependent on the nurse. Encourage client to become independent.
      b. Termination may recall client's previous separation experiences, causing feelings of abandonment, rejection, and depression. Discuss client's previous experiences.
   4. Discuss client's feelings about termination.

Focus of Relationship Therapy

A. Assume the role of facilitator in the relationship.
B. Accept the client as having value and worth as an individual.
C. Maintain relationship on a professional level.
D. Provide an environment conducive to the client's experiencing corrective emotional experiences.
E. Keep interaction reality oriented, that is, in the here and now.
F. Listen actively.
G. Use nonverbal communication to support and encourage the client.
   1. Recognize meaning and purpose of nonverbal communication.
   2. Keep verbal and nonverbal communication congruent.
H. Focus content and direction of conversation on client.
I. Interact on the client's intellectual, developmental, and emotional level.
J. Focus on "how, what, when, where, and who" rather than on "why."
K. Teach client problem solving to correct maladaptive patterns.
L. Help client to identify, express, and cope with feelings.
M. Help client develop alternative coping mechanisms.
N. Recognize a high level of anxiety and assist client to deal with it.
O. Use therapeutic communication techniques.

1. Use techniques to increase effective communication. (See section on therapeutic communication in Appendix 1, p. 464).
2. Recognize blocks to communication and work to remove them. (See section on nontherapeutic communication in Appendix 2, p. 465).

Communication Techniques

Definition: Communication is the process of sending and receiving messages by means of symbols, words, signs, gestures, or other action. It is a multilevel process consisting of the content or information of the message, and the part that defines the meaning of the message. Messages sent and received define the relationship between people.

Purpose of Communication

A. To transfer ideas from one person to another.
B. To create meaning through the process.
C. To reduce uncertainty, to act effectively, and to defend or strengthen one's ego.
D. To affect or influence others, one's physical environment, and one's self.

Characteristics

A. A person cannot *not* communicate.
B. Communication is a basic human need.
C. Communication includes verbal and nonverbal expression (also, tone, pace, and manner of dress).
D. Successful communication includes:
   1. Appropriateness.
   2. Efficiency.
   3. Flexibility.
   4. Feedback.
E. Communication skills are learned as the individual grows and develops.
F. The foundation of the person's perception of himself and the world is the result of communicated messages received from significant others.
G. Factors that affect communication.
   1. The intrapersonal framework of the person.
   2. The relationship between the participants.
   3. The purpose of the sender.
   4. The content.
   5. The context.
   6. The manner in which the message is sent.
   7. The effect on the receiver.

Goal-directed Communication

Definition: . Communication or transmission of facts, feelings, and meanings through words and gestures that is intended to accomplish a defined goal.

Interviewing Skills

A. As the first step in therapeutic interviewing, assess the client's condition.
B. Observe accurately what is happening with the client here and now.
C. Be aware of your own feelings, reactions, and level of anxiety.
   1. High anxiety in the nurse impedes communication.
   2. Self-awareness during the interview facilitates honest communication.
   3. Use "I" messages, not "you" messages (for example, "I feel uncomfortable," not "you make me feel uncomfortable").
D. Encourage the client to describe perceptions and feelings.
   1. Focus communication but use indirect approach.
   2. Use minimal verbal activity.
   3. Encourage spontaneity.
E. Assist client in clarifying feelings and events and placing them in time sequence.
   1. Focus on emotionally charged area.
   2. Maintain accepting, nonjudgmental attitude.
F. Give broad openings and ask open-ended questions to enable client to describe what is happening with him.
G. Use body language to convey empathy, interest, and encouragement to facilitate communication.
H. Use silence as a therapeutic tool; it enables client to pace and direct his own communications. Long periods of silence, however, may increase the client's anxiety level.
I. Define the limits of interview, determining the purpose and structuring the time and interaction patterns accordingly.
J. Never employ interviewing techniques as stereotyped responses.

1. Use of such responses negates open and honest communication.
2. Use of structured responses is counterproductive, as it presents nurse as a dishonest communicator.
3. Interaction must be alive and responsive, not dependent on a technique for continuance.

K. Provide safe, private, comfortable setting.

L. Allow the interview to take place any time the nurse and client have contact (bed bath, treatments, etc.).

Counseling

Definition: The process by which one individual with certain skills assists another individual who is having difficulties. May be a short- or long-term process.

Components of Counseling Process

A. Being present and allowing client to experience supportiveness.

B. Maintaining consistency with flexibility to provide security.

C. Giving information but not advice.

D. Assisting clients without persuading, admonishing, threatening, or compelling the client to change attitudes, beliefs, or behaviors.

E. Using the interviewing process to facilitate accomplishment of a goal.

F. Using active listening, therapeutic communication, and empathic understanding.

G. Setting limits and goals.

H. Enabling client to make fullest use of potential within his/her current experience to develop new ways of coping with life situations.

I. Assisting the client to build more effective coping mechanisms by:
   1. Gathering pertinent data.
   2. Defining the problem.
   3. Mutually agreeing about working toward a solution.
   4. Setting a goal.
   5. Selecting alternatives.
   6. Activating problem-solving behavior.
   7. Evaluating and modifying solution or goals.

Specific Communication Techniques

A. Therapeutic communication.
   1. Listening.
   2. Acknowledgment.
   3. Feedback.
   4. Mutual fit or congruence.
   5. Clarification.
   6. Focusing or refocusing.
   7. Validation.
   8. Reflection.
   9. Open-ended questions.
   10. Nonverbal encouragement.
   11. Restatement.
   12. Paraphrase.
   13. Neutral response.
   14. Incomplete sentences.
   15. Minimum verbal activity.
   16. Broad opening statements.

B. Blocks to therapeutic communication.
   1. Internal validation.
   2. Giving advice.
   3. Changing the subject.
   4. Social response.
   5. Invalidation.
   6. False reassurance agreement.
   7. Overloading.
   8. Underloading.
   9. Incongruence.
   10. Value judgments.

Note: Definitions of therapeutic and nontherapeutic techniques in Appendix 1 and 2, pp. 464–465.

Anxiety

Definition: Anxiety is an affective state subjectively experienced as a response to stress. It is experienced as painful, vague uneasiness, tension, or diffuse apprehension. It is a form of energy whose presence is inferred from its effect on attention, behavior, learning, and perception.

Characteristics

A. Anxiety is perceived subjectively by the conscious mind of the person experiencing it.

B. Anxiety is a result of conflicts between the personality and the environment or between different forces within the personality.

C. It may be a reaction to threats of deprivation of something biologically or emotionally vital to the person.

D. The causative conflicts and/or threats are undefined in the conscious mind of the person.

E. The amount or level of anxiety is related to the following factors:

1. Degree of threat to the self.
2. Degree to which behavior reduces anxiety.

F. Varying degrees of anxiety are common to all human beings at one time or another.

G. Anxiety is easily transmitted from one individual to another.

H. Constructive use of anxiety is healthy.

I. States of anxiety vary in degree, and can be assessed as follows:

1. Ataraxia—absence of anxiety.

   a. Uncommon.
   b. Can be seen in persons who take drugs.
   c. Indicates low motivation.

2. Mild.

   a. Senses are alert.
   b. Attentiveness is increased.
   c. Motivation is increased.

3. Moderate.

   a. Perception is narrowed, and attention is selective.
   b. Degree of pathology depends on individual.
   c. May be detected in complaining, arguing, teasing behaviors.
   d. Can be converted to physical symptoms such as headaches, low back pain, nausea, diarrhea.

4. Severe.

   a. All senses are gravely affected.
   b. Behavior becomes automatic.
   c. Energy is drained.
   d. Defense mechanisms are used to control it.
   e. Cannot be used constructively by person.
   f. Psychologically extremely painful.
   g. Nursing action always indicated for this state.

5. Panic.

   a. Individual is overwhelmed.
   b. Personality may disintegrate.
   c. Following behaviors can be observed.
      (1) Wild, desperate, ineffective.
      (2) Possible bodily harm to self and others.

   d. State cannot be tolerated very long.
      (1) Person cannot control his behavior.
      (2) Person feels helpless.
      (3) Person is momentarily psychotic.

   e. Condition is pathological.
   f. Immediate intervention is needed.
      (1) Physical restraint.
      (2) Tranquilizers.
      (3) Nonstimulating environment.
      (4) Constant presence of nurse.

J. Neurotic anxiety.

1. Anxiety is disproportionate to the danger.
2. Involves repression and dissociation.
3. Behavior is relatively ineffective and is inflexible.

K. Anxiety is always found in emotional disorders.

L. Physiological reactions to anxiety.

1. Increased heart rate.
2. Increased or decreased appetite.
3. Increased blood supply to skeletal muscles.
4. Tendency to void and defecate.
5. Dry mouth.
6. Butterflies in stomach, nausea, vomiting, cramps, diarrhea.
7. "Flight or fight" response.

Nursing Management

A. Long-term goals for client.

1. Recognize behavior that is related to anxiety.
2. Gain insight into cause of anxiety.
3. Increase tolerance for some anxiety.
4. Learn new ways of coping with anxiety.

B. Short-term goals.

1. Intervene when client unable to cope with anxiety.
2. Attempt to reduce anxiety and make client comfortable.
3. Help client tolerate some anxiety.
4. Assist client in channeling the anxiety-produced energy into constructive behavior.

C. Recognize anxiety in self.

D. Maintain appropriate attitudes toward client.

1. Acceptance.
2. Matter-of-fact approach.
3. Willingness to listen and help.
4. Calmness and support.

E. Recognize anxiety-produced behavior.

F. Provide activities that decrease anxiety and provide an outlet for energy.

G. Establish person-to-person relationship.
   1. Allow client to express his feelings.
   2. Proceed at client's pace.
   3. Avoid forcing client.
   4. Assist client in identifying anxiety.
   5. Assist client in learning new ways of dealing with anxiety.

H. Provide appropriate physical environment.
   1. Nonstimulating.
   2. Structured.
   3. Designed to prevent physical exhaustion or self-harm.

l. Administer medication as directed and needed.

Patterns of Adjustment (Defense Mechanisms)

Definition: Defense mechanisms are processes by which an individual relieves or decreases anxieties caused by uncomfortable situations that threaten self-esteem.

Characteristics

A. The purpose of defense mechanisms is to attempt to reduce anxiety and to reestablish equilibrium.

B. Adjustment depends on one's ability to vary responses so that anxiety is decreased.

C. Individuals use essentially the same mechanisms but may vary them.

D. Use of defense mechanisms may be a conscious process but usually takes place at the unconscious level.

E. Defense mechanisms are compromise solutions and include those listed on page 466.

F. Healthy adjustment.
   1. Healthy adjustment is characterized by:
      a. Infrequent use of defense mechanisms.
      b. Ability to form new responses.
      c. Ability to change the external environment.
      d. Ability to modify one's needs.
   2. Healthy adjustment patterns may include mechanisms such as rationalization, sublimation, compensation, and suppression.

G. Unhealthy adjustment.
   1. Unhealthy adjustment is characterized by:
      a. Undeveloped ability or loss of ability to vary responses.
      b. Retreat from problem or reality.
      c. Frequent use of defense mechanisms, which may interfere with maintenance of self-image.
   2. Unhealthy adjustment patterns may include mechanisms such as regression, repression, denial, projection, and isolation.

Specific Defense Mechanisms

A. Compensation.
B. Denial.
C. Displacement.
D. Fantasy.
E. Fixation.
F. Identification.
G. Insulation.
H. Isolation.
I. Introjection.
J. Projection.
K. Rationalization.
L. Reaction-formation.
M. Regression.
N. Repression.
O. Sublimation.
P. Substitution.
Q. Suppression.
R. Symbolization.
S. Undoing.

Note: Definitions of defense mechanisms are listed in Appendix 2.

Nursing Management

A. Be aware of own behavior and use of adjustment patterns.

B. Avoid criticizing the client's behavior and use of adjustment mechanisms.

C. Help client explore the underlying source of the anxiety that gives rise to an unhealthy adjustment.

D. Assist the client in learning new or alternative adjustment patterns for healthier adaptation.

E. Use techniques to alleviate the client's anxiety.

F. Use a firm supportive approach to explore any ineffective use of adjustment patterns.

G. Remember that defense mechanisms serve a purpose and cannot be arbitrarily eliminated without being replaced.

Psychosomatic Disorders

Definition: Psychosomatic disorders are physical diseases that may involve any organ system, and whose etiologies are in part related to emotional factors. These disorders are also called psychophysiologic disorders.

Characteristics

A. Man must adapt and adjust to stresses in life.
   1. The way a person adapts depends on the individual's characteristics.
   2. Emotional stress may exacerbate or precipitate an illness.

B. Psychosocial stress is an important factor in symptom formation.
   1. Stress imposes demands and requirements on the person.
   2. Symptoms reflect adaptive and coping patterns as well as the reaction of a particular organ system.
   3. The way an individual reacts to stress depends on his physiological and psychological make-up.

C. There is a synergistic relationship between repressed feelings and overexcited organs.

D. Any body system may be involved and result in a psychosomatic disorder.
   1. Gastrointestinal system.
      a. Peptic ulcer.
      b. Colic.
      c. Ulcerative colitis.
   2. Cardiovascular system.
      a. Hypertension.
      b. Tachycardia.
      c. Migraine headaches.
   3. Respiratory system.
      a. Asthma.
      b. Hay fever.
      c. Hiccoughs.
      d. Common cold.
      e. Hyperventilation.
   4. Skin—most expressive organ of emotion.
      a. Blushing.
      b. Flushing, perspiring.
      c. Dermatitis.
   5. Nervous system.
      a. Chronic general fatigue.
      b. Exhaustion.
   6. Endocrine.
      a. Dysmenorrhea.
      b. Hyperthyroidism.
   7. Musculoskeletal system.
      a. Cramps.
      b. Rheumatoid arthritis.
   8. Other.
      a. Diabetes mellitus.
      b. Obesity.
      c. Sexual dysfunctions.
      d. Hyperemesis gravidarum.
      e. Accident proneness.

E. Structural changes may take place and pose a life-threatening situation.

F. Defense mechanisms used (see page 466).
   1. Repression.
   2. Denial.
   3. Projection.
   4. Conversion.
   5. Introjection.

G. Psychosomatic illness provides individual with coping mechanisms.
   1. Means of coping with anxiety and stress.
   2. Means of gaining attention in socially acceptable way.
   3. Means of adjusting to dependency needs.
   4. Means of coping with anger and aggression.
   5. Rationalization for failures.
   6. Means of punishing self and others.

Nursing Management

A. Observe closely and assess the client's condition.
   1. Collect data about physical illness as well as psychosocial adjustment, life situation, natural stress, strengths, etc.
   2. Note if symptoms come and go.
   3. Assess what kinds of things aggravate or release the symptom.

4.   Consider and assess multiple sources of illness.
B.   Care for the "total" person—physical and emotional.
C.   Realize physical symptoms are real and that person is not faking.
D.   Recognize that treatment of physical problems does not relieve emotional problems.
E.   Reduce demands on the client.
F.   Develop nurse-client relationship.
   1.   Respect the person and his problems.
   2.   Help the client to express his feelings.
   3.   Help the client to express anxiety and explore new coping mechanisms.
   4.   Allow the client to meet dependency needs.
   5.   Allow the client to feel in control.
G.   Help the client to work through problems and learn new methods of responding to stress.
H.   Provide safe, nonthreatening environment.
   1.   Balance therapy and recreation.
   2.   Decrease stimuli.
   3.   Provide activities that deemphasize the client's physical symptoms.

Differences Between Psychosomatic and Psychoneurotic Disorders

Psychosomatic	*Psychoneurotic*
Autonomic nervous system involved	Voluntary nervous system and sensory systems involved
May be life-threatening	Usually not life-threatening
Actual physical changes occur	No actual physical changes occur
Gross organic dysfunction (ulcers, colitis) with no symbolic solution to anxiety	Symbolic solution to overwhelming anxiety

Neurotic Disorders

Definition of *neurosis:*   A mild to moderately severe personality disorder where the individual suppresses and represses unpleasant thoughts or feelings to alleviate the discomfort of the resulting anxiety. The resulting behav-

ior patterns include anxiety reaction, phobias, obsessive-compulsive reaction, dissociation, hypochondriasis, and neurasthenia.

Characteristics

A.   Repression and projection are common defense mechanisms.
B.   Patterns of behavior are used in a rather stereotyped way.
C.   Client becomes more dependent as time goes on.
D.   Client is almost always unaware of his behavior patterns.
E.   The neurosis is client's attempt to deal with anxiety.
F.   Secondary gains from neurosis become associated problems.
   1.   Secondary gains are those social and psychological uses (fringe benefits) that the client may make of his/her symptoms.
   2.   Client does not understand unconscious motivation.
   3.   Secondary gains reinforce neurotic behavior.
G.   Client has little difficulty talking, but conversation may be vague and unrevealing.
H.   Low self-esteem is often observable in disorder.
I.   Reality is not grossly distorted.
J.   Personality is not grossly disorganized.
K.   Attitude of martyrdom is common.
L.   Client is highly amenable to suggestion.

Nursing Management

A.   Recognize and understand own feelings.
   1.   Recognize and understand own anxiety.
   2.   Convey an attitude of acceptance and understanding to the client.
B.   Discourage client's reliance on nurse beyond that which is necessary.
C.   Plan activities for client that reduce anxiety and increase self-esteem.
D.   Remain with extremely anxious client.
E.   Deal with secondary gains.
   1.   Differentiate secondary gains from malingering.
   2.   Avoid reinforcing secondary gains.
   3.   Help client to understand unconscious motivation.
F.   Provide a safe, supportive environment.
G.   Be aware of the specific needs of each client as

demonstrated by his/her behavior.

H. Plan holistic nursing care; have staff use consistent approach.

Classifications of Neuroses

Anxiety Neurosis

A. Client has diffuse (free floating) anxiety.

B. Client cannot control anxiety by defense mechanisms.

C. Psychological symptoms.
1. Lack of concentration on work.
2. Feelings of depression and guilt.
3. Harbored fear of sudden death or insanity.
4. Dread of being alone.
5. Confusion.
6. Tension.
7. Agitation and restlessness.

D. Physiological symptoms.
1. Tremors.
2. Dyspnea.
3. Palpitations.
4. Tachycardia.
5. Numbness of extremities.

E. Specific nursing approaches.
1. Maintain calm, serene approach; nurse's anxiety reinforces client's anxiety.
2. Help client to develop conscious awareness of anxiety.
3. Help client to explore source of anxiety.
4. Provide physical outlet for anxiety.
5. Remain with client.
6. Decrease environmental stimuli.

Hysterical Neurosis, Dissociate Type

A. Client attempts to deal with anxiety through various disturbances or by walling off certain areas of the mind from consciousness.

B. Client remains in contact with reality.

C. Repression is used.

D. Symptoms.
1. Amnesia.
2. Fugue or physical flight.
3. Multiple personality.

E. Specific nursing approaches.
1. Encourage socialization.
2. Avoid sympathizing with client.
3. Redirect client's attention away from self.
4. Reduce anxiety-producing stimuli.

Hysterical Neurosis, Conversion Type

A. Client converts anxiety resulting from unconscious conflict into physical symptoms.

B. Type of physical symptoms is influenced by culture.

C. Repression is used.

D. Client exhibits relative lack of distress toward symptoms—"la belle indifference."

E. Primary gain is alleviation of anxiety.

F. Secondary gains are additional advantages (e.g., attention).

G. Types of conversions can involve any of the senses or parts of the body (e.g., blindness, paralysis, tics, tremors).

H. Client actually has the physical symptoms and is not malingering.

I. Symptoms disappear under hypnosis.

J. Specific nursing approaches.
1. Reduce pressure on client.
2. Control environment.
3. Provide recreational and social activities.
4. Do not confront client with his illness.
5. Divert client's attention from symptom.
6. Reassure and encourage client.
7. Use matter-of-fact approach.

Phobic Neurosis

A. Client transfers anxiety or fear from its source to a symbolic idea or situation.

B. Client has unrealistic, irrational fear.

C. Client uses projection, displacement, repression, and sublimation.

D. Symptoms: zoophobia, acrophobia, claustrophobia, etc.

E. Specific nursing approaches.
1. Draw client's attention away from phobia.
2. Have client focus on awareness of self.
3. Do not force client into situation feared.
4. Slowly develop sound relationship with client.
5. Desensitize client to the phobia.

Obsessive-Compulsive Neurosis

A. Client has anxiety associated with persisting undesired ideas or thoughts.

B. Client releases anxiety through a repetitive act.

C. Personality characteristics.
1. Insecure, guilt-ridden.
2. Sensitive, shy.
3. Straight-laced.
4. Fussy and meticulous.

D. Client uses repression, isolation, and undoing to control anxiety.

E. Client is unable to control feelings of hostility and aggression.

F. Specific nursing approaches.
1. Avoid punishment or criticism.
2. Protect client from harmful acts by setting limits.
3. Engage in alternative activities with client.
4. Limit decision-making for client.
5. Provide for client's physical needs.

Hypochondriacal Neurosis

A. Client has severe, morbid preoccupation with own body.

B. Client shows lack of interest in environment.

C. Client shows severe regression.

D. Neurosis borders on psychosis.

E. Client goes from doctor to doctor to find cure.

F. Client enjoys recounting medical history.

G. Specific nursing approaches.
1. Accept the client; recognize and understand that complaints are not conscious.
2. Provide diversionary activities in which the client can succeed.
3. Use friendly, supportive approach.
4. Help client to refocus interest.
5. Provide for client's physical needs; give correct information and correct any misinformation.

Neurasthenic Neurosis

A. Client avoids anxiety by becoming bored and fatigued.

B. Client does not use defense mechanisms.

C. Includes a number of physical complaints.
1. Insomnia.
2. Weakness.
3. Exhaustion.
4. Occasional backaches and headaches.

D. Specific nursing approaches.
1. Help client to redirect interests.
2. Involve client in successful activities.
3. Help client express feelings in more effective ways.

Personality Disorders

Definition: Personality disorders are those in which persons have difficulty adjusting to life situations and experience inadequate interactions with society. They exhibit behavioral problems rather than symptoms and have what is known as a psychopathic personality.

Characteristics

A. Client experiences difficulty in forming warm interpersonal relationships.
1. Shallow affective responses.
2. Inability to feel or express emotion.
3. Inability to form deep, meaningful relationships.

B. Client exhibits ineffectual response to intellectual and emotional demands made of him: poor concentration, minimal insight.

C. Behavior involves outward expression of aggressive and sexual impulses.

D. Client experiences low tolerance for anxiety; will go to any length to avoid anxiety-producing situations.
1. Behavior often stems from attempts to gain relief from anxiety.
2. No awareness of what behavior is contrary to society's expectations.

E. Client exhibits poor impulse control, poor judgment, and rejects all authority and regulations.

F. Assets involve social skills—intelligence, charm, and manipulation.

G. Behavior often viewed as direct or indirect attack on laws and mores of society.

H. Specific profiles.
1. Antisocial personality.
   a. Pathological lying, cheating, and stealing—diagnosis common in prisons.
   b. Emotional immaturity.
   c. Lack of judgment.
   d. Ability to rationalize behavior so that it appears justified.

2. Inadequate personality.
   a. Ineffectual response to intellectual and emotional demands.
   b. Poor judgment—does not learn from experience or punishment.
   c. Social instability.
   d. Lack of adaptability.
3. Characteristics of the so-called "social deviate."
   a. Sadism—inflicting pain on another.
   b. Masochism—inflicting pain on self.
   c. Voyeurism—peeping Tom.
   d. Exhibitionism—pleasure in exposing one's body.
4. Drug addiction and alcoholism (see section on substance abuse, p. 451).
5. Schizoid personality.
   a. Lack of close interpersonal relationships.
   b. Shy and withdrawn behavior.
   c. Viewed as eccentric.
   d. Flat affect and inability to express hostility.
6. Paranoid personality.
   a. Suspiciousness toward others.
   b. Inadequate interpersonal relationships—lack of trust.
   c. Feelings of jealousy and envy in relation to others.

Differentiation of Illnesses

A. Differ from psychotic illness.
   1. No ego disintegration (reality oriented).
   2. No impairment of thought processes.
B. Differ from neurotic disorders.
   1. No underlying anxiety, shame, or guilt.
   2. No primary defenses employed.

Nursing Management

A. Form therapeutic nurse-client relationship in which positive behavior is reinforced.
   1. Accept client as he is and where he is (in terms of his abilities).
      a. Set realistic expectations.
      b. Assess capabilities realistically so that failure will not be reinforced.
   2. Maintain control and protect other clients from client's antisocial behavior.
   3. Allow client to express frustration and hos-

tility.
   4. Help client tolerate frustration and postpone satisfaction.
   5. Explore new alternatives for living within society's boundaries.
   6. Be aware of own negative attitudes that may arise when working with these clients.
B. Be firm and consistent in setting limits.
   1. Do not be influenced by client's charming and manipulative ways.
   2. Understand that the client's anxiety will increase if manipulations do not work.
   3. Employ united staff approach to maintenance of limits.
C. Recognize that punishment does not resolve problems or change behavior.
   1. Behavior must be confronted, but the client should not be put down.
   2. Environment must be supportive.
      a. Provide the client with a sense of security.
      b. Provide opportunities for client to learn to cope with impulses.
D. Help formulate realistic future plans.
E. Maintain continuous staff interaction for support and to sustain consistent approach.

Affective Disorders

Definition: Any emotional disorder primarily associated with disturbances in emotional feeling tone.

Depression

Definition: The symptoms of depression may be mild and only slightly debilitating, or pathological, implying overwhelming intensity and long duration. Depression is a universal symptom that is probably experienced by 15 out of 100 adults in our society.

Characteristics

A. Mood is the fundamental disorder, called the "mean blues"; affect is sadness or gloom.
B. Behavior is slowed down with diminished purposeful movement and neglect of personal appearance.
C. Thought processes are slowed down until there is a paucity of thinking.

D. Attitudes are pessimistic and self-denigrating and focus is on the problems and uselessness of life. The client lacks inner resources and strengths to cope effectively.

E. Physical symptoms are usually a preoccupation with body and poor health accompanied by weight loss, insomnia, and general malaise.

F. Social interaction is reduced and inappropriate—the depressed person feels isolated on the one hand; on the other he cannot contribute to interpersonal relationships.

G. Common outcome of depression is suicide (refer to section on suicide, p. 445).

Psychodynamics of Depression

A. Thought to involve a severe blow to self-esteem, a punitive superego, and subsequent lowering of self-image.

B. Intense needs for love cannot be satisfied, which causes disappointment and alienation from others.

C. Exaggerated need for love and dependency makes individuals vulnerable to rejection.

D. Experienced anger is not expressed directly but is internalized.

E. Repression and denial of feelings are characteristic defense mechanisms.

Classifications of Depressive Illnesses

A. *Exogenous or neurotic depression* (also called reactive depression)—influenced by outside events such as the real or symbolic loss of a love object.

  1. Normal self-limited reaction to obvious loss is called grief. Grief reactions are usually brief and milder than pathological depressions.

  2. In neurotic depression, experience of loss results in anger and guilt feelings, which are repressed.

  3. Affective symptoms are sadness, unhappiness, inability to cope with life situations, inability to concentrate, and a general gloomy outlook for the future.

  4. Neurotic depression is milder than either endogenous or involutional depression.

  5. May vary in intensity from day to day.

  6. Usually occurs in the twenty to forty age group.

  7. Type of insomnia characteristic of neurotic depression involves difficulty in going to sleep and 25 percent less REM sleep.

  8. May require sleep medication, but must be monitored for drug dependency.

B. *Endogenous depression*—a state that occurs from within or for no apparent reason, and may result from early personality deficit. The term is used synonymously with manic-depressive illness but also may include categories of psychotic and postpartum depression.

  1. Manic-depressive illness may take clinical course of either depression or mania.

    a. Cyclical periods may last from hours to years.

    b. Cycles occur independent of outside factors.

  2. Onset of depressive illness may occur in early thirties.

  3. Characteristic symptoms of endogenous depression.

    a. Behavior symptoms of psychomotor retardation (in thoughts and actions).

    b. Affective symptoms of sadness, hopelessness, worthlessness, and guilt.

    c. Low verbal response or interactions with others.

    d. Inability to make decisions, concentrate, or complete tasks of daily living.

    e. Symptoms of depression are relatively constant and do not vary day by day.

C. *Involutional depression*—predisposing factors appear to be dissatisfaction with accomplishments in life plus awareness that the prime of life has passed.

  1. Most severe type of primary depression.

  2. Insidious onset occurs between ages of forty and sixty-five.

  3. Distinguishing clinical symptoms.

    a. Behavior is perfectionistic and compulsive.

    b. Many somatic concerns with progressive hypochondriasis.

    c. High anxiety state and frequent agitation.

    d. Physiological symptoms of insomnia, weight loss, anorexia, constipation, and fatigue.

    e. Suicidal impulses.

    f. Other behavioral symptoms are similar to those seen in endogenous depressions: sadness, hopelessness, self-doubt, indecision, inability to concentrate, and guilt feelings.

D. *Secondary depression*—occurs as secondary reaction to other illnesses.

1. Most common illnesses.
   a. Chronic physical disease, i.e., cancer, ulcerative colitis.
   b. Chronic alcoholism.
   c. Organic brain syndrome.
   d. Personality disorders.
   e. Schizophrenia.
2. Not classified as severe compared with the primary depressive states, which are totally debilitating.
3. Major characteristics are similar to general depression.
   a. Sadness, feelings of worthlessness and hopelessness.
   b. Indecisiveness.
   c. Inability to concentrate or to complete tasks of daily living.

Nursing Management

A. Provide a safe milieu and protect the client from self-injury (prevent suicide).
B. Provide a structured environment to mobilize the client.
   1. Allow time for daily activities.
   2. Stimulate recreational activity.
   3. Reactivate interests outside of the client's concerns.
   4. Motivate client for treatment.
   5. Introduce psychotherapy and occupational therapy.
C. Build trust through one-to-one relationship.
   1. Employ a supportive, unchallenging approach.
   2. Use accepting, nonjudgmental attitude and behavior.
   3. Show interest. Listen and give positive reinforcement.
   4. Redirect the client's monologue away from painful, depressing thoughts.
   5. Focus on the client's underlying anger and encourage expression of it.
D. Build the client's ego assets to increase his self-esteem.
   1. Lower standards to create successful experiences.
   2. Limit decision making with the severely depressed.
   3. Support use of defenses to alleviate suffering.
E. Be attentive to the client's physical needs: provide adequate nutrition, sleep, and exercise.
F. Recognize importance of considering differential diagnosis with depression.

Suicide

Characteristics

A. Suicide is the seventh most common cause of death for all ages in the United States today—second cause of death in college students.
B. Suicide statistics are probably low because of unknown cases such as car accidents.
   1. Suicide ranks fourth as the cause of death in the fifteen to forty age group.
   2. For every successful suicide, it is believed that there are five to ten attempted suicides.
   3. Women make more suicide attempts than men.
   4. Suicide is more common in the elderly age group.
   5. Suicide is increasing in the adolescent and elderly age group.
C. Factors that contribute to suicide attempts.
   1. The single most common cause is depression; alcohol is the second most common cause.
   2. Another common cause is that individuals feel overwhelmed by problems in living.
   3. A final cause may be the attempt to control others.
D. Depressed clients, when severely ill, rarely commit suicide.
   1. They do not have the drive and energy to make a plan and follow it through when severely depressed.
   2. Danger period is when depression begins to lift.
E. Eight out of ten known cases give warnings or messages through direct or indirect means.
F. Accompanying symptoms range from depression, disorientation, and defiance to intense dependence on another.

Nursing Management

A. Provide safe environment to protect client from self-destruction.
B. Observe client closely at all times, especially when depression is lifting.
C. Establish supportive relationship, letting the client know you are concerned for his welfare.

D. Encourage expression of feelings, especially anger.

E. Determine presence of suicide ideation (ideas).

1. Ask questions such as "Do you wish you were dead?" "Did you think you might do something about it?" "What?" "Have you taken any steps to prepare?" "What are they?"

2. Important to recognize a continued desire to commit suicide.

F. Focus on client's strengths and successful experiences to increase self-esteem.

G. Provide a structured schedule and involve the client in activities with others.

H. Structure a plan for the client to use as a means of coping when next confronted with suicide ideation.

I. Help the client plan for continued professional support after discharge.

Manic-Depressive Disorder

Definition: Manic-depression is an affective disorder involving cyclothymic mood swings, ranging from depression to acute elation or mania.

Incidence

A. 52.2 persons/100,000 population experience manic episodes.

B. Incidence of manic-depressive episodes is 25 times higher among siblings of manic-depressive clients as in general population.

C. There may be a biochemical connection between increased norepinephrine at the adrenergic receptor sites in the brain and episodes of elation.

D. Twice as many females as males experience manic-depressive disorders.

Characteristics

A. Underlying dynamics: hostility, guilt, and depression.

B. Although the manic client appears to be almost exactly the opposite from the depressed client, this appearance can best be understood as a defense against underlying depression.

C. Mood is one of euphoria, which can lead to grandiose behavior and delusions.

D. Client overresponds to stimuli.

1. Rapid talk, with play on words and flight of ideas.

2. Increased motor activity and thought processes.

E. Client exercises poor judgment (spends money foolishly, runs up charge accounts, etc.).

F. Client exhibits narcissistic attitude and intolerance of guidance or criticism.

G. Client pays little attention to physical health.

1. Poor sleep habits and no apparent fatigue.

2. Poor nutrition.

3. Poor or even bizarre habits of grooming.

H. Behavior varies from joyful and playful to restless, irritable, sarcastic, and even antagonistic and combative.

I. If behavior is not controlled, the client will become incoherent, overtly aggressive, and hostile.

Stages of Mania

A. Mild elation—difficult to detect as it may not progress. Persons are often referred to as "hypomanics."

1. Affect: feelings of happiness, freedom from worry, confidence, and noninhibition.

2. Thought: rapid association of ideas but with little evidence of introspection.

3. Behavior: increased motor activity (person always on the go) and increased sexual drives—superficial relationships.

B. Acute elation—symptoms of mild elation more intensified and observable. Person usually requires treatment.

1. Affect: feelings of exaltation and expansiveness with mood turning rapidly to anger; labile and spiraling mood.

2. Thought: flight of ideas, loquaciousness (pressured speech), loose associations; grandiose and persecutory delusions.

3. Behavior: constant and urgent motor activity; decreased appetite; disturbed sleep patterns; inappropriate dress and makeup; decreased inhibitions; sexual indiscretions; short attention span.

C. Delirium—state of extreme excitement. Person is disoriented, incoherent, agitated, and frenetic.

1. May experience visual or olfactory hallucinations.

2. Exhaustion, dehydration, injury, and death are real dangers and must be prevented by the nurse.

Nursing Management

A. Environmental.
  1. Reduce external stimuli—noise, people, and motion.
  2. Avoid competitive activities.
  3. Redirect energy into short, useful activities.
B. Interpersonal involvement.
  1. Maintain accepting, nonjudgmental attitude and create conditions where trust can develop in the relationship.
  2. Avoid entering into the client's playful, joking activity.
  3. Allow the client to verbalize his feelings, especially hostility.
C. Set realistic limits on behavior.
  1. Provide scope and limitations to behavior for a sense of security.
  2. Anticipate destructive behavior—set limits.
  3. Be firm and consistent.
  4. Involve client in setting own limits.
    a. Gives client sense of control.
    b. Client fears inability to control own behavior.
D. Give attention to physical needs.
  1. Be sure the client has a high calorie, vitamin, and fluid diet.
  2. Ensure adequate rest and sleep.

Psychotic Disorders

Schizophrenia

Definition: A psychiatric syndrome characterized by thought disturbance, withdrawal from reality, regressive behavior, ineffective communication, and severely impaired interpersonal relationships.

Characteristics

A. May result from many possible factors: genetic constellation, individual adaptive patterns, poor family relationships, lack of ego strength, past traumatic experiences, or a deficit in cognitive development.
B. Ego is weak and unable to function as mediator between the self and external reality.
C. Regression and repression are considered to be the primary mechanisms of schizophrenia.
D. Major maladaptive disturbances: impaired interpersonal relationships, inappropriate mental and emotional processes, and disturbances in overt behavior patterns.
E. Manifestations of the illness: acute psychosis involving the total personality or a group of symptoms circumscribed to one area of the personality.

Primary Disturbances

A. Disturbance in thought processes.
  1. Client's thoughts are confused and disorganized, and ability to communicate clearly is limited.
  2. Client manifests tangential or circumstantial speech and has problems with symbolic meaning of certain words.
    a. May be very concrete in thinking and demonstrate an inability to think in abstract terms.
    b. May live in a fantasy world, responding to reality in a bizarre or autistic manner, thereby having great difficulty in testing reality.
B. Disturbance of affect.
  1. Client has difficulty expressing emotions appropriately, and subjective emotional experience may be blunted or flattened.
  2. Client has difficulty expressing positive or warm emotions; when they are expressed, it is often in an inappropriate manner.
  3. While client's feelings may seem inappropriate to the thoughts expressed, they are appropriate to the client's inner experience and are meaningful to him.
  4. Client's inappropriate affect makes it difficult for him to establish close relationships with others.
C. Disturbance in behavior.
  1. Client's behavior is often disorganized and inappropriate and apparently lacks a purposeful activity.
  2. Client typically lacks motivation or drive for change in circumstances; general condition is one of apathy and listlessness.
  3. Client's behavior may appear to be bizarre and extremely inappropriate to the circumstances.
D. Disturbance in interpersonal relationships.

1. Client typically has great difficulty in relating to others.
   a. Cannot build close relationships; probably has not experienced close, meaningful relationships in the past.
   b. Has difficulty trusting others and experiences fear, ambivalence, and dependency that influences his relationships with others.
   c. Often learns to protect self from further hurt by maintaining distance, thus experiences lack of warmth, trust, and intimacy.
2. Client's relationships are impaired by inability to communicate clearly and to react in an appropriate and empathic manner.

Clinical Manifestations

A. The four "A's."
1. *Affect*—feelings or emotions minimal, i.e., flat, blunted, or inappropriate.
2. *Associative looseness*—no connection between thoughts or ideas expressed.
3. *Autistic thinking*—thoughts excessively involved with self; focused inward; unresponsive, mute with disintegrated thought processes.
4. *Ambivalence*—two equally strong feelings (love and hate) neutralizing each other and immobilizing client.

B. Other important symptoms.
1. Difficulty in *reality testing*—inability to distinguish between objective facts and wishes or fears.
2. *Delusions* (fixed misinterpretation of reality)—false beliefs maintained despite evidence to the contrary.
3. *Hallucinations* (unwilled sense perceptions with no basis in reality)—auditory, visual, olfactory, tactile, gustatory.
4. *Withdrawal*—adoption of more satisfying regressive behavior; focus on internal world (autism).
5. *Depersonalization*—feelings of estrangement or unconnectedness of body parts.

Nursing Management

A. General approaches.
1. Establish nurse-client relationship.
   a. Increase social contacts with others.
   b. Build positive and trusting relationship.
   c. Provide a safe and secure environment.
2. Stress reality; help the client to reality-test, to leave his fantasy world.
   a. Involve the client in reality-oriented activities.
   b. Help the client find satisfaction in the external environment.
3. Accept the client as he is.
   a. Do not invalidate disturbed thoughts or fantasies.
   b. Do not invalidate the client himself by inappropriate responses.
4. Use therapeutic communication techniques.
   a. Encourage expression of emotions, negative or positive.
   b. Encourage expression of thoughts, fears, and problems.
   c. Attempt to fit nonverbal with verbal communications.
   d. Focus on clear communication with the client.
5. Avoid fostering dependency relationship.
6. Avoid stressful situations or increasing the client's anxiety.

B. Nursing approaches to specific symptoms.
1. Dealing with delusions.
   a. Help the client recognize distorted views of reality.
   b. Focus on ego assets, strengths, etc.
   c. Provide a safe, nonthreatening milieu.
   d. Divert focus from delusional material to reality.
   e. Provide experiences in which client can feel success.
   f. Specific nursing responses:
      (1) Avoid confirming or feeding into delusion.
      (2) Stress reality by denying you believe the client's delusion.
      (3) Respond to feelings. For example, validate the feelings of the client by asking, "I sense you are afraid. Is this true?"
2. Dealing with withdrawn behavior.
   a. Assist client in developing satisfying relationships with others.
      (1) Initiate interaction.

(2) Build a trusting relationship by being consistent in keeping appointments, in attitudes, and in nursing practice.

(3) Be honest and direct in what is said and done.

(4) Deal with therapist's feelings in relation to client's hostility or rejection.

b. Help client to modify perception of self.

(1) Do not structure situation in which client will fail.

(2) Increase client's self-esteem by focusing on assets or strengths.

(3) Relieve client from decision making until he is able to make decisions.

c. Teach client renewal of social skills.

(1) Increase social contacts with staff and other clients.

(2) Increase social contacts with significant others when appropriate.

d. Focus on reality situations.

(1) Use nonthreatening approach.

(2) Provide safe, nonthreatening milieu.

e. Attend to physical needs, e.g., nutrition, sleep, exercise, occupational therapy.

3. Dealing with hallucinations.

a. Provide safe, structured environment with routine activities.

b. Protect client from self-injury prompted by "voices."

c. Initiate short, frequent interactions.

(1) Respond verbally to anything real that the client talks about.

(2) Avoid denying or arguing with the client about the hallucinations he is experiencing.

(3) Increase client's social interaction gradually from interaction with one person to interaction with small groups as the client can tolerate it.

C. Use real objects or activities (singing) to distract or redirect client.

D. Decrease the client's anxiety level.

E. Use warm, honest, matter-of-fact approach.

F. Recognize that the nurse and others influence the client even if he appears unresponsive, remote, and detached at times.

Schizophrenic Subtypes

A. Paranoid schizophrenia.

1. Persecutory or grandiose delusions are prominent.

2. Extreme suspiciousness and withdrawal common manifestation.

B. Catatonic schizophrenia.

1. Secondary symptoms of motor involvement are present.

a. Underactivity resulting in bizarre posturing.

b. Overactivity leading to agitation.

2. Negativism—doing the opposite of what is asked.

a. Rigidity is simplest form of negativism.

b. Mute behavior is another form of negativism.

C. Hebephrenic schizophrenia.

1. Inappropriate affect—giggling and silly laughter.

2. Hallucinations.

3. Regression.

4. Severe thought disturbance.

D. Simple schizophrenia.

1. Autism.

2. Flat affect.

3. Association disorders.

a. Delusions.

b. Hallucinations.

Paranoid Schizophrenia

Definition: Diagnosis of paranoid schizophrenia is made when paranoid features dominate the personality; other symptoms of maladaptive behavior may be absent. The majority of paranoid psychoses are classified under schizophrenia, but a paranoid reaction also occurs in organic, senile, alcoholic, and other mental illnesses.

Characteristics

A. Characterized by extreme suspiciousness and withdrawal from all emotional contact with others.

B. The onset is usually gradual.

C. The onset of paranoid reactions may be precipitated by certain stressful events in the client's life.

1. Real or imaginary loss of a love object.

2. Experiences of failure with subsequent loss of self-esteem.

D. Behavioral manifestation of illness seen with intense focus on hypochondriasis.
  1. Complaints of insomnia and weakness.
  2. Complaints of strange bodily sensations.
  3. The more common paranoid psychosis manifested by delusional thoughts.
     a. Most common delusions are of persecution (people are out to harm, injure, or destroy).
     b. Other delusions may center around grandeur, somatic complaints, or delusions of jealousy.

Clinical Manifestations

A. Extreme suspiciousness and mistrust of others.
B. Hostility toward others.
C. Delusions—persecution, grandeur, and/or hypochrondriasis.
D. Chronic insecurity, inadequate self-concept, and low self-esteem.
E. Chronic high anxiety level.
F. Denial of client role.

Nursing Management

A. Establish a trusting relationship.
  1. Be consistent and friendly despite client's hostility.
  2. Avoid talking and laughing when the client can see you but not hear you.
  3. If client very suspicious, use a one-to-one relationship, not group situation.
  4. Involve the client in the treatment plan.
  5. Give support by being nonpunitive.
B. Reduce client's anxiety associated with interpersonal interactions.
  1. Avoid power struggles—do not argue with the client; arguing increases anxiety and hostility.
  2. Do not proceed too fast with nursing therapy. Remember that a paranoid client is suspicious and mistrustful of others.
  3. Be consistent and honest.
C. Help differentiate delusion from reality (refer to section on delusions).
  1. Do not explain away false ideas. Ideas are real to the client.
  2. Any attempt to disagree with delusion may reinforce it.
  3. Use reality-testing when possible.
  4. Focus on reality situations in the environment.
  5. Attempt to engage in activities that require concentration.

Differentiation Between Psychosis and Neurosis

Psychosis	Neurosis
A. Major ego impairment. Includes faulty reality testing, delusions, hallucinations, and illusions.	No grave impairment of reality testing. No hallucinations or delusions.
B. Serious impairment of client's life, including social, vocational, and sexual.	Difficulty in relating, but interaction with others not prevented. Personality usually remains organized.
C. Little insight into problems and behavior. Client generally does not recognize he is ill.	Some awareness into problems. Keenly feels subjective suffering. Often unconsciously fights any change in status (getting well).
D. Severe personality disorganization, e.g., poor judgment, memory, and perceptions.	Less severe disorganization. Can function but with decreased efficiency.
E. May be caused by both physiological or psychological factors.	Always a functional disorder; not organic in origin.
F. Usually requires hospitalization and long-term treatment.	Usually does not require hospitalization. May require long-term hospitalization.
G. Maladaptive adjustment mechanisms used in rigid, fixed way. May be seen as severe regression.	Suppression and repression used to handle internal conflicts; defenses are largely symbolic.
H. No secondary gain received.	Symptoms generally exploited for secondary gain.

Schools of Thought

A. There are several schools of thought concerning the labels "psychosis" and "psychoneurosis."
B. Some make the distinction on the basis of the extent of involvement of the personality and the

individual's level of contact with reality.

C. Personality reactions.

1. Major reactions—psychosis.

2. Minor reactions—psychoneurosis.

D. No sharp line between the psychoneuroses and psychoses. The differences are largely descriptive and are of degree.

Substance Abuse

Definition: Substance abuse is the process by which people introduce various chemicals and substances into their bodies that produce physical symptoms of withdrawal when the use of the addictive agent is terminated.

Characteristics of Substance Abuse

A. Psychological dependence—emotional dependence, desire, or compulsion to continue taking the substance or drug.

B. Tolerance—the gradual increase of the amount required to obtain the desired effect.

C. Physical dependence—physical need for the substance manifested by appearance of withdrawal symptoms when substance not taken.

Alcoholism

Consumption of Alcohol

A. Permitted by law and supported by most people in our society as a recreational activity.

B. There is a fine line between the so-called "social drinker" and the addicted or problem drinker.

C. The greatest difference involves the degree of compulsion to drink and the inability to survive the trials of everyday living without the ingestion of alcohol.

D. Alcoholism is the third largest health problem in the United States (heart disease and cancer are first and second).

E. Alcoholism is involved in about 30,000 deaths and one-half million injuries (auto accidents) every year.

F. Alcoholism decreases life span 10 to 12 years.

G. Loss to industry caused by alcoholism is estimated at 15 billion dollars a year (affecting primarily the 35 to 55 age group).

Dynamics of Alcoholism

A. Alcoholic disease implies the consumption of alcohol to the point where it interferes with the individual's physical, emotional, and social functioning.

1. The syndrome consists of two phases: problem drinking and alcohol addiction.

2. Dependence on other drugs is very common.

B. No hereditary or organic basis for alcoholism has been proven to date.

C. Alcohol blocks synaptic transmission, depresses the central nervous system (CNS), and releases inhibitions. It acts initially as a stimulant but is actually a depressant.

1. Chronic excessive use can lead to brain damage (sedative effect on CNS).

2. High blood levels may cause malfunctions in cardiovascular and respiratory systems.

3. Large doses over a long period of time may lead to delirium tremens, alcohol intoxication, or Korsakoff's syndrome.

D. Psychological effects of alcohol appear to be gratification of oral impulses and reduction of superego forces; abuse leads to shame and guilt and impaired ego function.

E. Alcohol may be said to be a defense against anxiety; therefore, the client needs to work on problems causing his anxiety.

Characteristics of an Alcoholic

A. Dependent personality with resentment toward authority.

B. High self-expectations and low frustration tolerance.

C. Life usually characterized by patterns of failure.

D. False sense of success, power, and confidence from use of alcohol.

E. Apparent need to ease suffering, reduce anxiety, and cope with life stresses through use of alcohol.

F. Decreased ability to function intellectually, emotionally, and socially as need for alcohol increases.

Nursing Management

A. Reestablish the healthy physical condition of the client.

1. Supply adequate nutrition, including fluids and high vitamin, high calorie, high protein diet.

2. Promote adequate rest and sleep.

3. Observe client for symptoms of impending

delirium tremens.

B. Set up a controlled and structured environment until the client is able to manage his own circumstances.
   1. Set behavior limits and confront the client who is manipulative.
   2. Suggest group involvement for client who experiences loneliness.
   3. Remember that the client needs support, firmness, and a reality-oriented approach.

C. Treatment techniques.
   1. Client must first go through detoxification—intensive care to avoid the toxic state and to return to a nonalcoholic state.
   2. Help the client accept the fact that alcoholism is an illness.
   3. Help the client accept that life must be managed without the support of alcohol.
   4. Provide psychotherapy techniques such as group and family therapy and nurse-client relationship therapy.
      a. Focus on the underlying emotional problems.
      b. Offer assistance in handling anxiety.
      c. Focus on relieving feelings of inferiority and low self-esteem.
   5. Provide for rehabilitation or long-term supportive care.
      a. Continued psychotherapy on an out-client basis.
      b. Referral to Alcoholics Anonymous.
      c. Medication such as Antabuse (alcohol-sensitizing drug that causes vomiting and cardiovascular symptoms if the person drinks alcohol).
      d. Social or vocational rehabilitation community programs.

D. Nursing attitudes.
   1. Maintain a nonjudgmental attitude toward the alcoholic.
   2. Be firm and consistent in approach.
   3. Be accepting toward the individual—not his deviant behavior.
   4. Be supportive of attempts to change life patterns.

Acute Intoxication

A. Symptoms of alcohol intoxication are the same as those of overdosage with any CNS depressant.
   1. Drowsiness, ataxia, nystagmus.
   2. Respiratory depression, stupor, coma, and death in severe cases.

B. Delirium tremens.
   1. DT's is an acute condition usually manifested within 24 to 72 hours after the last ingestion of alcohol. May appear 7 to 10 days later or even during drinking periods when no food is ingested.
   2. There is a wide spectrum of withdrawal symptoms ranging from anxiety to full-blown DT's.
   3. Symptoms of DT's include mental confusion, tremors, visual hallucinations, delirium, rapid and weak pulse.
   4. DT's is a critical illness—death rate from heart failure is 10 to 15 percent.

C. Nursing concerns.
   1. Suspect alcohol withdrawal in every unexplained delirium, tremors or restlessness.
   2. Condition requires critical care—hospitalization.
   3. Condition requires CNS depressants to counteract CNS excitability resulting from cessation of alcohol.
   4. Condition requires high calorie fluids concurrent with vitamin supplements (B complex).
   5. Client needs environment with minimal stimulation—rest is important.
   6. Post-hospitalization plan of care and psychotherapy are important.

Drug Addiction

Definition: Drug addiction is dependency on drugs other than alcohol or tobacco that involve alteration of perception or mood.

Narcotic Addiction

A. The most common types of narcotics are heroin and morphine.
B. Emotional dependence on the drug (to alter mood) occurs first, followed by physical dependence on the drug.
C. Narcotics have a sedative effect on the CNS.
D. Tolerance level increases, so greater amounts of the drug are necessary to produce pleasurable effects.

E. Addiction tends to be chronic, with a high rate of relapse.

F. Withdrawal symptoms.
    1. Anxiety.
    2. Nausea and vomiting.
    3. Sneezing, yawning, and watery eyes.
    4. Tremor and profuse perspiration.
    5. Stomach cramps and dehydration.
    6. Convulsions and coma.

G. Characteristic personality of the narcotic addict.
    1. Emotional immaturity with feelings of inadequacy and inferiority.
    2. Inadequate interpersonal relationships, dishonesty, and insincerity.
    3. Poor judgment and inability to tolerate frustration.

Sedative Hypnotics Addiction

A. Common drugs include Librium, Valium, Quaalude, Equanil, Miltown, Seconal, Nembutal, and Sodium Amytal.

B. Barbiturates have CNS sedative effect—danger of death from overdose.

C. Psychological dependence occurs, followed by tolerance and physical dependence.

D. May be used originally as a "prescribed" drug for relief of chronic pain or sleeplessness.

E. Individual usually has emotional problems and an anxious temperament.

F. Sudden withdrawal of barbiturates may result in acute psychosis and seizures.

G. Overdoses and acute withdrawal from barbiturates are medical emergencies and require hospitalization.

Other Common Addictive Patterns

A. Amphetamines, Benzedrine, and Dexedrine.
    1. All effect or produce a "high."
    2. All are CNS stimulants, so overuse may result in brain damage.
    3. Large doses produce a hyperactive and agitated state.
    4. Amphetamines are emotionally addictive, especially for persons with insecure, inadequate personalities.
    5. Amphetamines affect individual's physical condition as the drug reduces appetite and awareness of body needs.

B. LSD, or "acid."
    1. LSD is a hallucinogenic drug and mimics hallucinations seen in psychoses.
    2. Produces changes in perception and logical thought processes.
    3. Not considered addictive per se, but individual may become emotionally dependent on drug.
    4. Experiences with LSD range from ecstasy to terror and the results are unpredictable.

C. Marijuana.
    1. Has low abuse potential since it produces neither tolerance nor physical dependence.
    2. Produces "dreamy" state and feelings of euphoria, hilarity, and well-being.
    3. Moods vary according to environmental stimuli.
    4. Changes perception of space and time—seems distorted and extendable.
    5. High dosage may produce hallucinations and delusions.

D. Cocaine.
    1. Classified as a stimulant.
    2. Usually sniffed or used I.V.
    3. May cause strong psychological dependence.
    4. Does not develop physical dependence or tolerance.

E. P.C.P.—"Crystal," "elephant tranquilizer."
    1. Usually smoked with marijuana. May also be ingested or injected.
    2. Reactions vary from sense of well-being to total disorientation and hallucinations.
    3. Considered an extremely dangerous "street" drug.
    4. Psychological dependence may occur.
    5. Cerebral cellular destruction and atrophy occur with even small amounts.
    6. Overdoses or "bad trips" are characterized by erratic, unpredictable behavior, withdrawal, disorientation, self-mutilation, or self-destructive behaviors.
    7. Overdoses are treated with sedatives, and by decreasing environmental stimuli and protecting the client from harming self and others.

Nursing Management

A. Nursing approaches and attitudes are similar to those enumerated in the previous section on alcoholism.

B. Specific treatment approach to drug addiction.

1. Withdrawal is the first step in treatment and may be accomplished abruptly ("cold turkey") or gradually over a period of days.
2. Often, a substitute drug (e.g., Methadone) is used to reduce the physical reaction to withdrawal.
3. Prolonged medical and psychiatric treatment for physical and emotional deterioration must be part of convalescence.
4. Resocialization process of client needs supportive treatment from professional or community resources.
5. Rehabilitation programs must be aimed at helping the person reenter the mainstream of society.
    a. Various self-help groups offer aid in rehabilitation.
    b. Therapeutic communities and group therapy programs also accomplish rehabilitation.

Organic Brain Syndrome (OBS)

Definition: Organic brain syndromes are psychiatric disorders with organic etiology which may be reversible (acute brain syndrome) or irreversible (chronic brain syndrome).

Acute Brain Syndrome

Characteristics

A. Sudden onset.
B. Rapid impairment of orientation, memory, intellectual function, judgment, and affect.
C. Client may be delirious or comatose—may experience hallucinations and delusions.
D. Cause is temporary and reversible with time and treatment.

Etiology

A. Any acute disease or injury that interferes with cerebral function.
B. Infections, circulatory disturbances, metabolic and endocrine disorders.
C. Brain trauma, neoplasms, tumors.
D. Poisons, drugs, or systemic intoxication.

Nursing Management

A. Provide for physical needs of client.
B. Implement treatment to combat specific etiology.
C. Eliminate irritating stimuli.
D. Provide protective measures to prevent accidents and self-injury.
E. Observe and report signs of fever, shock, increased intracranial pressure, acute anxiety, and restlessness.
F. Reassure client and family.

Chronic Brain Syndrome

Characteristics

A. Disorder affects the central nervous system, with damage or destruction of neurons.
B. Disorder interferes with normal functioning.
    1. It is irreversible.
    2. The symptoms may vary with the cause.
C. Onset is generally slow.
D. Illness may be stabilized (undergo remission).
E. Generally there is increasing deterioration.
F. Usual symptoms.
    1. Cognitive impairment.
        a. Disorientation.
        b. Severe loss of memory.
        c. Judgment impairment.
        d. Loss of capacity to learn.
        e. Perceptual disturbances.
        f. Decreased attention span.
        g. Paranoid ideation.
    2. Conative impairment.
        a. Decreased motivation, interests, and self-concern.
        b. Loss of normal inhibitions.
        c. Loss of insight.
    3. Affective impairment.
        a. Labile mood, irritableness, and explosiveness.
        b. Depression.
        c. Withdrawal.
        d. Anxiety.
    4. Behavioral impairment.
        a. Restlessness.
        b. Ritualistic, stereotyped behavior to deal with environment.

c. Possible combativeness.

d. Possible inappropriate and regressive behavior.

e. Alterations in sexual drives and activity.

f. As client's defenses break down, behavior may seem to be neurotic or psychotic.

Etiology

A. Prenatal: congenital cranial anomaly, congenital spastic paraplegia.

B. Infection: central nervous system (CNS), syphilis, meningoencephalitis.

C. Intoxication: drug or poison, alcohol.

D. Trauma: brain trauma gross force, brain operation.

E. Circulatory disorder: cerebral arteriosclerosis.

F. Disturbance of innervation: convulsions.

G. Disturbances of metabolism, growth, or nutrition.

1. Senile brain disease: dementia.

2. Glandular problems.

3. Pellagra.

H. New growths: brain neoplasm.

Progressive Degenerative Diseases

A. *Korsakoff's syndrome*—associated with chronic alcoholism and polyneuritis caused by thiamine deficiency.

B. *Alzheimer's disease*—onset at age 40 to 50 with diffuse degeneration of all layers of the cortex and atrophy of cerebrum. Death occurs from 1 to 10 years after onset.

C. *Pick's disease*—rare heredodegenerative process not associated with the normal aging process.

D. *Huntington's chorea*—genetically transmitted disorder.

1. Characterized by onset of symptoms after the age of 30.

2. Progressive mental and physical deterioration is inevitable.

E. *Multiple sclerosis*—demyelinating disease characterized by involuntary movements, dysarthria, ataxia, emotional lability, euphoria, depression, and irritability.

Psychological Reactions to COB Disorder

A. Change in self-concept.

B. Anger and frustration as reactions to forced change in life role.

C. Denial used as defense.

D. Depression.

E. Acceptance of limitations.

F. Assumption of "sick" role.

1. Dependency.

2. Lack of motivation.

Nursing Management

A. Meet both physical and psychological needs.

B. Help client maintain contact with reality.

1. Give feedback.

2. Avoid small chatter.

3. Personalize interaction.

4. Supply stimulation to motivate client.

5. Keep client from becoming bored and distracted.

C. Assist client in accepting the diagnosis.

1. Be supportive.

2. Maintain good communication.

3. During denial phase, listen and accept; do not argue.

4. Assist development of awareness.

5. Help client develop the ability to cope with his altered identity.

D. Focus of interactions with client.

1. Have short, frequent contacts with client.

2. Use concrete ideas in communicating with the client.

3. Maintain reality orientation by allowing the client to talk about his past and to confabulate.

4. Acknowledge the client as an individual.

E. Provide a safe, stable, consistent environment.

F. Assess the client's disabilities and develop a nursing plan to deal with them.

G. Become a member of the rehabilitation team.

Child Psychiatry

Emotionally Disturbed Child

Definition: Emotional disturbance in children encompasses any form of dysfunctional or maladaptive behavior. It can take as many forms as adult disturbance, ranging from healthy responses in situational or developmental crises to neurotic or psychotic disorders. Situational crises such as separation anxiety and developmental deviations are considered in the chapter on Pediatric Nursing.

Autistic Behavior in Children

A. Autism is complete self-involvement, withdrawal to "inner world."

B. It occurs in infancy and the etiology is not known at this time.

C. It may involve pathological or family dynamics.

D. It is generally thought that the autistic child manifests weak ego boundaries and fails to develop a separate concept of the "self."

    1. Early symbiotic relationship to the mother leads to the child's perception of self as an extension of the mother.

    2. The autistic child can neither distinguish himself from the world nor distinguish internal from external stimuli.

    3. Differentiated from childhood schizophrenia where the child has more sense of self and views self as separate from mother.

Characteristics

A. Somatic manifestations: enuresis; eating or sleeping difficulties.

B. Withdrawn behavior.

C. Bizarre responses, such as rocking, hand movements in the air, fecal smearing.

D. Absent or inappropriate communication.

E. Flat or inappropriate affect.

F. Tantrums or self-destructive behavior, such as head banging.

G. Aggressive behavior toward persons or objects.

H. Absence of "self" image, e.g., inability to identify parts of the body.

Nursing Management

A. To work effectively with autistic children, the nurse needs to know patterns of normal growth and development (Erikson and Piaget), basic principles of psychiatric intervention, communication techniques, and have self-awareness.

B. The nurse must also be able to assess totally the child's psychomotor skills, reactions to environment, interaction and communication patterns, emotional status, and body image.

C. The nurse must establish some method of relating to the child, either verbal or nonverbal.

    1. Communication is essential for the development of a relationship.

    2. Establishing a relationship with a mute and/or withdrawn child may be long and frustrating for the nurse because she must deal with her own feelings too.

    3. Genuine concern, warmth, and acceptance must be felt by the nurse toward the child in order for her interactions to be effective.

D. A primary objective is to teach and support the child in mastering beginning development tasks that were never completed.

E. The nurse must give good physical care and protect the child from self-destructive behavior.

F. The nurse must set firm limits and be consistent to provide a secure milieu.

G. The nurse must provide activities for participation, fun, and reeducation according to developmental level of the child.

Adolescent Adjustment Problems

Definition: Adolescent emotional disturbances occur in adolescents when their behavior becomes maladaptive and they cease to function effectively.

Characteristics

A. Adolescence is a period of ambivalence: dependence versus independence.

B. Influenced by peer group pressures, the adolescent may experience an identity crisis because his own identity has not yet been resolved.

C. The adolescent evidences an inability to resolve conflicts and to master developmental tasks (identity versus role diffusion). For a full discussion of Erikson's "Stages of Development," see the chapter on Pediatric Nursing.

D. Confusion may result in anxiety, depression, acting out, or antisocial behavior.

E. Specific behaviors observed in adolescent maladjustment:

    1. Defiance and hostility, especially toward authority figures.

    2. Sullenness and withdrawal.

    3. Sexual deviations.

4. Addiction to drugs or alcohol.
5. Depression and self-destructive impulses.
6. Acting out or testing.

Nursing Management

A. Set firm limits and be consistent in approach.

B. Be accepting and supportive without being maternal, judgmental, or punitive.

C. Confront maladaptive behavior and reinforce efforts to change it.

D. Avoid being manipulated or supportive of acting-out behavior.

E. Provide the experience of a positive relationship and encourage interaction with others.

Maladaptive Behavior—Nursing Management

Aggressive or Combative Behavior

A. Observe client acutely for clues that the client is getting out of control.
   1. Note rising anger—verbal and nonverbal behavior.
   2. Note erratic or unpredictable response to staff or other clients.

B. Intervene immediately when loss of control is imminent.

C. Use a nonthreatening approach to the client.

D. Set firm limits on unacceptable behavior.

E. Maintain calm manner and do not show fear.

F. Avoid engaging in an argument or provoking the client.

G. Summon assistance only when indicated; sudden involvement of many people will increase the client's agitation.

H. Remove the client from the situation as soon as possible.

I. Use seclusion and/or restraints only if necessary.

J. Attempt to calm the client so that he may regain control.

K. Be supportive and stay with the client.

L. Use problem-solving focus following outburst of aggressive or combative behavior.
   1. Encourage discussion of feelings surrounding incident.
   2. Attempt to look at causal factors of the behavior.
   3. Examine the client's response to stimulus and alternative responses.
   4. Point out consequences of aggressive behavior.
   5. Discuss the client's role of taking responsibility for his aggressive behavior.

Verbally Abusive Behavior

A. Do not respond in kind to abusive comments.

B. Try not to take abuse personally.

C. Interact with the client on a therapeutic basis.
   1. Help the client examine his feelings.
   2. Do not reject the client.
   3. Give client feedback concerning your reactions to abusive comments.
   4. Teach alternative ways to express his feelings.

D. Maintain a calm, accepting approach to client.

Demanding Behavior

A. Do not ignore demands, they will only increase in intensity.

B. Attempt to determine causal factors of behavior, e.g., high anxiety level.

C. Set limits to response patterns when client is demanding.

D. Control own feelings of anger and irritation.

E. Teach alternative means to getting needs met.

F. Plan nursing care to include frequent contacts initiated by the nurse.

G. Alert the staff to try to give client the reassurance he needs.

Psychotropic Drugs

Definition: Psychotropic drugs are those used in psychiatry in conjunction with other forms of therapy to temporarily modify behavior.

Characteristics

A. Affect both the central and autonomic nervous systems.

B. Affect behavior indirectly by chemically interacting with other chemicals, enzymes, or enzyme substrates.

1. Produce change in cellular, tissue, and organ functions.
2. Drug effects vary from cellular activity to psychosocial interaction.

Common Categories of Psychotropic Drugs

A. Antipsychotic drugs.
   1. Also known as ataractic, neuroleptic, or major tranquilizers.
   2. Came into use about 1953.
   3. Most common are the phenothiazine derivatives (Thorazine, Mellaril, Sparine, Compazine, Stelazine, Trilafon, Vesprin, and Prolixin).
      a. Antipsychotic drugs can calm an excited client without producing a marked impairment of motor function or sleep.
      b. Side effects.
         (1) Blood dyscrasias, agranulocytosis, and leukopenia.
         (2) Photosensitivity, dermatitis, melanin pigmentation, and corneal and lens deposits.
         (3) Extrapyramidal stimulation, affecting the voluntary movements and skeletal muscles.
            (a) Parkinsonism—signs are similar to classic parkinsonism: rigidity, a shuffling gait, pill-rolling hand movement, tremors, dyskinesia, and mask-like face.
            (b) Akathisia—uncontrolled motor restlessness, foot-tapping, agitation, pacing.
            (c) Dystonia—limb and neck spasms, difficulty in speaking and swallowing, and rigidity and spasm of muscles.
         (4) Hypotension.
         (5) Tachycardia.
         (6) Edema.
         (7) Impotence.
         (8) Decreased libido.
         (9) Dry mouth, blurred vision, nasal congestion, increased appetite, and insomnia.
   4. Butyrophenone derivative (Haldol).
      a. Less sedative than phenothiazines.
      b. Favored in Europe before coming into use

in the United States.
   5. Thioxanthene (Taractan, Navane).
B. Antianxiety drugs.
   1. Induce sedation, relax muscles, and inhibit convulsions; major use to reduce anxiety.
   2. Potentiate drug abuse. Greatest harm occurs when combined with alcohol.
   3. Used in neuroses, psychosomatic disorders, or functional psychiatric disorders, but do not modify psychotic behavior.
   4. Include Equanil, Miltown, Ultran, Librium, Valium, Serax, Atarax, and Vistaril.
   5. Side effects.
      a. Drowsiness (avoid driving or working around equipment).
      b. Blurred vision, constipation, dermatitis, mental confusion, anorexia, polyuria, menstrual irregularities, and edema.
      c. Habituation and increased tolerance.
      d. Pancytopenia, thrombocytopenia, and agranulocytopenia.
C. Antidepressant drugs.
   1. Tricyclics—Elavil, Norpramin, Tofranil, Aventyl, and Vivactil.
      a. Anticholinergic—take one to three weeks to be effective.
      b. Produce antagonism of the parasympathetic system.
      c. Side effects.
         (1) Muscular hypertension, drowsiness, dry mouth, tremors, fatigue, weakness, blurred vision, and headache.
         (2) Edema, mild extrapyramidal stimulation, and urinary retention.
   2. Monoamine oxidase inhibitors—Marplan, Niamid, Nardil, and Parnate.
      a. MAO inhibitors are toxic, potent, and produce many side effects.
      b. Should rarely be the first antidepressant drug used.
      c. Side effects.
         (1) Postural hypertension, headaches, constipation, anorexia, diarrhea, and chills.
         (2) Tachycardia, edema, impotence, dizziness, insomnia, and restlessness.
         (3) Manic episodes and anxiety.
         (4) Hypertensive crisis—the most dangerous reaction.

d. All clients must be warned not to eat foods with high tyramine content (aged cheese, wine, beer, chicken liver, yeast), drink alcohol, or take other drugs, especially sympathomimetic drugs (amphetamines, L-Dopa, epinephrine).

e. MAO inhibitors must not be used in combination with tricyclics.

D. Antimanic drugs.

1. Used to control mood disorders.

2. Must reach certain blood levels before they become effective.

3. Lithium carbonate.

a. Not effective for acute depression or schizophrenia.

b. Serum level can be simply and reliably measured in milliequivalents of lithium per liter of blood.

c. Side effects.

(1) More apt to appear at blood levels above 1.6 mEq./liter.

(2) Gastrointestinal disturbances, muscle weakness, sluggishness, thirst, polyuria, and fine hand tremors.

(3) Hypothyroidism.

d. Lithium toxicity.

(1) Appears when blood level exceeds 2.0 mEq./liter. May appear sooner.

(2) Central nervous system is chief target.

(3) Initial symptoms include drowsiness, tremors, and slurred speech.

(4) If drug is continued, coma, convulsions, and death may result.

E. Antiparkinson drugs.

1. The term "extrapyramidal disease" refers to motor disorders often associated with pathologic dysfunction in the basal ganglia.

a. Clinical symptoms of the disease include abnormal involuntary movement, changes in tone of the skeletal muscles, and a reduction of automatic associated movements.

b. Reversible extrapyramidal reactions may follow the use of certain drugs.

c. The most common drugs are the phenothiazine derivatives.

2. Antiparkinson drugs act on the extrapyramidal system to reduce disturbing symptoms.

a. Usually given in conjunction with anti-

psychotic drugs.

b. Two of the most common are Artane and Cogentin.

c. Side effects are dizziness, gastrointestinal disturbance, headaches, urinary hesitancy, and memory impairment.

F. General nursing responsibilities for drug administration in a psychiatric setting.

1. Give correct *drug* and *dose* at correct *time* to correct *client*.

2. Know specific actions and uses of drugs.

3. Be familiar with the side effects and precautions of major drug groups.

4. Observe client carefully for side effects.

5. Be aware that certain drug groups are not compatible.

6. Notify doctor of EPR side effects and lithium toxicity, and immediately implement nursing interventions.

Note: See Appendix 4: Drug Classification Table.

Treatment Modalities

Behavior Modification

Definition: Behavior modification is a process for dealing with problematic, ineffective human behavior through planned, systematic interventions. It is a three-staged process involving behavior assessment, intervention, and evaluation.

Characteristics

A. Behavior modification assumes that maladaptive behaviors have been learned or acquired through life's experiences.

B. The process draws on learning theory as an approach to the modification of behavior.

1. It involves stimulus-response type learning.

2. Techniques are drawn from Pavlov and Skinner.

3. It has been labeled "behavior conditioning."

4. It assumes that man's learned behavior is specifically connected with his environmental reinforcers, e.g., American eating patterns.

5. The appropriate location for behavioral intervention and change is the individual's environment.

C. Behavior cannot be thoroughly understood independent of events that precede or follow it.

D. The concept of contingency relationships is basic.

1. Relationships between behavior and reinforcing events.

2. Positive reinforcer—a desirable reward produced by a specific behavior; for example, salary is contingent on work: no work, no salary.

3. Negative reinforcer—punishment or negative reward; for example, the mother spanks the child for playing with matches.

4. Removal of a positive reinforcer; for example, the student is not allowed to watch TV until he finishes his homework.

5. Removal of a negative reinforcer; for example, the mother threatens the child until he cleans up his room. Removal produces avoidance behaviors.

6. Principle of extinction.

a. Reduce the frequency of a behavior by disrupting its contingency with the reinforcement.

b. Arrange conditions so that the reinforcing event which has been maintaining the behavior no longer occurs.

E. Goal: to arrange and manage reinforcement contingencies so that desired behaviors are increased in frequency and undesirable behaviors are decreased in frequency or removed.

F. Specific terminology.

1. Behavior problem—condemned, excessive, or deficient behavior.

2. Operant behavior—voluntary activities which are strongly influenced by events that follow them.

3. Reinforcer—a reward which positively or negatively influences and strengthens desired behavior.

a. Primary—inborn.

b. Acquired—not inborn.

4. Stimulus—any event impinging on, or affecting, an individual.

5. Accelerating behavior—increase in frequency of a desired behavior.

6. Decelerating behavior—decrease in frequency of an undesirable behavior.

7. Target behavior—particular activities that the nurse wants to accelerate.

Nursing Management

A. The nurse can be the major treatment agent because she has the most significant number of contacts with the client and his environment.

B. The nurse may be in charge of designing and implementing the program.

C. The nurse may be in charge of supervising a program that another staff member is putting into effect.

D. Proximity to the client enables the nurse to identify any specifically maladaptive behavior.

Crisis Intervention

Definition: Crisis intervention is the form of therapy aimed at immediate intervention in an acute episode or crisis that the individual is unable to cope with alone.

Crisis Situation

A. Person is typically in a state of equilibrium or homeostatic balance.

B. State is maintained by behavioral patterns involving interchange between the person and his environment.

C. When problems arise, the person uses learned coping mechanisms to deal with them.

D. When a problem becomes too great to be handled by previously learned coping techniques, the crisis situation develops.

1. Result is major disorganization in functioning.

2. In circumstances of inability to resolve crisis, the person is more amenable to intervention, and the potential for growth increases.

E. Precipitant factors in a crisis.

1. Threat to individual security: may be loss or threat of loss.

a. Situational crisis, which may be an actual or potential loss (job, friend, mate, etc.).

b. Developmental crisis, which could be any change (e.g., marriage, new baby).

c. Two or more severe problems arising concurrently.

2. Precipitants typically occur within two weeks of onset of disorganization.

Stages of Crisis Development

A. Initial perception of problem.

B. Rise in tension and anxiety; usual coping mechanisms are tried.

C. Usual situational supports are consulted.

D. Known methods prove unsuccessful and tension increases.

E. If new problem-solving methods are unsuccessful, the problem remains and cannot be avoided.

1. Person's functioning becomes disorganized.
2. Extreme anxiety is likely to be experienced.
3. Perception is narrowed.
4. Coping ability is further reduced.

F. Resolution usually occurs within six weeks with or without intervention.

Characteristics

A. Crisis is self-limiting, acute, lasting one to six weeks.

B. Crisis is initiated by triggering event (death, loss, etc.); usual coping mechanisms are inadequate for the situation.

C. Situation is dangerous to the person; he may harm self or others.

D. Individual will return to a state that is better, worse, or the same as before the crisis; therefore, intervention by the therapist is important.

E. Person is totally involved—hurts all over.

F. At this time person is most open for intervention; therefore, major changes can take place and the crisis can be the turning point for the person.

Crisis Assessment

A. Period of disorganization.

1. Degree of disorganization.
2. Length of time situation has existed.
3. Level of functioning.

B. Precipitant event.

1. Problem presented by the actual event triggering crisis.
2. Significance of the event to the individual.

C. Past coping mechanisms.

1. Past history in experiencing similar situations.
2. Past history in coping with similar situations.

D. Situational supports.

1. Significant others.
2. Agencies.

E. Alternative coping.

1. New coping alternatives.

2. Use of situational supports.

Principles of Crisis Intervention

A. Goal is to help person return to precrisis level and maintain functioning.

B. Immediate intervention is important because the possibility for intervention is time limited (six weeks).

C. Make accurate assessment of problem and focus on this problem; use reality-oriented therapy with "here and now" focus.

D. Set limits.

E. Stay with client or have significant persons available if necessary.

F. Explore available coping mechanisms.

1. Develop strengths and capitalize on them.
2. Do not focus on weakness or pathology.
3. Help explore the available situational supports.

G. Clarify the problem and help the individual understand the problem and integrate the events in his life.

H. When the above steps are completed, some plans for future support should be worked out by the therapist and the client.

Environmental Therapy

Definition: Environmental therapy is a broad term that encompasses several forms and mechanisms for treating the mentally ill.

Community Mental Health Act

A. The Community Mental Health Act of 1964 provides for the establishment of mental health centers to serve communities across the country.

B. Each community must provide full service for its population.

C. Services include in- and out-client treatment services, long-term hospitalization if necessary, emergency service, and consultation and educational services.

Characteristics

A. Hospitalization may be provided by private or public psychiatric hospitals or in psychiatric units of general hospitals.

B. Day-night hospitals provide structured treatment

programs for a specified part of each day, after which the client returns to his family.

C. Half-way houses provide live-in facilities with guidance and treatment available for clients who are not quite ready to return to the community and function independently.

D. Therapeutic communities provide milieu therapy, a therapy involving the total community (or unit). The staff formulates and, together with the clients, implements the treatment program. Emphasis is often on group therapies and group techniques.

Group Therapy

Definition: Group therapy refers to the psychotherapeutic processes that occur in formally organized groups designed to effect improvement in symptoms or behavior through group interactions.

Types of Groups

A. Structured group: group has predetermined goals and leader retains control. Group has directed focus; factual material is presented and format is clear and specific.

B. Unstructured group: responsibility for goals is shared by group and leader; leader is non-directive. Topics are not pre-selected, and discussion flows according to concerns of group members. Often emphasis is more on feelings than facts, and decision making is part of the group process.

Phases of Group Therapy

A. Initial phase: formation of group; clarification of goals and expectations; members becoming acquainted; superficial interactions.

B. Working phase: identification of problems; confrontation between members; problem-solving process; emergence of group cohesiveness.

C. Termination phase: evaluation; goal fulfillment; support for leave-taking.

Principles Underlying Group Work

A. Support: members gain support from others in group via sharing and interaction.

B. Verbalization: members express feelings, and group reinforces appropriate (versus inappropriate) communication.

C. Activity: verbalization and expression of feelings and problems are stimulated by activity.

D. Change: members have opportunity to try out new, more adaptive behaviors in group setting.

Methods of Focusing Group Therapy

A. Focus on here and now versus there and then. Help group members express inner experiences occurring right in the present rather than in the past. The past cannot be altered; the person can only report on it.

B. Focus on feelings versus ideas. Abstract or cognitive focus directs group away from dealing with here and now feelings and experiences, and allows no opportunity for exploring and coping with feelings.

C. Focus on telling versus questioning. Focus on the individual's reporting about himself rather than on his questioning of others, which is artificial and a defensive posture.

D. Focus on experience versus "ought" or "should." Avoid setting up "should" systems, which focus on judgmental and critical content rather than on supportiveness.

Leader Functions and Roles

A. Determine structure and format of group sessions.

B. Determine goals and work toward helping group achieve these goals.

C. Establish the psychological climate of group, e.g., acceptance, sharing, and nonpunitive interactions.

D. Set limits for the group and interpret group rules.

E. Facilitate group process to promote flow of clear communication.

F. Encourage participation from silent members and limit participation of monopolizers.

G. Exert leadership when group flounders; always maintain a degree of control.

H. Act as resource person and role model.

Advantages of Group Therapy

A. Economy in use of staff.

B. Increased socialization potential in group setting leading to increased interaction between clients.

C. Feedback from group members.
   1. Increases reality testing mechanisms.
   2. Builds self-confidence and self-image.
   3. Can correct distortions of problem, situation, or feelings by group pressure.

4. Gives information about how one's personality and actions appear to others.

D. Reduction in feelings of being alone with problem and being the only one experiencing despair.

E. Opportunity for practicing new alternative methods for coping with feelings such as anger and anxiety.

F. Increased feelings of closeness with others, thus reducing loneliness.

G. Potential development of insight into one's problems by expression of own experiences and by listening to others in group.

H. Therapeutic effect from attention to reality, from focus on the here and now rather than on own inner world.

Family Therapy

Definition: Family therapy is a form of group therapy based on the premise that it is the total family rather than the identified client that is dysfunctional.

Basic Assumptions

A. An identified client is not ill; rather, the total family is in need of and will benefit from treatment.

B. An identified client reflects disequilibrium in the family structure.

Focus

A. Family therapy focuses on exploration of patterns of interaction within the family rather than on individual pathology.

B. Conjoint family therapy (Virginia Satir) treats the family as a group. It was originally developed as a method of treatment for schizophrenics.

Therapist Behaviors

A. Models role of clear communicator.
1. Clarifies and validates communication.
2. Points out dysfunctional communication.

B. Acts as resource person.

C. Observes and reports on congruent and incongruent communications and behaviors.

D. Supports entire family as members attempt to change inappropriate patterns of relating and communicating with one another.

E. In general, follows the same therapeutic approaches as in nurse-client relationship therapy.

Death, Dying, and Grief Process

Psychological Impact of Dying Process

Physical Symptoms of Dying

A. Cardiovascular collapse.

B. Renal failure.

C. Physical and mental capacity decreased.

D. Gradual loss of consciousness.

Stages of Dying

(See Elisabeth Kübler-Ross, *Death and Dying*, New York, Macmillan Publishing Company, Inc., 1970).

A. Individual is stunned at the knowledge he is dying and denies it.

B. Anger and resentment usually follow as the individual questions, "Why me?"

C. With the beginning of acceptance of impending death comes the bargaining stage, that is, bargaining for time to complete some situation in his life.

D. Full acknowledgment usually brings depression; individual begins to work through his feelings and withdraw from his life and relationships.

E. Final stage is full acceptance and preparation for death.

F. Throughout the dying process, hope is an important element which should be supported but not reinforced unrealistically.

Psychosocial Clinical Manifestations

A. Depressed and withdrawn.

B. Fearful and anxious.

C. Internally focused.

D. Agitated and restless.

Nursing Management

A. Minimize physical discomfort.
1. Attend to all physical needs.
2. Make patient as comfortable as possible.

B. Recognize crisis situation.
1. Observe for changes in patient's condition.
2. Support the patient.

C. Be prepared to give the dying patient the emotional support he needs.

D. Encourage communication.
   1. Allow the patient to express feelings, to talk, or to cry.
   2. Pick up cues that the patient wants to talk, especially about fears.
   3. Be available to form a relationship with the patient.
   4. Communicate honestly.

E. Prepare and support the family for their impending loss.

F. Understand the grieving process of the patient and the family.

The Grief Process

Definition: Grief is a process an individual goes through in response to the loss of a significant or loved person in his life. Grieving process follows certain predictable phases—classic description originally done by Dr. Eric Lindeman. The normal grieving process is described by George Engle, M.D., in "Grief and Grieving," *American Journal of Nursing,* September 1964.

A. First response is shock and refusal to believe that the loved one is dead.
   1. Inability to comprehend the meaning of loss.
   2. Attempts to protect self against painful feelings.

B. As awareness increases, the bereaved experiences severe anguish.
   1. Crying is common in this stage.
   2. Anger directed toward those people or circumstances thought to be responsible.

C. Mourning is the next stage where the work of restitution takes place.
   1. Rituals of the funeral help the bereaved accept reality.
   2. Support from friends and spiritual guidance comfort the bereaved.

D. Resolution of the loss occurs as the mourner begins to deal with the void.

E. Idealization of the deceased occurs next where only the pleasant memories are remembered.

1. Characterized by the mourner's taking on certain qualities of the deceased.
2. This process takes many months as preoccupation with the deceased diminishes.

F. Outcome of the grief process takes a year or more.
   1. Indications of successful outcome are when the mourner remembers both the pleasant and unpleasant memories.
   2. Eventual outcome influenced by:
      a. Importance of the deceased in the life of mourner.
      b. The degree of dependence in the relationship.
      c. The amount of ambivalence toward the deceased.
      d. The more hostile the feelings that exist, the more guilt that interferes with the grieving process.
      e. Age of both mourner and deceased.
      f. Death of a child is more difficult to resolve than that of an aged loved one.
      g. Number and nature of previous grief experiences.
      h. Degree of preparation for the loss.

Nursing Management

A. Recognize that grief is a syndrome with somatic and psychological symptomology:
   1. Weeping, complaints of fatigue, digestive disturbance, and insomnia.
   2. Guilt, anger, and irritability.
   3. Restless, but unable to initiate meaningful activity.
   4. Depression and agitation.

B. Be prepared to support the family as they learn of the death.
   1. Know the general response to death by recognizing the stages of the grief process.
   2. Understand that the behavior of the mourner may be unstable and disturbed.

C. Use therapeutic communication techniques.
   1. Encourage the mourner to express feelings, especially tears.
   2. Attempt to meet the needs of the mourner for privacy, information, and support.
   3. Show respect for the religious and social customs of the family.

Appendix 1. Communication Techniques

Table 1. Therapeutic Communication Techniques

Listening	The process of consciously receiving another person's message. Includes listening eagerly, actively, responsively, and seriously.
Acknowledgment	Recognizing the other person without inserting your own values or judgments. Acknowledgment may be simple and with or without understanding. For example, in the response "I hear what you're saying," the person acknowledges a statement without agreeing with it. Acknowledgment may be verbal or nonverbal.
Feedback	The process the receiver uses to relay to the sender the effect the message has had, which either helps keep the sender on course or alters his course. It involves acknowledging, validating, clarifying, extending, and altering. *Nurse to client:* "You did that well."
Mutual Fit or Congruence	Harmony of verbal and nonverbal messages. For example, a client is crying, and the nurse says, "I want to help," and puts her hand on the client's shoulder.
Clarification	The process of checking out or making clear either the intent or hidden meaning of the message, or of determining if the message sent was the message received. *Nurse:* "You said it was hot in here. Would you like to open the window?"
Focusing or Refocusing	Picking up on central topics or "cues" given by the individual. *Nurse:* "You were telling me how hard it was to talk to your mother."
Validation	The process of verifying the accuracy of the sender's message. *Nurse:* "Yes, it is confusing with so many people around."
Reflection	Identifying and sending back a message acknowledging the feeling expressed rather than paraphrasing the verbal message. (Conveys acceptance and great understanding.) *Nurse:* "You distrust your doctor?"
Open-ended Questions	Asking questions that cannot be answered "Yes" or "No" or "Maybe," generally requiring an answer of several words in order to broaden conversational opportunities and to help the client communicate. *Nurse:* "What kind of job would you like to do?"
Nonverbal Encouragement	Using body language to communicate interest, attention, understanding, support, caring, and/or listening in order to promote data gathering. *Nurse:* Nods appropriately as someone talks.
Restatement	Echoing back the last few words the client says. *Nurse:* "You hear voices."
Paraphrase	Rewording what has been said. *Nurse:* "You mean you're unhappy."
Neutral Response	Showing interest and involvement without saying anything else. *Nurse:* "Yes . . . ." "Uh hm . . . ."
Incomplete Sentences	Encouraging client to continue. *Nurse:* "Then your life is . . . ."
Minimum Verbal Activity	Keeping your own verbalization minimal and letting the client lead the conversation. *Nurse:* "You feel . . . .?"
Broad Opening Statements	Opening the communication by allowing the client freedom to talk and to focus on himself. *Nurse:* "How have you been feeling?"

Table 2. Blocks to Communication

Internal Validation	(Jumping to conclusions.) Making an assumption about the meaning of someone else's behavior that is not validated by the other person. The nurse finds the suicidal client smiling and joking and tells the staff he's in a cheerful mood.
Giving Advice	Telling the client what to do. Giving your opinion, or making decisions for the client, implies he cannot handle his own life decisions and that you are accepting responsibility for him. *Nurse:* "If I were you . . . ."
Changing the Subject	Introducing new topics inappropriately, a pattern that may indicate anxiety. The client is crying and discussing her fear of surgery, when the nurse asks, "How many children do you have?"
Social Response	Responding in a way that focuses attention on the nurse instead of the client. *Nurse:* "This sunshine is good for my roses. I have a beautiful rose garden."
Invalidation	Ignoring or denying another's presence, thoughts, or feelings. *Client:* "Hi, how are you?" *Nurse:* "I can't talk now. I'm on my way to lunch."
False Reassurance Agreement	Using clichés, pat answers, "cheery" words, advice, and "comforting" statements as an attempt to reassure the patient. Most of what is called "reassurance" is really false reassurance. *Nurse:* "It's going to be all right."
Overloading	Talking rapidly, changing subjects, and giving more information than can be absorbed at one time. *Nurse:* "What's your name? I see you're forty-eight years old and that you like sports. Where do you come from?"
Underloading	Remaining silent and unresponsive, not picking up cues, and failing to give feedback. *Client:* "What's your name?" *Nurse:* Smiles and walks away.
Incongruence	Sending verbal and nonverbal messages that contradict one another; two or more messages, sent via different levels, seriously contradicting one another. The contradiction may be between the content, verbal, nonverbal, and/or content (time, space). This contradiction is a *double message*. *Client:* "I like your dress." *Nurse:* Annoyed, frowns and looks disgusted.
Value Judgments	(Evaluations.) Giving one's own opinion or moralizing or implying one's own values by using words such as "nice," "good," "bad," "right," "wrong," "should," and "ought." *Nurse:* "I think he's a very good doctor."

Appendix 2. Ego-Defense Mechanisms

Compensation	Covering up a lack or weakness by emphasizing a desirable trait, or making up for a frustration in one area by overemphasis in another area. This is learned early in childhood and may be easily recognized in adult behavior; for example, the physically handicapped individual who is an outstanding scholar.
Denial	Refusal to face reality. The ego protects itself from unpleasant pain or conflict by rejecting reality. Denial of illness is a common example; people wait to see a doctor because they don't want to know the truth. A more subtle example is the individual who avoids reality by getting "sick."
Displacement	Discharging pent-up feelings from one object to a less dangerous object. A fairly common mechanism; for example, your supervisor yells at you, you yell at your husband.
Fantasy	Gratification by imaginary achievements and wishful thinking; for example, children's play. Sometimes, in order to satisfy a need, one relieves the tension by anticipating the pleasure of gratification.
Fixation	The persistence into later life of interests and behavior patterns appropriate to an earlier age.
Identification	The process of taking on the desirable attributes in personalities of other people one admires. Identification plays an important role in the development of a child's personality; for example, the child who mimics mother or daddy. A kind of satisfaction can be derived from sharing the success or the experience of others, such as the nurse who feels sick watching a traumatic procedure on her client.
Insulation	Withdrawal into passivity, becoming inaccessible in order to avoid further threatening circumstances. Sometimes the individual appears cold and indifferent to his surroundings. Insulation may be used harmlessly at times, but becomes very serious if used so much it interferes with interaction with others.
Isolation	Excluding certain ideas, attitudes, or feelings from awareness. Isolation is separating the feelings from the intellect by putting emotions concerning a specific traumatic event into a lock-tight compartment; for example, the individual talks about a significant situation such as an accident or death without a display of feelings. This pattern can be positive if used temporarily to protect the ego from being overwhelmed.
Introjection	A type of identification in which there is a symbolic incorporation of a loved or hated object, belief system, or value into the individual's own ego structure; there is no absolute assimilation as in identification.
Projection	Placing blame for difficulties on others or attributing one's own undesirable traits to someone else; for example, the child who says to a parent, "You hate me," after the parent has spanked the child. In an adult, this mechanism is a predominant indicator of paranoia. The paranoid client projects his hate for others by saying that others are out to get him.
Rationalization	The mechanism that is almost universally employed to prove or justify behavior. It is face saving to give a reason that is acceptable rather than the real reason, as in remarks such as, "It wasn't worth it anyway," "It's all for the best." This mechanism relieves anxiety temporarily and helps the person avoid facing reality.
Reaction-Formation	Prevention of dangerous feelings and desires from being expressed by exaggerating the opposite attitude—a kind of denial. The overly neat, polite, conscientious individual may have an unconscious desire to be untidy and carefree. The behavior becomes pathological when it interferes with tasks or produces anxiety and frustration.
Regression	Resorting to an earlier developmental level in order to deal with reality. Regression is an immature way of responding, and it is frequently seen during a physical illness. It is sometimes used to an extreme degree by the mentally ill, who may regress all the way back to infancy.

Repression	The unconscious process whereby one keeps undesirable and unacceptable thoughts from entering the conscious. This repressed material may be the motivation for some behavior. The superego is largely responsible for repression; the stronger, more punitive the superego, the more emotion will be repressed. The child who is frustrated and downtrodden by a parent may rebel against authority in later life.
Sublimation	The mechanism by which a primitive or unacceptable tendency is redirected into socially constructive channels. This adjustment pattern is at least partly responsible for many artistic and cultural achievements, such as painting and poetry.
Substitution	The replacement of a highly valued unacceptable object with an object that is more acceptable to the ego.
Suppression	The act of keeping unpleasant feelings and experiences from awareness.
Symbolization	Use of an idea or object by the conscious mind to represent another actual event or object. Sometimes the meaning is not clear because the symbol may be representative of something unconscious. Children use symbolization in this way and have to learn to distinguish between the symbol and the thing being symbolized. Examples include obsessive thoughts or behavior (hand washing, cleansing) and the incoherent speech of the schizophrenic (by the time the painful thoughts reach the surface, they are so jumbled that they lose their painfulness).
Undoing	Closely related to reaction-formation—performance of a specific action that is considered to be the opposite of a previous unacceptable action. This action is felt to neutralize or "undo" the original action; for example, when Lady MacBeth rubbed and washed her hands.

Appendix 3. Psychiatric Assessment of Mental Status

Factors to be Assessed	Symptoms of Disturbance
General Appearance, Manner, and Attitude	
Grooming and mode of dress	Poor grooming, lack of cleanliness
Appropriateness to situation	Inappropriate dress or combination of clothes
Appropriateness to person's age and social circumstance	
Speech	
Speed, pressure, diction	Accelerated speech or retarded, poor or inappropriate diction
Relatedness in interview	Inappropriate responses, tangential or out-of-context replies
Expressive Aspects of Behavior	
General activity level	Overactivity: restlessness, agitation, impulsiveness
	Underactivity (psychomotor retardation): slowness in initiation; slowness in execution
Purpose	Repetitious activities: rituals or compulsions
	Command automatism
	Negativism
	Violence
	Thoughts of suicide
Consciousness	Disordered attention; distraction
	Clouding of consciousness
	Delirium
	Stupor
	Disorientation regarding time, place, and person
Perception	
Account of person's perceptual experiences and his reactions to them	Illusions
	Hallucinations: auditory, visual, olfactory, gustatory, tactile, kinesthetic
Thought Process	
Realism, logic, coherency	Disorders of form of thought: autistic (or dereistic), abstract, concrete
	Disorders of progression of thought: disordered tempo (flight of ideas, retardation); disordered progression (looseness, circumstantial, incoherent, irrelevant, blocking); distortion (neologisms, word salad, echolalia)
Thought Content and Mental Trend	
General themes that determine beliefs and conduct	Delusions (systematized or unsystematized): delusions of grandeur; delusions of persecution
	Ideas of reference
	Hypochondria
	Obsessions
	Phobias

Affect
    Prevailing mood

        Pleasurable affect: euphoria, elation, ecstasy
        Depression
        Anxiety
        Inadequate affect: dampened, flat
        Inappropriate affect
        Ambivalence
        Lability

Memory
    Registration and retention
    Recall (recent and remote)

        Hyperamnesia, amnesia, paramnesia
        Déjà vu
        Poor recall for immediate or past events

Judgment
    Correctness of estimates and
    interpretations

        Poor judgment, poor decision-making capability
        Inappropriate interpretation of events or situations

Insight

        Lack of insight into problems or situation

Intelligence and Fund of Information

Personal Maturity

Developmental Level

Appendix 4. Drug Classification Chart

Common Psychotropic Drugs

Major Tranquilizers

Drug	Method of Administration	Daily Dose
Thorazine	Tablets, concentrate, syrup, I.M., I.V., suppositories	25–1500 mg.
Sparine	Tablets, concentrate, syrup, capsules, I.M., I.V.	50–100 mg.
Mellaril	Tablets, concentrate	100–800 mg.
Serentil	Tablets, concentrate, I.M.	30–400 mg.
Trilafon	Tablets, concentrate, syrup, I.M., suppositories	6–64 mg.
Prolixin, Permitil	Tablets, concentrate, I.M.	0.5–20 mg.
Stelazine	Tablets, concentrate, I.M.	2–50 mg.
Quide	Tablets	10–180 mg.
Compazine	Tablets, capsules, syrup, concentrate, I.M., I.V., suppositories	15–150 mg.
Taractan	Tablets, concentrate, I.M.	30–600 mg.
Navane	Capsules, concentrate, I.M.	6–60 mg.
Haldol	Tablets, concentrate, I.M.	2–40 mg.

Minor Tranquilizers (Antianxiety)

Drug	Method of Administration	Daily Dose
Atarax	Tablets, syrup	50–400 mg.
Vistaril	Capsules, suspension, I.M. only	50–400 mg. 50–100 mg.
Librium, Librax	Tablets, capsules, I.M., I.V.	10–100 mg.
Valium	Tablets, I.M., I.V.	2–40 mg.
Serax	Capsules, tablets	30–120 mg.
Equanil	Tablets, capsules, suspension	400–1200 mg.
Miltown	Tablets	400–1200 mg.

Antidepressants (Mood Elevators)

MAO Inhibitors

Drug	Method of Administration	Daily Dose
Marplan	Tablets	10–30 mg.
Niamid	Tablets	125–200 mg.
Nardil	Tablets	15–75 mg.
Parnate	Tablets	20–30 mg.

Tricyclics

Tofranil	Tablets, I.M.	75–300 mg.
Elavil	Tablets, I.M.	50–200 mg.
Norpramin	Tablets	75–150 mg.
Aventyl	Capsules, liquid	20–100 mg.
Vivactil	Tablets	15–60 mg.
Sinequan	Capsules	25–300 mg.

Antimanic

Lithium carbonate, Lithane, Litho-Tabs, Lithonate	Tablets, capsules	600–1800 mg.

Antiparkinson

Cogentin	Tablets, I.M.	1–6 mg.
Artane	Tablets, elixir, capsules	1–10 mg.
Akineton	Tablets, I.M., I.V.	1–8 mg.
Kemadrin	Tablets	6–15 mg.

Appendix 5. Legal Issues in Psychiatric Nursing

Note: Legal rights for both psychiatric client and the community at large are an important aspect of psychiatric nursing.

Statutes of Protection

A. Laws of certain states protect individuals from themselves.
   1. These laws require that such persons be evaluated by competent psychiatric personnel.
   2. The laws protect the client's rights and civil liberties by not allowing them to be hospitalized inappropriately.
B. Laws also protect family members and the general community from persons who are dangerous or severely disturbed.

Admission Procedures

A. There are voluntary and involuntary admissions for psychiatric clients.

B. Voluntary admission occurs when an individual recognizes he needs treatment and signs himself into a hospital.
   1. After admission, the client is *not* free to leave before a specified period of time.
   2. Such a client may leave the hospital against the physician's advice if he gives notice of his intent at least one or two days prior to leaving.
   3. If the physician feels the client is too ill, he can legally assign the client to involuntary status.
   4. A voluntary client loses none of his civil rights.
C. Involuntary status occurs when the client is psychiatrically evaluated to be too ill to function outside the hospital.
   1. When a client is committed, he cannot leave the hospital against medical advice.
   2. Family members, a physician, a law officer, or a community member can institute commitment proceedings.
   3. The client is permitted to leave only when psychiatric evaluation indicates he is able to care for himself or is not dangerous to himself or others.

Appendix 6. Glossary

Abreaction Vivid recall of a painful experience with the expression of emotion appropriate to the original situation.

Acting out Expression of unconscious emotional conflicts of hostility or love in actions that the person does not consciously know are related to such conflicts of feelings.

Affect Generalized feeling, tone, or mood.

Aggression Any verbal/nonverbal activity that may be forceful abuse of self, another person, or thing.

Ambivalence The simultaneous existence of contradictory and contrasting emotions toward a person or object, that is, love and hate.

Amnesia A condition where the individual experiences a loss of memory because of physical or emotional trauma.

Anxiety A persistent feeling of tension and apprehension arising from within the individual. Response to vague, unspecific danger that may be real or imagined.

Apathy Pathological indifference.

Autism Detachment from reality when self-preoccupation and involvement is predominant.

Compulsion An irresistible urge to repeat an act that must be carried out to avoid anxiety.

Conflict A struggle between two or more opposing forces.

Covert Hidden, below the surface.

Cyclothymia Alternations in mood from high to low.

Defense mechanism Originally identified by Anna Freud as an activity by which the ego defends itself by not allowing unacceptable thoughts or feelings to come into awareness to cause anxiety.

Delusion A false belief maintained in spite of facts or evidence to the contrary.

Depression An unshakable feeling of sadness accompanied by feelings of hopelessness, worthlessness, and bleakness regarding future.

Disorientation A condition where the individual manifests loss of ability to recognize or locate himself in respect to time, place, or other persons.

Echolalia A condition where the individual constantly repeats what is heard.

Echopraxia A condition where the individual mimics what is done.

Ego A Freudian term denoting that aspect of the psyche which is conscious and most in touch with external reality; the "I" part of the person. Also, that part of the personality that makes decisions, is conscious, and represents the thinking-feeling part of a person.

Electroshock A medical procedure of applying electric current to certain areas in the brain. Used in the treatment of certain psychiatric disorders (especially depression).

Etiology The cause or causes of disease.

Euphoria A feeling of elation or joy.

Fear Response to an actual situation or person posing danger.

Fixation A stage in development when there is an abnormal attachment; inability to move on to later developmental tasks.

Frustration A feeling that may contain elements of anger, hopelessness, or defeat. It occurs when goals set by perceived needs are blocked.

Functional Used in psychiatry to denote mental illness existing without known physical causes or structural changes.

Fugue A condition experienced as a transient disorientation—patient is unaware that he has physically escaped or run to another place.

Hypochondriasis A state of morbid concern about one's body or health for which there is no physical evidence.

Hysteric Involves elements of both conscious and unconscious exaggerated reaction, often in a dramatic manner, to some stimuli.

Id A Freudian term denoting a division of the psyche from which comes blind, instinctual impulses that lead to immediate gratification of primitive needs, dominated by the pleasure principle.

Ideas of reference A distortion of reality where a person believes that activities of others have a personal reference to him.

Illusion Distorted perceptual experience where the individual misinterprets actual data from the environment. Examples: a mirage on the desert; seeing a lake when it is only light refraction.

Insight An individual's understanding of the origin and mechanisms of his attitudes and behavior.

Interpersonal Existing between two or more persons.

Intrapersonal Existing within one person.

Labile Refers to rapid shifts in emotions from high to low.

Manipulation The process by which one individual influences another individual to function in accordance with his needs without regard to the other's needs or goals.

Mental retardation A term for mental deficiency or lack of normal development of intelligence.

Milieu The total environment, emotional as well as physical.

Narcissistic Loving one's self excessively in a childish or infantile fashion.

Negativism A strong resistance to suggestions coming from others.

Neologism A term that refers to the coining of a new word, as seen in schizophrenia.

Obsession A persistent repetitive and unwanted thought.

Organic Based on structural alterations, gross or microscopic.

Overt Discernible; out in the open.

Parataxic A term coined by Sullivan to mean distorted perception.

Phobia The dread of an object, an act, or a situation that is not realistically dangerous but that has come to represent a danger.

Premorbid personality The status of an individual's personality (conflicts, defenses, strengths, weaknesses) before the onset of clinical illness.

Psyche A term meaning the mind or the mental and emotional "self."

Psychogenic Originating within the psyche or mind. Sometimes used to describe physical disorders that are believed to stem from the emotions.

Rapport A component of a relationship where one feels harmony or empathy with another.

Regression Reverting to types of behavior characteristic of an earlier level of development.

Resistance A mechanism an individual employs to avoid certain ideas or feelings coming into consciousness.

Schizoid A term used to describe a form of personality disorder characterized by an unsocial, withdrawn, shy type of personality.

Seclusive A term describing persons who are unsociable, reserved, secretive, and adverse to interacting with people.

Soma A term meaning body.

Superego A Freudian term referring to a system within the total psyche that is developed by incorporating parental standards such as moral values; the two components of superego are *conscience* and *ego ideal.*

Unconscious A term coined by Freud to refer to that part of the mind where mental activity is always going on, but not on a conscious level.

Undoing A defense mechanism aimed at the removal of a painful memory.

Waxy flexibility A condition associated with catatonic schizophrenia, where a posture is maintained for long periods of time.

Review Questions

1. During the initial phase of the nurse-patient relationship, it is most important that the nurse understand which of the following concepts?

    A. The focus is on mutual attempts to know each other and help the patient become oriented to his environment.
    B. Identifying expectations is important to accomplish before the relationship begins.
    C. Recognizing and testing attitudes of the nursing staff.
    D. The relationship is effected by the degree of comfort the nurse feels.

2. For the best therapeutic care of the psychiatric patient, the nurse must

    A. Like every patient she is responsible for.
    B. Accept the patient (as a human being) and reject the maladaptive behavior.
    C. Sympathize with the patient's problems and circumstances.
    D. Keep a distant, professional attitude.

3. Mr. Perks is a fifty-four-year-old alcoholic, who has been admitted to the ward for detoxification and treatment. Which of the following statements by him may be a barrier to the development of a therapeutic relationship?

    A. "Nurse, you said I reminded you of your alcoholic father."
    B. "You want to spend some time talking with me. Won't you just be wasting your time?"
    C. "I bet you love to see us old drunks come in!"
    D. "How many children do you have, nurse?"

4. A basic concept for psychiatric nurses who are beginning to establish a therapeutic relationship is

    A. All the needs of the emotionally disturbed individual are at times common to all human beings.
    B. All behavior has meaning and purpose.
    C. To assist others, the nurse must understand herself.
    D. Behavior is directed toward the elimination of threat with the greatest conservation of energy.

5. Which of the following is not a behavior that is evoked by anxiety?

    A. Anger.
    B. Withdrawal.
    C. Crying.
    D. Perspiring.

6. Mr. Oliver is unable to sleep. He is pacing the floor, head down, and wringing his hands. The nurse recognizes that he is anxious. In which way would she intervene?

    A. Help the patient talk about his behavior.
    B. Give him his p.r.n. sleeping medicine
    C. Let the patient know she is interested, is willing to listen, and wants to assist him.
    D. Explore with him alternatives to his problem.

7. Of the four levels of anxiety—mild, moderate, severe, and panic—which of the following statements is characteristic of severe anxiety?

    A. The senses become more alert.
    B. Experience inflicts pain that is difficult to bear.
    C. Perception narrows; person is unaware of peripheral activities (selective inattention).
    D. Sense of being overpowered and disintegrating control.

8. Jill, a patient of yours, has just been told that her father was in a bad automobile accident and is critically ill in the hospital. Her response is to smile and ask what time lunch is served. This is an example of

    A. Lack of affect.
    B. Inappropriate affect.
    C. Disturbed association of ideas.
    D. Primary disturbance.

9. Your most appropriate response to Jill's comment about when lunch will be served would be

    A. "Jill, did you hear what I said?"
    B. "Jill, your father is critically ill. Don't you want to talk about it?"
    C. "Jill, you are blocking and I think you need to talk about your feelings."
    D. "Jill, I told you your father was critically ill and you asked what time lunch would be served."

10. The purpose or function of adjustment mechanisms is to

    A. Increase self-esteem.
    B. Decrease anxiety.
    C. Conserve energy.
    D. Cope with internal conflicts in an efficient manner.

11. Defense mechanisms can reduce anxiety by

    A. Moving away from anxiety (flight).
    B. Moving against anxiety (fight).
    C. Moving toward anxiety (problem solving).
    D. All of the above.

12. The most common adjustment mechanism used is

    A. Rationalization.
    B. Undoing.
    C. Sublimation.
    D. Projection.

13. Jennifer is a thirty-year-old mother of two, who was brought to the hospital by her husband. He complained that Jennifer could not manage the house, was easily distracted, and was constantly in motion. The nurse noticed that Jennifer was unable to converse rationally and changed the subject frequently. This is most clearly an example of

A. Delusions.
B. Associative looseness.
C. Flight of ideas.
D. Echolalia.

14. Jennifer's diagnosis is manic-depressive-manic illness. She manifests an excess of energy, and it is difficult for her to sit still. The most useful activity for Jennifer that the nurse might suggest would be

A. Playing volleyball outside.
B. Occupational therapy that is group exercises.
C. Emptying wastebaskets.
D. Delivering linen to the rooms.

15. Jennifer's disruptive behavior on the ward has been increasingly annoying to the other patients. One approach by the nurse might be to

A. Tell Jennifer she is annoying others and confine her to her room.
B. Ignore her behavior, realizing it is consistent with her illness.
C. Set limits on her behavior and be consistent in approach.
D. Make a rigid, structured plan that Jennifer will have to follow.

16. Jennifer's illness can best be understood as the ego's attempt to compensate for an assault against it and fear of the punitive superego. What underlying condition would be the source of the mania?

A. Delusions of grandeur.
B. Depression.
C. Fear of loss.
D. Malformed superego.

17. Jennifer frequently exhibits bizarre and inappropriate behavior. Such behavior may be best explained by all of the following *except*

A. One purpose of the behavior may be to attract attention.
B. Jennifer has little or no control over her impulsive behavior.
C. Her behavior is a method of expressing herself in a symbolic way.
D. Her behavior is caused by a genetic imbalance.

18. Mrs. Long, age thirty-four, has been on 5 mg t.i.d. chlordiazepoxide (Librium) for the past six months. Which of the following is not an appropriate statement about antianxiety drugs?

A. Antianxiety drugs may become habitual as the patient acquires an increased tolerance.
B. Mrs. Long may experience extrapyramidal side effects.
C. Librium is one of the most widely abused drugs because the public sees it as "aspirin for nervousness."
D. Sudden, abrupt drug withdrawal may create marked changes in behavior with physiological complications.

19. Lithium carbonate is used to treat manic-type behavior disorders. Which of the following symptoms is *not* a common side effect?

A. Gastrointestinal disturbances (nausea, vomiting, diarrhea, abdominal pain).
B. Muscle weakness.
C. A sluggish, dazed feeling.
D. Anuria.

20. Mr. Braner, a sixty-year-old retired tool-and-die maker, has been admitted to your ward, a short-term acute center for the care and treatment of psychiatric disorders. His symptoms are fatigue, an inability to concentrate, and an inability to complete everyday tasks. Mr. Braner is assigned to you and refuses to care for himself, doesn't eat, and prefers to sleep all day. Your first priority would be to

A. Develop a good nursing care plan.
B. Talk to his wife for cues to help him.
C. Encourage him to join activities on the unit.
D. Develop a structured routine for him to follow.

21. Mr. Braner, while talking with you, becomes very dejected and states that life isn't meaningful and no one really cares what happens to him. The best response from the nurse would be

A. "Of course, people care. Your wife comes to visit every day."
B. "Let's not talk about sad things. Why don't we play Ping-pong?"
C. "I care about you, Mr. Braner, and I am concerned that you feel so down."
D. "Tell me, who doesn't care about you?"

22. Mr. Braner has been in the hospital a week and you notice a sudden improvement in his state of depression. He says to you that things are beginning to fall into place and he feels better. Your understanding of the syndrome of depression leads you to which one of the following conclusions?

A. Mr. Braner is finally coming out of the depression and you can begin to consider discharge plans.
B. Mr. Braner may be planning to commit suicide so he should be watched carefully.
C. Now that Mr. Braner feels better, you should begin to discuss the source of his depression.
D. You should notify his wife so that family therapy sessions can begin.

23. Depressed persons exhibit which of the following overt expressions of depressed affect?

A. Unable to concentrate.
B. Sad and hopeless.
C. Unable to complete everyday tasks.
D. Guilty and agitated.

24. Which of the following drugs are antidepressants?

A. Mellaril (thioridazine).
B. Tofranil (imipramine).

C. Librium (chlordiazepoxide).
D. Cogentin (benztropine mesylate).

25. Electrotherapy is a possible method of treating severe depression, especially if other methods have failed. All of the following are potential side effects of ECT except
A. Fractures.
B. Degeneration of brain cells.
C. Cardiac arrest.
D. Loss of recent memory and anxiety.

26. The two main drugs (a curare-like drug and a barbiturate) given to patients before ECT are aimed at reducing which of the following side effects?
A. Cardiac arrest and loss of memory.
B. Convulsions and fractures.
C. Fractures and anxiety.
D. Anxiety and loss of memory.

27. Mrs. Brown, admitted to a psychiatric unit two days previously with a diagnosis of acute depression, made a suicide attempt on the evening shift. The staff intervened in time to prevent Mrs. Brown from harming herself. What would be the most important rationale for the staff to use in discussing this situation after the fact?
A. They need to re-enact the attempt so that they understand exactly what happened.
B. The staff needs to file an accident report so that the hospital administration is kept informed.
C. The staff needs to discuss the patient's behavior prior to the attempt to determine what cues in her behavior might have warned them that she was contemplating suicide.
D. Because Mrs. Brown made one suicide attempt, there is a high probability she will make a second attempt in the immediate future.

28. There is a major difference between affective disorders and thought disorders for people who are emotionally disturbed. The major difference in nursing approaches to dealing with these two categories would be
A. In thought disorders, a nursing approach emphasis would be on reality orientation.
B. Thought disorders imply a fundamental problem with the patient's intellectual development; thus, the nurse focuses on the thinking process.
C. There is no difference in the nursing approaches for the two categories.
D. In affective disorders, the nursing emphasis is on teaching control of feelings.

29. Which one of the following characteristics distinguish neurotic depression from the depressive cycle of manic-depressive reaction?
A. Neurotic depression is milder than manic depression.

B. Neurotic depression is more variable in mood by day.
C. Neurotic depression is more easily influenced by outside events.
D. Neurotic depression characteristically is accompanied by evening insomnia.

30. Angela, age fourteen, was admitted to the pediatric unit with complaints of lower limb paralysis. She seemed to have little or no anxiety about her paralysis. She came from a difficult home situation where her two older sisters ran away from home. She was the last child at home and had a very domineering mother. Medical tests revealed no physical cause for her paralysis. In formulating an effective plan of care for Angela, the nurse needs to have an understanding of psychodynamic principles related to conversion reactions. Which one of the following reactions is not a correct principle?
A. Conversion symptoms tend to reflect the patient's concept of disease and her cultural background.
B. Conversion symptoms actually serve an unconscious purpose and are responsible for the relative lack of distress toward the symptoms (la belle indifference).
C. Conversion is a strong emotional conflict that is expressed or is converted to physical symptoms.
D. The patient is consciously aware of the cause of her symptoms.

31. Angela's *primary* gain is to
A. Get attention.
B. Handle her anxiety.
C. Manipulate her mother.
D. Avoid her responsibilities at home.

32. The most effective nursing approach would be to
A. Focus on the symptom—try to make Angela walk.
B. Develop a warm, open approach to the patient.
C. Tell the patient she is just "faking" and she could walk if she wanted to.
D. Plan activities that would encourage Angela to use her legs.

33. Mr. Chew, fifty-two years old, has begun a daily ritual for the past five weeks of washing and straightening everything in his room before he can participate in his planned activities for the day. The first week he missed breakfast because of his compulsive behavior. Now the nursing staff is unable to get him to attend morning psychotherapy at 11:00 A.M. An assessment and intervention team meeting was held in order to discuss Mr. Chew's behavior and possible interventions. The psychotherapy team should be aware that Mr. Chew's compulsive room cleaning is probably an attempt to

A. Keep his room cleaner than the rooms of the other patients on the ward.
B. Avoid going to psychotherapy.
C. Reduce his anxiety.
D. Manipulate the team members.

34. In planning nursing care for Mr. Chew, which concept or principle is incorrect and should not form the foundation of a nursing care plan?
    A. The obsessive individual is involved in a conflict between obedience and defiance.
    B. Unbearable tension is momentarily relieved through compulsive behavior.
    C. Ritualistic behavior provides a way for the individual to remain detached and isolated from his own emotions and relationships with others.
    D. The patient will usually no longer need the ritualistic behavior once the tension has been released by performing the necessary act.

35. To assist the patient and reduce his anxiety the nurse could
    A. Manipulate the environment to minimize the opportunities for anxiety-provoking stimuli and to increase self-esteem.
    B. Initiate a close interpersonal relationship with the patient.
    C. Set definite limits on the patient's behavior.
    D. Use humor to help the patient realize how maladaptive his behavior is.

36. Jane failed her psychology final exam and spent the entire evening berating the teacher and the course. This behavior is an example of
    A. Reaction-formation.
    B. Compensation.
    C. Projection.
    D. Acting out.

37. One adjustment mechanism used by psychiatric patients is regression. Which of the following best describes this mechanism?
    A. It is an immature way of responding.
    B. It works most effectively to reduce the anxiety.
    C. It fosters dependence.
    D. It provides attention through child-like behavior.

38. A terminally ill twenty-four-year-old female says to the nurse, "I don't know why you are all so concerned; I'm not that sick." She is using which adjustment mechanism?
    A. Denial.
    B. Rationalization.
    C. Projection.
    D. Regression.

39. Isolation can best be described as
    A. An idea or thought used by the conscious mind to represent an idea or object.

B. A withdrawal into passivity.
C. The discharge of pent-up emotions on a less dangerous object.
D. A walling-up of certain ideas, attitudes, or feelings.

40. Persons with overly suspicious behavior patterns tend to use projection. What is the purpose of using this mechanism?
    A. To handle the feelings of inadequacy and low self-esteem.
    B. To manipulate others.
    C. To avoid reality.
    D. To keep out painful memories.

41. Doug, a new patient on the psychiatric ward where you work, had just spent twenty minutes telling you his sad history. He told you that he had been wounded in Vietnam, his wife had left him, and his friends had deserted him. After checking his chart, you learned that all these stories were untrue. You would suspect which of the following diagnoses?
    A. Depressive personality.
    B. Paranoid personality.
    C. Sociopathic personality.
    D. Neurotic personality.

42. Doug has been certified for fourteen days on the locked unit. While there he becomes friendly with a very disturbed young woman and convinces her to escape with him when a visitor comes through the locked door. This is an example of impairment in which of the following areas?
    A. Judgment.
    B. Emotional response to others.
    C. Unconscious processes.
    D. Intellectual development.

43. Doug is constantly trying to manipulate the staff as a way of getting his needs met. Which response to Doug would indicate that the nurse understands the psychodynamic principle behind the manipulation?
    A. "Doug, I won't allow you to manipulate me."
    B. "Doug, I won't be able to do as you ask, but I will stay with you and talk."
    C. "Doug, if this behavior doesn't stop, I shall have to tell your doctor."
    D. "Doug, let's focus on your anxiety so we can deal with all this manipulation."

44. While persons convicted of felonies are usually put in prisons, many of them have underlying emotional problems. Probably the most common diagnosis seen in prisons would be
    A. Psychotic personality.
    B. Personality disorder.
    C. Paranoid personality.
    D. Adolescent adjustment.

45. Ellen, a nineteen-year-old medical student, is brought into the hospital by her roommate, who is worried about her lack of interest in anything, her loss of weight, somatic complaints, and constant tiredness. Ellen says that her major problem is her indecision about continuing to pursue her medical career or changing fields entirely. You are the nurse assigned to interview new patients for a nursing history and diagnosis. In light of her presenting symptoms, how would you expect Ellen to answer the question, "How does the future look to you"?
    A. "It looks pretty bleak and miserable."
    B. Noncommital.
    C. "Oh, I'm sure I'll be able to make a decision soon."
    D. A tangential response, since ambivalence has an immobilizing effect.

46. Of the following categories, which is the one most likely not to be associated with suicidal potential?
    A. Depression.
    B. Chronic alcoholism.
    C. Organic brain disease.
    D. Psychoneurotic syndrome.

47. Antidepressive drugs act on the brain's chemistry. Therefore, they would be more useful in which form of depression?
    A. Endogenous depression.
    B. Exogenous depression.
    C. Reactive depression.
    D. Secondary depression.

48. Which of the following drugs is used to reduce the extrapyramidal side effects that are common with use of the phenothiazines?
    A. Cogentin.
    B. Niamid.
    C. Ritalin.
    D. Miltown.

49. In providing nursing care for the individual with a psychosomatic illness, the nurse needs to know which of the following general concepts?
    A. The nurse must incorporate concepts of adaptation, stress, body image, and anxiety.
    B. The area of symptom formation may be symbolic to the patient.
    C. Psychosomatic illnesses may be life threatening.
    D. All of the above concepts are important.

50. Gerry, an eighteen-year-old unemployed male laborer, was admitted to the hospital vomiting red blood. A tentative diagnosis of a peptic ulcer was made. Gerry is married and has twin eighteen-month-old sons. He continually refuses the ulcer diet and criticizes the nursing staff. What might Gerry's behavior indicate?
    A. He is not interested in getting well.
    B. He does not understand what is expected of him.
    C. He is concerned about his family and his economic problems that have been complicated by his illness.
    D. He needs some attention and to be able to trust and rely on the nursing staff.

51. During visiting hours Gerry becomes very agitated and asks his mother to leave. This behavior may indicate
    A. An emotional conflict between his role as an independent adult and his need to be dependent.
    B. Gerry is allowing his hostility to become conscious and he is handling it in a more effective manner.
    C. Gerry's behavior has become worse.
    D. A conflict exists, and there is a need for clarification and exploration.

52. Which would be the most effective nursing approach to Gerry's behavior?
    A. Restrict his mother from visiting.
    B. Approach Gerry in a warm, supportive manner and assist him in exploring his feelings.
    C. Confront Gerry with his rudeness to his mother.
    D. Ask Gerry if he would like his p.r.n. sedative.

53. Gerry's family is making plans for his discharge. What will have the greatest effect on his further recovery?
    A. His wife's clear understanding of Gerry's dietary needs.
    B. The amount of emotional support he receives from his family.
    C. His understanding of the causes and treatment of his illness.
    D. His expectations of himself to assume his share of responsibility in his family.

54. Gerry is primarily using which of the following defense mechanisms?
    A. Repression.
    B. Reaction formation.
    C. Sublimation.
    D. Projection.

55. Mrs. Rain is a patient who never discusses her problems or her illness. Occasionally, the nurse observes Mrs. Rain's crying as she passes the door. A response using an effective communication technique would be:
    A. Ignore the crying as you realize she wants to let down alone.
    B. As you pass the door, acknowledge her by saying, "Good morning, Mrs. Rain."
    C. Go in the room and ask her to tell you why she is crying.
    D. Go in the room, sit down, and stay quietly with her.

56. Phobic reactions differ from obsessive compulsive reactions in which of the following ways?

    A. Phobias are beyond voluntary control and cannot adequately or logically be explained by the patient.
    B. With phobic reactions, the patient's behavior is directed toward reducing tension and anxiety.
    C. Phobias interfere with the patient's everyday life.
    D. Phobias may be associated with an unreasonable fear of specific objects or situations.

57. Mrs. Jones, age forty-seven, was referred to the community mental health center by her family physician with an initial diagnosis of hypochondriacal neurosis. In the past seven years she has been examined by numerous physicians for vague complaints of abdominal pains and chronic constipation. Mrs. Jones spends a great deal of time reading and collecting articles on possible causes for her complaint. Gradually, the amount of time she spends being ill has increased, which has interfered with her family life. Finally, her husband has convinced her to keep her initial appointment at the mental health center. Which of the following would be the most effective approach to Mrs. Jones?

    A. Sympathize with her physical complaints.
    B. Involve her in activities she can succeed at, such as hobbies and recreation.
    C. Convince her that her complaints have no physical basis.
    D. Use a matter-of-fact but nonempathic approach.

58. The nurse needs to understand which of the following psychodynamic concepts are true in order to provide care for Mrs. Jones.

    A. The physical complaints are used to create interest and attention.
    B. Specific symptom choice is not symbolic but directly related to the patient's faulty identification with a parent.
    C. Regression is the primary coping mechanism.
    D. The patient's symptoms are faked and are used to gain sympathy.

59. Which of the following behaviors may indicate that the individual who uses psychoneurotic behavior patterns is dealing more effectively with his problems?

    A. Verbalizes his thoughts and feelings rather than demonstrating them through physiological symptoms or maladaptive behavior.
    B. Openly expresses hostility.
    C. Freely chooses activities that include other people.
    D. Initiates contact with others.

60. Mary is standing in front of the mirror and as you enter the room says, "Look, my face is disintegrating." This is an example of

A. Amnesia.
B. Multiple personality.
C. Depersonalization.
D. Fugue.

61. Mr. Allen, seventy-two years old, has been hospitalized in a long-term nursing care facility for the past six months. He is confused and disoriented most of the time. His behavior alternates between calling for his deceased wife and screaming and sobbing uncontrollably. Mr. Allen shuffles up to the station, crying and screaming, "Nobody cares if I live or die! You all hate me! You all hate me!" Which response by the nurse would be most therapeutic?

    A. "Mr. Allen, what makes you think we hate you?"
    B. "Pete, you are always saying that and you know we all love you."
    C. "Pete, here is a cigarette. Now go in the dayroom and watch TV."
    D. "Mr. Allen, you seem very upset. Let's take a walk and we can talk."

62. In planning Mr. Allen's daily schedule, it is important for the nurse to understand which of the following principles?

    A. The patient may have moderate to severe memory impairment and short periods of concentration.
    B. The more rigid his daily schedule, the more comfortable he will be.
    C. The patient is more likely to be able to remember current experiences than past ones.
    D. The patient can usually be trusted to be responsible for his daily care needs.

63. Mrs. Maring was brought to a county medical center locked unit by the police. She was found wandering around the streets, incoherent, and her behavior appeared to be inappropriate. She was tentatively diagnosed as schizophrenic and held in the hospital for a three-day evaluation. Miss James, a nurse on the locked unit, is assigned to Mrs. Maring. The nurse knows that a diagnosis of schizophrenia implies that a patient would manifest which of the following behaviors?

    A. Inability to concentrate.
    B. Loss of contact with reality.
    C. Guilt feelings.
    D. Feelings of worthlessness.

64. Mrs. Maring says that the voices are telling her to do things and she can't stop listening. The best response from the nurse would be

    A. "Never mind the voices; let's just concentrate on the game."
    B. "The voices will go away soon."
    C. "I don't hear any voices. I think the voices are part of your illness. Try to listen to what I'm saying."

D. "Just stop listening to what is in your head and they will go away."

65. On the second day of Mrs. Maring's stay in the hospital, she appears withdrawn and spends most of her time alone in her room staring at the wall. The nurse recognizes that this behavior is a symptom of schizophrenia known as
A. Social withdrawal.
B. Autism.
C. Loose associations.
D. Stress.

66. Mrs. Maring, after a two-week stay, appears much better. She is in contact with reality and is able to interact with others in an appropriate way. The doctor is sending her home with medication. The most common medications given for schizophrenia are
A. ECT.
B. Phenothiazines.
C. MAO inhibitors.
D. Antidepressants.

67. While it is important to consider people as individuals with their own patterns of behavior, we have classified certain behaviors or symptoms as indicative of the mental illness known as schizophrenia. Which of the following symptoms does not belong in this category?
A. Loose associations.
B. Depersonalization.
C. Affective disturbance.
D. Cyclothymic.

68. The nursing staff is planning an all-day picnic and outing for a group of patients. All the patients are on large doses of phenothiazines. Which precautionary measure is most important for the nursing staff to enforce?
A. All patients should be kept in the shade as much as possible and should wear clothing or hats to protect exposed skin areas.
B. Avoid excessive stimuli.
C. Take along a first-aid kit, because psychiatric patients are accident prone.
D. Avoid foods such as cheese, coke, coffee, or wine that are high in tyramine.

69. Drug addiction is a major social problem in our society. Aside from the physical deterioration of the individual and the subculture participation that may lead to crime, a further result of the addiction may be
A. The development of psychosis.
B. The disintegration of family relationships.
C. Addiction to other substances such as alcohol.
D. Intellectual dependence on the drug.

70. The treatment for delirium tremens may include all

of the following except
A. High calorie, vitamin, and fluid diet.
B. Tranquilization.
C. Side rails for client protection.
D. Morphine to induce rest.

71. Paranoid symptoms can be observed as secondary symptoms to schizophrenia. In which of the following disorders would you also be apt to observe paranoid symptoms?
A. Organic syndromes.
B. Involutional melancholia.
C. Alcoholism.
D. All of the above.

72. Mr. Davis has been admitted to your hospital unit with a tentative diagnosis of paranoid schizophrenia. He tells you the story that he was walking down the corridor at work and saw two friends talking and laughing. He assumed they were talking about him, but was willing to consider other reasons for their conversation. Mr. Davis has expressed a symptom known as
A. Delusion of reference.
B. Idea of reference.
C. Illusion.
D. Suspicious response.

73. Mr. Davis continues to be suspicious toward others in his immediate environment. His ideas of reference become fixed, and he manifests symptoms of paranoid schizophrenia known as delusions. The most common delusions associated with this illness are
A. Delusions of grandeur.
B. Delusions of persecution.
C. Delusions of jealousy.
D. Litigiousness.

74. The nurse may expect Mr. Davis to exhibit all of the following characteristics along with his paranoid ideation except
A. Jealousy.
B. Tendency to violence.
C. Tendency to flight.
D. Alcoholism.

75. The nurse, in caring for Mr. Davis, would evaluate his discharge plans in terms of his ability to function in society. In order for Mr. Davis to return to society, she knows that
A. His paranoid ideas must be completely absent.
B. As long as Mr. Davis can keep his paranoid ideas to himself, he can be discharged.
C. The family must have therapy, because the family is the source of his paranoid ideation.
D. The paranoid ideas have to be investigated to insure that there is no truth in them.

76. An important nursing goal in planning care for the

individual with chronic brain syndrome is

A. To allow the patient to function as independently as therapeutically possible.
B. To continually orient the patient to reality.
C. To provide a safe, structured environment with appropriate recreational activities.
D. All of the above.

77. Which of the following best describes the general characteristics of the individual with chronic brain syndrome?

A. Ritualistic about daily activities.
B. Impaired judgment.
C. All areas of the personality and mental functioning may be affected.
D. Uses confabulation to compensate for memory impairment.

78. The aged, senile individual should be

A. Allowed to be responsible for his own nutritional needs.
B. Kept active through plenty of exercise.
C. Kept in his room to avoid potentially unsafe situations.
D. Given opportunities to be useful.

79. Which of the following is not appropriate in caring for a confused, incoherent person?

A. Engage the individual in reality-oriented conversations.
B. Hurry him through the daily activities so he may rest sooner.
C. Be firm and gentle and assist the patient where needed.
D. Only help the patient as often as is appropriate.

80. The mental health of the aged is most influenced by

A. Basic personality structure and make-up.
B. Philosophical point of view and attitudes about life and death.
C. Family attitudes toward the aged.
D. Cultural and environmental factors.

81. Which of the following is not a possible cause for organic brain syndrome?

A. Senility.
B. Arteriosclerosis.
C. Trauma.
D. Intoxication.

82. Confabulation is a symptom frequently seen in Korsakoff's psychosis, a syndrome of chronic alcoholism. Confabulation can best be defined as

A. Amnesia for recent events.
B. A defense mechanism to control anxiety.
C. Falsifying facts to fill in memory gaps.
D. A mechanism to raise self-esteem.

83. Mr. Meteress has been admitted to an alcohol detoxification unit. He sits dejected in a corner and, when approached by the nurse, he says, "I'm really no good. I drink and don't take care of my family, and I'm a rotten father." A response by the nurse using an effective communication technique would be

A. "But now you are doing something about your problem, Mr. Meteress."
B. "Sounds as though you are feeling pretty guilty about drinking."
C. "I'm sure that you are a good father, Mr. Meteress."
D. "What makes you think you are no good?"

84. Alcoholics who have been heavy drinkers for a number of years are prone to experience all of the following *except*

A. Some brain cell destruction.
B. Esophageal varacies.
C. Malnutrition.
D. Serum hepatitus.

85. Mrs. Jones has been a patient on the oncology unit for two months. She has become a favorite with the staff, and although her condition is deteriorating, she remains cheerful and pleasant. One day she says to you, "Well, I've given up all hope. I know I'm going to die soon." What would be the most therapeutic response you could make?

A. "Now, Mrs. Jones, one should never give up all hope. We are finding new cures every day."
B. "Mrs. Jones, would you like to talk about dying?"
C. "You've given up all hope?"
D. "You know, your doctor will be here soon. Why don't you talk to him about your feelings and giving up all hope?"

86. Mrs. Jones's condition is critical, and you are assigned to care for her. Of the following tasks, which one would have lowest priority?

A. Attending to her physical needs and assessing the situation for changes.
B. Contacting the family and giving them needed support.
C. Encouraging Mrs. Jones to express and talk about her fears of dying.
D. Contacting her lawyer so she can tie up loose ends.

87. One year ago Mrs. Brown lost her husband to whom she had been married for ten years. They had had a stormy marriage, punctuated by frequent disagreements and several separations. Mrs. Brown is experiencing intense grief, which she seems unable to work through. To understand this behavior, the nurse should be familiar with which of the following principles?

A. The longer the marriage, the more intense the grief.
B. The more dependent the relationship, the more

difficult the grief process.

   C. The more ambivalent the relationship, the more intense the grief.

   D. It is too soon to expect Mrs. Brown to have worked through the grief process.

88. Mrs. Kelly is a forty-two-year-old patient diagnosed as a chronic schizophrenic. She has been hospitalized for nine years. Mrs. Kelly presented a nursing problem because she stole food and hoarded linen. Methods used to discourage the hoarding failed. The nurse began to give Mrs. Kelly linen on a noncontingent basis instead of removing it. Using behavior modification theory, which of the following is *not* an appropriate concept in altering Mrs. Kelly's behavior?

   A. The target behavior would be to eliminate the undesirable behavior.

   B. Each behavior should be dealt with separately.

   C. Decelerating procedures are appropriate.

   D. To accelerate desirable behavior, the behavior needs to be continually reinforced.

89. Positive reinforcers are used to produce behaviors in several ways. Which of the following is not used to produce desired change in behavior?

   A. Present a pleasant event contingent on the occurrence of the behavior.

   B. The positive reinforcers depend on the individual.

   C. The relationship between the desired behavior and its consequence must be a planned, contingent one.

   D. Rewarded behavior is more likely to increase in frequency.

90 Reinforcement practice can be useful in which of the following areas?

   A. A parents' group for autistic children.

   B. Teaching self-care to a diabetic patient.

   C. Working with a patient with the condition anorexia nervosa.

   D. All of the above.

91. Susan, a twenty-year-old female, comes into the crisis clinic, and you are assigned to interview her. From your knowledge of crisis theory, you know that success of her crisis therapy would be most influenced by which of the following factors?

   A. Past history of her illness.

   B. Availability of support systems.

   C. Previous unsatisfactory relationships.

   D. Financial resources available.

92. Before working with Susan, it would be important for you to obtain a history containing all of the following information *except*

   A. The identification of the problem from Susan's point of view.

   B. The coping mechanisms Susan has available to

handle the crisis.

   C. The triggering event leading to the crisis.

   D. The life experiences she has had in the past.

93. Sadness of brief duration that follows an obvious loss should be termed

   A. Crisis.

   B. Grief.

   C. Melancholia.

   D. Neurotic depression.

94. A recent trend that nurses should be aware of focuses on follow-up care for clients returned to the community after a period of hospitalization for mental illness. This treatment is called

   A. Primary prevention of psychiatric illness.

   B. Secondary prevention.

   C. Crisis intervention.

   D. Community psychiatry.

95. Group therapy has been an accepted method of treatment for psychiatric patients for several years. The best rationale for this form of treatment is

   A. It is the most economical—one staff member can treat many patients.

   B. The format of the therapy is not psychoanalytically based and does not deal with unconscious material.

   C. It enables patients to become aware that others have problems and that they are not alone in their suffering.

   D. It provides a social milieu similar to society in general, where the patient can relate to others and validate perceptions in realistic settings.

96. The therapist role(s) that a nurse would assume if she were designated as group leader for a group therapy session would be

   A. Role model for effective communication.

   B. Clarifier and validator of patient responses.

   C. Facilitator and interpreter.

   D. All of the above.

97. You are assigned to work with an autistic child and have had no previous experience with emotionally disturbed children. Which basic principles of psychiatric nursing could you transfer to caring for children?

   A. Principles of acceptance of the person at his individual level of development.

   B. Principles of relationship therapy where frequent interactions are indicated.

   C. Principles of limit setting and consistency in approach to build security and trust.

   D. All of the above.

98. Of the following categories of illness, which one would you not include in group therapy?

   A. Chronic brain syndrome patients.

   B. Paranoid patients.

C. Psychoneurotic patients.

D. Acutely psychotic patients.

99. A very attractive young man with whom you have a nurse-patient relationship continues to make sexual advances toward you that make you very uncomfortable. The best approach would be to

A. Ignore the advances, for you know that lack of reinforcement usually extinguishes the behavior.

B. Don't reject the young man, for you know this will reinforce his negative self-image.

C. Be direct in communicating your discomfort with his advances and set limits on his behavior.

D. Tell his doctor, who should be informed of his inappropriate behavior on the unit.

100. A nurse on your unit was caught stealing narcotics from the locked cabinet. She was charged with a felony and let out on bail to await trial. Her R.N. license was suspended by which of the following agencies?

A. The county judicial system.

B. The district attorney who charged her with the felony.

C. The American Nurses' Association.

D. The State Board of Nurse Registration.

Answers and Rationale

1. (A) Both the nurse and patient need to become comfortable with each other in the initial phase before the working phase can begin.

2. (B) While the behavior is maladaptive, the patient must feel that the nurse sees him/her as a worthwhile individual. Most of the time, patients have low self-esteem. Answer A is incorrect because the nurse must realize that she is a human being with her own point of view and prejudices; therefore, she cannot like everyone. She must be aware of her feelings so that they do not interfere and block the patient's treatments. Sympathizing with the patient meets the nurse's needs, not the patient's. The nurse must maintain a therapeutic, professional attitude but allow her humanness to show; it is important to be able to relate as one human being to another.

3. (A) The nurse's unresolved attitudes and feelings toward her father may spill over and influence her relationship with the patient. If the nurse is not aware of her attitudes, she may lose her objectivity.

4. (B) It encompasses the other answers and is more fundamental.

5. (D) Perspiring is not a behavior but a physiological reaction to anxiety. A, B, and C are behaviors that may be seen as a result of moderate to severe anxiety.

6. (C) It includes the other three answers. Sleeping medicine should be avoided if at all possible or unless absolutely necessary, because it helps suppress the patient's feelings only temporarily.

7. (B) Severe anxiety cannot be used to serve the patient and requires nursing intervention to lower it. As this anxiety becomes more unbearable, it is likely an adjustment mechanism will come into play. A is mild anxiety; C is moderate anxiety; and D is panic.

8. (B) The response is inappropriate to the situation. This is an example of one of the two forms of abnormal affect. The other form is lack of affect, where no response (including facial expression) would be present.

9. (D) Simply restating the interaction is the best response so that Jill may see the connection and her inappropriate reply. She may or may not choose to talk about her feelings. Your restatement will give her an opportunity but not force her to do so.

10. (D) All of the choices are true, but D includes the basic idea of the others and is more comprehensive.

11. (D) The mind is set up to handle threats to the self in which every way learned is more effective and serves the purpose of the individual.

12. (A) Undoing and projection are fairly ineffective ways of adjusting to anxiety and if used repeatedly may indicate problems. Sublimation is also a common mechanism but not as common as rationalization.

13. (C) The symptom is a characteristic flow of ideas in which one idea rapidly triggers another.

14. (D) This activity would channel her energy, but not increase the external stimuli as the group activities would do.

15. (C) Setting limits is important to avoid rejection of the other patients with subsequent lowering of self-esteem.

16. (B) Depression is a result of the assault on the ego (loss or injury) and the mania covers the depression.

17. (D) While one may speculate that mania is caused by a chemical imbalance and transmitted through the genes, it is only a theory.

18. (B) Extrapyramidal side effects are associated with the antipsychotic drugs. The other answers are important to be aware of when monitoring the use of antianxiety drugs.

19. (D) The usual side effect is polyuria, not anuria.

20. (D) While a good nursing care plan is important, the priority would be to get Mr. Braner mobilized so that his focus will not be centered on internal suffering.

21. (C) A depressed person needs to experience that someone cares for him, is concerned for his welfare, and is someone he can relate to during his hospitalization.

22. (B) When depression lifts, the patient has enough energy to commit suicide. Satisfaction may well indicate a well-formulated plan.

23. (B) The other answers do not refer to depressed affect (feelings), but rather to behavior—also characteristic of a depressed person.

24. (B) Elavil, Triavil, Aventyl, Vivactil, and Sinequan are also antidepressant drugs. Answer A (Mellaril) is an antipsychotic drug. Answer C is an antianxiety drug. Answer D is an antiparkinson agent used in conjunction with the antipsychotic drugs.

25. (B) As far as is known, the electric current (75 to 150 volts, 60 cycle) does not destroy brain cells. All of the other answers are side effects.

26. (C) The curare-like drug lessens strong muscular contraction during the convulsion, and the barbiturate is given to reduce anxiety by putting the patient to sleep for 5 to 10 minutes.

27. (C) Even though all of the reasons are important and should not be ignored, the most important task is that the staff should learn to assess the patient's behavior and to identify cues that might indicate an impending suicide attempt.

28. (A) With thought disorders, the individual has difficulty in keeping in touch with reality, which is not usually a problem with people experiencing problems in the affective area.

29. (C) A main characteristic of neurotic depression is that it is easily influenced by events in the outside world—the word used to describe this condition is exogenous depression.

30. (D) It is incorrect because neurosis is an unconscious process. The patient is aware he has a problem but is not conscious of its cause.

31. (B) The symptom is formed to alleviate a high level of anxiety. Selections A, C, and D are secondary gains.

32. (B) An observant, warm, nonthreatening approach is more effective. A is incorrect, because focusing on the symptom will only increase the anxiety level. C and D are incorrect because the patient is actually experiencing the symptom in conversion reaction even though there are no physiological reasons for the problem.

33. (C) Symptom formation is to avoid the anxiety and its discomfort.

34. (D) It is incorrect because ritualistic behavior does not disappear until the underlying basic conflict is resolved. Through the behavior, the anxiety is

temporarily relieved, but the cause is not resolved.

35. (A) The nurse needs to keep environmental stimuli nonthreatening. B is incorrect, because close intimate contact increases the patient's anxiety. He wants and needs the contact but is afraid of it as it is a source of "hurt" and "disappointment" for him. C is incorrect. Rigidly defended limits again increase this obsessive–compulsive anxiety level. D is incorrect. Humor is inappropriate and may be misinterpreted by the patient as an attack to his already low self-esteem.

36. (C) Jane is placing blame on others and not taking responsibility for her own behavior.

37. (B) It includes A, B, and C. Regression is a way to reduce anxiety and cope with different situations.

38. (A) The patient is simply refusing to accept her terminal illness to protect herself from the unpleasant reality of death.

39. (D) A is symbolization. B is insulation. C is displacement.

40. (A) The main goal of an adjustment mechanism is to protect the self-image. The others may be true, but they fit within the framework of answer A.

41. (C) Characteristics such as pathological lying, manipulation, and deception are common to sociopathic character disorders.

42. (A) Psychopathic personalities evidence poor judgment, poor superego control, as well as poor emotional responses to others. The only area unimpaired is the intellect.

43. (B) It is important to set limits but not to reinforce low self-esteem, so staying with Doug would be therapeutic.

44. (B) These persons exercise poor judgment and do not learn from experience.

45. (A) Ellen's symptoms are indicative of depression, and typically these patients feel the future is bleak and hopeless.

46. (D) While all patients who are impulsive may be potentially suicidal, the least likely category is neurosis.

47. (A) Endogenous depression is more related to internal chemical changes than depressions influenced by external events.

48. (A) The others are incorrect—Niamid and Ritalin are antidepressant drugs and Miltown is classified as an antianxiety drug.

49. (D) Psychosomatic illnesses focus on the "holism" of the individual.

50. (D) It is more basic and includes selections B and C.

51. (D) Selections A, B, and C are drawing conclusions without validation. Selection D provides the

validation intervention.

52. (B) This approach would help decrease Gerry's anxiety and assist him in gaining insights. Selection A and D deny the problem, whereas C may increase his anxiety and prolong his illness.

53. (B) Selections A, C, and D are important but the emotional support of his family is vital. Intellectual understanding may not effect an improvement in his condition, inasmuch as it may be used to avoid the underlying feelings and conflicts.

54. (A) The patient is keeping his undesirable and painful thoughts and feelings on an unconscious level and is handling them through his body.

55. (D) The most effective communication technique in this case would be silence; support the patient nonverbally, accept her and open up the opportunity for an expression of feelings.

56. (D) Phobias involve unreasonable fears of specific objects or situations. Obsessions are recurring thoughts that create discomfort. Both involve a high level of anxiety.

57. (B) The hypochondriac has a severe, morbid preoccupation with the state of his own body. Approaches and activities that increase self-esteem and direct the patient's attention outward are therapeutic.

58. (C) Hypochondriasis is the rarest and most serious of the psychoneuroses. Narcissistic body preoccupation and severe regression are common.

59. (A) Verbalizing thoughts and feelings is indicative of effectively dealing with problems. This answer encompasses the other selections.

60. (C) Depersonalization is a dissociative reaction where the client perceives that parts of his body are separating or changing. It is a symptom of the person losing touch with reality and is usually seen in regressed schizophrenics.

61. (D) The nurse acknowledges the patient and his feelings without focusing directly on them. A asks for an analysis of feelings. B is making light of the patient's feelings. C is ignoring the problem.

62. (A) It is important to remember that patients usually have some memory and concentration impairment. The degree depends upon the individual and is influenced by the basic personality structure and the cause of the problem.

63. (B) Loss of contact with reality is a symptom of schizophrenia. All of the other symptoms are indicative of depression.

64. (C) It is the best answer, for it helps the patient cope with reality by validating that another person does not hear them, as well as directing the patient to focus on reality content.

65. (B) Autistic behavior is the basic social isolation of schizophrenics when they withdraw into their own inner world.

66. (B) Tranquilizing drugs help patients to cope with reality by modifying their symptoms.

67. (D) Cyclothymic personality is one in which the individual experiences mood swings and is most often seen in past histories of manic-depressives.

68. (A) One of the major side effects of the phenothiazine drug group is photosensitivity. Skin burns and irritations may be caused by even short exposure to direct sunlight. B is correct, but is not the most important precaution. C is incorrect, in that psychiatric patients are no more accident prone than the general population; however, it would be appropriate to include a first-aid kit. D is incorrect, because avoidance of those foods is important when using antiparkinsonian drugs.

69. (B) Family relationships generally suffer or cease entirely when a person becomes addicted to hard drugs.

70. (D) Morphine, a C.N.S. depressant, would be contraindicated.

71. (D) Paranoid symptoms can accompany all of the disorders, but not necessarily.

72. (B) A delusion of reference refers to a fixed belief when no amount of evidence can alter the belief.

73. (B) Feelings of persecution or extreme suspicion or mistrust are the most common manifestation of the paranoid position.

74. (D) Alcoholism may be accompanied by paranoid delusions, but alcoholism per se is not a characteristic of paranoid conditions.

75. (B) Even though his paranoid ideas have not disappeared, if they are localized to a small area of his life and kept to himself, he can return and continue to function in society.

76. (D) Each answer is important in providing care for the patient.

77. (C) All the other answers are correct, but C includes them and is therefore more comprehensive.

78. (D) This allows the patient to function at an optimum level for as long as possible and also assists in maintaining his self-esteem. The other answers are incorrect.

79. (B) Hurrying tends to exhaust the patient physically and emotionally, thus adding to his confusion.

80. (A) It broadly encompasses the other answers.

81. (A) Senility is not a cause but a label for behaviors associated with organic brain syndrome. B, C, and D are a few of the common causes of organic brain syndrome.

82. (C) As the patient experiences memory gaps, he fills them in with stories unsubstantiated by facts to preserve his self-esteem.

83. (B) The nurse paraphrases the patient's comments to give feedback, to show she understands what he has said and to encourage him to continue expressing his feelings.

84. (D) Serum hepatitis is caused by the use of unsterile instruments used in injections and would be a more common result of heroin addiction.

85. (C) This reflective response will open up communication and enable the patient to express whatever concerns or feelings she has without confining her to a discussion of dying (answer B).

86. (D) Contacting her family and supporting them is part of your role as a professional nurse, but contacting her lawyer is not necessarily your responsibility.

87. (C) When both positive and negative feelings are felt toward the deceased, the grief process is more difficult to resolve because of guilt arising from the negative feelings.

88. (D) The modifying procedure used was satiation, which is a decelerating procedure. Choice D is incorrect, in that the goal is to eliminate the behavior, not accelerate it.

89. (C) It is dealing with the target behavior rather than a positive reinforcement factor.

90. (D) Behavior modification can be useful in any area where the nurse is working with behaviors and their consequences.

91. (B) The more supports the client has available during a crisis period, the more easily she may develop coping mechanisms to handle the crisis.

92. (D) All of the other choices would be important ingredients of a crisis history which is "here and now" focused.

93. (B) Grief occurs following an obvious loss, is a normal reaction to the loss, and is of short duration, while the other depressed states are abnormal reactions to loss.

94. (B) It refers to the focus on preventing a reoccurrence of the primary illness.

95. (D) Since many people's problems occur in an interpersonal framework, the group setting is a way to correct faulty perceptions as well as work on ineffective ways of relating to others.

96. (D) The nurse must assume all these roles if she is to be an effective (therapeutic) group leader. (See the section on communication in this chapter.)

97. (D) While working with autistic children may involve some specific approaches, the basic principles still apply.

98. (B) When patients are acutely paranoid, they are too suspicious and mistrustful of others to relate in a group setting.

99. (C) This patient needs direct feedback and clear delineation of limits to the relationship.

100. (D) The same agency that issues the license has the power to suspend or revoke it.

Legal Issues
in Nursing

This chapter reviews important legal issues in nursing. Topics covered include the Nurse Practice Act, patients' rights, nurses' liability, key legal terms, drugs and the nurse, and grounds for professional misconduct.

Like many other professions, nursing is becoming more regulated and more involved with legal proceedings. Each state has the authority to regulate and administrate health care professionals. While the provisions of the Nurse Practice Acts are quite similar from state to state, it is imperative that the nurse knows the licensing requirements and the grounds for license revocation as defined by the state in which he or she works.

Legal and ethical standards for nurses are complicated by a myriad of federal and state statutes and the continually changing interpretation of them by the courts of law. Nurses are faced today with the threat of legal action based on malpractice, invasion of privacy, and other grounds.

Nurse Practice Act

Definition: A series of statutes enacted by each state's legislature to regulate the practice of nursing in that state. Subjects covered by the Nurse Practice Acts include definition of scope of practice, education, licensure, grounds for disciplinary actions, and related topics. The Nurse Practice Acts are quite similar throughout the United States, but the professional nurse is held legally responsible for the specific requirements for licensure and regulations of practice as defined by the state in which he or she is working.

The Practice of Nursing

A. Professional nursing.
   1. Responsibilities.
      a. Performance, for compensation, of a defined range of health care services including assessment, implementation, and evaluation of nursing action as well as teaching and counseling.
      b. Administration of medications and treatments as prescribed by a licensed physician or other designated licensed professional.
      c. Supervision of other nursing personnel.
   2. Requirements: specialized skills taught by and acquired at an accredited nursing school.
B. Major functions of registered nurses.
   1. Direct and indirect patient care services.
   2. Performance of basic health care, testing, and prevention procedures.
   3. Observation of signs and symptoms of illness, treatment reactions, and general physical or mental conditions.
   4. Documentation of nursing care.

Board of Registered Nursing (BRN)

A. Each state has a Board of Registered Nursing (or its equivalent) organized within the executive branch of the state government. Primary responsibilities of the BRN include administration of the state's Nurse Practice Act as applied to registered nurses.
B. Functions of state Boards of Registered Nursing.
   1. Establishing educational and professional standards for licensure.
   2. Conducting examinations, registering, and licensing applicants.
   3. Conducting investigations of violations of statutes and regulations.
   4. Issuing citations and holding disciplinary hearings for possible suspension or revocation of licenses.
   5. Imposing penalties following disciplinary hearings.
   6. Formulating regulations to implement the Nurse Practice Act.

Authorization to Practice Nursing

A. To legally engage in the practice of nursing, an individual must hold an active license issued by the state in which he or she intends to work.
B. The licensing process.
   1. The applicant must pass a licensing examination administered by the state Board of Registered Nursing, or the BRN may grant reciprocity to an applicant who holds a current license in another state.
   2. The applicant for R.N. licensure examination must have attended an accredited state school of nursing, must be a qualified related nursing professional or para-professional, or must meet specified prerequisites if licensed in a foreign country.
   3. Boards of Registered Nursing contract with the National Council of State Boards of Nursing, Inc., for use of the State Board Test Pool Examination.

Professional Misconduct and Potential Penalties

Grounds for Professional Misconduct

A. Licensed professional nurses are regulated and disciplined by the state in which they work.
B. The practicing nurse should know how his or her state defines professional misconduct.
C. Common grounds for professional misconduct.
   1. Obtaining R.N. license through fraudulent methods.
   2. Practicing in an incompetent and/or negligent manner.

3. Practicing when ability to practice is impaired by mental or physical disability, drugs, or alcohol.
4. Being habitually drunk or being dependent on or a habitual user of drugs.
5. Conviction of or committing an act constituting a crime under federal or state law.
6. Refusing to provide health care services on the grounds of race, color, creed, or national origin.
7. Permitting or aiding an unlicensed person to perform activities requiring a license.
8. Practicing nursing while license is suspended.
9. Practicing medicine without a license.

Penalties for Professional Misconduct

A. The state's Board of Registered Nursing has the authority to impose penalties for professional misconduct.
B. Types of discipline include:
1. Probation.
2. Censure and reprimand.
3. Suspension of license.
4. Revocation of license.

Nature of the Law

Definition: A system of principles and processes by which people who live in a society deal with their disputes and problems. They are rules of human conduct.

Types of Laws

A. Criminal.
1. The harm is against society and guilt requires proof beyond a reasonable doubt.
2. Punishment may be a fine or imprisonment.
B. Civil.
1. The harm is against another individual and guilt requires proof by a preponderance of the evidence.
2. Punishment is generally the payment of monetary compensation.

Elements for Liability

A. There must be a legal basis such as statutory law for finding liability.

B. A causal relationship must exist between the harm to the patient and the act or omission to act by the nurse.
C. There must be some damage or harm sustained by the patient.

Table 1. Nursing Liability

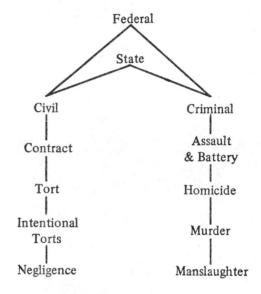

Key Legal Terms

Negligence

A. The key elements of negligence are based on:
1. The duty of the nurse to provide patients with due care.
2. A breach of that duty which is the cause of a compensatory injury to the patient.
B. Malpractice is negligence on the part of a nurse, physician, or other health care professional.
C. Classifications of malpractice: criminal, civil, and ethical.

Liability

A. A nurse has a personal, legal obligation to provide a standard of patient care expected of a reasonably competent professional nurse.
B. Professional nurses are held responsible (liable) for harm resulting from their negligent acts, or omissions to act.

Respondeat Superior

A. Legal doctrine which holds an employer liable for negligent acts of employees in the course and scope of employment.

B. Physicians, hospitals, clinics, and other employers may be held liable for negligent acts of their employees.

C. This doctrine does not support acts of gross negligence or acts which are outside the scope of employment.

Table 2. Classifications of Law Related to Nursing

Classification	Example
Constitutional	Patients' rights to equal treatment
Administrative	Licensure and the state BRN
Labor Relations	Union negotiations
Contract	Relationship with employer
Criminal	Handling of narcotics
Tort	
1. Medical Malpractice	Reasonable and prudent patient care
2. Product Liability	Warranty on medical equipment

Risk Areas

Definition: Certain areas of practice which increase the risk of potential liability for the nurse because of an increased nursing involvement, a hazard potential involved in the function and/or an increased social awareness.

Patient's Rights

A. A right or claim may be moral and/or legal.
   1. A legal right can be enforced in a court of law.

   2. Within the health care system, all patients retain their basic constitutional rights such as freedom of expression, due process of law, freedom from cruel and inhumane punishment, equal protection, and so forth.

B. Patient rights may conflict with nursing function.
   1. Key elements of a patient's rights with which nurses should be thoroughly familiar include consent, confidentiality, and involuntary commitment.
   2. The patient's right may be modified by his or her mental or physical condition as well as his or her social status.

Consent to Receive Health Services

A. Consent is the patient's approval to have his body touched by specific individuals (such as doctor, nurse, laboratory technician).
   1. Types of consent: expressed or implied—verbal or written.
   2. Informed consent: prior to granting a consent, the patient must be fully informed regarding treatment, tests, surgery, etc., and must understand both the intended outcome and the potentially harmful results.
   3. The patient may rescind a prior consent verbally or in writing.

B. Authority to consent.
   1. A mentally competent adult patient must give his or her own consent.
   2. In emergency situations, if the patient is in immediate danger of serious harm or death, action may be taken to preserve life without the patient's consent.
   3. Parents or legal guardians may give consent for minors.
   4. Court-authorized persons may give consent for mentally incompetent patients.

C. Voluntary admission.
   1. A person freely consents to enter an institution for purposes of receiving psychiatric care and treatment.
   2. Patients who enter on a voluntary basis may leave at will.

D. Involuntary admission.
   1. An individual may legally be admitted to an institution without his or her own consent

when the individual does not have the mental capacity or competency to understand his or her own acts.

2. Occurs when the patient is judged by a court of law to be mentally ill, dangerous to him- or herself and others, and requiring admission to a psychiatric ward or center.

E. Nurse's liability.

1. The nurse who asks a patient to sign a consent form may be held personally liable if the nurse knows or should know that the patient has not been fully informed by the physicians, hospital staff, or others regarding potentially harmful effects of treatments, tests, surgery, and other acts.

2. Nurses must respect the right of a mentally competent adult patient to refuse health care. However, a life-threatening situation may alter the patient's right to refuse treatment.

Patient's Right to Privacy

A. Confidential information.

1. Patients are protected by law (invasion of privacy) against unauthorized release of personal clinical data such as symptoms, diagnoses, and treatments.

2. Nurses, as well as other health care professionals and their employers, may be held personally liable for invasion of privacy as well as other torts should litigation arise from unauthorized release of patient data.

3. Nurses have a legal and ethical responsibility to become familiar with their employers' policies and procedures regarding protection of patients' information.

4. Confidential information may be released by consent of the patient.

5. Information release is mandatory when ordered by a court or when state statutes require reporting child abuse, communicable diseases, or other incidents.

B. Patient care: nurses have an ethical responsibility to protect the patient's personal privacy during treatment or hospitalization by means of gowns, screens, closed doors, etc.

C. Medical records.

1. As the key written account of patient information such as signs and symptoms, diagnosis, treatment, etc., the medical record fulfills many functions both within the hospital or clinic and with outside parties.

a. Documents care given the patient.

b. Provides effective means of communication among health care personnel.

c. Contains important data for insurance and other expense claims.

d. May be utilized in court in the event of litigation.

2. Nurses have a strong ethical and legal obligation to maintain complete and timely records, and to sign or countersign only those documents which are accurate and complete.

Drugs and the Nurse

Definition: In their daily work, most nurses handle a wide variety of drugs. Failure to give the correct medication or improper handling of drugs may result in serious problems for the nurse due to strict federal and state statutes relating to drugs.

Regulation

A. The Comprehensive Drug Abuse Prevention Act of 1970 provides the fundamental regulations (federal) for the compounding, sale, and dispensing of narcotics, stimulants, depressants, and other controlled items.

B. Each state has a similar set of regulations for the same purpose.

Violation

A. State pharmacy acts provide standards for dispensing drugs.

B. Noncompliance with federal or state drug regulations can result in liability.

C. Violation of the state's drug regulations or licensing laws are grounds for BRN administrative disciplinary action.

Annotated Bibliography

Chapter 1. Nursing Through the Life Cycle

Birchenall, Joan, and Streight, Mary Eileen. *Care of the Older Adult.* Philadelphia: J. B. Lippincott Company, 1973.

A basic text for nursing care of the aged. Emphasis is placed on the role of nurse in preventive aspects of geriatric care. The normal aging process is discussed. Good basic text for all levels of nursing education.

Brink, Pamela J., ed. *Transcultural Nursing.* Englewood Cliffs, New Jersey: Prentice-Hall, Inc., 1976.

A collection of readings which deal with cultural differences among people. Combines nursing and anthropology to provide a knowledge base for nursing care of patients of other cultures. Appropriate for baccalaureate and graduate nursing students.

Burnside, Irene Mortenson. *Nursing and the Aged.* New York: McGraw-Hill Cook Company, 1976.

In this text, the contributing authors have covered aging from philosophy and the normal aging process through pathophysiology and psychosocial development. A clear, well-written text that has as an added attraction—the nursing process and its relationship to the aging process.

Food and Nutrition Board, National Research Council, National Academy of Sciences. *Recommended Dietary Allowances.* Rev. ed. Washington, D.C.: 1968.

Scientifically designed "for the maintenance of practically all healthy people in the U.S.A." The values of the caloric and nutrient requirements are used in assessing nutritional states.

Hall, Joanne E., and Weaver, Barbara. *Nursing of Families in Crisis.* Philadelphia: J. B. Lippincott Company, 1974.

Families in Crisis covers material from birth to the aged. It focuses on the maturational and situational crises, as well as crisis theory and nursing interventions. An excellent text written by and for nurses.

Luckman, Joan, and Sorensen, Karen Creason. *Medical-Surgical Nursing—A Psychophysiological Approach.* Philadelphia: W. B. Saunders Company, 1979.

A basic medical-surgical text with a psychophysiological approach. Includes comprehensive chapters on stress, adaptation, and homeostasis, theories of disease causation, understanding illness, psychophysiological imbalances, and the body's response to homeostasis imbalances. Appropriate for all levels of nursing education.

Turner, Jeffrey S., and Helms, Donald B. *Contemporary Adulthood.* Philadelphia: W. B. Saunders Company, 1979.

A comprehensive textbook focusing on the dynamics behind growing old and the nature of adulthood in a contemporary society. This is an excellent, readable book, dealing with young adulthood, the middle years of adulthood, the retirement years, and death and dying. Appropriate for all levels of nursing education.

U.S. Department of Agriculture. *A Daily Food Guide: The Basic Four.* Rev. ed. Washington, D.C.: Government Printing Office, 1973.

Offers choices in four food groups to meet the nutrient recommendations during the life cycle. Caloric requirement is not included.

Williams, Sue Rodwell. *Essentials of Nutrition and Diet Therapy.* St. Louis: The C. V. Mosby Company, 1977.

An excellent all-around nutrition text encompassing general principles of nutrition, therapeutic nutrition, and coverage of diseases requiring special diets.

Woods, Nancy Fugate. *Human Sexuality in Health and Illness.* St. Louis: The C. V. Mosby Company, 1979.

An excellent reference book on normal sexual behavior with nursing management principles. This book also includes care and nursing care of handicapped persons.

Chapter 2. Medical Nursing

Armstrong, Margaret, and others. *McGraw-Hill Handbook of Clinical Nursing.* New York: McGraw-Hill Book Company, 1979.

A comprehensive handbook of all clinical nursing in outline format written in a nursing process framework. An excellent resource and reference book for student nurses.

Brooks, Stewart. *Basic Facts of Body Water and Ions.* New York: Springer Publishing Company, Inc., 1973.

Excellent presentation in a basic manner. Recommended for students who need clarification and help in understanding fluid and electrolyte balance in the body.

Broughton, Joseph O. "Understanding Blood Gases." Ohio Medical Products Article Reprint Library, August 1971.

Excellent detailed explanation of acid-base balance. Recommended for students who need help in understanding the theoretical gases of acid-base balance in the body.

Brunner, Lillian Sholtis, and Suddarth, Doris Smith. *Textbook of Medical-Surgical Nursing.* 3rd ed. Philadelphia: J. B. Lippincott Company, 1975.

Presents an overview of all body systems and includes physiology, diseases, treatment, and nursing management. It is particularly useful for its emphasis on nursing interventions for medical disorders.

Bushnell, Sharon Spaeth. *Respiratory Intensive Care Nursing.* Boston: Little, Brown & Company, 1973.

Anatomy, physiology, and nursing interventions presented in outline format. Easy to follow and to comprehend; a good resource book for nurses.

Cherniack, R. M., Cherniack, L., and Naimark, A. *Respiration in Health and Disease.* Philadelphia, London, and Toronto: W. B. Saunders Company, 1972.

Intermediate level presentation, but the format is easy to follow and very informative in its explanations of the respiratory system.

French, Ruth. *Guide to Diagnostic Procedures.* New York: McGraw-Hill Book Company, 1975.

A general reference book on common diagnostic procedures. The content is clearly presented and the most important diagnostic examinations are included, focusing on fundamental principles, definitions, and the role of the nurse in the administration of each test.

Gardner, Ernest, and others. *Anatomy: A Regional Study of Human Structure.* 4th ed. Philadelphia: W. B. Saunders Company, 1975.

A clear, concise explanation of the structure of human body systems. This book includes the major function of each structural part and is presented in a way that students can easily grasp the major concepts.

Guyton, Arthur C. *Textbook of Medical Physiology.* Philadelphia: W. B. Saunders Company, 1971.

A basic textbook covering all aspects of medical physiology. This book is extensive in its coverage of all body processes. The clear and concise presentation of principles and facts makes it easy to understand and to apply to disease processes. An excel-

lent resource for students having difficulty understanding the theory of physiology.

Krueger, Judith A., and Ray, Janis C. *Endocrine Problems in Nursing.* St. Louis: The C. V. Mosby Company, 1976.

A comprehensive book that focuses on a physiologic approach to nursing problems encountered with endocrine disorders of patients.

Krupp, Marcus A., and Chatton, Milton J. *Current Medical Diagnosis and Treatment.* Los Altos, California: Lange Medical Publications, 1978.

A desk reference intended primarily for physicians, but it is also an excellent resource for nurses. This book includes a concise description of various medical disorders and processes in medical diagnosis and treatment. The material is current, inclusive, and succinctly presented.

Luckmann, Joan, and Sorensen, Karen Creason. *Medical-Surgical Nursing: A Psychophysiological Approach.* Philadelphia: W. B. Saunders Company, 1979.

Extensive presentation of all body systems—pathophysiology, medical treatment regimes, and nursing interventions. Excellent source of information on medical-surgical nursing concepts, principles, and therapeutic applications.

Physicians' Desk Reference To Pharmaceutical Specialities and Biologicals. Oradell, New Jersey: Medical Economics, Inc., 1978.

Includes the latest available information on over two thousand drug products. The format is arranged so that the drugs, by generic, chemical, and brand name, can be easily located and identified. An excellent drug resource book for nurses.

Shafer, Kathleen Newton, and others. *Medical-Surgical Nursing.* 4th ed. St. Louis: The C. V. Mosby Company, 1975.

Good source of information on nursing care of patients with all disorders. For students interested in material related to endocrine disorders, it is a useful text.

Williams, Robert H., ed. *Textbook of Endocrinology.* 5th ed. Philadelphia: W. B. Saunders Company, 1974.

A good source of information related to the endocrine system. Although the information included is quite technical, the clear and concise presentation makes this text a useful resource for nurses.

Chapter 3. Surgical Nursing

Beland, Irene L., and Passos, Joyce Y. *Clinical Nursing: Pathophysiological and Psychosocial Approaches.* 3rd ed. New York: Macmillan Publishing Company, Inc., 1975.

This is an excellent resource for pathophysiology. It is written in depth, although at times the organization of the book makes it difficult to find the exact information desired.

Brunner, Lillian Sholtis, and Suddarth, Doris Smith. *The Lippincott Manual of Nursing Practice.* Philadelphia: J. B. Lippincott Company, 1978.

An excellent standard text for nursing interventions, the "what to do" aspect. Although it usually does not give explanations as to "why" the nursing interventions are carried out, it gives a quick review of what the essential interventions should be for major nursing care problems.

Brunner, Lillian Sholtis, and Suddarth, Doris Smith. *Textbook of Medical-Surgical Nursing.* 3rd ed. Philadelphia: J. B. Lippincott Company, 1975.

Nursing management is well defined in an easily understood format. It is well written and contains factual, pertinent information. The sections on gastric and intestinal disorders and disorders of the liver and biliary tract are especially well written.

Dunphy, J. Englebert, and Way, Lawrence W. *Current Surgical Diagnosis and Treatment.* 2nd ed. Los Altos, California: Lange Medical Publications, 1975.

This book, intended primarily for physicians and surgeons, presents material covering recent developments in all fields of surgery. It focuses on common surgical problems and presents the essentials of diagnosis and treatment. An excellent resource book for nurses.

Fluid and Electrolytes: Some Practical Guides to Clinical Use. Chicago: Abbott Laboratories, 1970.

A simplified version of fluid and electrolytes which is clear, concise and easy to understand.

Luckmann, Joan, and Sorensen, Karen. *Medical-Surgical Nursing: A Psychophysiologic Approach.* Philadelphia: W. B. Saunders Company, 1979.

The study guide and questions listed for each chapter can be utilized to test knowledge. Nursing principles are well stated throughout the book. Pathophysiology is easy to comprehend, and the neurosurgical section is particularly good.

Orthopedic Nurses Association, Inc. *Manual of Orthopedic Nursing Care Plans.* Atlanta, Georgia: May 1975.

Excellent resource for pertinent nursing interventions. Pathophysiology is not included and validation is not provided, so it does not provide complete coverage of the content area.

Chapter 4. Emergency Interventions and Nursing Procedures

Barry, Jean. *Emergency Nursing.* New York: McGraw-Hill Book Company, 1978.

A current emergency text that covers the primary emergency situations and gives nursing principles. Written in a clear, concise manner with workable format.

Underwood, JoAnn R. *Basic Cardiopulmonary Life Support; Theory and Technique.* Los Altos, CA: Applied Medical Training, Inc., 1978.

A manual for professional health personnel describing anatomy, electrophysiology and pathology of the cardiovascular system. This text emphasizes recognition and systematic management of life-threatening emergencies.

Chapter 5. Maternity Nursing

Babson, S. Gorham, and Benson, Ralph. *Management of High-Risk Pregnancy and Intensive Care of the Neonate.* St. Louis: The C.V. Mosby Company, 1975.

This is a very readable text, containing general information about high-risk conditions in pregnancy and infancy. Students who wish to supplement their knowledge of maternity nursing will find it helpful.

Greenhill, J. P., and Friedman, Emanuel A. *Biological Principles and Modern Practice of Obstetrics.* Philadelphia: W. B. Saunders Company, 1974.

This is a revised edition of a medical text first authored by Joseph B. De Lee sixty years ago. It covers a wide range of information on normal physiology and conduct of pregnancy, labor, and puerperium, as well as pathological conditions of pregnancy, labor, and puerperium.

Jensen, Margaret, Benson, Ralph, and Bobak, Irene M. *Maternity Care: The Nurse and the Family.* St. Louis: The C. V. Mosby Company, 1977.

An extensive comprehensive text that goes into much detail, and for review is better used as a reference than a textbook.

Karones, Shelton B. *High-Risk Newborn Infants.* St. Louis: The C. V. Mosby Company, 1975.

Clear, well written text with a focus on the nursing aspects of high-risk infants. Provides basic concepts of neonatal care.

Wilson, Robert J., and others. *Obstetrics and Gynecology.* St. Louis: The C. V. Mosby Company, 1975.

Basic medical text containing up-to-date information in the areas of obstetrics and gynecology. It includes sections on abortion, contraception, maternal and fetal physiology, and management of normal and abnormal pregnancy and of puerperium, as well as information on gynecological conditions.

Ziegle, Erna, and Van Blarcom, Carolyn Conant. *Obstetric Nursing.* New York: Macmillan Publishing Company, Inc., 1972.

Presents comprehensive, current information on normal physiologic and pathological conditions of pregnancy and infants. Includes information on the reproductive organs and the menstrual cycle.

Chapter 6. Pediatric Nursing

Blake, F. G., and others. *Nursing Care of Children.* Philadelphia: J. B. Lippincott, 1978.

A basic comprehensive textbook that covers all aspects of pediatric nursing: from pediatric techniques through all the major childhood diseases. A good resource for nurses who wish to review pediatric concepts as well as nursing care.

Chinn, Peggy L. *Child Health Maintenance: Concepts in Family Centered Care.* St. Louis: The C. V. Mosby Company, 1979.

An excellent text covering child health concepts from prenatal development to health problems of the adolescent. Study questions, many illustrations, and a clear readable format make this book a useful resource for students.

Gillies, Dee Ann, and Alyn, Irene Barrett. *Saunders Tests for Self-Evaluation of Nursing Competence.* Philadelphia: W. B. Saunders Company, 1978.

A text covering psychiatry, maternity, medical-surgical as well as pediatric nursing that focuses on self-evaluation of nursing competence in the various areas. Since the text is designed for undergraduate and graduate nurses, the questions vary in degree of difficulty and may be above the level of questions asked on State Board Examinations. However, for pediatric nursing concepts, this book adequately tests mastery of the content.

Marlow, D. *Textbook of Pediatric Nursing.* Philadelphia: W. B. Saunders Company, 1979.

A general textbook of pediatric nursing that covers the basic content in a systematic and thorough manner. Useful as a general review book, but not enough depth for a comprehensive textbook.

Pellitteri, Adele. *Nursing Care of the Growing Family: A Child Health Text.* Boston: Little, Brown & Company, 1977.

A comprehensive yet easy to read and understand text that enables the student to get a clear picture of pediatric nursing principles with a focus on growth and development levels.

Scipien, Gladys, and others. *Comprehensive Pediatric Nursing.* New York: McGraw-Hill Book Company, 1979.

A comprehensive, sophisticated, detailed, nursing oriented text. It is divided by systems, includes an excellent pathophysiology section, and deals with diseases by age group which makes it both a complete and in-depth text. A classic of nursing textbooks.

Chapter 7. Psychiatric Nursing

Beckett, Peter, Edward, E. D., and Bleakley, Thomas. *A Teaching Program in Psychiatry*, Vol. I., *Schizophrenia, Paranoid Conditions,* and Vol. II, *Psychoneurosis, Organic Brain Disease and Psychopharmacology.* Detroit: Wayne State University Press, 1969.

In a didactic format, these two volumes extensively cover psychiatric knowledge, including clinical conditions, treatment, and case histories. Comprehensive in approach and excellent for foreign-trained nurses who are deficient in psychiatric content.

Burgess, Ann Wolbert, and Lazare, Aaron. *Psychiatric Nursing in the Hospital and the Community.* 2nd ed. Englewood Cliffs, New Jersey: Prentice-Hall, Inc., 1976.

This new edition of a basic psychiatric textbook presents all essential psychiatric nursing content in a clear, organized, and stimulating format. Excellent general resource book for students.

Haber, Judith, Leach, Anita M., Schudy, Sylvia M., and Sidelean, Barbara Flynn. *Comprehensive Psychiatric Nursing*. New York: McGraw-Hill Book Company, 1978.

A conceptual approach to psychiatric nursing based on the nursing process. This book utilizes psychiatric mental health principles to formulate an integrated approach to care of clients. An excellent high-level nursing text more suited to baccalaureate and graduate programs than review of basic concepts or principles for State Board Examinations.

Hays, J. S., and Larson, K. *Interacting with Patients*. New York: Macmillan Publishing Company, 1965.

A basic text focusing on nurse-client interactions and communication techniques. For students who have difficulty mastering nursing responses and therapeutic communication techniques, an excellent reference.

MacKinnan, Roger, and Michels, Robert. *The Psychiatric Interview in Clinical Practice*. Philadelphia: W. B. Saunders Company, 1971.

While the focus is on interviewing, this comprehensive text gives excellent content in psychopathology and psychodynamics of clinical disorders. The format is easy to read and comprehend. This is an excellent basic text for nurses attempting to master content in psychiatric nursing.

Marram, Gwen D. *The Group Approach in Nursing Practice*. St. Louis: The C. V. Mosby Company, 1978.

An excellent resource text for nurses that presents the scope of group work as well as the theory and practice of group psychotherapies.

Mendels, Joseph. *Concepts of Depression*. New York: John Wiley & Sons, Inc., 1970.

This book gives a comprehensive view of depression, covering clinical features, classification, and treatment.

Payne, Dorris B. *Psychiatric Mental Health Nursing. Nursing Outline Series*. Flushing, New York: Medical Examination Publishing Company, Inc., 1974.

A clear, concise, comprehensive text outline of all the major psychiatric disorders and nursing interventions. Excellent for review of psychiatric nursing.

Saxton, Dolores, and Haring, Phyllis. *Care of Patients With Emotional Problems*. St. Louis: The C. V. Mosby Company, 1979.

A basic psychiatric nursing text with a narrow focus more appropriate for foreign trained nurses or as a quick review for basic students on the major emotional disorders and nursing principles of care.

Wilson, Holly Skodal, and Kneisl, Carol Ren. *Psychiatric Nursing*. Menlo Park, California: Addison-Wesley Publishing Company, 1979.

A comprehensive, theoretically based text for contemporary psychiatry nursing practice. Unique in this text are chapters on psychiatric nursing ethics, parenting, human sexuality, group dynamics, alternative therapies, and private practice versus institutional practice models. Well organized and easy to understand, which makes this text appropriate for psychiatric nursing review.

Chapter 8. Legal Issues in Professional Nursing

Cazalas, Mary W. *Nursing and the Law*. Germantown: Aspen Systems Corporation, 1978.

This book clearly explains the important legal implications of professional nursing. Major subjects covered are nurses and their patients, nurses and their employers, and the nurse and society. The appendices are both comprehensive and helpful.

Hemelt, Mary Dolores, and Mackert, Mary Ellen. *Dynamics of Law in Nursing and Health Care*. Reston: Reston Publishing Company, 1978.

Written on a more technical level, this text describes the law as applied to health care and discusses current medical-legal issues such as abortion, child abuse, dignified death, and others. A series of "vignettes" is presented to illustrate how the law is applied to common situations. The appendices are a useful reference source.

Bibliography

Aguilera, Donna. *Crises Intervention: Theory and Methodology.* St. Louis: The C. V. Mosby Company, 1978.

Amas, George. *The Rights of the Hospital Patients.* ACLU Handbook. Avon Books, 1975.

Anderson, Betty Ann, and others. *The Childbearing Family,* Vol. I, *Pregnancy and Family Health.* New York: McGraw-Hill Book Company, 1974.

Andreoli, Kathleen, and others. *Comprehensive Cardiac Care: A Textbook for Nurses, Physicians, and Other Health Practitioners.* 3rd ed. St. Louis: The C. V. Mosby Company, 1975.

Arieti, Silvano, ed. *American Handbook of Psychiatry,* Vols. I, II, and III. New York: Basic Books, Inc., Publishers, 1974.

Armstrong, Margaret, and others. *McGraw-Hill Handbook of Clinical Nursing.* New York: McGraw-Hill Book Company, 1979.

Ayres, Stephen. "Pulmonary Physiology at the Bedside: Oxygen and Carbon Dioxide Abnormalities." *Cardiovascular Nursing,* January-February, 1973.

Babson, S. Gorham, and Benson, Ralph. *Management of High-Risk Pregnancy and Intensive Care of the Neonate.* St. Louis: The C. V. Mosby Company, 1975.

Barnard, Martha U., and others. *Human Sexuality for Health Professionals.* Philadelphia: W. B. Saunders Company, 1978.

Barry, Jean. *Emergency Nursing.* New York: McGraw-Hill Book Company, 1978.

Beckett, Peter, Edward, E. D., and Bleakley, Thomas. *A Teaching Program in Psychiatry,* Vol. I, *Schizophrenia, Paranoid Conditions,* and Vol. II, *Psychoneurosis, Organic Brain Disease and Psychopharmacology.* Detroit: Wayne State University Press, 1969.

Beland, Irene, and Passos, Joyce. *Clinical Nursing.* 3rd ed. New York: Macmillan Publishing Company, Inc., 1975.

Bergersen, Betty S. *Pharmacology in Nursing.* 12th ed. St. Louis: The C. V. Mosby Company, 1973.

Birchenall, Joan, and Streight, Mary Eileen. *Care of the Older Adult.* Philadelphia: J. B. Lippincott Company, 1973.

Blake, F. G., and others. *Nursing Care of Children.* Philadelphia: J. B. Lippincott Company, 1978.

Bleier, Inge J. *Workbook in Bedside Maternity Nursing.* Philadelphia: W. B. Saunders Company, 1974.

Bordick, Katherine. *Patterns of Shock: Implications for Nursing Care.* New York: Macmillan Publishing Company, Inc., 1965.

Brink, Pamela J., ed. *Transcultural Nursing.* Englewood Cliffs, N.J.: Prentice-Hall, Inc., 1976.

Brooks, Stewart. *Basic Facts of Body Water and Ions.* New York: Springer Publishing Company, Inc., 1973.

Broughton, Joseph O. "Chest Physical Diagnosis for Nurses and Respiratory Therapists." *Heart and Lung,* March-April, 1972.

Broughton, Joseph O. "Understanding Blood Gases." Ohio Medical Products Article Reprint Library, August 1971.

Brunner, Lillian Sholtis, and Suddarth, Doris Smith. *Textbook of Medical Surgical Nursing.* 3rd ed. Philadelphia: J. B. Lippincott Company, 1975.

Brunner, Lillian Sholtis, and Suddarth, Doris Smith. *The Lippincott Manual of Nursing Practice.* Philadelphia: J. B. Lippincott Company, 1978.

Bullough, Bonnie. *The Law and the Expanding Nursing Role.* New York: Appleton Century Croft, 1975.

Burgess, Ann Wolbert, and Lazare, Aaron. *Psychiatric Nursing in the Hospital and the Community.* 2nd ed. Englewood Cliffs, N.J.: Prentice-Hall, Inc., 1976.

Burnside, Irene Mortenson. *Nursing and the Aged.* New York: McGraw-Hill Book Company, 1976.

Bushnell, Sharon Spaeth. *Respiratory Intensive Care Nursing.* Boston: Little, Brown & Company, 1973.

Carini, Esta, and Owens, Guy. *Neurological and Neurosurgical Nursing.* St. Louis: The C. V. Mosby Company, 1974.

Cazalas, Mary W. *Nursing and the Law.* Germantown: Aspen Systems Corporation, 1978.

Cherniack, R. M., Cherniack, L., and Naimark, A. *Respiration in Health and Disease.* Philadelphia, London and Toronto: W. B. Saunders Company, 1972.

Chinn, Peggy L. *Child Health Maintenance: Concepts in Family Centered Care.* St. Louis: The C. V. Mosby Company, 1979.

Dickason, Elizabeth J., and Schultz, Martha Olsen. *Maternal and Infant Care.* New York: McGraw-Hill Book Company, 1975.

Dunphy, J. Englebert, and Way, Lawrence L. *Current Surgical Diagnosis and Treatment.* Los Altos, Calif.: Lange Medical Publications, 1975.

Dutcher, I., and Fielo, S. *Water and Electrolytes: Implications for Nursing Practice.* New York and London: Macmillan Publishing Company, Inc., 1967.

Engle, George L. "Grief and Grieving." *American Journal of Nursing* (September, 1964).

Erikson, Erik H. *Childhood and Society*. New York: W. W. Norton and Company, Inc., 1963.

Fitzpatric, Elise, and others. *Maternity Nursing*. Philadelphia: J. B. Lippincott Company, 1971.

Fluid and Electrolytes: Some Practical Guides to Clinical Use. Chicago: Abbott Laboratories, 1970.

Food and Nutrition Board, National Research Council, National Academy of Sciences. *Recommended Dietary Allowances*. Washington, D.C.: 1968.

French, Ruth. *Guide to Diagnostic Procedures*. New York: McGraw-Hill Book Company, 1975.

Gardner, Ernest, and others. *Anatomy: A Regional Study of Human Structure*. 4th ed. Philadelphia: W. B. Saunders Company, 1975.

Garvey, Judith. "Infant Respiratory Distress Syndrome." *American Journal of Nursing*, April 1975.

Gillies, Dee Ann, and Alyn, Irene Barrett. *Saunders Tests for Self-Evaluation of Nursing Competence*. Philadelphia: W. B. Saunders Company, 1978.

Greenhill, J. P., and Friedman, Emanuel A. *Biological Principles and Modern Practice of Obstetrics*. Philadelphia: W. B. Saunders Company, 1974.

Guthrie, Helen Andrews. *Introduction to Nutrition*. 2nd ed. St. Louis: The C. V. Mosby Company, 1971.

Guyton, Arthur C. *Textbook of Medical Physiology*. Philadelphia: W. B. Saunders Company, 1971.

Haber, Judith, Leach, Anita M., Schudy, Sylvia M., and Sidelean, Barbara Flynn. *Comprehensive Psychiatric Nursing*. New York: McGraw-Hill Book Company, 1978.

Hall, Joanne E., and Weaver, Barbara. *Nursing of Families in Crisis*. Philadelphia: J. B. Lippincott Company, 1974.

Hays, J. S., and Larson, K. *Interacting with Patients*. New York: Macmillan Publishing Company, 1965.

Hemelt, Mary Dolores, and Mackert, Mary Ellen. *Dynamics of Law in Nursing and Health Care*. Reston: Reston Publishing Company, 1978.

Hudak, Carolyn M., and others. *Critical Care Nursing*. Philadelphia: J. B. Lippincott Company, 1973.

Jensen, Margaret, Benson, Ralph, and Bobak, Irene M. *Maternity Care: The Nurse and the Family*. St. Louis: The C. V. Mosby Company, 1977

Kalkman, Marion, and Davis, Ann. *New Dimensions in Mental-Health Psychiatric Nursing*. 4th ed. New York: McGraw-Hill Book Company, 1974.

Karones, Shelton B. *High-Risk Newborn Infants*. St. Louis: The C. V. Mosby Company, 1975.

Kentzel, Kay Carmen. *Advanced Concepts in Clinical Nursing*. Philadelphia and Toronto: J. B. Lippincott Company, 1971.

King, Quida. *Care of the Cardiac Surgical Patient*. St. Louis: The C. V. Mosby Company, 1975.

Krizinofski, Marian T. "Human Sexuality and Nursing Practice." *Nursing Clinics of North America*, December 1973.

Krueger, Judith A., and Ray, Janis C. *Endocrine Problems in Nursing*. St. Louis: The C. V. Mosby Company, 1976.

Krupp, Marcus A., and Chatton, Milton J. *Current Medical Diagnosis and Treatment*. Los Altos, Calif.: Lange Medical Publications, 1978.

Kübler-Ross, Elisabeth. *On Death and Dying*. New York: Macmillan Publishing Company, Inc., 1969.

Lepkin, Gladys B. *Psychosocial Aspects of Maternal-Child Nursing*. St. Louis: The C. V. Mosby Company, 1974.

Luckmann, Joan, and Sorensen, Karen Creason. *Medical-Surgical Nursing: A Psychophysiologic Approach*. Philadelphia: W. B. Saunders Company, 1979.

Luft, Joseph. *Group Dynamics: An Introduction to Group Dynamics*. 2nd ed. Palo Alto, Calif.: National Press, 1970.

MacKinnan, Roger, and Michels, Robert. *The Psychiatric Interview in Clinical Practice*. Philadelphia: W. B. Saunders Company, 1971.

Marlow, D. R. *Textbook of Pediatric Nursing*. Philadelphia: W. B. Saunders Company, 1979.

Marram, Gwen D. *The Group Approach in Nursing Practice*. St. Louis: The C. V. Mosby Company, 1979.

McCalister, Donald, and others. *Readings in Family Planning*. St. Louis: The C. V. Mosby Company, 1973.

Mendels, Joseph. *Concepts of Depression*. New York: John Wiley & Sons, Inc., 1970.

Mereness, Dorothy. *Psychiatric Nursing*. Dubuque, Iowa: W. C. Brown Company, 1966.

Mims, Fern H., ed. "Symposium on Human Sexuality." *Nursing Clinics of North America*, September 1975.

Mooney, Thomas O., and others. *Sexual Options for Paraplegics and Quadraplegics*. Boston: Little, Brown & Company, 1975.

Nelson, W. *Textbook of Pediatrics.* Philadelphia: W. B. Saunders Company, 1969.

Oakes, Annalee, and Morrow, Helen. "Understanding Blood Gases." *Nursing 73,* September 1973.

Orthopedic Nurses Association, Inc. *Manual of Orthopedic Nursing Care Plans.* Atlanta, Ga.: May 1975.

Payne, Dorris B. *Psychiatric Mental Health Nursing.* Nursing Outline Series. Flushing, N.Y.: Medical Examination Publishing Company, Inc., 1974.

Pellitteri, Adele. *Nursing Care of the Growing Family: A Child Health Text.* Boston: Little, Brown & Company, 1977.

Peplau, Hildegarde. "Talking With Patients." *American Journal of Nursing,* 1960.

Petrillo, M., and Sanger, S. *Emotional Care of Hospitalized Children.* Philadelphia: J. B. Lippincott Company, 1972.

Petty, Thomas L. *Intensive and Rehabilitative Respiratory Care.* Philadelphia: Lea and Febiger, 1974.

Physician's Desk Reference To Pharmaceutical Specialties and Biologicals. Oradell, N.J.: Medical Economics, Inc., 1978.

Reusch, Jurgen. *Therapeutic Communication.* New York: W. W. Norton & Company, Inc., 1961.

Rodman, Morton, and Smith, Dorothy. *Clinical Pharmacology in Nursing.* Philadelphia: J. B. Lippincott Company, 1974.

Sanderson, Richard. *The Cardiac Patient, a Comprehensive Approach.* Philadelphia: W. B. Saunders Company, 1972.

Satir, Virginia. *Conjoint Family Therapy.* Palo Alto, Calif.: Science & Behavior Books, Inc., 1967.

Saxton, Dolores, and Haring, Phyllis. *Care of Patients With Emotional Problems.* St. Louis: The C. V. Mosby Company, 1979.

Schwartz, Morris S., and Shockley, Emmy Lanning. *The Nurse and Mental Patient: A Study in Interpersonal Relations.* New York: John Wiley & Sons, Inc., 1956.

Scipien, Gladys, and others. *Comprehensive Pediatric Nursing.* New York: McGraw-Hill Book Company, 1979.

Selye, Hans. *The Stress of Life.* New York: McGraw-Hill Book Company, 1965.

Shafer, Kathleen Newton, and others. *Medical Surgical Nursing.* 4th ed. St. Louis: The C. V. Mosby Company, 1975.

Silver, H. K., and others. *Handbook of Pediatrics.* Los Altos, Calif.: Lange Medical Publications, 1974.

Solnick, Robert L., ed. *Sexuality and Aging.* Los Angeles Ethel Percy Andrus Gerontology Center, 1978.

Stoot, Violet R., Lee, Carla A., and Schaper, C. Ann. *Fluids and Electrolytes: A Practical Approach.* Philadelphia: F. A. Davis Company, 1974.

Travelbee, Joyce. *Intervention in Psychiatric Nursing. Process in the One-to-One Relationship.* Philadelphia: F. A. Davis Company, 1969.

Traver, Gayle. "Assessment of Thorax and Lungs." *American Journal of Nursing.* March 1973.

Traver, Gayle. "Symposium on Care in Respiratory Disease." *Nursing Clinics of North America,* March, 1974.

Tucker, Susan Martin, and others. *Patient Care Standards.* St. Louis: The C. V. Mosby Company, 1975.

Turner, Jeffrey S., and Helms, Donald B. *Contemporary Adulthood.* Philadelphia: W. B. Saunders Company, 1979.

U. S. Department of Agriculture. *A Daily Food Guide: The Basic Four.* Rev. ed. Washington, D.C.: Government Printing Office, 1973.

Underwood, JoAnn R. *Basic Cardiopulmonary Life Support; Theory and Technique.* Los Altos, CA: Applied Medical Training, Inc., 1978.

Wade, Jacqueline. *Respiratory Nursing Care: Physiology and Technique.* St. Louis: The C. V. Mosby Company, 1973.

Wasserman, Edward, and Slobody, Laurence B. *Survey of Clinical Pediatrics.* New York: McGraw-Hill Book Company, 1974.

West, John. *Respiratory Physiology—The Essentials.* Baltimore: Williams & Wilkins Company, 1974.

Widmann, Frances. *Goodale's Clinical Interpretation of Laboratory Tests.* Philadelphia: F. A. Davis Company, 1973.

Williams, Robert H., ed. *Textbook of Endocrinology.* 5th ed. Philadelphia: W. B. Saunders Company, 1974.

Williams, Sue Rodwell. *Essentials of Nutrition and Diet Therapy.* St. Louis: The C. V. Mosby Company, 1978.

Wilson, Holly Skodal, and Kneisl, Carol Ren. *Psychiatric Nursing.* Menlo Park, Calif.: Addison-Wesley Publishing Company, 1979.

Wilson, Robert J., and others. *Obstetrics and Gynecology.* St. Louis: The C. V. Mosby Company, 1975.

Wing, Kenneth. *The Law and The Public's Health.* The C. V. Mosby Company, 1976.

Woods, Nancy Fugate. *Human Sexuality in Health and Illness.* St. Louis: The C. V. Mosby Company, 1979.

Yalom, Irvin D. *The Theory and Practice of Group Psychotherapy.* New York: Basic Books, Inc., 1970.

Ziegle, Erna, and Van Blarcom, Carolyn Conant. *Obstetric Nursing.* New York: Macmillan Publishing Company, Inc., 1972.

Index

National Nursing Review

We Assist Student Nurses To Prepare for R.N. State Board Examinations

☐ A Second Book to Help You Increase Your Test Scores

Practice Tests for State Board Examinations

edited by
Sandra F. Smith, R.N., M.S.

☐ Multiple Choice Questions on the Five Key Nursing Areas
☐ Answers with Extensive Rationale
☐ The Art of Effective Test Taking

published by
National Nursing Review, Inc.

☐ Anxiety Control Techniques
☐ Review Guidelines & Strategies
☐ Useful for Both School Exams and State Board Preparation

☐ Audio Cassette To Help You Reduce Anxiety

The National Nursing Review is offering a new audio cassette to help you anticipate the State Board Examinations with increased self-confidence. The cassette's side #1, "Tension Relaxation," is a simple, but powerful relaxation experience which will help you eliminate stress-related tension and its symptoms. Side #2, "Successfully Confronting State Board Examinations," leads you through a visualization process and provides you with a positive image rehearsal of taking State Boards. This cassette was designed and recorded by Emmett E. Miller, M.D., who also directed the musical accompaniment.

☐ Review Courses for RN State Board Examinations

The National Nursing Review gives review courses for State Board Exams each year in several locations in New York, New England, the Midwest, California, Washington, D.C. and the Southeast. The five-day courses are highly concentrated, complete reviews of nursing content. Each day is devoted to a different subject: medicine, surgery, maternity, pediatrics, and psychiatry. Also, time is allocated for practice questions and a discussion of the rationale for their answers. The review lecturers are selected from major schools of nursing throughout the U.S. Each instructor is highly qualified in her area of clinical specialization. *Review of Nursing for State Board Examinations* is the recommended review course text.

ORDER FORM

Mail this card to **National Nursing Review**, P.O. Box 806, Los Altos, CA 94022.

☐ I am ordering *Practice Tests for State Board Examinations*.
$6.95 + $1.00 postage & handling = $7.95
California residents add $.42 sales tax = $8.37

Allow 3 weeks for delivery. For RUSH delivery, first class mail, add $1.50.

☐ I am ordering the audio cassette.
$6.95 + $.55 postage & handling = $7.50
California residents add $.42 sales tax = $7.92

Allow 3 weeks for delivery. For RUSH delivery, first class mail, add $.50.

Please send me review information for the **National Nursing Review**'s courses for the:

_____ February Boards (California, New York)
_____ July Boards (California, Midwest, New York, New England, Washington, D.C., Southeast)

Name _____
Address _____
City/State _____ Zip _____
School _____
Taking State Boards (mo/yr) _____